MIKE GIMBEL'S
BASEBALL PLAYER AND TEAM RATINGS
- 1993 EDITION

Mike Gimbel's

BASEBALL PLAYER AND TEAM RATINGS

1993 EDITION

BOERUM STREET PRESS

NEW YORK

January 1993

Distributed by:

Boerum Street Press   National Book Network, Inc.
131 Boerum Street   and   4720 Boston Way
Brooklyn, NY 11206   Lanham, MD 20706

Gimbel, Mike, 1944-
    Mike Gimbel's baseball player and team ratings / Mike Gimbel. --
4th ed.
    p. cm.
    Includes player index.
    ISBN 0-9626748-3-4

    1. Baseball players--United States--Rating of. 2. Baseball
players--United States--Statistics. 3. Baseball--United States--
Statistics.   I. Title. II. Title: Baseball player and team
ratings.

    GV877   796.357

Library of Congress Catalog Number: 90-167749

ACKNOWLEDGEMENTS

To Bob Mecca of STATS, Inc. who provided the raw data on the major leagues upon which this book is based. STATS, Inc. maintains a database which contains detailed information on every pitch of every major league game. For those who wish to pursue their own statistical investigations you can reach them at:

STATS, Inc.
7250 N. Cicero
Lincolnwood, Il. 60646
Tel: (708)676-3322

To Howe Sportsdata International, Inc. for providing the minor league raw data upon which the minor league player ratings were based. They can be reached at:

Howe Sportsdata International, Inc.
Boston Fish Pier, West Building #2, Suite 306
Boston, MA. 02210
Tel: (617)951-0070

To the Society for American Baseball Research (SABR) for their efforts in baseball research and the annual conventions which bring together so many who love our beautiful game:

The Society for American Baseball Research
Box 93183
Cleveland, Ohio 44101
Tel: (216)575-0500

CONTENTS

	Author's Preface	**1**
	Introduction	**5**
SECTION I	**EXPLANATION OF METHODS 17**	
	Explanation of player statistics	19
	How values determined	19
	The linear weight values	20
	The Set-up RPA	20
	Age: the moving target	21
	A little more mathematics	23
	A team RPA formula work-up	24
	Individual player adjustments	26
	The defensive rating	27
	The stadium adjustment	29
	The rotisserie rating	30
	More on the defensive rating	31
	Assigned defensive areas listed	33
	STATS, Inc. chart of field	34
	Stadium run adjustments for the 1991 season	35
	The use of player age changes to make better RPA forecasts	39
	List of RPA age adjustments	43
SECTION II	**PLAYER RANKINGS**	**47**
	First Base	48
	Second Base	50
	Third Base	52
	Shortstop	54
	Left Field	56
	Center Field	58
	Right Field	60
	Catcher	62
	Catcher defensive data	64
	DH	66
SECTION III	**PITCHER RANKINGS**	**67**
	Starting pitchers -110 innings +	68
	Starting pitchers - 75 innings +	70
	Starting pitchers - less than 75 innings	71
	Relief pitchers - 50 innings +	72
	Relief pitchers - less than 50 innings	74

CONTENTS

SECTION IV

TOP MINOR LEAGUE PLAYERS   **75**
Top AAA hitters in 1991   76
Top AAA pitchers in 1991   77
Top AA hitters in 1991   78
Top AA pitchers in 1991   79

SECTION V

THE TEAMS   **81**
How to read the data in this section   82

AMERICAN LEAGUE EAST:
Baltimore Orioles   83
Boston Red Sox   91
Cleveland Indians   99
Detroit Tigers   107
Milwaukee Brewers   115
New York Yankees   123
Toronto Blue Jays   131

AMERICAN LEAGUE WEST:
California Angels   139
Chicago White Sox   147
Kansas City Royals   155
Minnesota Twins   163
Oakland Athletics   171
Seattle Mariners   179
Texas Rangers   187

NATIONAL LEAGUE EAST:
Chicago Cubs   195
Montreal Expos   203
New York Mets   211
Philadelphia Phillies   219
Pittsburgh Pirates   227
St. Louis Cardinals   235

NATIONAL LEAGUE WEST:
Atlanta Braves   243
Cincinnati Reds   251
Houston Astros   259
Los Angeles Dodgers   267
San Diego Padres   275
San Francisco Giants   283

CONTENTS

SECTION VI

SECTION VII

THE EXPANSION TEAMS **291**
Colorado Rockies 292
Florida Marlins 293

ESSAYS **295**
Who were the real MVP's in 1991? 297

My batting average means nothing. 299

The players and pitchers with the
greatest platoon difference. 301

The myth of the good old days 303

Can we tell when a hitter is
beginning to lose it? 305

The list of reverse-type pitchers. 307

The accuracy of minor league RPA's. 309

PLAYER INDEX **313**

AUTHOR'S PREFACE

The 1992 season was an incredibly eventful one for me. For the first time I became an active participant in the behind-the-scenes events which were reflected in the on-the-field playing of the 1992 baseball season. In the fall of 1991 I was hired as player evaluation consultant by Dan Duquette, the newly appointed General Manager and Vice-President of the Montreal Expos.

This is the 4th annual edition of the *Baseball Player & Team Ratings,* which began its publication life virtually by accident, and this publication has now led me to an area of work which was entirely unanticipated when I began this adventurous journey during the winter prior to the 1990 season.

At the end of the 1991 season and after the end of the selling season for the second edition, I became utterly convinced that I needed to take my data beyond the publication stage. It was clear to me that my ratings were the most accurate and useful ratings available and that this ought to bear some weight in the baseball front offices. I had no idea what response I would get or even whether I would get any response at all, but I felt that being an active participant in helping to shape a Major League franchise would bring more public attention to the real value of the **RPA**™ in assessing player talent and its value to the serious baseball fan's enjoyment of our wonderful national game.

I must admit that the continuously ignorant articles in the media and the usually silly comments by TV and radio "experts" or "color" commentators had some effect on my decision to expand into being an active participant. The written or verbal remarks of these so-called "experts" was so irksome that I felt almost propelled into making this decision just to set the record straight. Too many player careers were being negatively affected by these ignorant, superficial and glib reporters. The success of my rating system could be put to the ultimate test by having practical on-field effects. Of course, I had no idea how my data would be put to use even if I were hired by a Major League team, but I felt it was necessary to at least test the waters.

The question was how to proceed. I did not want to approach an established "contender" since there can be no question of earning a reputation based upon helping a team that is already a powerhouse or has been in contention most recently. In order to "prove" the value of my system I decided that I needed to approach a team at the bottom of the barrel. I decided to first approach the Cleveland Indians but was not able to meet with their General Manager, and in fact, after arranging to meet with the Cleveland GM on the field at Yankee Stadium prior to a game with the Indians, the meeting was effectively blocked by their media relations chief with whom I ended up in a shouting match in the hallway outside the Yankee Stadium press box.

I really had my heart set on Cleveland, since they were virtually the symbol of futility for over a third of a century, as well as the fact that my wife is from Cleveland, and I was a Cleveland Browns fan during the Jim Brown era. But it was clear that I would get no hearing from the Indians, so I looked around and determined that the next team that ought to be contacted was the Montreal Expos. They had finished last the previous year and were in serious financial difficulty, and there were some questions in the media as to whether the Expos would be able to remain in Montreal. It was a franchise in serious trouble, according to the press.

The Expos had never been in a World Series, although they did have considerable success for several years in the late '70's and early '80's. I new from my mailing list that Dan Duquette, a member of the Expos front office, had purchased my first two editions, but I was unaware that he was in line to become General Manager. The Expos were my next logical choice and so I contacted Dan Duquette and he agreed to meet me at his hotel in early September, 1991 when the Expos were in Philadelphia for a weekend series.

After my bad Cleveland Indians experience, I was stunned at how easy it was to set up the meeting with Duquette. I was even more pleased after actually meeting with Dan. He used the time of our meeting to ask questions and to listen carefully to my answers. There was no impermeable "baseball insider" moat around him and the organization, as I feared would be the case after the Cleveland debacle.

I don't think I learned about Duquette's impending appointment as Expos GM until shortly after our meeting, although my memory could be mistaken on this point. In any case, shortly after Dan Duquette was promoted to GM, just one month after our meeting, he hired me as a consultant on player evaluation.

I can't reveal the internal discussions that I and Dan have had since that time, since it affects the careers of various players and possible future transactions, but our working relationship is very good and I am beginning to get a real education in the internal thinking and judgment processes of a Major League front office. I can say, however, that things have gone even better than I could have anticipated at the time, although not everything can be perfect, of course, and sometimes I was admittedly a little frustrated since the GM is the one who makes the decisions and not myself. I can only give advice. But I must say that, on the whole, our working relationship has been very beneficial to both the Expos as well as to myself. The nicest thing is to have several players placed on the Expos roster as a result of my efforts and advice over the past year. This is Dan Duquette's team, but in a certain sense I also feel , at least in part and with some justification, that it's my team too.

I can't resist two last parting shots at the media. The Andres Galarraga for Ken Hill trade was the first major move by Duquette after he and I came aboard. He took a real pounding from the Montreal media over the trade during the winter months prior to the 1992 season. It may look silly now, but it didn't seem silly to Duquette at the time, since he was taking all the hits from the media. I told him at the time to pay no attention to the attacks since the media will completely forget what they said in the winter because we were going to be contenders in 1992, which is exactly what happened. By the way, has any of the media apologized? I doubt it. They may now hail the Galarraga for Hill trade as the biggest steal of the 1992 season, but that isn't what they said then.

I am also saddened at the Expos loss of Bret Barberie in the expansion draft. The media can take some credit for this loss since Barberie was not permitted by them to settle in at third base. Its hard enough for a kid to make the transition from the minor leagues to the Majors without having the additional burden of the media attacks which are then picked up by the fans who then make life miserable for the kid, especially a kid who's

taking the job of a long-time and well-liked veteran like Tim Wallach. The reason I am so saddened is not so much for Bret, since he'll have an outstanding career in spite of the Montreal media, but for the Expos who have lost a terrific talent, who, I am convinced, will be one of the top leadoff hitters in the Majors for years to come. He certainly would have been a huge asset to the Expos in the coming years.

Fortunately the Expos have sufficient young talent in the minor leagues to overcome the losses in the expansion draft, and also fortunately for the Expos, there are still a number of Major League front offices that appear to have no understanding of the quality of the young talent that they possess. While many teams are throwing around megabucks like so much monopoly money, the Expos are proceeding to utilized their deeper understanding of young player talent so as to make smart trades of older "established" players for young talented players. In other words, what other teams grow, we can sometimes reap. In this manner, the Expos can expect to field competitive teams for many years to come, while other organizations throw money around for quick-fix solutions to their problems. I really find it ironic that the one team (the Expos) that has stayed almost completely out of the free agent market for these past two years is the team expected to be the favorite to win the Eastern division of the National League after having finished last just two years ago.

I look forward to the 1993 season with real anticipation. With all the money being thrown around and all the wild swings created in player rosters on many teams, I anticipate a lot of surprises for the fans in the coming year. While many fans are discouraged by these numerous changes, it's grist for the mill of a publication like this and ought to provide the serious fan with many things to discuss since there will be so many more unknowns to ponder.

As I write this preface, I've completed all my player ratings but I have yet to make my team-by-team analysis. I am as intrigued as you are as to how this upcoming season will proceed. I wonder how my team-by-team analysis will end up. Will my Expos still be the favorites after I run the numbers through? I don't know, but I soon will and so will you. All you have to do is read these pages to find out what the results of my analysis were.

> ## On to 1993!

INTRODUCTION

Note: most of this introduction (although not all) is relatively similar to last year's since this part of the book is intended primarily for first time readers who are unfamiliar with the RPA and what it means and how it is used. For previous readers, it is not necessary to read this introduction, and you can safely skip it, although it should be helpful reading as a "refresher course".

The ratings in this book are the result of testing years of detailed player data for performances done under varying conditions. This testing would not have been possible without the advent of the personal computer and without the existence of an organization like STATS, Inc. which has an individual at each stadium for each game who charts the complete detail of every pitch and every resulting play and every player on the field at the time. These mounds of data are far too complex to be analyzed through the use of a mere calculator.

You may object that fans or professional baseball front office personnel can't or even shouldn't make judgment based on "mere" statistics. Those individuals who have spent their lives making subjective judgments in assessing player abilities are often suspicious of "outside advisors" who are baseball "nonprofessionals" and who are simply "number-crunchers" with their "objective" but "weird" or "over-complicated" statistically based ratings. Truth be told, these long-time professional baseball insiders were often correct in their suspicions, since the science of baseball statistics is only beginning to become fully mature through the publication of this series of books. The shoe is on the other foot now, however, for the long-time baseball professional. Since the objective technique developed in this book has matured to the point where better judgments on player ability can be usually made through these statistically-based ratings than through the old seat-of-the-pants subjective judgments, it now becomes incumbent upon the working professionals to integrate the RPA rating into their work. The best results will be gotten by those individual professionals and Major League organizations that can integrate these subjective and objective judgments into their decision making system.

WHAT MAKES THIS BOOK VALUABLE?

This book rates players on a *quality*, not a *quantity* basis. This book evaluates each player's total ability in terms of how many runs a player produces each time he walks to the plate or how many runs a pitcher surrenders to each batter faced.

The quantity of runs created or surrendered by each player or pitcher is not a simple thing to determine. There are many variables. Tests must be done to see how each variable fits into the overall picture of player ability. The final result is a tested formula for the offense, the defense and the pitchers. All these ratings are done on the same scale so that you, the reader, can evaluate a trade of a pitcher for a hitter, or the value of a glove-man versus the value of a strong hitter. The formulas utilized are not hidden from you. They are fully worked out so that you can see how they actually perform what they claim to perform.

THE ILLUSION OF COMPETENCE

One of the "charms" of baseball is the fact that the previous purely subjective methods of evaluating player performance have been subject to all sorts of illusion which created many mistakes in judgment. Today's terrific player can be tomorrow's waived reject, or vice versa. An example in point: Jerome Walton was the National League rookie-of-the-year in 1989. It was clear, when I examined the data for my 1990 book, that Walton was not all he was cooked up to be. In my first book I gave him a below average rating and his ratings have plummeted each year since. Just prior to the 1991 season at the Baseball Coaches Association convention in New Orleans that January, I was talking to some Chicago Cubs scouts who were very upset at my extremely low rating for Walton in my newly published

1991 edition. I could only shrug my shoulders and hope they later would give it some more thought, as their judgments on Walton would surely to be shown to be false over time.

My first edition (1990) of these player ratings proved that even the same player's statistics can be highly misleading from year to year. I used an essay (entitled: *An Illustrative Illusion*) on Howard Johnson to prove my point. His raw stats from the 1987 and 1988 were highly misleading, causing the Mets to try to unload him during the winter prior to the 1989 season, which would have been a huge mistake on their part had they gotten any takers.

In last year's edition I had an essay (entitled: *My Batting Average Means Nothing, part II*) which listed Rob Deer as having the greatest variance in the Major Leagues between his batting average and his actual production, once the proper analysis is done by the use of the RPA formula. In fact, I would startle radio listeners when doing live interviews with the statement that Rob Deer's offensive production during the 1991 season, with a batting average of .179, the lowest average ever for anyone with so many at-bats, was actually ***more productive*** than Tony Gwynn's who had a .317 batting average that very same year!

The use of the batting average as a measure of offensive ability is one of my pet peeves, since it usually creates more illusions than it clears up. The Deer/Gwynn comparison was as extreme an example as I could find. I used the Deer/Gwynn comparison to illustrate the seriousness of the problem.

In evaluating a hitter, the primary things you want to know, to put it in its simplest terms, is: (1) did he get on base, and (2) if he got on base, where did he place himself, on first base, second base, third base, or did he clear the bases? These two items above can be loosely termed as (1) on-base average and (2) power. Both of these items are extremely important in evaluating a hitter.

In the Deer/Gwynn comparison there is no question as to whom to give the edge to as to power: it's Rob Deer by a country mile. It's the on-base part that really illustrates my point. Despite the enormous difference in batting averages between Deer and Gwynn in 1991 the *effective* on-base percentages of the two players were not significantly in favor of Gwynn. In 530 at-bats, Gwynn had only 26 walks while hitting into 11 double plays and stealing 8 bases while being caught 9 times. In other words, after taking the batting average into account, he only added 6 base runners (26 walks less the 11 runners removed on the double-plays and 9 runners removed by the caught stealing), or 15 runners if you include the 9 times he reached on an error. The 11 extra outs created by the double-plays also lowers Gwynn's *effective* on-base percentage since it increases Gwynn's *effective* plate appearance total by those 11 extra outs created.

Deer, on the other hand, was a virtual mirror-image of Gwynn. In 1991 he had 88 walks in just 448 at-bats, while hitting into only 3 double-plays. He stole 1 base and was caught stealing 3 times. In other words, he added a whopping 82 runners (or 85 if you include the 3 times he reached on an error), after taking into account his batting average.

Lets put it another way: Rob Deer accounted for 371 outs in 1991 with an effective plate appearance total of 539 (448+88+3) while Tony Gwynn accounted for 382 outs with an effective plate appearance total of 567 (530+26+11). That's a miniscule on-base advantage for Gwynn over Deer when Gwynn had only 4 homers in 1991 compared to Deer's 25.

Defense has its illusions as well. A highly skilled defensive player is praised by all, even though he may actually be a defensive liability when put to the proper tests. Likewise, a player who makes many spectacular defensive plays may also be a defensive liability, while another player who occasionally bobbles routine plays and never dives for a ball may actually be a superior defensive player. *This book will tell you who has been good and who has been poor on defense over these past two years.* Some of the ratings will greatly surprise you.

GO ELSEWHERE FOR TRIVIA!

This is a serious study of player talent. For those who wish for the trivia that the *Elias*

Baseball Analyst produces, this book is not for you. This book deals with tested formulas and significant data only!

The fact that a particular hitter is 3 for 19 against a particular pitcher has little, if any, statistical significance. Statistical significance means the threshold number of occurrences of an event in order to draw reliable conclusions. This book rates hitters with at least 100 at-bats or 25 innings pitched (over the last three seasons) because fewer at-bats or innings pitched would produce totally unreliable data upon which to base conclusions. Even this minimum amount is merely a threshold where conclusions can only *start* to be made. A guy could get 4 bloop base hits one day and completely skew the data when you utilize too few data points. A Mark Lemke has had fabulous play-offs and World Series for 1991 and 1992, while Barry Bonds' stats have been poor. Does this mean that Lemke is a better clutch hitter than Bonds? No way! Lemke's "hot bat" was merely the result of a statistical chance variation, i.e., *he got lucky* while Bonds was equally unlucky. That is why I won't rate players who don't meet the minimum requirements of 100 at-bats or 25 innings pitched. Does this mean that there are a lot of players just entering the Major Leagues that I can't give a rating for? Not at all. The AAA and AA minor league performances of all players meeting the above requirements are also rated and these ratings are the Major League equivalents for their minor league performances. Don't

think for a moment that you can't equate these minor league performances with their Major League ability. You can do it at least as well as for the year-to-year Major League performances, as was proved in last year's edition.

In fact, since I've already proved that we can safely use these minor league stats to project Major League performance, I've integrated this data into the RPA ratings for all Major League players who spent time in the minor leagues over the past two years. In other words, if a player had 450 computed plate appearances in the Major Leagues over the past two years and 200 computed plate appearances at AAA over the same period, the RPA rating will reflect the combined overall rating.

Most of the *Elias* data is trivia. Their data is what I would term simple facts without much meaning or usefulness. It is simple raw data for people who don't want to dig very hard to get at the substance beneath the data. What you get in this book is real analysis, based on tested formulas, which covers all aspects of a player's performance under the varying circumstances under which the play occurred.

Hard data means tested data. That does not mean that it is perfect data. Tested formulas can always be improved through further testing. In addition, *statistical studies deal with probability, not certainty.* That's why we play the game. One team may be superior to another team, yet the inferior team may sweep a series from the superior team or even finish ahead of the superior team in the final standings due to injuries or just plain luck. *Luck is a very important and highly underestimated part of our beautiful national pastime.* The difference between the best and worst teams in baseball is generally so small that luck plays a huge role in the fates of both teams and players!

Hard data also requires explanation -- something that can't be done in 20 second sound bytes or two paragraphs in a daily newspaper column. This unfortunate fact may not be helpful in popularizing the findings contained herein, but the alternative would destroy the integrity of the data.

The ratings in this book are not limited to a few chosen players. This would be playing it very safe. By limiting the number of players I rate, I could reduce any potential criticism of my rating formula. But that would limit the value of these ratings. This book attempts, and I believe quite successfully, to eliminate any subjective bias that could enter our system -- even the bias as to whom to rate. *Every major league and minor league player meeting the minimum requirements is rated in this book! Each year I rate approximately 1750 players!*

IS IT PREDICTABLE?

What is meant by a tested formula and why is it needed? A tested formula is one that after taking all the known factors into account most accurately reflects reality. A tested formula is required because we need to know how many runs a player produces or a pitcher gives up after we eliminate all illusions and all data which is dependent upon other players' performances. Without testing the formula we wouldn't know if the formula actually works in the real world.

Runs are what wins games. A team can have 13 hits in a game and still not score a single run. This team will lose the game and there won't be a consolation prize for the number of hits gotten. Runs is all that counts and my formula, therefore, has to be able to accurately rate players on their ability to produce these runs.

Before I could accurately rate each individual baseball player listed in this book in terms of run production, it was necessary to develop a formula that would most accurately reflect run scoring at the league and team level.

In other words, if you were to be given the total number of singles, doubles, triples, etc., that a team received during the year, then you ought to be able to estimate with some reasonable level of accuracy the total number of runs scored by that team that year.

The RPA formula usually produces results which are within 10 or 20 or at most 30 runs (with few exceptions) of the actual run production for each team in any particular year. When applied to the league as a whole, however, the formula's prediction accuracy improves even more. This is because smaller samples, i.e., individual team run scoring, is more subject to chance variation than the larger aggregate scoring of an entire league. My formula produced projected American League and National League run scoring totals for each of the five years prior to the last edition of my book that were almost dead-on!

As a new advance in this book over the previous editions, I decided that for the purposes of my rating system that, since the formula predicting run scoring was clearly accurate, and since the total number of runs scored at any particular stadium in any particular year was a relatively small number subject to relatively large chance variation effects, that I would use the **_predicted_** number of runs for each stadium as derived by the RPA formula, rather than the actual number of runs scored at a stadium as the working stadium variant utilized in this book and used by the RPA formula for determining individual player ratings.

In other words, if at stadium "A" there were 700 runs scored, and 680 runs were scored on the road during the 1992 season, and my formula predicted that there should have been 721 runs scored at stadium "A" and 668 runs scored on the road, the latter figures would be used for the new stadium variants utilized by the RPA formula and listed in this book, since the RPA formula uses

thousands of data points to get its results, i.e. all the walks, all the hits, all the errors, all the stolen bases, etc., to reach its conclusion. The raw run totals usually are around 700 for a season for both teams at each Major League stadium, and can more easily be affected by chance variation than the thousands of data points used by the RPA formula.

Since three years of ratings for each player are listed in this book, previous readers may notice that there are small changes from the previously reported ratings. The reason is the use of these new stadium variants. It doesn't mean that the old ratings were wrong, especially since the differences are very minor. It just means that every year, as new data becomes available and new studies based on them are made, we can be assured that the RPA formula will grow and mature and get better and better.

THE DEFENSIVE RATING

The defensive ratings for each Major League player are based on very accurate data maintained by STATS, Inc. Defensive ratings are not included for the minor leaguers since adequate and accurate defensive data is presently not available at the minor league level. It would require an organization like Stats, Inc. to have a person at each stadium for each minor league game. That would be an enormous undertaking that I am certain is not being contemplated by anyone at the present time, although it would have enormous benefit for the evaluation of minor league player talent if it were to be undertaken.

AGE IS IMPORTANT

These RPA ratings are solely based on the actual performance of each player, and not on their supposed "potential" except as it pertains to the age related deltas. The age of a player is very important in assessing how they may perform in the coming season. A new study based upon the previously reported RPA ratings was done by Brom Keifetz. Brom will explain his results in the essay in this book which is entitled "Using Age Changes to Make Better RPA Forecasts", and I've utilized his age-related RPA changes to adjust each players' RPA in the position-by-position rating section.

I leave to the front-office management of the major league teams the responsibility of figuring out which players may have hidden talents not revealed by the RPA ratings. But they (and you!) need to begin the assessment of player talent with these RPA figures! How can a team's management rate their own players and prospects if they don't even know how well these players have actually performed? My ratings are tested, accurate and the best available!

THE RPA RATING

The RPA rating is not a simple thing to determine, however. We cannot take the raw data such as is found in the daily box scores and accept it as is. It's much easier to hit .300 at Fenway Park than at Shea Stadium. In effect, a single at Fenway Parrk does not have as much value as a single at Shea Stadium when we are figuring a particular player's RPA, since hits are so much easier to come by at this hitter's paradise. In other words, batting averages and run production are heavily dependent on the stadium played in, and, in addition, individual runs scored or knocked-in are also heavily dependent on the player's teammates who precede or follow him in the line-up.

Even the year in which the performance took place is important. Some summers are hot, some are cold. Some years the wind blows in at Wrigley, while most other years it blows out. The weather, in other words, has a big effect on player stats from one year to the next. I therefore normalize all the ratings for the year of the performance as well, basing this adjustment on the total number of runs scored at all stadiums in a particular year, while using the average number of runs scored per year over the last three years as my baseline.

THE INDIVIDUAL PLAYER

For each player we need all the available and relevant raw data which is not dependent on other players' performances. For instance, a player's ability to get on first base through walks, hit-by-pitch or even errors are important factors in a player's rating. His power is extremely important, as well as his speed, stolen-base ability, and whether or not he hits into lots of double plays.

What is needed is a tested formula that takes all these factors into account so as to come up with accurate player ratings which will be equalized no matter under what conditions the player performed!

In addition, it is advantageous to have individual player ratings which eliminate, as much as is possible, the year-to-year fluctuations in player performance. In other words, a player's performance fluctuates greatly from year-to-year. One year he could be an "All-Star". The next year no one even notices he's around. Which one is the "real" player? The answer is neither, or rather the answer is a little bit of both. This additional player rating adjustment is easily accomplished by simply utilizing the RPA ratings which **combine the last two years performance data** for each player in order to get our overall rating.

I have found two year averaging to be the most reliable method of evaluating players. Three separate years of RPA ratings are listed for each player so that we can see trends. Any records more than three years old cannot be relied upon as being very useful. They may be interesting for historical purposes *but this book seeks to rate current talent*, and including more than three years of past performance data will only confuse the issue.

THE STARTER

Once we know how many runs a player produces (offensively and defensively and after adjusting for age) we can then compare him to all the other players at his position. There are now 14 teams in each league. This means that there are 14 positions available for starting players at any particular position other than pitcher. To be qualified to be a Major League starting position player, a player at first base, for instance, would have to have a total RPA rating that would place him in the top 14 rated players at that particular position in his league.

THE PREMIER PLAYER

The object of baseball, however, is to win a pennant. Merely being qualified to start at a particular position is not what a team ought to be looking for. Premier players are the stuff of pennants.

In order to determine the premier players and the extent of their value to a particular team this book compares players to the *median rating* for these major league starting players. The median rating is the point at which half the qualified *starting* players at a particular position fall above and half fall below. Those players at or above this median point are your *premier players* at any particular position. Since each league has 14 teams, this median is the average RPA of the 7th and 8th highest rated players at any particular position.

RATING THE PITCHER

The method for rating pitchers is almost the same as for the position players, except that pitchers want to keep their RPA's low while the hitters want theirs high. A single by a hitter is a single off of a pitcher, therefore the value in terms of runs credited to the hitter is equally ascribed to the pitcher. There are only a few minor pieces of raw data, such as the wild pitch and the balk, which can be ascribed to a pitcher and not to a hitter. The pitcher's RPA is adjusted to include these items. The hitter's RPA rating, however, includes his base running ability in the form of the number of extra bases taken while running the base paths, which has no comparable counterpart in the pitcher data.

In addition, the pitcher rating is adjusted by taking into account the quality of the defense behind each pitcher during a particular season.

You may not think that the defensive abilities of a team is a big influence on a pitcher's apparent ability, but this would be a big mistake! Just ask Dwight Gooden and the rest of the Mets pitchers if the horrendous defense behind them for the past two seasons did not affect their stats! Just ask the Los Angeles Dodger pitchers if the disastrous defense behind them last year didn't contribute to bloating their E.R.A.'s.

Should these pitchers be penalized in our ratings because of the failings of their teammates? All these pitchers can do is get the hitters to put the ball in play where a fielder has a chance to make a play. These pitchers can't be held accountable if the players behind them treated every ball as if it were a live hand-grenade! Should other pitchers benefit because they pitch in front of a marvelous defensive squad? No -- not if we want to rate each player or pitcher on the same scale so as to be able to judge their actual value to a team or to the team to which they are traded.

EIGHT IS ENOUGH

In today's game, while there are eight positions on the field for the regular players for each team, the single position of pitcher is usually held by eight regulars for each team, i.e., 5 starters plus either one long reliever and two stoppers -- one of whom is a lefty and the other a righty or two set-up men leading to the big stopper who gets every save possibility available.

Determining the number of qualified starters and premier pitchers, therefore, is merely a matter of multiplication. For the starters in each league there are 14 teams with 5 starting positions each. This gives a total of 70 available positions to be filled in these starting rotations, of which the top 35 would be your premier starters.

DISSECTING HITTER PERFORMANCE

In this book, each hitter's performance has

been broken down into its component parts. A hitter has two main responsibilities: (1) to the runners already on the base paths, and (2) to the hitters following him in the line-up. An RPA rating is given for each hitter for each of these responsibilities. They are termed the Set-Up and Drive-In RPA's. These Set-Up and Drive-In RPA's are extremely important when assessing where a particular hitter ought to bat in any particular line-up. You want the player with better Set-Up RPA's to bat in front of the player with the better Drive-In RPA's.

In addition to the above, the RPA's for each hitter against each type of pitcher faced are listed. There are six types of pitchers (or more accurately 12 when accounting for reverse-type pitchers), groundball, flyball and neutral type lefties and righties. The RPA ratings for each hitter when facing left-handed, right-handed, groundball, flyball and neutral type pitchers ought to be used by every major league manager in each and every game played! Just because they may not (yet) use this rating does not mean that you can't do your own assessments based on these figures and be several steps ahead of them!

WATCH FOR THE REVERSE

Pay special attention to the reverse-type pitchers like Sid Fernandez. These are pitchers who throw as if they were throwing with the opposite arm. Sid is a terrific lefty pitcher. Opposing teams stack their line-ups with righty hitters as is the tradition. There is only one slight problem. Sid murders righty hitters while he's much more human against lefty hitters. In other words, Major League managers have been stacking their line-up in exactly the wrong manner when facing Sid. Sid is not an isolated example. There are many in his category, some of whom are much more extreme than Sid. In fact this year's edition of the hitter's lefty-righty splits were not compiled as they were last year when I utilized the traditional manner of categorizing the pitchers faced.

This year I treated all reverse-type pitchers as if they actually were throwing with the other arm when I had the data for the hitters compiled.

As stated earlier, the formulas used in this book are not secrets. The following chapter of this book fully demonstrates and explains these formulas and shows you how they work. *If you are unfamiliar with the RPA you ought to read it before proceeding to the main body of this work.* Once the meaning of the formulas are grasped, everything in this book becomes easy to understand.

One final note: this book packs so much information that even I have trouble keeping track of all the players listed and rated and of remembering even a fraction of the data, or even parts of the formulas enclosed within these pages. It is for this reason that a player index is included. This index has been very helpful to me, especially with all the trades, signings and roster changes that take place on an almost constant basis. With all the player moves this winter, this index becomes doubly necessary.

The beauty of this book is that it is not a static list of batting averages or other "trivia". This book is a dynamic tool with which we can understand and judge the performance of individual players and entire teams. Players may not always perform exactly as the RPA would predict, and exact predictability is utterly impossible where so much chance is involved, but this book can give you an understanding of the dynamics of these player performances so as to make educated estimates of where the trend lines are for both players and teams alike. In other words, this book is a tool that can be used both before and during the season for making, understanding, or criticizing the many strategic and tactical moves of the game.

SECTION I

EXPLANATION OF METHODS

EXPLANATION OF PLAYER STATISTICS

[As with the introduction, much of this section will be very familiar, and in part will contain some of the exact same words as in those previous books. Those of you who have read the previous editions of this annual ratings book can safely skip it, although there will be a few new additions, such as the inclusion of the age adjustment, but much of what is included here will otherwise not have changed at all since last year's edition.]

Before we can rate any individual player we need to be able to find out the value, in terms of runs produced, of the individual offensive acts in which the player is involved. This means we need to know what the run production value of a single is as compared to the value of a double or the value of a stolen base or the value of a walk, etc.

HOW DO WE DETERMINE THESE VALUES?

Each year, in each league, and for each team, there are accurate records of the number of occurrences of each offensive and defensive event as well as the number of runs which resulted. The Stats, Inc. organization has an individual in every major league ball park's press section who records every pitch thrown and every ball put in play with each ball's direction, distance and outcome, and every player on the field at the time.

Utilizing several years of the above data for all 26 major league teams, it becomes a matter of experimenting with different linear weight values for the various events (singles, doubles, etc.) until I arrived at values which were accurate enough to use in estimating the approximate number of runs that should have been scored during a full season by any major league team in any particular year. A linear weight value, for those unfamiliar with the term as used in this book, simply means that a specific run value has been determined for a particular event that takes place on the playing field. As an example from this book, a single has a linear weight value of 0.29 runs.

The resulting values, which have been arrived at through statistical testing for each of the individual events, are not static values, however. These values change with the opportunities available. The greater the number of opportunities, the greater the opportunity of scoring runs per each offensive act. If a team gets only one single or one walk per game and nothing more, then this single or walk will probably have no value in terms of runs, since no one would likely score. If however, every hitter who comes to the plate either singles or gets a walk or hits a home run, then these singles and walks would be exactly equal to home runs since every hitter would score. Run scoring and the values of individual offensive events, therefore, vary with team and individual on-base percentage.

The **Run Production Average** is the result of statistical experimentation. The **RPA** is the product of a testable formula which results in our ability to rate each player or pitcher on a per plate appearance basis.

Here then are the linear weight values determined through the above testing:

Single =	.29 runs
Double =	.41 runs
Triple =	.70 runs
Home Run =	1.44 runs
Walk, Hit-By-Pitch (HBP) &	
Reached-on-an-error =	.165 runs
Extra Base taken as a runner &	
Stolen Base, Wild Pitch & Balk =	.10 runs
Caught Stealing & Picked-off =	-.165 runs
Ground into Double Play* =	-.165 runs
*plus one added plate appearance.	

The value of the intentional walk is not listed since it affects only the team totals when we use the formula to predict run scoring for the team and league. We won't use it in our individual player ratings.

THE SET-UP RPA

The linear weights listed above are not static values. The values of these singles, doubles, triples, etc., are dependent upon how often people are on base. In addition, each batter is responsible for driving-in or moving up the runners already on base as well as placing himself on the base paths in order to set-up the hitters coming after him in the line-up.

The RPA formula, therefore, is split up into two main parts: a **set-up** and a **drive-in** RPA rating. It is the set-up portion that reflects a batter's ability to get on base. *This is the portion of the formula which is not linear since the percentage of times a batter gets on base increases or decreases the linear values of each individual offensive act.*

When the result of the on-base production adjustment is applied to the individual player it will be listed separately as the **set-up RPA**. This will show how many runs a hitter sets up, as compared to how many he has driven-in, on average, for each computed plate appearance.

For example, if a player, prior to the on-base adjustment, has a production figure of 100 runs, then one-half (50 runs) is his figure for driving in runs and will not be adjusted by the on-base percentage. The other 50 runs will be adjusted to reflect the on-base ability of the hitter. We can then divide each of these run totals by the total number of computed plate appearances to get an RPA rating for setting-up runs and an RPA rating for driving-in runs.

If, in this example, the player had a computed plate appearance total of 500, then his **drive-in RPA** would be .100 (50 runs divided by 500). If, after adjusting for this player's on-base ability, his computed set-up runs were 45, then his Set-up RPA would be .090. His total offensive RPA would be .190 (.100 plus .090). To this will be added (or subtracted) his RPA based on his defensive ability. In other words, if the above player had a -.013 defensive rating, compared to the median rated starter at his primary position, then his total RPA would now be .177 (.190 less .013). This is still a very good overall rating and such a player would be a valuable addition to any team despite his poor fielding. If his team can move him to an easier defensive position or to DH (if he's in the American League) then they may be able to maximize his offensive assets without incurring his defensive liabilities.

In many cases, however, the defensive liabilities of a player can entirely negate his offensive contributions and, vice versa, a very ordinary hitter may turn out to be an extraordinary asset based solely on his defensive abilities.

The Set-up RPA and the Drive-in RPA figures
can be used to see how each batter does his job. It will enable us to indicate the location the hitter should occupy in a particular line-up. If he is particularly adept at setting up runs, we will want to place him in front of those hitters that are particularly good at driving him in. As indicated in last year's edition there should be two or more "bumps" in each properly designed line-up, i.e., two sets of set-up and drive-in hitters: a stronger set at the top of the line-up and a lesser set after that.

AGE: THE MOVING TARGET

For the first time since the publication of the *Baseball Player and Team Ratings* began in the Winter of 1990, a guest article is appearing in this annual work. As the reader can tell, this publication does not contain "fluff" pieces. It is not meant as a place to locate trivia. It is a place where serious statistical investigations and the results of these investigations are put into print. In order for a guest article to appear in this work it must meet these standards.

The essay entitled "Using Age Changes to Make Better RPA Forecasts", by Brom Keifetz is an extremely valuable contribution to the investigation of how to measure *current* player ability. It may be the most important new feature added for this edition.

This year, more than almost any other year I can think of, has shown the value of making proper estimates of age changes in player ability. I listen to the media and am stunned by some of the free agent signing's and some of the trades, some of which make sense, but so many of which don't make any sense whatever. So many older free agents, either just past their prime or even far past their prime, have received whopping, multi-year contracts as if they were the same players they were a few years ago or as if they will remain the same players they are today for years down the road. This may happen in a few lucky cases, but the abilities of most individual players change relatively rapidly over time. Player abilities are truly moving targets, and it is vitally important to understand this when one is estimating how a player will perform in a coming season. The greatest single variable is age, and Brom Keifetz's article is truly a welcome addition to the RPA tool chest.

Keifetz's article is printed here exactly as he sent it to me, with only one addition, since I did not feel, due to its importance and the quality of the work, that I should tamper with his article in any way. In his article he proposes a method for handling my two-year averaged RPA's which is quite serviceable and not contradictory to my methodology. If you prefer his method, please use it. The only addition I made to his article is to list alongside his one-year RPA age deltas my two-year RPA age deltas which, in turn, are based on his one-year age deltas.

I prefer a slightly different method for using

the results of his research from the one he proposes, and it is the one I used in the position-by-position ratings section. Since Keifetz's research shows the expected change in RPA from one year to the next year, this poses a problem when the basic RPA rating that I use is based on two-year averaging. Let's say that we are dealing with a hitter who is listed in the current (1993) edition as being 33 years old. His expected change in RPA from 32 years old, according to Keifetz's study, will be -3.8 basis points.

The two-year RPA, however, is an average RPA for this 33 year old player which includes his performances both as a 31 year old and a 32 year old. In other words, this two-year combination RPA rating contains the player's rating from a year, 31, when his play was, on average, of better quality than at the age of 32. We, therefore, must make a further adjustment to the -3.8 basis points. We cannot simply add up the changes of one year and the next. In this case you would have -2.6 (31 to 32) plus -3.8 (32 to 33) for a total of -6.4 basis points since that would be wrong, because this player is not going directly from 31 years old to 33 years old.

A player age 33 in this book, when considering a two year averaged RPA change, will have his age delta figured in the following manner: the sum of the RPA changes for year #1 + year #2 divided by 2 (for the two year averaging) *plus* the year #2 change divided by 2. Since we are using 2 years to divide each half of the above, the formula can be simplified to: the sum of the changes for Year #1 + Year #2 + Year #2 divided by 2.

Now let's figure the age delta for this 33 year old hitter. We add -2.6, -3.8 and -3.8 for a total of -10.2 basis points and then divide this total by 2. The resultant expected change in RPA that I will use in this book for a currently listed 33 year old hitter will be -5.1 basis points (-10.2 divided by 2). An even simpler way to figure the age delta is simply to add one-half the age delta for year #1 to the age delta for year #2. In this case you would divide -2.6 by 2 then add -3.8. The result is -1.3 plus -3.8 = -5.1, exactly the same result as above. These results will be rounded off for our purposes to -5 basis points. The eliminated fractional excess is too small a figure to merit giving any real consideration. This rounded figure of -5 points equals -.005, or 5/1000. That is already a very small figure. It would be pointless to break it down any further.

A LITTLE MORE MATHEMATICS

The on-base ability of a hitter is a little complicated to determine but, like most everything else in this book, it does not require a higher math education to understand. *What we need to know is how many runners are left on base after a particular hitter bats for the rest of the line-up to knock in.*

In order to determine the number of runners on base at the completion of a plate appearance it is necessary to make *subtractions* for some of the offensive acts listed in the earlier listed shaded box. A home run, for instance, has a *negative* effect on the number of players on base. In fact, there never is anyone on base after a home run. Yet the on-base averages listed in all the newspapers and books include homers. These on-base averages listed in the newspapers are not wrong, they just aren't useful as tools. They are flat statistics just sort of lying there doing nothing very useful. What we want and need is a tool for understanding the internal dynamics of a line-up. Yes, the homer should be awarded a plus in the standard on-base percentages for historical purposes, but for our purposes of attempting to understand how to structure a line-up we must have a tool which as accurately as possible can tell us how many runners will be on base after a particular hitter finishes his turn at bat.

Remember, the purpose of this part of the formula is to determine how many runs a player sets up for those batters that follow him in the line-up. Let's look at the home run as an example of such a subtraction. It is true that the homer puts the batter on the bases for his trip around them, for which we must certainly account. Our on-base part of the formula will add the batter as a base runner as is traditionally done. We need, however, to account for the fact that the home run hitter also removed himself from these same base paths -- and even more important -- that he removed whoever was already on base. This results in a plus 1 runner minus 1.44 runners (see above values) for a net on-base production of minus 0.44 for a home run.

Here are the on-base adjustment values needed to determine a hitter's Set-up RPA:

Add: total of walks + hits; to this add .10 (to account for the extra base) times the number of doubles, stolen bases, wild pitches and balks plus .20 times the number of triples.

Subtract: the number of times caught stealing and picked-off and the number of double plays grounded into and .29 times the number of singles, .41 times the number of doubles, .70 times the number of triples and 1.44 times the number of home runs.

After getting the total for the above on-base production, we need to divide this figure by the number of computed plate appearances to get a *per plate appearance average.* A hitter with an on-base total of 110 in 500 computed plate appearances would have a .220 plate appearance average.

The recent year-to-year major league computed per plate appearance average is about a .208 rating per batter (I use a lower average for the pitcher due to some differences in the types of data involved). The individual player, pitcher or team per plate appearance average can then be compared to this major league average to get the individual player or team on-base

adjustment figure.

Say that a batter's computed on-base production rating is .200 per plate appearance. This is poorer than the .208 average. We divide the player's .200 rating by the league average .208 rating to get an adjustment figure of .9615. This figure is then multiplied against one-half of the total run production determined by the linear weights listed on the previous page. The reason that we multiply it against only one-half is because we are adjusting for one-half of a batter's responsibility, i.e., his ability to set up runs as opposed to driving in runs.

A TEAM RPA FORMULA WORK-UP

Here is an example of a team's actual run scoring as compared to the estimated result created by use of the RPA formula:

**Atlanta Braves (1990 season)
Actual runs scored = 682**

Hits:

Singles = 925:   925 x .29 = 268.3 runs
Doubles = 263:   263 x .41 = 107.8 runs
Triples = 26:   26 x .70 = 18.2 runs
Home Runs = 162: 162 x 1.44 = 233.3 runs

Hit subtotal = 627.6 runs

To the above we add:

Walks + HBP = 500: 500 x .165 = 82.5 runs

Stolen Bases + Wild Pitches
+ Balks = 162:   162 x .10 = 16.2 runs

> *Adjusted subtotal = 726.3 runs*

> TOTAL OF COMPUTED RUNS FOR THE ATLANTA BRAVES DURING THE 1990 SEASON (PRIOR TO THE ON-BASE ADJUSTMENT) = 698.9

THE ON-BASE ADJUSTMENT

Atlanta's on-base Production:

Singles:	925
Doubles:	263
Triples:	26
Home Runs:	162
Walks:	473
Hit-By-Pitch:	27

> *Total = 1876 hitters who reached base*

From the above we subtract the following:

Caught Stealing + Ground into Double Play (GDP) = 157: 157 x -.165 = -25.9 runs

> *new subtotal = 700.4 runs*

Before we adjust for on-base production we need to add or subtract the value of the intentional walk. *This is used for team computations only.* The American League value for the intentional walk is plus .165 runs, which is the same value as a regular walk. There is little or no advantage to the intentional walk in the American League, due to the existence of the DH rule, since a regular hitter almost always follows.

The National League value is considerably different due to the fact that the intentional walk usually precedes the pitcher, which results in the waste of many scoring opportunities. The value of the intentional walk, therefore, is minus .04 runs (plus .3 plate appearances):

Adding the value of the intentional walk:

Intentional Walks = 37:

          37 x -.04   = -1.5 runs

To the 1876 that reached base we add the following adjustments:

Stolen Bases + Wild Pitches + Balks + Doubles = 425:   425 x .10 = 42.5
Triples = 26:   26 x .20 = 5.2

> *Adjusted on-base subtotal = 1923.7*

From this subtotal we subtract:

Caught Stealing + GIDP =   157
Hit subtotal (from pg. 15) =   627.6

> *On-base Production Total =   1139.1*

The on-base production total will be divided by the computed plate appearance total which is worked out as follows:

At-bats (less home runs) =   5342

Walks + HBP =	500
Intentional Walks (37 x .3) =	11.1
GIDP =	102

Plate Appearance Total: 5955.1

No plate appearance is charged for home runs since we are only dealing with that half of the run production formula dealing with setting up runs. The home run hitter is almost like the ghost who was never there but managed to leave his mark by causing runners who may have been on base at the time to "disappear". As explained in previous years, this non-inclusion of the home run in plate appearances is mostly a subjective judgment on my part. **In any case, the hitter is still charged with a plate appearance for the rest of the formula.**

On-base production results:

Total on-base production =	1139.1
Divided by plate appearances =	5955.1

Atlanta's On-base Rating for 1990 = .191

This rating is lower than the .208 rating which makes it below normal. We'll have to make a subtraction for this poorer rating:

Atlanta's On-Base Rating =	.191
Divided by Normal Rating =	.208

Atlanta's On-Base Production Variant = .918

Computed Runs (see above) =	698.9

Multiplied by On-Base Production
 Variant (698.9 x 0.918) = 641.6

Difference = - 57.3 runs

Remember: this is an example using 1990 Atlanta Braves' data to determine that portion of the formula dealing with on-base production. We must cut the above subtotal in half, since we are only modifying that half of the run production for each team which is accounted for by the on-base setting up of runs:

Divide -57.3 by 2:   = **-28.6 runs**

We then subtract the 28.6 runs from the previously listed total of Atlanta's computed runs for 1990 which equaled 698.9 to get a **final total of 670.3** runs as estimated by the formula. Since the actual runs scored by Atlanta were 682, we are only off by a little less than 12 runs.

INDIVIDUAL PLAYER ADJUSTMENTS

It is important to know how each hitter fares against the different types of pitchers he may face. There are 3 types of lefty and 3 types of righty pitchers: Groundball, flyball and neutral type. **Groundball and flyball match-ups are very important, although not as much as lefty-righty match-ups.** *In this book there are proposed line-ups for each major league team for all 6 types of pitchers these teams may face. There is one serious proviso, however. There really are* ***twelve*** types of pitchers since there is a very substantial group of pitchers who throw as if they were pitching from the opposite side. These pitchers I refer to as "reverse-type" pitchers. Therefore, there are six types each of standard and of reverse-type pitchers for anyone contemplating the correct setting-up of any particular lineup. As a new feature in this book, instead of simply saying "lefty" or "righty" after each pitcher's name following the word "Throws:", I've put in a more complete description such as "Groundball type, extreme reverse lefty" for Jim Abbott. The meaning of this cryptic remark is that Jim Abbott throws from the left side, but actually pitches like an extreme right-hander, and he's a primarily groundball producing pitcher.

We will include the Set-up and the Drive-in RPA ratings for each hitter against each of the 6 types of pitchers faced and include these ratings (but with the new adjustments for age) in the above-mentioned proposed line-ups. These Set-up and Drive-in ratings for each hitter against each type of pitcher to be faced are in the team section of this book. *Be prepared for many surprises!* These line-ups are anything but traditional. As stated last year, for example, I don't go along with the belief that you have to have a speedy runner at the top of the line-up. Speed is only a bonus. You can't steal first base. An even worse practice, in my view, is placing a slow contact hitter in the number two position. This is a prescription for the worst of all offensive disasters: the double

play! Better the slow hitter hits in front of the speedy one, but only if he makes up for his slow speed by getting on base frequently. Otherwise he should be farther back in the lineup.

THE DEFENSIVE RATING

The defensive rating, as used in this book, was introduced two years ago. *It is, unquestionably, my proudest contribution to the rating of player talent.* While there are various methods that exist, at least in part, for the rating of the offensive abilities of baseball players, this cannot be said for rating players defensively. There is no other method in existence that in any way approaches a realistic evaluation of defensive ability.

Let me say this loud and clear: the defensive ratings in this book are at least as good as the offensive ratings, if not better.

How can I be so certain of this? Isn't defensive ability more difficult to quantify than offensive ability? I certainly used to think so myself.

As it turns out, defense may actually be easier to quantify and rate. For instance, there are no walks, no hit-by-pitch on defense and the stolen base only affects the catcher's rating. It's somewhat simpler to rate defense since all we need to really know is how to determine the stadium and position variants on defense, and the direction, distance and outcome for every batted ball into a particular player's defensive area of responsibility. *Note:* I even published a proof of the defensive rating system in last year's edition.

In last year's edition I included the original explanation for how I determined the defensive ratings for each individual player. The thing was, however, that I had simplified the method used to determine defensive ability considerably, but it was too late to revise the explanation in time for the publication of the book.

The reason that there was a simplified method was because the stats I received from Stats, Inc. for the original method were not sufficiently broken down, and therefore I had to go through some necessary permutations to get my answers. The defensive data for last year's edition was the last section of data I received from Stats, Inc., and this was very late in the process of putting the book together. The new data, however, was much easier to work with since it had the defensive data broken down much more clearly. It was much easier and simpler to see how an individual defensive performer was doing his job.

As with all my data, I used all available defensive statistics for the previous two years. If a player, say Ozzie Smith, is playing shortstop for a particular team in a particular stadium, in this case the St. Louis Cardinals in Busch Stadium, I take the total

defensive computed RPA's of all the visiting shortstops playing against the Cardinals at shortstop at Busch Stadium and directly use this total average RPA of these shortstops as the measuring stick with which to judge Ozzie Smith's performance. I then do the same comparison for Ozzie Smith against all these other shortstops for all the away parks for when the Cardinals are on the road.

As an example, let's take player fictional player A. If the average defensive RPA for all visiting players who played his position at his stadium was .080 per batted ball through his position, which this player's defensive RPA worked out to .095 per batted ball, then this player would be rated negatively on defense at his home park. Let's say that, on average he would be expected to have 275 balls hit through his position in any one season for the 81 games at his home park. He would be giving away .015 runs (.095 minus .080) on each and every ball hit through his area. Multiply .015 by the total number of expected balls through his area (275) and you get a total of 4.125 runs given up by this fielder over the 81 games at his home park. Let's say we did the same thing for the 81 games where he played at the visitor's park, and using the RPA's garnered at those parks it turned out that his deficit was not as bad, say 2.200 runs given away. The total gift to the opposing team from this porous defender would come to 6.325 runs over a 162 game season if he were to play as a regular with such a defensive RPA. If we divide the 6.325 runs by the standard used here of 600 computed plate appearances, we end up with a defensive RPA of minus .01054 which we can safely round off to -.011 or in its shorthand form: -11 basis points. In other words this player gives up .011 runs on defense for each time he comes to the plate.

ADJUSTING FOR THE STADIUM

Since the defensive RPA's, as demonstrated above, already include the stadium and the position played at that stadium in computing them, no further stadium adjustment need be made. There will be some adjustments in terms of finding the median rating for players at that position, but nothing more than that is required.

The offensive RPA formula, as it is applied to individual players and pitchers, is further adjusted by the use of stadium variants. *The purpose of these variants is to enable us to equalize the offensive ratings for all the players regardless of the stadium in which they play.* Some stadiums greatly enhance offensive production and others reduce this production. A single or homer at Wrigley Field cannot have the same value as a single or homer at Shea Stadium, since Wrigley Field is a tremendous hitters' ballpark and Shea Stadium is a pitchers' ballpark.

Stadium variants are not constant from year-to-year due to many factors -- primarily the weather. *This is why combining multiple year stadium variants are incorrect.* In this year's introduction I again referred to my

article in the 1990 edition on Howard Johnson's illusion of having a bad year in 1988 when, in fact, he had actually improved as a hitter. Had I combined the stadium variants for the high-scoring 1987 season and the low-scoring 1988 season, I would never have discovered this fact. I would have been just like the Mets management and would have thought he had a poor year *(although I would never have tried to trade him after that season as they tried to do!)*. The weather can have an enormous effect on offensive production from one year to the next. It is usually quite cold in April and sometimes even well into May in many parts of this country. Those of you who have had the decidedly unenjoyable experience of hitting a baseball on very cold days know how the ball clangs off the bat and the bat rattles in your hand, and you should easily appreciate how cold weather reduces the number of home runs.

How is our stadium adjustment accomplished? Each major league team plays the exact same number of games at home, against the exact same teams as it plays on the road. Therefore, if you use the RPA formula on all the offensive acts at a particular stadium over the course of a full season by both the home and visiting teams so as to compute the total number of runs that should have been produced, as opposed to the total number of runs that should have been produced by the same teams when the home team goes on the road, you will be able to determine the stadium adjustment as it pertains to run scoring.

In the past I've used only the total runs actually scored, but I've come to the conclusion that the computed runs, i.e., the number of runs that should have been scored, given the number of singles, doubles, triples, etc., is the better number to use since it contains a far smaller amount of possible chance variation based on the far, far larger number of data points. Using this massive amount of internal offensive data for each park means that, after computing the amount of runs that should have been scored, we can then divide this computed figure by the number of computed plate appearances at that park so as to get the average RPA for each plate appearance at that stadium as opposed to the average RPA for each plate appearance for the same two teams when they went to the visitor's home ballpark.

Let's look at an example of a pitcher's park: the Houston Astrodome, 1992.

Computed runs at Astrodome:	639.4
Computed Plate Appearances:	6269
Average RPA per Plate Appearance:	.1020

Computed runs at Visitor Park:	668.3
Computed Plate Appearances:	6037
Average RPA per Plate Appearance:	.1107

Stadium Variant for Astrodome: 1.0853
(.1107 divided by .1020).

This means that the Astrodome was a pitcher's heaven in 1992 as compared to when the Astros and their opponents went on the road. The difference for play at the Astrodome was almost 9 RPA points lower per plate appearance. When evaluating two players, these 9 points can be quite significant, especially if the player being compared to performed at a hitter's park where the player RPA's were shifted several points in the opposite direction. Without adjusting for the stadium, a person could get a wildly inaccurate idea of the ability of a particular player.

Stadium variants can be applied only to one-half of a player's rating since he plays only half his games at his home park. In addition, stadium variants are further reduced by 10% because we don't want to unduly reward or penalize the home team player. A Red Sox player would still play several games at Fenway Park if he were on another American League team's roster. Therefore, stadium variants cannot be applied to the entire 81 games he played at any team's home park.

THE ROTISSERIE RATING

Many baseball fans are involved in rotisserie leagues. Equalizing player ratings by the use of these stadium variants is not what they are looking for. They want to know whom to draft. For that reason they want to know who'll produce the best figures for "their" team. If a Chicago Cub, playing in the friendly confines of Wrigley Field, can hit 40 home runs, then that is all they need to know. The fact that his production may be drastically curtailed if he were to play at Shea Stadium is irrelevant to rotisserie fans. This book, therefore, will provide these fans with a Rotisserie League rating (RL#) which will not include the stadium adjustment. *A word of caution:* A rotisserie league participant will still have to figure out who actually will be chosen to play, and these fans will still have to choose an occasional inferior player based on some of the quirky rules in his or her league.

Another reminder to rotisserie league participants: don't confuse good rotisserie league player-value with the actual on-the-field abilities of players! While managing your own team may be very exciting, fulfilling and highly enjoyable, if not downright addicting, *it isn't the same game as played on the field all across the world.* I have heard that some leagues try to come as close as possible to having rules which will approximate actual playing skills. These leagues which are the most serious deserve praise for their efforts. They should find the ratings in this book of the greatest help.

MORE ON THE DEFENSIVE RATING

Baseball is a sport filled with illusions, and nowhere else are these illusions more evident than on defense. In baseball, only one team takes the field at a time. This is the main source of the illusions created in our wonderful game. In other team sports both teams take the field at the same time and any player unable to perform in some fundamental way will be undressed publicly by his opponent. It's the most direct measure of skill, and easy to spot, even for the untrained eye. In baseball, however, the player guards territory, not another player. The player, therefore, who can guard the most territory will be the most valuable on defense -- *regardless of skills.* Skills help make the fast and quick player even better but usually cannot rescue a lead-footed player from being rated a defensive liability in these pages. In most cases, skills only create the *illusion of competence* in the slow-footed player.

The linear weights for singles, doubles, etc., as listed previously, are used to determine the number of runs given up at a particular fielding position at each stadium. For instance, the Dodger Stadium infield was the most difficult infield to play in the major leagues in 1990. More runs were produced by the fielding conditions in the infield at Dodger Stadium than at any other stadium in the major leagues! This means that when the very same players who played a particular infield position, both for the Dodgers and the visitors, went to the visitor's home stadium, these same fielders were turning batted balls into outs that were hits or errors at Dodger Stadium.

This data can be further broken down to show how each infield position contributed to this effect in that particular year or over a period of years. In the team section I will list the approximate difficulty for each position at each stadium, based on the last three years of data.

For the purposes of this study, the individual player defensive statistics I have utilized are limited to direction and outcome and have been proven sufficient for our needs. I only utilize ground ball data for the infielders and fly ball data for the outfielders in making these ratings.

Why not break the defensive data down further? **Because, in statistics, as you break the data down into smaller units you fall prey to subjective judgments based on too few occurrences.**

What causes stadium differences on defense? The causes are many. At some parks it is more obvious than at others. Left fielders at Fenway obviously cannot be adequately rated against left fielders at other ball parks without a huge stadium variant. A third baseman playing on a grass field will often encounter defensive differences from playing conditions at other grass fields and even bigger differences when moving onto a plastic surface.

Some infields are harder and/or more liable to bad bounces than others. Some have their grass cut lower than others. Some have their foul lines more sloped than others. Even the plastic infields can play differently from each other. Some are faster and others slower. Some are new and others old and worn. The lighting conditions and background and noise can have a noticeable affect. Heat, moisture, wind, glare, altitude and weather conditions all vary from stadium to stadium. All these elements can come into play to create peculiar playing conditions at every position at every ballpark.

One of the most beautiful aspects of baseball are these varied conditions. It is part of the **real charm** of this game. It would be a true shame, in my eyes, if the lords of baseball ever got it into their minds to attempt to homogenize our beautiful national pastime by eliminating these stadium differences. Judging from the construction of the newest ball parks, like Camden Yards, we won't have to worry, since it is clear that this uniqueness is consciously being preserved.

Stats, Inc.'s directional chart (see page 34) for all batted balls is very logical. This is the actual chart used by all the Stats, Inc. scorers to record direction and distance for all batted balls. The directional areas start from the foul territory adjacent to the left field stands (letter "A") over to the right field foul territory adjacent to those stands (letter "Z") in a fan shaped pattern.

Note: In the position-by-position ratings you will find the defensive rating for each player in the column headed "**DEF**", which is short for "Defense."

Here then are the assigned defensive areas for each defensive position, utilizing the lettering system on the previously referred to Stats, Inc. chart located on page 35:

First Base: U to X.
Second Base: N to T
Shortstop: H to M plus 90% of G.
Third Base: C to F plus 10% of G.
Left Field: C to I plus 60% of J.
Center Field: K to P plus 40% of J and 75% of Q.
Right Field: 25% of Q plus R to X.

The catcher's defensive ratings are much simpler. We merely add up all the stolen bases plus passed balls and multiply this figure by 0.10 runs and then subtract by 0.165 runs the number of caught stealing + picked off. We take the difference and average it out over the number of outs produced while he was catching and add 8 points. We add 8 points since the median rating on defense for the catcher position gave away 8 points and we need to compare individual catcher values to the median values of players at other positions. All the other positions, including the pitcher, are judged by the median of all players at their position. Their (+) or (-) rating is a comparison to this median for all players at that position. Adding 8 points establishes the proper relationship of each catcher to the median value for all catchers and to the median values of all other players. In fact, each defensive position, when I look at the defensive ratings, will find the median rated

player will be somewhat away from a zero (neutral) rating, and I adjusted each player's rating at each position so as to place the median rated defensive player at the zero point on my scale.

Another new addition to the current edition is the inclusion of the AAA and AA minor league data in the individual player and pitcher ratings. These minor league ratings have been adjusted to correspond to their Major League equivalents, after taking all the necessary factors into account. The important thing to remember is that these minor league ratings do work, as was shown in last year's essay.

In the individual player data in the team section, for Nelson Santovenia of the White Sox for instance, on the top line (above the line which breaks down the hitter's RPA vs. the six types of pitchers and the set-up/drive-in and overall two-year RPA) after "Bats Left", there's a series of numbers which indicate that Nelson has had 126 plate appearances against lefties (125L), 153 against righties (153R), 96 against groundball type pitchers (96G) and 62 plate appearances against flyball-type pitchers (62F) over the past three years. Three years of data are used to get the lefty-righty, groundball-flyball RPA ratings because two years of data would elicit too small a database in most cases, since we are taking pieces of the whole and analyzing these smaller pieces as against the whole. To the right of this data for Santovenia is the figure

549ML, which means that for the purposes of the overall two-year RPA rating, he had his 549 minor league computed plate appearances over the past two years integrated into his rating.

The RPA is a comprehensive rating that takes into account offensive ability, defensive ability, pitching, the position played, the stadium where the performance took place, the age of the player and AAA & AA minor league performance.

The most complete and accurate picture of player ability ever produced!

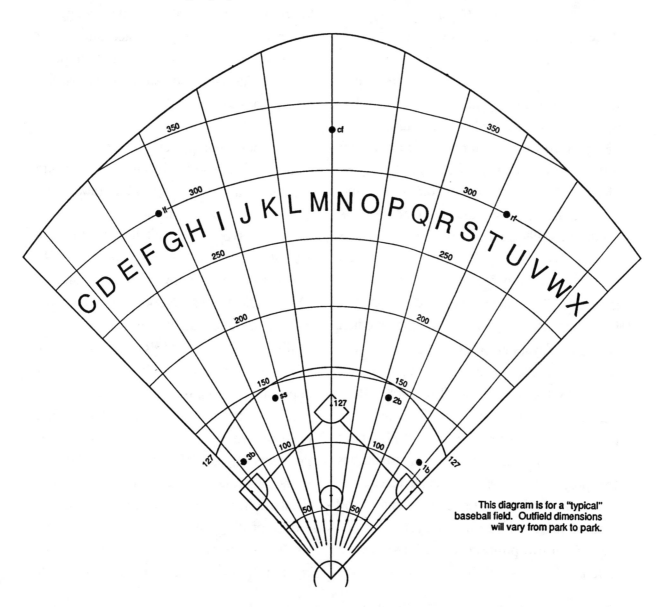

This diagram is for a "typical" baseball field. Outfield dimensions will vary from park to park.

STADIUM RUN ADJUSTMENTS FOR THE 1992 SEASON

In making the adjustments for park effects there is a basic assumption: Each league whether it be either major league, or AAA or AA minor league, is equivalent to any other league at the same level of play. In addition, it is possible to adjust the RPA ratings for player performance in the minor leagues to what its major league equivalent should be.

This means that the National League play is equivalent to the play in the American League. It means that the level of play in the AAA Pacific Coast League is equivalent in quality of play to the play of the AAA International League. It means that the offensive production in each league at the same level is equivalent, at least for our purposes. When stated in this way it is clear that this can't be 100% correct. There will be some difference between leagues, even at the same level of play. My assumption, and I believe it to be obviously correct, is that this difference is not significant enough to invalidate the method used.

When rating the AAA or AA minor leagues I first needed to adjust the run scoring to a figure equalized across each of the three leagues at each level. Denver and Omaha are both in the AAA American Association. Las Vegas and Portland are in the AAA

Pacific Coast League. The run scoring at each of these stadiums cannot be adjusted for home versus away and compared to each other until we can make a comparison of how much run scoring occurred in each of the three AAA leagues as a whole and compare these leagues against each other.

In 1992 the International League for AAA and the Eastern League for AA were, once again, the benchmark leagues against which the other leagues were measured because run scoring was held to a premium in these leagues. The 1991 season had been exceptional, due to the hot weather in the east, causing these two leagues to abdicate their normal position as the premier pitcher's leagues for AAA and AA. In 1991 the best pitcher's leagues were the American Association for AAA and the Southern League for AA. In 1992, however, the cold summer in the east returned the International League and the Eastern League to their usual position as pitcher's leagues. I always choose the best pitcher's leagues as the benchmark from which to measure the performances of minor league players since they provide us with an RPA figure that needs the least numerical adjustment in order to make the minor league RPA's equivalent to major league RPA's.

In other words, before I compared data from some of the extremely high scoring stadiums in the Pacific Coast League to what it would be in terms of the major leagues, I first "shrank" the data to the level of the best pitcher's league in AAA, i.e., the International League last year.

These "pitcher's" leagues became the standard against which the other leagues at their level were measured. This means that the league adjustment for these two pitcher's leagues should be 1.000, i.e., there is no downward adjustment of run scoring when compared to the other two leagues at the same level of play.

After determining the league adjustments for AAA and AA we can then make a park adjustment just as was described in the *Explanation of Player Statistics*.

A COMPLICATION

There is one proviso, however. The three AAA leagues do not play equal amounts of games with each team in their respective leagues. The PCL has a northern and a southern division. Most of the games are played within a team's division and the difference in run production is very significant between these divisions. The northern division has a number of pitcher's parks while the southern division is a hitter's paradise. In American Association there are eastern and western divisions. Sometimes, even within a division or league,

there are "irregular schedules". Sometimes these are simply games lost which are never made up. In any case, there is sometimes a wild variation in how these schedules are made up. This means that there are going to be different road variants for each team, depending on where they played when on the road in the AAA and AA minor leagues (except for the International League and the Eastern League whose road variant is standardized at 1.000). These road variants have to be made alongside a home park variant for any particular team. Both the road and home variants listed below already include the league adjustment in them.

Once we have determined the home and road variants we can then rate each minor league player's performance on the same scale regardless of the league or stadium where the performance took place. It is then a matter of comparing this performance with the actual performances of those players that went to the major leagues, or in the case of AA players, those that moved up to AAA, in order to determine the necessary RPA adjustment when a player moves up to the next level.

On the pages which follow are the stadium variant adjustments for each ballpark in the Major Leagues, the three AAA minor leagues and the three AA minor leagues together with the road variants, where necessary. All these variants, including the minor league variants, were produced by the RPA formula utilizing the entire spectrum

of offensive production in the process of determing these variants.

Please note that those stadiums with a higher variant than 1.000, e.g., a variant of 1.040, indicates a pitcher's park (or league) where offensive production, as per the RPA formula, has to be adjusted _**upwards**_ by multiplying this offensive production by this variant (1.040). A park (or league) with an adjustment of 0.920 is a hitter's park (or league) where offensive production has to be adjusted _**downwards**_ utilizing this (0.920) particular park or league variant:

***** MAJOR LEAGUE PARK VARIANTS FOR 1992 *****

AMERICAN LEAGUE:		NATIONAL LEAGUE:	
Baltimore:	1.0011	Atlanta:	0.9798
Boston:	0.9394	Chicago:	1.0036
California:	1.0190	Cincinnati:	0.9622
Chicago:	1.0652	Houston:	1.0853
Cleveland:	0.9261	Los Angeles:	1.0808
Detroit:	0.9507	Montreal:	0.9636
Kansas City:	1.0724	New York:	1.0531
Milwaukee:	1.1323	Philadelphia:	0.9954
Minnesota:	0.9728	Pittsburgh:	1.0103
New York:	0.9608	St. Louis:	1.0064
Oakland:	0.9961	San Diego:	0.8740
Seattle:	0.9772	San Francisco:	1.0130
Texas:	1.0230		
Toronto:	1.0059		

***** AAA MINOR LEAGUE PARK VARIANTS FOR 1992 *****

INTERNATIONAL LEAGUE:
League Variant (used for Away Park variant): 1.000

Columbus:	0.992	Scranton Wilkes-Barre:	0.927
Pawtucket:	0.953	Syracuse:	1.004
Richmond:	1.023	Tidewater:	1.090
Rochester:	0.966	Toledo:	1.060

AMERICAN ASSOCIATION:

	Home	Away		Home	Away
Buffalo:	1.083	0.923	Louisville:	0.926	0.950
Denver:	0.815	0.952	Nashville:	0.956	0.944
Indianapolis:	0.984	0.940	Oklahoma City:	0.882	0.940
Iowa:	0.893	0.939	Omaha:	0.973	0.925

PACIFIC COAST LEAGUE:

Northern Division:

	Home	Away
Calgary:	0.798	0.996
Edmonton:	0.860	0.984
Portland:	1.067	0.946
Tacoma:	1.063	0.947
Vancouver:	1.076	0.946

Southern Division:

	Home	Away
Albuquerque:	0.894	0.955
Colorado Springs:	0.905	0.954
Las Vegas:	0.831	0.966
Phoenix:	1.071	0.922
Tucson:	0.982	0.939

***** AA MINOR LEAGUE PARK VARIANTS FOR 1992 *****

EASTERN LEAGUE:
League Variant: 1.0000

Albany:	1.190
Binghampton:	1.050
Canton/Akron:	1.048
Hagerstown:	0.899
Harrisburg:	1.048
London:	0.822
New Britain:	1.129
Reading:	0.888

TEXAS LEAGUE:

	Home	Away
Arkansas:	0.971	1.001
El. Paso:	0.861	0.994
Jackson:	1.079	0.973
Midland:	0.865	0.994
San Antonio:	1.022	0.956
Shreveport:	1.000	0.992
Tulsa:	0.967	0.999
Wichita:	1.082	0.942

SOUTHERN LEAGUE:

	Home	Away		Home	Away
Birmingham:	1.187	0.934	Huntsville:	0.972	0.960
Carolina:	0.951	0.951	Jacksonville:	0.906	0.955
Charlotte:	0.886	0.963	Knoxville:	0.934	0.964
Chattanooga:	0.925	0.980	Memphis:	0.978	0.959
Greenville:	0.972	0.952	Orlando:	0.866	0.958

The Use of Player Age Changes to Make Better RPA Forecasts

By Brom Keifetz

I first met Mike Gimbel at the 1991 SABR convention in New York. He was hawking the 1990 and 1991 editions of his **Baseball Player and Team Ratings,** calling out to anyone who would listen: "this is a serious baseball inquiry; this is not a rotisserie book!" I walked up to him, introduced myself, and admitted it: "I enjoy rotisserie baseball." He said, "I know, I know, I just gotta get their attention." Maybe so, but I don't think he meant it. I still think Mike considers rotisserie baseball to be a thin trivialization of something important.

Well--*and I know Mike is going to hate having to read this*--I originally bought his book to give myself an edge in rotisserie. I had been tinkering with my own performance rating model. This model, I thought, might give me some advantage in pricing players for rotisserie auctions. When I saw the ad for Mike's book in **Baseball America,** I suspected that I had found the milk-and-honey-land. I spent the twelve bucks and change and got a better set of ratings than I could ever have generated myself. And I saved all that time. As it turned out, the RPA gave me more than just an edge in rotisserie, it gave me the feeling that I had "The Answer".

Unfortunately, good feelings don't last forever. Despite having these accurate ratings, the prediction problem never went away. Past performance may be the best indicator of future results, but where do you hang your hat? Steve Avery may have turned in a .096 last year, but what's he going to do this year? Danny Tartabull's first year with the Yankees yielded a .182; what did the Rockies and Marlins miss out on for 1993? What's the truer 1993 expectation for Randy Velarde--rotisserie-relevant with Charlie Hayes in Denver--the .090 or the .116 of 1993? What can the Japanese expect from Mel Hall? So much uncertainty remains.

Mike deals with the year to year variability in RPAs by forming a composite score of the player's last two years, with the assumption that most things in time return to the center. As far as I'm concerned, that's absolutely the right thing to do. There's too much variability in any player's one-year RPA, and to reach back three years exposes the analyst to the risk of using ratings which are irrelevant to a dynamic process. There is a shortcoming to the *uncorrected* two-year composite approach, however. It treats each player as a wholly abstract quantity, fixed in time, as opposed to the living, breathing, *aging* being he is. We all accept the notion that in the vast majority of cases, players improve for a while, hit a peak, then decline in ability to the point that they have to leave major league baseball. (Forget about Fisk, Ryan and Winfield. They're the exceptions, which is why they're so famous.) I wanted to get at some of the seemingly unexplainable flukiness. I wanted to know how the aging process is reflected in Mike Gimbel's RPAs, and I wanted to work out a way to combine that information with the RPAs in his book to make better forecasts. It's for those who, like myself, enjoy rotisserie baseball *and* consider themselves serious students of baseball, that I offer the results of my inquiries.

THE FIRST STEP

The key pieces of information for my study were the *incremental change* in RPA, i.e., the amount and direction of absolute change in a player's rating from one year to the next, and the age at which the change happened. I used RPA data from the 1987 through 1992 seasons. I only used the incremental changes for players with representative numbers of Computed Plate Appearances

or outs recorded. RPAs generated for 50 at-bat seasons weren't going to do me any good, although for players who split their seasons between two major league clubs, or between the majors and minors, I used an average RPA weighted by Computed Plate Appearances for hitters, outs recorded for pitchers. When the data were available, I also included performance changes that happened from year to year between minor league seasons--players going from AA to AAA, repeating at AA, repeating at AAA, and so forth. Because I wanted large samples and wanted them quickly, I made no distinctions between regulars and reserves, starters and relievers. I used the players' ages as reported in the 1990-1993 editions of the book, and for computational and typing ease multiplied all RPA by 1000 to get whole numbers. (I will refer on-and-off to these whole numbers as RPA "basis points" to distinguish them from real RPA values.) For example, for the 1992 baseball year, Carlos Baerga's incremental RPA change was +7 basis points: his 136 RPA from 1992 minus his 129 RPA from 1991. That 7 point RPA improvement was considered to have taken place from age 25 to age 26. I looked at the same data for pitchers. *(note: improvement for a pitcher is in the minus direction. The exact opposite of the hitter. -- editor)* For example, Charles Nagy's change was -30: 73 from 1992 minus 103 from 1991; age 24 to age 25. Bill Gullickson's change was +13: 109 from 1992 minus 96 from 1991; age 32 to age 33. Starting with the 1987 season, I separated hitters and pitchers, segmented each group by age change, age 20-to-age-21 through age 38-to-age-39, and added on a separate 40-plus category because I didn't want Fisk and Ryan to skew the results too much. For each age change category, I averaged up the performance changes.

	HITTERS			PITCHERS	
Age Change	Number in Sample	Average RPA Change		Number in Sample	Average RPA Change
20-to-21	7	+12		3	-32
21-to-22	15	+10		12	-19
22-to-23	46	+7		48	+2
23-to-24	84	+9		68	0
24-to-25	111	+6		114	-3
25-to-26	137	+6		112	-3
26-to-27	156	+5		112	0
27-to-28	142	-2		99	+5
28-to-29	137	+2		95	+1
29-to-30	125	-2		89	+10
30-to-31	113	-4		68	0
31-to-32	89	-2		65	0
32-to-33	63	-4		52	+5
33-to-34	45	-1		43	+5
34-to-35	32	-6		37	+5
35-to-36	25	-6		27	+5
36-to-37	19	-3		16	+3
37-to-38	14	-12		12	+1
38-to-39	9	-4		5	+16
40+	19	-5		16	+19

The expected trend obtained for both hitters and pitchers. The players got better for a while, hit their peaks, and then started to get worse. The absolute values of the year to year RPA changes got bigger as the ages moved away from the peak performance ages. The data as presented in these tables, however, were way too bouncy to use. The trends in sample sizes by age were pretty smooth. The average rates of change, however, were another story, jagged not only for the small samples of very young and very old players, but also for the larger samples at the mid-level ages. I believed that there was a trend, but I didn't believe that the jaggedness could be useful. How could pitchers get worse, on the average, by +10 basis points between ages 29 and 30 and not at all between ages 30 and 31? In order to be informative and useful as predictive devices, the results had to be smoothed out in some way.

THE REFINEMENT

I decided to use a simple linear regression analysis. The incremental performance changes were used as the dependent (Y) variable, while the associated ages of the changes were used as the independent, predictor, (X) variable. This is just good old XY-coordinate geometry with a twist. I plotted 1388 hitter-points and 1093 pitcher-points on the XY-graphs. Continuing with the Baerga, Belle, Nagy and Gulickson examples, Baerga's 1992 season was plotted with age 24--his age over the course of the most recent performance change--as the X-value, and +7--the change itself--as the Y-value. Belle's 1992 season

was (26, -2), Nagy's (25, -30), and Gullickson's (33, +13). Once the points were plotted, a line--the prediction line--was fit for each graph such as to minimize the squared distance between all the points in the graph and the line itself. The analysis also provided some useful information such as the probability that any linear association between the two variables obtained purely by accident (virtually no chance of that). It told how much of the overall variation in incremental RPA changes was explained by aging (3% for hitters, 2% for pitchers). It also told me how much error there was in the estimate (25 points for hitters, 24 basis points for pitchers).

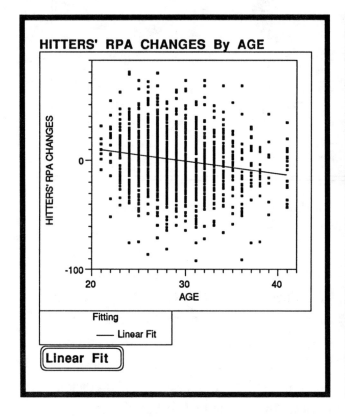

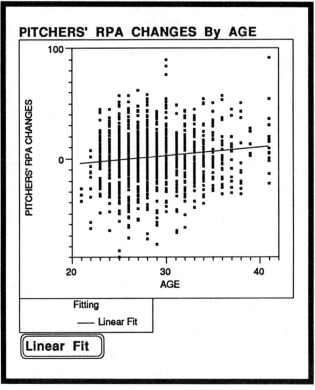

	WHAT THE LINES PREDICTED					
	Hitters:			**Pitchers:**		
	Expected	**2 Year***		**Expected**	**2 Year***	
	Change	**Averaged**		**Change**	**Averaged**	
New Age	**in RPA**	**RPA Changes**	**New Age**	**in RPA**	**RPA Changes**	
21	+10.2	+16	21	-4.3	-7	
22	+9.1	+14	22	-3.5	-6	
23	+7.9	+12	23	-2.7	-4	
24	+6.7	+11	24	-2.0	-3	
25	+5.6	+9	25	-1.2	-2	
26	+4.4	+7	26	-0.4	-1	
27	+3.2	+5	27	+0.3	0	
28	+2.2	+4	28	+1.1	+1	
29	+0.9	+2	29	+1.9	+2	
30	-0.3	0	30	+2.6	+3	
31	-1.4	-2	31	+3.4	+5	
32	-2.6	-4	32	+4.1	+6	
33	-3.8	-5	33	+4.9	+7	
34	-5.0	-7	34	+5.7	+8	
35	-6.1	-9	35	+6.5	+9	
36	-7.3	-11	36	+7.2	+10	
37	-8.5	-12	37	+8.0	+12	
38	-9.6	-14	38	+8.8	+13	
39	-10.8	-16	39	+9.5	+14	
40	-12.0	-17	40	+10.3	+15	
41	-13.1	-19	41	+11.1	+16	
42	-14.3	-21	42	+11.8	+17	
43	-15.4	-23	43	+12.6	+18	
44	-16.7	-24	44	+13.4	+20	
45	-17.8	-26	45	+14.1	+21	

* Rounded off (in Basis points) and used by Mike Gimbel in the position-by-position ratings.

HERE ARE SOME DETAILS

The equations (prediction formulas) of the hitters' and pitchers' lines came out as follows:

For hitters: **Predicted Incremental RPA Change = 34.81 - [1.169 times Age].**

For pitchers: **Predicted Incremental RPA Change = -20.345 = [0.765 times Age].**

These equations are, of course, in the old, familiar Y=mX+b form. Focus in on the slope terms in these equations, -1.169 for hitters and +0.765 for pitchers. These represent the movement in incremental

RPA performance changes predicted by the unit change--one year--in age. In other words, for hitters, the predicted incremental RPA change should move by approximately -1.17 RPA basis points from one year to the next for each position player or DH. For pitchers, the predicted incremental RPA change should move by approximately +.765 RPA basis points from one year to the next.

WHAT DOES ALL THIS MEAN?

1) It means that, *all other things being equal,* a hitter who is now 21 years old is expected in terms of Mike Gimbel's RPA to produce about .010 more runs per Computed Plate Appearance (CPA) than he did at age 20 *(Please note: I'm abandoning the big basis points and am going back to the true RPA scale now).* A 21-year-old pitcher should expect to allow about .004 fewer runs per batter faced than he allowed at age 20. A 31-year-old hitter should produce about .001 fewer runs per CPA than he did at age 30, while a 31-year-old pitcher should allow about .003 more runs per batter faced than he did at 30.

2) It means that, *all other things being equal,* a hitter who delivers a .120 season at age 24 should expect to peak out at .136 at age 29. If he stays healthy, he should recede to about .117 by age 35. Similarly, a pitcher who delivers a .100 season at age 24 should expect to peak out two years later with a .098. If he stays healthy (a pitcher? hah!), he should enjoy his last few moments in the afternoon sun and under the halogen lamps at 35 with a .129 RPA.

3) It means that, given these observations, we can assume for the time being that hitters tend to peak out at some point just after age 29, and pitchers tend to peak out at some point between 26 and 27. This contrasts somewhat with Bill James' findings. He found that hitters tend to peak at 26, while pitchers tend to peak at 27 *(Bill James Baseball Abstract, 1982)*. I'm definitely not saying that he's wrong and I'm right. I wouldn't dare. This article is not intended to be a critique of his work. The contrasting findings could be a result of measurement differences, differences in sample sizes, study design problems, randomness or any combination thereof. Until I make a follow-up study for the next edition of Mike Gimbel's book, however, I'll stick by the results as I have laid them out.

4) It means that the overall results obtained for pitchers in my study as well as in the Bill James study were counter-intuitive. Didn't we all expect that pitchers would peak later in life than hitters would? Haven't we been told about pitchers "learning hitters", "gaining maturity and smarts", becoming "wily veterans" and all that other stuff over and over again by sportscasters and writers, players and club officials? There may be a great deal less to all of that than meets the eye. Take a star pitcher who peaks out at age 27 with a .075 RPA. Using the results of this study, we can expect him to deliver

something like a .112 at 36. A .112 RPA at age 36 for a winning ball club is hardly inconsistent with, say, a 16-15 record and an ERA of 4.47. That's Rick Sutcliffe and his .110 1992 RPA! How about a 21-6 record, and a 4.04 ERA for a great club? That's Jack Morris and his .106 1992 RPA! A couple of "gutsy" pennant-race performances against divisional rivals on national TV and--voila!--you've got the "wily veteran" who "really knows the hitters", who has "really stabilized the young staff", who has "gotten better with age". Chose your cliche. We listen to that stuff and end up with very bad intuition. In RPA terms, Sutcliffe and Morris are formerly star pitchers whose abilities have decayed with age such that they are now eminently replaceable, no matter what the sportscasters say about "gutsiness" or "smarts" or "aging like vintage wines".

I think something else is going on here. Look at the slope terms of the prediction formulas--1.17 for hitters, 0.76 for pitchers--and you might be able to guess where I'm going with this. What's happening is probably just this: the abilities of both hitters and pitchers are decaying over time, but pitchers are decaying a little slower, thus they are hanging on to acceptable performance levels later on in their careers than are hitters. For whatever reason--the nature of the task, the required development of skills necessary to the task, the phases of the moon, you tell me--pitchers seem to be avoiding what Bill James calls "the white

space" (oblivion) better than hitters are.

HOW TO USE THE TABLES

Returning to the Avery, Tartabull, Velarde and Hall examples, here's how I would use the results of the study to make reasonable forecasts of 1993 RPAs. I'd start by looking at the two-year composite box. Avery has a composite rating of .093. He accomplished this by age 22, so I would consider the 1993 season to be his 23rd year, and therefore add the age 23 pitcher correction (-.003) to the two-year composite, for a forecasted performance of .090 for 1993. Tartabull's composite is .186. He accomplished this by age 30, so I would consider the 1993 season to be his 31st year, and therefore add the age 31 hitter correction (-.001) to his composite for a forecasted performance of .185 for 1993. Velarde, .108 composite and age 30, gets the same correction as Tartabull did, giving the probable Yankee third baseman a forecasted RPA of .1097. Hall, .122 composite and age 33, gets the 34-year-old hitter correction (-.005), for a .117 forecasted rating in Japan. Probably good enough for him to put up Cromartie-like numbers.

SOME CAVEATS

1. *All other things are never equal!* The age formula explained only 2 to 3 percent of the total variation in incremental RPAs among the 1388 year to year RPA changes for hitters and the 1093 year to year RPA changes for pitchers. You can explain the

rest of the variation with any other factor or factors you like: injuries, psychological factors, changes in personal lives, or just plain old randomness. As players age, all of those other things are going on as well, and there's not a damned thing that a rotisserie player or serious baseball analyst can do about them. There's probably not a great deal more that a club official or team physician can do either.

2. *Variable estimates.* The RPA changes predicted by age were quite conservative (plus or minus 0, .001 and .002 for the important mid-range ages), which is not surprising considering how important to winning and losing seemingly small differences in abilities are. There was also a lot of error--the political polling kind, not the careless kind--in the estimates. For hitters, the standard error of the estimate was plus or minus .025 runs per CPA. For Pitchers, it was .024. This means that obtaining an actual 1993 performance of up to .024 or .025 runs away from the estimate should be quite normal for any player. In truth, one can only expect to get about 2 or 3 RPA exact estimates out of any hundred. Don't forget that the RPA itself is not *reality*, but instead just a *close representation of reality*, and as such must contain some error. This hardly invalidates the formulas, however. In general, the formulas should help an analyst work out the general

direction of things, but please don't expect to be able to forecast performance with 1/1000 run accuracy. That cannot be done.

3. *This is only a first pass at a very thorny problem.* Next year's edition will have the results of a bigger, more comprehensive, better designed study. I may segment players by role and by quality as well as by age. I decided against that approach for this study because I needed large samples quickly and wanted to avoid introducing too much subjectivity--*is he a reliever or a spot starter?*--into the study. I suspected I would have to deal with enough randomness as it was. With any luck, I'll be able to work out those classification kinks in some sort of pseudo-realistic and user-friendly way. Next year, I may also look at relative--that is, percentage--changes in ability by age. Anyway, the analyses cannot help but get better with time and effort. "All models are wrong. Some are useful" Or so said G.E.P. Box. The Run Production Average in *Mike Gimbel's Baseball player and Team Ratings* is the most useful model for understanding baseball that I've come across. I only hope that my work with performance and aging has added value and will continue to add value to his outstanding model.

Brom Keifetz
Los Angeles, California
December 1992

SECTION II

PLAYER RANKINGS

FIRST BASE
AMERICAN LEAGUE

NAME	TEAM	SET-UP	DRIVE-IN	DEFENSE	AGE	TOTAL RPA
Premier Players:						
Frank Thomas	Chicago	.112	.079	-3	+11	.199
Mark McGwire	Oakland	.083	.077	+1	+2	.163
Rafael Palmeiro	Texas	.081	.071	-2	+4	.154
John Olerud	Toronto	.071	.063	+4	+11	.149
John Jaha	Milwaukee	.071	.066	**	+7	.144
Cecil Fielder	Detroit	.069	.074	-5	+2	.140
Wally Joyner	Kansas City	.068	.064	+2	0	.134
Qualified Starting Players:						
Kent Hrbek	Minnesota	.067	.063	+5	-4	.131
Tino Martinez	Seattle	.049	.063	+9	+9	.130
Paul Sorrento	Cleveland	.058	.065	-1	+5	.127
Reggie Jefferson	Cleveland	.056	.058	**	+11	.125
Scott Cooper	Boston	.064	.052	**	+9	.125
Randy Milligan	Baltimore	.069	.058	-1	-2	.124
Mo Vaughn	Boston	.060	.062	-10	+9	.121
Job in Danger or not yet ready for prime time:						
Don Mattingly	New York	.057	.056	-1	-2	.110
Franklin Stubbs	Milwaukee	.053	.059	+1	-4	.109
David Segui	Baltimore	.046	.046	+6	+4	.102
Lee Stevens	California	.048	.052	-10	+9	.099
Pete O'Brien	Seattle	.048	.056	-5	-7	.092
Carlos Martinez	Cleveland	.047	.054	-17	+5	.089
Pat Tabler	Toronto	.044	.040	**	-7	.077
Dave Bergman	Detroit	.060	.051	-19	-16	.076

Median qualified starter rating: .133

FIRST BASE
NATIONAL LEAGUE

NAME	TEAM	SET-UP	DRIVE-IN	DEFENSE	AGE	TOTAL RPA
Premier Players:						
Jeff Bagwell	Houston	.083	.068	+2	+11	.164
Will Clark	San Francisco	.085	.076	-3	+4	.162
Fred McGriff	San Diego	.085	.077	-6	+4	.160
John Kruk	Philadelphia	.087	.068	+5	-2	.158
Mark Grace	Chicago	.071	.057	+7	+4	.139
Orlando Merced	Pittsburgh	.071	.061	-1	+7	.138
Brian Hunter	Atlanta	.053	.064	+4	+11	.132
Qualified Starting Players:						
Eric Karros	Los Angeles	.054	.065	+1	+9	.129
Hal Morris	Cincinnati	.067	.059	-3	+5	.128
Jeff Conine	Florida	.061	.059	**	+7	.127
Archi Cianfrocco	Montreal	.058	.058	+2	+7	.125
Greg Colbrunn	Montreal	.058	.054	**	+12	.124
Ricky Jordan	Philadelphia	.051	.058	+10	+5	.124
Gary Redus	Pittsburgh	.072	.064	-2	-11	.123
Job in Danger or not yet ready for prime time:						
Sid Bream	Atlanta	.063	.061	-4	-4	.116
Rod Brewer	St. Louis	.053	.046	**	+7	.106
Eddie Murray	New York	.058	.060	-5	-11	.102
Andres Galarraga	Colorado	.042	.055	-1	-2	.094
Gerald Perry	St. Louis	.048	.054	-7	-4	.091
Todd Benzinger	Los Angeles	.043	.049	-9	+2	.085
Pedro Guerrero	St. Louis	.050	.051	-18	-11	.072

Median qualified starter rating: .131

SECOND BASE
AMERICAN LEAGUE

AME	TEAM	SET-UP	DRIVE-IN	DEFENSE	AGE	TOTAL RPA
Premier Players:						
Lou Whitaker	Detroit	.093	.071	+3	-7	.160
Roberto Alomar	Toronto	.085	.064	-1	+11	.159
Tony Phillips	Detroit	.082	.061	+19	-5	.157
Chuck Knoblauch	Minnesota	.071	.054	+15	+11	.151
Julio Franco	Texas	.080	.069	-6	-2	.141
Carlos Baerga	Cleveland	.070	.063	-6[1]	+11	.138
Randy Ready	Oakland	.068	.051	+19	-4	.134
Lance Blankenship	Oakland	.074	.056	+2	+2	.134
Qualified Starting Players:						
Keith Miller	Kansas City	.075	.060	-4	+2	.133
Pat Kelly	New York	.051	.055	+4	+9	.119
Mike Gallego	New York	.063	.057	+2	-4	.118
Bret Boone	Seattle	.046	.060	-1	+12	.117
Bobby Rose	California	.049	.050	+8	+9	.116
Donnie Hill	Minnesota	.065	.050	0	-4	.111
Job in Danger or not yet ready for prime time:						
Dave Rohde	Cleveland	.052	.054	**	+4	.110
Scott Fletcher	Boston	.056	.050	+5	-7	.104
Curt Wilkerson	Kansas City	.045	.047	+13[2]	-2	.103
Joey Cora	Chicago	.061	.048	-12	+5	.102
Luis Sojo	Toronto	.041	.048	+6	+7	.102
Luis Quinones	Minnesota	.047	.050	**	0	.097
Jeff Frye	Texas	.055	.043	-10	+7	.095
Harold Reynolds	Baltimore	.055	.049	-11	-4	.089
Steve Sax	Chicago	.052	.052	-12	-4	.088
Jose Lind	Kansas City	.035	.043	+4	+4	.086
Jim Gantner	Milwaukee	.042	.047	+11	-14	.086
Ken Oberkfell	California	.049	.044	**	-11	.082
Billy Ripken	Baltimore	.031	.039	+6	+4	.080
Terry Shumpert	Kansas City	.030	.043	-2	+7	.078
Al Newman	Texas	.030	.044	+5	-4	.075
Mark McLemore	Baltimore	.038	.039	-13	+4	.068

Median qualified starter rating: .134

[1] Carlos Baerga seems to have had a breakthrough year defensively in 1992 and was above average defensively. Baerga's defensive rating combines this positive 1992 defensive data with his poor 1991 defensive data, however, since I rely on two-year totals for my ratings.

[2] Curtis Wilkerson had a few more opportunities over these last two seasons at shortstop (with a rating of +1) but has a better rating at second base. That is why he's listed here, rather than shortstop.

SECOND BASE
NATIONAL LEAGUE

NAME	TEAM	SET-UP	DRIVE-IN	DEFENSE	AGE	TOTAL RPA
Premier Players:						
Ryne Sandberg	Chicago	.087	.074	+11	-5	.167
Geronimo Pena	St. Louis	.075	.069	+12	+9	.165
Robby Thompson	San Francisco	.076	.068	+7	0	.151
Luis Alicea	St. Louis	.057	.056	+22	+5	.140
Craig Biggio	Houston	.081	.061	-8	+5	.139
Jeff Kent	New York	.061	.064	-2	+11	.134
Delino DeShields	Montreal	.065	.058	-2	+12	.133
Qualified Starting Players:						
Jose Oquendo	St. Louis	.063	.049	+10	+4	.126
Willie Randolph	New York	.075	.053	-1	-14	.113
Jeff Treadway	Atlanta	.053	.050	+7	+2	.112
Mark Lemke	Atlanta	.047	.045	+13	+5	.110
Mickey Morandini	Philadelphia	.054	.050	-2	+7	.109
Jody Reed	Los Angeles	.054	.048	+6	0	.108
Juan Samuel	Cincinnati	.061	.057	-7	-4	.107
Job in Danger or not yet ready for prime time:						
Billy Doran	Cincinnati	.062	.053	-5	-7	.103
Jeff McKnight	New York	.044	.056	**	+2	.102
Lenny Harris	Los Angeles	.050	.048	-2[1]	+4	.100
John Patterson	San Francisco	.040	.050	**	+9	.099
Jeff Branson	Cincinnati	.042	.046	**	+9	.097
Greg Litton	San Francisco	.043	.051	-4[2]	+5	.095
Wally Backman	Philadelphia	.056	.044	**	-5	.095
Eric Young	Colorado	.047	.045	-14	+9	.087
Paul Faries	San Francisco	.039	.041	**	+5	.085
Tim Teufel	San Diego	.055	.055	-22	-7	.081
Rex Hudler	St. Louis	.035	.048	**	-4	.079
Junior Noboa	Cincinnati	.031	.044	**	+4	.079
Kurt Stillwell	San Diego	.046	.047	-32	+5	.066

Median qualified starter rating: .130

[1] Lenny Harris is a much better defensive third baseman than second baseman and may get to play at third more often (as a substitute or in a platoon with Mike Sharperson) now that the Dodgers have acquired Jody Reed.

[2] Based on just 99 ground balls through his position in 1991 & 1992. I violated my minimum standards since one more chance was not likely to make much of a difference in his rating.

THIRD BASE
AMERICAN LEAGUE

NAME	TEAM	SET-UP	DRIVE-IN	DEFENSE	AGE	TOTAL RPA
Premier Players:						
Robin Ventura	Chicago	.075	.064	+15	+9	.163
Edgar Martinez	Seattle	.090	.070	-6	+2	.156
Jerry Browne	Oakland	.057	.048	+15	+7	.127
Leo Gomez	Baltimore	.067	.063	-12	+9	.127
Scott Leius	Minnesota	.057	.051	+11	+5	.124
Wade Boggs	New York	.073	.056	+2	-7	.124
Skeeter Barnes	Detroit	.062	.068	+3	-9	.124
Qualified Starting Players:						
Dean Palmer	Texas	.064	.068	-21	+11	.122
Gregg Jefferies	Kansas City	.055	.056	-2	+9	.118
Hensley Meulens	New York	.050	.057	**	+9	.116
Kevin Seitzer	Milwaukee	.059	.054	+3	0	.116
Tony Perezchica	Cleveland	.053	.054	**	+7	.114
Scott Brosius	Oakland	.047	.060	**	+7	.114
Scott Livingstone	Detroit	.057	.053	-2	+5	.113
Jim Thome	Cleveland	.054	.059	-14	+14	.113
Job in Danger or not yet ready for prime time:						
Darnell Coles	Toronto	.055	.057	**	0	.112
Kelly Gruber	California	.049	.058	+3	0	.110
Mike Pagliarulo	Minnesota	.048	.049	+15	-4	.108
Tim Hulett	Baltimore	.044	.054	+12	-4	.106
Rene Gonzales	California	.057	.053	-4	-2	.104
Rich Amaral	Seattle	.046	.058	**	0	.104
Mike Blowers	Seattle	.046	.052	**	+5	.103
Carney Lansford	Oakland	.061	.054	-4	-9	.102
Gary Gaetti	California	.048	.056	+4	-7	.101
Damion Easley	California	.037	.039	+2	+12	.090
Craig Worthington	Cleveland	.047	.052	-15	+5	.089
Brook Jacoby	Cleveland	.039	.043	-12	-5	.065

Median qualified starter rating: .123

THIRD BASE
NATIONAL LEAGUE

NAME	TEAM	SET-UP	DRIVE-IN	DEFENSE	AGE	TOTAL RPA
Premier Players:						
Dave Hollins	Philadelphia	.090	.075	+1	+7	.173
Bret Barberie	Florida	.082	.064	+13	+9	.168
Gary Sheffield	San Diego	.069	.071	+2	+11	.153
Terry Pendleton	Atlanta	.068	.069	+7	-4	.140
Matt D. Williams	San Francisco	.053	.070	+6	+5	.134
Mike Sharperson	Los Angeles	.074	.057	+2	-2	.131
Willie Greene	Cincinnati	.057	.058	**	+16	.131
Qualified Starting Players:						
Steve Buechele	Chicago	.063	.061	+6	-2	.128
Ken Caminiti	Houston	.054	.060	+11	+2	.127
Chris Sabo	Cincinnati	.060	.065	-1	0	.124
Dave Magadan	Florida	.079	.053	-8	0	.124
Chris Donnels	Houston	.065	.057	-8	+7	.121
John Wehner	Pittsburgh	.054	.044	+14	+9	.121
Todd Zeile	St. Louis	.066	.058	-9	+5	.120
Job in Danger or not yet ready for prime time:						
Jeff King	Pittsburgh	.049	.060	+6	+4	.119
Sean Berry	Montreal	.053	.056	**	+7	.116
Bill Pecota	New York	.054	.053	+5	-4	.108
Dave Hansen	Los Angeles	.044	.050	-2	+11	.103
Doug Strange	Chicago	.052	.045	**	+4	.101
Tim Wallach	Los Angeles	.048	.051	+6	-9	.096
Ernest Riles	Houston	.046	.052	+1	-4	.095
Charlie Hayes	Colorado	.042	.055	-9	+5	.093
Chico Walker	New York	.058	.053	-12	-7	.092
Tracy Woodson	St. Louis	.050	.040	**	0	.090
Craig Wilson	St. Louis	.041	.042	**	+4	.087
Dave Anderson	Los Angeles	.035	.050	**	-4	.081
Gary Scott	Florida	.038	.041	-12	+11	.078
Luis Salazar	Chicago	.036	.053	-3	-11	.075
Denny Walling	Houston	.025	.029	**	-14	.040

Median qualified starter rating: .130

SHORTSTOP
AMERICAN LEAGUE

NAME	TEAM	SET-UP	DRIVE-IN	DEFENSE	AGE	TOTAL RPA
Premier Players:						
Craig Grebeck	Chicago	.073	.059	+22	+4	.158
Cal Ripken	Baltimore	.071	.070	+5	-4	.142
Pat Listach	Milwaukee	.061	.049	+18	+9	.137
Travis Fryman	Detroit	.058	.062	+1	+12	.133
Mike Bordick	Oakland	.058	.051	+17	+5	.131
Jeff Reboulet	Minnesota	.055	.044	+23	+4	.126
Bill Spiers	Milwaukee	.062	.059	-10[1]	+7	.118
Qualified Starting Players:						
Jeff Huson	Texas	.057	.052	+2	+4	.115
Greg Gagne	Kansas City	.042	.050	+23	-2	.113
Manuel Lee	Texas	.049	.045	+12	+5	.111
Andy Stankiewicz	New York	.051	.045	+11	+4	.111
Randy Velarde	New York	.055	.053	+2	0	.110
Omar Vizquel	Seattle	.048	.045	+8	+9	.110
Tim Naehring	Boston	.052	.047	-3	+9	.105
Spike Owen	New York	.057	.053	-3	-2	.105
Job in Danger or not yet ready for prime time:						
Gary DiSarcina	California	.038	.043	+14	+9	.104
Ozzie Guillen	Chicago	.038	.045	+16	+4	.103
Alan Trammell	Detroit	.058	.054	-5	-7	.100
Rico Rossy	Kansas City	.046	.046	+1	+4	.097
Luis Rivera	Boston	.047	.047	-3	+4	.095
Dickie Thon	Texas	.048	.052	-1	-7	.092
Mark Lewis	Cleveland	.040	.045	-5	+12	.092
John Valentin	Boston	.060	.050	-27	+9	.092
Dave Howard	Kansas City	.041	.043	-2	+9	.091
Jose Hernandez	Cleveland	.033	.044	**	+12	.089
Dale Sveum	Chicago	.043	.047	-4	+2	.088
Alfredo Griffin	Toronto	.038	.039	+18	-9	.086
Felix Fermin	Cleveland	.040	.043	-6	+2	.079
Esteban Beltre	Chicago	.027	.042	-3	+9	.075
Jeff Schaefer	Cleveland	.025	.039	-9	-4	.051
Mario Diaz	Texas	.038	.041	-49	0	.030

Median qualified starter rating: .117

[1] Carryover from last year's rating since he had no opportunities at shortstop in 1992.

SHORTSTOP
NATIONAL LEAGUE

NAME	TEAM	SET-UP	DRIVE-IN	DEFENSE	AGE	TOTAL RPA
Premier Players:						
Barry Larkin	Cincinnati	.083	.068	+6	+4	.161
Jeff Blauser	Atlanta	.075	.065	-2[1]	+5	.143
Ozzie Smith	St. Louis	.069	.056	+16	-14	.127
Juan Guerrero	Houston	.056	.058	**	+9	.123
Jay Bell	Pittsburgh	.062	.061	-5	+5	.123
Juan Bell	Philadelphia	.033	.040	+37	+11	.121
Rey Sanchez	Chicago	.048	.045	+17	+9	.119
Qualified Starting Players:						
Jose Offerman	Los Angeles	.050	.045	0	+11	.106
Wilfredo Cordero	Montreal	.062	.050	-23	+16	.105
Jose Vizcaino	Chicago	.039	.043	+10	+11	.103
Tony Fernandez	New York	.054	.050	-4	0	.100
Dick Schofield	New York	.050	.045	+5	0	.100
Casey Candaele	Houston	.050	.049	0	-2	.097
Royce Clayton	San Francisco	.039	.047	-4	+14	.096
Job in Danger or not yet ready for prime time:						
Mike Benjamin	San Francisco	.027	.042	+20	+5	.094
Shawon Dunston	Chicago	.050	.057	-16	+2	.093
Rafael Belliard	Atlanta	.037	.039	+19	-2	.093
Tim Jones	St. Louis	.037	.043	+11	0	.091
Kevin Elster	New York	.049	.049	-11	+4	.091
Jose Uribe	San Francisco	.041	.047	+7	-5	.090
Andujar Cedeno	Houston	.040	.054	-16	+12	.090
Alex Arias	Florida	.058	.043	-21	+9	.089
Freddie Benavides	Colorado	.030	.034	+15	+7	.086
Kim Batiste	Philadelphia	.030	.042	-16	+11	.067
Rafael Ramirez	Houston	.039	.044	-12	-5	.066
Jeff Kunkel	Cincinnati	.027	.039	**	0	.066
Tom Foley	Pittsburgh	.029	.035	+7	-5	.066
Walt Weiss	Florida	.041	.040	-19	+2	.064
Eric Yelding	Cincinnati	.032	.040	-15[2]	+5	.062
Gary Green	Cincinnati	.027	.032	**	0	.059
Craig Shipley	San Diego	.037	.042	-23	+2	.058

Median qualified starter rating: .113

[1] Blauser's 1992 defensive data indicate a big breakthrough. He was a +7, but his poor defensive rating from the 1991 season prevents him from garnering a superior rating in this book until he shows that 1992 was no fluke by repeating his success in 1993.

[2] Yelding had no defensive opportunities at shortstop in 1992. The above rating is a carryover from the previous year.

LEFT FIELD
AMERICAN LEAGUE

NAME	TEAM	SET-UP	DRIVE-IN	DEFENSE	AGE	TOTAL RPA
Premier Players:						
Rickey Henderson[1]	Oakland	.105	.074	+3	-7	.175
Greg Vaughn	Milwaukee	.065	.069	+31	+5	.170
Shane Mack	Minnesota	.086	.072	+7	+2	.167
Brady Anderson	Baltimore	.082	.066	+6	+4	.158
Ivan Calderon	Boston	.073	.070	+5	0	.148
Tim Raines	Chicago	.079	.061	+9	-5	.144
Mike Felder	Seattle	.061	.056	+26	0	.143
Qualified Starting Players:						
Derek Bell	Toronto	.059	.057	+15	+11	.142
Henry Cotto	Seattle	.062	.062	-3	-2	.119
Thomas Howard	Cleveland	.050	.049	+15	+4	.118
Kevin McReynolds	Kansas City	.071	.063	-11	-5	.118
Rob Ducey	Texas	.054	.054	+4	+5	.117
Mel Hall	New York	.059	.063	-3	-4	.115
Bob Zupcic	Boston	.056	.053	-2	+7	.114
Kevin Reimer	Milwaukee	.060	.066	-16	+4	.114
Job in Danger or not yet ready for prime time:						
Glenallen Hill	Cleveland	.044	.065	-8	+5	.106
John Cangelosi	Detroit	.052	.048	**	+2	.102
Mike Greenwell	Boston	.056	.053	-10	+2	.101
Dan Gladden	Detroit	.048	.050	+8	-9	.097
Luis Polonia	California	.053	.053	-16	+4	.094
Greg Briley	Seattle	.044	.051	-7	+5	.093
Mark Carreon	Detroit	.038	.049	-1	+2	.088
Jack Daugherty	Texas	.045	.041	+1	-4	.083
Billy Hatcher	Boston	.041	.045	-6	-4	.076
John Moses	Seattle	.044	.035	**	-9	.070

Median qualified starter rating: .143

[1]The 1993 season could be the 'Last Hurrah' for Rickey Henderson's long tenure as the top left fielder in the American League. 1994 looks like the season when someone finally overtakes this magnificent performer. Either Greg Vaughn or Shane Mack appear to be the most likely candidates, although my money is on Vaughn. Vaughn's improvement over the last two years has been relentless while Rickey's defensive ability seems to be slipping as age and injuries begin to take its usual toll.

LEFT FIELD
NATIONAL LEAGUE

NAME	TEAM	SET-UP	DRIVE-IN	DEFENSE	AGE	TOTAL RPA
Premier Players:						
Barry Bonds	San Francisco	.115	.090	+5	+4	.214
Bip Roberts	Cincinnati	.073	.059	+36	+2	.170
Luis Gonzalez	Houston	.056	.064	+28	+9	.157
Milt Thompson	Philadelphia	.074	.067	+17	-5	.153
Bernard Gilkey	St. Louis	.060	.057	+29	+7	.153
Moises Alou	Montreal	.068	.066	+12	+7	.153
John VanderWal	Montreal	.065	.065	+14	+7	.151
Qualified Starting Players:						
Kevin Mitchell	Cincinnati	.079	.075	-14	0	.140
Roberto Kelly	Cincinnati	.057	.061	+9	+4	.131
Ron Gant	Atlanta	.067	.068	-18	+5	.122
Candy Maldonado	Chicago	.072	.067	-13	-4	.122
Glenn Braggs	Cincinnati	.059	.060	0	0	.119
Lonnie Smith	Atlanta	.081	.060	-18	-12	.111
Pete Incaviglia	Philadelphia	.056	.059	-11	+4	.108
Mariano Duncan	Philadelphia	.048	.057	-1	+2	.106
Job in Danger or not yet ready for prime time:						
Daryl Boston	Colorado	.066	.063	-26	+2	.105
Jerald Clark	Colorado	.045	.053	+3	+2	.103
Kevin Bass	New York	.048	.058	-3	-5	.098
Phil Stephenson	San Diego	.055	.047	**	-4	.098
Derrick May	Chicago	.043	.057	-16	+11	.095
Mark Leonard	San Francisco	.058	.058	-25	+4	.095
Jerome Walton	Chicago	.042	.046	**	+5	.093
Alex Cole	Colorado	.059	.052	-24	+5	.092
Kal Daniels	Chicago	.061	.060	-34	+2	.089
Eric Davis	Los Angeles	.063	.057	-36	0	.084
Chris James	San Francisco	.045	.050	-13	0	.082
Oscar Azocar	San Diego	.031	.037	+4	+5	.077
Monty Fariss	Florida	.059	.057	-55	+9	.070
Kevin Ward	San Diego	.032	.045	-10	-2	.065

Median qualified starter rating: .146

CENTERFIELD
AMERICAN LEAGUE

NAME	TEAM	SET-UP	DRIVE-IN	DEFENSE	AGE	TOTAL RPA
Premier Players:						
Ken Griffey, Jr.[1]	Seattle	.078	.077	-6	+12	.161
Devon White	Toronto	.065	.063	+26	0	.154
Juan Gonzalez	Texas	.060	.078	0	+12	.150
Kenny Lofton	Cleveland	.058	.051	+18	+9	.136
Kirby Puckett	Minnesota	.069	.067	-1	-2	.133
Mike Devereaux	Baltimore	.059	.066	+5	+2	.132
Ellis Burks	Boston	.060	.060	-2	+4	.122
Qualified Starting Players:						
Shawn Abner	Chicago	.045	.047	+20	+7	.119
Robin Yount	Milwaukee	.063	.058	+10	-12	.119
Bernie Williams	New York	.063	.058	-14	+11	.118
Dave Henderson	Oakland	.067	.066	-19	-7	.107
Brian McRae	Kansas City	.044	.051	+1	+9	.105
Lance Johnson	Chicago	.044	.050	+6	+2	.102
Eric Fox	Oakland	.051	.049	**	+2	.102
Job in Danger or not yet ready for prime time:						
Chad Curtis	California	.057	.055	-23	+11	.100
Steve Lyons	Boston	.043	.044	+16	-4	.099
Gary Pettis	Oakland	.055	.047	+3	-7	.098
Milt Cuyler	Detroit	.057	.050	-20	+11	.098
Willie Wilson	Oakland	.046	.047	+7	-12	.088
Herm Winningham	Boston	.033	.040	+6	-2	.077

Median qualified starter rating: .121

[1]1992 was a big breakthrough year defensively for Griffey. In the 1992 book I had been
negative about his defense since I had expected this breakthrough to take place in 1991.
Young players often have trouble defensively in their first year, but Griffey's problems had
extended through two full seasons, which I took to be a bad sign. Fortunately, my
apprehensions were misplaced. The reason that the defensive rating for Griffey shows a
minus six points is because all my ratings include two years of data. In this case it included
both the very poor 1991 defensive rating and the good 1992 defensive rating. Griffey's
rating in next year's book ought to be very positive, provided he maintains the 1992
defensive level of play.

CENTERFIELD
NATIONAL LEAGUE

NAME	TEAM	SET-UP	DRIVE-IN	DEFENSE	AGE	TOTAL RPA
Premier Players:						
Lenny Dykstra	Philadelphia	.093	.066	-4	+2	.157
Andy Van Slyke	Pittsburgh	.090	.073	-7	-4	.152
Deion Sanders	Atlanta	.064	.067	+10	+9	.150
Ray Lankford	St. Louis	.065	.067	+7	+9	.148
Reggie Sanders	Cincinnati	.073	.066	-1	+9	.147
Marquis Grissom	Montreal	.061	.062	+4	+9	.136
Brett Butler	Los Angeles	.084	.059	0	-9	.134
Qualified Starting Players:						
Steve Finley	Houston	.068	.062	-5	+5	.130
Dave Gallagher	New York	.055	.050	+28	-4	.129
Otis Nixon	Atlanta	.065	.054	+10	-5	.124
Willie McGee	San Francisco	.063	.056	+9	-7	.121
Dave Martinez	San Francisco	.061	.057	-2	+4	.120
Stan Javier	Philadelphia	.057	.048	+8	+4	.117
Junior Felix	Florida	.051	.053	+2	+9	.115
Job in Danger or not yet ready for prime time:						
Darrin Jackson	San Diego	.049	.062	0	+2	.113
Darren Lewis	San Francisco	.053	.044	+6	+9	.112
Tommy Gregg	Atlanta	.053	.054	**	+2	.109
Sammy Sosa	Chicago	.041	.057	-2	+11	.107
Dwight Smith	Chicago	.048	.053	-2	+2	.101
Vince Coleman	New York	.063	.055	-21	-2	.095
Howard Johnson[1]	New York	.067	.070	-43	-4	.090
Doug Dascenzo	Chicago	.047	.046	-7	+4	.090
Gerald Young	Houston	.051	.047	-17	+4	.085
Ryan Thompson	New York	.045	.053	-38	+9	.069

Median qualified starter rating: .132

[1]HoJo belongs in the infield where he would get a much higher rating. Whoever came up with the brilliant idea of moving him to centerfield gets the 'dunce-of-the-year' award.

RIGHT FIELD
AMERICAN LEAGUE

NAME	TEAM	SET-UP	DRIVE-IN	DEFENSE	AGE	TOTAL RPA
Premier Players:						
Danny Tartabull	New York	.103	.083	-9	0	.177
Ruben Sierra	Oakland	.068	.068	+12	+5	.153
Rob Deer	Detroit	.073	.071	+13	-4	.153
Paul O'Neill	New York	.063	.063	+17	+2	.145
Jay Buhner	Seattle	.067	.069	+5	+4	.145
Chito Martinez	Baltimore	.069	.075	-4	+5	.145
Joe Carter	Toronto	.062	.074	+12	-4	.144
Qualified Starting Players:						
Kevin Koslofski	Kansas City	.059	.058	+17	+7	.141
Jose Canseco	Texas	.074	.079	-19	+4	.138
Turner Ward	Toronto	.060	.053	+15	+5	.133
Dan Pasqua	Chicago	.069	.063	0	-2	.130
Daryl Hamilton	Milwaukee	.067	.060	-2	+4	.129
Mark Whiten	Cleveland	.053	.054	+14	+7	.128
Warren Newson	Chicago	.083	.059	-18	+4	.128
Job in Danger or not yet ready for prime time:						
Pedro Munoz	Minnesota	.048	.061	+5	+11	.125
Mike Huff	Chicago	.051	.054	+14	+2	.121
Dion James	New York	.064	.054	**	0	.118
Gary Thurman	Kansas City	.042	.049	+23	+4	.118
Tom Brunansky	Boston	.061	.060	-1	-4	.116
Jim Eisenreich	Kansas City	.052	.053	+14	-5	.114
Luis Mercedes	Baltimore	.050	.051	**	+11	.112
Dann Howitt	Seattle	.048	.055	**	+4	.107
Joe Orsulak	Baltimore	.060	.055	-10	0	.105
Gene Larkin	Minnesota	.053	.050	0	0	.103
Von Hayes	California	.045	.046	+13	-7	.097
Jose Gonzalez	California	.037	.045	+10	+4	.096
Chris Gwynn	Kansas City	.056	.060	-27	+4	.093
Jesse Barfield	New York	.037	.058	0	-5	.090
Andre Dawson	Boston	.058	.070	-27	-14	.087
Mike Kingery	Oakland	.040	.043	**	-2	.081

Median qualified starter rating: .143

RIGHT FIELD
NATIONAL LEAGUE

NAME	TEAM	SET-UP	DRIVE-IN	DEFENSE	AGE	TOTAL RPA
Premier Players:						
Dave Justice	Atlanta	.084	.071	+19	+7	.181
Phil Plantier	San Diego	.081	.071	+2	+12	.166
Larry Walker	Montreal	.072	.073	+13	+7	.165
Bobby Bonilla	New York	.081	.070	+4	+2	.157
Felix Jose	St. Louis	.065	.063	+9	+5	.142
Lloyd McClendon	Pittsburgh	.076	.063	+6	-5	.140
Kirk Gibson	Pittsburgh	.066	.063	+13	-9	.133[1]
Qualified Starting Players:						
Darryl Strawberry	Los Angeles	.074	.072	-14	0	.132
Ruben Amaro	Philadelphia	.048	.051	+22	+5	.126
Jim Lindeman	Philadelphia	.068	.054	**	0	.122
Tony Gwynn	San Diego	.061	.057	+7	-4	.121
Dave Clark	Pittsburgh	.057	.064	**	0	.121
Mike Simms	Houston	.057	.054	**	+9	.120
Cecil Espy	Cincinnati	.056	.056	+3	+2	.117
Job in Danger or not yet ready for prime time:						
Mitch Webster	Los Angeles	.059	.058	+4	-5	.116
Billy Ashley	Los Angeles	.045	.056	**	+14	.115
Gary Varsho	Cincinnati	.060	.062	-7	-2	.113
Braulio Castillo	Colorado	.043	.054	**	+11	.108
Jim Vatcher	San Diego	.055	.043	**	+7	.105
Brian Jordan	St. Louis	.035	.060	**	+9	.104
Tom Marsh	Philadelphia	.029	.050	+18	+5	.102
Cory Snyder	Los Angeles	.047	.056	-4	0	.099
Dale Murphy	Philadelphia	.048	.056	+6	-11	.099
Karl Rhodes	Houston	.045	.045	-2	+11	.099
Wes Chamberlain	Philadelphia	.049	.059	-19	+7	.096
Chris Jones	Houston	.042	.048	**	+5	.095
Dante Bichette	Colorado	.042	.057	-6	+2	.095
Darren Reed	New York	.037	.048	**	+5	.090
Eric Anthony	Houston	.050	.060	-34	+9	.085
Henry Rodriguez	Los Angeles	.038	.050	-45	+9	.052

Median qualified starter rating: .133

[1] Gibson's retirement was more a question of pride and injuries, rather than loss of skills.

CATCHER
AMERICAN LEAGUE

NAME	TEAM	SET-UP	DRIVE-IN	DEFENSE	AGE	TOTAL RPA

Premier Players:

NAME	TEAM	SET-UP	DRIVE-IN	DEFENSE	AGE	TOTAL RPA
Mickey Tettleton	Detroit	.086	.073	-1	-4	.154
Chris Hoiles	Baltimore	.071	.068	-3	+5	.141
Mike MacFarlane	Kansas City	.066	.071	-1	+4	.140
Dave Nilsson	Milwaukee	.056	.057	+7	+12	.132
Ron Karkovice	Chicago	.060	.063	+7	+2	.132
Ed Sprague	Toronto	.065	.057	**	+9	.131
Mike Stanley	New York	.079	.061	-11	+2	.131

Qualified Starting Players:

NAME	TEAM	SET-UP	DRIVE-IN	DEFENSE	AGE	TOTAL RPA
Jim Leyritz	New York	.066	.060	+2	+2	.130
Ivan Rodriguez	Texas	.038	.047	+15	+16	.116
Terry Steinbach	Oakland	.054	.056	+4	0	.114
Matt Nokes	New York	.050	.067	-8	+2	.111
Lance Parrish	Seattle	.049	.062	+8	-11	.108
Brian Harper	Minnesota	.060	.058	-6	-5	.107
B.J. Surhoff	Milwaukee	.047	.050	0	+4	.101

Job in Danger or not yet ready for prime time:

NAME	TEAM	SET-UP	DRIVE-IN	DEFENSE	AGE	TOTAL RPA
John Orton	California	.046	.042	+7	+5	.100
Pat Borders	Toronto	.043	.053	+2	+2	.100
Chad Kreuter	Detroit	.045	.045	+6	+4	.100
Mark Parent	Baltimore	.052	.055	-5	-2	.100
Greg Myers	California	.041	.050	-6	+7	.092
Brent Mayne	Kansas City	.037	.042	+1	+11	.091
Dave Cochrane	Seattle	.044	.044	***	+2	.090
Ron Tingley	California	.039	.044	+12	-5	.090
Lenny Webster	Minnesota	.045	.044	-5	+5	.089
Dave Valle	Seattle	.045	.048	-1	-4	.088
Jeff Tackett	Baltimore	.035	.045	+2	+5	.087
Geno Petralli	Texas	.044	.044	+3	-4	.087
Sandy Alomar, Jr.	Cleveland	.036	.041	+3	+7	.087
Bob Melvin	Boston	.040	.044	0	-2	.082
Carlton Fisk	Chicago	.045	.054	+2	-20	.081
Jamie Quirk	Oakland	.042	.044	+6	-14	.078
Andy Allanson	Milwaukee	.035	.041	+4	-2	.078
Mike Fitzgerald	California	.043	.050	-12	-4	.077
Matt Merullo	Chicago	.038	.045	-15	+5	.073
Nelson Santovenia	Kansas City	.032	.057	-14	-2	.073
Junior Ortiz	Cleveland	.036	.037	+5	-5	.073
Rick Dempsey	Baltimore	.045	.048	-2	-18	.073
John Russell	Texas	.050	.050	-26	-2	.072
John Marzano	Boston	.036	.034	0	+2	.072
Tony Pena	Boston	.037	.042	+1	-9	.071

Median qualified starter rating: .131

CATCHER
NATIONAL LEAGUE

NAME	TEAM	SET-UP	DRIVE-IN	DEFENSE	AGE	TOTAL RPA
Premier Players:						
Darren Daulton	Philadelphia	.085	.074	0	0	.159
Rick Wilkins	Chicago	.058	.059	+4	+9	.130
Don Slaught	Pittsburgh	.074	.062	+1	-7	.130
Hector Villanueva	St. Louis	.060	.058	-3	+4	.119
Eddie Taubensee	Houston	.052	.054	-1	+11	.116
Francisco Cabrera	Atlanta	.044	.060	**	+7	.111
Tom Prince	Pittsburgh	.051	.050	+1	+4	.106
Qualified Starting Players:						
Kirt Manwaring	San Francisco	.046	.047	+7	+5	.105
Todd Hundley	New York	.042	.055	-7	+12	.102
Tom Lampkin	San Diego	.046	.046	+3	+4	.099
Mike LaValliere	Pittsburgh	.054	.051	-2	-4	.099
Dan Walters	San Diego	.046	.050	-5	+7	.098
Carlos Hernandez	Los Angeles	.041	.050	-3	+9	.097
Mike Scioscia	Los Angeles	.056	.051	-4	-7	.096
Tom Pagnozzi	St. Louis	.040	.049	+7	0	.096
Benito Santiago	Florida	.036	.053	+2	+5	.096
Joe Girardi	Colorado	.046	.045	+1	+4	.096
Rick Cerone	Montreal	.056	.050	+4	-14	.096
Job in Danger or not yet ready for prime time:						
Steve Decker	Florida	.040	.048	+1	+5	.094
Joe Oliver	Cincinnati	.037	.051	0	+5	.093
Greg Olson	Atlanta	.049	.047	-6	-4	.086
Scott Servais	Houston	.038	.042	-4	+9	.085
Charlie O'Brien	New York	.038	.042	+7	-2	.085
Jeff Reed	Cincinnati	.046	.045	-9	0	.082
Mackey Sasser	New York	.042	.051	-11	0	.082
Damon Berryhill	Atlanta	.036	.053	-12	+2	.081
Dann Bilardello	San Diego	.039	.042	+4	-5	.080
Darrin Fletcher	Montreal	.037	.047	-11	+7	.080
Craig Colbert	San Francisco	.034	.039	**	+5	.078
Gary Carter	Montreal	.048	.049	-7	-14	.076
Scott Bradley	Cincinnati	.043	.038	-9	-4	.068
Steve Lake	Chicago	.030	.040	+4	-9	.065
Rich Gedman	St. Louis	.030	.040	-14	-5	.051

Median qualified starter rating: .106

CATCHER DATA*
AMERICAN LEAGUE

NAME	OUTS	STOLEN BASES	CAUGHT STEALING	PICKED -OFF	PASSED BALLS	PITCHER E.R.A.
Premier Players:						
Mickey Tettleton	8131	193	70	0	17	4.47
Chris Hoiles	4782	140	44	0	7	3.97
Mike MacFarlane	7003	156	51	3	20	3.92
Dave Nilsson	1164	21	12	0	0	3.60
Ron Karkovice	5546	112	62	6	9	3.66
Ed Sprague	279	7	1	0	1	2.52
Mike Stanley	3434	116	29	0	20	4.27
Qualified Starting Players:						
Jim Leyritz	664	18	11	0	6	4.31
Ivan Rodriguez	5000	89	85	7	18	4.05
Terry Steinbach	7888	187	98	2	19	3.88
Matt Nokes	7017	248	70	4	26	4.46
Lance Parrish	7280	174	99	3	35	3.57
Brian Harper	9269	302	90	0	26	4.01
B.J. Surhoff	9088	232	91	2	21	3.88
Job in Danger or not yet ready for prime time:						
John Orton	2316	53	30	1	3	3.95
Pat Borders	7983	220	106	5	30	3.76
Chad Kreuter	1688	32	18	1	5	4.66
Mark Parent	1736	59	16	2	2	3.68
Greg Myers	4731	135	38	0	19	3.85
Brent Mayne	3301	84	34	0	6	3.70
Dave Cochrane	496	10	5	0	7	5.28
Ron Tingley	2259	48	38	1	4	3.77
Lenny Webster	1265	36	8	1	2	3.24
Dave Valle	8225	195	73	3	28	4.08
Jeff Tackett	1641	36	17	2	10	3.62
Geno Petralli	4795	116	61	3	26	4.15
Sandy Alomar, Jr.	6532	141	71	0	19	4.09
Bob Melvin	4075	106	40	1	6	4.40
Carlton Fisk	6582	166	83	1	26	3.85
Jamie Quirk	3222	89	51	0	4	4.15
Andy Allanson	1388	27	12	1	3	4.81
Mike Fitzgerald	5005	205	45	0	8	3.59
Matt Merullo	731	25	5	0	6	3.70
Nelson Santovenia	1691	68	17	0	12	3.50
Junior Ortiz	4366	95	48	6	14	3.96
Rick Dempsey	2260	67	27	1	10	4.07
John Russell	646	30	3	0	5	3.47
John Marzano	1869	50	22	0	7	4.06
Tony Pena	10280	260	106	5	18	3.71

* *Based on 3-year totals.*

CATCHER DATA*
NATIONAL LEAGUE

NAME	OUTS	STOLEN BASES	CAUGHT STEALING	PICKED -OFF	PASSED BALLS	PITCHER E.R.A.
Premier Players:						
Darren Daulton	9098	250	97	3	20	4.15
Rick Wilkins	3385	95	51	2	9	4.08
Don Slaught	5011	145	64	1	13	3.49
Hector Villanueva	2296	65	25	1	11	3.37
Eddie Taubensee	2956	86	35	2	13	4.13
Francisco Cabrera	353	10	4	0	3	4.29
Tom Prince	673	19	9	0	2	3.85
Qualified Starting Players:						
Kirt Manwaring	4143	85	52	1	9	3.82
Todd Hundley	3686	123	35	1	13	3.28
Tom Lampkin	822	27	15	0	3	3.84
Mike LaValliere	7112	229	86	2	12	3.34
Dan Walters	1297	47	16	0	2	3.50
Carlos Hernandez	1572	48	18	1	7	3.73
Mike Scioscia	8523	268	88	3	22	3.34
Tom Pagnozzi	8596	213	129	0	11	3.64
Benito Santiago	8971	226	96	5	14	3.64
Joe Girardi	5567	140	69	0	25	3.95
Rick Cerone	2920	67	36	2	13	3.77
Job in Danger or not yet ready for prime time:						
Steve Decker	2463	63	29	0	9	3.98
Joe Oliver	8458	221	93	4	32	3.58
Greg Olson	7450	240	64	0	11	3.68
Scott Servais	1854	53	14	1	3	3.40
Charlie O'Brien	4524	131	76	5	7	3.78
Jeff Reed	3657	128	31	0	10	3.52
Mackey Sasser	2810	138	45	1	11	3.98
Damon Berryhill	3414	116	25	0	19	3.32
Dann Bilardello	813	29	16	0	2	2.36
Darrin Fletcher	2709	112	27	0	4	2.99
Craig Colbert	651	16	8	0	6	3.98
Gary Carter	5091	223	77	1	9	3.20
Scott Bradley	2574	80	18	0	11	3.86
Steve Lake	2171	55	30	1	7	4.15
Rich Gedman	2622	115	30	0	13	3.48

* Based on 3-year totals.

DESIGNATED HITTER
AMERICAN LEAGUE

NAME	TEAM	SET-UP	DRIVE-IN	AGE	TOTAL RPA
Premier Players:					
Paul Molitor	Toronto	.089	.072	-11	.150
Chili Davis	California	.083	.069	-4	.148
Brian Downing	Texas	.091	.070	-18	.143
Albert Belle	Cleveland	.055	.074	+7	.136
Kevin Maas	New York	.066	.063	+5	.134
Glenn Davis	Baltimore	.068	.067	-2	.133
Harold Baines	Oakland	.069	.065	-5	.129
Dave Winfield	Minnesota	.074	.074	-19	.129
Qualified Starting Players:					
Sam Horn	Baltimore	.056	.070	+2	.128
Jack Clark	Boston	.074	.062	-12	.124
George Bell	Chicago	.048	.064	-5	.107
Randy Bush	Minnesota	.052	.053	-7	.098
Rance Mulliniks	Toronto	.060	.046	-11	.095
George Brett	Kansas City	.054	.056	-16	.094
Job in Danger or not yet ready for prime time:					
Hubie Brooks	California	.046	.057	-11	.092
Alvin Davis	California	.048	.047	-4	.091
John Morris	California	.040	.044	-2	.082

Median qualified starter rating: .129

SECTION III

PITCHER RANKINGS

STARTING PITCHERS - 110 INNINGS PLUS
AMERICAN LEAGUE

NAME	TEAM	AGE	RPA	NAME	TEAM	AGE	RPA
Premier Starting Pitchers:				*Continued from column #1:*			
Roger Clemens	Boston	+3	.072	Julio Valera	California	-3	.113
Jim Abbott	New York	-2	.084	Scott Sanderson	New York	+10	.113
Mike Mussina	Baltimore	-3	.085	Eric King	Detroit	+1	.113
Charles Nagy	Cleveland	-2	.086	Bob Welch	Oakland	+10	.113
Melido Perez	New York	-1	.087	Kelly Downs	Oakland	+6	.114
Juan Guzman	Toronto	-1	.090	Kirk McKaskill	Chicago	+5	.115
Kevin Appier	Kansas City	-2	.091	Walt Terrell	Detroit	+8	.116
John Smiley	Minnesota	0	.091	Rick Sutcliffe	Baltimore	+10	.116
Scott Erickson	Minnesota	-3	.092	Bobby Witt	Oakland	+1	.116
David Cone	Kansas City	+2	.093	Bob Milacki	Baltimore	+1	.116
Kevin Brown	Texas	0	.093	Todd Stottlemyre	Toronto	0	.116
Mark Langston	California	+6	.094				
Frank Viola	Boston	+6	.094	*Job in Danger or not yet ready:*			
John Doherty	Detroit	-2	.095	Mark Gubicza	Kansas City	+3	.117
Jack McDowell	Chicago	-1	.096	Jose Mesa	Cleveland	-1	.118
Jaime Navarro	Milwaukee	-2	.096	Frank Tanana	Detroit	+14	.119
Chris Bosio	Seattle	+2	.097	Rich DeLucia	Seattle	+1	.119
Dave Fleming	Seattle	-4	.097	Ricky Bones	Milwaukee	-4	.120
Jose Guzman	Texas	+2	.099	Hipolito Pichardo	Kansas City	-4	.120
Kevin Tapani	Minnesota	+1	.099	Danny Darwin	Boston	+12	.121
Mark Leiter	Detroit	+2	.102	Mike Boddicker	Kansas City	+9	.121
Bill Wegman	Milwaukee	+3	.102	Dave Stewart	Toronto	+9	.125
John Dopson	Boston	+2	.102	Bert Blyleven	California	+16	.131
Erik Hanson	Seattle	0	.102	Tim Leary	Seattle	+8	.132
Scott Kamieniecki	New York	+1	.103				
Mike Gardiner	Boston	0	.104				
Luis Aquino	Kansas City	0	.104				
Craig Lefferts	Baltimore	+9	.104				
Randy Johnson	Seattle	+2	.105	*Median qualified starter rating: .105*			
Qualified Starting Pitchers:							
Jimmy Key	New York	+5	.106				
Dennis Cook	Cleveland	+3	.107				
Mike Moore	Detroit	+7	.108				
Tom Gordon	Kansas City	-2	.109				
Chuck Finley	California	+3	.109				
Rod Nichols	Cleveland	0	.109				
Ben McDonald	Baltimore	-2	.110				
Joe Hesketh	Boston	+7	.110				
Bill Gullickson	Detroit	+7	.110				
Ron Darling	Oakland	+6	.110				
Alex Fernandez	Chicago	-4	.111				
Nolan Ryan	Texas	+20	.112				
Jack Morris	Toronto	+12	.113				
David Wells	Toronto	+2	.113				

Note: The above list includes all pitchers with at least 110 innings pitched in 1992 <u>or</u> at least 220 innings pitched in 1991 & 1992 combined (includes innings as a reliever).

STARTING PITCHERS - 110 INNINGS PLUS
NATIONAL LEAGUE

NAME	TEAM	AGE	RPA	NAME	TEAM	AGE	RPA
Premier Starting Pitchers:				*Continued from column #1:*			
Bill Swift	San Francisco	+5	.070	Rheal Cormier	St. Louis	-2	.106
Greg Maddux	Atlanta	-1	.073	Greg Hibbard	Chicago	+1	.106
Jose Rijo	Cincinnati	0	.075	Brian Barnes	Montreal	-2	.107
Tom Glavine	Atlanta	-1	.078	Mark Clark	St. Louis	-3	.108
Bret Saberhagen	New York	+1	.081	Kyle Abbott	Philadelphia	-3	.109
Mike Morgan	Chicago	+7	.082	Bud Black	San Francisco	+9	.110
Curt Schilling	Philadelphia	-1	.083	Mark Gardner	Montreal	+3	.111
Sid Fernandez	New York	+3	.084	Jimmy Jones	Houston	+1	.112
Dwight Gooden	New York	+1	.085	Danny Jackson	Philadelphia	+3	.113
Steve Avery	Atlanta	-6	.087	Tom Browning	Cincinnati	+6	.114
Zane Smith	Pittsburgh	+6	.088	Bob Walk	Pittsburgh	+10	.115
Andy Benes	San Diego	-2	.088				
Terry Mulholland	Philadelphia	+2	.089	*Job in Danger or not yet ready:*			
Greg Swindell	Houston	0	.089	Bryn Smith	Colorado	+12	.116
John Smoltz	Atlanta	-2	.089	Jose DeLeon	Philadelphia	+6	.116
Wally Whitehurst	San Diego	+1	.090	Shawn Boskie	Chicago	0	.117
Chris Nabholz	Montreal	-2	.091	Bill Krueger	Montreal	+8	.117
Dennis Martinez	Montreal	+12	.092	Butch Henry	Colorado	-3	.117
Doug Drabek	Houston	+3	.092	Anthony Young	New York	-1	.120
Frank Castillo	Chicago	-4	.092	Jack Armstrong	Florida	0	.120
Randy Tomlin	Pittsburgh	-1	.095	Darryl Kile	Houston	-3	.123
Ken Hill	Montreal	0	.096	Charlie Hough	Florida	-20	.134
Bob Tewksbury	St. Louis	+6	.096				
Chris Hammond	Cincinnati	-1	.096				
Greg W. Harris	San Diego	+2	.097				
Tom Candiotti	Los Angeles	+9	.098				
Tim Belcher	Cincinnati	+5	.098				
Ramon Martinez	Los Angeles	-3	.098	*Median qualified starter rating: .100*			
Donovan Osborne	St. Louis	-4	.099				
Trevor Wilson	San Francisco	-1	.099				
Mark Portugal	Houston	+3	.100				
Mike Bielecki	Atlanta	+7	.100				
Bruce Hurst	San Diego	+8	.100				
Qualified Starting Pitchers:							
Omar Olivares	St. Louis	-2	.101				
Charlie Leibrandt	Atlanta	+10	.102				
Orel Hershiser	Los Angeles	+8	.102				
Pete Harnisch	Houston	-1	.102				
Tommy Greene	Philadelphia	-2	.103				
Pete Schourek	New York	-4	.104				
Kevin Gross	Los Angeles	+5	.104				
Bob Ojeda	Los Angeles	+9	.105				
Jim DeShaies	San Diego	+6	.105				
John Burkett	San Francisco	+1	.105				

STARTING PITCHERS - 75 INNINGS PLUS
BOTH LEAGUES

NAME	TEAM	AGE	RPA	NAME	TEAM	AGE	RPA
AMERICAN LEAGUE:				**NATIONAL LEAGUE:**			
Premier Starting Pitchers:				*Premier Starting Pitchers:*			
Cal Eldred	Milwaukee	-2	.103	None			
Arthur Rhodes	Baltimore	-4	.103				
Joe Grahe	California	-2	.104	*Qualified Starting Pitchers:*			
Rick Reed	Kansas City	+1	.105	Cliff Brantley	Philadelphia	-3	.104
				Tim Wakefield	Pittsburgh	-1	.110
Qualified Starting Pitchers:				Frank Seminara	San Diego	-2	.110
Todd Burns	Texas	+2	.106	Pete Smith	Atlanta	-1	.111
Scott Scudder	Cleveland	-3	.109	Willie Blair	Colorado	0	.112
Dennis Rasmussen	Kansas City	+7	.109	Pedro Astacio	Los Angeles	-4	.114
Mike Magnante	Kansas City	0	.109				
Jeff Johnson	New York	-1	.110	*Job in Danger or not yet ready:*			
Dave Stieb	Chicago	+9	.111	Danny Cox	Pittsburgh	+7	.118
Dave Otto	Cleveland	+1	.111	Brian Williams	Houston	-4	.120
Mark Grant	Seattle	+2	.111	Ben Rivera	Philadelphia	-4	.125
Wilson Alvarez	Chicago	-6	.112	Don Robinson	Philadelphia	+9	.126
Shawn Hillegas	Oakland	+1	.114	Jeff M. Robinson	Pittsburgh	+5	.127
				Jim Bullinger	Chicago	0	.127
Job in Danger or not yet ready:				Tom Bolton	Cincinnati	+3	.129
Matt Young	Boston	+8	.117				
Bruce Ruffin	Milwaukee	+2	.119				
Chris Haney	Kansas City	-3	.122				
Brian Fisher	Seattle	+3	.126				
Joe Slusarski	Oakland	-1	.129				
Kevin Ritz	Detroit	0	.134				

Note: The above list includes all pitchers with at least 75 innings pitched in 1992 or at least 150 innings pitched in 1991 & 1992 combined (includes innings as a reliever).

STARTING PITCHERS - LESS THAN 75 INNINGS
BOTH LEAGUES

NAME	TEAM	AGE	RPA	NAME	TEAM	AGE	RPA
AMERICAN LEAGUE:				**NATIONAL LEAGUE:**			
Premier Starting Pitchers:				*Premier Starting Pitchers:*			
Sam Militello	New York	-4	.098	Scott Chiamparino	Florida	-1	.091
Pat Mahomes	Minnesota	-6	.104	Gil Heredia	Montreal	0	.096
				Mike Williams	Philadelphia	-3	.096
Qualified Starting Pitchers:				Francisco Oliveras	San Francisco	+2	.097
Roger Pavlik	Texas	-2	.108				
Tim Fortugno	California	+3	.111	*Qualified Starting Pitchers:*			
Mike Trombley	Minnesota	-2	.113	Kip Gross	Los Angeles	+1	.104
Ron Robinson	Milwaukee	+3	.113	Tim Pugh	Cincinnati	-2	.110
				Joe Magrane	St. Louis	+1	.110
Job in Danger or not yet ready:				Dave Eiland	San Diego	-1	.112
Curt Young	Oakland	+6	.118	Mickey Weston	Philadelphia	+5	.113
Brian Bohanon	Texas	-3	.119	Vince Palacios	Pittsburgh	+2	.115
Bob Wickman	New York	-4	.121				
Scott Lewis	California	0	.122	*Job in Danger or not yet ready:*			
Dave Mlicki	Cleveland	-3	.122	Denis Boucher	Colorado	-3	.116
Clay Parker	Seattle	+3	.123	Mike Harkey	Chicago	-1	.117
Jeff Mutis	Cleveland	-1	.124	Armando Reynoso	Colorado	-1	.118
Willie Banks	Minnesota	-4	.130	Kent Bottenfield	Montreal	-3	.119
Kevin D. Brown	Seattle	-1	.131	Kevin Rogers	San Francisco	-3	.119
Buddy Groom	Detroit	0	.131	Brad Brink	Philadelphia	0	.121
Mike Jeffcoat	Texas	+7	.134	Dave Burba	San Francisco	-1	.121
David West	Minnesota	+1	.138	Andy Ashby	Colorado	-2	.124
Doug Linton	Toronto	0	.144	Larry Carter	San Francisco	0	.127
Randy Kramer	Seattle	+6	.145	Shane Reynolds	Houston	-3	.127
Dave Haas	Detroit	0	.145	Greg Mathews	Philadelphia	+3	.128
				Pat Combs	Philadelphia	-1	.129
				Victor Cole	Pittsburgh	-3	.132
				Tom Filer	New York	+10	.137
				Bobby Ayala	Cincinnati	-4	.137
				Ryan Bowen	Florida	-3	.137
				Eric Hillman	New York	-1	.139
				Scott Aldred	Colorado	-3	.143

Note: **The above list includes all pitchers with less than 75 innings pitched in 1992 and less than 150 innings pitched in 1991 & 1992 combined (includes innings as a reliever).**

RELIEF PITCHERS - 50 INNINGS PLUS
AMERICAN LEAGUE

NAME	TEAM	AGE	RPA	NAME	TEAM	AGE	RPA
Premier Relief Pitchers:				*Continued from column #1:*			
Todd Frohwirth	Baltimore	+3	.076	Calvin Jones	Seattle	+2	.110
John Habyan	New York	+1	.078	Alan Mills	Baltimore	-1	.111
Duane Ward	Toronto	+1	.080	Dan Plesac	Milwaukee	+3	.112
Steve Olin	Cleveland	0	.080	Kevin Campbell	Oakland	+1	.114
Carl Willis	Minnesota	+6	.081	Bill Sampen	Kansas City	+2	.115
Steve Farr	New York	+10	.082	Jeff Parrett	Oakland	+5	.116
Mark Eichhorn	Toronto	+6	.084	Mike Flanagan	Baltimore	+16	.117
Bryan Harvey	California	+2	.086	Dennis Powell	Seattle	+2	.117
Gregg Olson	Baltimore	-1	.087	Kenny Rogers	Texas	+1	.117
Mike Henneman	Detroit	+5	.088	Juan Berenguer	Kansas City	+13	.118
Rick Aguilera	Minnesota	+5	.089	Pat Hentgen	Toronto	-3	.118
Tom Henke	Texas	+9	.091	Bob MacDonald	Toronto	0	.121
Scott Radinsky	Chicago	-3	.091	Juan Agosto	Seattle	+8	.121
Jim Corsi	Oakland	+5	.091	Chuck Crim	California	+5	.124
Rich Monteleone	New York	+2	.092	Neal Heaton	Milwaukee	+6	.125
Mike Timlin	Toronto	-1	.093	Bobby Thigpen	Chicago	+2	.125
Dennis Eckersley	Oakland	+13	.093	Eric Plunk	Cleveland	+2	.127
Jeff Montgomery	Kansas City	+3	.094	Jim Acker	Seattle	+8	.132
				Edwin Nunez	Texas	+2	.139
Qualified Relief Pitchers:				Gene Nelson	Oakland	+6	.151
Jeff Russell	Oakland	+5	.096				
Steve Shifflett	Kansas City	-1	.097				
Greg Harris	Boston	+12	.098				
Roberto Hernandez	Chicago	+1	.098				
Ted Power	Cleveland	+12	.101				
Donn Pall	Chicago	+3	.101				
Darren Holmes	Milwaukee	-1	.101				
Jeff Nelson	Seattle	-1	.101				
Jim Austin	Milwaukee	+2	.102				
Tim Burke	New York	+7	.102				
Russ Swan	Seattle	+1	.102				
Mike Fetters	Milwaukee	+2	.103				
Terry Leach	Chicago	+13	.104				
Mark Guthrie	Minnesota	0	.104				
Derek Lilliquist	Cleveland	-1	.104				
Les Lancaster	Detroit	+3	.105	*Median qualified reliever rating: .095*			

Job in Danger or not yet ready:

NAME	TEAM	AGE	RPA
Doug Henry	Milwaukee	+2	.106
Tom Edens	Minnesota	+5	.107
Rusty Meacham	Kansas City	-3	.107
John Kiely	Detroit	+1	.108
Mike Schooler	Seattle	+3	.109
Storm Davis	Oakland	+5	.109
Kurt Knudsen	Detroit	-2	.109

Note: The above list includes all pitchers with at least 50 innings pitched in 1992 or at least 100 innings pitched in 1991 & 1992 combined (includes innings as a starter).

RELIEF PITCHERS - 50 INNINGS PLUS
NATIONAL LEAGUE

NAME	TEAM	AGE	RPA	NAME	TEAM	AGE	RPA
Premier Relief Pitchers:				*Continued from column #1:*			
Rod Beck	San Francisco	-3	.072	Steve Wilson	Los Angeles	+1	.114
Jeff Innis	New York	+3	.074	Ken Patterson	Chicago	+1	.114
Mike Maddux	New York	+5	.078	Rob Murphy	Houston	+6	.114
Rich Rodriguez	San Diego	+2	.081	Scott Bankhead	Cincinnati	+2	.115
Mike Stanton	Atlanta	-2	.082	Jeff Reardon	Atlanta	+12	.116
Bob Scanlan	Chicago	-1	.084	Lee Guetterman	New York	+8	.117
Rob Dibble	Cincinnati	+1	.084	Scott Ruskin	Cincinnati	+2	.119
Marvin Freeman	Atlanta	+2	.087	Jeff Robinson	Chicago	+6	.120
Mike Jackson	San Francisco	+1	.087	Dennis Lamp	Pittsburgh	+15	.121
Jose Melendez	San Diego	0	.088	Paul Gibson	New York	+6	.121
Jeff Fassero	Montreal	+2	.090	Denny Neagle	Pittsburgh	-3	.122
Norm Charlton	Cincinnati	+2	.090	Roger Mason	San Diego	+8	.128
Cris Carpenter	Florida	0	.090	Bob McClure	Florida	+14	.128
Alejandro Pena	Pittsburgh	+7	.091	Mike Hartley	Philadelphia	+5	.130
Chuck McElroy	Chicago	0	.091	Mark Davis	Atlanta	+6	.146
Jim Gott	Los Angeles	+7	.091				
Mel Rojas	Montreal	-1	.092				
John Wetteland	Montreal	-1	.092				
Qualified Relief Pitchers:							
Kent Mercker	Atlanta	-3	.094				
Bryan Hickerson	San Francisco	+2	.095				
Randy Myers	Chicago	+3	.097				
Xavier Hernandez	Houston	0	.097				
Todd Worrell	Los Angeles	+7	.099	*Median qualified reliever rating: .093*			
Barry Jones	New York	+2	.100				
Dwayne Henry	Cincinnati	+3	.102				
Roger McDowell	Los Angeles	+6	.103				
Bob Patterson	Pittsburgh	+7	.105				
Stan Belinda	Pittsburgh	-1	.106				
Paul Assenmacher	Chicago	+6	.106				
Jeff Brantley	San Francisco	+2	.106				
Lee Smith	St. Louis	+9	.106				
Doug Jones	Houston	+9	.106				
Tim Crews	Los Angeles	+5	.107				
Dave Righetti	San Francisco	+8	.107				
Job in Danger or not yet ready:							
Joe Boever	Houston	+6	.108				
Al Osuna	Houston	0	.108				
Greg Cadaret	Cincinnati	+3	.109				
Mike Perez	St. Louis	+1	.109				
Jerry Don Gleaton	Pittsburgh	+9	.111				
Steve Foster	Cincinnati	-1	.111				
Mitch Williams	Philadelphia	+1	.111				

RELIEF PITCHERS - LESS THAN 50 INNINGS
BOTH LEAGUES

NAME	TEAM	AGE	RPA	NAME	TEAM	AGE	RPA

AMERICAN LEAGUE:

Premier Relief Pitchers:

Steve Howe	New York	+8	.057
Pat Clements	Baltimore	+3	.085
Vince Horsman	Oakland	-2	.093
Tony Fossas	Boston	+9	.094
Matt Whiteside	Texas	-2	.094

Qualified Relief Pitchers:

Lance McCullers	Texas	+1	.097
Jim Poole	Baltimore	-1	.101
Kevin Wickander	Cleveland	0	.105
Larry Casian	Minnesota	0	.105

Job in Danger or not yet ready:

Brian Drahman	Chicago	-1	.107
Steve Frey	California	+2	.108
Jeff Shaw	Cleveland	-1	.111
Daryl Irvine	Boston	+1	.113
Bruce Walton	Oakland	+3	.114
Mike Butcher	California	0	.114
Jesse Orosco	Milwaukee	+9	.115
Terry Mathews	Texas	+1	.115
Mike Munoz	Detroit	0	.115
Mark Williamson	Baltimore	+7	.117
Goose Gossage	Oakland	+16	.119
Gary Wayne	Minnesota	+3	.118
Paul Abbott	Minnesota	-2	.120
Eric Bell	Cleveland	+2	.120
Gerald Alexander	Texas	-3	.120
Bob Kipper	Minnesota	+1	.122
Rick Honeycutt	Oakland	+13	.121
Paul Quantrill	Boston	-3	.125
Don Carman	Texas	+7	.126
Floyd Bannister	Texas	+12	.129
Mike Dunne	Chicago	+3	.132
Eric Gunderson	Seattle	-1	.137
Wayne Rosenthal	Texas	0	.139
Scott Bailes	California	+3	.139
Dave Schmidt	Seattle	+9	.149
Brad Arnsberg	Cleveland	+2	.155
John Briscoe	Oakland	-2	.158

NATIONAL LEAGUE:

Premier Relief Pitchers:

John Franco	New York	+6	.079
Larry Anderson	Philadelphia	+14	.082
Milt Hill	Cincinnati	0	.091

Qualified Relief Pitchers:

Mark Wohlers	Atlanta	-6	.095
John Candelaria	Los Angeles	+14	.096
Jay Howell	Los Angeles	+12	.096
Jeremy Hernandez	San Diego	-1	.096
Sergio Valdez	Montreal	0	.097
Wally Ritchie	Philadelphia	0	.101
Tim Scott	San Diego	-1	.105
Doug Simons	Montreal	-1	.107
Heathcliff Slocumb	Chicago	-1	.107

Job in Danger or not yet ready:

Randy St. Claire	Atlanta	+6	.113
Rob Mallicoat	Houston	+1	.113
Bill Landrum	Cincinnati	+8	.119
Gene Harris	San Diego	+1	.120
Mark Dewey	New York	0	.121
Keith Brown	Cincinnati	+1	.122
Bob Ayrault	Philadelphia	-1	.122
Dave Smith	Chicago	+12	.129
Frank DiPino	St. Louis	+10	.129
Jim Pena	San Diego	+1	.136
Steve Searcy	Los Angeles	+1	.146

SECTION IV

TOP MINOR LEAGUE PLAYERS

THE BEST AAA MINOR LEAGUE HITTERS IN 1992

PLAYER & AGE	TEAM	POSITION	CPA	RUNS	SET-UP	DRIVE-IN	RPA
Todd Pratt,25	Scranton (Phillies)	C	317	51.0	.096	.065	.161
Mike Piazza,24	Albuquerque (Dodgers)	C	535	77.9	.078	.068	.146
Brian Deak,25	Richmond (Braves)	C	304	42.4	.084	.056	.140
Eric Wedge,24	Pawtucket (Red Sox)	C	250	33.8	.072	.063	.135
Jesse Levis,24	Colorado Springs (Indians)	C	300	39.0	.075	.055	.130
Tim Spehr,26	Omaha (Royals)	C	413	52.5	.071	.056	.127
Ed Sprague,25	Syracuse (Blue Jays)	C	424	52.0	.063	.060	.123
John Jaha,26	Denver (Brewers)	1B	333	53.1	.092	.067	.159
George Canale,27	Colorado Springs (Indians)	1B	407	61.1	.080	.070	.150
Jeff Conine,26	Omaha (Royals)	1B	459	62.5	.072	.064	.136
Mike Twardoski,28	Pawtucket (Red Sox)	1B	492	66.8	.080	.056	.136
Chris Cron,28	Vancouver (White Sox)	1B	619	84.2	.081	.055	.136
Bob Hamelin,25	Omaha (Royals)	1B	258	34.6	.074	.060	.134
J.T. Snow,24	Columbus (Yankees)	1B	572	75.9	.074	.059	.133
Reggie Jefferson,24	Colorado Springs (Indians)	1B	254	33.5	.068	.064	.132
Torey LoVullo,27	Columbus (Yankees)	2B	543	73.7	.073	.063	.136
Todd Haney,27	Indianapolis (Expos)	2B	240	29.5	.071	.052	.123
Bret Boone,23	Calgary (Mariners)	2B	516	58.9	.061	.053	.114
Jeff Gardner,28	Las Vegas (Padres)	2B	517	58.2	.068	.045	.113
Nelson Liriano,28	Colorado Springs (Indians)	2B	417	46.6	.061	.051	.112
Kevin Flora,23	Edmonton (Angels)	2B	206	22.2	.060	.051	.111
John Wehner,25	Buffalo (Pirates)	2B	260	27.5	.052	.054	.106
Rico Rossy,28	Omaha (Royals)	SS	213	25.3	.068	.051	.119
Carlos Garcia,25	Buffalo (Pirates)	SS	461	54.3	.057	.061	.118
Dave Silvestri,25	Columbus (Yankees)	SS	496	58.1	.061	.056	.117
Rich Amaral,30	Calgary (Mariners)	SS	478	52.3	.064	.045	.109
Jeff Reboulet,28	Portland (Twins)	SS	204	22.2	.062	.047	.109
Wil Cordero,21	Indianapolis (Expos)	SS	235	24.8	.052	.053	.105
John Valentin,25	Pawtucket (Red Sox)	SS	391	40.4	.054	.049	.103
Chris Donnels,26	Tidewater (Mets)	3B	345	47.3	.082	.055	.137
Boi Rodriguez,26	Richmond (Braves)	3B	315	42.6	.067	.068	.135
Frank Bolick,26	Calgary (Mariners)	3B	586	77.0	.069	.062	.131
Jeff Manto,28	Richmond (Braves)	3B	522	63.9	.067	.055	.122
Kevin Young,23	Buffalo (Pirates)	3B	579	70.1	.068	.053	.121
Russ McGinnis,29	Oklahoma City (Rangers)	3B	431	52.3	.066	.055	.121
Hensley Meulens,25	Columbus (Yankees)	3B	613	72.5	.057	.061	.118
Tim Salmon,24	Edmonton (Angels)	OF	515	93.8	.109	.073	.182
Troy Neel,27	Tacoma (Athletics)	OF	470	76.7	.095	.068	.163
Mark Leonard,28	Phoenix (Giants)	OF	164	25.1	.092	.061	.153
Al Martin,25	Buffalo (Pirates)	OF	462	68.9	.076	.073	.149
Dave Clark,30	Buffalo (Pirates)	OF	293	41.9	.076	.067	.143
Ozzie Canseco,28	Louisville (Cardinals)	OF	356	49.1	.069	.069	.138
Shawn Hare,25	Toledo (Tigers)	OF	242	32.3	.074	.059	.133
Phil Stephenson,32	Las Vegas (Padres)	OF	246	31.9	.073	.057	.130
Eddie Zambrano,26	Buffalo (Pirates)	OF	456	58.7	.068	.061	.129
Monty Fariss,25	Oklahoma City (Rangers)	OF	223	28.5	.067	.061	.128
Darrell Sherman,25	Las Vegas (Padres)	OF	592	75.2	.075	.052	.127
Geronimo Berroa,27	Nashville (Reds)	OF	511	646	.062	.065	.127
Bernie Williams,24	Columbus (Yankees)	OF	424	53.8	.069	.058	.127
Wayne Kirby,28	Colorado Springs (Indians)	OF	515	63.7	.063	.061	.124
Jack Voigt,26	Rochester (Orioles)	OF	515	63.2	.065	.058	.123
D.J. Dozier,27	Tidewater (Mets)	OF	239	29.2	.065	.057	.122
Beau Allred,27	Colorado Springs (Indians)	OF	509	62.2	.064	.058	.122

Note: At least 150 computed plate appearances required to make this list.

THE BEST AAA MINOR LEAGUE PITCHERS IN 1992

PLAYER & AGE	TEAM	OUTS		RPA
Pete Smith,26	Richmond (Braves)	328		.086
Kip Gross,28	Albuquerque (Dodgers)	323		.093
Rick Huismann,23	Phoenix (Giants)	478		.096
Sam Militello,23	Columbus (Yankees)	424		.097
Cal Eldred,25	Denver (Brewers)	423		.098
Denis Boucher,24	Colorado Springs (Indians)	372		.101
Rich Sauveur,29	Omaha (Royals)	352	*300+*	.102
Roger Pavlik,25	Oklahoma City (Rangers)	353		.104
Doug Simons,26	Indianapolis (Expos)	360	*Outs*	.105
Pat Rapp,25	Phoenix (Giants)	363		.106
Rene Arocha,26	Louisville (Cardinals)	500		.107
Kevin Rogers,24	Phoenix (Giants)	512		.107
Matt Turner,25	Tucson (Astros)	300		.108
Ross Powell,24	Nashville (Reds)	452		.108
Mickey Weston,31	Scranton (Phillies)	512		.108
Mike Williams,24	Scranton (Phillies)	325		.111
John O'Donoghue,23	Rochester (Orioles)	546		.112
Steve Cooke,22	Buffalo (Pirates)	331		.113
David Nied,24	Richmond (Braves)	504		.113
Tim Worrell,25	Las Vegas (Padres)	567		.113
Jamie Moyer,30	Toledo (Tigers)	416		.113
Scott Service,25	Nashville (Reds)	285		.090
Blas Minor,26	Buffalo (Pirates)	289		.097
Mark Grater,28	Louisville (Cardinals)	228		.099
Brett Merriman,26	Edmonton (Angels)	254		.101
Joey Vierra,26	Nashville (Reds)	263	*225+*	.103
Mike Capel,31	Tucson (Astros)	247		.103
Mike Ignasiak,26	Denver (Brewers)	276	*Outs*	.104
Tom McCarthy,31	Richmond (Braves)	278		.107
Terry Bross,26	Las Vegas (Padres)	257		.107
Gil Heredia,27	Indianapolis (Expos)	295		.108
Willie Banks,23	Portland (Twins)	225		.108
Joe Ausanio,27	Buffalo (Pirates)	251		.109
Jeff Johnson,26	Columbus (Yankees)	174		.081
Rob Mallicoat,28	Tucson (Astros)	151		.085
Jay Baller,32	Scranton (Phillies)	190		.087
Steve Reed,26	Phoenix (Giants)	180		.089
Larry Casian,27	Portland (Twins)	186	*150+*	.090
Mike Dalton,29	Buffalo (Pirates)	214		.095
Milt Hill,27	Nashville (Reds)	223	*Outs*	.095
Jeff Schwarz,28	Vancouver (White Sox)	224		.095
Scott Chiamparino,26	Oklahoma City (Rangers)	150		.096
Brad Pennington,23	Rochester (Orioles)	202		.097
Mike Christopher,29	Colorado Springs (Indians)	176		.099
Lance McCullers,28	Albuquerque (Dodgers)	208		.100
Alex Fernandez,23	Vancouver (White Sox)	86		.055
Tim Scott,26	Las Vegas (Padres)	84		.071
Dave Otto,28	Colorado Springs (Indians)	140	*75+*	.074
Steve Shifflett,26	Omaha (Royals)	131		.075
Kyle Abbott,24	Scranton (Phillies)	105	*Outs*	.075
Daryl Irvine,28	Pawtucket (Red Sox)	123		.078
John Dopson,29	Pawtucket (Red Sox)	114		.081
Brett Backlund,?	Buffalo (Pirates)	132		.082

THE BEST AA MINOR LEAGUE HITTERS IN 1992

PLAYER & AGE	TEAM	POSITION	CPA	RUNS	SET-UP	DRIVE-IN	RPA
Javy Lopez,22	Greenville (Braves)	C	479	57.6	.060	.060	.120
John Russell,31	Tulsa (Rangers)	C	191	20.8	.048	.061	.109
Scott Makarewicz,25	Jackson (Astros)	C	379	39.1	.052	.051	.103
Tim Laker,23	Harrisburg (Expos)	C	463	46.8	.047	.054	.101
Brook Fordyce,22	Binghampton (Mets)	C	479	48.3	.049	.052	.101
Kiki Hernandez,23	Albany (Yankees)	C	382	38.0	.052	.048	.100
Brian Johnson,24	Wichita (Padres)	C	277	27.7	.052	.048	.100
Tony Eusebio,25	Jackson (Astros)	C	378	38.0	.051	.049	.100
Kevin Garner,27	Chattanooga (Reds)	DH (1B?)	271	36.5	.067	.068	.135
Jay Gainer,26	Wichita (Padres)	1B	426	55.3	.063	.067	.130
Sherman Obando,22	Albany (Yankees)	1B	432	54.8	.061	.066	.127
Don Sparks,26	Albany (Yankees)	1B	551	65.1	.058	.060	.118
Tim Costo,23	Chattanooga (Reds)	1B	493	56.1	.052	.062	.114
Alan Zinter,24	Binghampton (Mets)	1B	511	57.6	.059	.054	.113
Willie Tatum,26	New Britain (Red Sox)	1B	551	61.9	.063	.049	.112
Hector Vargas,26	Albany (Yankees)	2B	474	53.6	.061	.052	.113
John Finn,25	El Paso (Brewers)	2B	528	51.4	.056	.041	.097
Edgar Alfonzo,25	Midland (Angels)	2B	259	25.2	.051	.046	.097
Darryl Vice,26	Huntsville (Athletics)	2B	58.7	55.7	.055	.040	.095
Terry Taylor,24	Midland (Angels)	2B	312	29.0	.055	.038	.093
Kevin Castleberry,24	Birmingham (White Sox)	2B	436	40.7	.049	.044	.093
Brian Turang,25	Jacksonville (Mariners)	2B	550	49.7	.043	.047	.090
Ty Griffin,25	Chattanooga (Reds)	2B	420	38.0	.048	.042	.090
Chipper Jones,20	Greenville (Braves)	SS	282	38.8	.069	.069	.138
Tom Allison,25	Binghampton (Mets)	SS	149*	16.0	.059	.048	.107
Mike Lansing,24	Harrisburg (Expos)	SS	554	56.3	.052	.050	.102
Ray Holbert,22	Wichita (Padres)	SS	354	35.1	.053	.046	.099
Tim Barker,24	San Antonio (Dodgers)	SS	389	36.8	.051	.044	.095
Steve Bethea,25	Wichita (Padres)	SS	297	28.3	.052	.043	.095
Edgar Caceres,28	El Paso (Brewers)	SS	411	37.9	.048	.044	.092
Jim Thome,22	Canton-Akron (Indians)	3B	190	27.8	.090	.056	.146
Russ Davis,23	Albany (Yankees)	3B	558	74.2	.066	.066	.132
Adell Davenport,25	Shreveport (Giants)	3B	483	58.0	.057	.063	.120
Willie Greene,21	Chattanooga (Reds)	3B	406	45.8	.056	.057	.113
Joe Oliva,21	Tulsa (Rangers)	3B	494	55.8	.055	.058	.113
Paul Gonzalez,23	Wichita (Padres)	3B	494	51.7	.051	.054	.105
Bobby Holley,25	Jacksonville (Mariners)	3B	452	45.9	.053	.049	.102
Lance Madsen,24	Jackson (Astros)	3B	378	38.6	.048	.054	.102
Aubrey Waggoner,26	Greenville (Braves)	OF	334	53.4	.094	.066	.160
Melvin Nieves,21	Greenville (Braves)	OF	412	57.8	.075	.065	.140
Ken Ramos,25	Canton-Akron (Indians)	OF	532	74.1	.085	.054	.139
Scott Lydy,24	Huntsville (Athletics)	OF	461	61.7	.080	.054	.134
Greg Blosser,21	New Britain (Red Sox)	OF	506	65.6	.065	.065	.130
Tracy Sanders,23	Canton-Akron (Indians)	OF	470	61.2	.068	.062	.130
Kevin Belcher,25	Tulsa (Rangers)	OF	473	58.6	.066	.058	.124
Dan Rumsey,25	Midland (Angels)	OF	25.7	31.0	.067	.054	.121
Jeff Kipila,27	Midland (Angels)	OF	477	57.1	.061	.059	.120
Scott Jaster,27	Birmingham (White Sox)	OF	461	54.8	.067	.052	.119
Nigel Wilson,22	Knoxville (Blue Jays)	OF	563	66.4	.055	.063	.118
Garey Ingram,22	San Antonio (Dodgers)	OF	242	28.2	.067	.050	.117
Dave McCarty,23	Orlando (Twins)	OF	562	64.0	.061	.053	.114
Troy O'Leary,23	El Paso (Brewers)	OF	573	64.8	.063	.050	.113
Rex DeLaNuez,24	Orlando (Twins)	OF	524	58.0	.061	.050	.111

Note: At least 150 computed plate appearances required to make this list

*Tom Allison's CPA total of 149 qualifies since one more out would not have lowered his ranking.

THE BEST AA MINOR LEAGUE PITCHERS IN 1992

PLAYER & AGE	TEAM	OUTS		RPA
Dan Smith,23	Tulsa (Rangers)	439		.092
Allen Watson,22	Arkansas (Cardinals)	326		.095
Andy Nezelek,27	Greenville (Braves)	341		.095
Nate Minchey,23	New Britain (Red Sox)	537		.097
Larry Thomas,23	Birmingham (White Sox)	362		.101
Bobby Jones,22	Binghampton (Mets)	474		.101
Mike Farrell,23	El Paso (Brewers)	319	**300+**	.104
Kip Yaughn,23	Hagerstown (Orioles)	349		.105
Mike Mathile,24	Harrisburg (Expos)	557		.110
Paul Fletcher,25	Reading (Phillies)	449	**Outs**	.112
Steve Peck,25	Midland (Angels)	334		.112
Donnie Elliot,24	Greenville (Braves)	418		.114
Mike Anderson,26	Chattanooga (Reds)	515		.114
Bo Kennedy,24	Birmingham (White Sox)	433		.115
Steve Trachsel,22	Charlotte (Cubs)	573		.115
Brian Warren,25	London (Tigers)	442		.117
Rafael Novoa,25	El Paso (Brewers)	439		.117
Richard Robertson,24	Carolina (Pirates)	374		.118
Ed Puig,27	Memphis (Royals)	226		.079
Bill Wertz,25	Canton-Akron (Indians)	292		.082
Jeff Tabaka,28	El Paso (Brewers)	246		.089
Steve Allen,26	San Antonio (Dodgers)	237		.093
Hilly Hathaway,23	Midland (Angels)	286		.094
Doug Bochtler,22	Harrisburg (Expos)	233		.094
Keith Shepherd,24	Reading (Phillies)	282		.094
Alan Embree,22	Canton-Akron (Indians)	237	**225+**	.102
Jeff Braley,25	London (Tigers)	245		.103
Carl Hanselman,22	Shreveport (Giants)	240		.103
Graeme Lloyd,25	Knoxville (Blue Jays)	276	**Outs**	.105
Gab Ozuna,23	Arkansas (Cardinals)	234		.107
Jeff Bronkey,27	Tulsa (Rangers)	259		.108
Mario Brito,26	Harrisburg (Expos)	248		.108
Dennis Tafoya,28	Carolina (Pirates)	257		.109
Pedro Borbon,26	Greenville (Braves)	282		.109
Brian Shouse,24	Carolina (Pirates)	232		.110
Mike Lumley,25	London (Tigers)	225		.110
Terry Burrows,24	Tulsa (Rangers)	252		.112
Jerry Spradlin,25	Chattanooga (Reds)	196		.071
Jerry Nielsen,26	Albany (Yankees)	174		.086
Don Strange,25	Greenville (Braves)	180		.086
Todd Revenig,23	Huntsville (Athletics)	191	**150+**	.089
David Lynch,27	Chattanooga (Reds)	157		.096
Mark Ohlms,25	Knoxville (Blue Jays)	209		.096
Jose Martinez,21	Binghampton (Mets)	174	**Outs**	.096
Steve Dixon,23	Arkansas (Cardinals)	206		.101
Jason Bere,21	Birmingham (White Sox)	165		.103
Rick Shackle,25	Arkansas (Cardinals)	216		.104
Danilo Leon,25	Tulsa (Rangers)	104		.067
Louis Pote,21	Shreveport (Giants)	113	**75+**	.080
Matt Rambo,25	Jackson (Astros)	100		.080
Brad Woodall,23	Greenville (Braves)	118		.084
Rusty Kilgo,26	Chattanooga (Reds)	95	**Outs**	.098
Matt Whiteside,25	Tulsa (Rangers)	135		.100

SECTION V

THE
TEAMS

HOW TO READ THE DATA IN THIS SECTION

Hitter Example:

| | Bats Left | 298L | 584R | 107G | 139F | 359ML |

Eric Anthony, 25

L= .092G .098L .106F [(.050/.060) .110] .110G .116R .124F = R

ATBATS 1B 2B 3B HR HBP BB GDP SB CS ROE XB RUNS EOB% RL# SET-UP DR-IN RPA

Top line (after Bats Left) gives the major league totals for at-bats against the different types of pitchers faced over the last three (3) years. For instance, the 298L means than Anthony had 298 at-bats against lefties. The 584R means 584 at-bats against righties. The 107G & 139F gives the number of at-bats against Groundball and Flyball type pitchers, respectively. I use three year totals to get the proper splits since this would give me a larger sample from which to rate the player's tendencies. The 359ML is the total of minor league Computed Plate Appearances over the last two seasons. These 359 plate appearances were used in computing the two-year overall combined RPA rating.

The next line (after the player's age) is the most important line in the player's record. This line lists the RPA's against each type of pitcher faced as well as the set-up and drive-in RPA figures for the *average* pitcher faced. This line reads from left (L=) to right (=R). The box in the middle [(.050/.060) .110] lists the overall combined Set-up RPA (.050), the Drive-in RPA (.060) and the total offensive RPA (.110) against the average pitcher for the last two years. The L= side of this box gives the RPA against the three types of lefties: Groundball, Flyball and neutral lefties. The central figure with an L after it is the figure against neutral lefties. The =R side of this box gives the player's RPA against Groundball and Flyball righties with the central figure with an R after it being the RPA against neutral righties. In other words, Anthony's offensive RPA against left-handed, groundball type pitchers is a puny .092 but is a much stronger .124 against right-handed, flyball type pitchers.

The next line (shaded) is the data label line:

> The 1B, 2B, and 3B are short for single, double and triple. HBP is Hit-By-Pitch.
> BB is Bases-on-Balls (not including Intentional Walks).
> GDP is Grounded-into-Double-Plays.
> SB & CS is Stolen Bases and Caught Stealing, respectively.
> ROE is Reached-On-Error. XB is eXtra-Bases taken as a base runner.
> Runs is the total of the computed runs produced as per the RPA formula.
> EOB% is the player's *Effective* On-Base percentage.
> RL# is the Rotisserie League RPA. (The standard RPA less the stadium variant).
> SET-UP is the Set-Up RPA. DR-IN is the Drive-In RPA.
> RPA = the total of the Set-Up and Drive-In RPA which results in this final, overall, rating.

Pitcher Example: Throws: Groundball type, moderate to severe righty

Mark Wohlers, 22   [(.113/.090) .101]   99L 106R   378ML

OUTS RO 1B 2B 3B HR HBP BB GDP SB CS PO WP BK RUNS EOB% RL# RPA

The top line indicates that this pitcher (Wohlers) is a righty who is moderately to severely more difficult against righty hitters in comparison to lefty hitters and gets the bulk of his outs through groundballs. After the pitcher's name and age comes a box similar to the hitter's example, above. This set of numbers has a slightly different meaning. The [.113/.090] in this box reflects the pitcher's effectiveness against lefty hitters and righty hitters. In other words, Wohlers is tougher on righty hitters. They have averaged only a .090 RPA against him over the past two years. Left-handed batters, however, have a very respectable .113 RPA against him. The .101 is Wohler's overall combined two-year RPA when left-handed and right-handed batters are combined. The two sets of numbers to the right of the box, 99L and 106R are the number of Left-handed and Right-handed hitters faced, respectively. Again, this is the three (3) year major league total which is used so as to get the largest possible sample size. A young pitcher like Wohlers, however, may not have more than parts of one or, in this case, two Major League seasons under their belt. In this case the bulk of Wohler's rating comes from the next entry on this line: 378ML. This is the number of AAA and/or AA minor league batter's faced by Wohlers over the last two years. Three years of minor league data are not used.

The next line (shaded area data label line):

> Outs = Total outs created as a pitcher. Divide by 3 to get the innings pitched.
> RO = Total outs created as a reliever. This figure is a subset of the Outs column.
> PO, WP & BK = Picked-Off, Wild Pitches and Balks.
> Runs = Total runs surrendered as per RPA formula.
> EOB% = Opposition *Effective* On-Base percentage.

82   *Data Reference Sheet*

BALTIMORE ORIOLES

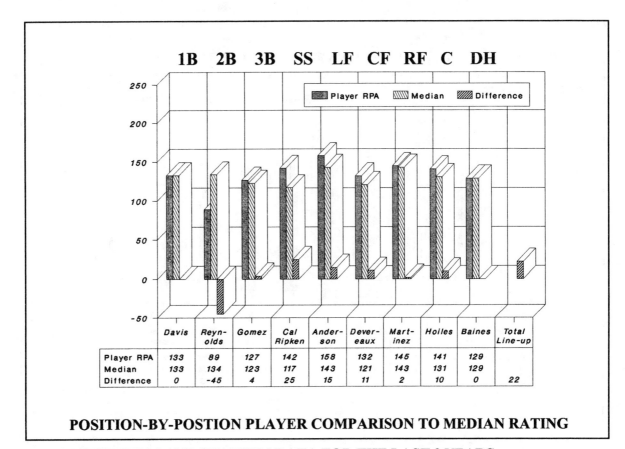

	Davis	Reyn-olds	Gomez	Cal Ripken	Ander-son	Dever-eaux	Mart-inez	Hoiles	Baines	Total Line-up
Player RPA	133	89	127	142	158	132	145	141	129	
Median	133	134	123	117	143	121	143	131	129	
Difference	0	-45	4	25	15	11	2	10	0	22

POSITION-BY-POSTION PLAYER COMPARISON TO MEDIAN RATING

DEFENSIVE TEAM AND STADIUM DATA FOR THE LAST 3 YEARS:

TEAM DEFENSE BY POSITION:

		1990	1991	1992	POSITION-BY-POSITION STADIUM CHARACTERISTICS:
1B:	Home	-0.9	-0.8	-1.0	Easy to play*
	Away	-0.2	+3.9	+0.8	
2B:	Home	+3.0	-0.1	+1.4	Slightly easy to play*
	Away	-1.7	+1.2	-3.2	
3B:	Home	+3.6	+0.2	-2.3	Average*
	Away	+0.1	-2.1	-3.5	
SS:	Home	+2.5	+1.3	+0.3	Easy to play*
	Away	+0.9	+4.1	-4.4	
LF:	Home	-2.2	-8.3	+6.1	Slightly easy to play*
	Away	-0.1	-7.7	+5.9	
CF:	Home	-1.5	-0.1	-1.6	Very easy to play*
	Away	-0.1	+2.6	+1.0	
RF:	Home	+1.8	-2.9	-0.6	Average*
	Away	+6.2	-5.9	-7.2	
Total Home:		+6.3	-10.7	+2.4	The new stadium appears to be a real treat for
Total Away:		+5.1	-3.9	-10.5	the defensive players.

Comments: The + or - figures represent the number of <u>runs</u> the home team was better or worse than its opponents at that position during that season. Whatever defensive improvement the Orioles had in 1992 can be attributed to Brady Anderson's play in left field. Without him, the 1991 defensive collapse would have continued and even gotten worse in 1992 due to Cal Ripken's sudden defensive decline this past season. *Based on only one year of defensive data.*

BALTIMORE ORIOLES

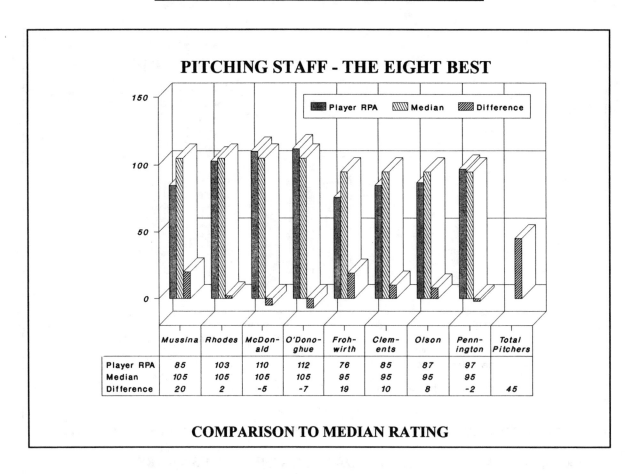

PITCHING STAFF - THE EIGHT BEST

	Mussina	Rhodes	McDon-ald	O'Dono-ghue	Froh-wirth	Clem-ents	Olson	Penn-ington	Total Pitchers
Player RPA	85	103	110	112	76	85	87	97	
Median	105	105	105	105	95	95	95	95	
Difference	20	2	-5	-7	19	10	8	-2	45

COMPARISON TO MEDIAN RATING

SUGGESTED LINE-UPS (with set-up RPA & drive-in RPA ratings):

Vs: Left-handed Groundball
LF:	B. Anderson	83-68
3B:	L. Gomez	78-72
C:	C. Hoiles	100-94
1B:	S. Obando	73-73
CF:	M. Devereaux	71-79
SS:	C. Ripken	65-64
RF:	L. Mercedes	61-61
DH:	G. Davis	60-60
2B:	H. Reynolds	55-49

Vs: Neutral Lefty Pitchers
LF:	B. Anderson	76-61
3B:	L. Gomez	74-69
C:	C. Hoiles	72-68
DH:	G. Davis	72-71
SS:	C. Ripken	74-73
1B:	S. Obando	73-73
CF:	M. Devereaux	72-79
RF:	C. Martinez	58-56
2B:	S. Scarsone	50-60

Vs: Left-handed Flyball
LF:	B. Anderson	66-53
3B:	L. Gomez	70-66
1B:	D. Segui	69-69
DH:	G. Davis	90-89
SS:	C. Ripken	85-85
C:	M. Parent	83-87
RF:	C. Martinez	82-91
CF:	M. Devereaux	73-80
2B:	S. Scarsone	50-60

Vs: Right-handed Groundball
LF:	B. Anderson	94-77
2B:	H. Reynolds	61-55
3B:	L. Gomez	74-69
C:	C. Hoiles	103-97
DH:	S. Horn	63-77
SS:	C. Ripken	58-57
1B:	G. Davis	53-53
CF:	M. Devereaux	55-61
RF:	C. Martinez	51-56

Vs: Neutral Righty Pitchers
LF:	B. Anderson	87-70
3B:	L. Gomez	71-66
C:	C. Hoiles	75-71
1B:	G. Davis	65-64
SS:	C. Ripken	67-66
RF:	C. Martinez	73-81
DH:	S. Horn	59-74
CF:	M. Devereaux	55-62
2B:	H. Reynolds	55-49

Vs: Right-handed Flyball
LF:	B. Anderson	77-62
3B:	L. Gomez	67-62
DH:	G. Davis	82-81
SS:	C. Ripken	78-78
RF:	C. Martinez	97-107
1B:	D. Segui	66-65
CF:	M. Devereaux	56-63
2B:	S. Scarsone	40-50
C:	M. Parent	41-44

Comments: At this point it doesn't appear that the Orioles will re-sign Sam Horn, but I was at a bit of a loss as to who could fill the DH position against neutral and groundball type righties, so I included him there since I had no other present choice. Even with Horn this offense is slightly below average in strength in the AL. Harold Reynolds is only a band-aid solution to the Oriole offensive problems at second base. Sherman Obando was the best Rule 5 selection taken.

BALTIMORE ORIOLES

I picked the '92 Oriole team as one of my two "sleeper" teams and they didn't disappoint. The make-up of the '93 squad, however, does seem to be a real disappointment. This team was very close, but this winter has served to erode some of the gains made last season.

Randy Milligan and Sam Horn are not now premier players, but they are a lot better than what the O's have as their replacements. David Segui is no answer. The Orioles did make one excellent move over the winter and it wasn't the signing of Harold Reynolds, who is merely a band-aid solution to the Orioles perennial problems at second base. The excellent move was the selection of Sherman Obando in the Rule 5 draft. He's a terrific hitter, although he may need a couple of months seasoning at AAA, which the O's can't do under the rules of the Rule 5 draft. The "loss" of Joe Orsulak is a case of addition by subtraction. In fact the '92 team only had a chance at the pennant if they had played Chito Martinez, which they failed to do by playing Orsulak. Luis Mercedes is just a younger version of Orsulak. His only role seems to be to keep power hitter Chito Martinez out of the batter's box. That's a big mistake.

This is still a solid team, however, despite the backsliding over the winter. With the decimation of the Blue Jays over this winter it opens up the division and the Orioles figure to contend. Unfortunately for them, the Yankees have taken full advantage of Toronto's decline and should blow past the Orioles quite easily.

With the aging Cal Ripken at shortstop and the aging Harold Reynolds at second base and the poor fielding Leo Gomez at third base, the Orioles defense appears to headed in the wrong direction, particularly in the infield.

The Oriole pitching staff, however, is still very strong. It is tied with the Red Sox staff as the second best in the AL. The O's staff is keyed by the marvelous Mike Mussina as a starter and the almost equally marvelous Todd Frohwirth out of the bullpen. Unfortunately for the Orioles, they are in the same division with the Yankees, who have improved their pitching staff to be far and away the best in baseball.

The Orioles lost an excellent pitching prospect in Kip Yaughn to the Florida Marlins in the first round of the expansion draft. I would have protected him and pitching prospect John O'Donoghue (pulled back after Yaughn's selection) before I would have protected Segui and Mercedes.

The Orioles were really lucky that Chito Martinez wasn't selected in the expansion draft. If he had been lost in the draft it would have virtually sealed the Orioles fate for '93. The two expansion clubs made a big mistake in passing him by.

Steve Scarsone, provided he's halfway decent defensively, needs to be platooned with Harold Reynolds as indicated in the line-ups on the opposite page.

Brad Pennington looks like a super pitching prospect who's ready right now. Other prospects: Doug Robbins (catcher\1B) and Jack Voigt (OF\1B).

Baltimore's Projected record for 1993: 84--78, good for second place in the division.

BALTIMORE ORIOLES

Brady Anderson, 28

Bats Left   327L   964R   356G   291F

L= .147G .133L .115F (.082/.066) .148 .167G .153R .135F = R

		ATBATS	1B	2B	3B	HR	HBP	BB	GDP	SB	CS	ROE	XB	RUNS	EOB%	RL#	SET-UP	DR-IN	RPA
Baltimore	1990	234	44	5	2	3	5	29	4	15	2	4	19	31	.252	.114	.063	.052	.115
Baltimore	1991	256	42	12	3	2	5	38	1	12	5	2	27	36	.265	.116	.066	.052	.118
Baltimore	1992	623	110	28	10	21	9	84	2	53	20	5	68	115	.250	.160	.088	.072	.160

Glenn Davis, 31

Bats Right   313L   702R   308G   210F

L= .122G .145L .179F (.068/.067) .135 .108G .131R .165F = R

		ATBATS	1B	2B	3B	HR	HBP	BB	GDP	SB	CS	ROE	XB	RUNS	EOB%	RL#	SET-UP	DR-IN	RPA
Houston	1990	327	41	15	4	22	8	29	5	8	3	6	26	65	.195	.148	.080	.086	.166
Baltimore	1991	176	20	9	1	10	5	16	2	4	1	4	6	29	.206	.142	.072	.073	.145
Baltimore	1992	398	80	15	2	13	2	35	12	1	0	6	19	58	.216	.130	.066	.064	.130

Rick Dempsey, 43

Bats Right   237L   110R   130G   78F

L= .113G .100L .078F (.045/.048) .093 .092G .079R .057F = R

		ATBATS	1B	2B	3B	HR	HBP	BB	GDP	SB	CS	ROE	XB	RUNS	EOB%	RL#	SET-UP	DR-IN	RPA
Los Angeles	1990	128	18	5	0	2	0	23	8	1	0	0	3	13	.194	.078	.039	.041	.080
Milwaukee	1991	147	25	5	0	4	0	22	7	0	2	2	1	17	.200	.096	.047	.049	.096
Baltimore	1992	9	1	0	0	0	0	2	1	0	0	0	2	0	.142	.040	.016	.024	.040

Mike Devereaux, 29

Bats Right   539L   1248R   487G   402F

L= .148G .149L .151F (.059/.066) .125 .114G .115R .117F = R

		ATBATS	1B	2B	3B	HR	HBP	BB	GDP	SB	CS	ROE	XB	RUNS	EOB%	RL#	SET-UP	DR-IN	RPA
Baltimore	1990	367	57	18	1	12	0	28	10	13	14	10	39	42	.161	.103	.045	.059	.104
Baltimore	1991	608	102	27	10	19	2	45	13	16	11	8	48	80	.185	.117	.057	.063	.120
Baltimore	1992	653	116	29	11	24	4	43	14	10	9	5	40	93	.185	.130	.061	.069	.130

Leo Gomez, 25

Bats Right   281L   761R   308G   219F   120ML

L= .141G .135L .127F (.067/.063) .130 .134G .128R .120F = R

		ATBATS	1B	2B	3B	HR	HBP	BB	GDP	SB	CS	ROE	XB	RUNS	EOB%	RL#	SET-UP	DR-IN	RPA
Baltimore	1990	39	9	0	0	0	0	8	2	0	0	0	4	4	.253	.085	.047	.039	.086
Baltimore	1991	391	56	17	2	16	2	40	11	1	1	8	18	54	.195	.118	.059	.062	.121
Baltimore	1992	468	83	24	0	17	8	59	14	2	3	3	33	74	.228	.135	.071	.064	.135

Chris Hoiles, 27

Bats Right   260L   561R   231G   179F

L= .189G .135L .065F (.071/.068) .139 .195G .141R .071F = R

		ATBATS	1B	2B	3B	HR	HBP	BB	GDP	SB	CS	ROE	XB	RUNS	EOB%	RL#	SET-UP	DR-IN	RPA
Baltimore	1990	63	8	3	0	1	0	4	0	0	0	1	7	6	.187	.087	.041	.047	.088
Baltimore	1991	341	57	15	0	11	1	28	11	0	2	4	18	40	.178	.102	.048	.057	.105
Baltimore	1992	310	54	10	1	20	2	53	8	0	2	3	21	64	.241	.173	.093	.080	.173

Sam Horn, 29

Bats Left   41L   801R   250G   175F

L= ....G .030L ....F (.056/.070) .126 .138G .131R .121F = R

		ATBATS	1B	2B	3B	HR	HBP	BB	GDP	SB	CS	ROE	XB	RUNS	EOB%	RL#	SET-UP	DR-IN	RPA
Baltimore	1990	246	34	13	0	14	0	31	8	0	0	3	16	39	.195	.137	.067	.071	.138
Baltimore	1991	317	35	16	0	23	3	37	10	0	0	1	13	50	.165	.133	.061	.076	.137
Baltimore	1992	162	22	10	1	5	1	19	8	0	0	1	5	20	.183	.105	.049	.056	.105

Tim Hulett, 32

Bats Right   218L   334R   118G   161F

L= .093G .096L .098F (.044/.054) .098 .097G .100R .102F = R

		ATBATS	1B	2B	3B	HR	HBP	BB	GDP	SB	CS	ROE	XB	RUNS	EOB%	RL#	SET-UP	DR-IN	RPA
Baltimore	1990	153	28	7	1	3	0	15	2	1	0	2	14	21	.233	.120	.064	.057	.121
Baltimore	1991	206	26	9	0	7	1	13	3	0	1	4	13	22	.165	.096	.043	.055	.098
Baltimore	1992	142	30	7	2	2	1	9	7	0	1	0	5	16	.180	.099	.046	.053	.099

BALTIMORE ORIOLES

Chito Martinez, 27

Bats Left   78L   386R   119G   110F   240ML

L= .071G .118L .168F   (.069/.075) .144   .102G .149R .199F = R

		ATBATS	1B	2B	3B	HR	HBP	BB	GDP	SB	CS	ROE	XB	RUNS	EOB%	RL#	SET-UP	DR-IN	RPA
Baltimore	1991	216	32	12	1	13	0	11	2	1	1	4	15	34	.175	.144	.068	.080	.148
Baltimore	1992	198	37	10	1	5	2	27	9	0	1	0	18	28	.218	.119	.061	.058	.119

Mark McLemore, 28

Bats Both   117L   270R   119G   96F

L= .089G .078L .064F   (.038/.039) .077   .087G .076R .062F = R

		ATBATS	1B	2B	3B	HR	HBP	BB	GDP	SB	CS	ROE	XB	RUNS	EOB%	RL#	SET-UP	DR-IN	RPA
California	1990	48	5	2	0	0	0	4	1	1	0	1	5	3	.170	.056	.025	.030	.055
Cleveland	1990	12	2	0	0	0	0	0	0	0	0	0	2	1	.118	.044	.016	.028	.044
Houston	1991	61	8	1	0	0	0	6	1	0	2	0	6	3	.138	.040	.018	.027	.045
Baltimore	1992	228	47	7	2	0	0	20	6	11	5	0	31	22	.194	.086	.042	.044	.086

Luis Mercedes, 24

Bats Right   78L   42R   33G   27F   919ML

L= ....G .100L ....F   (.050/.051) .101   ....G .103R ....F = R

		ATBATS	1B	2B	3B	HR	HBP	BB	GDP	SB	CS	ROE	XB	RUNS	EOB%	RL#	SET-UP	DR-IN	RPA
Baltimore	1991	54	9	2	0	0	0	4	1	0	0	2	6	5	.216	.077	.041	.039	.080
Baltimore	1992	50	5	2	0	0	1	8	2	0	1	0	4	3	.179	.054	.025	.029	.054

Randy Milligan, 31

Bats Right   450L   1185R   441G   362F

L= .118G .159L .210F   (.069/.058) .127   .074G .115R .166F = R

		ATBATS	1B	2B	3B	HR	HBP	BB	GDP	SB	CS	ROE	XB	RUNS	EOB%	RL#	SET-UP	DR-IN	RPA
Baltimore	1990	362	55	20	1	20	2	85	11	6	3	7	41	82	.284	.178	.103	.076	.179
Baltimore	1991	483	92	17	2	16	2	80	23	0	7	1	25	70	.217	.116	.061	.058	.119
Baltimore	1992	462	78	21	1	11	4	106	15	0	1	4	30	79	.284	.135	.078	.057	.135

Joe Orsulak, 30

Bats Left   237L   1168R   411G   287F

L= .079G .095L .119F   (.060/.055) .115   .103G .119R .143F = R

		ATBATS	1B	2B	3B	HR	HBP	BB	GDP	SB	CS	ROE	XB	RUNS	EOB%	RL#	SET-UP	DR-IN	RPA
Baltimore	1990	413	83	14	3	11	1	37	7	6	8	2	32	54	.203	.116	.058	.059	.117
Baltimore	1991	486	107	22	1	5	4	27	9	6	2	5	35	57	.221	.105	.055	.053	.108
Baltimore	1992	391	88	18	3	4	4	23	3	5	5	6	32	52	.240	.123	.066	.057	.123

Mark Parent, 31

Bats Right   105L   138R   99G   57F   405ML

L= .145G .155L .172F   (.052/.055) .107   .060G .070R .087F = R

		ATBATS	1B	2B	3B	HR	HBP	BB	GDP	SB	CS	ROE	XB	RUNS	EOB%	RL#	SET-UP	DR-IN	RPA
San Diego	1990	189	28	11	0	3	0	13	2	1	0	2	9	19	.195	.093	.045	.048	.093
Texas	1991	1	0	0	0	0	0	0	0	0	0	0	0	0	.000	.000	.000	.000	.000
Baltimore	1992	34	5	1	0	2	1	3	0	0	0	0	3	6	.204	.149	.074	.075	.149

Billy Ripken, 28

Bats Right   383L   736R   306G   228F

L= .069G .081L .097F   (.031/.039) .070   .052G .064R .080F = R

		ATBATS	1B	2B	3B	HR	HBP	BB	GDP	SB	CS	ROE	XB	RUNS	EOB%	RL#	SET-UP	DR-IN	RPA
Baltimore	1990	406	86	28	1	3	4	26	7	5	2	12	39	55	.257	.124	.069	.056	.125
Baltimore	1991	287	50	11	1	0	0	15	14	0	1	3	15	18	.147	.056	.024	.033	.057
Baltimore	1992	330	57	15	0	4	3	17	10	2	3	5	18	30	.172	.082	.037	.045	.082

Cal Ripken, 32

Bats Right   569L   1531R   568G   458F

L= .133G .151L .174F   (.071/.070) .141   .119G .137R .160F = R

		ATBATS	1B	2B	3B	HR	HBP	BB	GDP	SB	CS	ROE	XB	RUNS	EOB%	RL#	SET-UP	DR-IN	RPA
Baltimore	1990	600	97	28	4	21	5	64	12	3	1	12	47	91	.226	.132	.069	.064	.133
Baltimore	1991	650	125	46	5	34	5	38	19	6	1	17	39	121	.219	.165	.087	.083	.170
Baltimore	1992	637	116	29	1	14	7	50	13	4	3	5	49	79	.207	.111	.055	.056	.111

BALTIMORE ORIOLES

David Segui, 26

Bats Both   238L   346R   170G   107F

L= .072G .096L .134F   (.046/.046) .092 .065G .089R .127F = R

		ATBATS	1B	2B	3B	HR	HBP	BB	GDP	SB	CS	ROE	XB	RUNS	EOB%	RL#	SET-UP	DR-IN	RPA
Baltimore	1990	123	21	7	0	2	1	9	12	0	0	1	12	10	.125	.067	.026	.042	.068
Baltimore	1991	212	50	7	0	2	0	10	7	1	1	5	8	22	.205	.093	.048	.048	.096
Baltimore	1992	189	34	9	0	1	0	17	4	1	0	0	17	18	.206	.088	.044	.044	.088

Jeff Tackett, 27

Bats Right   66L   152R   52G   52F   504ML

L= .146G .148L .150F   (.035/.045) .080 .048G .050R .052F = R

		ATBATS	1B	2B	3B	HR	HBP	BB	GDP	SB	CS	ROE	XB	RUNS	EOB%	RL#	SET-UP	DR-IN	RPA
Baltimore	1991	8	1	0	0	0	0	2	0	0	0	0	1	1	.271	.076	.044	.033	.077
Baltimore	1992	179	29	8	1	5	2	16	11	0	0	1	18	20	.160	.095	.041	.054	.095

PITCHERS

Throws: Groundball type, extreme lefty

Pat Clements, 30

(.041/.114) .082   134L   174R

		OUTS	RO	1B	2B	3B	HR	HBP	BB	GDP	SB	CS	PO	WP	BK	RUNS	EOB%	RL#	RPA
San Diego	1990	39	39	11	7	1	1	0	6	2	0	0	0	1	0	10	.234	.154	.153
San Diego	1991	43	43	10	3	0	0	0	5	3	0	0	0	0	0	4	.140	.066	.067
San Diego	1992	71	71	21	4	0	0	2	8	3	5	1	0	0	0	9	.197	.087	.083
Baltimore	1992	74	74	20	3	0	0	2	11	3	0	0	0	1	0	9	.218	.086	.088

Throws: Neutral type, neutral righty

Storm Davis, 31

(.105/.104) .104   644L   667R

		OUTS	RO	1B	2B	3B	HR	HBP	BB	GDP	SB	CS	PO	WP	BK	RUNS	EOB%	RL#	RPA
Kansas City	1990	336	12	91	27	2	9	0	34	8	3	0	0	8	1	60	.202	.118	.123
Kansas City	1991	343	188	105	21	3	11	1	37	16	2	2	0	1	0	58	.174	.114	.116
Baltimore	1992	268	239	65	8	1	5	2	30	10	9	2	0	4	0	32	.161	.086	.087

Throws: Neutral type, extreme lefty

Mike Flanagan, 41

(.064/.119) .101   211L   417R

		OUTS	RO	1B	2B	3B	HR	HBP	BB	GDP	SB	CS	PO	WP	BK	RUNS	EOB%	RL#	RPA
Toronto	1990	61	0	22	3	0	3	0	8	1	1	3	0	0	0	12	.177	.130	.126
Baltimore	1991	295	283	65	13	0	6	3	19	12	6	3	0	2	2	28	.117	.072	.071
Baltimore	1992	104	104	40	6	1	3	5	22	5	2	0	0	4	0	29	.280	.161	.164

Throws: Groundball type, moderate to severe righty

Todd Frohwirth, 30

(.086/.065) .073   296L   487R

		OUTS	RO	1B	2B	3B	HR	HBP	BB	GDP	SB	CS	PO	WP	BK	RUNS	EOB%	RL#	RPA
Philadelphia	1990	3	3	3	0	0	0	0	4	0	1	0	0	1	0	4	.633	.365	.365
Baltimore	1991	289	289	45	14	3	2	1	26	9	10	4	1	0	0	21	.115	.058	.058
Baltimore	1992	318	318	78	15	0	4	3	37	14	11	2	0	1	0	37	.166	.083	.085

Throws: Neutral type, moderate to severe lefty

Craig Lefferts, 35

(.069/.102) .095   281L   1080R

		OUTS	RO	1B	2B	3B	HR	HBP	BB	GDP	SB	CS	PO	WP	BK	RUNS	EOB%	RL#	RPA
San Diego	1990	236	236	51	7	0	10	1	18	5	3	2	0	1	0	29	.133	.091	.090
San Diego	1991	207	207	55	11	3	5	1	11	4	6	4	0	3	1	28	.150	.096	.098
San Diego	1992	490	0	131	29	4	16	0	33	13	14	8	1	4	1	68	.145	.098	.096
Baltimore	1992	99	0	27	4	0	3	0	6	4	6	2	0	1	0	12	.115	.087	.088

Throws: Neutral type, moderate to severe reverse righty

Ben McDonald, 25

(.101/.124) .112   951L   949R

		OUTS	RO	1B	2B	3B	HR	HBP	BB	GDP	SB	CS	PO	WP	BK	RUNS	EOB%	RL#	RPA
Baltimore	1990	356	29	65	14	0	9	0	35	5	10	2	1	5	0	40	.153	.082	.084
Baltimore	1991	379	0	85	22	3	16	1	41	11	14	3	0	3	0	59	.160	.111	.111
Baltimore	1992	681	0	132	44	5	32	9	69	14	20	8	0	3	2	108	.156	.111	.113

BALTIMORE ORIOLES

Bob Milacki, 28

Throws: Neutral type, moderate reverse righty

(.110/.120) .115   894L   903R   250ML

		OUTS	RO	1B	2B	3B	HR	HBP	BB	GDP	SB	CS	PO	WP	BK	RUNS	EOB%	RL#	RPA
Baltimore	1990	406	18	95	30	0	18	0	59	13	19	3	0	2	1	74	.184	.123	.126
Baltimore	1991	552	63	119	39	0	17	1	50	18	12	6	0	1	2	69	.143	.093	.092
Baltimore	1992	347	28	89	31	4	16	2	42	13	11	1	0	7	1	71	.188	.135	.137

Alan Mills, 26

Throws: Neutral type, moderate righty

(.118/.106) .112   313L   337R   522ML

		OUTS	RO	1B	2B	3B	HR	HBP	BB	GDP	SB	CS	PO	WP	BK	RUNS	EOB%	RL#	RPA
N.Y. Yankees	1990	125	125	32	10	2	4	1	27	5	4	1	0	3	0	26	.233	.138	.133
N.Y. Yankees	1991	49	22	13	2	0	1	0	8	1	3	0	1	2	0	7	.206	.106	.100
Baltimore	1992	310	270	55	16	2	5	1	44	11	12	4	0	2	0	34	.156	.081	.082

Mike Mussina, 24

Throws: Flyball type, moderate to severe reverse righty

(.077/.099) .088   634L   619R   497ML

		OUTS	RO	1B	2B	3B	HR	HBP	BB	GDP	SB	CS	PO	WP	BK	RUNS	EOB%	RL#	RPA
Baltimore	1991	263	0	55	14	1	7	1	21	9	4	4	0	3	1	28	.123	.081	.080
Baltimore	1992	723	0	152	39	5	16	2	46	18	9	9	1	6	0	77	.129	.079	.080

Gregg Olson, 26

Throws: Neutral type, moderate to severe reverse righty

(.077/.100) .088   433L   396R

		OUTS	RO	1B	2B	3B	HR	HBP	BB	GDP	SB	CS	PO	WP	BK	RUNS	EOB%	RL#	RPA
Baltimore	1990	223	223	46	8	0	3	3	28	6	11	2	0	5	0	26	.176	.082	.084
Baltimore	1991	221	221	66	5	2	1	1	24	5	13	1	0	8	1	30	.210	.097	.096
Baltimore	1992	184	184	38	4	1	3	0	24	8	10	0	2	4	0	19	.140	.075	.076

Jim Poole, 26

Throws: Neutral type, moderate to severe lefty

(.072/.107) .102   87L   123R   396ML

		OUTS	RO	1B	2B	3B	HR	HBP	BB	GDP	SB	CS	PO	WP	BK	RUNS	EOB%	RL#	RPA
Los Angeles	1990	32	32	4	2	0	1	0	4	2	0	0	0	1	0	3	.094	.068	.072
Texas	1991	18	18	8	2	0	0	0	3	0	0	0	0	0	0	5	.324	.156	.156
Baltimore	1991	108	108	14	2	0	3	0	7	2	0	1	0	2	0	7	.085	.055	.055
Baltimore	1992	10	10	3	0	0	0	0	1	0	2	1	0	0	0	1	.102	.062	.063

Arthur Rhodes, 23

Throws: Neutral type, lefty

(..../.111) .107   61L   482R   862ML

		OUTS	RO	1B	2B	3B	HR	HBP	BB	GDP	SB	CS	PO	WP	BK	RUNS	EOB%	RL#	RPA
Baltimore	1991	108	0	34	8	1	4	0	23	2	7	2	0	2	0	27	.254	.156	.154
Baltimore	1992	283	0	57	20	4	6	1	36	10	4	4	0	2	1	38	.161	.094	.095

Rick Sutcliffe, 36

Throws: Neutral type, moderate righty

(.115/.097) .106   754L   711R

		OUTS	RO	1B	2B	3B	HR	HBP	BB	GDP	SB	CS	PO	WP	BK	RUNS	EOB%	RL#	RPA
Chicago Cubs	1990	64	0	18	5	0	2	0	12	1	3	2	0	4	0	12	.225	.133	.123
Chicago Cubs	1991	290	2	67	20	5	4	0	43	12	21	2	0	2	2	40	.191	.104	.095
Baltimore	1992	712	0	187	37	7	20	7	70	20	22	5	0	7	2	112	.180	.108	.110

Mark Williamson, 33

Throws: Neutral type, extreme reverse righty

(.079/.132) .110   300L   428R

		OUTS	RO	1B	2B	3B	HR	HBP	BB	GDP	SB	CS	PO	WP	BK	RUNS	EOB%	RL#	RPA
Baltimore	1990	256	256	42	13	2	8	0	26	9	5	2	0	1	0	28	.121	.080	.082
Baltimore	1991	241	241	60	16	2	9	0	28	8	10	3	0	7	0	40	.169	.115	.115
Baltimore	1992	56	56	13	1	1	1	0	9	3	2	1	0	1	0	7	.146	.084	.085

Baltimore Orioles AAA & AA Minor League Ratings

AAA (ROCHESTER)	AGE	BATS	POSITION	CPA	RUNS	SET-UP	DRIVE-IN	RPA
Damon Buford	22	R	OF	594	50.2	.043	.042	.085
Bobby Dickerson	27	R	SS	267	18.4	.029	.040	.069
Ricky Gutierrez	22	R	2B\SS	496	34.9	.035	.035	.070
Doug Jennings	28	L	1B\OF	483	61.9	.071	.057	.128
Dave Liddell	26	R	C	164	9.2	.024	.032	.056
Rod Lofton	25	R	2B	331	18.4	.024	.032	.056
Scott Meadows	26	R	OF	449	44.6	.056	.043	.099
Luis Mercedes	24	R	OF	465	45.4	.051	.047	.098
Mark Parent	31	R	C	405	44.5	.051	.059	.110
Doug Robbins	26	R	C\1B	343	41.2	.067	.053	.120
Steve Scarsone	26	R	2B	452	43.1	.043	.052	.095
Tommy Shields	28	R	3B	472	52.2	.057	.054	.111
Jack Voigt	26	R	OF\1B	515	63.2	.065	.058	.123
Melvin Wearing	25	R	DH\1B	559	58.5	.057	.048	.105
Ed Yacopino	27	B	OF	485	43.5	.045	.045	.090

AA (HAGERSTOWN)	AGE	BATS	POSITION	CPA	RUNS	SET-UP	DRIVE-IN	RPA
Manny Alexander	21	R	SS	564	42.5	.034	.041	.075
Sergio Cairo	22	R	OF	454	35.1	.038	.039	.077
Paul Carey	24	L	1B	280	24.7	.043	.045	.088
Cesar DeVarez	23	R	C	345	21.3	.029	.033	.062
Sam Ferretti	27	R	3B\2B\SS	230	15.4	.031	.036	.067
Tim Holland	23	R	3B	288	16.4	.024	.033	.057
Brent Miller	22	L	1B\3B	476	33.0	.031	.038	.069
Greg Roth	26	L	3B\2B	202	12.1	.028	.032	.060
Mark Smith	22	R	OF	536	49.3	.047	.045	.092
Brad Tyler	23	L	2B	296	23.7	.041	.039	.080
Kyle Washington	23	R	SS	441	38.2	.046	.041	.087

AAA Pitchers	Age	Throws	Outs	RPA	AA Pitchers	Age	Throws	Outs	RPA
Tim Layana	28	R	217	.147	Jeff Bumgarner	25	R	83	.192
Pat Leinen	25	L	166	.172	Tim Drummond	28	R	388	.136
Jim Lewis	28	R	181	.148	Grady Hall	28	L	239	.122
Richie Lewis	26	R	478	.122	Mike Hook	24	L	91	.145
Bob Milacki	28	R	183	.139	Stacey Jones	25	R	211	.127
Dave Miller	26	R	374	.131	Daryl Moore	24	L	81	.106
John O'Donoghue	23	L	546	.112	John Pawlowski	29	R	195	.199
Mike Oquist	24	R	460	.139	Jeff Pico	26	R	82	.161
Brad Pennington	23	L	202	.097	John Polasek	24	L	134	.189
Jim Poole	26	L	166	.137	Chuck Ricci	24	R	173	.177
Arthur Rhodes	23	L	305	.116	Jeff Williams	23	R	369	.180
Todd Stephan	26	R	259	.139	Brian Wood	27	R	198	.159
Anthony Telford	26	R	543	.132	Kip Yaughn	23	R	349	.105

BOSTON RED SOX

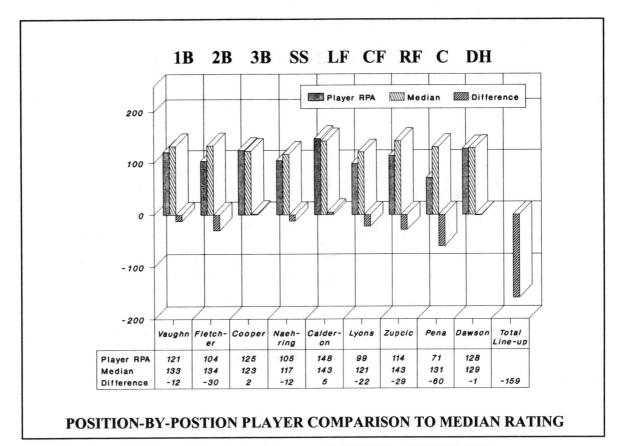

| | 1B | 2B | 3B | SS | LF | CF | RF | C | DH |
	Vaughn	Fletch-er	Cooper	Naeh-ring	Calder-on	Lyons	Zupcic	Pena	Dawson	Total Line-up
Player RPA	121	104	125	105	148	99	114	71	128	
Median	133	134	123	117	143	121	143	131	129	
Difference	-12	-30	2	-12	5	-22	-29	-60	-1	-159

POSITION-BY-POSTION PLAYER COMPARISON TO MEDIAN RATING

DEFENSIVE TEAM AND STADIUM DATA FOR THE LAST 3 YEARS:

TEAM DEFENSE BY POSITION:

POSITION-BY-POSITION STADIUM CHARACTERISTICS:

		1990	1991	1992	
1B:	Home	-1.1	-0.3	-3.1	Slightly easy to play
	Away	+4.0	+1.9	+0.3	
2B:	Home	+0.4	+6.4	+0.2	Very hard to play
	Away	-2.5	-1.0	+2.4	
3B:	Home	+0.1	+0.3	-1.7	Average
	Away	-8.4	+1.9	+2.9	
SS:	Home	-0.2	-3.9	-6.3	Slightly hard to play
	Away	-5.0	+2.1	-3.9	
LF:	Home	+1.7	-3.9	-3.7	Extremely hard to play. A H/A variant of 28.5
	Away	+1.7	-5.1	-3.7	RPA pts. per ball put in play over the 3 yrs!
CF:	Home	+0.8	+2.0	-6.2	Average
	Away	-5.4	+2.1	-3.2	
RF:	Home	+5.0	-0.3	+8.8	Slightly hard to play.
	Away	-4.5	-1.8	-5.2	
Total Home:		+6.7	+0.3	-12.0	RF & CF are not as difficult to play as they
Total Away:		-20.1	+0.1	-10.4	were in former years.

Comments: Boston's 1992 defense collapsed at shortstop and centerfield while continuing to be horrid in left field. With the addition of the immobile Andre Dawson to the right field defense for 1993 it should only get worse for this awful defensive team. The position-by-position 3-year stadium ratings are based upon the home vs. away difference in RPA per ball put in play. (*Translation:* Slightly > 5 pt. RPA difference; hard/easy > 10 pts.; very > 15 pts; extremely > 20 pts.)

BOSTON RED SOX

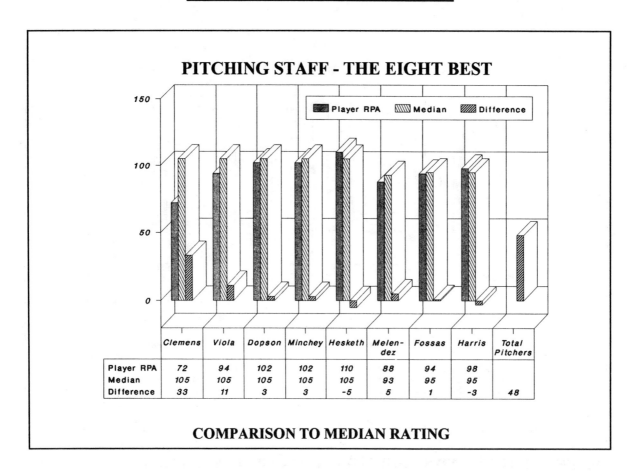

PITCHING STAFF - THE EIGHT BEST

Legend: ■ Player RPA ▨ Median ▨ Difference

	Clemens	Viola	Dopson	Minchey	Hesketh	Melen-dez	Fossas	Harris	Total Pitchers
Player RPA	72	94	102	102	110	88	94	98	
Median	105	105	105	105	105	93	95	95	
Difference	33	11	3	3	-5	5	1	-3	48

COMPARISON TO MEDIAN RATING

SUGGESTED LINE-UPS (with set-up RPA & drive-in RPA ratings):

Vs: Left-handed Groundball
3B:	S. Cooper	64-51
RF:	B. Zupcic	68-64
DH:	J. Clark	96-91
LF:	I. Calderon	91-88
1B:	M. Vaughn	73-77
2B:	S. Fletcher	57-52
SS:	T. Naehring	55-49
C:	B. Melvin	55-59
CF:	S. Lyons	37-37

Vs: Neutral Lefty Pitchers
3B:	S. Cooper	64-51
SS:	T. Naehring	70-64
DH:	J. Clark	100-87
LF:	I. Calderon	89-86
RF:	R. Zupcic	64-60
1B:	M. Vaughn	61-63
2B:	S. Fletcher	58-52
C:	B. Melvin	53-57
CF:	S. Lyons	34-35

Vs: Left-handed Flyball
3B:	S. Cooper	64-51
SS:	T. Naehring	92-85
DH:	J. Clark	106-93
LF:	I. Calderon	86-83
RF:	B. Zupcic	60-56
2B:	S. Fletcher	59-53
1B:	M. Vaughn	50-53
C:	B. Melvin	51-55
CF:	S. Lyons	32-32

Vs: Right-handed Groundball
3B:	S. Cooper	74-61
RF:	B. Zupcic	62-57
DH:	G. Blosser	73-73
1B:	M. Vaughn	77-82
LF:	I. Calderon	66-64
2B:	S. Fletcher	49-44
CF:	S. Lyons	45-45
C:	J. Marzano	41-38

Vs: Neutral Righty Pitchers
3B:	S. Cooper	74-61
LF:	I. Calderon	64-62
DH:	G. Blosser	73-73
1B:	M. Vaughn	77-82
RF:	B. Zupcic	58-53
2B:	S. Fletcher	50-44
SS:	L. Rivera	48-48
CF:	S. Lyons	42-43
C:	T. Pena	30-33

Vs: Right-handed Flyball
3B:	S. Cooper	74-61
LF:	I. Calderon	61-59
DH:	G. Blosser	73-73
1B:	M. Vaughn	55-57
RF:	B. Zupcic	54-49
SS:	L. Rivera	52-52
2B:	S. Fletcher	51-45
CF:	S. Lyons	40-40
C:	T. Pena	37-41

Comments: There's a reason I left Mike Greenwell & Andre Dawson off of the above proposed lineups. The reason is that neither can play defense & this team would be even more pitiful if I included them. I also left off John Valentin, despite his strong hitting ability, due to his extremely poor defensive stats for his short stint at shortstop in '92. Hopefully he will improve enough defensively so that I can include him next year in these proposed lineups.

BOSTON RED SOX

What in the world is going on in the Red Sox front office? I cannot think of more disastrous personnel decisions than have been made by this front office over this fall and winter. It almost reminds one of the movie "Major League" where management purposely attempted to destroy the team in order to get a new stadium.

I don't think these disastrous moves were done with the purpose of destroying this team for some ulterior purpose. My impression is that the moves made are the signature of a front office in a total panic after a disastrous season.

Why am I so hard on the Red Sox front office? The Red Sox, prior to these disastrous moves, had some of the best young hitting talent in all of baseball in the persons of Phil Plantier, Eric Wedge and Greg Blosser. These three could have been the core around which the Red Sox could have quickly grown into contenders. Only the Braves possess a set of young power hitters to match these three.

The Red Sox inexplicably failed to protect Wedge in the expansion draft while protecting over-the-hill players Tony Pena and Mike Greenwell. Unfortunately for the Red Sox, Wedge was selected by the Rockies in one of their only selections that made any sense whatsoever. Then the Red Sox traded Plantier. They got a very good reliever in Jose Melendez, but there is absolutely no way I make that trade.

While protecting their over-the-hill players, the Red Sox waste money signing Billy Hatcher(!) to a multi-year contract, sign Steve Lyons(!) and signed a very old, immobile outfielder, Andre Dawson, to a huge multi-year contract. The trade of Ivan Calderon for Mike Gardiner might have been a plus on a contending team, but not here. This team has done exactly the opposite of what they ought to be doing. Haven't they noticed what Cleveland, Houston and Montreal have accomplished by emphasizing young talent in their rebuilding plans? When you're down, unless you sign a Barry Bonds, it's the only way to go. This team has thrown away its future trying to get immediate band-aid solutions. The irony is that this team would have been much stronger even this season, let alone the future, had this front office not panicked and simply gone with the kids.

The signing of Scott Fletcher is a minor plus, but it won't in any way stop the bleeding. He's only a journeyman player.

The only asset this team possesses is its pitching staff. That's not nearly enough to be a contender or even respectable. Pitching isn't 90% of the game. Just look at the pitching rich Red Sox and Mets. Just look at the Oakland A's with their truly awful pitching staff. Pitching, as stated many times before, is only a part of the defense. And defense, by definition, is exactly 50% of the game. I would estimate that pitching is no more than 1/3 of the game. The most valuable players in the game are your big hitters like Barry Bonds and Rickey Henderson. That's why it was such an awful decision when the Red Sox traded away two of their three young power hitters.

Nate Minchey looks like a good young pitching prospect.

Boston's Projected record for 1993: 73--89, good for last place in the division.

BOSTON RED SOX

Wade Boggs, 34

Bats Left   625L   1286R   509G   462F

L= .092G .095L .099F (.073/.056) .129 .141G .145R .149F = R

		ATBATS	1B	2B	3B	HR	HBP	BB	GDP	SB	CS	ROE	XB	RUNS	EOB%	RL#	SET-UP	DR-IN	RPA
Boston	1990	619	132	44	5	6	1	68	14	0	1	8	60	90	.267	.132	.072	.056	.128
Boston	1991	546	129	42	2	8	0	64	16	1	2	11	41	90	.283	.147	.083	.060	.143
Boston	1992	514	100	22	4	7	4	55	10	1	3	7	33	66	.240	.116	.061	.052	.113

Tom Brunansky, 32

Bats Right   513L   1131R   467G   388F

L= .145G .137L .128F (.061/.060) .121 .122G .114R .105F = R

		ATBATS	1B	2B	3B	HR	HBP	BB	GDP	SB	CS	ROE	XB	RUNS	EOB%	RL#	SET-UP	DR-IN	RPA
St. Louis	1990	57	5	3	0	1	1	12	1	0	0	0	3	7	.245	.094	.051	.043	.094
Boston	1990	461	79	24	5	15	3	47	12	5	10	3	29	61	.197	.120	.057	.059	.116
Boston	1991	459	64	24	1	16	3	47	8	1	2	2	22	56	.195	.111	.052	.056	.108
Boston	1992	458	73	31	3	15	0	64	11	2	6	4	23	71	.230	.137	.070	.063	.133

Ellis Burks, 28

Bats Right   439L   1000R   396G   352F

L= .108G .111L .115F (.060/.060) .120 .121G .124R .128F = R

		ATBATS	1B	2B	3B	HR	HBP	BB	GDP	SB	CS	ROE	XB	RUNS	EOB%	RL#	SET-UP	DR-IN	RPA
Boston	1990	588	112	33	8	21	1	44	18	9	12	8	51	83	.192	.131	.061	.066	.127
Boston	1991	474	69	33	3	14	6	37	7	6	12	10	38	60	.199	.117	.056	.058	.114
Boston	1992	235	41	8	3	8	1	23	5	5	2	5	20	35	.215	.134	.067	.064	.131

Jack Clark, 37

Bats Right   430L   922R   402G   291F

L= .191G .199L .211F (.074/.062) .136 .099G .107R .119F = R

		ATBATS	1B	2B	3B	HR	HBP	BB	GDP	SB	CS	ROE	XB	RUNS	EOB%	RL#	SET-UP	DR-IN	RPA
San Diego	1990	334	51	12	1	25	2	93	12	4	3	5	30	86	.287	.192	.112	.080	.192
Boston	1991	481	73	18	1	28	3	93	17	0	3	4	25	85	.234	.148	.076	.068	.144
Boston	1992	257	38	11	0	5	2	53	4	1	1	4	19	38	.278	.124	.069	.052	.121

Scott Cooper, 25

Bats Left   55L   362R   96G   134F   553ML

L= .190G .176L .166F (.064/.052) .116 .121G .107R .097F = R

		ATBATS	1B	2B	3B	HR	HBP	BB	GDP	SB	CS	ROE	XB	RUNS	EOB%	RL#	SET-UP	DR-IN	RPA
Boston	1990	1	0	0	0	0	0	0	0	0	0	0	1	0	.000	.000	.000	.000	.000
Boston	1991	35	10	4	2	0	0	2	0	0	0	0	7	8	.348	.235	.141	.085	.226
Boston	1992	337	67	21	0	5	0	37	5	1	1	3	23	46	.251	.126	.067	.056	.123

Mike Greenwell, 29

Bats Left   480L   1008R   406G   342F

L= .096G .100L .104F (.056/.053) .109 .109G .113R .117F = R

		ATBATS	1B	2B	3B	HR	HBP	BB	GDP	SB	CS	ROE	XB	RUNS	EOB%	RL#	SET-UP	DR-IN	RPA
Boston	1990	610	131	30	6	14	4	53	19	8	7	10	49	85	.227	.128	.065	.059	.124
Boston	1991	544	122	26	6	9	3	37	11	15	7	7	33	72	.229	.123	.063	.057	.120
Boston	1992	180	38	2	0	2	2	17	8	2	3	1	9	16	.179	.078	.035	.041	.076

Billy Hatcher, 32

Bats Right   513L   953R   487G   311F

L= .081G .082L .084F (.041/.045) .086 .087G .088R .090F = R

		ATBATS	1B	2B	3B	HR	HBP	BB	GDP	SB	CS	ROE	XB	RUNS	EOB%	RL#	SET-UP	DR-IN	RPA
Cincinnati	1990	504	101	28	5	5	6	28	4	30	10	12	57	65	.235	.123	.064	.056	.120
Cincinnati	1991	442	84	25	3	4	7	22	9	11	9	6	33	45	.199	.093	.044	.046	.090
Cincinnati	1992	94	22	3	0	2	0	5	2	0	2	0	4	10	.180	.101	.047	.055	.102
Boston	1992	315	56	16	2	1	3	16	9	4	6	2	29	26	.169	.077	.034	.041	.075

BOSTON RED SOX

		Bats Left		46L	393R	129G	111F		146ML

Steve Lyons, 32

L= ....G .069L ....F **(.043/.044) .087** .094G .089R .084F = R

		ATBATS	1B	2B	3B	HR	HBP	BB	GDP	SB	CS	ROE	XB	RUNS	EOB%	RL#	SET-UP	DR-IN	RPA
White Sox	1990	146	20	6	1	1	1	9	1	1	0	4	12	13	.202	.083	.041	.042	.083
Boston	1991	212	36	10	1	4	0	9	1	10	3	1	11	21	.175	.096	.043	.050	.093
Atlanta	1992	14	0	0	1	0	0	0	1	0	0	0	0	0	.033	.015	.000	.015	.015
Montreal	1992	13	3	0	0	0	0	1	1	1	2	0	0	0	.015	.024	.002	.021	.023
Boston	1992	28	6	0	1	0	0	2	0	0	1	0	3	3	.192	.091	.042	.046	.088

		Bats Right		74L	188R	98G	53F		68ML

John Marzano, 29

L= .102G .088L .063F **(.036/.034) .070** .077G .063R .038F = R

		ATBATS	1B	2B	3B	HR	HBP	BB	GDP	SB	CS	ROE	XB	RUNS	EOB%	RL#	SET-UP	DR-IN	RPA
Boston	1990	83	16	4	0	0	0	5	0	0	1	1	3	7	.217	.084	.042	.040	.082
Boston	1991	114	22	8	0	0	1	1	5	0	0	2	6	8	.166	.072	.031	.039	.070
Boston	1992	50	1	2	1	0	1	2	0	0	1	1	4	2	.124	.041	.015	.026	.041

		Bats Right		126L	237R	107G	74F		44ML

Tim Naehring, 25

L= .095G .125L .168F **(.052/.047) .099** .055G .085R .128F = R

		ATBATS	1B	2B	3B	HR	HBP	BB	GDP	SB	CS	ROE	XB	RUNS	EOB%	RL#	SET-UP	DR-IN	RPA
Boston	1990	85	15	6	0	2	0	7	2	0	0	2	6	11	.227	.123	.063	.059	.122
Boston	1991	55	5	1	0	0	0	6	0	0	0	1	2	3	.184	.047	.022	.024	.046
Boston	1992	186	32	8	0	3	3	18	1	0	0	1	10	22	.234	.109	.056	.051	.107

		Bats Right		412L	1116R	396G	374F		

Tony Pena, 35

L= .084G .098L .113F **(.037/.042) .079** .058G .072R .087F = R

		ATBATS	1B	2B	3B	HR	HBP	BB	GDP	SB	CS	ROE	XB	RUNS	EOB%	RL#	SET-UP	DR-IN	RPA
Boston	1990	491	102	19	1	7	1	40	23	8	6	9	38	50	.191	.093	.043	.048	.091
Boston	1991	464	77	23	2	5	4	36	23	8	4	6	28	40	.171	.078	.034	.042	.076
Boston	1992	410	76	21	1	1	1	24	11	3	2	7	30	37	.197	.085	.040	.042	.082

		Bats Left		111L	478R	159G	147F		419ML

Phil Plantier, 23

L= .085G .095L .105F **(.081/.071) .152** .155G .165R .175F = R

		ATBATS	1B	2B	3B	HR	HBP	BB	GDP	SB	CS	ROE	XB	RUNS	EOB%	RL#	SET-UP	DR-IN	RPA
Boston	1990	15	1	1	0	0	1	4	1	0	0	0	0	1	.257	.072	.039	.032	.071
Boston	1991	148	30	7	1	11	1	21	2	1	0	0	15	35	.260	.207	.112	.090	.202
Boston	1992	349	60	19	0	7	2	36	9	2	3	4	23	42	.213	.109	.053	.053	.106

		Bats Right		578L	1436R	530G	497F		

Jody Reed, 30

L= .105G .108L .111F **(.054/.048) .102** .111G .114R .117F = R

		ATBATS	1B	2B	3B	HR	HBP	BB	GDP	SB	CS	ROE	XB	RUNS	EOB%	RL#	SET-UP	DR-IN	RPA
Boston	1990	598	123	45	0	5	4	71	19	4	5	9	57	80	.257	.120	.064	.052	.114
Boston	1991	618	126	42	2	5	4	58	15	6	5	9	54	77	.245	.114	.060	.051	.111
Boston	1992	550	105	27	1	3	0	60	17	7	10	8	51	57	.215	.094	.046	.045	.091

		Bats Right		334L	832R	296G	283F		

Luis Rivera, 28

L= .091G .098L .106F **(.047/.047) .094** .085G .092R .100F = R

		ATBATS	1B	2B	3B	HR	HBP	BB	GDP	SB	CS	ROE	XB	RUNS	EOB%	RL#	SET-UP	DR-IN	RPA
Boston	1990	346	51	20	0	7	1	25	10	4	3	3	32	33	.169	.089	.039	.047	.086
Boston	1991	414	74	22	3	8	3	35	10	4	4	6	38	50	.212	.110	.054	.053	.107
Boston	1992	288	50	11	1	0	3	26	5	4	3	1	12	24	.205	.077	.037	.038	.075

		Bats Right		43L	169R	53G	75F		880ML

John Valentin, 25

L= .063G .121L .162F **(.060/.050) .110** .049G .107R .148F = R

		ATBATS	1B	2B	3B	HR	HBP	BB	GDP	SB	CS	ROE	XB	RUNS	EOB%	RL#	SET-UP	DR-IN	RPA
Boston	1992	185	33	13	0	5	2	20	5	1	0	3	12	28	.243	.137	.072	.061	.133

Mo Vaughn, 25

Bats Left   126L   532R   136G   170F   475ML

L= .141G .115L .094F (.060/.062) .122 .150G .124R .103F = R

		ATBATS	1B	2B	3B	HR	HBP	BB	GDP	SB	CS	ROE	XB	RUNS	EOB%	RL#	SET-UP	DR-IN	RPA
Boston	1991	219	41	12	0	4	2	24	7	2	1	0	13	26	.217	.105	.052	.051	.103
Boston	1992	355	52	16	2	13	3	40	8	3	4	2	26	47	.195	.119	.056	.060	.116

Herm Winningham, 31

Bats Left   66L   535R   165G   175F

L= .010G .016L .021F (.033/.040) .073 .074G .080R .085F = R

		ATBATS	1B	2B	3B	HR	HBP	BB	GDP	SB	CS	ROE	XB	RUNS	EOB%	RL#	SET-UP	DR-IN	RPA
Cincinnati	1990	160	25	8	5	3	0	13	0	6	5	2	13	20	.206	.123	.059	.060	.119
Cincinnati	1991	169	30	6	1	1	0	10	2	4	4	3	13	14	.183	.077	.035	.039	.074
Boston	1992	234	45	8	1	1	0	10	3	6	6	1	14	18	.163	.075	.032	.040	.072

Bob Zupcic, 26

Bats Right   160L   292R   125G   125F   523ML

L= .125G .117L .109F (.056/.053) .109 .112G .104R .096F = R

		ATBATS	1B	2B	3B	HR	HBP	BB	GDP	SB	CS	ROE	XB	RUNS	EOB%	RL#	SET-UP	DR-IN	RPA
Boston	1991	25	3	0	0	1	0	1	0	0	0	0	0	2	.108	.071	.024	.045	.069
Boston	1992	392	85	19	1	3	4	24	6	2	2	4	32	45	.229	.109	.056	.050	.106

PITCHERS

Throws: Neutral type, neutral righty

Roger Clemens, 30

(.071/.066) .069   1520L 1352R

		OUTS	RO	1B	2B	3B	HR	HBP	BB	GDP	SB	CS	PO	WP	BK	RUNS	EOB%	RL#	RPA
Boston	1990	685	0	146	35	5	7	7	51	11	14	14	1	8	0	65	.148	.075	.071
Boston	1991	814	0	150	46	8	15	5	53	18	23	16	1	6	0	74	.119	.073	.070
Boston	1992	740	0	151	39	2	11	9	57	28	24	12	1	3	0	66	.120	.070	.067

Throws: Flyball type, moderate to severe righty

Danny Darwin, 37

(.126/.091) .109   825L   750R

		OUTS	RO	1B	2B	3B	HR	HBP	BB	GDP	SB	CS	PO	WP	BK	RUNS	EOB%	RL#	RPA
Houston	1990	488	135	94	31	0	11	4	27	8	17	6	1	0	2	56	.134	.076	.083
Boston	1991	204	0	38	17	1	15	4	14	1	5	1	0	2	0	38	.162	.137	.130
Boston	1992	484	163	111	31	6	11	5	44	7	14	6	0	5	0	68	.181	.103	.100

Throws: Groundball type, moderate to severe reverse righty

John Dopson, 29

(.085/.112) .100   298L   355R   153ML

		OUTS	RO	1B	2B	3B	HR	HBP	BB	GDP	SB	CS	PO	WP	BK	RUNS	EOB%	RL#	RPA
Boston	1990	53	0	10	1	0	2	0	9	1	1	1	0	0	0	6	.164	.094	.088
Boston	1991	3	3	1	1	0	0	0	1	0	0	0	0	0	0	1	.400	.219	.205
Boston	1992	424	0	111	30	1	17	2	36	17	17	7	0	3	3	62	.142	.107	.103

Throws: Groundball type, extreme lefty

Tony Fossas, 35

(.044/.111) .085   190L   291R

		OUTS	RO	1B	2B	3B	HR	HBP	BB	GDP	SB	CS	PO	WP	BK	RUNS	EOB%	RL#	RPA
Milwaukee	1990	88	88	32	6	1	5	0	8	2	2	0	0	0	0	22	.212	.157	.157
Boston	1991	171	171	36	10	0	3	3	19	9	5	2	0	2	0	18	.137	.078	.076
Boston	1992	89	89	19	10	1	1	1	11	2	4	2	0	0	0	13	.194	.105	.101

Throws: Neutral type, moderate reverse righty

Mike Gardiner, 27

(.095/.111) .104   532L   620R   358ML

		OUTS	RO	1B	2B	3B	HR	HBP	BB	GDP	SB	CS	PO	WP	BK	RUNS	EOB%	RL#	RPA
Seattle	1990	38	13	16	3	2	1	2	5	2	0	1	0	0	0	10	.234	.160	.157
Boston	1991	390	0	94	26	2	18	0	45	11	11	5	1	1	0	62	.161	.116	.111
Boston	1992	392	84	93	15	6	12	2	56	12	3	2	1	8	0	59	.183	.107	.105

BOSTON RED SOX

Greg Harris, 37

Throws: Groundball type, moderate to severe lefty

(.070/.097) .086   855L   1028R

		OUTS	RO	1B	2B	3B	HR	HBP	BB	GDP	SB	CS	PO	WP	BK	RUNS	EOB%	RL#	RPA
Boston	1990	553	15	133	37	3	13	6	70	17	15	7	3	8	1	77	.177	.103	.097
Boston	1991	519	157	110	30	4	13	5	64	17	1	6	3	6	1	64	.156	.092	.088
Boston	1992	323	284	61	11	4	6	4	49	11	3	6	0	5	0	35	.158	.083	.080

Joe Hesketh, 33

Throws: Groundball type, moderate lefty

(.095/.105) .103   282L   1206R

		OUTS	RO	1B	2B	3B	HR	HBP	BB	GDP	SB	CS	PO	WP	BK	RUNS	EOB%	RL#	RPA
Montreal	1990	9	9	2	0	0	0	0	1	0	1	0	0	0	0	1	.209	.071	.078
Atlanta	1990	93	93	16	8	1	5	1	12	4	0	0	1	5	0	14	.142	.113	.107
Boston	1990	77	45	29	6	0	2	0	10	2	1	0	0	3	0	16	.247	.143	.134
Boston	1991	460	130	86	32	5	19	0	50	19	7	8	1	8	0	57	.116	.095	.091
Boston	1992	446	31	106	39	2	15	2	49	10	17	4	0	6	0	75	.188	.118	.115

Daryl Irvine, 28

Throws: Groundball type, moderate righty

(.114/.111) .112   116L   157R   296ML

		OUTS	RO	1B	2B	3B	HR	HBP	BB	GDP	SB	CS	PO	WP	BK	RUNS	EOB%	RL#	RPA
Boston	1990	52	52	13	2	0	0	0	7	3	0	0	0	1	1	5	.166	.071	.066
Boston	1991	54	54	14	8	1	2	2	8	1	1	0	0	1	0	14	.264	.168	.160
Boston	1992	84	84	25	4	1	1	2	12	1	0	1	0	3	0	14	.243	.117	.113

Paul Quantrill, 24

Throws: Neutral type, righty

(..../.138) .128   76L   122R   1291ML

		OUTS	RO	1B	2B	3B	HR	HBP	BB	GDP	SB	CS	PO	WP	BK	RUNS	EOB%	RL#	RPA
Boston	1992	148	148	47	6	1	1	1	10	4	3	2	0	1	0	18	.177	.089	.086

Frank Viola, 32

Throws: Neutral type, moderate lefty

(.081/.090) .088   517L   2353R

		OUTS	RO	1B	2B	3B	HR	HBP	BB	GDP	SB	CS	PO	WP	BK	RUNS	EOB%	RL#	RPA
New York Mets	1990	749	0	174	36	2	15	2	58	17	25	15	1	11	0	82	.139	.079	.079
New York Mets	1991	694	0	189	41	4	25	1	50	16	6	16	0	6	1	89	.145	.104	.092
Boston	1992	714	0	161	40	0	13	7	85	29	12	5	1	12	2	83	.163	.087	.084

Matt Young, 34

Throws: Groundball type, moderate to severe lefty

(.091/.112) .109   228L   1381R

		OUTS	RO	1B	2B	3B	HR	HBP	BB	GDP	SB	CS	PO	WP	BK	RUNS	EOB%	RL#	RPA
Seattle	1990	676	3	155	25	3	15	6	100	27	20	14	0	16	0	83	.159	.090	.088
Boston	1991	266	11	76	12	0	4	2	51	11	8	3	0	5	0	41	.218	.108	.103
Boston	1992	212	111	50	12	0	7	3	40	6	10	3	0	2	0	37	.212	.120	.117

Boston Red Sox AAA & AA Minor League Ratings

AAA (PAWTUCKET)	AGE	BATS	POSITION	CPA	RUNS	SET-UP	DRIVE-IN	RPA
Luis Aguayo	33	R	3B	269	30.1	.062	.050	.112
Tom Barrett	32	B	2B	383	34.8	.050	.041	.091
Mike Brumley	29	B	OF\2B	415	34.4	.040	.043	.083
Jim Byrd	24	R	2B\SS	330	18.7	.024	.033	.057
John Flaherty	25	R	C	116	5.9	.022	.029	.051
Bob Geren	31	R	C	235	18.1	.031	.046	.077
Denny Gonzalez	29	R	3B	143	12.2	.042	.043	.085
Wayne Housie	27	B	OF	498	33.1	.030	.036	.066
Steve Lyons	32	L	3B\OF	146	13.4	.044	.048	.092
Dave Milstein	24	R	3B	289	17.3	.027	.033	.060
Juan Paris	26	R	OF	120	4.8	.015	.025	.040
John Shelby	34	B	OF	527	43.8	.036	.047	.083
Van Snider	29	L	OF	417	34.0	.035	.047	.082
Mike Twardoski	28	L	1B\OF	492	66.8	.080	.056	.136
John Valentin	25	R	SS	391	40.4	.054	.049	.103
Mo Vaughn	25	L	1B	172	19.1	.055	.056	.111
Eric Wedge	24	R	C	250	33.8	.072	.063	.135

AA (NEW BRITAIN)	AGE	BATS	POSITION	CPA	RUNS	SET-UP	DRIVE-IN	RPA
Mike Beams	25	R	OF	301	26.8	.038	.051	.089
Scott Bethea	23	L	SS\2B	388	30.3	.042	.036	.078
Greg Blosser	21	L	OF	506	65.6	.065	.065	.130
Bruce Chick	23	R	OF	470	37.1	.035	.044	.079
Mike DeKneef	23	R	2B	451	27.8	.026	.036	.062
Colin Dixon	24	R	3B\1B	290	17.4	.027	.033	.060
Greg Graham	23	B	SS	389	23.1	.027	.032	.059
Scott Hatteberg	23	L	C	346	28.6	.043	.040	.083
Jeff McNeely	23	R	OF	298	21.3	.033	.039	.072
Bill Norris	23	L	3B	425	25.6	.027	.033	.060
Ruben Rodriguez	28	R	C	174	12.6	.034	.038	.072
Willie Tatum	26	B	1B	551	61.9	.063	.049	.112
Paul Thoutsis	27	L	OF	362	29.5	.037	.044	.081

AAA Pitchers	Age	Throws	Outs	RPA	AA Pitchers	Age	Throws	Outs	RPA
Brian Conroy	24	R	483	.148	Gar Finnvold	24	R	495	.132
John Dopson	29	R	114	.081	Don Florence	25	L	224	.112
Mike Gardiner	27	R	98	.121	Nate Minchey	23	R	537	.097
Tom Fischer	25	L	212	.162	Tony Mosley	23	L	264	.164
Peter Hoy	26	R	219	.150	Gary Painter	24	R	285	.142
Daryl Irvine	28	R	123	.078	Ed Riley	22	L	381	.121
Derek Livernois	25	R	478	.157	Ken Ryan	24	R	178	.129
Kevin Morton	24	L	416	.163	Al Sanders	25	R	341	.175
Jeff Plympton	27	R	244	.133	Aaron Sele	22	R	99	.222
Paul Quantrill	24	R	357	.144	Tim Smith	24	R	462	.163
Larry Shikles	29	R	448	.135	Kevin Uhrhan	26	R	251	.142
Scott Taylor	25	L	486	.138					
Dave Walters	29	B	230	.195					

CLEVELAND INDIANS

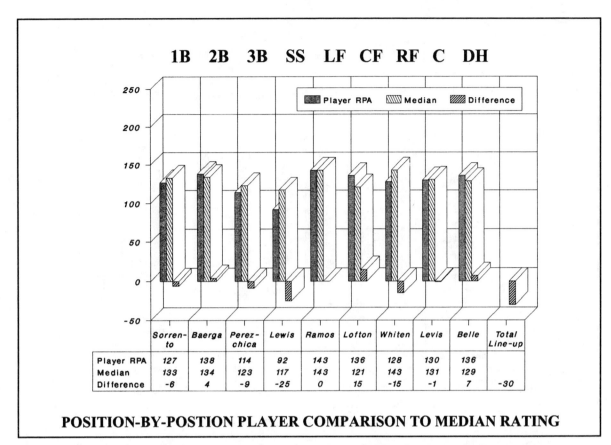

	1B	2B	3B	SS	LF	CF	RF	C	DH	Total Line-up
	Sorrento	Baerga	Perez-chica	Lewis	Ramos	Lofton	Whiten	Levis	Belle	
Player RPA	127	138	114	92	143	136	128	130	136	
Median	133	134	123	117	143	121	143	131	129	
Difference	-6	4	-9	-25	0	15	-15	-1	7	-30

POSITION-BY-POSTION PLAYER COMPARISON TO MEDIAN RATING

DEFENSIVE TEAM AND STADIUM DATA FOR THE LAST 3 YEARS:

TEAM DEFENSE BY POSITION:

		1990	1991	1992	POSITION-BY-POSITION STADIUM CHARACTERISTICS:
1B:	Home	+1.5	-5.0	+1.8	Easy to play
	Away	+0.3	-1.4	+0.9	
2B:	Home	+0.9	-4.7	+5.8	Average
	Away	-1.8	-4.7	-3.7	
3B:	Home	+0.6	-1.4	-2.2	Slightly hard to play
	Away	+1.1	-0.1	-4.8	
SS:	Home	-0.4	-1.2	-4.1	Slightly hard to play
	Away	+0.2	-5.3	-3.0	
LF:	Home	+4.4	-0.8	-5.4	Slightly hard to play
	Away	-3.0	-3.6	+0.3	
CF:	Home	+10.5	+3.8	+7.7	Average
	Away	+6.9	-1.5	+1.5	
RF:	Home	-7.1	-1.8	+2.9	Average
	Away	-4.7	-5.0	-1.5	
Total Home:		+10.4	-11.1	+6.6	
Total Away:		-1.0	-21.6	-10.4	

Comments: There seems to be a home-field advantage for the Indians while on defense with more than a 10 run advantage at home vs. away in each of the last 4 years. Unfortunately for the Tribe in 1992, however, only Kenny Lofton in centerfield provided them with enough superior defense to make the advantage really work in their favor. The left side of the infield is the Indians' major defensive weakness. Will Mark Lewis mature into an adequate defensive shortstop?

CLEVELAND INDIANS

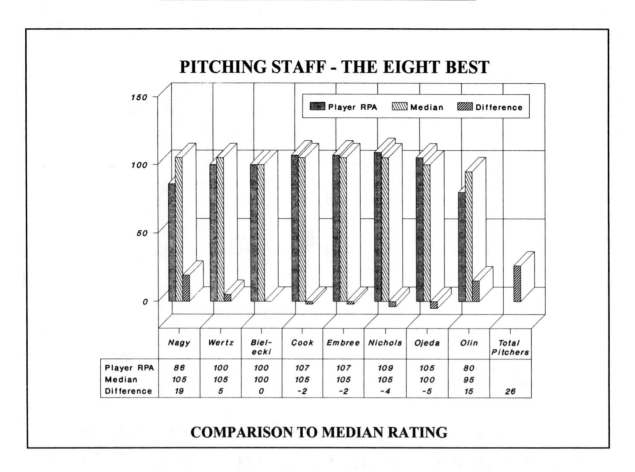

PITCHING STAFF - THE EIGHT BEST

	Nagy	Wertz	Biel-ecki	Cook	Embree	Nichols	Ojeda	Olin	Total Pitchers
Player RPA	86	100	100	107	107	109	105	80	
Median	105	105	100	105	105	105	100	95	
Difference	19	5	0	-2	-2	-4	-5	15	26

COMPARISON TO MEDIAN RATING

SUGGESTED LINE-UPS (with set-up RPA & drive-in RPA ratings):

Vs: Left-handed Groundball

C:	J. Levis	72-52
CF:	K. Lofton	78-68
2B:	C. Baerga	69-62
RF:	T. Howard	68-67
3B:	T. Perezchica	62-62
LF:	G. Hill	60-89
1B:	R. Jefferson	61-64
SS:	M. Lewis	56-62
DH:	A. Belle	43-59

Vs: Neutral Lefty Pitchers

C:	J. Levis	72-52
CF:	K. Lofton	85-75
2B:	C. Baerga	77-68
RF:	M. Whiten	71-71
3B:	T. Perezchica	62-62
LF:	T. Howard	60-60
1B:	R. Jefferson	61-64
SS:	M. Lewis	57-64
DH:	A. Belle	54-74

Vs: Left-handed Flyball

C:	J. Levis	72-52
CF:	K. Lofton	91-80
2B:	C. Baerga	86-77
RF:	M. Whiten	94-93
3B:	T. Perezchica	62-62
1B:	R. Jefferson	61-64
DH:	A. Belle	67-88
SS:	M. Lewis	58-65
LF:	T. Howard	51-50

Vs: Right-handed Groundball

LF:	K. Ramos	92-61
C:	J. Levis	82-62
2B:	C. Baerga	68-61
3B:	J. Thome	69-74
1B:	P. Sorrento	60-69
RF:	T. Howard	57-56
DH:	A. Belle	48-65
CF:	K. Lofton	48-43
SS:	M. Lewis	41-45

Vs: Neutral Righty Pitchers

LF:	K. Ramos	92-61
C:	J. Levis	82-62
2B:	C. Baerga	76-67
3B:	J. Thome	66-71
1B:	Paul Sorrento	62-71
DH:	Albert Belle	59-80
CF:	K. Lofton	56-49
RF:	M. Whiten	52-52
SS:	M. Lewis	42-47

Vs: Right-handed Flyball

LF:	K. Ramos	92-61
C:	J. Levis	82-62
2B:	C. Baerga	85-76
RF:	M. Whiten	75-74
1B:	P. Sorrento	64-73
DH:	A. Belle	72-94
3B:	J. Thome	62-68
CF:	K. Lofton	62-54
SS:	M. Lewis	43-48

Comments: The Indians have lots of good young talent and I didn't hesitate to put them in the above lineups. Sandy Alomar, Jr. is completely left off for two reasons: he's been a terrible hitter and Jesse Levis looks like he's ready and is already a much better offensive threat than is Alomar. Ken Ramos and Jim Thome seem to be ready also, but could need a couple of months of seasoning at AAA.

CLEVELAND INDIANS

This team, as everyone knows, is quickly improving. The Indians, however, are not yet ready to contend. Their signings of veteran pitchers Bob Ojeda and Mike Bielecki can only help this young team, but they should only expect to be respectable as a result. There is nothing wrong with being respectable, however, since it is a lot more than could be expected of past Indian teams.

I'm a little concerned as to how some of the Indians youngsters fit into their future plans. Quite often with rebuilding teams they get to the point of respectability and then promptly forget how they got there. They start fooling around with aging veterans or failing to quickly move up talented youngsters that would have moved up earlier in the rebuilding process.

The reason I've got this concern was when I saw that Jesse Levis, Ken Ramos and Tracy Sanders were all left unprotected in the Expansion draft. Only Ramos was even a pullback during the actual draft! It is not to the Indians credit that they lucked through the draft. They could have, and should have, lost at least two of the three. Ramos and Sanders may need a little seasoning at AAA, but Levis seems ready and should replace Alomar immediately due to Alomar's offensive liabilities. Alomar could come back from his injuries and have a big year, and if I were the Indians I'd certainly give him some opportunities to show if he's recovered, but I'd plan on putting Levis behind the plate.

As you can see by my high rating for Kenny Lofton, I agree with those who say he's a very good player, but that doesn't mean that I agree that the trade of Taubensee was a one-sided affair in favor of the Indians, as so many pundits have written. Taubensee is just as good a player as Lofton, and plays a generally harder to fill position. In addition, if it weren't for the presence of Jesse Levis (or if Levis doesn't replace Alomar), I'd have to give the edge to Houston in this trade since the catcher position has been one of the biggest problems for the Indians and the Indians possess a number of good young outfielders.

I think that Jim Thome is ready to fulfill his promise and will become a very good Major League hitter. '93 should be his breakthrough year. I think, however, that Tony Perezchica (see line-ups) should platoon with him until he shows that he can handle lefties.

I would have pulled Denis Boucher back in the second round of pullbacks at the expansion draft. He's got ability and I think he may be ready to at least be an adequate starter at the Major League level right now.

Another major problem is shortstop with Mark Lewis. Hopefully he'll take a big step forward this year, but it's not likely. Until the Indians solve this problem it will be a major part of holding them back from moving up in the standings. Felix Fermin isn't the answer, either. He can't hit a lick and his defensive range is beginning to shrink. Even weak hitting Alvaro Espinoza is far superior to Fermin.

Alan Embree, Chad Ogea and Bill Wertz look like real good pitching prospects. They all probably need a little time at AAA, however.

Cleveland's Projected record for 1993: 78--84, good for 6th place in the division.

CLEVELAND INDIANS

Sandy Alomar, Jr, 26
Bats Right   238L   762R   319G   231F

L= .082G .091L   .103F   (.036/.041) .077   .063G   .072R   .084F = R

		ATBATS	1B	2B	3B	HR	HBP	BB	GDP	SB	CS	ROE	XB	RUNS	EOB%	RL#	SET-UP	DR-IN	RPA
Cleveland	1990	445	92	26	2	9	2	23	10	4	1	4	49	57	.210	.120	.060	.059	.119
Cleveland	1991	184	31	9	0	0	4	7	4	0	4	3	8	13	.172	.063	.030	.036	.066
Cleveland	1992	299	57	16	0	2	5	10	7	3	3	4	15	27	.188	.087	.040	.044	.084

Carlos Baerga, 24
Bats Both   462L   1236R   504G   408F

L= .120G .134L   .152F   (.070/.063) .133   .118G   .132R   .150F = R

		ATBATS	1B	2B	3B	HR	HBP	BB	GDP	SB	CS	ROE	XB	RUNS	EOB%	RL#	SET-UP	DR-IN	RPA
Cleveland	1990	312	55	17	2	7	4	14	4	0	2	5	26	37	.201	.113	.055	.057	.112
Cleveland	1991	593	130	28	2	11	6	43	12	3	2	9	52	84	.237	.123	.069	.060	.129
Cleveland	1992	657	152	32	1	20	13	25	15	10	3	9	45	97	.220	.141	.070	.066	.136

Albert Belle, 26
Bats Right   306L   886R   325G   313F

L= .095G .121L   .148F   (.055/.074) .129   .106G   .132R   .159F = R

		ATBATS	1B	2B	3B	HR	HBP	BB	GDP	SB	CS	ROE	XB	RUNS	B-AVG	RL#	SET-UP	DR-IN	RPA
Cleveland	1990	23	3	0	0	1	0	1	1	0	0	2	1	2	.154	.093	.039	.054	.093
Cleveland	1991	461	69	31	2	28	5	23	24	3	2	6	28	67	.139	.124	.052	.078	.130
Cleveland	1992	585	94	23	1	34	4	47	18	8	2	2	37	84	.164	.133	.057	.071	.128

Felix Fermin, 29
Bats Right   332L   830R   379G   255F

L= .091G .092L   .093F   (.040/.043) .083   .078G   .079R   .080F = R

		ATBATS	1B	2B	3B	HR	HBP	BB	GDP	SB	CS	ROE	XB	RUNS	EOB%	RL#	SET-UP	DR-IN	RPA
Cleveland	1990	414	90	13	2	1	0	26	13	3	3	4	42	37	.194	.083	.040	.042	.082
Cleveland	1991	424	96	13	2	0	3	26	17	5	5	2	24	37	.186	.075	.037	.042	.079
Cleveland	1992	215	49	7	2	0	1	17	7	0	0	1	20	22	.219	.094	.047	.044	.091

Jose Hernandez, 23
Bats Right   30L   77R   20G   27F   451ML

L= ....G L   ....F   (.033/.044) .077   ....G   .070R   ....F = R

		ATBATS	1B	2B	3B	HR	HBP	BB	GDP	SB	CS	ROE	XB	RUNS	EOB%	RL#	SET-UP	DR-IN	RPA
Texas	1991	98	15	2	1	0	0	3	2	0	1	1	10	5	.131	.051	.020	.031	.051
Cleveland	1992	4	0	0	0	0	0	0	0	0	0	0	0	0	.000	.000	.000	.000	.000

Glenallen Hill, 27
Bats Right   382L   556R   263G   214F

L= .144G .123L   .097F   (.044/.065) .109   .121G   .100R   .074F = R

		ATBATS	1B	2B	3B	HR	HBP	BB	GDP	SB	CS	ROE	XB	RUNS	EOB%	RL#	SET-UP	DR-IN	RPA
Toronto	1990	260	34	11	3	12	0	18	5	8	3	2	30	32	.150	.114	.047	.064	.111
Toronto	1991	99	15	5	2	3	0	7	2	2	2	0	9	11	.162	.106	.044	.057	.101
Cleveland	1991	122	24	3	0	5	0	16	5	4	3	0	10	17	.183	.114	.056	.063	.119
Cleveland	1992	369	54	16	1	18	4	20	11	9	6	3	22	43	.137	.111	.042	.065	.107

Thomas Howard, 28
Bats Both   162L   570R   215G   174F

L= .131G .116L   .097F   (.050/.049) .099   .109G   .094R   .075F = R

		ATBATS	1B	2B	3B	HR	HBP	BB	GDP	SB	CS	ROE	XB	RUNS	EOB%	RL#	SET-UP	DR-IN	RPA
San Diego	1990	44	10	2	0	0	0	0	1	0	1	1	0	3	.166	.070	.031	.039	.070
San Diego	1991	281	51	12	3	4	1	20	4	10	7	2	20	30	.190	.095	.046	.050	.096
San Diego	1992	3	1	0	0	0	0	0	0	0	0	0	0	0	.237	.101	.052	.046	.098
Cleveland	1992	358	80	15	2	2	0	16	4	15	8	7	26	38	.212	.105	.051	.050	.101

Brook Jacoby, 33
Bats Right   420L   1002R   449G   335F

L= .085G .088L   .092F   (.039/.043) .082   .077G   .080R   .084F = R

		ATBATS	1B	2B	3B	HR	HBP	BB	GDP	SB	CS	ROE	XB	RUNS	EOB%	RL#	SET-UP	DR-IN	RPA
Cleveland	1990	553	120	24	4	14	2	57	20	1	4	7	42	79	.226	.126	.065	.060	.125
Cleveland	1991	231	40	9	1	4	2	14	7	0	1	3	10	23	.177	.086	.041	.049	.090
Oakland	1991	188	28	12	0	0	1	10	6	2	0	1	8	14	.168	.060	.029	.036	.065
Cleveland	1992	291	65	7	0	4	1	26	13	0	3	1	17	29	.187	.089	.041	.046	.087

Reggie Jefferson, 24
Bats Both   46L   160R   61G   64F   556ML

L= ....G   .090L   ....F   (.056/.058) .114   .103G   .121R   .138F = R

		ATBATS	1B	2B	3B	HR	HBP	BB	GDP	SB	CS	ROE	XB	RUNS	EOB%	RL#	SET-UP	DR-IN	RPA
Cincinnati	1991	7	0	0	0	1	0	1	0	0	0	1	1	2	.223	.219	.106	.099	.205
Cleveland	1991	101	15	3	0	2	0	3	1	0	0	1	6	8	.144	.073	.031	.046	.077
Cleveland	1992	89	21	6	2	1	1	1	2	0	0	0	4	12	.213	.130	.063	.061	.124

CLEVELAND INDIANS

Mark Lewis, 23

Bats Right   202L   591R   200G   214F   201ML

L= .106G .109L .111F   (.040/.045) .085   .074G   .077R   .079F = R

		ATBATS	1B	2B	3B	HR	HBP	BB	GDP	SB	CS	ROE	XB	RUNS	EOB%	RL#	SET-UP	DR-IN	RPA
Cleveland	1991	314	67	15	1	0	0	15	12	2	2	3	21	27	.184	.076	.038	.042	.080
Cleveland	1992	413	83	21	0	5	3	24	12	4	6	3	29	41	.187	.094	.043	.048	.091

Bats Left   169L   560R   176G   211F   599ML

Kenny Lofton, 25

L= .137G .151L .162F   (.058/.051) .109   .082G   .096R   .107F = R

		ATBATS	1B	2B	3B	HR	HBP	BB	GDP	SB	CS	ROE	XB	RUNS	EOB%	RL#	SET-UP	DR-IN	RPA
Houston	1991	74	14	1	0	0	0	5	0	2	2	2	6	6	.200	.068	.036	.038	.074
Cleveland	1992	576	136	15	8	5	2	65	7	66	20	5	82	83	.249	.133	.070	.058	.128

Bats Right   336L   470R   186G   206F

Carlos Martinez, 27

L= .127G .111L .097F   (.047/.054) .101   .110G   .094R   .080F = R

		ATBATS	1B	2B	3B	HR	HBP	BB	GDP	SB	CS	ROE	XB	RUNS	EOB%	RL#	SET-UP	DR-IN	RPA
White Sox	1990	272	46	6	5	4	0	8	8	0	4	2	15	20	.125	.070	.027	.044	.071
Cleveland	1991	257	54	14	0	5	2	8	10	3	2	1	10	27	.166	.093	.044	.054	.098
Cleveland	1992	228	45	9	1	5	1	7	5	1	2	6	11	25	.185	.106	.049	.054	.103

Bats Right   181L   430R   153G   133F

Junior Ortiz, 33

L= .077G .079L .081F   (.036/.037) .073   .069G   .071R   .073F = R

		ATBATS	1B	2B	3B	HR	HBP	BB	GDP	SB	CS	ROE	XB	RUNS	EOB%	RL#	SET-UP	DR-IN	RPA
Minnesota	1990	170	49	7	1	0	2	12	4	0	4	3	17	22	.261	.120	.065	.051	.116
Minnesota	1991	134	22	5	1	0	1	15	6	0	1	2	7	10	.196	.071	.033	.034	.067
Cleveland	1992	244	54	7	0	0	4	12	7	1	3	4	13	20	.200	.079	.037	.039	.076

Bats Right   37L   64R   24G   23F   219ML

Tony Perezchica, 26

L= ....G .087L ....F   (.053/.054) .107   ....G   .118R   ....F = R

		ATBATS	1B	2B	3B	HR	HBP	BB	GDP	SB	CS	ROE	XB	RUNS	EOB%	RL#	SET-UP	DR-IN	RPA
San Francisco	1990	3	1	0	0	0	0	1	0	0	0	0	1	1	.428	.189	.127	.062	.189
San Francisco	1991	48	6	4	1	0	0	2	0	0	1	0	3	4	.170	.077	.036	.044	.080
Cleveland	1991	22	6	2	0	0	0	3	0	0	0	0	5	5	.346	.173	.113	.068	.181
Cleveland	1992	20	1	1	0	0	0	2	0	0	0	1	2	1	.200	.059	.028	.029	.057

Bats Both   70L   98R   73G   32F   830ML

Dave Rohde, 28

L= .090G .114L ....F   (.052/.054) .106   .077G   .101R   ....F = R

		ATBATS	1B	2B	3B	HR	HBP	BB	GDP	SB	CS	ROE	XB	RUNS	EOB%	RL#	SET-UP	DR-IN	RPA
Houston	1990	98	14	4	0	0	5	7	3	0	0	2	7	9	.210	.066	.036	.037	.073
Houston	1991	41	5	0	0	0	0	5	1	0	0	0	2	2	.161	.038	.019	.024	.043
Cleveland	1992	7	0	0	0	0	0	1	0	0	0	0	0	0	.125	.017	.006	.010	.016

Bats Left   63L   642R   178G   193F   494ML

Paul Sorrento, 27

L= .065G .069L .073F   (.058/.065) .123   .124G   .128R   .132F = R

		ATBATS	1B	2B	3B	HR	HBP	BB	GDP	SB	CS	ROE	XB	RUNS	EOB%	RL#	SET-UP	DR-IN	RPA
Minnesota	1990	121	15	4	1	5	1	12	3	1	1	1	7	14	.165	.104	.045	.056	.101
Minnesota	1991	47	6	2	0	4	0	2	3	0	0	0	1	5	.060	.103	.022	.076	.098
Cleveland	1992	458	80	24	1	18	1	44	13	0	3	0	29	63	.191	.126	.058	.063	.121

Bats Left   34L   203R   68G   63F   706ML

Jim Thome, 22

L= ....G .054L ....F   (.054/.059) .113   .129G   .123R   .116F = R

		ATBATS	1B	2B	3B	HR	HBP	BB	GDP	SB	CS	ROE	XB	RUNS	EOB%	RL#	SET-UP	DR-IN	RPA
Cleveland	1991	98	18	4	2	1	1	4	4	1	1	1	3	9	.162	.083	.038	.049	.087
Cleveland	1992	117	18	3	1	2	2	8	3	2	0	3	9	12	.193	.094	.043	.046	.089

Bats Both   310L   821R   323G   257F

Mark Whiten, 26

L= .099G .135L .180F   (.053/.054) .107   .061G   .097R   .142F = R

		ATBATS	1B	2B	3B	HR	HBP	BB	GDP	SB	CS	ROE	XB	RUNS	EOB%	RL#	SET-UP	DR-IN	RPA
Toronto	1990	88	20	1	1	2	0	7	2	2	0	0	9	11	.207	.115	.056	.057	.113
Toronto	1991	149	24	4	3	2	1	10	5	0	2	2	10	13	.162	.080	.033	.043	.076
Cleveland	1991	258	41	14	4	7	2	18	8	4	4	4	30	33	.180	.110	.053	.062	.115
Cleveland	1992	508	97	19	4	9	2	62	12	16	12	6	61	65	.222	.116	.058	.054	.112

Bats Right   209L   437R   185G   117F   367ML

Craig Worthington, 27

L= .115G .120L .127F   (.047/.052) .099   .084G   .089R   .096F = R

		ATBATS	1B	2B	3B	HR	HBP	BB	GDP	SB	CS	ROE	XB	RUNS	EOB%	RL#	SET-UP	DR-IN	RPA
Baltimore	1990	425	71	17	0	8	3	61	13	1	2	5	26	52	.228	.102	.054	.049	.103
Baltimore	1991	102	16	3	0	4	1	12	3	0	1	2	3	13	.199	.111	.055	.059	.114
Cleveland	1992	24	4	0	0	0	0	2	0	0	1	0	0	1	.148	.045	.018	.024	.042

CLEVELAND INDIANS

PITCHERS

Jack Armstrong, 27

Throws: Neutral type, moderate righty

(.128/.110) .120   1058L 919R 143ML

		OUTS	RO	1B	2B	3B	HR	HBP	BB	GDP	SB	CS	PO	WP	BK	RUNS	EOB%	RL#	RPA
Cincinnati	1990	498	8	106	30	6	9	6	52	9	14	6	0	7	5	69	.181	.098	.100
Cincinnati	1991	419	17	105	24	4	25	2	52	7	12	8	6	2	1	74	.156	.123	.117
Cleveland	1992	500	93	121	28	4	23	3	67	8	15	9	2	6	3	89	.180	.122	.122

Brad Arnsberg, 29

Throws: Neutral type, moderate righty

(.157/.151) .153   128L 234R 461ML

		OUTS	RO	1B	2B	3B	HR	HBP	BB	GDP	SB	CS	PO	WP	BK	RUNS	EOB%	RL#	RPA
Texas	1990	188	188	41	11	0	4	2	32	3	1	0	2	8	0	30	.219	.104	.106
Texas	1991	29	29	5	0	0	5	0	5	1	0	0	0	1	1	7	.105	.168	.168
Cleveland	1992	32	32	6	1	0	6	2	11	4	0	0	0	2	0	11	.139	.195	.196

Eric Bell, 29

Throws: Neutral type, extreme lefty

(..../.154) .118   42L 87R 1085ML

		OUTS	RO	1B	2B	3B	HR	HBP	BB	GDP	SB	CS	PO	WP	BK	RUNS	EOB%	RL#	RPA
Cleveland	1991	54	54	5	0	0	0	1	5	3	2	0	0	0	0	1	.060	.022	.022
Cleveland	1992	46	35	16	5	0	1	1	9	2	4	1	0	1	0	11	.251	.149	.144

Denis Boucher, 24

Throws: Neutral type, extreme reverse lefty

(..../.110) .119   64L 370R 797ML

		OUTS	RO	1B	2B	3B	HR	HBP	BB	GDP	SB	CS	PO	WP	BK	RUNS	EOB%	RL#	RPA
Toronto	1991	106	0	21	12	0	6	2	15	2	1	1	0	0	4	22	.201	.143	.141
Cleveland	1991	68	0	19	9	1	6	0	8	2	2	0	0	1	0	19	.200	.184	.175
Cleveland	1992	123	10	33	5	1	9	1	20	7	0	1	1	1	0	24	.144	.130	.131

Dennis Cook, 30

Throws: Flyball type, neutral reverse lefty

(.106/.104) .104   275L 1072R 580ML

		OUTS	RO	1B	2B	3B	HR	HBP	BB	GDP	SB	CS	PO	WP	BK	RUNS	EOB%	RL#	RPA
Philadelphia	1990	425	177	98	19	2	13	2	45	10	14	3	2	6	3	59	.165	.102	.101
Los Angeles	1990	43	3	11	4	1	7	0	2	0	2	1	0	0	0	14	.122	.192	.204
Los Angeles	1991	53	36	9	3	0	0	0	6	2	1	1	2	0	0	3	.069	.043	.042
Cleveland	1992	474	60	90	34	3	29	2	48	7	8	10	2	4	5	76	.135	.116	.114

Derek Lilliquist, 26

Throws: Flyball type, moderate reverse lefty

(.115/.102) .105   213L 584R 491ML

		OUTS	RO	1B	2B	3B	HR	HBP	BB	GDP	SB	CS	PO	WP	BK	RUNS	EOB%	RL#	RPA
Atlanta	1990	185	3	50	15	0	10	1	15	4	9	1	0	0	2	34	.179	.131	.123
San Diego	1990	181	57	45	10	0	6	2	22	5	3	2	0	2	1	28	.180	.107	.107
San Diego	1991	43	17	16	6	0	3	0	3	0	0	1	0	0	0	13	.216	.175	.178
Cleveland	1992	185	185	24	10	0	5	2	12	4	4	2	0	2	0	15	.104	.067	.066

Jose Mesa, 26

Throws: Flyball type, neutral reverse righty

(.119/.120) .119   738L 677R 216ML

		OUTS	RO	1B	2B	3B	HR	HBP	BB	GDP	SB	CS	PO	WP	BK	RUNS	EOB%	RL#	RPA
Baltimore	1990	140	0	26	9	0	2	1	25	4	1	1	0	1	1	19	.202	.092	.094
Baltimore	1991	371	0	105	33	2	11	3	60	9	12	5	0	3	0	76	.227	.134	.133
Baltimore	1992	203	7	49	19	0	9	2	26	5	8	5	0	2	0	38	.177	.124	.127
Cleveland	1992	279	0	72	14	1	5	2	43	10	6	3	1	0	0	39	.190	.098	.097

Dave Mlicki, 24

Throws: Flyball type, righty

(..../....) .125   54L 43R 718ML

		OUTS	RO	1B	2B	3B	HR	HBP	BB	GDP	SB	CS	PO	WP	BK	RUNS	EOB%	RL#	RPA
Cleveland	1992	65	0	16	3	1	3	1	16	2	7	1	0	1	0	15	.239	.152	.151

Jeff Mutis, 26

Throws: Neutral type, lefty

(..../.121) .125   16L 110R 1334ML

		OUTS	RO	1B	2B	3B	HR	HBP	BB	GDP	SB	CS	PO	WP	BK	RUNS	EOB%	RL#	RPA
Cleveland	1991	37	0	15	5	2	1	0	6	0	0	0	0	1	0	13	.314	.204	.203
Cleveland	1992	34	12	15	3	2	4	0	6	0	0	0	0	2	0	16	.283	.267	.258

CLEVELAND INDIANS

Charles Nagy, 25
Throws: Groundball type, moderate righty

(.095/.080) .088   1038L 1000R

		OUTS	RO	1B	2B	3B	HR	HBP	BB	GDP	SB	CS	PO	WP	BK	RUNS	EOB%	RL#	RPA
Cleveland	1990	137	5	42	9	0	7	1	20	6	2	2	0	1	1	28	.184	.133	.134
Cleveland	1991	634	0	160	45	8	15	6	59	22	23	7	0	6	2	93	.169	.105	.103
Cleveland	1992	756	0	189	41	4	11	2	56	34	12	15	0	7	0	75	.120	.074	.073

Rod Nichols, 28
Throws: Flyball type, extreme righty

(.132/.089) .109   506L 570R 233ML

		OUTS	RO	1B	2B	3B	HR	HBP	BB	GDP	SB	CS	PO	WP	BK	RUNS	EOB%	RL#	RPA
Cleveland	1990	48	19	9	6	4	5	2	6	0	0	1	0	0	0	17	.206	.211	.213
Cleveland	1991	412	120	120	18	1	6	6	27	10	16	8	0	3	0	51	.164	.090	.089
Cleveland	1992	316	144	80	16	5	13	2	30	6	6	2	1	3	0	53	.175	.118	.117

Steve Olin, 27
Throws: Groundball type, extreme righty

(.112/.056) .080   403L 531R 190ML

		OUTS	RO	1B	2B	3B	HR	HBP	BB	GDP	SB	CS	PO	WP	BK	RUNS	EOB%	RL#	RPA
Cleveland	1990	277	256	79	13	1	3	6	24	13	9	3	1	0	0	33	.158	.085	.085
Cleveland	1991	169	169	48	10	1	2	1	16	9	3	2	0	0	0	20	.152	.086	.084
Cleveland	1992	265	265	63	8	1	8	4	21	15	2	4	0	1	1	26	.098	.075	.074

Dave Otto, 28
Throws: Groundball type, neutral reverse lefty

(.111/.110) .110   130L 626R 584ML

		OUTS	RO	1B	2B	3B	HR	HBP	BB	GDP	SB	CS	PO	WP	BK	RUNS	EOB%	RL#	RPA
Oakland	1990	7	7	3	0	0	0	0	3	1	0	0	0	0	0	1	.260	.115	.122
Cleveland	1991	300	25	83	14	4	7	4	21	11	4	4	1	3	0	39	.146	.094	.093
Cleveland	1992	241	5	81	17	0	12	1	33	16	11	2	0	5	0	49	.173	.133	.132

Eric Plunk, 29
Throws: Flyball type, moderate to severe righty

(.138/.115) .125   485L 611R

		OUTS	RO	1B	2B	3B	HR	HBP	BB	GDP	SB	CS	PO	WP	BK	RUNS	EOB%	RL#	RPA
N.Y. Yankees	1990	218	218	43	6	3	6	2	39	4	4	8	2	4	2	27	.156	.092	.088
N.Y. Yankees	1991	335	200	83	22	5	18	1	61	7	28	3	1	6	2	74	.218	.149	.141
Cleveland	1992	215	215	47	9	0	5	0	36	4	3	2	1	5	0	30	.197	.099	.097

Ted Power, 37
Throws: Neutral type, moderate to severe righty

(.106/.076) .089   413L 513R

		OUTS	RO	1B	2B	3B	HR	HBP	BB	GDP	SB	CS	PO	WP	BK	RUNS	EOB%	RL#	RPA
Pittsburgh	1990	155	155	37	7	1	5	0	11	4	4	2	0	1	0	21	.137	.092	.098
Cincinnati	1991	261	261	61	18	2	6	2	26	5	12	4	0	6	1	36	.179	.105	.098
Cleveland	1992	298	298	67	14	0	7	4	26	13	8	3	0	2	1	32	.133	.081	.079

Scott Scudder, 24
Throws: Neutral type, moderate to severe righty

(.122/.100) .112   601L 510R

		OUTS	RO	1B	2B	3B	HR	HBP	BB	GDP	SB	CS	PO	WP	BK	RUNS	EOB%	RL#	RPA
Cincinnati	1990	215	68	45	14	3	12	3	26	4	10	4	0	2	2	41	.168	.130	.132
Cincinnati	1991	304	75	63	19	3	6	6	52	6	12	6	0	7	0	45	.209	.104	.099
Cleveland	1992	327	3	99	23	2	10	2	55	14	14	7	0	7	0	62	.200	.126	.125

Jeff Shaw, 26
Throws: Neutral type, moderate to severe righty

(.130/.096) .112   249L 288R 1002ML

		OUTS	RO	1B	2B	3B	HR	HBP	BB	GDP	SB	CS	PO	WP	BK	RUNS	EOB%	RL#	RPA
Cleveland	1990	146	28	45	16	1	11	0	20	6	4	1	0	3	0	39	.195	.168	.169
Cleveland	1991	217	203	55	10	1	6	4	22	13	1	3	0	6	0	26	.128	.088	.087
Cleveland	1992	23	10	5	0	0	2	0	4	1	1	0	0	0	0	4	.144	.129	.124

Kevin Wickander, 27
Throws: Flyball type, extreme reverse lefty

(.168/.064) .105   88L 137R 155ML

		OUTS	RO	1B	2B	3B	HR	HBP	BB	GDP	SB	CS	PO	WP	BK	RUNS	EOB%	RL#	RPA
Cleveland	1990	37	37	11	2	1	0	1	4	0	0	1	0	0	0	6	.230	.106	.107
Cleveland	1992	123	123	32	5	1	1	4	25	5	3	0	0	1	1	20	.245	.108	.108

Cleveland Indians AAA & AA Minor League Ratings

AAA (COL. SPRINGS)	AGE	BATS	POSITION	CPA	RUNS	SET-UP	DRIVE-IN	RPA
Mike Aldrete	31	L	1B\OF	538	66.7	.073	.051	.124
Beau Allred	27	L	OF	509	62.2	.064	.058	.122
George Canale	27	L	1B	407	61.1	.080	.070	.150
Alan Cockrell	30	R	OF	291	23.2	.037	.043	.080
Mark Davidson	31	R	OF	347	34.3	.051	.048	.099
Alvaro Espinoza	30	R	SS	523	46.2	.041	.047	.088
Reggie Jefferson	24	B	1B	254	33.5	.068	.064	.132
Brian Johnson	26	R	C	180	14.4	.039	.041	.080
Wayne Kirby	28	L	OF	515	63.7	.063	.061	.124
Jesse Levis	24	L	C	300	39.0	.075	.055	.130
Nelson Liriano	28	B	2B\3B	417	46.6	.061	.051	.112
Dave Rohde	28	B	2B\3B\SS	516	54.0	.058	.047	.105
Craig Worthington	27	R	3B	367	35.4	.050	.046	.096

AA (CANTON-AKRON)	AGE	BATS	POSITION	CPA	RUNS	SET-UP	DRIVE-IN	RPA
Carlo Colombino	28	R	3B	345	28.5	.038	.045	.083
Terry Crowley	24	B	3B\2B\SS	252	17.5	.033	.036	.069
Tom Eiterman	25	R	OF	205	13.9	.032	.036	.068
Daren Epley	25	L	1B	444	47.2	.059	.047	.106
Miguel Flores	22	R	2B	516	38.5	.035	.040	.075
Jose Hernandez	19	R	SS	451	37.9	.042	.042	.084
Carlos Mota	24	R	C	229	13.8	.027	.033	.060
Donell Nixon	31	R	OF	130	11.2	.039	.047	.086
Ken Ramos	25	L	OF	532	74.1	.085	.054	.139
Tracy Sanders	23	L	OF	470	61.2	.068	.062	.130
Mike Sarbaugh	25	R	1B\3B	132	10.1	.035	.041	.076
Kelly Stinnett	22	R	C	324	28.6	.041	.047	.088
Jim Thome	22	L	3B	190	27.8	.090	.056	.146
Lee Tinsley	23	B	OF	506	49.1	.050	.047	.097

AAA Pitchers	Age	Throws	Outs	RPA	AA Pitchers	Age	Throws	Outs	RPA
Eric Bell	29	L	413	.125	Chad Allen	24	R	112	.186
Denis Boucher	24	L	372	.101	Paul Byrd	22	R	457	.131
Mike Christopher	29	R	176	.099	Colin Charland	27	L	215	.156
Terry Clark	32	R	179	.110	Alan Embree	22	L	237	.102
Jerry DiPoto	24	R	366	.148	Victor Garcia	26	L	307	.172
Tom Kramer	24	R	227	.134	Mike Gardella	25	L	219	.156
Jeff Mutis	26	L	436	.139	Garland Kiser	24	L	160	.159
Rod Nichols	28	R	162	.143	Dave Mlicki	24	R	518	.121
Dave Otto	28	L	140	.074	Chad Ogea	22	R	147	.106
Greg Roscoe	28	R	383	.118	Mike Soper	26	R	192	.165
Jeff Shaw	26	R	465	.129	Wally Trice	26	L	334	.183
Willie Smith	25	R	223	.134	Joe Turek	26	R	226	.132
					Bill Wertz	25	R	292	.082

DETROIT TIGERS

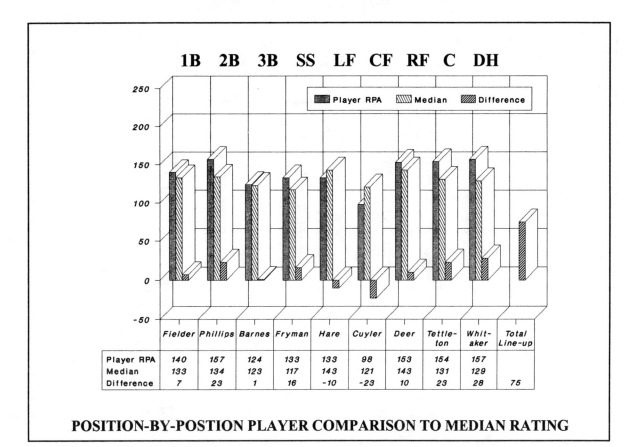

	Fielder	Phillips	Barnes	Fryman	Hare	Cuyler	Deer	Tettle-ton	Whit-aker	Total Line-up
Player RPA	140	157	124	133	133	98	153	154	157	
Median	133	134	123	117	143	121	143	131	129	
Difference	7	23	1	16	-10	-23	10	23	28	75

POSITION-BY-POSTION PLAYER COMPARISON TO MEDIAN RATING

DEFENSIVE TEAM AND STADIUM DATA FOR THE LAST 3 YEARS:

TEAM DEFENSE BY POSITION:

		1990	1991	1992
1B:	Home	-1.1	-0.2	-1.6
	Away	-1.2	-4.3	-1.7
2B:	Home	+7.2	+2.2	-1.8
	Away	+4.2	+2.0	+4.6
3B:	Home	-1.4	-2.2	+2.9
	Away	+0.3	-3.1	-2.7
SS:	Home	+3.1	+2.4	-2.3
	Away	-0.2	+1.4	-1.6
LF:	Home	-9.6	+7.0	+5.6
	Away	-7.8	-0.2	+1.6
CF:	Home	+1.0	-6.8	-10.5
	Away	-0.9	-0.7	-9.9
RF:	Home	+7.0	+2.6	+8.4
	Away	+11.2	-0.6	+4.3
Total Home:		+6.2	+5.0	+0.7
Total Away:		+5.6	-5.5	-5.4

POSITION-BY-POSITION STADIUM CHARACTERISTICS:

1B:	Easy to play
2B:	Average
3B:	Average
SS:	Average
LF:	Slightly easy to play
CF:	Average
RF:	Average

Comments: This could be a pretty good defensive team if it could solve its massive problems in centerfield. In addition, Lou Whitaker, while still a superior defensive second baseman, is beginning to noticeably lose range. My lineups will show him as a DH since Tony Phillips is an even better defensive second baseman than is Whitaker.

DETROIT TIGERS

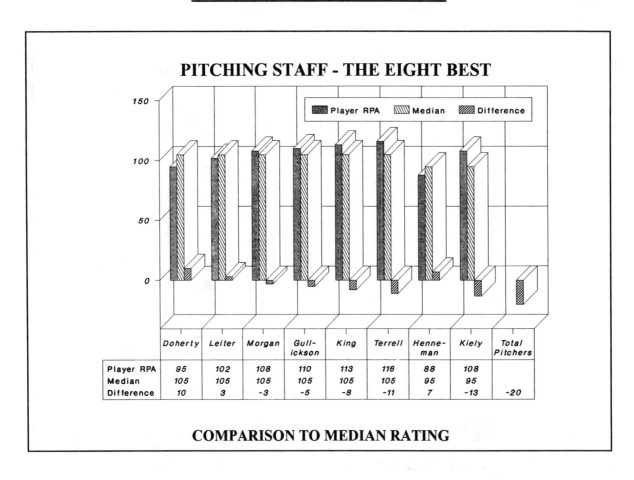

PITCHING STAFF - THE EIGHT BEST

	Doherty	Leiter	Morgan	Gull-ickson	King	Terrell	Henne-man	Kiely	Total Pitchers
Player RPA	95	102	108	110	113	116	88	108	
Median	105	105	105	105	105	105	95	95	
Difference	10	3	-3	-5	-8	-11	7	-13	-20

COMPARISON TO MEDIAN RATING

SUGGESTED LINE-UPS (with set-up RPA & drive-in RPA ratings):

Vs: Left-handed Groundball

DH:	Lou Whitaker	71-53
2B:	T. Phillips	88-67
C:	M. Tettleton	83-71
RF:	R. Deer	105-103
1B:	C. Fielder	94-101
SS:	T. Fryman	72-76
3B:	S. Barnes	68-74
CF:	S. Hare	70-55
LF:	D. Gladden	57-58

Vs: Neutral Lefty Pitchers

DH:	L. Whitaker	78-59
2B:	T. Phillips	91-69
C:	M. Tettleton	80-68
RF:	R. Deer	100-98
1B:	C. Fielder	102-109
SS:	T. Fryman	78-82
LF:	S. Hare	70-55
CF:	M. Cuyler	70-63
3B:	S. Barnes	60-65

Vs: Left-handed Flyball

DH:	L. Whitaker	87-66
2B:	T. Phillips	94-71
CF:	M. Cuyler	88-79
RF:	R. Deer	94-91
1B:	C. Fielder	111-119
SS:	T. Fryman	84-89
C:	M. Tettleton	76-64
LF:	S. Hare	70-55
3B:	S. Barnes	51-56

Vs: Right-handed Groundball

2B:	T. Phillips	71-52
DH:	L. Whitaker	87-66
CF:	S. Hare	80-65
C:	M. Tettleton	88-75
RF:	R. Deer	64-62
3B:	S. Barnes	63-68
LF:	J. Hurst	56-50
SS:	T. Fryman	53-57
1B:	C. Fielder	50-55

Vs: Neutral Righty Pitchers

2B:	T. Phillips	74-54
DH:	L. Whitaker	92-70
CF:	S. Hare	80-65
C:	M. Tettleton	85-72
RF:	R. Deer	59-57
SS:	T. Fryman	59-63
1B:	C. Fielder	58-63
LF:	J. Hurst	56-50
3B:	S. Barnes	55-59

Vs: Right-handed Flyball

2B:	T. Phillips	76-57
DH:	L. Whitaker	100-78
LF:	S. Hare	80-65
C:	M. Tettleton	81-68
CF:	M. Cuyler	77-69
SS:	T. Fryman	65-70
1B:	C. Fielder	66-71
3B:	S. Livingstone	66-60
RF:	R. Deer	52-51

Comments: A terrific line-up against all lefties, but rather ordinary vs. neutral & groundball type righties. The Tigers offense is second in strength only to the A's in the AL. Rob Deer is the only legitimate outfielder on the Tiger roster. That's why I projected Shawn Hare and Jody Hurst into these lineups. They have to be better than Dan Gladden and Milt Cuyler in their overall ability. If they're not better, then this team has big outfield problems.

DETROIT TIGERS

The Tigers are going to move up in the standings in '93. They are not likely to actually contend, but they could throw a scare into the division before fading in the end. This team, which has had so much offensive power without any pitching to compliment that power, has finally begun to put together a pitching staff that can get more than the occasional batter out.

The signing of pitcher Mike Moore, together with the development of John Doherty and Mark Leiter are the key changes. If they could add a solid reliever to complement Mike Henneman or another top-notch starter like Moore, then they would become serious contenders. They are very close and if they can hold together the nucleus of their offense for one more season, they ought to be able to get that pitcher they need and become serious contenders in '94.

The signing's of Bill Krueger and Tom Bolton are not likely to be the answer, although Krueger has shown ability at times.

I really didn't understand why the Tigers didn't protect Mark Leiter, Shawn Hare, and AA pitching prospects Jeff Braley and Mike Lumley in the Expansion draft. I'd have protected them over Chad Kreuter, Milt Cuyler, David Haas and Greg Gohr. As it turned out, however, the Tigers skated through the draft totally unscathed. They "lost" Scott Aldred and Kevin Ritz. Why the Colorado Rockies wanted their services is beyond me. Do they need a couple of batting practice pitchers?

I'm a little concerned about Cecil Fielder's RPA downward slide. Big guys with a lot of weight on their body tend to have shortened careers. He's a marvelous power hitter, but he could be giving signs that his career might be shortly over.

Rico Brogna is about two years away from the Majors even though he played at AAA in '92. He looks like a good prospect but he shouldn't be rushed since he doesn't appear to be ready yet.

Rich Rowland had only a so-so year at AAA in '92 after having a very promising season in '91. I think that '93 is going to be the year which will tell us if he will ever fulfill his earlier promise or only become a journeyman Major Leaguer.

Milt Cuyler has some promise, but he'll never fulfill that promise until he improves his defense in centerfield or is moved to left field where his defensive liabilities may be less pronounced. Phil Clark and Jody Hurst, at this point, appear to be at least the equal of Cuyler on offense and they couldn't be much worse on defense. If either one can play centerfield I'd quickly have them take over from Cuyler if he were to show no defensive improvement this year.

In addition to the AA pitchers previously mentioned, AA pitchers Brian Warren and Sean Bergman also appear to have some promise.

Detroit's Projected record for 1993: 83--79, good for 3rd place in the division.

DETROIT TIGERS

Skeeter Barnes, 35

Bats Right   215L   133R   98G   92F   266ML

L= .151G .134L .116F   (.062/.068) .130   .140G   .123R   .105F = R

		ATBATS	1B	2B	3B	HR	HBP	BB	GDP	SB	CS	ROE	XB	RUNS	EOB%	RL#	SET-UP	DR-IN	RPA
Detroit	1991	159	26	13	2	5	0	8	1	10	7	3	18	22	.185	.132	.061	.069	.130
Detroit	1992	165	33	8	1	3	2	9	4	3	3	1	14	19	.189	.107	.050	.055	.105

Dave Bergman, 39

Bats Left   52L   623R   222G   165F

L= .066G .059L .049F   (.060/.051) .111   .122G   .115R   .105F = R

		ATBATS	1B	2B	3B	HR	HBP	BB	GDP	SB	CS	ROE	XB	RUNS	EOB%	RL#	SET-UP	DR-IN	RPA
Detroit	1990	205	44	10	1	2	0	30	7	3	2	5	12	29	.267	.120	.067	.052	.119
Detroit	1991	194	28	10	1	7	0	33	2	1	1	2	8	31	.254	.137	.074	.060	.134
Detroit	1992	181	38	3	0	1	0	19	4	1	0	1	7	17	.220	.087	.044	.041	.085

John Cangelosi, 29

Bats Both   74L   119R   64G   39F   567ML

L= .087G .106L ....F   (.052/.048) .100   .077G   .096R   ....F = R

		ATBATS	1B	2B	3B	HR	HBP	BB	GDP	SB	CS	ROE	XB	RUNS	EOB%	RL#	SET-UP	DR-IN	RPA
Pittsburgh	1990	76	13	2	0	0	1	11	2	7	2	2	5	8	.237	.085	.047	.042	.089
Texas	1992	85	13	2	0	1	0	18	0	6	7	0	9	9	.213	.090	.046	.044	.090

Mark Carreon, 29

Bats Right   424L   431R   238G   216F

L= .100G .083L .065F   (.038/.049) .087   .107G   .090R   .072F = R

		ATBATS	1B	2B	3B	HR	HBP	BB	GDP	SB	CS	ROE	XB	RUNS	EOB%	RL#	SET-UP	DR-IN	RPA
Mets	1990	188	25	12	0	10	2	15	1	1	0	4	20	33	.213	.146	.078	.076	.154
Mets	1991	254	56	6	0	4	2	10	13	2	2	5	8	22	.161	.080	.034	.044	.078
Detroit	1992	336	56	11	1	10	1	20	12	3	1	5	15	35	.158	.096	.040	.054	.094

Milt Cuyler, 24

Bats Both   243L   659R   285G   200F

L= .098G .122L .156F   (.057/.050) .107   .077G   .101R   .135F = R

		ATBATS	1B	2B	3B	HR	HBP	BB	GDP	SB	CS	ROE	XB	RUNS	EOB%	RL#	SET-UP	DR-IN	RPA
Detroit	1990	51	9	3	1	0	0	5	1	1	2	0	8	5	.194	.090	.043	.047	.090
Detroit	1991	475	97	15	7	3	5	52	4	41	10	7	46	62	.254	.118	.064	.052	.116
Detroit	1992	291	55	11	1	3	4	10	4	8	6	8	17	28	.192	.093	.044	.047	.091

Rob Deer, 32

Bats Right   439L   1056R   435G   364F

L= .212G .202L .189F   (.073/.071) .144   .130G   .120R   .107F = R

		ATBATS	1B	2B	3B	HR	HBP	BB	GDP	SB	CS	ROE	XB	RUNS	EOB%	RL#	SET-UP	DR-IN	RPA
Milwaukee	1990	440	49	15	1	27	4	58	0	2	3	3	29	72	.202	.140	.071	.073	.144
Detroit	1991	448	39	14	2	25	0	88	3	1	3	3	21	68	.219	.130	.065	.062	.127
Detroit	1992	393	44	20	1	32	3	50	8	4	2	5	22	74	.189	.167	.078	.085	.163

Cecil Fielder, 29

Bats Right   553L   1507R   599G   502F

L= .193G .209L .228F   (.069/.074) .143   .103G   .119R   .135F = R

		ATBATS	1B	2B	3B	HR	HBP	BB	GDP	SB	CS	ROE	XB	RUNS	EOB%	RL#	SET-UP	DR-IN	RPA
Detroit	1990	573	82	25	1	51	5	79	15	0	1	9	33	122	.210	.182	.091	.090	.181
Detroit	1991	624	94	25	0	44	6	66	17	0	0	10	30	105	.194	.150	.071	.076	.147
Detroit	1992	594	88	22	0	35	2	65	14	0	0	10	19	94	.196	.142	.067	.072	.139

Travis Fryman, 23

Bats Right   437L   1151R   457G   421F

L= .136G .148L .161F   (.058/.062) .120   .098G   .110R   .123F = R

		ATBATS	1B	2B	3B	HR	HBP	BB	GDP	SB	CS	ROE	XB	RUNS	EOB%	RL#	SET-UP	DR-IN	RPA
Detroit	1990	232	48	11	1	9	1	17	3	3	3	7	16	38	.236	.152	.080	.071	.151
Detroit	1991	557	84	36	3	21	3	40	13	12	6	6	33	71	.182	.119	.054	.062	.116
Detroit	1992	659	120	31	4	20	6	44	13	8	5	12	38	89	.206	.126	.061	.062	.123

DETROIT TIGERS

Dan Gladden, 35

Bats Right   450L 1104R 441G 347F

L= .124G .113L .099F **(.048/.050) .098** .103G .092R .078F = R

		ATBATS	1B	2B	3B	HR	HBP	BB	GDP	SB	CS	ROE	XB	RUNS	EOB%	RL#	SET-UP	DR-IN	RPA
Minnesota	1990	534	109	27	6	5	6	24	17	25	9	7	44	56	.192	.100	.046	.051	.097
Minnesota	1991	461	85	14	9	6	5	35	13	15	12	4	55	46	.182	.097	.043	.049	.092
Detroit	1992	417	78	20	1	7	2	30	10	4	2	7	35	49	.208	.108	.053	.053	.106

Chad Kreuter, 28

Bats Both   102L 149R 59G 79F   253ML

L= .089G .067L .051F **(.045/.045) .090** .128G .106R .090F = R

		ATBATS	1B	2B	3B	HR	HBP	BB	GDP	SB	CS	ROE	XB	RUNS	EOB%	RL#	SET-UP	DR-IN	RPA
Texas	1990	22	0	1	0	0	0	8	0	0	0	0	1	2	.290	.069	.040	.029	.069
Texas	1991	4	0	0	0	0	0	0	0	0	0	0	0	0	.000	.000	.000	.000	.000
Detroit	1992	190	37	9	0	2	0	19	8	0	1	2	12	20	.203	.093	.045	.046	.091

Scott Livingstone, 27

Bats Left   65L 454R 122G 157F   382ML

L= .129G .152L .169F **(.057/.053) .110** .081G .104R .121F = R

		ATBATS	1B	2B	3B	HR	HBP	BB	GDP	SB	CS	ROE	XB	RUNS	EOB%	RL#	SET-UP	DR-IN	RPA
Detroit	1991	127	30	5	0	2	0	10	0	2	1	1	12	17	.252	.128	.069	.056	.125
Detroit	1992	354	75	21	0	4	0	20	8	1	3	4	25	40	.209	.107	.052	.052	.104

Gary Pettis, 34

Bats Both   325L 696R 295G 263F

L= .088G .098L .109F **(.055/.047) .102** .094G .104R .115F = R

		ATBATS	1B	2B	3B	HR	HBP	BB	GDP	SB	CS	ROE	XB	RUNS	EOB%	RL#	SET-UP	DR-IN	RPA
Texas	1990	423	74	16	8	3	4	57	6	38	15	3	51	54	.232	.107	.057	.051	.108
Texas	1991	282	49	7	5	0	0	54	4	29	14	5	30	35	.253	.102	.056	.047	.103
San Diego	1992	30	5	1	0	0	0	2	0	1	0	0	1	2	.198	.071	.034	.036	.070
Detroit	1992	129	18	4	3	1	0	27	3	13	5	1	17	17	.240	.110	.058	.050	.108

Tony Phillips, 33

Bats Both   441L 1360R 503G 435F

L= .160G .165L .170F **(.082/.061) .143** .128G .133R .138F = R

		ATBATS	1B	2B	3B	HR	HBP	BB	GDP	SB	CS	ROE	XB	RUNS	EOB%	RL#	SET-UP	DR-IN	RPA
Detroit	1990	573	108	23	5	8	4	99	10	19	9	10	58	88	.276	.128	.073	.055	.128
Detroit	1991	564	111	28	4	17	3	74	8	10	5	9	47	94	.264	.148	.081	.063	.144
Detroit	1992	606	122	32	3	10	1	112	13	12	10	10	75	103	.287	.144	.082	.059	.141

Mickey Tettleton, 32

Bats Right   355L 822R 358G 252F

L= .158G .152L .144F **(.086/.073) .159** .167G .161R .153F = R

		ATBATS	1B	2B	3B	HR	HBP	BB	GDP	SB	CS	ROE	XB	RUNS	EOB%	RL#	SET-UP	DR-IN	RPA
Baltimore	1990	444	61	21	2	15	5	103	7	2	5	4	39	80	.280	.142	.082	.061	.143
Detroit	1991	501	82	17	2	31	2	92	12	3	3	4	32	96	.244	.162	.086	.073	.159
Detroit	1992	525	68	25	0	32	1	104	5	0	6	2	23	102	.245	.164	.086	.074	.160

Alan Trammell, 34

Bats Left   305L 1342R 458G 379F

L= .114G .115L .117F **(.058/.054) .112** .109G .110R .112F = R

		ATBATS	1B	2B	3B	HR	HBP	BB	GDP	SB	CS	ROE	XB	RUNS	EOB%	RL#	SET-UP	DR-IN	RPA
Detroit	1990	559	118	37	1	14	1	61	11	12	10	7	51	89	.247	.141	.076	.064	.140
Detroit	1991	375	64	20	0	9	3	36	7	11	2	7	25	48	.227	.117	.059	.055	.114
Detroit	1992	102	19	7	1	1	1	15	6	2	2	1	7	13	.224	.108	.055	.051	.106

Lou Whitaker, 35

L= .131G .144L .160F **(.093/.071) .164** .160G .169R .185F = R

		ATBATS	1B	2B	3B	HR	HBP	BB	GDP	SB	CS	ROE	XB	RUNS	EOB%	RL#	SET-UP	DR-IN	RPA
Detroit	1990	472	70	22	2	18	0	67	10	8	3	4	46	70	.220	.129	.066	.062	.128
Detroit	1991	470	80	26	2	23	2	84	3	4	2	6	33	96	.285	.177	.100	.072	.172
Detroit	1992	453	81	26	0	19	1	76	9	6	4	2	34	84	.257	.159	.086	.069	.155

DETROIT TIGERS

PITCHERS

Scott Aldred, 24

Throws: Flyball type, extreme lefty

(.074/.148) .146

95L 489R 973ML

		OUTS	RO	1B	2B	3B	HR	HBP	BB	GDP	SB	CS	PO	WP	BK	RUNS	EOB%	RL#	RPA
Detroit	1990	43	2	11	2	0	0	1	9	4	3	0	0	0	0	5	.185	.083	.080
Detroit	1991	172	0	42	6	1	9	0	28	5	5	2	1	3	1	29	.173	.122	.117
Detroit	1992	195	18	50	17	1	12	3	29	5	7	4	0	1	0	44	.192	.146	.147

John Doherty, 25

Throws: Groundball type, extreme reverse righty

(.050/.132) .097

194L 265R 281ML

		OUTS	RO	1B	2B	3B	HR	HBP	BB	GDP	SB	CS	PO	WP	BK	RUNS	EOB%	RL#	RPA
Detroit	1992	348	164	113	13	1	4	4	20	22	4	4	0	5	0	37	.127	.078	.078

Buddy Groom, 27

Throws: Groundball type, lefty

(..../.120) .131

36L 128R 983ML

		OUTS	RO	1B	2B	3B	HR	HBP	BB	GDP	SB	CS	PO	WP	BK	RUNS	EOB%	RL#	RPA
Detroit	1992	116	10	32	10	2	4	0	18	4	0	2	0	0	1	23	.198	.129	.130

Bill Gullickson, 33

Throws: Neutral type, moderate to severe righty

(.116/.087) .103

1414L 1172R

		OUTS	RO	1B	2B	3B	HR	HBP	BB	GDP	SB	CS	PO	WP	BK	RUNS	EOB%	RL#	RPA
Houston	1990	580	0	154	37	9	21	2	47	18	23	9	0	3	2	103	.155	.104	.117
Detroit	1991	679	0	176	51	7	22	4	31	22	15	8	1	4	0	91	.137	.100	.096
Detroit	1992	665	0	150	38	5	35	0	45	15	20	8	0	6	0	100	.132	.109	.109

Dave Haas, 27

Throws: Neutral type, moderate righty

(.150/.141) .145

133L 165R 1354ML

		OUTS	RO	1B	2B	3B	HR	HBP	BB	GDP	SB	CS	PO	WP	BK	RUNS	EOB%	RL#	RPA
Detroit	1991	32	32	6	1	0	1	1	9	3	0	1	0	1	0	4	.143	.088	.083
Detroit	1992	185	3	50	9	1	8	1	15	4	1	1	0	2	0	30	.170	.115	.115

Mike Henneman, 31

Throws: Groundball type, moderate righty

(.094/.074) .083

432L 561R

		OUTS	RO	1B	2B	3B	HR	HBP	BB	GDP	SB	CS	PO	WP	BK	RUNS	EOB%	RL#	RPA
Detroit	1990	283	283	70	15	1	4	3	21	13	7	2	0	3	0	30	.140	.079	.077
Detroit	1991	253	253	60	17	2	2	0	26	10	3	2	0	5	0	28	.164	.084	.080
Detroit	1992	232	232	56	11	2	6	0	10	7	2	1	0	7	0	27	.131	.086	.086

John Kiely, 28

Throws: Neutral type, extreme reverse righty

(.072/.132) .107

104L 147R 426ML

		OUTS	RO	1B	2B	3B	HR	HBP	BB	GDP	SB	CS	PO	WP	BK	RUNS	EOB%	RL#	RPA
Detroit	1991	20	20	9	4	0	0	1	7	0	0	0	0	1	0	9	.420	.218	.213
Detroit	1992	165	165	32	10	0	2	0	25	7	2	1	0	0	0	18	.167	.079	.079

Eric King, 28

Throws: Neutral type, moderate righty

(.119/.104) .112

790L 781R

		OUTS	RO	1B	2B	3B	HR	HBP	BB	GDP	SB	CS	PO	WP	BK	RUNS	EOB%	RL#	RPA
Chi. White Sox	1990	453	0	104	17	4	10	6	40	12	8	5	0	2	3	56	.156	.088	.090
Cleveland	1991	452	7	122	33	4	7	3	40	9	8	3	0	2	2	67	.198	.105	.103
Detroit	1992	238	36	64	12	2	12	1	27	5	8	3	0	3	0	45	.179	.128	.129

Kurt Knudsen, 25

Throws: Flyball type, moderate reverse righty

(.100/.119) .111

118L 176R 387ML

		OUTS	RO	1B	2B	3B	HR	HBP	BB	GDP	SB	CS	PO	WP	BK	RUNS	EOB%	RL#	RPA
Detroit	1992	212	206	47	13	1	9	1	32	4	6	5	0	5	0	36	.179	.118	.118

DETROIT TIGERS

Throws: Neutral type, moderate to severe righty

Les Lancaster, 30   (.119/.085) .102   723L   735R

		OUTS	RO	1B	2B	3B	HR	HBP	BB	GDP	SB	CS	PO	WP	BK	RUNS	EOB%	RL#	RPA
Chicago Cubs	1990	327	231	89	20	1	11	1	32	7	4	3	1	7	0	49	.180	.112	.103
Chicago Cubs	1991	468	251	108	26	3	13	4	42	6	14	14	1	2	2	56	.149	.093	.085
Detroit	1992	260	246	69	21	0	11	3	39	8	3	3	0	2	0	51	.201	.129	.129

Throws: Flyball type, moderate to severe righty

Mark Leiter, 29   (.117/.086) .100   515L   603R

		OUTS	RO	1B	2B	3B	HR	HBP	BB	GDP	SB	CS	PO	WP	BK	RUNS	EOB%	RL#	RPA
N.Y. Yankees	1990	79	24	22	6	0	5	2	9	2	3	1	1	0	0	16	.175	.139	.137
Detroit	1991	404	128	84	20	5	16	6	46	8	6	6	0	2	0	58	.165	.107	.103
Detroit	1992	336	112	82	19	6	9	3	38	11	7	9	3	3	0	45	.141	.096	.096

Throws: Groundball type, extreme lefty

Mike Munoz, 27   (.076/.140) .115   102L   157R   235ML

		OUTS	RO	1B	2B	3B	HR	HBP	BB	GDP	SB	CS	PO	WP	BK	RUNS	EOB%	RL#	RPA
Los Angeles	1990	17	17	6	0	0	0	0	3	2	0	0	0	0	0	2	.135	.067	.068
Detroit	1991	28	28	12	2	0	0	0	5	1	0	1	0	1	0	5	.244	.122	.117
Detroit	1992	144	144	34	6	1	3	0	19	4	3	1	0	2	0	20	.182	.096	.096

Throws: Groundball type, extreme righty

Kevin Ritz, 27   (.171/.108) .134   202L   280R   535ML

		OUTS	RO	1B	2B	3B	HR	HBP	BB	GDP	SB	CS	PO	WP	BK	RUNS	EOB%	RL#	RPA
Detroit	1990	22	0	12	2	0	0	0	12	1	3	0	0	3	0	11	.436	.231	.224
Detroit	1991	46	19	13	3	0	1	2	21	2	3	0	0	0	0	14	.359	.172	.166
Detroit	1992	241	82	70	14	0	4	3	40	3	11	5	0	7	1	43	.237	.120	.119

Throws: Neutral type, extreme lefty

Frank Tanana, 39   (.060/.114) .105   404L   1981R

		OUTS	RO	1B	2B	3B	HR	HBP	BB	GDP	SB	CS	PO	WP	BK	RUNS	EOB%	RL#	RPA
Detroit	1990	529	32	124	40	1	25	9	59	14	9	15	0	5	1	84	.153	.114	..111
Detroit	1991	652	0	153	34	4	26	2	69	17	17	14	0	3	1	90	.147	.103	.098
Detroit	1992	560	6	130	34	2	22	7	81	21	21	11	1	11	1	90	.164	.111	.112

Throws: Groundball type, moderate to severe righty

Walt Terrell, 34   (.118/.097) .108   1099L   1040R

		OUTS	RO	1B	2B	3B	HR	HBP	BB	GDP	SB	CS	PO	WP	BK	RUNS	EOB%	RL#	RPA
Pittsburgh	1990	248	0	62	20	3	13	4	32	11	3	4	0	7	2	50	.165	.130	.137
Detroit	1990	226	6	62	16	1	7	8	21	10	7	2	0	0	0	36	.176	.112	.109
Detroit	1991	656	11	185	48	8	16	2	69	35	6	5	0	8	0	95	.162	.105	.101
Detroit	1992	410	178	120	27	2	14	3	38	11	7	3	0	3	0	72	.187	.119	.119

Detroit Tigers AAA & AA Minor League Ratings

AAA (TOLEDO)	AGE	BATS	POSITION	CPA	RUNS	SET-UP	DRIVE-IN	RPA
Karl Allaire	29	L	3B\SS	551	49.4	.046	.044	.090
Rico Brogna	22	L	1B	426	42.6	.048	.052	.100
Steve Carter	28	L	OF	510	51.5	.049	.052	.101
Phil Clark	24	R	OF\C	297	31.0	.047	.057	.104
Dean DeCillis	25	R	1B\2B\3B	293	19.0	.029	.036	.065
Shawn Hare	25	L	OF\1B	242	32.3	.074	.059	.133
Jody Hurst	25	R	OF	473	53.1	.059	.053	.112
Riccardo Ingram	26	R	OF	457	39.6	.040	.047	.087
Marty Pevey	31	L	C	144	15.5	.053	.054	.107
Rod Robertson	24	B	3B\OF	507	38.8	.034	.043	.077
Victor Rosario	26	R	SS	353	17.1	.019	.029	.048
Rich Rowland	25	R	C	552	56.3	.045	.057	.102
Greg Smith	25	B	2B	506	43.4	.042	.044	.086

AA (LONDON)	AGE	BATS	POSITION	CPA	RUNS	SET-UP	DRIVE-IN	RPA
Brian Cornelius	25	L	OF	328	26.1	.037	.043	.080
Ivan Cruz	24	L	1B	580	50.7	.041	.046	.087
Mike DeButch	29	R	SS\2B\OF	381	32.7	.046	.040	.086
Lou Frazier	27	B	OF	575	51.4	.051	.038	.089
Mike Gillette	25	R	C	225	13.9	.029	.033	.062
Chris Gomez	?	?	SS	254	17.2	.032	.036	.068
Tyrone Kingwood	27	R	OF	412	37.0	.044	.046	.090
Kirk Mendenhall	25	R	SS\2B\3B	427	34.0	.041	.039	.080
Rob Reimink	25	B	3B	563	51.9	.051	.041	.092
Rick Sellers	25	R	C	374	36.4	.049	.048	.097
Greg Sparks	28	L	1B	525	57.3	.052	.057	.109

AAA Pitchers	Age	Throws	Outs	RPA	AA Pitchers	Age	Throws	Outs	RPA
Scott Aldred	24	L	258	.174	Don August	29	R	203	.128
Tony Castillo	29	L	134	.138	Sean Bergman	22	R	265	.124
Greg Gohr	25	R	392	.127	Jeff Braley	25	R	245	.103
Frank Gonzales	24	L	492	.130	Sherm Corbett	30	L	167	.132
Buddy Groom	27	L	328	.115	John DeSilva	25	R	214	.146
David Haas	27	R	446	.136	Mike Garcia	24	R	410	.130
Dave Johnson	33	R	164	.149	Jim Henry	22	L	241	.147
Jeff Kaiser	32	L	92	.114	Mike Lumley	25	R	225	.110
John Kiely	28	R	95	.092	Ricky Rojas	26	R	122	.172
Doug Kline	27	R	139	.128	Brian Warren	25	R	442	.117
Vance Lovelace	29	L	76	.180	Marty Willis	27	R	311	.163
Jamie Moyer	30	L	416	.113	Steve Wolf	24	R	364	.134
Ron Rightnowar	28	R	171	.174					
Mike Walker	26	R	236	.174					

MILWAUKEE BREWERS

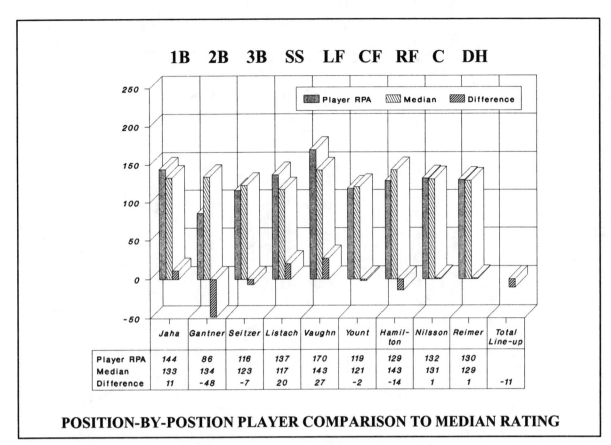

	1B	2B	3B	SS	LF	CF	RF	C	DH
	Jaha	Gantner	Seitzer	Listach	Vaughn	Yount	Hamil-ton	Nilsson	Reimer	Total Line-up
Player RPA	144	86	116	137	170	119	129	132	130	
Median	133	134	123	117	143	121	143	131	129	
Difference	11	-48	-7	20	27	-2	-14	1	1	-11

POSITION-BY-POSTION PLAYER COMPARISON TO MEDIAN RATING

DEFENSIVE TEAM AND STADIUM DATA FOR THE LAST 3 YEARS:

TEAM DEFENSE BY POSITION:

POSITION-BY-POSITION STADIUM CHARACTERISTICS:

		1990	1991	1992	
1B:	Home	+2.2	+2.0	-1.0	Slightly easy to play
	Away	-1.6	-2.1	+1.5	
2B:	Home	-1.8	+3.5	-0.1	Slightly easy to play
	Away	+1.8	+0.8	+7.0	
3B:	Home	-0.9	+1.5	+4.3	Average
	Away	-1.0	-4.4	-4.1	
SS:	Home	-3.1	-7.9	+2.7	Average
	Away	-0.8	0.0	+4.9	
LF:	Home	-5.6	+10.7	+2.9	Average
	Away	-1.3	+4.5	+7.0	
CF:	Home	+2.6	-3.5	+7.9	Slightly easy to play
	Away	-9.1	+8.6	+4.3	
RF:	Home	+1.8	+0.8	-1.7	Average
	Away	+0.3	-2.3	-7.5	
Total Home:		-4.8	+7.1	+15.1	
Total Away:		-11.7	+5.1	+13.0	

Comments: This was the 4th best defense in the Major Leagues in 1992. The Brewers were a very poor defensive squad in 1990, improved to be good in 1991 and to be outstanding in 1992. The biggest single improvement (+15.5 runs) between 1991 and 1992 was at shortstop with the introduction of Pat Listach.

MILWAUKEE BREWERS

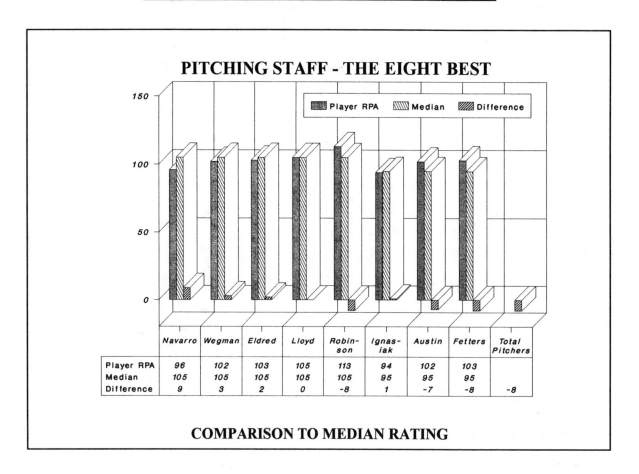

PITCHING STAFF - THE EIGHT BEST

	Navarro	Wegman	Eldred	Lloyd	Robin-son	Ignas-iak	Austin	Fetters	Total Pitchers
Player RPA	96	102	103	105	113	94	102	103	
Median	105	105	105	105	105	95	95	95	
Difference	9	3	2	0	-8	1	-7	-8	-8

COMPARISON TO MEDIAN RATING

SUGGESTED LINE-UPS (with set-up RPA & drive-in RPA ratings):

Vs: Left-handed Groundball

SS:	P. Listach	72-59
3B:	K. Seitzer	74-68
1B:	J. Jaha	77-70
C:	D. Nilsson	57-58
LF:	G. Vaughn	59-63
2B:	C. Montoyo	63-47
CF:	R. Yount	59-53
RF:	M. Mieske	47-58
DH:	K. Reimer	48-53

Vs: Neutral Lefty Pitchers

SS:	P. Listach	86-70
CF:	R. Yount	65-58
3B:	K. Seitzer	77-70
1B:	J. Jaha	68-63
LF:	G. Vaughn	62-66
2B:	B. Spiers	57-53
C:	D. Nilsson	57-58
DH:	B.J. Surhoff	53-56
RF:	M. Mieske	47-58

Vs: Left-handed Flyball

SS:	P. Listach	98-79
CF:	R. Yount	72-64
RF:	D. Hamilton	72-65
3B:	K. Seitzer	80-72
2B:	B. Spiers	66-62
LF:	G. Vaughn	65-70
DH:	B.J. Surhoff	62-66
1B:	J. Jaha	61-57
C:	D. Nilsson	57-58

Vs: Right-handed Groundball

RF:	T. O'Leary	70-57
CF:	D. Hamilton	58-53
2B:	B. Spiers	63-60
1B:	J. Jaha	87-80
C:	D. Nilsson	67-68
LF:	G. Vaughn	66-71
DH:	K. Reimer	66-72
3B:	J. Tatum	56-54
SS:	P. Listach	46-36

Vs: Neutral Righty Pitchers

RF:	T. O'Leary	70-57
CF:	D. Hamilton	73-66
2B:	B. Spiers	69-65
1B:	J. Jaha	79-72
C:	D. Nilsson	67-68
LF:	G. Vaughn	69-74
DH:	K. Reimer	65-70
SS:	P. Listach	60-47
3B:	J. Tatum	56-54

Vs: Right-handed Flyball

SS:	P. Listach	71-57
1B:	J. Jaha	72-66
RF:	D. Hamilton	94-85
2B:	B. Spiers	78-74
C:	D. Nilsson	67-68
LF:	G. Vaughn	72-78
DH:	K. Reimer	63-69
CF:	R. Yount	62-55
3B:	K. Seitzer	54-50

Comments: Only the 11th best offense in the AL, even with figuring in some youngsters who may not get a chance, like Matt Mieske and Charlie Montoyo, or, in the case of Troy O'Leary, who may be a year away. The Brewers are particularly vulnerable to groundball-type pitchers. Jaha and Nilsson are budding stars with extremely bright futures.

MILWAUKEE BREWERS

The Milwaukee Brewers, a small-market team, were not able to compete in this winter's wild bidding wars. As such, they were hurt by the losses of front line performers Paul Molitor, Chris Bosio, and, to a lesser extent, journeyman infielder Scott Fletcher.

In exchange for these three all the Brewers have to show for their efforts is AA pitcher Graeme Lloyd. Lloyd is a very good prospect and could be pitching in Milwaukee very soon, but the promise shown by Milwaukee's late run at the pennant in '92 is not likely to be fulfilled in '93.

That isn't to say that the Brewers are totally without hope. This team had a deserving rookie-of-the-year in Pat Listach, a fabulous young veteran player in Greg Vaughn, and has two of the best young players just beginning their Major League careers in catcher Dave Nilsson and first baseman John Jaha. If this team could have held together its veteran nucleus, then these young players would certainly have projected this team into at least serious contenders, if not favorites to win the division this year.

The "Lords of Baseball" are killing the game by protecting the big market teams from so-called "socialistic" methods. It's ridiculous to term the needed reforms "socialist" since we are talking about multi-millionaire owners even in the case of the very smallest of the small-market teams. All that's involved is making a modest effort at creating a level playing field for all the franchises. Without this level playing field why would a fan continue to have loyalty to our beautiful game? Instead, it seems that the "Lords of Baseball" are more interested in protecting the profits of a few wealthy investors than in providing quality competitive baseball at all 28 Major League stadiums.

By the way: we shouldn't forget that Bill Spiers is another excellent young talent who has been held back by injuries. If he can overcome these injuries and make the transition to second base, then this team could have a quality double-play combination for years to come.

There was a deal this winter that did heavily favor the Brewers. It was the trade of Dante Bichette for Kevin Reimer. What Colorado wants with Bichette is beyond me, but Reimer can hit righty pitching quite decently and can be used to fill the DH role against these righties. The Brewers need to find someone to DH against lefties. I've proposed B.J. Surhoff and Reimer in the line-ups listed opposite, but that's only be a band-aid solution to a massive problem.

I'm not a particular Doug Henry fan, although he clearly has some talent. I would have protected Darren Holmes over him in the Expansion draft. I would also have pulled back Jeff Tabaka no later than the first round of pullbacks. The loss of AAA third baseman Jim Tatum was also a bad break. He would have been a better solution to the DH problems against lefty pitching and I would have protected him over Angel Miranda in the first pullback at the Expansion draft. The Brewers as it turns out, were amongst the hardest hit teams in the Expansion draft in losing three good players in Holmes, Tabaka and Tatum.

Milwaukee's Projected record for 1993: 79--83, good for 5th place in the division.

MILWAUKEE BREWERS

Andy Allanson, 31

Bats Right 130L 58R 66G 39F

L= .040G .047L ....F (.035/.041) .076 .134G .141R ....F = R

		ATBATS	1B	2B	3B	HR	HBP	BB	GDP	SB	CS	ROE	XB	RUNS	EOB%	RL#	SET-UP	DR-IN	RPA
Detroit	1991	151	24	10	0	1	0	7	3	0	1	0	6	11	.166	.073	.032	.039	.071
Milwaukee	1992	25	7	1	0	0	0	1	1	3	1	0	2	3	.184	.096	.047	.054	.101

Dante Bichette, 29

Bats Right 452L 813R 340G 286F

L= .118G .109L .099F (.042/.057) .099 .102G .093R .083F = R

		ATBATS	1B	2B	3B	HR	HBP	BB	GDP	SB	CS	ROE	XB	RUNS	EOB%	RL#	SET-UP	DR-IN	RPA
California	1990	349	58	15	1	15	3	15	9	5	2	3	21	41	.155	.112	.047	.063	.110
Milwaukee	1991	445	70	18	3	15	1	18	9	14	9	4	21	45	.138	.095	.038	.056	.094
Milwaukee	1992	387	77	27	2	5	3	13	13	18	9	1	26	43	.168	.099	.046	.058	.104

Scott Fletcher, 34

Bats Right 417L 844R 350G 322F

L= .116G .117L .119F (.056/.050) .106 .100G .101R .103F = R

		ATBATS	1B	2B	3B	HR	HBP	BB	GDP	SB	CS	ROE	XB	RUNS	EOB%	RL#	SET-UP	DR-IN	RPA
White Sox	1990	509	98	18	3	4	3	42	10	1	3	6	53	53	.214	.094	.048	.046	.094
White Sox	1991	248	39	10	1	1	3	17	3	0	2	3	8	20	.195	.073	.035	.037	.072
Milwaukee	1992	386	82	18	3	3	7	29	4	17	10	9	33	54	.245	.121	.069	.058	.127

Jim Gantner, 38

Bats Left 192L 911R 340G 246F

L= .102G .094L .083F (.042/.047) .089 .096G .088R .077F = R

		ATBATS	1B	2B	3B	HR	HBP	BB	GDP	SB	CS	ROE	XB	RUNS	EOB%	RL#	SET-UP	DR-IN	RPA
Milwaukee	1990	323	72	8	5	0	2	29	10	18	3	7	38	39	.236	.103	.056	.050	.106
Milwaukee	1991	526	116	27	4	2	3	22	13	4	7	2	38	51	.195	.091	.044	.047	.091
Milwaukee	1992	256	49	12	1	1	0	10	9	6	2	5	11	23	.174	.079	.038	.046	.084

Daryl Hamilton, 28

Bats Left 206L 932R 343G 238F

L= .065G .093L .133F (.067/.060) .127 .107G .135R .175F = R

		ATBATS	1B	2B	3B	HR	HBP	BB	GDP	SB	CS	ROE	XB	RUNS	EOB%	RL#	SET-UP	DR-IN	RPA
Milwaukee	1990	156	40	5	0	1	0	9	2	10	5	4	22	20	.231	.114	.062	.055	.117
Milwaukee	1991	405	104	15	6	1	0	31	10	16	9	4	47	51	.234	.114	.060	.054	.114
Milwaukee	1992	470	109	19	7	5	1	45	10	41	16	9	42	73	.240	.131	.074	.065	.139

John Jaha, 26

Bats Right 54L 93R 36G 43F 914ML

L= .140G .124L .111F (.071/.066) .137 .160G .144R .131F = R

		ATBATS	1B	2B	3B	HR	HBP	BB	GDP	SB	CS	ROE	XB	RUNS	EOB%	RL#	SET-UP	DR-IN	RPA
Milwaukee	1992	133	24	3	1	2	2	11	1	10	0	1	10	18	.226	.112	.063	.058	.121

Pat Listach, 25

Bats Both 157L 481R 147G 177F 552ML

L= .122G .147L .168F (.061/.049) .110 .073G .098R .119F = R

		ATBATS	1B	2B	3B	HR	HBP	BB	GDP	SB	CS	ROE	XB	RUNS	EOB%	RL#	SET-UP	DR-IN	RPA
Milwaukee	1992	579	142	19	6	1	1	55	3	54	18	7	73	85	.257	.127	.074	.060	.134

Paul Molitor, 36

Bats Right 457L 1430R 515G 440F

L= .208G .203L .198F (.089/.072) .161 .153G .148R .143F = R

		ATBATS	1B	2B	3B	HR	HBP	BB	GDP	SB	CS	ROE	XB	RUNS	EOB%	RL#	SET-UP	DR-IN	RPA
Milwaukee	1990	418	74	27	6	12	1	33	7	18	3	7	35	67	.227	.142	.076	.069	.145
Milwaukee	1991	665	154	32	13	17	6	61	11	19	8	5	91	116	.255	.157	.086	.071	.157
Milwaukee	1992	609	140	36	7	12	3	61	13	31	6	7	62	113	.263	.157	.092	.073	.165

Dave Nilsson, 23

Bats Left 29L 152R 39G 65F 661ML

L= ....G ....L ....F (.056/.057) .113 .148G .119R .101F = R

		ATBATS	1B	2B	3B	HR	HBP	BB	GDP	SB	CS	ROE	XB	RUNS	EOB%	RL#	SET-UP	DR-IN	RPA
Milwaukee	1992	164	26	8	0	4	0	16	1	2	2	1	3	20	.206	.109	.056	.057	.113

MILWAUKEE BREWERS

Kevin Seitzer, 30

Bats Right 460L 1117R 423G 398F

L= .142G .147L .152F (.059/.054) .113 .094G .099R .104F = R

		ATBATS	1B	2B	3B	HR	HBP	BB	GDP	SB	CS	ROE	XB	RUNS	EOB%	RL#	SET-UP	DR-IN	RPA
Kansas City	1990	622	129	31	6	2	2	65	11	7	6	9	67	85	.249	.118	.066	.055	.121
Kansas City	1991	234	47	11	3	1	2	26	4	4	1	2	19	31	.254	.111	.063	.052	.115
Milwaukee	1992	540	105	35	1	5	2	53	16	13	11	6	45	69	.218	.107	.058	.055	.113

Bill Spiers, 26

Bats Left 225L 643R 271G 165F

L= .092G .103L .121F (.062/.059) .121 .116G .127R .145F = R

		ATBATS	1B	2B	3B	HR	HBP	BB	GDP	SB	CS	ROE	XB	RUNS	EOB%	RL#	SET-UP	DR-IN	RPA
Milwaukee	1990	363	68	15	3	2	1	16	12	11	6	4	35	31	.162	.077	.035	.044	.079
Milwaukee	1991	414	90	13	6	8	2	34	9	14	8	7	42	56	.221	.121	.062	.059	.121
Milwaukee	1992	16	3	2	0	0	0	1	0	1	1	0	4	2	.212	.121	.064	.063	.127

Franklin Stubbs, 32

Bats Left 305L 909R 343G 235F

L= .088G .095L .104F (.053/.059) .112 .111G .118R .127F = R

		ATBATS	1B	2B	3B	HR	HBP	BB	GDP	SB	CS	ROE	XB	RUNS	EOB%	RL#	SET-UP	DR-IN	RPA
Houston	1990	448	69	23	2	23	2	45	4	19	6	7	41	84	.214	.144	.081	.079	.160
Milwaukee	1991	362	48	16	2	11	2	32	4	13	4	6	22	43	.192	.107	.051	.056	.107
Milwaukee	1992	288	45	11	1	9	1	24	2	11	8	4	25	37	.184	.113	.055	.062	.117

B. J. Surhoff, 28

Bats Left 367L 1230R 437G 363F

L= .090G .105L .124F (.047/.050) .097 .080G .095R .114F = R

		ATBATS	1B	2B	3B	HR	HBP	BB	GDP	SB	CS	ROE	XB	RUNS	EOB%	RL#	SET-UP	DR-IN	RPA
Milwaukee	1990	474	100	21	4	6	1	36	8	18	8	10	48	63	.229	.117	.063	.057	.120
Milwaukee	1991	505	118	19	4	5	0	24	21	5	8	6	44	50	.180	.091	.042	.049	.091
Milwaukee	1992	480	97	19	1	4	2	38	9	14	8	5	38	55	.210	.098	.052	.052	.104

Greg Vaughn, 27

Bats Right 444L 1163R 430G 376F

L= .117G .123L .130F (.065/.069) .134 .132G .138R .145F = R

		ATBATS	1B	2B	3B	HR	HBP	BB	GDP	SB	CS	ROE	XB	RUNS	EOB%	RL#	SET-UP	DR-IN	RPA
Milwaukee	1990	382	39	26	2	17	1	32	11	7	4	5	29	48	.154	.109	.048	.064	.112
Milwaukee	1991	542	76	24	5	27	1	60	5	2	3	5	40	84	.205	.138	.069	.069	.138
Milwaukee	1992	501	71	18	2	23	5	59	8	15	18	5	43	74	.179	.122	.060	.069	.129

Robin Yount, 37

Bats Right 468L 1383R 510G 426F

L= .124G .135L .148F (.063/.058) .121 .105G .116R .129F = R

		ATBATS	1B	2B	3B	HR	HBP	BB	GDP	SB	CS	ROE	XB	RUNS	EOB%	RL#	SET-UP	DR-IN	RPA
Milwaukee	1990	587	106	17	5	17	6	72	7	15	8	8	66	89	.236	.130	.071	.062	.133
Milwaukee	1991	503	97	20	4	10	4	46	13	6	4	10	43	64	.223	.114	.059	.055	.114
Milwaukee	1992	557	96	40	3	8	3	44	9	15	6	12	39	78	.230	.121	.067	.061	.128

PITCHERS

Throws: Flyball type, moderate reverse righty

Jim Austin, 29

(.096/.103) .100 107L 153R 184ML

		OUTS	RO	1B	2B	3B	HR	HBP	BB	GDP	SB	CS	PO	WP	BK	RUNS	EOB%	RL#	RPA
Milwaukee	1991	26	26	5	2	0	1	3	10	2	0	0	0	1	0	7	.302	.159	.159
Milwaukee	1992	175	175	27	9	0	2	2	26	7	2	4	0	1	0	17	.133	.064	.073

Throws: Neutral type, moderate reverse righty

Ricky Bones, 23

(.120/.128) .124 446L 467R 611ML

		OUTS	RO	1B	2B	3B	HR	HBP	BB	GDP	SB	CS	PO	WP	BK	RUNS	EOB%	RL#	RPA
San Diego	1991	162	0	46	7	1	3	0	18	4	3	1	0	4	0	25	.195	.101	.104
Milwaukee	1992	490	25	110	27	5	27	9	48	11	13	2	1	3	2	101	.168	.124	.143

MILWAUKEE BREWERS

Chris Bosio, 29

Throws: Neutral type, moderate to severe righty

(.106/.083) .095   1160L 1088R

		OUTS	RO	1B	2B	3B	HR	HBP	BB	GDP	SB	CS	PO	WP	BK	RUNS	EOB%	RL#	RPA
Milwaukee	1990	398	0	88	23	5	15	3	37	10	7	4	1	7	0	59	.154	.106	.106
Milwaukee	1991	614	0	140	28	4	15	8	58	22	9	4	2	5	0	74	.149	.088	.088
Milwaukee	1992	694	0	161	38	3	21	4	43	25	12	7	0	8	2	93	.126	.087	.100

Cal Eldred, 25

Throws: Flyball type, moderate to severe reverse righty

(.087/.120) .105   202L 257R 1354ML

		OUTS	RO	1B	2B	3B	HR	HBP	BB	GDP	SB	CS	PO	WP	BK	RUNS	EOB%	RL#	RPA
Milwaukee	1991	48	0	17	1	0	2	0	6	1	3	1	0	0	0	9	.196	.128	.128
Milwaukee	1992	301	0	59	10	3	4	2	23	5	8	4	1	3	0	32	.139	.071	.081

Mike Fetters, 28

Throws: Groundball type, moderate righty

(.105/.098) .101   306L 398R 264ML

		OUTS	RO	1B	2B	3B	HR	HBP	BB	GDP	SB	CS	PO	WP	BK	RUNS	EOB%	RL#	RPA
California	1990	203	175	61	6	1	9	2	20	7	6	3	0	3	0	31	.160	.114	.107
California	1991	134	87	42	7	0	4	3	26	8	6	4	0	4	0	24	.190	.119	.119
Milwaukee	1992	188	188	27	8	0	3	7	22	8	4	3	0	4	1	18	.128	.065	.074

Neal Heaton, 32

Throws: Neutral type, extreme reverse lefty

(.164/.105) .119   247L 781R 98ML

		OUTS	RO	1B	2B	3B	HR	HBP	BB	GDP	SB	CS	PO	WP	BK	RUNS	EOB%	RL#	RPA
Pittsburgh	1990	438	30	98	26	2	17	2	37	10	15	13	0	4	1	61	.127	.096	.102
Pittsburgh	1991	206	194	51	15	0	6	4	19	6	9	2	0	0	1	32	.177	.107	.109
Kansas City	1992	123	123	32	6	0	5	1	20	5	9	0	0	3	1	25	.203	.128	.138
Milwaukee	1992	3	3	0	0	0	0	0	1	0	0	0	0	0	0	0	.250	.047	.056

Doug Henry, 29

Throws: Flyball type, extreme righty

(.129/.083) .104   185L 215R 234ML

		OUTS	RO	1B	2B	3B	HR	HBP	BB	GDP	SB	CS	PO	WP	BK	RUNS	EOB%	RL#	RPA
Milwaukee	1991	108	108	9	6	0	1	0	13	1	0	1	0	0	0	7	.141	.053	.053
Milwaukee	1992	195	195	42	14	2	6	0	20	2	4	3	0	4	0	34	.177	.108	.124

Darren Holmes, 26

Throws: Neutral type, moderate to severe reverse righty

(.087/.116) .102   262L 298R 48ML

		OUTS	RO	1B	2B	3B	HR	HBP	BB	GDP	SB	CS	PO	WP	BK	RUNS	EOB%	RL#	RPA
Los Angeles	1990	52	52	11	3	0	1	0	8	0	4	2	0	1	0	8	.190	.099	.104
Milwaukee	1991	229	229	68	15	1	6	1	26	5	1	3	0	6	0	40	.201	.117	.117
Milwaukee	1992	127	127	26	6	2	1	2	7	3	4	1	0	0	0	14	.147	.073	.083

Jaime Navarro, 25

Throws: Neutral type, moderate righty

(.108/.088) .098   1308L 1239R

		OUTS	RO	1B	2B	3B	HR	HBP	BB	GDP	SB	CS	PO	WP	BK	RUNS	EOB%	RL#	RPA
Milwaukee	1990	448	69	136	25	4	11	4	38	14	11	4	0	6	5	72	.183	.111	.111
Milwaukee	1991	702	0	177	39	3	18	6	70	20	23	7	0	10	0	101	.173	.102	.102
Milwaukee	1992	738	0	162	42	6	14	6	60	23	17	11	0	6	0	94	.141	.083	.094

Jesse Orosco, 35

Throws: Flyball type, moderate reverse lefty

(.114/.102) .106   200L 409R

		OUTS	RO	1B	2B	3B	HR	HBP	BB	GDP	SB	CS	PO	WP	BK	RUNS	EOB%	RL#	RPA
Cleveland	1990	194	194	37	10	2	9	0	31	5	3	1	0	1	0	32	.179	.116	.117
Cleveland	1991	137	137	40	8	0	4	1	7	2	5	0	0	1	1	22	.189	.112	.111
Milwaukee	1992	117	117	24	4	0	5	1	12	3	3	4	0	2	0	15	.109	.086	.099

MILWAUKEE BREWERS

Dan Plesac, 30

Throws: Flyball type, neutral reverse lefty

(.113/.108) .109   213L   757R

		OUTS	RO	1B	2B	3B	HR	HBP	BB	GDP	SB	CS	PO	WP	BK	RUNS	EOB%	RL#	RPA
Milwaukee	1990	207	207	48	13	1	5	3	25	8	8	1	0	2	0	30	.178	.102	.102
Milwaukee	1991	277	133	58	20	2	12	3	38	7	4	5	0	2	1	46	.171	.116	.116
Milwaukee	1992	237	174	42	17	0	5	3	30	6	2	3	0	3	1	32	.169	.088	.099

Ron Robinson, 30

Throws: Neutral type, moderate reverse righty

(.107/.114) .110   491L   435R

		OUTS	RO	1B	2B	3B	HR	HBP	BB	GDP	SB	CS	PO	WP	BK	RUNS	EOB%	RL#	RPA
Cincinnati	1990	94	14	25	9	0	2	0	14	4	2	3	0	1	0	15	.170	.105	.107
Milwaukee	1990	445	0	125	27	1	5	6	36	10	13	8	1	2	0	57	.177	.093	.092
Milwaukee	1991	13	0	3	2	1	0	1	2	1	1	0	0	0	0	3	.243	.150	.151
Milwaukee	1992	106	0	35	12	1	3	2	14	1	3	1	0	0	0	30	.260	.155	.173

Bruce Ruffin, 29

Throws: Groundball type, moderate to severe lefty

(.090/.125) .117   325L   1058R   456ML

		OUTS	RO	1B	2B	3B	HR	HBP	BB	GDP	SB	CS	PO	WP	BK	RUNS	EOB%	RL#	RPA
Philadelphia	1990	447	50	115	45	4	14	1	55	10	3	4	0	3	2	84	.205	.129	.128
Philadelphia	1991	357	96	88	28	3	6	1	35	12	7	4	0	4	0	49	.170	.093	.094
Milwaukee	1992	174	111	46	11	2	7	0	38	8	5	3	0	2	0	39	.205	.132	.147

Bill Wegman, 30

Throws: Neutral type, extreme reverse righty

(.066/.130) .099   937L   991R

		OUTS	RO	1B	2B	3B	HR	HBP	BB	GDP	SB	CS	PO	WP	BK	RUNS	EOB%	RL#	RPA
Milwaukee	1990	89	19	23	7	1	6	0	5	2	1	0	1	0	0	16	.141	.130	.129
Milwaukee	1991	580	0	128	29	3	16	7	40	17	10	7	1	6	0	67	.133	.085	.085
Milwaukee	1992	785	0	171	50	2	28	9	52	22	18	6	2	1	2	116	.138	.095	.109

Milwaukee Brewers AAA & AA Minor League Ratings

AAA (DENVER)	AGE	BATS	POSITION	CPA	RUNS	SET-UP	DRIVE-IN	RPA
Andy Allanson	31	R	C\1B	294	27.9	.049	.046	.095
Alex Diaz	24	B	OF	496	33.7	.032	.036	.068
Sandy Guerrero	26	L	1B\2B	300	28.6	.046	.049	.095
Kenny Jackson	28	R	OF	374	34.1	.043	.048	.091
John Jaha	26	R	1B	333	53.1	.092	.067	.159
Joe Kmak	29	R	C	252	24.6	.051	.047	.098
Cedric Landrum	29	L	OF	183	16.3	.048	.041	.089
Matt Mieske	24	R	OF	581	52.2	.040	.050	.090
Charlie Montoyo	27	R	2B\3B	317	31.8	.058	.042	.100
Dave Nilsson	23	L	C\1B	266	28.8	.058	.050	.108
Jim Olander	29	R	OF	94	15.7	.097	.070	.167
Ken Shamburg	25	R	1B	272	19.8	.032	.041	.073
William Suero	26	R	2B	313	24.4	.039	.039	.078
Jim Tatum	25	R	3B	553	64.2	.059	.057	.116
Jose Valentin	23	B	SS	558	42.5	.039	.037	.076
Kenny Williams	28	R	OF	152	14.3	.046	.048	.094

AA (EL PASO)	AGE	BATS	POSITION	CPA	RUNS	SET-UP	DRIVE-IN	RPA
John Byington	25	R	3B\2B	522	45.2	.043	.044	.087
Edgar Caceres	28	B	SS\2B	411	37.9	.048	.044	.092
Mike Carter	23	R	OF	184	13.2	.033	.039	.072
Vince Castaldo	25	L	OF	476	45.3	.049	.046	.095
Tony Diggs	25	B	OF	319	20.4	.031	.033	.064
Bo Dodson	22	L	1B	414	40.2	.054	.043	.097
Craig Faulkner	27	R	C\1B	366	26.6	.033	.040	.073
John Finn	25	R	2B\OF	528	51.4	.056	.041	.097
Mike Guerrero	24	R	SS	291	23.0	.041	.038	.079
Charlie Hillemann	26	R	OF	189	15.7	.043	.040	.083
Bob Kapesser	25	R	C	264	16.3	.029	.033	.062
Alan Lewis	26	L	3B	377	35.8	.050	.045	.095
Troy O'Leary	23	L	OF	573	64.8	.063	.050	.113

AAA Pitchers	Age	Throws	Outs	RPA	AA Pitchers	Age	Throws	Outs	RPA
Cal Eldred	25	R	423	.098	Glenn Carter	25	R	234	.144
Chris George	26	R	128	.129	Jim Czajkowski	29	R	238	.145
Otis Green	28	L	457	.129	Tim Dell	25	R	263	.152
Jim Hunter	28	R	458	.119	Mike Farrell	23	L	319	.104
Mike Ignasiak	26	R	276	.104	Dave Fitzgerald	27	L	127	.184
Mark Kiefer	24	R	488	.140	Steve Lienhard	28	R	90	.149
Mark Lee	28	L	206	.124	David Martinez	29	R	242	.155
Paul McClellan	26	R	288	.163	Tom McGraw	25	L	208	.125
Angel Miranda	23	L	481	.141	Rafael Novoa	25	L	439	.117
Eric Nolte	28	L	216	.128	Dave Richards	25	L	189	.132
Bruce Ruffin	29	L	86	.119	Steve Sparks	27	R	422	.141
Efrain Valdez	26	L	204	.134	Jeff Tabaka	28	L	246	.089
Rob Wishnevski	25	R	283	.114	Scott Taylor	26	R	280	.140
					Brandy Vann	26	R	231	.158

NEW YORK YANKEES

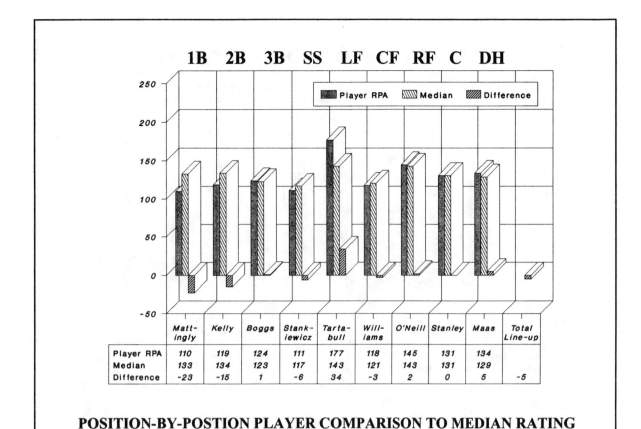

	1B	2B	3B	SS	LF	CF	RF	C	DH	Total Line-up
	Matt-ingly	Kelly	Boggs	Stank-iewicz	Tarta-bull	Will-iams	O'Neill	Stanley	Maas	
Player RPA	110	119	124	111	177	118	145	131	134	
Median	133	134	123	117	143	121	143	131	129	
Difference	-23	-15	1	-6	34	-3	2	0	5	-5

POSITION-BY-POSTION PLAYER COMPARISON TO MEDIAN RATING

DEFENSIVE TEAM AND STADIUM DATA FOR THE LAST 3 YEARS:

TEAM DEFENSE BY POSITION:

		1990	1991	1992	POSITION-BY-POSITION STADIUM CHARACTERISTICS:
1B:	Home	-0.3	-1.9	-1.3	Slightly hard to play
	Away	-1.4	-0.1	+0.9	
2B:	Home	-0.6	-4.2	+2.0	Average
	Away	-5.8	-1.6	+0.9	
3B:	Home	-4.1	-2.4	-0.5	Hard to play
	Away	-5.2	-5.6	-2.0	
SS:	Home	+2.1	+4.7	-1.2	Average
	Away	+1.8	-0.9	0.0	
LF:	Home	+1.3	+5.3	+1.4	Easy to play
	Away	-9.5	-7.9	+10.0	
CF:	Home	-1.0	-8.4	-4.7	Extremely easy to play. The H/A difference
	Away	-7.8	-4.6	-6.4	over 3 yrs. was 25.3 pts. of RPA per chance.
RF:	Home	-3.3	+1.5	-3.3	Slightly easy to play
	Away	-5.8	-3.6	-3.2	
Total Home:		-5.9	-5.4	-7.7	
Total Away:		-33.7	-24.3	+0.2	

Comments: Even though the Yankee defense in '92 was below average, it still represented a whopping improvement over the awful defense of '91 and the even worse defense of '90. Centerfield remains the biggest problem area. Perhaps Bernie Williams, as he gains experience, will begin to turn this around. If not, then this team needs to look for a solution. Giving away 11 runs at one position is an awful lot of generosity to the opponent.

American League East

NEW YORK YANKEES

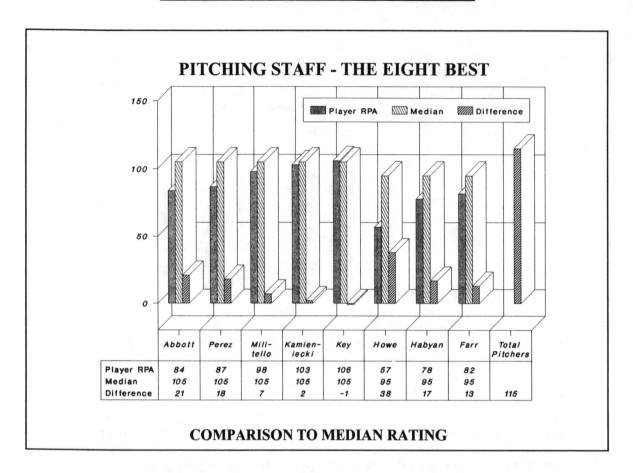

PITCHING STAFF - THE EIGHT BEST

Legend: ■ Player RPA ▨ Median ▨ Difference

	Abbott	Perez	Mili-tello	Kamien-iecki	Key	Howe	Habyan	Farr	Total Pitchers
Player RPA	84	87	98	103	106	57	78	82	
Median	105	105	105	105	105	95	95	95	
Difference	21	18	7	2	-1	38	17	13	115

COMPARISON TO MEDIAN RATING

SUGGESTED LINE-UPS (with set-up RPA & drive-in RPA ratings):

Vs: Left-handed Groundball
DH:	M. Stanley	73-56
RF:	D. Tartabull	102-82
C:	J. Leyritz	84-77
3B:	R. Davis	75-75
SS:	S. Owen	62-57
CF:	B. Williams	63-58
2B:	M. Gallego	60-54
LF:	G. Williams	55-62
1B:	D. Mattingly	46-46

Vs: Neutral Lefty Pitchers
DH:	M. Stanley	89-69
RF:	D. Tartabull	122-98
C:	J. Leyritz	81-74
3B:	R. Davis	75-75
2B:	M. Gallego	68-62
CF:	B. Williams	67-62
SS:	R. Velarde	64-62
LF:	G. Williams	55-62
1B:	D. Mattingly	55-55

Vs: Left-handed Flyball
DH:	M. Stanley	107-85
CF:	B. Williams	73-67
RF:	D. Tartabull	143-116
C:	J. Leyritz	77-71
SS:	R. Velarde	72-70
2B:	P. Kelly	72-78
3B:	H. Meulens	72-82
1B:	D. Mattingly	66-65
LF:	G. Williams	55-62

Vs: Right-handed Groundball
3B:	W. Boggs	76-58
LF:	D. Tartabull	74-60
1B:	K. Maas	74-67
RF:	P. O'Neill	72-72
DH:	R. Davis	65-65
CF:	B. Williams	66-60
C:	J. Leyritz	58-52
2B:	M. Gallego	50-45
SS:	A. Stankiewicz	48-42

Vs: Neutral Righty Pitchers
3B:	W. Boggs	78-60
LF:	D. Tartabull	94-76
CF:	B. Williams	70-64
1B:	K. Maas	75-70
RF:	P. O'Neill	74-74
DH:	R. Davis	65-65
2B:	P. Kelly	55-60
C:	J. Leyritz	55-49
SS:	A. Stankiewicz	55-48

Vs: Right-handed Flyball
3B:	W. Boggs	80-62
C:	M. Stanley	83-65
LF:	D. Tartabull	116-93
DH:	K. Maas	80-75
CF:	B. Williams	76-69
RF:	P. O'Neill	77-77
2B:	P. Kelly	72-78
1B:	D. Mattingly	67-66
SS:	A. Stankiewicz	61-54

nts: 5th best offense in the AL, provided they make the above moves. Boggs can't hit lefties and it would be a big
allow him to face them. Russ Davis is a better hitter than Dave Silvestri and is very important in the above
may need a couple of months at AAA. Spike Owen and Paul O'Neill are valuable *platoon* players, not
epends upon Tartabull staying healthy. This team can win it all if he does stay healthy.

NEW YORK YANKEES

Was I in for a shock when I did my spreadsheet calculations for each Major League team in order to project their records in the coming season based on the talent each team possessed! There were three "sleeper" teams, and totally unexpectedly, the New York Yankees were probably the best bet amongst the three to win their division. In fact, I'd say that the Yankees are the best bet amongst all the 28 Major League teams to win a pennant in 1993.

The key to this team's fortune in '93 is its magnificent pitching staff. There is nothing to compare it to. Not even the fabulous Atlanta Braves pitching staff, even with the addition of the marvelous Greg Maddux, can hold a candle to what has been assembled at Yankee Stadium.

The 5 starters and 3 relievers, listed on the graph on the opposite page, are all quality performers. In fact, this team has pitching depth even beyond these 8 quality performers. The Yankee offense will only be the 5th best in the league and its defense will remain below average, but this team should blow past everyone in the division due to its magnificent pitching and the decimation of the Toronto Blue Jays this winter.

Can you believe the utter idiocy of the New York media? The "loss" of Charlie Hayes in the expansion draft was headline news. *Newsday* called it "The Hayes Heist", which was probably one of the milder terms used in the New York press to describe this event. *Give me a break!* Charlie Hayes was, is, and will remain a purely journeyman player, and not a very good one at that. If I were Gene Michael, sitting on a massive amount of young talent, I would have danced a jig at the idiocy of the Colorado Rockies in taking Hayes.

I don't have a line on Expansion draftee Carl Everett, whom the press has labelled a huge talent, but going by my experience with the press, let's just say I'm skeptical.

The press has also labelled the loss of Brad Ausmus as catastrophic, and quickly attacked the Yankee front office for exposing him. Am I missing something here? Ausmus has shown no ability to hit whatsoever. Where is this great talent hidden? What fortune teller have the press been visiting? I think they've been peering into a very cracked ball!

This team could have lost Danny Tartabull and that would truly have cost them a chance at the pennant. Why they protected Mattingly over him, I believe, has more to do with the color of Mattingly's skin than ability. This team could have lost a valuable utility man in Randy Velarde. They could have lost the bat of Kevin Maas and a good hitting catcher in Jim leyritz. The Yankees could have lost quality pitchers Scott Kamieniecki, Steve Farr, John Habyan and Rich Monteleone.

The Yankees lost a top hitting prospect in the Rule 5 draft when the Orioles selected power hitter Sherman Obando. AA player Russ Davis is the Yanks third baseman of the future.

New York's Projected record for 1993: 89--73, good for 1st place in the division.

NEW YORK YANKEES

Jesse Barfield, 33

Bats Right   360L   637R   186G   208F

L= .091G .139L .182F   (.037/.058) .095   .022G   .070R   .113F = R

		ATBATS	1B	2B	3B	HR	HBP	BB	GDP	SB	CS	ROE	XB	RUNS	EOB%	RL#	SET-UP	DR-IN	RPA
Yankees	1990	476	69	21	2	25	5	78	6	4	3	5	40	91	.246	.155	.086	.073	.159
Yankees	1991	284	35	12	0	17	0	30	11	1	0	1	19	37	.149	.111	.046	.065	.111
Yankees	1992	95	9	2	0	2	0	7	5	1	0	0	8	5	.077	.046	.012	.033	.045

Mike Gallego, 32

Bats Right   334L   868R   389G   250F

L= .118G .134L .159F   (.063/.057) .120   .099G   .115R   .140F = R

		ATBATS	1B	2B	3B	HR	HBP	BB	GDP	SB	CS	ROE	XB	RUNS	EOB%	RL#	SET-UP	DR-IN	RPA
Oakland	1990	389	62	13	2	3	4	35	13	5	5	9	28	37	.190	.076	.039	.043	.082
Oakland	1991	482	88	15	4	12	5	64	8	6	9	6	36	71	.234	.114	.064	.058	.122
Yankees	1992	173	33	7	1	3	4	20	5	0	1	2	15	24	.238	.115	.062	.053	.115

Mel Hall, 32

Bats Left   424L   1091R   411G   371F

L= .114G .110L .105F   (.059/.063) .122   .131G   .127R   .122F = R

		ATBATS	1B	2B	3B	HR	HBP	BB	GDP	SB	CS	ROE	XB	RUNS	EOB%	RL#	SET-UP	DR-IN	RPA
Yankees	1990	360	56	23	2	12	2	4	7	0	0	2	27	40	.145	.103	.043	.062	.105
Yankees	1991	492	96	23	2	19	3	20	6	0	1	9	32	69	.203	.131	.064	.067	.131
Yankees	1992	583	109	36	3	15	1	25	13	4	2	5	36	72	.187	.115	.055	.060	.115

Charlie Hayes, 27

Bats Right   572L   1067R   550G   378F

L= .090G .099L .112F   (.042/.055) .097   .087G   .096R   .109F = R

		ATBATS	1B	2B	3B	HR	HBP	BB	GDP	SB	CS	ROE	XB	RUNS	EOB%	RL#	SET-UP	DR-IN	RPA
Philadelphia	1990	561	115	20	0	10	2	25	12	4	4	15	44	61	.199	.103	.050	.052	.102
Philadelphia	1991	460	70	23	1	12	1	13	13	3	3	6	19	42	.137	.080	.033	.049	.082
Yankees	1992	509	92	19	2	18	3	28	12	3	5	5	21	61	.170	.111	.050	.060	.110

Dion James, 30

Bats Left   29L   421R   147G   115F

L= ....G ....L ....F   (.064/.054) .118   .138G   .115R   .086F = R

		ATBATS	1B	2B	3B	HR	HBP	BB	GDP	SB	CS	ROE	XB	RUNS	EOB%	RL#	SET-UP	DR-IN	RPA
Cleveland	1990	248	50	15	2	1	1	24	6	5	3	4	19	30	.241	.108	.058	.050	.108
Yankees	1992	145	27	8	0	3	1	22	3	1	1	2	20	23	.265	.135	.075	.060	.135

Pat Kelly, 25

Bats Right   232L   449R   189G   161F   126ML

L= .076G .106L .141F   (.051/.055) .106   .076G   .108R   .141F = R

		ATBATS	1B	2B	3B	HR	HBP	BB	GDP	SB	CS	ROE	XB	RUNS	EOB%	RL#	SET-UP	DR-IN	RPA
Yankees	1991	298	53	12	4	3	5	15	5	12	3	3	24	31	.196	.093	.045	.048	.093
Yankees	1992	318	41	22	2	7	10	24	6	8	6	3	28	38	.194	.106	.051	.054	.105

Jim Leyritz, 29

Bats Right   282L   320R   169G   125F   321ML

L= .159G .153L .146F   (.066/.060) .126   .108G   .102R   .095F = R

		ATBATS	1B	2B	3B	HR	HBP	BB	GDP	SB	CS	ROE	XB	RUNS	EOB%	RL#	SET-UP	DR-IN	RPA
Yankees	1990	303	59	13	1	5	7	26	11	2	3	3	17	36	.209	.099	.051	.051	.102
Yankees	1991	77	11	3	0	0	0	13	0	0	2	1	3	7	.243	.078	.041	.036	.077
Yankees	1992	144	24	6	0	7	6	13	2	0	1	2	5	24	.228	.147	.076	.070	.146

Kevin Maas, 27

Bats Left   349L   839R   342G   269F

L= .096G .103L .113F   (.066/.063) .129   .133G   .140R   .150F = R

		ATBATS	1B	2B	3B	HR	HBP	BB	GDP	SB	CS	ROE	XB	RUNS	EOB%	RL#	SET-UP	DR-IN	RPA
Yankees	1990	254	34	9	0	21	3	33	2	1	2	1	15	50	.200	.165	.083	.087	.170
	1991	500	72	14	1	23	4	80	4	5	1	1	36	79	.233	.132	.070	.062	.132
	1992	286	48	12	0	11	0	21	1	3	2	2	14	38	.195	.125	.060	.064	.124

NEW YORK YANKEES

Don Mattingly, 31

Bats Left   607L   1149R   484G   403F

L= .094G .112L .133F   (.057/.056) .113   .096G .114R .135F = R

		ATBATS	1B	2B	3B	HR	HBP	BB	GDP	SB	CS	ROE	XB	RUNS	EOB%	RL#	SET-UP	DR-IN	RPA
Yankees	1990	394	80	16	0	5	3	15	13	1	0	3	27	37	.176	.085	.040	.047	.087
Yankees	1991	587	125	35	0	9	4	35	21	2	0	5	33	68	.207	.103	.051	.052	.103
Yankees	1992	640	130	40	0	14	1	32	11	3	0	7	57	85	.213	.124	.062	.061	.123

Hensley Meulens, 25

Bats Right   232L   189R   103G   96F   613ML

L= .079G .111L .145F   (.050/.057) .107   .069G .101R .135F = R

		ATBATS	1B	2B	3B	HR	HBP	BB	GDP	SB	CS	ROE	XB	RUNS	EOB%	RL#	SET-UP	DR-IN	RPA
Yankees	1990	83	10	7	0	3	3	9	3	1	0	4	8	14	.250	.140	.079	.065	.144
Yankees	1991	288	49	8	1	6	4	17	7	3	1	5	18	29	.182	.088	.041	.047	.088
Yankees	1992	5	2	0	0	1	0	1	1	0	0	0	0	2	.163	.258	.112	.143	.255

Matt Nokes, 29

Bats Left   219L   1081R   387G   298F

L= .109G .116L .125F   (.050/.067) .118   .110G .117R .126F = R

		ATBATS	1B	2B	3B	HR	HBP	BB	GDP	SB	CS	ROE	XB	RUNS	EOB%	RL#	SET-UP	DR-IN	RPA
Detroit	1990	111	21	5	1	3	2	1	5	0	0	0	7	11	.134	.090	.035	.055	.090
Yankees	1990	240	45	4	0	8	4	17	6	2	2	2	12	28	.179	.102	.048	.056	.104
Yankees	1991	456	78	20	0	24	5	20	6	3	2	6	16	64	.177	.129	.059	.070	.129
Yankees	1992	384	54	9	1	22	3	26	13	0	1	1	6	45	.127	.105	.040	.064	.104

Paul O'Neill, 29

Bats Left   534L   1194R   575G   395F

L= .078G .082L .088F   (.063/.063) .126   .142G .146R .152F = R

		ATBATS	1B	2B	3B	HR	HBP	BB	GDP	SB	CS	ROE	XB	RUNS	EOB%	RL#	SET-UP	DR-IN	RPA
Cincinnati	1990	503	92	28	0	16	2	40	12	13	11	1	37	62	.183	.113	.052	.059	.111
Cincinnati	1991	532	72	36	0	28	1	59	8	12	8	3	37	80	.196	.133	.062	.066	.128
Cincinnati	1992	496	88	19	1	14	2	62	10	6	4	7	35	72	.229	.122	.064	.059	.123

Andy Stankiewicz, 28

Bats Right   153L   303R   124G   127F   418ML

L= .077G .090L .102F   (.051/.045) .096   .086G .099R .111F = R

		ATBATS	1B	2B	3B	HR	HBP	BB	GDP	SB	CS	ROE	XB	RUNS	EOB%	RL#	SET-UP	DR-IN	RPA
Yankees	1992	400	81	22	2	2	5	38	13	9	6	8	48	49	.233	.107	.056	.050	.106

Mike Stanley, 29

Bats Right   415L   238R   173G   152F

L= .126G .155L .189F   (.079/.060) .139   .082G .111R .145F = R

		ATBATS	1B	2B	3B	HR	HBP	BB	GDP	SB	CS	ROE	XB	RUNS	EOB%	RL#	SET-UP	DR-IN	RPA
Texas	1990	189	36	8	1	2	0	28	4	1	0	2	12	25	.259	.110	.061	.049	.110
Texas	1991	181	28	13	1	3	2	34	2	0	0	2	9	30	.296	.135	.080	.057	.137
Yankees	1992	173	28	7	0	8	1	33	6	0	0	1	6	31	.245	.143	.077	.065	.142

Danny Tartabull, 30

Bats Right   455L   975R   386G   364F

L= .184G .220L .259F   (.103/.083) .186   .134G .170R .209F = R

		ATBATS	1B	2B	3B	HR	HBP	BB	GDP	SB	CS	ROE	XB	RUNS	EOB%	RL#	SET-UP	DR-IN	RPA
Kansas City	1990	313	50	19	0	15	0	36	9	1	1	4	22	51	.210	.140	.072	.070	.142
Kansas City	1991	484	84	35	3	31	3	59	9	6	3	4	33	105	.241	.184	.102	.088	.190
Yankees	1992	421	68	19	0	25	0	89	7	2	2	7	32	95	.280	.183	.104	.078	.182

Randy Velarde, 30

Bats Right   320L   611R   270G   249F

L= .112G .126L .142F   (.055/.053) .108   .085G .099R .115F = R

		ATBATS	1B	2B	3B	HR	HBP	BB	GDP	SB	CS	ROE	XB	RUNS	EOB%	RL#	SET-UP	DR-IN	RPA
Yankees	1990	229	35	6	2	5	1	20	6	0	3	5	18	24	.178	.089	.042	.049	.091
Yankees	1991	184	32	11	1	1	3	18	6	3	1	1	13	19	.217	.090	.046	.044	.090
Yankees	1992	412	80	24	1	7	2	37	13	7	2	6	40	54	.222	.117	.060	.056	.116

NEW YORK YANKEES

Bernie Williams, 24

		Bats Both		220L	448R	202G	143F		775ML

L= .110G   .118L   .129F   (.063/.058) .121   .115G   .123R   .134F = R

		ATBATS	1B	2B	3B	HR	HBP	BB	GDP	SB	CS	ROE	XB	RUNS	EOB%	RL#	SET-UP	DR-IN	RPA
Yankees	1991	320	50	19	4	3	1	48	4	10	7	2	28	41	.244	.107	.058	.049	.107
Yankees	1992	261	52	14	2	5	1	28	5	7	7	3	31	37	.228	.126	.065	.060	.125

PITCHERS

Throws: Groundball type, neutral righty

Tim Burke, 33

(.097/.094) .095   423L   453R

		OUTS	RO	1B	2B	3B	HR	HBP	BB	GDP	SB	CS	PO	WP	BK	RUNS	EOB%	RL#	RPA
Montreal	1990	225	225	56	8	1	6	2	15	7	5	1	0	1	1	29	.147	.088	.093
Montreal	1991	138	138	29	7	2	3	4	8	8	7	1	0	1	0	16	.109	.076	.083
New York Mets	1991	167	167	40	9	1	5	0	10	6	1	0	0	2	0	18	.138	.092	.081
New York Mets	1992	47	47	21	3	1	1	0	3	1	1	0	0	2	0	11	.244	.149	.146
N.Y. Yankees	1992	83	83	13	11	0	2	1	11	2	4	1	1	2	0	13	.175	.104	.105

Throws: Neutral type, moderate to severe righty

Steve Farr, 36

(.084/.062) .072   436L   521R

		OUTS	RO	1B	2B	3B	HR	HBP	BB	GDP	SB	CS	PO	WP	BK	RUNS	EOB%	RL#	RPA
Kansas City	1990	381	271	79	12	2	6	5	39	13	8	3	1	2	0	39	.145	.074	.076
N.Y. Yankees	1991	210	210	41	12	0	4	5	17	8	2	2	0	2	0	20	.136	.074	.070
N.Y. Yankees	1992	156	156	28	4	0	2	2	19	3	7	0	0	0	0	16	.180	.075	.075

Throws: Groundball type, extreme righty

John Habyan, 28

(.104/.059) .077   259L   402R

		OUTS	RO	1B	2B	3B	HR	HBP	BB	GDP	SB	CS	PO	WP	BK	RUNS	EOB%	RL#	RPA
N.Y. Yankees	1990	26	26	5	4	1	0	1	2	2	0	0	0	1	0	4	.159	.099	.094
N.Y. Yankees	1991	270	270	51	17	3	2	2	18	10	4	1	4	1	2	21	.112	.063	.059
N.Y. Yankees	1992	218	218	63	13	2	6	2	16	11	5	0	3	2	1	30	.140	.097	.098

Throws: Groundball type, moderate to severe lefty

Steve Howe, 34

(.033/.055) .049   69L   183R

		OUTS	RO	1B	2B	3B	HR	HBP	BB	GDP	SB	CS	PO	WP	BK	RUNS	EOB%	RL#	RPA
N.Y. Yankees	1991	145	145	30	8	0	1	3	5	7	1	0	0	2	0	10	.111	.058	.054
N.Y. Yankees	1992	66	66	8	0	0	1	0	2	1	0	0	0	1	0	3	.070	.036	.036

Throws: Groundball type, extreme lefty

Jeff Johnson, 26

(.080/.116) .111   97L   672R   490ML

		OUTS	RO	1B	2B	3B	HR	HBP	BB	GDP	SB	CS	PO	WP	BK	RUNS	EOB%	RL#	RPA
N.Y. Yankees	1991	381	0	115	21	5	15	6	32	13	18	4	1	5	1	65	.173	.120	.113
N.Y. Yankees	1992	158	37	48	17	2	4	2	23	9	4	2	1	1	0	31	.192	.123	.125

Throws: Neutral type, moderate righty

Scott Kamieniecki, 28

(.108/.097) .102   487L   511R   358ML

		OUTS	RO	1B	2B	3B	HR	HBP	BB	GDP	SB	CS	PO	WP	BK	RUNS	EOB%	RL#	RPA
N.Y. Yankees	1991	166	0	31	12	3	8	3	21	5	4	2	2	1	0	25	.147	.112	.105
N.Y. Yankees	1992	564	0	141	38	1	13	5	65	19	29	6	1	9	1	84	.178	.102	.103

Throws: Flyball type, extreme righty

Sam Militello, 23

(.142/.066) .102   118L   132R   767ML

		OUTS	RO	1B	2B	3B	HR	HBP	BB	GDP	SB	CS	PO	WP	BK	RUNS	EOB%	RL#	RPA
...es	1992	180	0	24	13	0	6	2	31	4	7	0	1	1	0	26	.187	.101	.102

NEW YORK YANKEES

Throws: Neutral type, neutral reverse righty

Rich Monteleone, 29   (.088/.091) .090   245L   347R

		OUTS	RO	1B	2B	3B	HR	HBP	BB	GDP	SB	CS	PO	WP	BK	RUNS	EOB%	RL#	RPA
N.Y. Yankees	1990	22	22	5	3	0	0	0	2	0	0	1	0	0	0	3	.181	.088	.085
N.Y. Yankees	1991	141	141	27	10	0	5	0	16	3	2	2	0	1	1	18	.156	.097	.091
N.Y. Yankees	1992	278	278	58	13	4	7	0	24	3	3	5	0	0	3	34	.153	.089	.090

Throws: Neutral type, moderate righty

Melido Perez, 26   (.091/.085) .088   1124L   1191R

		OUTS	RO	1B	2B	3B	HR	HBP	BB	GDP	SB	CS	PO	WP	BK	RUNS	EOB%	RL#	RPA
Chi. White Sox	1990	591	0	122	31	10	14	2	85	20	12	11	1	8	4	81	.160	.096	.098
Chi. White Sox	1991	407	267	79	16	1	15	1	52	10	15	5	1	11	1	55	.152	.097	.099
N.Y. Yankees	1992	743	0	160	33	3	16	5	88	19	18	18	9	13	0	82	.134	.080	.081

Throws: Flyball type, moderate righty

Scott Sanderson, 36   (.108/.098) .103   1281L   1207R

		OUTS	RO	1B	2B	3B	HR	HBP	BB	GDP	SB	CS	PO	WP	BK	RUNS	EOB%	RL#	RPA
Oakland	1990	619	0	132	39	7	27	4	64	6	13	5	0	7	1	117	.182	.118	.130
N.Y. Yankees	1991	624	0	127	46	5	22	3	29	19	16	7	0	4	1	71	.116	.088	.083
N.Y. Yankees	1992	580	0	148	35	9	28	4	59	17	18	8	1	4	1	103	.160	.121	.122

Throws: Groundball type, moderate to severe righty

Bob Wickman, 23   (.139/.113) .125   96L   104R   1213ML

		OUTS	RO	1B	2B	3B	HR	HBP	BB	GDP	SB	CS	PO	WP	BK	RUNS	EOB%	RL#	RPA
N.Y. Yankees	1992	151	0	37	9	3	2	2	20	9	8	1	1	3	0	21	.160	.094	.095

Throws: Neutral type, extreme lefty

Curt Young, 32   (.084/.121) .112   268L   812R   111ML

		OUTS	RO	1B	2B	3B	HR	HBP	BB	GDP	SB	CS	PO	WP	BK	RUNS	EOB%	RL#	RPA
Oakland	1990	373	45	87	20	0	17	2	52	12	9	11	0	3	0	63	.146	.104	.117
Oakland	1991	205	188	53	11	2	8	2	32	8	4	3	0	2	1	37	.183	.113	.117
Kansas City	1992	73	51	20	7	1	1	0	6	2	2	1	0	0	0	12	.183	.106	.114
N.Y. Yankees	1992	130	34	37	13	0	1	2	9	5	3	1	0	0	0	18	.183	.096	.096

New York Yankees AAA & AA Minor League Ratings

AAA (COLUMBUS)	AGE	BATS	POSITION	CPA	RUNS	SET-UP	DRIVE-IN	RPA
Brad Ausmus	23	R	C	440	31.7	.034	.038	.072
Bobby DeJardin	25	B	2B\SS	470	33.2	.033	.038	.071
Mike Humphreys	25	R	OF	477	51.4	.057	.051	.108
Jay Knoblauh	27	R	OF	379	35.4	.044	.049	.093
Torey LoVullo	27	B	2B\3B	543	73.7	.073	.063	.136
Billy Masse	26	R	OF	426	44.8	.053	.052	.105
Hensley Meulens	25	R	3B	613	72.5	.057	.061	.118
Dave Sax	34	R	C\1B	216	16.9	.037	.041	.078
Dave Silvestri	25	R	SS	496	58.1	.061	.056	.117
J.T. Snow	24	B	1B	572	75.9	.074	.059	.133
Bernie Williams	24	B	OF	424	53.8	.069	.058	.127
Gerald Williams	26	R	OF	602	63.0	.049	.056	.105

AA (ALBANY)	AGE	BATS	POSITION	CPA	RUNS	SET-UP	DRIVE-IN	RPA
Richard Barnwell	24	R	OF	498	50.0	.052	.048	.100
Bubba Carpenter	24	L	OF	256	22.8	.041	.048	.089
Russ Davis	23	R	3B	558	74.2	.066	.066	.132
Robert Eenhoorn	24	R	SS	214	14.5	.029	.038	.067
Kiki Hernandez	23	R	C	382	38.0	.052	.048	.100
Lyle Mouton	23	R	OF	248	18.1	.033	.040	.073
Sherman Obando	22	R	1B	432	54.8	.061	.066	.127
Jason Robertson	21	L	OF	221	15.9	.030	.042	.072
Carlos Rodriguez	25	B	SS\2B	423	36.8	.043	.044	.087
Don Sparks	26	R	1B\3B	551	65.1	.058	.060	.118
Hector Vargas	26	R	2B	474	53.6	.061	.052	.113
John Viera	25	L	OF	200	19.2	.046	.050	.096

AAA Pitchers	Age	Throws	Outs	RPA	AA Pitchers	Age	Throws	Outs	RPA
Royal Clayton	27	R	392	.121	Richard Batchelor	25	R	212	.165
Andy Cook	25	R	299	.118	Mark Carper	24	R	400	.132
Francisco DeLaRosa	26	R	167	.115	Ken Greer	25	R	209	.110
Mike Draper	26	R	240	.110	Sterling Hitchcock	21	L	440	.128
Shawn Hillegas	28	R	82	.104	Darren Hodges	23	R	192	.205
Jeff Johnson	26	L	174	.081	Jeff Hoffman	25	R	363	.153
Ed Martel	23	R	452	.146	Scott Holcomb	24	L	160	.154
Sam Militello	23	R	424	.097	Mark Hutton	22	R	511	.138
Dave Rosario	26	L	220	.116	Ramon Manon	24	R	98	.156
Russ Springer	24	R	371	.114	Roberto Munoz	24	R	337	.142
Don Stanford	27	R	247	.132	Jerry Nielsen	26	L	174	.086
Bob Wickman	23	R	471	.116	Kirt Ojala	24	L	455	.145
Curt Young	32	L	78	.138	Tom Popplewell	25	R	170	.204

TORONTO BLUE JAYS

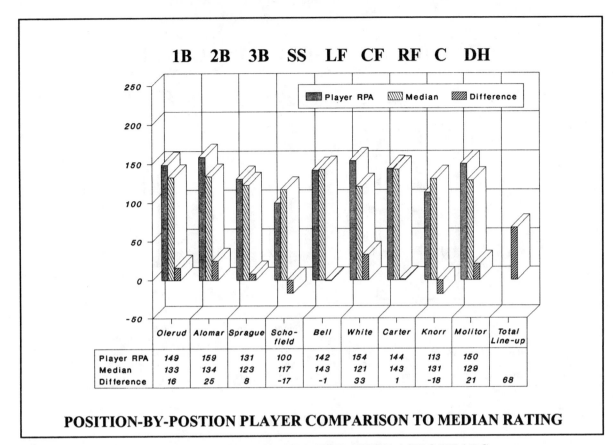

	1B	2B	3B	SS	LF	CF	RF	C	DH
	Olerud	Alomar	Sprague	Scho-field	Bell	White	Carter	Knorr	Molitor
Player RPA	149	159	131	100	142	154	144	113	150
Median	133	134	123	117	143	121	143	131	129
Difference	16	25	8	-17	-1	33	1	-18	21

Total Line-up
68

POSITION-BY-POSTION PLAYER COMPARISON TO MEDIAN RATING

DEFENSIVE TEAM AND STADIUM DATA FOR THE LAST 3 YEARS:

TEAM DEFENSE BY POSITION:

		1990	1991	1992	POSITION-BY-POSITION STADIUM CHARACTERISTICS:
1B:	Home	-0.1	+5.4	+0.7	Slightly hard to play
	Away	-0.2	-1.1	+2.2	
2B:	Home	-3.0	-1.3	-2.2	Average
	Away	+4.7	+4.5	+1.0	
3B:	Home	-0.5	-1.4	+1.2	Average
	Away	-0.1	-2.3	-1.6	
SS:	Home	+2.2	+0.3	+5.2	Average
	Away	+2.4	-1.3	+9.2	
LF:	Home	+1.5	+1.5	-2.5	Average
	Away	+1.0	+5.4	-3.5	
CF:	Home	+3.9	+6.5	+7.2	Slightly hard to play
	Away	+1.3	+4.5	+8.0	
RF:	Home	+4.6	+11.2	+3.5	Average (to slightly hard)
	Away	-0.4	+4.2	+2.5	
Total Home:		+8.6	+22.2	+13.1	
Total Away:		+8.7	+13.9	+17.7	

Comments: The Blue Jays had the best defensive team in the American League in 1992 despite the handicap of Candy Maldonado in left field. Derek Bell, taking the place of Maldonado, appears to be a very good defensive outfielder, which could make the Blue Jays outfield the best in the Major Leagues in 1993.

TORONTO BLUE JAYS

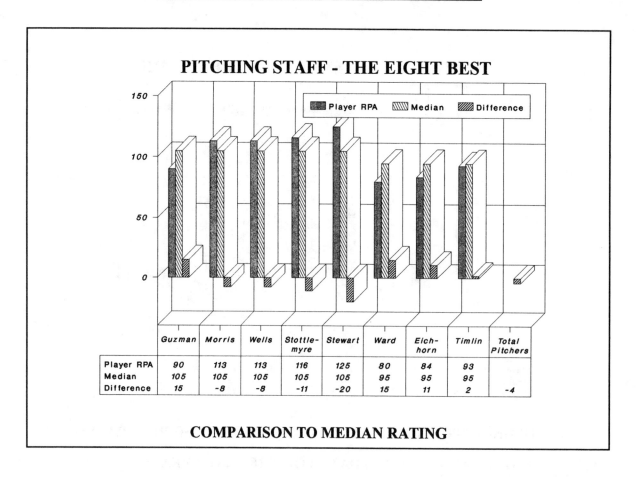

PITCHING STAFF - THE EIGHT BEST

Player RPA   Median   Difference

	Guzman	Morris	Wells	Stottle-myre	Stewart	Ward	Eich-horn	Timlin	Total Pitchers
Player RPA	90	113	113	116	125	80	84	93	
Median	105	105	105	105	105	95	95	95	
Difference	15	-8	-8	-11	-20	15	11	2	-4

COMPARISON TO MEDIAN RATING

SUGGESTED LINE-UPS (with set-up RPA & drive-in RPA ratings):

Vs: Left-handed Groundball

2B:	R. Alomar	82-61
DH:	P. Molitor	110-87
3B:	E. Sprague	73-63
1B:	J. Olerud	80-70
LF:	D. Bell	70-67
C:	R. Knorr	60-69
CF:	D. White	64-63
RF:	J. Carter	56-67
SS:	A. Griffin	40-39

Vs: Neutral Lefty Pitchers

2B:	R. Alomar	90-69
DH:	P. Molitor	107-85
3B:	E. Sprague	74-65
1B:	J. Olerud	88-77
LF:	D. Bell	70-67
RF:	J. Carter	61-73
CF:	D. White	64-63
C:	R. Knorr	60-69
SS:	A. Griffin	41-41

Vs: Left-handed Flyball

2B:	R. Alomar	103-78
DH:	P. Molitor	104-83
3B:	E. Sprague	76-66
1B:	J. Olerud	100-88
RF:	J. Carter	68-82
LF:	D. Bell	70-67
CF:	D. White	65-63
C:	R. Knorr	60-69
SS:	A. Griffin	43-43

Vs: Right-handed Groundball

2B:	R. Alomar	83-61
DH:	P. Molitor	79-63
1B:	J. Olerud	66-59
3B:	E. Sprague	64-56
CF:	D. White	66-63
LF:	D. Bell	60-57
RF:	J. Carter	54-66
C:	R. Knorr	50-59
SS:	A. Griffin	29-28

Vs: Neutral Righty Pitchers

2B:	R. Alomar	91-69
DH:	P. Molitor	76-61
1B:	J. Olerud	74-66
CF:	D. White	66-63
RF:	J. Carter	60-71
3B:	E. Sprague	66-57
LF:	D. Bell	60-57
C:	R. Knorr	50-59
SS:	A. Griffin	30-30

Vs: Right-handed Flyball

2B:	R. Alomar	104-78
DH:	P. Molitor	73-59
1B:	J. Olerud	87-76
CF:	D. White	66-64
RF:	J. Carter	67-80
3B:	E. Sprague	67-59
LF:	D. Bell	60-57
C:	R. Knorr	50-59
SS:	A. Griffin	32-32

Comments: A very weak offense, with only 3 teams in the AL having weaker offenses. There is decent strength against lefty pitching, but terrible weakness vs. all types of righties, particularly groundball-type righties. Alfredo Griffin is excellent on defense, but murders the offense. As a result, the loss of Manuel Lee hurts more than many people realize.

TORONTO BLUE JAYS

What gives? No sooner does Toronto win its first World Series, than it starts to self-destruct. David Cone leaves. Jimmy Key leaves. Tom Henke leaves. Manuel Lee leaves. That's a huge set of quality player losses.

I'm not including the departure of Dave Winfield in the above group since he was replaced by Paul Molitor. I'm also not including the trade of Kelly Gruber since Gruber's play has eroded badly in recent years.

What was only a year ago the best pitching staff in baseball is now a below average staff. The bullpen will remain relatively strong, but the starting staff has only one premier pitcher left: Juan Guzman. The signing's of Dave Stewart and Danny Cox are not answers. They're not even band-aid solutions.

Then comes the potentially disastrous situation at shortstop caused by Manuel Lee's departure. Alfredo Griffin can play excellent defense, but can't hit at all. Eddie Zosky has shown himself to be allergic to his bat and there are questions about his glove. Unless Zosky and his bat become closer friends the Blue Jays are in big trouble at shortstop.

This is not to say that the Blue Jays won't be respectable. They will. They could even stay in the race for a little while. They have, now that Derek Bell is taking over from Candy Maldonado, the best defensive outfield in the Major Leagues. The right side of the infield, with John Olerud and Roberto Alomar, is very strong. With both Randy Knorr and Ed Sprague ready, both the catching and third base positions should be strengthened. (It's a question whether Sprague can handle third base, but his hitting ought to allow him time to settle in). DH, with Paul Molitor swinging his potent bat should be even stronger than last year with Winfield.

Unfortunately for the Blue Jays, however, their problems on the mound and at shortstop will most likely lead them down to the level of mediocrity in '93.

The Blue Jays lost a real good prospect in Nigel Wilson in the Expansion draft. I certainly would have protected him over Todd Stottlemyre. Wilson could be a real steal on for the Marlins. He's probably at least a year away from the Majors, but don't be surprised if he gets there sooner.

The Blue Jays did get one break when pitcher Mark Ohlms slipped through the draft. He's at least a year away, but he appears to have real ability.

This is the year we ought to find out if Carlos Delgado is everything he appeared to be last year. His numbers were fabulous in A ball. Will they continue to look good as he climbs up the ladder of minor league ball? The Blue Jays think so. I also think so. He's for real. You can't put up those numbers with mirrors. The Blue Jays just need to be patient with him.

Toronto's Projected record for 1993: 82--80, good for 4th place in the division.

TORONTO BLUE JAYS

Roberto Alomar, 24

Bats Both   623L   1394R   648G   462F

L= .132G   .148L   .170F   (.085/.064) .149   .133G   .149R   .171F = R

		ATBATS	1B	2B	3B	HR	HBP	BB	GDP	SB	CS	ROE	XB	RUNS	EOB%	RL#	SET-UP	DR-IN	RPA
San Diego	1990	586	130	27	5	6	2	47	16	24	10	8	73	74	.224	.113	.059	.054	.113
Toronto	1991	637	127	41	11	9	4	54	5	53	14	9	59	94	.251	.139	.072	.061	.133
Toronto	1992	571	134	27	8	8	5	82	8	49	10	7	51	109	.297	.166	.098	.069	.167

Bats Right   80L   141R   68G   70F   539ML

Derek Bell, 24

L= .090G   .127L   .162F   (.059/.057) .116   .072G   .109R   .144F = R

		ATBATS	1B	2B	3B	HR	HBP	BB	GDP	SB	CS	ROE	XB	RUNS	EOB%	RL#	SET-UP	DR-IN	RPA
Toronto	1991	28	4	0	0	0	1	6	0	3	2	0	3	2	.233	.071	.036	.032	.068
Toronto	1992	161	28	6	3	2	5	14	6	7	3	4	15	20	.214	.110	.056	.055	.111

Bats Right   506L   706R   348G   279F

Pat Borders, 29

L= .098G   .095L   .092F   (.044/.053) .097   .101G   .098R   .095F = R

		ATBATS	1B	2B	3B	HR	HBP	BB	GDP	SB	CS	ROE	XB	RUNS	EOB%	RL#	SET-UP	DR-IN	RPA
Toronto	1990	346	58	24	2	15	0	16	17	0	1	3	13	42	.146	.112	.045	.064	.109
Toronto	1991	291	49	17	0	5	1	10	8	0	1	1	10	24	.155	.080	.033	.044	.077
Toronto	1992	480	75	26	2	13	2	30	11	1	1	5	29	56	.180	.108	.051	.058	.109

Bats Right   587L   1467R   662G   466F

Joe Carter, 32

L= .127G   .138L   .154F   (.062/.074) .136   .124G   .135R   .151F = R

		ATBATS	1B	2B	3B	HR	HBP	BB	GDP	SB	CS	ROE	XB	RUNS	EOB%	RL#	SET-UP	DR-IN	RPA
San Diego	1990	634	95	27	1	24	7	30	12	22	6	15	54	76	.170	.111	.050	.061	.111
Toronto	1991	638	96	42	3	33	10	37	6	20	10	7	43	94	.189	.141	.064	.071	.135
Toronto	1992	622	93	30	7	34	11	32	14	12	6	4	37	92	.160	.137	.060	.078	.138

Bats Both   370L   651R   325G   214F

Alfredo Griffin, 35

L= .089G   .092L   .096F   (.038/.039) .077   .067G   .070R   .074F = R

		ATBATS	1B	2B	3B	HR	HBP	BB	GDP	SB	CS	ROE	XB	RUNS	EOB%	RL#	SET-UP	DR-IN	RPA
Los Angeles	1990	461	82	11	3	1	2	18	5	6	3	9	45	37	.182	.073	.035	.040	.075
Los Angeles	1991	350	77	6	2	0	1	17	5	5	4	5	17	29	.199	.076	.038	.039	.077
Toronto	1992	150	28	7	0	0	0	9	3	3	3	2	13	12	.185	.077	.037	.041	.078

Bats Right   422L   1193R   496G   360F

Kelly Gruber, 30

L= .125G   .135L   .148F   (.049/.058) .107   .087G   .097R   .110F = R

		ATBATS	1B	2B	3B	HR	HBP	BB	GDP	SB	CS	ROE	XB	RUNS	EOB%	RL#	SET-UP	DR-IN	RPA
Toronto	1990	592	89	36	6	31	8	46	14	14	3	7	55	94	.195	.147	.069	.074	.143
Toronto	1991	429	68	18	2	20	6	26	7	12	8	11	26	57	.183	.126	.056	.064	.120
Toronto	1992	446	72	16	3	11	4	23	14	7	7	7	36	45	.152	.093	.040	.054	.094

Bats Both   484L   877R   408G   312F

Manuel Lee, 27

L= .091G   .093L   .095F   (.049/.045) .094   .092G   .094R   .096F = R

		ATBATS	1B	2B	3B	HR	HBP	BB	GDP	SB	CS	ROE	XB	RUNS	EOB%	RL#	SET-UP	DR-IN	RPA
Toronto	1990	391	73	12	4	6	0	26	9	3	1	7	36	41	.197	.099	.047	.049	.096
Toronto	1991	445	83	18	3	0	2	24	11	7	2	10	29	36	.200	.078	.037	.038	.075
Toronto	1992	396	90	10	1	3	0	50	8	6	2	4	31	51	.254	.114	.063	.052	.115

Bats Right   432L   1120R   499G   337F

Candy Maldonado, 32

L= .149G   .159L   .174F   (.072/.067) .139   .120G   .130R   .145F = R

		ATBATS	1B	2B	3B	HR	HBP	BB	GDP	SB	CS	ROE	XB	RUNS	EOB%	RL#	SET-UP	DR-IN	RPA
Cleveland	1990	590	105	32	2	22	5	45	13	3	5	10	39	85	.206	.130	.065	.065	.130
Milwaukee	1991	111	12	6	0	5	0	13	4	1	0	2	4	14	.175	.108	.049	.059	.108
Toronto	1991	177	33	9	0	7	6	19	4	3	1	0	11	28	.235	.139	.071	.062	.133
Toronto	1992	489	84	25	4	20	7	56	13	2	2	5	25	82	.226	.147	.077	.071	.148

Rance Mulliniks, 36

Bats Left   24L   389R   143G   73F

L= ....G L   ....F   **(.060/.046) .106**   .110G   .104R   .091F = R

		ATBATS	1B	2B	3B	HR	HBP	BB	GDP	SB	CS	ROE	XB	RUNS	EOB%	RL#	SET-UP	DR-IN	RPA
Toronto	1990	97	22	4	0	2	0	20	2	2	1	0	7	17	.297	.144	.083	.058	.141
Toronto	1991	240	45	12	1	2	0	42	9	0	0	4	18	31	.266	.109	.058	.046	.104
Toronto	1992	2	1	0	0	0	0	1	0	0	0	0	0	1	.570	.302	.225	.082	.307

John Olerud, 24

Bats Left   318L   1161R   466G   305F

L= .139G   .154L   .177F   **(.071/.063) .134**   .114G   .129R   .152F = R

		ATBATS	1B	2B	3B	HR	HBP	BB	GDP	SB	CS	ROE	XB	RUNS	EOB%	RL#	SET-UP	DR-IN	RPA
Toronto	1990	358	65	15	1	14	1	51	5	0	2	4	19	58	.249	.144	.076	.064	.140
Toronto	1991	454	68	30	1	17	6	59	12	0	2	0	28	65	.220	.126	.062	.059	.121
Toronto	1992	458	86	28	0	16	1	59	15	1	0	7	28	78	.243	.148	.080	.069	.149

Ed Sprague, 25

Bats Right   111L   121R   58G   48F   424ML

L= .127G   .130L   .133F   **(.065/.057) .122**   .111G   .114R   .117F = R

		ATBATS	1B	2B	3B	HR	HBP	BB	GDP	SB	CS	ROE	XB	RUNS	EOB%	RL#	SET-UP	DR-IN	RPA
Toronto	1991	160	33	7	0	4	3	17	2	0	3	0	14	21	.233	.121	.061	.055	.116
Toronto	1992	47	8	2	0	1	0	3	0	0	0	3	3	7	.258	.133	.075	.060	.135

Pat Tabler, 34

Bats Right   364L   270R   195G   151F

L= .079G   .076L   .073F   **(.044/.040) .084**   .097G   .094R   .091F = R

		ATBATS	1B	2B	3B	HR	HBP	BB	GDP	SB	CS	ROE	XB	RUNS	EOB%	RL#	SET-UP	DR-IN	RPA
Kansas City	1990	195	38	14	0	1	1	18	8	0	2	2	14	21	.214	.094	.049	.047	.096
Mets	1990	43	9	1	1	1	1	3	0	0	0	0	0	7	.242	.130	.073	.062	.135
Toronto	1991	185	33	5	1	1	1	24	3	0	0	3	7	19	.245	.092	.047	.040	.087
Toronto	1992	135	29	5	0	0	0	11	6	0	0	1	7	12	.198	.079	.039	.040	.079

Turner Ward, 27

Bats Both   59L   151R   69G   40F   662ML

L= .156G   .137L   ....F   **(.060/.053) .113**   .123G   .104R   ....F = R

		ATBATS	1B	2B	3B	HR	HBP	BB	GDP	SB	CS	ROE	XB	RUNS	EOB%	RL#	SET-UP	DR-IN	RPA
Cleveland	1990	46	12	2	1	1	0	3	1	3	0	0	8	8	.250	.163	.089	.074	.163
Cleveland	1991	100	16	7	0	0	0	10	1	0	0	2	8	11	.245	.094	.052	.045	.097
Toronto	1991	13	4	0	0	0	0	1	1	0	0	0	0	1	.189	.072	.033	.036	.069
Toronto	1992	29	6	3	0	1	0	4	1	0	1	0	2	5	.239	.160	.087	.075	.162

Devon White, 30

Bats Both   559L   1343R   551G   435F

L= .127G   .127L   .128F   **(.065/.063) .128**   .129G   .129R   .130F = R

		ATBATS	1B	2B	3B	HR	HBP	BB	GDP	SB	CS	ROE	XB	RUNS	EOB%	RL#	SET-UP	DR-IN	RPA
California	1990	443	65	17	3	11	3	39	6	21	8	12	45	52	.201	.109	.052	.055	.107
Toronto	1991	642	114	40	10	17	7	54	7	33	14	7	65	93	.226	.136	.068	.062	.130
Toronto	1992	641	109	26	7	17	5	47	9	37	4	6	52	88	.204	.126	.063	.064	.127

Dave Winfield, 41

Bats Right   531L   1321R   509G   412F

L= .179G   .172L   .164F   **(.074/.074) .148**   .144G   .137R   .129F = R

		ATBATS	1B	2B	3B	HR	HBP	BB	GDP	SB	CS	ROE	XB	RUNS	EOB%	RL#	SET-UP	DR-IN	RPA
Yankees	1990	61	8	3	0	2	1	4	2	0	0	1	3	7	.165	.094	.043	.053	.096
California	1990	414	75	18	2	19	1	45	15	0	1	8	35	65	.211	.139	.069	.067	.136
California	1991	568	90	27	4	28	1	52	21	7	2	6	35	83	.177	.126	.059	.070	.129
Toronto	1992	583	107	33	3	26	1	72	10	2	3	7	39	109	.244	.166	.090	.077	.167

TORONTO BLUE JAYS

PITCHERS

David Cone, 29
Throws: Neutral type, moderate righty

(.096/.084) .091   1661L 1138R

		OUTS	RO	1B	2B	3B	HR	HBP	BB	GDP	SB	CS	PO	WP	BK	RUNS	EOB%	RL#	RPA
New York Mets	1990	635	3	118	31	7	21	1	64	9	23	9	3	10	4	81	.147	.092	.092
New York Mets	1991	698	0	155	29	7	13	5	71	8	27	13	1	17	1	78	.171	.093	.082
New York Mets	1992	590	0	119	24	7	12	9	77	8	34	6	2	9	1	79	.191	.099	.096
Toronto	1992	159	6	28	6	2	3	3	27	1	15	4	0	3	0	25	.204	.103	.113

Mark Eichhorn, 32
Throws: Groundball type, extreme righty

(.112/.053) .078   431L 572R

		OUTS	RO	1B	2B	3B	HR	HBP	BB	GDP	SB	CS	PO	WP	BK	RUNS	EOB%	RL#	RPA
California	1990	254	254	81	14	1	2	6	23	6	4	3	2	2	0	35	.201	.099	.093
California	1991	245	245	43	16	2	2	2	12	11	3	3	0	0	0	18	.090	.056	.056
California	1992	170	170	40	7	2	2	0	10	4	3	2	0	3	1	18	.142	.077	.078
Toronto	1992	93	93	28	4	2	1	2	7	2	3	0	0	6	0	17	.215	.114	.124

Juan Guzman, 26
Throws: Neutral type, moderate reverse righty

(.086/.095) .091   623L 653R 287ML

		OUTS	RO	1B	2B	3B	HR	HBP	BB	GDP	SB	CS	PO	WP	BK	RUNS	EOB%	RL#	RPA
Toronto	1991	416	0	77	13	2	6	4	66	7	11	6	0	10	0	48	.189	.083	.083
Toronto	1992	542	0	104	24	1	6	1	70	7	27	8	2	14	2	65	.177	.083	.090

Tom Henke, 35
Throws: Flyball type, moderate righty

(.086/.077) .082   362L 328R

		OUTS	RO	1B	2B	3B	HR	HBP	BB	GDP	SB	CS	PO	WP	BK	RUNS	EOB%	RL#	RPA
Toronto	1990	224	224	40	9	1	8	1	17	4	5	0	0	6	0	27	.144	.090	.089
Toronto	1991	151	151	20	8	1	4	0	9	4	2	0	1	1	0	12	.094	.065	.064
Toronto	1992	167	167	26	9	0	5	0	20	3	2	1	0	4	0	21	.157	.089	.097

Pat Hentgen, 24
Throws: Flyball type, moderate righty

(.130/.114) .121   106L 137R 810ML

		OUTS	RO	1B	2B	3B	HR	HBP	BB	GDP	SB	CS	PO	WP	BK	RUNS	EOB%	RL#	RPA
Toronto	1991	22	7	2	2	0	1	2	3	1	1	0	0	1	0	4	.179	.112	.113
Toronto	1992	151	127	30	11	1	7	0	27	5	5	0	0	2	1	31	.198	.132	.143

Jimmy Key, 31
Throws: Neutral type, extreme lefty

(.070/.106) .101   344L 1987R

		OUTS	RO	1B	2B	3B	HR	HBP	BB	GDP	SB	CS	PO	WP	BK	RUNS	EOB%	RL#	RPA
Toronto	1990	464	0	116	31	2	20	1	20	17	6	4	0	0	1	61	.119	.098	.096
Toronto	1991	628	0	157	36	2	12	3	41	14	6	2	0	1	0	77	.167	.090	.089
Toronto	1992	650	0	135	45	1	24	0	59	11	14	9	0	5	0	100	.157	.104	.113

Doug Linton, 27
Throws: Flyball type, righty

(..../....) .144   45L 66R 1451ML

		OUTS	RO	1B	2B	3B	HR	HBP	BB	GDP	SB	CS	PO	WP	BK	RUNS	EOB%	RL#	RPA
Toronto	1992	72	34	21	5	0	5	0	17	2	0	2	0	2	0	20	.218	.163	.177

Bob MacDonald, 27
Throws: Flyball type, extreme lefty

(.096/.135) .121   151L 274R 104ML

		OUTS	RO	1B	2B	3B	HR	HBP	BB	GDP	SB	CS	PO	WP	BK	RUNS	EOB%	RL#	RPA
Toronto	1990	7	7	0	0	0	0	0	2	1	0	0	0	0	0	0	.000	.010	.010
Toronto	1991	161	161	39	7	0	5	0	21	3	5	4	0	1	1	22	.168	.099	.097
Toronto	1992	142	142	32	12	2	4	1	13	1	4	0	0	0	0	27	.208	.122	.133

TORONTO BLUE JAYS

Jack Morris, 37

Throws: Neutral type, extreme righty

(.120/.081) .101   1496L 1410R

		OUTS	RO	1B	2B	3B	HR	HBP	BB	GDP	SB	CS	PO	WP	BK	RUNS	EOB%	RL#	RPA
Detroit	1990	749	0	160	42	3	26	6	84	23	45	6	0	16	2	107	.164	.105	.103
Minnesota	1991	740	0	174	28	6	18	5	87	23	32	8	0	15	1	97	.168	.100	.097
Toronto	1992	722	0	160	41	3	18	10	78	15	22	16	0	9	2	104	.164	.097	.106

Dave Stieb, 35

Throws: Neutral type, moderate to severe righty

(.115/.089) .102   760L 708R

		OUTS	RO	1B	2B	3B	HR	HBP	BB	GDP	SB	CS	PO	WP	BK	RUNS	EOB%	RL#	RPA
Toronto	1990	626	0	134	31	3	11	10	64	7	6	8	1	5	0	76	.181	.089	.088
Toronto	1991	179	0	39	8	1	4	2	23	7	5	5	2	0	0	19	.121	.078	.078
Toronto	1992	289	52	66	21	2	9	4	40	10	3	6	2	4	0	47	.162	.106	.116

Todd Stottlemyre, 27

Throws: Neutral type, moderate to severe righty

(.127/.105) .116   1196L 1274R

		OUTS	RO	1B	2B	3B	HR	HBP	BB	GDP	SB	CS	PO	WP	BK	RUNS	EOB%	RL#	RPA
Toronto	1990	609	0	152	36	8	18	8	65	13	23	13	1	6	1	94	.173	.109	.108
Toronto	1991	657	0	141	27	5	21	12	72	11	24	3	0	4	0	96	.185	.104	.103
Toronto	1992	522	3	124	31	0	20	10	59	8	17	3	0	7	0	98	.198	.121	.132

Mike Timlin, 26

Throws: Groundball type, extreme righty

(.131/.066) .094   262L 352R 51ML

		OUTS	RO	1B	2B	3B	HR	HBP	BB	GDP	SB	CS	PO	WP	BK	RUNS	EOB%	RL#	RPA
Toronto	1991	325	281	81	6	1	6	1	39	8	11	5	0	5	0	38	.168	.086	.084
Toronto	1992	131	131	39	6	0	0	1	15	4	4	3	0	0	0	17	.185	.084	.091

Duane Ward, 28

Throws: Groundball type, extreme righty

(.101/.059) .079   614L 672R

		OUTS	RO	1B	2B	3B	HR	HBP	BB	GDP	SB	CS	PO	WP	BK	RUNS	EOB%	RL#	RPA
Toronto	1990	383	383	76	13	3	9	1	32	14	12	6	0	5	0	36	.111	.074	.072
Toronto	1991	322	322	66	10	1	3	2	30	7	7	4	0	6	0	29	.151	.069	.067
Toronto	1992	304	304	59	10	2	5	1	36	5	14	4	0	7	0	37	.168	.085	.092

David Wells, 29

Throws: Flyball type, neutral lefty

(.113/.110) .111   353L 1677R

		OUTS	RO	1B	2B	3B	HR	HBP	BB	GDP	SB	CS	PO	WP	BK	RUNS	EOB%	RL#	RPA
Toronto	1990	567	64	105	39	7	14	2	42	9	11	11	1	7	1	65	.136	.087	.086
Toronto	1991	595	55	125	37	2	24	2	48	11	8	13	3	10	3	77	.127	.094	.094
Toronto	1992	360	132	85	35	2	16	8	30	8	14	6	1	3	1	70	.169	.125	.136

Toronto Blue Jays AAA & AA Minor League Ratings

AAA (SYRACUSE)	AGE	BATS	POSITION	CPA	RUNS	SET-UP	DRIVE-IN	RPA
Bruce Crabbe	30	R	2B	191	18.5	.050	.047	.097
Butch Davis	34	R	OF	605	53.8	.041	.048	.089
Ray Giannelli	26	L	OF	301	30.4	.055	.046	.101
Randy Knorr	24	R	C	250	28.2	.052	.061	.113
Mike Maksudian	26	L	C\1B	379	43.3	.056	.058	.114
Domingo Martinez	25	R	1B	490	56.5	.054	.061	.115
Rob Montalvo	22	R	2B\SS\3B	277	18.9	.033	.035	.068
Stu Pederson	32	L	OF	298	31.2	.055	.050	.105
Tom Quinlan	24	R	3B	413	32.8	.039	.040	.079
Jerry Schunk	27	R	2B\SS\3B	450	29.8	.030	.036	.066
Ed Sprague	25	R	C\1B	424	52.0	.063	.060	.123
Ryan Thompson	25	R	OF	480	57.8	.061	.059	.120
Turner Ward	27	B	OF	334	34.4	.051	.052	.103
Eddie Zosky	24	R	SS	372	24.7	.028	.038	.066

AA (KNOXVILLE)	AGE	BATS	POSITION	CPA	RUNS	SET-UP	DRIVE-IN	RPA
Domingo Cedeno	24	B	2B\SS	426	25.0	.026	.033	.059
Juan DeLaRosa	24	R	OF	544	57.1	.049	.056	.105
Brad Mengel	25	R	3B\2B\1B	318	18.7	.027	.032	.059
Jose Monzon	24	R	C	216	12.2	.026	.030	.056
Greg O'Halloran	24	L	C	450	34.0	.036	.039	.075
Robert Perez	23	R	OF	551	39.4	.030	.042	.072
Shawn Scott	23	B	OF\2B	383	22.1	.026	.032	.058
David Tollison	23	R	3B\2B	386	24.4	.030	.033	.063
Jason Townley	23	R	C\1B	201	15.1	.037	.038	.075
Nigel Wilson	22	L	OF	563	66.4	.055	.063	.118
Julian Yan	27	R	1B	438	42.6	.043	.054	.097

AAA Pitchers	Age	Throws	Outs	RPA	AA Pitchers	Age	Throws	Outs	RPA
Jose Alvarez	36	R	124	.129	Daren Brown	25	B	246	.146
Pete Blohm	27	R	387	.148	Tim Brown	24	R	504	.137
Wayne Edwards	28	L	392	.153	Nate Cromwell	24	L	303	.155
Darren Hall	28	R	207	.134	Jesse Cross	24	R	462	.134
Al Leiter	27	L	490	.128	Daren Kizziah	25	R	248	.175
Doug Linton	27	R	512	.145	Graeme Lloyd	25	L	276	.105
John Shea	26	L	354	.160	Paul Menhart	23	R	533	.127
Rick Trlicek	23	R	130	.135	Marcus Moore	22	R	319	.175
Gene Walter	32	L	172	.123	Mike Ogliaruso	22	R	81	.242
Anthony Ward	25	L	279	.181	Mark Ohlms	25	R	209	.096
Dave Weathers	23	R	145	.132	Aaron Small	21	R	405	.169
Woody Williams	26	R	362	.115					

CALIFORNIA ANGELS

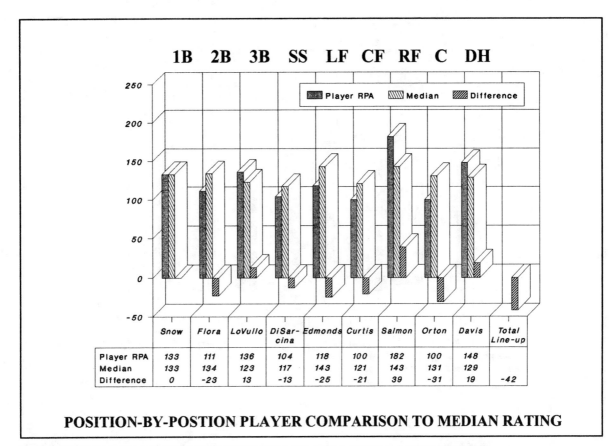

	Snow	Flora	LoVullo	DiSar-cina	Edmonds	Curtis	Salmon	Orton	Davis	Total Line-up
Player RPA	133	111	136	104	118	100	182	100	148	
Median	133	134	123	117	143	121	143	131	129	
Difference	0	-23	13	-13	-25	-21	39	-31	19	-42

POSITION-BY-POSTION PLAYER COMPARISON TO MEDIAN RATING

DEFENSIVE TEAM AND STADIUM DATA FOR THE LAST 3 YEARS:

TEAM DEFENSE BY POSITION:

		1990	1991	1992	POSITION-BY-POSITION STADIUM CHARACTERISTICS:
1B:	Home	-0.2	+4.2	-1.6	Average
	Away	-1.1	-2.8	-1.3	
2B:	Home	-5.6	-1.5	-3.0	Average
	Away	-3.0	+2.2	+2.2	
3B:	Home	+3.4	+0.9	+0.4	Slightly hard to play
	Away	-4.5	+3.7	-1.4	
SS:	Home	+7.4	+5.3	+4.9	Average
	Away	-4.1	+3.2	-0.1	
LF:	Home	-10.7	-4.4	-1.6	Slightly easy to play
	Away	-3.1	-5.2	-9.0	
CF:	Home	-2.9	-4.9	+3.1	Very easy to play
	Away	+1.5	+3.8	-2.4	
RF:	Home	-10.0	-1.9	-0.2	Easy to play
	Away	+3.1	-1.7	-0.4	
Total Home:		-18.6	-2.3	+1.9	One of the easiest outfields to play!
Total Away:		-11.2	+3.2	-12.4	

Comments: As I state every year, Polonia is a disaster in left field. He's not much offensively either. I don't know how well Jim Edmonds can play defense, but it can't be much worse than Polonia, and Edmonds ought to develop into a better hitter than Polonia, as well. I'd certainly give him a shot.

CALIFORNIA ANGELS

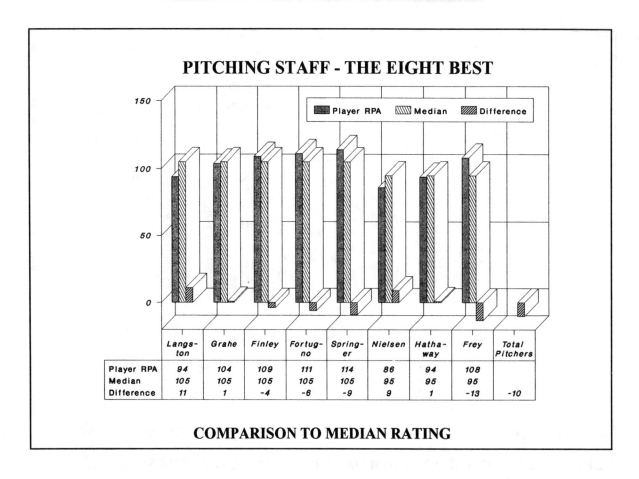

PITCHING STAFF - THE EIGHT BEST

	Langs-ton	Grahe	Finley	Fortug-no	Spring-er	Nielsen	Hatha-way	Frey	Total Pitchers
Player RPA	94	104	109	111	114	86	94	108	
Median	105	105	105	105	105	95	95	95	
Difference	11	1	-4	-6	-9	9	1	-13	-10

COMPARISON TO MEDIAN RATING

SUGGESTED LINE-UPS (with set-up RPA & drive-in RPA ratings):

Vs: Left-handed Groundball
2B:	K. Flora	68-59
1B:	J. T. Snow	77-62
RF:	T. Salmon	117-81
DH:	C. Davis	65-56
CF:	C. Curtis	69-65
3B:	K. Gruber	57-68
LF:	J. Edmonds	61-53
C:	J. Orton	54-49
SS:	G. DiSarcina	40-46

Vs: Neutral Lefty Pitchers
2B:	K. Flora	68-59
1B:	J. T. Snow	77-62
RF:	T. Salmon	117-81
DH:	C. Davis	73-60
CF:	C. Curtis	94-89
3B:	K. Gruber	62-73
LF:	J. Edmonds	61-53
C:	J. Orton	54-49
SS:	G. DiSarcina	38-43

Vs: Left-handed Flyball
1B:	J. T. Snow	77-62
RF:	T. Salmon	117-81
DH:	C. Davis	80-67
CF:	C. Curtis	114-108
3B:	K. Gruber	68-80
2B:	K. Flora	68-59
LF:	J. Edmonds	61-53
C:	J. Orton	54-49
SS:	G. DiSarcina	36-41

Vs: Right-handed Groundball
1B:	J. T. Snow	77-62
RF:	T. Salmon	107-71
DH:	C. Davis	78-65
3B:	T. LoVullo	73-63
CF(?):	D. Rumsey	70-57
LF:	J. Edmonds	71-63
2B:	K. Flora	58-49
C:	R. Tingley	42-47
SS:	G. DiSarcina	46-52

Vs: Neutral Righty Pitchers
1B:	J. T. Snow	77-62
RF:	T. Salmon	107-71
DH:	C. Davis	85-70
3B:	T. LoVullo	73-63
CF(?):	D. Rumsey	70-57
LF:	J. Edmonds	71-63
2B:	K. Flora	58-49
C:	G. Myers	46-56
SS:	G. DiSarcina	43-50

Vs: Right-handed Flyball
1B:	J. T. Snow	77-62
RF:	T. Salmon	107-71
DH:	C. Davis	92-77
3B:	T. LoVullo	73-63
LF:	J. Edmonds	71-63
CF:	C. Curtis	70-67
C:	G. Myers	57-70
2B:	K. Flora	58-49
SS:	G. DiSarcina	41-48

Comments: A much improved offense from last year's disaster. I hope they decide to go with most of these kids, since they could be contenders in the not-too-distant future based upon all the young talent they have. They'll just have to be patient. Dan Rumsey will probably require some time at AAA and I don't know if Rumsey can play CF, but Chad Curtis is no prize out there either, nor is Flora likely to be a good centerfielder if they try him out there.

CALIFORNIA ANGELS

While the Angels are still far from being legitimate contenders, this team is doing what it takes to position itself for the future. It has some of the best young talent around, including my top-rated minor leaguer of '92: Tim Salmon.

It was unfortunate that this team had to give up such a fabulous pitcher as Jim Abbott, but Angel fans shouldn't cry about it. They got three excellent young players in exchange. I just don't understand why the Angels left Junior Felix out there after the first pullback in the Expansion draft while pulling back Luis Polonia. Polonia is an albatross around this team's neck. He's awful defensively, and his offense is mostly smoke and mirrors. Once you get past the illusions created by his batting average, you find nothing there. I also don't know why Brett Merriman wasn't pulled back in the first set of pullbacks at the Expansion draft. He looks about ready right now.

The Angel offense in '92, more offensive to the nostrils than to the opposing team, will be much improved in '93. The arrival of Chili Davis as DH and Tim Salmon in the outfield will create some real excitement.

I really like the Angels signing of six-year minor league free-agent third baseman Torey LoVullo. I think he's a better hitter than Kelly Gruber.

First Baseman J.T. Snow, acquired in the Abbott trade, should have no trouble adjusting to Major League pitching. I don't know what the Angels will do with Don Barbara who now is effectively blocked by Snow. Barbara seems no more than a year away but may end up only as Snow's sub.

AAA outfielder Jim Edmonds looks like a real comer. He could be one of the best prospects around. I don't see any reason for him to spend much more time in the minors.

Kevin Flora looks like a good hitter, but, at this point, only as a second baseman. I think it's a mistake if they try to move him to the outfield. He's not a big enough hitter to merit the move and his defense would probably suffer as well.

Chad Curtis is another terrific hitting youngster. Hopefully his centerfield defensive range will improve as he gains experience. The Angels may have to pay very close attention to this problem.

Hilly Hathaway and Jerry Nielsen (acquired in the Abbott trade) both look like super young pitchers. Both probably need some time at AAA. I think it might be a mistake if they're rushed to the Majors this spring.

Pitcher Russ Springer (also acquired in the Abbott trade), while a little lower in talent than the above two, appears a little closer to being ready for the Majors since he was at AAA last year while the above duo both were at AA.

This division is going to be so wide open in '93 that no team, including California, should consider itself definitely out of the running. It would be a very long shot, but it isn't impossible that California could sneak in.

California's Projected record for 1993: 78--84, good for 6th place in the division.

CALIFORNIA ANGELS

Hubie Brooks, 36

Bats Right   457L   882R   441G   292F

L= .106G .102L .095F [(.046/.057) .103] .107G .103R .096F = R

		ATBATS	1B	2B	3B	HR	HBP	BB	GDP	SB	CS	ROE	XB	RUNS	EOB%	RL#	SET-UP	DR-IN	RPA
Los Angeles	1990	568	102	28	1	20	6	23	13	2	5	11	43	73	.179	.115	.055	.064	.119
Mets	1991	357	57	11	1	16	3	36	7	3	1	3	24	49	.196	.124	.059	.062	.121
California	1992	306	45	13	0	8	1	9	10	3	3	6	18	26	.128	.080	.031	.050	.081

Bats Right   149L   357R   123G   154F   495ML

Chad Curtis, 24

L= .123G .172L .211F [(.057/.055) .112] .038G .087R .126F = R

		ATBATS	1B	2B	3B	HR	HBP	BB	GDP	SB	CS	ROE	XB	RUNS	EOB%	RL#	SET-UP	DR-IN	RPA
California	1992	441	86	16	2	10	6	49	10	43	19	7	41	62	.214	.122	.062	.060	.122

Bats Left   334L   882R   313G   278F

Alvin Davis, 32

L= .118G .102L .083F [(.048/.047) .095] .108G .092R .073F = R

		ATBATS	1B	2B	3B	HR	HBP	BB	GDP	SB	CS	ROE	XB	RUNS	EOB%	RL#	SET-UP	DR-IN	RPA
Seattle	1990	494	102	21	0	17	4	75	9	0	2	4	30	87	.268	.149	.084	.065	.149
Seattle	1991	462	74	15	1	12	0	47	8	0	4	3	12	51	.190	.091	.045	.049	.094
California	1992	104	18	8	0	0	0	11	2	0	0	1	2	11	.242	.097	.053	.045	.098

Bats Right   153L   532R   177G   181F   440ML

Gary DiSarcina, 25

L= .077G .072L .068F [(.038/.043) .081] .089G .084R .080F = R

		ATBATS	1B	2B	3B	HR	HBP	BB	GDP	SB	CS	ROE	XB	RUNS	EOB%	RL#	SET-UP	DR-IN	RPA
California	1990	57	6	1	1	0	0	3	3	1	0	2	5	3	.120	.044	.016	.027	.043
California	1991	57	10	2	0	0	2	3	0	0	0	0	5	5	.217	.078	.041	.039	.080
California	1992	518	106	19	0	3	7	20	15	9	7	5	43	45	.176	.080	.037	.044	.081

Bats Left   31L   191R   59G   69F   318ML

Rob Ducey, 27

L= ....G ....L ....F [(.054/.054) .108] .167G .104R .051F = R

		ATBATS	1B	2B	3B	HR	HBP	BB	GDP	SB	CS	ROE	XB	RUNS	EOB%	RL#	SET-UP	DR-IN	RPA
Toronto	1990	53	11	5	0	0	1	7	0	1	1	0	7	8	.301	.136	.078	.054	.132
Toronto	1991	68	11	2	2	1	0	6	1	2	0	0	6	8	.202	.105	.049	.051	.100
Toronto	1992	21	0	1	0	0	0	0	0	0	1	0	1	0	.015	.007	.000	.007	.007
California	1992	59	11	3	0	0	0	5	1	2	3	1	4	5	.186	.077	.037	.041	.078

Bats Right   38L   126R   35G   59F   1007ML

Damion Easley, 23

L= ....G .080L ....F [(.037/.039) .076] ....G .075R .087F = R

		ATBATS	1B	2B	3B	HR	HBP	BB	GDP	SB	CS	ROE	XB	RUNS	EOB%	RL#	SET-UP	DR-IN	RPA
California	1992	151	33	5	0	1	3	8	2	9	6	2	9	15	.198	.093	.046	.048	.094

Bats Both   346L   965R   335G   336F

Junior Felix, 25

L= .116G .111L .106F [(.051/.053) .104] .106G .101R .096F = R

		ATBATS	1B	2B	3B	HR	HBP	BB	GDP	SB	CS	ROE	XB	RUNS	EOB%	RL#	SET-UP	DR-IN	RPA
Toronto	1990	463	77	23	7	15	2	45	4	13	8	6	53	69	.220	.137	.068	.065	.133
California	1991	230	51	10	2	2	3	11	5	7	6	3	19	26	.202	.100	.051	.052	.103
California	1992	509	89	22	5	9	2	28	9	8	8	11	36	57	.189	.103	.050	.054	.104

Bats Right   344L   470R   284G   185F

Mike Fitzgerald, 32

L= .096G .117L .150F [(.043/.050) .093] .055G .076R .109F = R

		ATBATS	1B	2B	3B	HR	HBP	BB	GDP	SB	CS	ROE	XB	RUNS	EOB%	RL#	SET-UP	DR-IN	RPA
Montreal	1990	313	48	18	1	9	2	58	5	8	1	3	14	54	.273	.138	.080	.062	.142
Montreal	1991	198	29	5	2	4	0	18	5	4	2	2	14	20	.169	.082	.040	.048	.088
California	1992	189	32	2	0	6	0	22	4	2	3	1	6	21	.180	.098	.046	.052	.098

Bats Right   491L   1271R   496G   404F

Gary Gaetti, 34

L= .096G .116L .140F [(.048/.056) .104] .080G .100R .124F = R

		ATBATS	1B	2B	3B	HR	HBP	BB	GDP	SB	CS	ROE	XB	RUNS	EOB%	RL#	SET-UP	DR-IN	RPA
Minnesota	1990	577	84	27	5	16	3	35	22	6	2	14	32	60	.165	.096	.041	.053	.094
California	1991	586	103	22	1	18	8	30	13	5	5	13	30	70	.185	.106	.051	.058	.109
California	1992	456	76	13	2	12	6	17	9	3	1	7	23	47	.166	.096	.043	.054	.097

CALIFORNIA ANGELS

Rene Gonzales, 31

Bats Right   166L 481R   185G   164F

L= .099G .128L .160F   (.057/.053) .110   .075G .104R .136F = R

		ATBATS	1B	2B	3B	HR	HBP	BB	GDP	SB	CS	ROE	XB	RUNS	EOB%	RL#	SET-UP	DR-IN	RPA
Baltimore	1990	103	17	3	1	1	0	12	3	1	2	2	12	10	.199	.086	.043	.044	.087
Toronto	1991	118	19	3	0	1	4	12	5	0	0	3	6	10	.211	.077	.037	.037	.074
California	1992	329	66	17	1	7	4	40	17	7	5	8	32	48	.226	.121	.064	.058	.122

Jose Gonzalez, 28

Bats Right   206L 96R   86G   71F   159ML

L= .085G .065L .040F   (.037/.045) .082   .139G .119R .094F = R

		ATBATS	1B	2B	3B	HR	HBP	BB	GDP	SB	CS	ROE	XB	RUNS	EOB%	RL#	SET-UP	DR-IN	RPA
Los Angeles	1990	99	13	5	3	2	1	5	1	3	2	1	15	12	.169	.105	.049	.060	.109
Los Angeles	1991	28	0	0	0	0	0	2	0	0	0	0	3	0	.067	.006	.003	.007	.010
Pittsburgh	1991	20	1	0	0	1	0	0	0	0	0	0	0	1	.014	.045	.003	.043	.046
Cleveland	1991	69	7	2	1	1	1	11	2	8	0	0	10	8	.210	.094	.050	.049	.099
California	1992	55	8	2	0	0	0	6	2	0	1	0	5	4	.160	.056	.024	.032	.056

Von Hayes, 34

Bats Left   362L 862R   400G   279F

L= .089G .095L .104F   (.045/.046) .091   .084G .090R .099F = R

		ATBATS	1B	2B	3B	HR	HBP	BB	GDP	SB	CS	ROE	XB	RUNS	EOB%	RL#	SET-UP	DR-IN	RPA
Philadelphia	1990	467	88	14	3	17	4	71	10	16	11	5	43	75	.237	.139	.073	.065	.138
Philadelphia	1991	284	48	15	1	0	3	30	6	9	2	5	32	30	.235	.089	.048	.043	.091
California	1992	307	47	17	1	4	0	33	9	11	8	3	26	32	.185	.091	.043	.048	.091

John Morris, 31

Bats Left   19L 200R   63G   51F

L= ....G ....L ....F   (.040/.044) .084   .077G .080R .084F = R

		ATBATS	1B	2B	3B	HR	HBP	BB	GDP	SB	CS	ROE	XB	RUNS	EOB%	RL#	SET-UP	DR-IN	RPA
St. Louis	1990	18	2	0	0	0	0	3	0	0	0	0	0	1	.210	.051	.025	.025	.050
Philadelphia	1991	127	24	2	1	1	1	8	1	2	1	2	7	12	.204	.082	.042	.042	.084
California	1992	57	9	1	0	1	1	3	0	1	0	0	3	5	.179	.084	.039	.046	.085

Greg Myers, 26

Bats Left   70L 637R   222G   154F

L= .038G .056L .081F   (.041/.050) .091   .077G .095R .120F = R

		ATBATS	1B	2B	3B	HR	HBP	BB	GDP	SB	CS	ROE	XB	RUNS	EOB%	RL#	SET-UP	DR-IN	RPA
Toronto	1990	250	46	7	1	5	0	22	12	0	1	6	19	25	.182	.090	.041	.047	.088
Toronto	1991	309	51	22	0	8	0	17	13	0	0	3	10	31	.166	.095	.041	.050	.091
Toronto	1992	61	7	6	0	1	0	5	2	0	0	0	5	6	.174	.095	.043	.052	.095
California	1992	17	3	1	0	0	0	0	0	0	0	0	0	1	.166	.069	.031	.039	.070

Ken Oberkfell, 36

Bats Left   35L 312R   105G   100F   237ML

L= ....G .026L ....F   (.049/.044) .093   .113G .102R .090F = R

		ATBATS	1B	2B	3B	HR	HBP	BB	GDP	SB	CS	ROE	XB	RUNS	EOB%	RL#	SET-UP	DR-IN	RPA
Houston	1990	150	23	6	1	1	1	14	2	1	1	1	6	15	.203	.077	.042	.042	.084
Houston	1991	70	12	4	0	0	0	10	0	0	0	1	4	9	.279	.098	.061	.045	.106
California	1992	91	23	1	0	0	0	6	2	0	1	0	6	8	.202	.081	.040	.041	.081

John Orton, 27

Bats Right   78L 220R   75G   79F   468ML

L= .110G .085L .062F   (.046/.042) .088   .114G .089R .066F = R

		ATBATS	1B	2B	3B	HR	HBP	BB	GDP	SB	CS	ROE	XB	RUNS	EOB%	RL#	SET-UP	DR-IN	RPA
California	1990	84	10	5	0	1	1	5	2	0	1	2	5	7	.166	.073	.032	.039	.071
California	1991	69	10	4	0	0	1	10	2	0	1	2	4	7	.242	.083	.045	.040	.085
California	1992	114	20	3	0	2	2	7	1	1	1	2	6	12	.201	.096	.048	.049	.097

Luis Polonia, 28

Bats Left   386L 1349R   458G   398F

L= .057G .072L .089F   (.053/.053) .106   .101G .116R .133F = R

		ATBATS	1B	2B	3B	HR	HBP	BB	GDP	SB	CS	ROE	XB	RUNS	EOB%	RL#	SET-UP	DR-IN	RPA
Yankees	1990	22	7	0	0	0	0	0	1	1	0	0	1	2	.177	.080	.038	.044	.082
California	1990	381	110	7	9	2	1	24	8	20	15	2	41	49	.225	.121	.062	.057	.119
California	1991	604	141	28	8	2	1	48	11	48	27	10	74	76	.224	.112	.060	.055	.115
California	1992	577	144	17	4	0	1	39	18	51	26	8	72	61	.197	.096	.047	.050	.097

CALIFORNIA ANGELS

Bobby Rose, 25

Bats Right   79L   100R   50G   42F   355ML

L= .161G .144L .123F (.049/.050) .099 .080G .063R .042F = R

		ATBATS	1B	2B	3B	HR	HBP	BB	GDP	SB	CS	ROE	XB	RUNS	EOB%	RL#	SET-UP	DR-IN	RPA
California	1990	13	4	0	0	1	0	2	0	0	0	0	4	4	.314	.260	.153	.102	.255
California	1991	65	11	5	1	1	0	3	1	0	0	1	4	8	.211	.116	.060	.059	.119
California	1992	84	11	5	0	2	2	7	2	1	1	1	7	10	.188	.100	.048	.053	.101

Luis Sojo, 26

Bats Right   266L   612R   234G   208F   160ML

L= .067G .077L .089F (.041/.048) .089 .084G .094R .106F = R

		ATBATS	1B	2B	3B	HR	HBP	BB	GDP	SB	CS	ROE	XB	RUNS	EOB%	RL#	SET-UP	DR-IN	RPA
Toronto	1990	80	14	3	0	1	0	5	1	1	1	3	8	8	.208	.095	.047	.047	.094
California	1991	364	76	14	1	3	5	14	12	4	2	7	22	35	.192	.087	.043	.046	.089
California	1992	368	78	12	3	7	1	14	14	7	12	8	25	37	.153	.092	.040	.053	.093

Lee Stevens, 25

Bats left   130L   547R   161G   190F   532ML

L= .058G .066L .072F (.048/.052) .100 .100G .108R .114F = R

		ATBATS	1B	2B	3B	HR	HBP	BB	GDP	SB	CS	ROE	XB	RUNS	EOB%	RL#	SET-UP	DR-IN	RPA
California	1990	248	36	10	0	7	0	19	8	1	2	3	16	23	.155	.087	.036	.049	.085
California	1991	58	10	7	0	0	0	4	0	1	2	0	4	7	.226	.106	.057	.052	.109
California	1992	312	43	19	0	7	1	23	4	1	4	5	11	34	.185	.098	.047	.052	.099

Ron Tingley, 33

Bats Right   76L   200R   77G   55F

L= .079G .072L .062F (.039/.044) .083 .094G .087R .077F = R

		ATBATS	1B	2B	3B	HR	HBP	BB	GDP	SB	CS	ROE	XB	RUNS	EOB%	RL#	SET-UP	DR-IN	RPA
California	1990	3	0	0	0	0	0	1	1	0	0	0	0	0	.000	.000	.000	.000	.000
California	1991	115	15	7	0	1	1	8	1	1	1	0	7	10	.179	.075	.036	.041	.077
California	1992	127	19	2	1	3	2	13	4	0	1	1	5	13	.175	.087	.040	.047	.087

PITCHERS

Jim Abbott, 25

Throws: Groundball type, extreme reverse lefty

(.119/.080) .086   411L   2263R

		OUTS	RO	1B	2B	3B	HR	HBP	BB	GDP	SB	CS	PO	WP	BK	RUNS	EOB%	RL#	RPA
California	1990	635	0	192	36	2	16	5	66	27	15	4	0	4	3	93	.180	.108	.101
California	1991	729	0	170	35	3	14	5	67	21	12	14	1	1	4	82	.143	.082	.083
California	1992	633	0	166	28	2	12	4	65	22	14	13	1	2	0	77	.150	.086	.088

Scott Bailes, 30

Throws: Neutral type, extreme lefty

(.111/.149) .136   193L   368R

		OUTS	RO	1B	2B	3B	HR	HBP	BB	GDP	SB	CS	PO	WP	BK	RUNS	EOB%	RL#	RPA
California	1990	106	106	33	3	2	8	1	20	2	5	0	0	0	0	28	.236	.177	.166
California	1991	155	155	28	7	1	5	4	17	2	2	3	0	2	0	20	.162	.094	.095
California	1992	116	116	45	7	0	7	1	24	4	4	1	0	2	1	35	.253	.176	.180

Bert Blyleven, 41

Throws: Neutral type, moderate reverse type righty

(.106/.119) .115   542L   565R   177ML

		OUTS	RO	1B	2B	3B	HR	HBP	BB	GDP	SB	CS	PO	WP	BK	RUNS	EOB%	RL#	RPA
California	1990	402	0	111	33	4	15	7	25	10	4	9	1	6	0	61	.155	.114	.106
California	1992	399	3	106	24	3	17	5	27	11	10	4	0	3	1	66	.157	.114	.116

Mike Butcher, 27

Throws: Flyball type, righty

(..../.088) .114   37L   85R   524ML

		OUTS	RO	1B	2B	3B	HR	HBP	BB	GDP	SB	CS	PO	WP	BK	RUNS	EOB%	RL#	RPA
California	1992	83	83	24	2	0	3	2	12	2	3	0	1	0	0	15	.206	.118	.121

CALIFORNIA ANGELS

Chuck Crim, 31

Throws: Groundball type, extreme reverse righty

(.092/.139) .119   464L 637R

		OUTS	RO	1B	2B	3B	HR	HBP	BB	GDP	SB	CS	PO	WP	BK	RUNS	EOB%	RL#	RPA
Milwaukee	1990	257	257	67	12	2	7	2	19	7	5	0	0	0	1	36	.170	.101	.101
Milwaukee	1991	274	274	91	15	0	9	2	16	7	12	1	0	3	3	48	.187	.120	.120
California	1992	261	261	73	15	1	11	6	23	8	7	5	0	4	0	45	.164	.116	.118

Chuck Finley, 30

Throws: Neutral type, moderate to severe reverse lefty

(.125/.103) .106   342L 2338R

		OUTS	RO	1B	2B	3B	HR	HBP	BB	GDP	SB	CS	PO	WP	BK	RUNS	EOB%	RL#	RPA
California	1990	708	0	154	36	3	17	2	78	23	15	18	0	9	0	75	.134	.083	.077
California	1991	682	0	136	43	3	23	8	100	21	15	14	0	6	3	100	.164	.102	.104
California	1992	613	0	151	34	3	24	3	96	28	21	18	1	6	0	95	.147	.105	.108

Tim Fortugno, 30

Throws: Flyball type, lefty

(..../.100) .108   31L 143R 697ML

		OUTS	RO	1B	2B	3B	HR	HBP	BB	GDP	SB	CS	PO	WP	BK	RUNS	EOB%	RL#	RPA
California	1992	125	46	28	4	0	5	0	19	2	5	2	1	2	1	19	.171	.107	.110

Steve Frey, 29

Throws: Neutral type, moderate reverse lefty

(.117/.100) .106   189L 381R 145ML

		OUTS	RO	1B	2B	3B	HR	HBP	BB	GDP	SB	CS	PO	WP	BK	RUNS	EOB%	RL#	RPA
Montreal	1990	167	167	32	8	0	4	1	23	4	7	1	1	0	0	22	.171	.089	.095
Montreal	1991	119	119	35	5	0	3	1	19	6	3	2	0	3	1	20	.182	.103	.112
California	1992	136	136	29	4	0	6	2	19	3	3	3	0	1	0	20	.158	.102	.105

Joe Grahe, 25

Throws: Groundball type, extreme righty

(.127/.087) .106   414L 479R 506ML

		OUTS	RO	1B	2B	3B	HR	HBP	BB	GDP	SB	CS	PO	WP	BK	RUNS	EOB%	RL#	RPA
California	1990	130	0	34	12	2	3	3	22	7	3	1	2	1	0	22	.191	.118	.111
California	1991	219	58	59	20	3	2	3	33	4	9	5	0	2	0	40	.228	.117	.120
California	1992	284	165	68	12	0	5	6	37	12	7	5	0	3	0	35	.162	.086	.087

Bryan Harvey, 29

Throws: Neutral type, moderate reverse righty

(.079/.089) .084   351L 311R

		OUTS	RO	1B	2B	3B	HR	HBP	BB	GDP	SB	CS	PO	WP	BK	RUNS	EOB%	RL#	RPA
California	1990	193	193	33	7	1	4	0	29	4	3	2	0	7	1	21	.172	.085	.080
California	1991	236	236	38	7	0	6	1	14	3	12	0	0	2	2	22	.133	.073	.074
California	1992	86	86	16	2	0	4	0	10	1	2	0	0	4	0	13	.167	.105	.108

Mark Langston, 32

Throws: Neutral type, moderate lefty

(.072/.091) .088   413L 2374R

		OUTS	RO	1B	2B	3B	HR	HBP	BB	GDP	SB	CS	PO	WP	BK	RUNS	EOB%	RL#	RPA
California	1990	669	0	154	40	8	13	5	103	20	22	14	5	8	0	89	.176	.099	.092
California	1991	739	0	124	34	2	30	2	93	16	10	15	4	6	0	89	.127	.088	.089
California	1992	687	0	151	38	3	14	6	72	23	21	10	5	5	0	80	.142	.084	.086

Scott Lewis, 27

Throws: Flyball type, extreme reverse righty

(.094/.149) .122   242L 247R 1119ML

		OUTS	RO	1B	2B	3B	HR	HBP	BB	GDP	SB	CS	PO	WP	BK	RUNS	EOB%	RL#	RPA
California	1990	49	0	5	3	0	2	0	2	0	0	1	0	0	0	4	.079	.067	.062
California	1991	181	19	56	16	0	9	2	21	2	6	2	0	3	0	43	.223	.151	.154
California	1992	115	79	31	2	0	3	2	13	4	2	3	0	1	1	14	.147	.087	.089

Julio Valera, 24

Throws: Neutral type, moderate to severe righty

(.127/.106) .116   396L 441R 739ML

		OUTS	RO	1B	2B	3B	HR	HBP	BB	GDP	SB	CS	PO	WP	BK	RUNS	EOB%	RL#	RPA
New York Mets	1990	39	0	14	5	0	1	0	7	1	0	2	0	0	0	9	.221	.133	.137
New York Mets	1991	6	6	1	0	0	0	0	3	0	1	0	0	0	0	1	.380	.132	.115
California	1992	564	18	132	38	3	15	2	59	15	14	4	1	5	0	83	.173	.102	.105

California Angels AAA & AA Minor League Ratings

AAA (EDMONTON)	AGE	BATS	POSITION	CPA	RUNS	SET-UP	DRIVE-IN	RPA
Don Barbara	24	L	1B	489	53.4	.065	.044	.109
Billy Bean	28	L	OF	159	10.8	.031	.037	.068
Pete Coachman	31	R	2B\3B	398	32.5	.040	.042	.082
Damion Easley	23	R	SS	478	38.4	.039	.041	.080
Jim Edmonds	22	L	OF	506	59.5	.063	.055	.118
Kevin Flora	23	R	2B	206	22.8	.060	.051	.111
Larry Gonzales	25	R	C\3B	289	31.3	.063	.045	.108
Ray Martinez	24	R	2B\SS	449	39.8	.044	.045	.089
Walt McConnell	28	L	3B	370	30.5	.045	.037	.082
Mike Musolino	25	L	C	174	15.3	.047	.041	.088
Ken Oberkfell	36	L	3B\2B	237	22.6	.053	.042	.095
John Orton	27	R	C	183	18.7	.055	.047	.102
Tim Salmon	24	R	OF	515	93.8	.109	.073	.182
Luis Sojo	26	R	3B	160	12.8	.039	.041	.080
Ty Van Burkleo	29	L	1B\OF	548	68.1	.066	.058	.124
Mark Wasinger	31	R	3B	185	13.2	.035	.036	.071
Reggie Williams	26	B	OF	619	61.6	.055	.044	.099

AA (MIDLAND)	AGE	BATS	POSITION	CPA	RUNS	SET-UP	DRIVE-IN	RPA
Edgar Alfonzo	25	R	2B	259	25.2	.051	.046	.097
Garret Anderson	20	L	OF	164	10.4	.027	.036	.063
Tony Brown	30	L	OF	196	15.6	.035	.044	.079
Ron Correia	25	R	SS	532	43.3	.039	.042	.081
John Jackson	25	L	OF	179	13.9	.039	.039	.078
Bobby Jones	25	B	OF	371	30.0	.043	.038	.081
Jeff Kipila	27	R	OF	477	57.1	.061	.059	.120
Marcus Lawton	27	B	OF	179	12.8	.034	.038	.072
Eduardo Perez	23	R	3B	264	18.1	.031	.038	.069
J.R. Phillips	22	L	1B	539	44.5	.037	.046	.083
Dan Rumsey	25	L	OF	257	31.0	.067	.054	.121
Terry Taylor	24	L	2B	312	29.0	.055	.038	.093
Fausto Tejero	24	R	C	309	14.8	.021	.027	.048

AAA Pitchers	Age	Throws	Outs	RPA	AA Pitchers	Age	Throws	Outs	RPA
Doug Bair	43	R	106	.155	Dave Adams	25	R	506	.127
Chris Beasley	30	R	100	.157	Erik Bennett	24	R	138	.124
Bert Blyleven	41	R	134	.107	Marvin Cobb	25	R	86	.233
Mike Butcher	27	R	88	.120	Ken Edenfield	25	R	149	.151
Tim Fortugno	30	L	220	.121	Hilly Hathaway	23	L	286	.094
Willie Fraser	28	R	270	.136	Phillip Leftwich	23	R	363	.163
Mark Holzemer	23	R	401	.163	Steve Peck	25	R	334	.112
Todd James	24	L	177	.219	Paul Swingle	26	R	449	.146
Joe Kraemer	28	L	241	.154					
Scott Lewis	27	R	440	.121					
Brett Merriman	26	R	254	.101					
Dana Ridenour	27	R	171	.115					
Darryl Scott	24	R	198	.122					
Ray Searage	37	L	147	.162					
Ray Soff	34	R	500	.132					
Don Vidmar	26	R	378	.144					
Cliff Young	28	L	430	.138					
Mark Zappelli	26	R	481	.136					

CHICAGO WHITE SOX

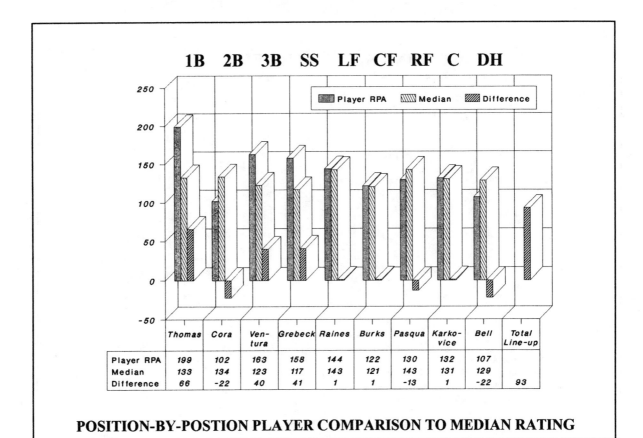

	1B	2B	3B	SS	LF	CF	RF	C	DH	Total Line-up
	Thomas	Cora	Ventura	Grebeck	Raines	Burks	Pasqua	Karko-vice	Bell	
Player RPA	199	102	163	158	144	122	130	132	107	
Median	133	134	123	117	143	121	143	131	129	
Difference	66	-22	40	41	1	1	-13	1	-22	93

POSITION-BY-POSTION PLAYER COMPARISON TO MEDIAN RATING

DEFENSIVE TEAM AND STADIUM DATA FOR THE LAST 3 YEARS:

TEAM DEFENSE BY POSITION:

POSITION-BY-POSITION STADIUM CHARACTERISTICS:

		1990	1991	1992	
1B:	Home	+2.0	+2.1	-1.0	Hard to play
	Away	-2.6	+1.5	+2.4	
2B:	Home	+0.3	-2.2	-3.2	Easy to play
	Away	-6.2	-3.6	-7.8	
3B:	Home	+6.3	+7.6	+5.5	Slightly easy to play
	Away	+4.5	+1.6	+6.2	
SS:	Home	+7.1	+4.4	+1.3	Slightly easy to play
	Away	+2.4	+1.8	+3.0	
LF:	Home	+2.9	+0.2	+8.0	Average
	Away	+0.1	+0.6	-0.9	
CF:	Home	+4.2	+7.3	-6.1	Easy to play
	Away	+3.8	+12.7	-4.4	
RF:	Home	+3.9	+2.8	+9.2	Average
	Away	-7.0	+6.4	+0.8	
Total Home:		+26.7	+22.2	+13.7	Position-to-position stadium characteristics
Total Away:		-5.0	+21.0	-0.7	based on 2 yrs. of defensive data only.

Comments: What happened to Lance Johnson in centerfield? Why the massive defensive drop-off? This team would have been my choice to win the pennant if they had done something this winter to replace the awful Steve Sax at second base. Even with him present, this team is almost dead-equal in my calculations with the A's.

CHICAGO WHITE SOX

PITCHING STAFF - THE EIGHT BEST

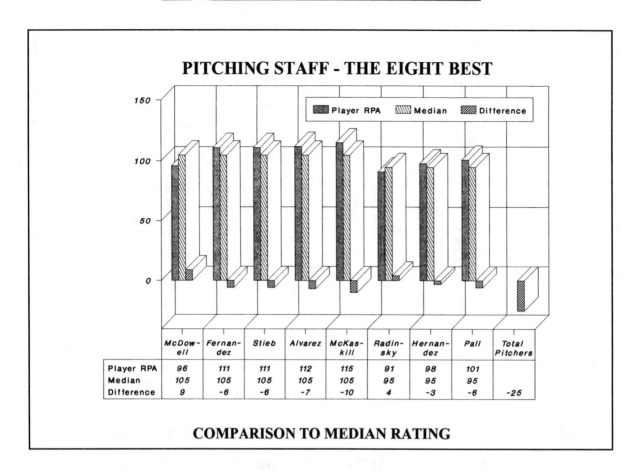

	McDow- ell	Fernan- dez	Stieb	Alvarez	McKas- kill	Radin- sky	Hernan- dez	Pall	Total Pitchers
Player RPA	96	111	111	112	115	91	98	101	
Median	105	105	105	105	105	95	95	95	
Difference	9	-6	-6	-7	-10	4	-3	-6	-25

COMPARISON TO MEDIAN RATING

SUGGESTED LINE-UPS (with set-up RPA & drive-in RPA ratings):

Vs: Left-handed Groundball
SS:	C. Grebeck	60-49
3B:	R. Ventura	68-58
1B:	F. Thomas	138-100
C:	R. Karkovice	67-70
DH:	G. Bell	47-63
RF:	M. Huff	52-55
LF:	T. Raines	57-45
2B:	J. Cora	58-46
CF:	S. Abner	48-50

Vs: Neutral Lefty Pitchers
2B:	J. Cora	66-51
LF:	T. Raines	64-51
SS:	C. Grebeck	75-61
1B:	F. Thomas	148-108
3B:	R. Ventura	67-57
C:	R. Karkovice	65-69
DH:	G. Bell	54-73
RF:	M. Huff	51-54
CF:	S. Abner	47-49

Vs: Left-handed Flyball
2B:	J. Cora	75-58
LF:	T. Raines	76-59
SS:	C. Grebeck	93-75
1B:	F. Thomas	161-118
RF:	D. Pasqua	71-64
C:	R. Karkovice	63-67
DH:	G. Bell	62-83
3B:	R. Ventura	65-56
CF:	E. Burks	60-59

Vs: Right-handed Groundball
LF:	T. Raines	74-58
1B:	F. Thomas	95-68
3B:	R. Ventura	87-74
CF:	E. Burks	63-62
C:	R. Karkovice	60-63
RF:	M. Huff	54-57
SS:	C. Grebeck	60-49
2B:	J. Cora	56-44
DH:	W. Newson	51-40

Vs: Neutral Righty Pitchers
DH:	W. Newson	85-61
LF:	T. Raines	82-63
3B:	R. Ventura	86-73
1B:	F. Thomas	106-75
SS:	C. Grebeck	75-61
RF:	D. Pasqua	70-63
CF:	E. Burks	64-64
C:	R. Karkovice	59-61
2B:	J. Cora	64-49

Vs: Right-handed Flyball
LF:	T. Raines	94-71
SS:	C. Grebeck	93-75
1B:	F. Thomas	119-85
DH:	W. Newson	134-98
3B:	R. Ventura	84-72
RF:	D. Pasqua	85-77
CF:	E. Burks	66-66
2B:	J. Cora	73-56
C:	R. Karkovice	57-59

Comments: The signing of Ellis Burks made this team the favorite to win the division, according to my figures. Now if they could just do something about second base! Only the A's and the Tigers have better offenses in the AL. These lineups are particularly strong against flyball-type pitchers, but very ordinary vs. groundball-type pitchers.

CHICAGO WHITE SOX

Writing about the White Sox is somewhat difficult since they have the most talent in the division but will probably blow the opportunity presented by this winter's weakening of their two main rivals: Oakland and Minnesota.

Why do I think they'll probably blow this chance? Any team that made those two terrible trades of 1992 in order to acquire Steve Sax and George Bell can't have much of an idea as to who ought to play and who ought to sit.

If Sax and Bell get anything like the playing time they got in '92 I can't see how this team can win the division. This team possesses the top rated player in the AL at three of the four infield positions: Frank Thomas at first base, Robin Ventura at third base and Craig Grebeck at shortstop. They have a cavernous hole at second base, however. Over this past winter, as far as I could tell, they did absolutely nothing to try to address their problem at second. As for George Bell, all I hear from Chicago is how great a year Bell had in '92. Folks, he had an awful year!

For some reason many teams and the media get locked into looking at only one piece of data and ignore the rest when making judgments on players. With some players it's their batting average. With some others it's the number of errors made in the field. With some relief pitchers it's the number of saves. With George Bell in '92 it's his 25 homers.

Isn't 25 homers a good indication that Bell had a good year? No it isn't. First of all, he had 627 official at-bats. That's a lot. Yet he had only 23 walks and 6 hit-by-pitch in those 627 at-bats,

while hitting into an incredible 29 double-plays. If you look on the following page at Bell's Effective On-Base% you will see that it plummeted to a microscopic .133 in 1992. Your average light-hitting Major League shortstop would have been a more effective DH for the Chisox in '92. George Bell will be 33 in 1993. That does not bode well for the Sox since his offensive production is more likely to be heading south than north this coming season.

I can't believe I'm still picking this team to win their division! What other choice do I have? This has got to be my most halfhearted selection in the 4 years I've been putting out this annual publication. I'm choosing the White Sox, but I'll be rooting with my heart for my "sleeper" team: The Seattle Mariners. They, at least, seem to have finally straightened themselves out and are beginning to make all the right moves.

I shouldn't be completely negative about the recent moves the Chisox have made. I almost completely agree with how they handled the Expansion draft, except I would have pulled back AA pitcher Larry Thomas in the first round of pullbacks. As it turned out he wasn't taken in any case.

I'm not a huge fan of Ellis Burks, but his signing really addressed a serious need and was the reason why I'm choosing this team to squeak through in the wide open western division.

Contrary to general belief, the only team with a worse pitching staff than the Chisox in the AL is Oakland. The Chisox have the third best offense, however.

Chicago's Projected record for 1993: 85--77, good for 1st place in the division.

CHICAGO WHITE SOX

Shawn Abner, 26

Bats Right   322L   328R   189G   149F   93ML

L= .093G .091L .088F   (.045/.047) .092   .095G .093R .090F = R

		ATBATS	1B	2B	3B	HR	HBP	BB	GDP	SB	CS	ROE	XB	RUNS	EOB%	RL#	SET-UP	DR-IN	RPA
San Diego	1990	184	35	9	0	1	2	8	3	2	4	5	16	17	.198	.086	.042	.044	.086
San Diego	1991	115	13	4	1	1	1	3	3	0	0	3	10	7	.133	.056	.022	.035	.057
California	1991	101	14	6	1	2	0	4	3	1	2	1	6	9	.130	.078	.031	.048	.079
White Sox	1992	208	46	10	1	1	3	10	3	1	2	7	14	26	.245	.114	.064	.054	.118

George Bell, 33

Bats Right   546L   1341R   514G   491F

L= .115G .132L .150F   (.048/.064) .112   .087G .104R .122F = R

		ATBATS	1B	2B	3B	HR	HBP	BB	GDP	SB	CS	ROE	XB	RUNS	EOB%	RL#	SET-UP	DR-IN	RPA
Toronto	1990	562	103	25	0	21	3	25	14	3	2	10	39	68	.177	.116	.052	.061	.113
Cubs	1991	558	107	27	0	25	4	26	10	2	6	6	33	74	.181	.127	.057	.066	.123
White Sox	1992	627	108	27	0	25	6	23	29	5	2	5	28	70	.133	.099	.040	.062	.102

Esteban Beltre, 25

Bats Right   54L   69R   29G   30F   639ML

L= ....G .093L ....F   (.027/.042) .069   ....G .051R ....F = R

		ATBATS	1B	2B	3B	HR	HBP	BB	GDP	SB	CS	ROE	XB	RUNS	EOB%	RL#	SET-UP	DR-IN	RPA
White Sox	1991	6	1	0	0	0	0	1	0	1	0	0	0	1	.259	.087	.048	.038	.086
White Sox	1992	110	18	2	0	1	0	3	3	1	0	0	16	7	.120	.059	.022	.039	.061

Joey Cora, 27

Bats Both   127L   382R   144G   121F

L= .099G .112L .128F   (.061/.048) .109   .095G .108R .124F = R

		ATBATS	1B	2B	3B	HR	HBP	BB	GDP	SB	CS	ROE	XB	RUNS	EOB%	RL#	SET-UP	DR-IN	RPA
San Diego	1990	100	24	3	0	0	0	5	1	8	3	1	14	10	.207	.093	.046	.047	.093
White Sox	1991	228	50	2	3	0	5	20	1	11	6	4	31	25	.242	.099	.052	.045	.097
White Sox	1992	122	22	7	1	0	4	21	2	10	4	2	19	19	.288	.126	.075	.054	.129

Carlton Fisk, 45

Bats Right   232L   823R   356G   266F

L= .071G .092L .120F   (.045/.054) .099   .080G .101R .129F = R

		ATBATS	1B	2B	3B	HR	HBP	BB	GDP	SB	CS	ROE	XB	RUNS	EOB%	RL#	SET-UP	DR-IN	RPA
White Sox	1990	452	90	21	0	18	7	53	12	7	3	3	32	75	.236	.143	.076	.068	.144
White Sox	1991	460	68	25	0	18	7	28	19	1	2	3	19	50	.151	.098	.041	.055	.096
White Sox	1992	188	35	4	1	3	1	18	2	3	0	1	5	22	.219	.102	.054	.051	.105

Craig Grebeck, 28

Bats Right   326L   396R   213G   181F

L= .105G .132L .164F   (.073/.059) .132   .105G .132R .164F = R

		ATBATS	1B	2B	3B	HR	HBP	BB	GDP	SB	CS	ROE	XB	RUNS	EOB%	RL#	SET-UP	DR-IN	RPA
White Sox	1990	119	15	3	1	1	2	8	2	0	0	3	8	9	.183	.071	.033	.038	.071
White Sox	1991	224	38	16	3	6	1	38	3	1	3	1	20	39	.273	.150	.083	.064	.147
White Sox	1992	287	51	21	2	3	3	30	5	0	3	1	19	39	.237	.116	.064	.055	.119

Ozzie Guillen, 28

Bats Left   398L   726R   336G   248F

L= .065G .066L .067F   (.038/.045) .083   .092G .093R .094F = R

		ATBATS	1B	2B	3B	HR	HBP	BB	GDP	SB	CS	ROE	XB	RUNS	EOB%	RL#	SET-UP	DR-IN	RPA
White Sox	1990	516	118	21	4	1	1	18	6	13	17	6	55	49	.191	.091	.044	.047	.091
White Sox	1991	524	117	20	3	3	0	10	7	21	15	7	37	46	.175	.086	.039	.046	.085
White Sox	1992	40	4	4	0	0	0	1	1	1	0	0	3	3	.136	.062	.025	.038	.063

Mike Huff, 29

Bats Right   240L   178R   131G   78F

L= .105G .103L .100F   (.051/.054) .105   .109G .107R .104F = R

		ATBATS	1B	2B	3B	HR	HBP	BB	GDP	SB	CS	ROE	XB	RUNS	EOB%	RL#	SET-UP	DR-IN	RPA
Cleveland	1991	146	26	6	1	2	4	25	2	11	4	2	25	24	.276	.129	.078	.059	.137
White Sox	1991	97	20	4	1	1	2	10	5	3	2	0	12	11	.198	.095	.045	.048	.093
White Sox	1992	115	19	5	0	0	1	9	2	1	2	0	9	9	.181	.069	.033	.038	.071

CHICAGO WHITE SOX

Lance Johnson, 29

Bats Left   521L   1308R   551G   436F

L= .074G .088L .105F   (.044/.050) .094   .082G   .096R   .113F = R

		ATBATS	1B	2B	3B	HR	HBP	BB	GDP	SB	CS	ROE	XB	RUNS	EOB%	RL#	SET-UP	DR-IN	RPA
White Sox	1990	541	126	18	9	1	1	31	12	36	22	11	64	59	.203	.101	.050	.051	.101
White Sox	1991	588	134	14	13	0	1	24	14	26	11	2	49	54	.185	.087	.040	.046	.086
White Sox	1992	567	128	15	12	3	1	30	20	41	15	7	51	63	.184	.099	.048	.054	.102

Ron Karkovice, 29

Bats Right   259L   502R   228G   205F

L= .135G .132L .128F   (.060/.063) .123   .121G   .118R   .114F = R

		ATBATS	1B	2B	3B	HR	HBP	BB	GDP	SB	CS	ROE	XB	RUNS	EOB%	RL#	SET-UP	DR-IN	RPA
White Sox	1990	183	29	10	0	6	1	15	1	2	0	2	19	26	.217	.127	.065	.063	.128
White Sox	1991	167	23	13	0	5	1	14	2	0	0	3	15	22	.218	.124	.062	.059	.121
White Sox	1992	342	55	12	1	13	3	29	3	10	5	1	22	47	.187	.120	.059	.065	.124

Matt Merullo, 27

Bats Left   12L   189R   52G   57F   49ML

L= ....G ....L ....F   (.038/.045) .083   .084G   .085R   .087F = R

		ATBATS	1B	2B	3B	HR	HBP	BB	GDP	SB	CS	ROE	XB	RUNS	EOB%	RL#	SET-UP	DR-IN	RPA
White Sox	1991	140	26	1	0	5	0	8	1	0	0	2	5	15	.180	.104	.047	.055	.102
White Sox	1992	50	7	1	1	0	1	1	0	0	0	1	1	4	.176	.067	.032	.037	.069

Warren Newson, 28

Bats Left   15L   323R   112G   72F   219ML

L= ....G ....L ....F   (.083/.059) .142   .087G   .142R   .228F = R

		ATBATS	1B	2B	3B	HR	HBP	BB	GDP	SB	CS	ROE	XB	RUNS	EOB%	RL#	SET-UP	DR-IN	RPA
White Sox	1991	132	30	5	0	4	0	27	4	2	2	2	9	24	.291	.151	.086	.062	.148
White Sox	1992	136	26	3	0	1	0	35	4	3	0	2	17	22	.307	.122	.075	.050	.125

Dan Pasqua, 31

Bats Left   115L   1038R   337G   282F

L= .083G .108L .137F   (.069/.063) .132   .110G   .135R   .164F = R

		ATBATS	1B	2B	3B	HR	HBP	BB	GDP	SB	CS	ROE	XB	RUNS	EOB%	RL#	SET-UP	DR-IN	RPA
White Sox	1990	325	46	27	3	13	2	30	4	1	1	3	25	53	.222	.146	.076	.071	.147
White Sox	1991	417	63	22	5	18	3	58	9	0	3	8	27	70	.238	.146	.076	.067	.143
White Sox	1992	265	33	16	1	6	1	35	4	0	1	3	15	35	.222	.111	.059	.055	.114

Tim Raines, 33

Bats Both   595L   1264R   599G   397F

L= .107G .120L .140F   (.079/.061) .140   .137G   .150R   .170F = R

		ATBATS	1B	2B	3B	HR	HBP	BB	GDP	SB	CS	ROE	XB	RUNS	EOB%	RL#	SET-UP	DR-IN	RPA
Montreal	1990	457	106	11	5	9	3	62	9	49	16	8	45	76	.257	.138	.078	.064	.142
White Sox	1991	609	132	20	6	5	5	74	7	51	16	7	67	82	.256	.121	.065	.054	.119
White Sox	1992	551	124	22	9	7	0	77	5	45	6	8	70	104	.293	.159	.096	.068	.164

Nelson Santovenia, 31

Bats Right   126L   153R   96G   62F   549ML

L= .064G .068L .074F   (.032/.057) .089   .103G   .107R   .113F = R

		ATBATS	1B	2B	3B	HR	HBP	BB	GDP	SB	CS	ROE	XB	RUNS	EOB%	RL#	SET-UP	DR-IN	RPA
Montreal	1990	163	21	3	1	6	0	8	5	0	3	2	1	13	.099	.070	.023	.049	.072
Montreal	1991	96	17	5	0	2	0	0	4	0	0	0	4	7	.109	.069	.025	.047	.072
White Sox	1992	3	0	0	0	1	0	0	0	0	0	0	0	0	.000	.220	.000	.220	.220

Steve Sax, 32

Bats Right   602L   1409R   578G   454F

L= .111G .118L .126F   (.052/.052) .104   .091G   .098R   .106F = R

		ATBATS	1B	2B	3B	HR	HBP	BB	GDP	SB	CS	ROE	XB	RUNS	EOB%	RL#	SET-UP	DR-IN	RPA
Yankees	1990	615	130	24	2	4	4	46	13	43	10	5	54	69	.214	.099	.051	.050	.101
Yankees	1991	652	148	38	2	10	3	39	15	31	11	7	66	85	.220	.119	.061	.057	.118
White Sox	1992	567	100	26	4	4	2	39	17	30	14	7	50	55	.176	.086	.040	.048	.088

CHICAGO WHITE SOX

Dale Sveum, 29

Bats Both   274L   441R   217G   152F

L= .117G .105L .087F (.043/.047) .090 .093G .081R .063F = R

		ATBATS	1B	2B	3B	HR	HBP	BB	GDP	SB	CS	ROE	XB	RUNS	EOB%	RL#	SET-UP	DR-IN	RPA
Milwaukee	1990	117	15	7	0	1	2	12	2	0	1	1	7	11	.205	.081	.042	.042	.084
Milwaukee	1991	266	40	19	1	4	1	32	8	2	4	1	16	30	.206	.097	.048	.049	.097
Philadelphia	1992	135	18	4	0	2	0	12	5	0	0	0	3	10	.144	.060	.026	.037	.063
White Sox	1992	114	14	9	0	2	0	12	1	1	1	1	5	14	.211	.104	.054	.053	.107

Frank Thomas, 24

Bats Right   469L   1191R   484G   371F

L= .227G .245L .268F (.112/.079) .191 .152G .170R .193F = R

		ATBATS	1B	2B	3B	HR	HBP	BB	GDP	SB	CS	ROE	XB	RUNS	EOB%	RL#	SET-UP	DR-IN	RPA
White Sox	1990	191	42	11	3	7	2	44	5	0	1	0	23	47	.323	.192	.117	.075	.192
White Sox	1991	559	113	31	2	32	1	125	20	1	3	6	39	131	.294	.190	.109	.077	.186
White Sox	1992	573	113	46	2	24	5	116	19	6	3	4	60	139	.299	.190	.115	.080	.195

Robin Ventura, 25

Bats Left   627L   1326R   545G   470F

L= .117G .115L .112F (.075/.064) .139 .152G .150R .147F = R

		ATBATS	1B	2B	3B	HR	HBP	BB	GDP	SB	CS	ROE	XB	RUNS	EOB%	RL#	SET-UP	DR-IN	RPA
White Sox	1990	493	100	17	1	5	1	53	5	1	4	6	37	58	.242	.105	.057	.049	.106
White Sox	1991	606	123	25	1	23	4	77	22	2	4	11	41	95	.235	.137	.071	.063	.134
White Sox	1992	592	112	38	1	16	0	84	14	2	4	3	46	100	.250	.140	.079	.065	.144

PITCHERS

Throws: Neutral type, extreme lefty

Wilson Alvarez, 22

(.082/.126) .118   123L   534R   634ML

		OUTS	RO	1B	2B	3B	HR	HBP	BB	GDP	SB	CS	PO	WP	BK	RUNS	EOB%	RL#	RPA
Chi. White Sox	1991	169	16	30	7	1	9	0	29	9	0	4	0	2	0	23	.111	.095	.098
Chi. White Sox	1992	301	155	78	13	0	12	4	63	13	9	8	1	2	0	56	.185	.116	.125

Throws: Neutral type, righty

Brian Dahman, 26

(..../.104) .108   48L   99R   242ML

		OUTS	RO	1B	2B	3B	HR	HBP	BB	GDP	SB	CS	PO	WP	BK	RUNS	EOB%	RL#	RPA
Chi. White Sox	1991	92	92	13	3	1	4	0	12	2	0	1	0	0	0	11	.131	.088	.091
Chi. White Sox	1992	21	21	5	1	0	0	0	2	1	1	0	0	1	0	2	.158	.072	.077

Throws: Groundball type, extreme reverse righty

Mike Dunne, 30

(.100/.160) .129   96L   88R   816ML

		OUTS	RO	1B	2B	3B	HR	HBP	BB	GDP	SB	CS	PO	WP	BK	RUNS	EOB%	RL#	RPA
San Diego	1990	86	23	20	4	0	4	0	17	1	4	0	0	4	1	18	.239	.140	.139
Chi. White Sox	1992	38	23	11	1	0	0	1	5	1	3	0	0	0	0	6	.232	.094	.101

Throws: Neutral type, moderate reverse righty

Alex Fernandez, 23

(.102/.121) .112   927L   1011R   109ML

		OUTS	RO	1B	2B	3B	HR	HBP	BB	GDP	SB	CS	PO	WP	BK	RUNS	EOB%	RL#	RPA
Chi. White Sox	1990	263	0	71	10	2	6	3	34	5	1	4	1	1	0	40	.192	.103	.106
Chi. White Sox	1991	575	8	131	33	6	16	2	86	13	15	11	1	4	1	91	.184	.107	.110
Chi. White Sox	1992	563	0	145	30	3	21	8	47	15	15	4	0	3	0	95	.168	.110	.120

Throws: Neutral type, neutral reverse righty

Roberto Hernandez, 28

(.096/.097) .097   154L   184R   366ML

		OUTS	RO	1B	2B	3B	HR	HBP	BB	GDP	SB	CS	PO	WP	BK	RUNS	EOB%	RL#	RPA
Chi. White Sox	1991	45	11	13	4	0	1	0	7	2	2	0	0	1	0	9	.218	.124	.127
Chi. White Sox	1992	213	213	30	11	0	4	4	19	2	4	4	0	2	0	21	.140	.070	.075

CHICAGO WHITE SOX

Charlie Hough, 44

Throws: Neutral type, neutral righty

(.114/.114) .114   1089L 1376R 142ML

		OUTS	RO	1B	2B	3B	HR	HBP	BB	GDP	SB	CS	PO	WP	BK	RUNS	EOB%	RL#	RPA
Texas	1990	656	0	134	28	4	24	11	117	20	33	6	3	4	0	108	.190	.109	.111
Chi. White Sox	1991	598	17	108	28	10	21	11	94	12	10	9	1	5	1	94	.182	.108	.111
Chi. White Sox	1992	529	0	112	25	4	19	7	64	13	17	3	1	10	1	87	.175	.108	.117

Terry Leach, 38

Throws: Groundball type, extreme righty

(.116/.073) .091   366L 514R

		OUTS	RO	1B	2B	3B	HR	HBP	BB	GDP	SB	CS	PO	WP	BK	RUNS	EOB%	RL#	RPA
Minnesota	1990	245	245	61	18	3	2	1	11	4	6	1	0	1	1	29	.176	.090	.087
Minnesota	1991	202	202	60	19	0	3	0	9	4	10	2	0	1	0	29	.182	.109	.105
Chi. White Sox	1992	221	221	43	9	3	2	4	15	4	7	3	1	0	0	22	.142	.070	.075

Kirk McCaskill, 31

Throws: Neutral type, moderate to severe righty

(.122/.099) .110   1136L 1185R

		OUTS	RO	1B	2B	3B	HR	HBP	BB	GDP	SB	CS	PO	WP	BK	RUNS	EOB%	RL#	RPA
California	1990	523	0	127	19	6	9	2	71	19	6	10	4	6	1	58	.152	.085	.080
California	1991	533	0	133	36	5	19	3	65	22	8	6	1	6	0	86	.163	.110	.112
Chi. White Sox	1992	627	0	143	31	8	11	6	90	12	12	9	3	6	2	96	.192	.099	.108

Jack McDowell, 26

Throws: Neutral type, neutral righty

(.098/.096) .097   1480L 1414R

		OUTS	RO	1B	2B	3B	HR	HBP	BB	GDP	SB	CS	PO	WP	BK	RUNS	EOB%	RL#	RPA
Chi. White Sox	1990	615	0	130	32	7	20	7	77	12	23	11	2	7	1	94	.169	.105	.109
Chi. White Sox	1991	761	0	144	44	5	19	4	80	12	22	10	5	10	1	95	.155	.090	.092
Chi. White Sox	1992	782	0	172	45	9	21	7	66	12	29	16	4	6	0	110	.150	.095	.102

Donn Pall, 30

Throws: Groundball type, neutral righty

(.099/.097) .098   336L 511R

		OUTS	RO	1B	2B	3B	HR	HBP	BB	GDP	SB	CS	PO	WP	BK	RUNS	EOB%	RL#	RPA
Chi. White Sox	1990	228	228	41	11	4	7	4	16	13	7	3	0	2	0	23	.083	.074	.076
Chi. White Sox	1991	213	213	46	6	0	7	3	17	8	4	5	0	2	0	22	.101	.075	.077
Chi. White Sox	1992	219	219	57	13	0	9	2	19	10	10	1	0	1	2	36	.148	.108	.117

Scott Radinsky, 24

Throws: Neutral type, extreme lefty

(.058/.109) .094   222L 529R

		OUTS	RO	1B	2B	3B	HR	HBP	BB	GDP	SB	CS	PO	WP	BK	RUNS	EOB%	RL#	RPA
Chi. White Sox	1990	157	157	39	6	1	1	2	35	5	2	0	0	2	1	26	.251	.105	.108
Chi. White Sox	1991	214	214	40	9	0	4	1	21	4	1	0	0	0	0	23	.164	.078	.079
Chi. White Sox	1992	178	178	38	11	2	3	2	29	4	1	3	0	3	0	28	.201	.101	.110

Bobby Thigpen, 29

Throws: Neutral type, moderate to severe righty

(.138/.110) .123   396L 453R

		OUTS	RO	1B	2B	3B	HR	HBP	BB	GDP	SB	CS	PO	WP	BK	RUNS	EOB%	RL#	RPA
Chi. White Sox	1990	266	266	45	8	2	5	1	29	12	3	0	0	2	0	24	.124	.067	.069
Chi. White Sox	1991	209	209	43	8	2	10	4	30	4	8	5	0	2	0	35	.167	.114	.118
Chi. White Sox	1992	165	165	45	9	0	4	3	28	5	3	0	0	0	0	32	.231	.119	.128

Chicago White Sox AAA & AA Minor League Ratings

AAA (VANCOUVER)	AGE	BATS	POSITION	CPA	RUNS	SET-UP	DRIVE-IN	RPA
Esteban Beltre	25	R	SS	173	12.1	.033	.037	.070
Ron Coomer	26	R	3B	290	22.0	.031	.045	.076
Chris Cron	28	R	1B	619	84.2	.081	.055	.136
Drew Denson	27	R	1B	395	43.8	.055	.056	.111
Brian Guinn	32	B	SS	109	10.5	.055	.041	.096
Joe Hall	26	R	3B\OF	447	48.0	.057	.050	.107
Shawn Jeter	26	L	OF	425	43.4	.054	.048	.102
Tracy Jones	31	R	OF	269	23.9	.048	.041	.089
Brad Komminsk	31	R	OF	494	54.3	.057	.053	.110
Derek Lee	26	L	OF	454	49.4	.058	.051	.109
Ever Magallanes	27	L	SS\2B	276	24.1	.044	.043	.087
Norberto Martin	26	B	2B	539	43.6	.040	.041	.081
Erik Pappas	26	R	C	283	28.3	.053	.047	.100
Nelson Santovenia	31	R	C	324	33.2	.054	.048	.102
Eric Yelding	27	R	SS\OF	372	27.3	.034	.039	.073

AA (BIRMINGHAM)	AGE	BATS	POSITION	CPA	RUNS	SET-UP	DRIVE-IN	RPA
Clemente Alvarez	24	R	C	186	7.3	.015	.024	.039
James Bishop	29	R	3B\1B	34.6	30.7	.044	.045	.089
Wayne Busby	25	R	SS\2B\3B	211	9.6	.019	.026	.045
Darrin Campbell	25	R	C	277	21.6	.035	.043	.078
Kevin Castleberry	24	L	2B	436	40.7	.049	.044	.093
Scott Cepicky	26	L	1B	557	57.0	.050	.052	.102
Lindsay Foster	25	B	SS	231	13.6	.026	.033	.059
Robert Harris	26	R	OF	304	21.6	.030	.041	.071
Scott Jaster	27	R	OF	461	54.8	.067	.052	.119
Al Liebert	25	L	C	240	21.9	.045	.046	.091
Greg Lonigro	27	R	SS\3B	275	21.2	.037	.040	.077
Kinnis Pledger	24	L	OF	215	11.3	.023	.030	.053
Tom Redington	23	R	3B	290	24.6	.041	.044	.085
Scott Tedder	26	L	OF	503	42.2	.045	.039	.084
Charlie White	25	R	OF	284	17.9	.027	.036	.063
Brandon Wilson	23	R	SS	112	9.1	.040	.041	.081
Jerry Wolak	22	R	OF	183	16.3	.044	.045	.089

AAA Pitchers	Age	Throws	Outs	RPA	AA Pitchers	Age	Throws	Outs	RPA
Rodney Bolton	24	R	562	.114	Jason Bere	21	R	165	.103
Jeff Carter	28	R	379	.137	Frank Campos	24	R	161	.174
Brian Drahman	26	R	175	.119	Fred Dabney	25	L	316	.164
Mike Dunne	30	L	398	.115	Bo Kennedy	24	R	433	.115
Alex Fernandez	23	R	86	.055	Brian Keyser	26	R	550	.129
Ramon Garcia	23	R	510	.123	Frank Merigliano	26	R	272	.130
John Hudek	26	B	291	.116	Mike Mongiello	24	R	247	.129
Greg Perschke	25	R	495	.123	Steve Olsen	23	R	232	.130
Jeff Schwarz	28	R	224	.095	Johnny Ruffin	21	R	143	.213
Ron Stephens	25	R	244	.130	Larry Thomas	23	L	362	.101
Steve Wapnick	27	R	214	.139					

KANSAS CITY ROYALS

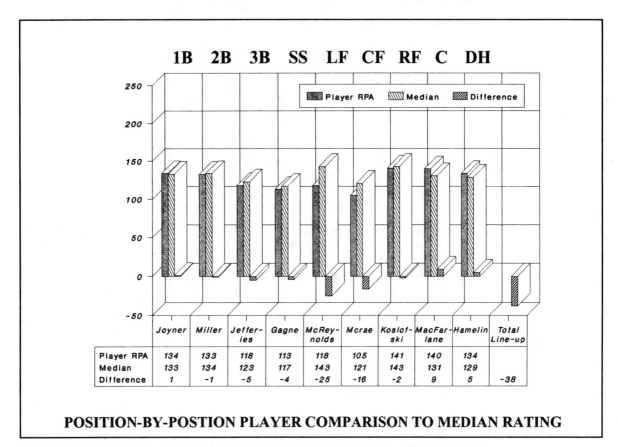

	1B	2B	3B	SS	LF	CF	RF	C	DH	Total Line-up
	Joyner	Miller	Jeffer-ies	Gagne	McRey-nolds	Mcrae	Koslof-ski	MacFar-lane	Hamelin	
Player RPA	134	133	118	113	118	105	141	140	134	
Median	133	134	123	117	143	121	143	131	129	
Difference	1	-1	-5	-4	-25	-16	-2	9	5	-38

POSITION-BY-POSTION PLAYER COMPARISON TO MEDIAN RATING

DEFENSIVE TEAM AND STADIUM DATA FOR THE LAST 3 YEARS:

TEAM DEFENSE BY POSITION:

		1990	1991	1992	POSITION-BY-POSITION STADIUM CHARACTERISTICS:
1B:	Home	+2.8	+0.9	+2.4	Hard to play
	Away	+3.7	+1.2	-0.5	
2B:	Home	+3.0	+3.5	-0.6	Slightly hard to play
	Away	-1.2	-4.0	+6.3	
3B:	Home	+1.2	+5.3	+1.6	Average
	Away	-0.9	-0.5	-2.6	
SS:	Home	-4.2	-3.5	+2.5	Average
	Away	-7.4	-8.9	-4.9	
LF:	Home	+2.9	+1.8	-4.5	Average
	Away	+4.6	0.0	+2.9	
CF:	Home	-1.3	-3.4	+3.9	Slightly hard to play
	Away	+2.6	+6.9	-1.5	
RF:	Home	+5.7	+1.4	+3.2	Average
	Away	-4.8	-0.1	+3.8	
Total Home:		+10.1	+6.0	+8.5	
Total Away:		-3.4	-5.4	+3.4	

Comments: A relatively good defensive squad without any particular "Star" position, unless you stretch the definition a little for the right fielders. Jefferies appears to be settling in at third base in a satisfactory manner. It's his hitting that's the big questionmark in my mind. McReynolds wasn't as bad defensively as he'd been in New York. The arrival of Gagne & Lind will improve the infield defense, but at an enormous (and unacceptable) cost to the offense.

KANSAS CITY ROYALS

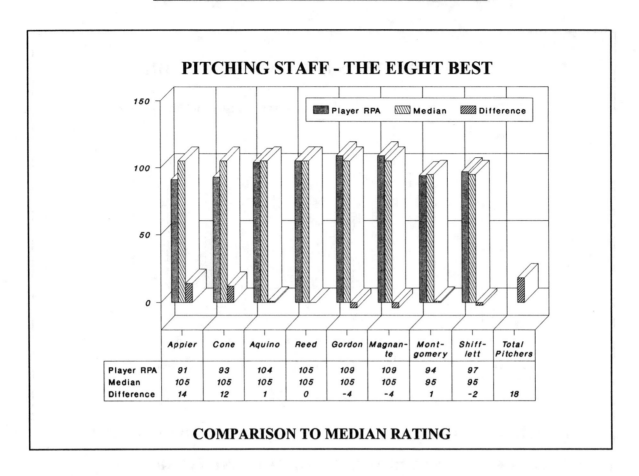

PITCHING STAFF - THE EIGHT BEST

	Appier	Cone	Aquino	Reed	Gordon	Magnan-te	Mont-gomery	Shiff-lett	Total Pitchers
Player RPA	91	93	104	105	109	109	94	97	
Median	105	105	105	105	105	105	95	95	
Difference	14	12	1	0	-4	-4	1	-2	18

COMPARISON TO MEDIAN RATING

SUGGESTED LINE-UPS (with set-up RPA & drive-in RPA ratings):

Vs: Left-handed Groundball
2B:	K. Miller	65-53
DH:	B. Hamelin	71-57
1B:	R. McGinnis	71-60
C:	M. MacFarlane	76-81
RF:	K. Koslofski	57-57
CF:	B. McRae	54-62
3B:	G. Jefferies	55-54
LF:	G. Thurman	50-58
SS:	G. Gagne	44-52

Vs: Neutral Lefty Pitchers
2B:	K. Miller	66-53
DH:	B. Hamelin	71-57
1B:	R. McGinnis	71-60
LF:	K. McReynolds	70-62
C:	M. MacFarlane	76-81
CF:	B. McRae	56-65
3B:	G. Jefferies	58-57
RF:	K. Koslofski	57-57
SS:	G. Gagne	46-55

Vs: Left-handed Flyball
DH:	B. Hamelin	71-57
1B:	R. McGinnis	71-60
LF:	K. McReynolds	77-69
C:	M. MacFarlane	76-81
3B:	G. Jefferies	61-60
2B:	C. Wilkerson	65-67
CF:	B. McRae	58-67
RF:	K. Koslofski	57-57
SS:	G. Gagne	49-58

Vs: Right-handed Groundball
2B:	K. Miller	84-67
DH:	B. Hamelin	81-67
1B:	W. Joyner	69-65
CF:	K. Koslofski	67-67
C:	M. MacFarlane	64-68
LF:	K. McReynolds	62-55
3B:	G. Jefferies	58-58
SS:	D. Howard	56-59
RF:	G. Thurman	45-53

Vs: Neutral Righty Pitchers
2B:	K. Miller	84-68
DH:	B. Hamelin	81-67
LF:	K. McReynolds	68-60
1B:	W. Joyner	76-71
CF:	K. Koslofski	67-67
C:	M. MacFarlane	64-68
3B:	G. Jefferies	61-61
RF:	G. Thurman	41-48
SS:	G. Gagne	39-47

Vs: Right-handed Flyball
2B:	K. Miller	84-68
DH:	B. Hamelin	81-67
LF:	K. McReynolds	75-67
1B:	W. Joyner	83-77
RF:	K. Koslofski	67-67
C:	M. MacFarlane	64-68
3B:	G. Jefferies	64-64
CF:	B. McRae	46-54
SS:	G. Gagne	42-50

Comments: Only the Red Sox have a weaker offense in the AL than the one listed above. The problem is, is that the actual line-ups used by the Royals in the coming season will probably be considerably weaker still. They will play Jose Lind, one of the worst hitters in the Majors. They will play an over-the-hill George Brett, and they won't platoon Joyner and McRae.

KANSAS CITY ROYALS

The only thing the Royals have going for them this season is that they'll be playing in the most wide-open division in baseball. This situation could keep everybody in the hunt well into the second half of the season.

Every time I see a reference to the trade for Jose Lind all I see is praise for the savvy of the Royals and condemnation of the Pirates' house cleaning. The Pirates lost the pennant when they lost Barry Bonds. They were hurt, but to a lesser extent, by the loss of Doug Drabek. The "loss" of Lind was a case of addition by subtraction. The big losers in this trade are the Royals. Okay, so Lind is a very good defensive player. But that is no answer to that fact that he's an awful hitter. This is another case of looking at a player on a one-dimensional basis. What's worse, the Lind trade will force Keith Miller off of second base. Miller could out-hit Lind in his sleep or on crutches. Miller may be a little rough around the edges defensively, but he makes up for that with his defensive range and quickness.

The signing of Gagne was a lot better than the trade for Lind, but only due to the comparison. Once we take a look at the whole picture, however, he doesn't bring all that much more to the table. Sure, he's a marvelous defensive player. But he can't hit! Unless they changed the rules while I was asleep, a player is still required to take his turn in the line-up.

Some teams, like the Texas Rangers and the New York Mets, get enamored with big hitters but forget that these players also have to take the field and that the gloves they bring to the ball park aren't mere ornaments. Some teams, like the Kansas City Royals, seem to be enamored with defensive ability and fail to recognize that baseball bats are more than mere ornaments. Each player is unique and each player brings these unique characteristics to the ball park. We shouldn't be prejudging players based on some half-baked prejudices which are really only based on an individuals' hunch as to what makes for a good player. Look at the whole player, not part of a player.

The signing of David Cone was a big plus, of course. The signing of 6-year minor league free-agent first baseman Russ McGinnis should add a little sock to the offense. But these additions can't offset the Royals' problems.

The trade of Tim Spehr to the Expos was a huge steal for Montreal. Mark Gardner is only a journeyman pitcher at best. Why Brent Mayne was in the Majors while Spehr was at Omaha is beyond my comprehension.

If George Brett is such a team player why didn't he volunteer to step aside so that the Royals could protect another player in the Expansion draft? Why did the Royals protect David Howard and Brent Mayne? While protecting these empty vessels, the Royals left talented players like Jeff Conine, Bob Hamelin, Kevin Koslofski, Tim Spehr, Luis Aquino, Steve Shifflett, Ed Puig and Mike Magnante unprotected.

With all that talent available, why did Florida take Andres Berumen in the Expansion draft?

Kansas City's Projected record for 1993: 76--86, good for last place in the division.

American League West *American League West*   **157**

KANSAS CITY ROYALS

George Brett, 39

Bats Left   599L   1219R   476G   486F

L= .094G .100L .105F   (.054/.056) .110   .109G   .115R   .120F = R

		ATBATS	1B	2B	3B	HR	HBP	BB	GDP	SB	CS	ROE	XB	RUNS	EOB%	RL#	SET-UP	DR-IN	RPA
Kansas City	1990	544	113	45	7	14	0	42	18	9	2	2	57	89	.226	.144	.077	.071	.148
Kansas City	1991	505	77	40	2	10	0	48	20	2	0	3	43	61	.196	.103	.051	.055	.106
Kansas City	1992	592	122	35	5	7	6	29	15	8	7	5	34	72	.203	.109	.056	.056	.112

Jeff Conine, 26

Bats Right   40L   82R   23G   46F   660ML

L= ....G   .175L   ....F   (.061/.059) .120   ....G   .093R   .070F = R

		ATBATS	1B	2B	3B	HR	HBP	BB	GDP	SB	CS	ROE	XB	RUNS	EOB%	RL#	SET-UP	DR-IN	RPA
Kansas City	1990	20	3	2	0	0	0	2	1	0	0	0	4	2	.196	.086	.042	.044	.086
Kansas City	1992	91	16	5	2	0	0	7	1	0	0	0	9	10	.220	.102	.053	.051	.104

Jim Eisenreich, 33

Bats Left   311L   988R   293G   347F

L= .075G .090L .102F   (.052/.053) .105   .095G   .110R   .122F = R

		ATBATS	1B	2B	3B	HR	HBP	BB	GDP	SB	CS	ROE	XB	RUNS	EOB%	RL#	SET-UP	DR-IN	RPA
Kansas City	1990	496	98	29	7	5	1	40	7	12	14	9	43	64	.225	.115	.061	.056	.117
Kansas City	1991	375	86	22	3	2	1	19	10	5	3	2	39	44	.214	.106	.055	.054	.109
Kansas City	1992	353	77	13	3	2	0	20	6	11	8	4	32	38	.200	.098	.050	.051	.101

Chris Gwynn, 28

Bats Left   37L   353R   105G   105F

L= ....G   .063L   ....F   (.056/.060) .116   .121G   .122R   .123F = R

		ATBATS	1B	2B	3B	HR	HBP	BB	GDP	SB	CS	ROE	XB	RUNS	EOB%	RL#	SET-UP	DR-IN	RPA
Los Angeles	1990	141	32	2	1	5	0	5	2	0	1	0	12	18	.171	.115	.053	.065	.118
Los Angeles	1991	139	24	5	1	5	1	9	5	1	0	2	11	17	.174	.109	.050	.060	.110
Kansas City	1992	84	18	3	2	1	0	3	1	0	0	2	6	11	.223	.124	.066	.061	.127

Dave Howard, 25

Bats Both   162L   329R   121G   143F

L= .098G .079L .063F   (.041/.043) .084   .106G   .087R   .071F = R

		ATBATS	1B	2B	3B	HR	HBP	BB	GDP	SB	CS	ROE	XB	RUNS	EOB%	RL#	SET-UP	DR-IN	RPA
Kansas City	1991	236	43	7	0	1	1	16	1	3	2	3	13	21	.206	.079	.041	.041	.082
Kansas City	1992	219	40	6	2	1	0	15	3	3	4	4	13	20	.192	.083	.041	.045	.086

Gregg Jefferies, 25

Bats Both   621L   1258R   542G   470F

L= .100G .106L .112F   (.055/.056) .111   .107G   .113R   .119F = R

		ATBATS	1B	2B	3B	HR	HBP	BB	GDP	SB	CS	ROE	XB	RUNS	EOB%	RL#	SET-UP	DR-IN	RPA
Mets	1990	604	113	40	3	15	5	44	12	11	2	12	60	94	.232	.130	.072	.065	.137
Mets	1991	486	102	19	2	9	2	45	12	26	7	3	34	60	.217	.114	.057	.054	.111
Kansas City	1992	604	123	36	3	10	1	39	24	19	10	7	58	74	.189	.108	.053	.058	.111

Wally Joyner, 30

Bats Left   538L   1077R   424G   429F

L= .090G .103L .116F   (.068/.064) .132   .134G   .147R   .160F = R

		ATBATS	1B	2B	3B	HR	HBP	BB	GDP	SB	CS	ROE	XB	RUNS	EOB%	RL#	SET-UP	DR-IN	RPA
California	1990	310	60	15	0	8	1	37	10	2	1	5	28	43	.233	.123	.064	.057	.121
California	1991	551	108	34	3	21	1	48	11	2	0	2	43	91	.225	.145	.077	.072	.149
Kansas City	1992	572	107	36	2	9	4	51	19	11	6	6	51	75	.212	.112	.058	.057	.115

Kevin Koslofski, 26

Bats Left   18L   130R   24G   58F   742ML

L= ....G L   ....F   (.059/.058) .117   ....G   .101R   .119F = R

		ATBATS	1B	2B	3B	HR	HBP	BB	GDP	SB	CS	ROE	XB	RUNS	EOB%	RL#	SET-UP	DR-IN	RPA
Kansas City	1992	133	28	0	2	3	1	12	2	2	1	1	11	18	.212	.115	.060	.059	.119

KANSAS CITY ROYALS

Bats Right   434L   752R   338G   329F

Mike MacFarlane, 28

L= .153G .153L .153F [(.066/.071) .137] .128G .128R .128F = R

		ATBATS	1B	2B	3B	HR	HBP	BB	GDP	SB	CS	ROE	XB	RUNS	EOB%	RL#	SET-UP	DR-IN	RPA
Kansas City	1990	400	68	24	4	6	7	23	9	1	0	2	30	46	.202	.103	.052	.054	.106
Kansas City	1991	267	41	18	2	13	6	17	4	1	0	3	19	45	.210	.148	.076	.076	.152
Kansas City	1992	402	46	28	3	17	15	28	8	1	5	4	20	58	.184	.124	.060	.068	.128

Bats Left   51L   450R   137G   153F

Brent Mayne, 24

L= .021G .026L .031F [(.037/.042) .079] .080G .085R .090F = R

		ATBATS	1B	2B	3B	HR	HBP	BB	GDP	SB	CS	ROE	XB	RUNS	EOB%	RL#	SET-UP	DR-IN	RPA
Kansas City	1990	13	3	0	0	0	0	3	0	0	1	0	0	1	.258	.084	.047	.037	.084
Kansas City	1991	231	47	8	0	3	0	19	6	2	4	0	13	23	.185	.085	.042	.046	.088
Kansas City	1992	213	38	10	0	0	0	11	5	0	4	2	10	16	.165	.066	.030	.038	.068

Bats Both   471L   967R   382G   400F

Brian McRae, 25

L= .107G .112L .116F [(.044/.051) .095] .082G .087R .091F = R

		ATBATS	1B	2B	3B	HR	HBP	BB	GDP	SB	CS	ROE	XB	RUNS	EOB%	RL#	SET-UP	DR-IN	RPA
Kansas City	1990	168	35	8	3	2	0	9	5	4	3	2	13	19	.191	.105	.051	.056	.107
Kansas City	1991	629	119	28	9	8	2	23	12	20	12	5	57	64	.171	.094	.044	.053	.097
Kansas City	1992	533	87	23	5	4	6	41	10	18	6	4	41	55	.197	.091	.045	.048	.093

Bats Right   561L   1046R   469G   390F

Kevin McReynolds, 33

L= .126G .137L .151F [(.071/.063) .134] .122G .133R .147F = R

		ATBATS	1B	2B	3B	HR	HBP	BB	GDP	SB	CS	ROE	XB	RUNS	EOB%	RL#	SET-UP	DR-IN	RPA
Mets	1990	521	92	23	1	24	1	60	8	9	3	10	53	94	.233	.147	.082	.073	.155
Mets	1991	522	86	32	1	16	2	42	8	6	6	6	38	67	.203	.119	.058	.059	.117
Kansas City	1992	373	54	25	0	13	0	64	6	7	1	8	27	70	.269	.152	.089	.068	.157

Bats Right   303L   336R   152G   187F

Bob Melvin, 31

L= .116G .112L .108F [(.040/.044) .084] .063G .059R .055F = R

		ATBATS	1B	2B	3B	HR	HBP	BB	GDP	SB	CS	ROE	XB	RUNS	EOB%	RL#	SET-UP	DR-IN	RPA
Baltimore	1990	301	53	14	1	5	0	10	8	0	1	1	11	26	.152	.080	.034	.047	.081
Baltimore	1991	228	46	10	0	1	0	9	5	0	0	2	4	19	.187	.077	.038	.042	.080
Kansas City	1992	70	17	5	0	0	0	5	3	0	1	0	2	8	.212	.096	.050	.049	.099

Bats Right   451L   575R   269G   275F

Keith Miller, 29

L= .116G .117L .117F [(.075/.060) .135] .149G .150R .150F = R

		ATBATS	1B	2B	3B	HR	HBP	BB	GDP	SB	CS	ROE	XB	RUNS	EOB%	RL#	SET-UP	DR-IN	RPA
Mets	1990	233	51	8	0	1	2	22	2	16	3	4	41	31	.255	.112	.065	.053	.118
Mets	1991	275	50	22	1	4	5	23	2	14	4	2	29	39	.249	.131	.070	.058	.128
Kansas City	1992	416	86	24	4	4	14	31	1	16	7	4	41	64	.263	.135	.078	.061	.139

Bats Right   60L   116R   55G   49F   779ML

Rico Rossy, 28

L= .101G .089L .076F [(.046/.046) .092] .106G .094R .081F = R

		ATBATS	1B	2B	3B	HR	HBP	BB	GDP	SB	CS	ROE	XB	RUNS	EOB%	RL#	SET-UP	DR-IN	RPA
Atlanta	1991	1	0	0	0	0	0	0	0	0	0	0	0	0	.000	.000	.000	.000	.000
Kansas City	1992	149	22	8	1	1	1	19	6	0	3	3	18	16	.202	.087	.044	.045	.089

Bats Right   575L   864R   422G   334F

Juan Samuel, 32

L= .149G .135L .117F [(.061/.057) .118] .121G .107R .089F = R

		ATBATS	1B	2B	3B	HR	HBP	BB	GDP	SB	CS	ROE	XB	RUNS	EOB%	RL#	SET-UP	DR-IN	RPA
Los Angeles	1990	492	79	24	3	13	5	46	8	38	22	7	42	62	.186	.109	.053	.059	.112
Los Angeles	1991	594	121	22	6	12	3	45	8	23	8	12	42	81	.227	.120	.064	.058	.122
Los Angeles	1992	122	28	3	1	0	1	4	0	2	2	1	7	12	.210	.089	.047	.047	.094
Kansas City	1992	102	21	5	3	0	1	6	2	6	2	1	9	13	.220	.114	.060	.057	.117

KANSAS CITY ROYALS

Terry Shumpert, 26

Bats Right   214L   397R   174G   162F   228ML

L= .057G .079L .103F   (.030/.043) .073   .047G   .069R   .093F = R

		ATBATS	1B	2B	3B	HR	HBP	BB	GDP	SB	CS	ROE	XB	RUNS	EOB%	RL#	SET-UP	DR-IN	RPA
Kansas City	1990	91	18	6	1	0	1	2	4	3	3	0	7	7	.140	.071	.029	.043	.072
Kansas City	1991	369	55	16	4	5	5	30	10	17	12	5	35	36	.170	.084	.039	.048	.087
Kansas City	1992	94	7	5	1	1	0	3	2	2	2	0	3	5	.078	.046	.013	.034	.047

Gary Thurman, 28

Bats Right   293L   184R   126G   138F

L= .104G .095L .087F   (.042/.049) .091   .094G   .085R   .077F = R

		ATBATS	1B	2B	3B	HR	HBP	BB	GDP	SB	CS	ROE	XB	RUNS	EOB%	RL#	SET-UP	DR-IN	RPA
Kansas City	1990	60	11	3	0	0	0	2	2	1	1	0	4	4	.140	.059	.024	.037	.061
Kansas City	1991	184	40	9	0	2	1	11	4	15	6	0	21	20	.188	.098	.048	.054	.102
Kansas City	1992	200	40	6	3	0	1	9	3	9	7	0	21	17	.164	.078	.035	.045	.080

Curt Wilkerson, 31

Bats Both   190L   529R   218G   195F

L= .087G .109L .134F   (.045/.047) .092   .064G   .086R   .111F = R

		ATBATS	1B	2B	3B	HR	HBP	BB	GDP	SB	CS	ROE	XB	RUNS	EOB%	RL#	SET-UP	DR-IN	RPA
Cubs	1990	186	35	5	1	0	0	5	4	2	2	1	18	11	.149	.061	.024	.034	.058
Pittsburgh	1991	191	24	9	1	2	0	15	2	2	1	2	13	16	.180	.077	.037	.042	.079
Kansas City	1992	296	61	10	1	2	1	15	4	18	7	8	21	32	.206	.098	.051	.051	.102

PITCHERS

Kevin Appier, 25

Throws: Neutral type, moderate to severe righty

(.107/.080) .093   1170L   1252R

		OUTS	RO	1B	2B	3B	HR	HBP	BB	GDP	SB	CS	PO	WP	BK	RUNS	EOB%	RL#	RPA
Kansas City	1990	557	47	148	17	1	13	6	52	21	13	1	0	6	1	73	.165	.092	.094
Kansas City	1991	623	22	150	41	1	13	2	58	12	10	8	0	7	1	85	.174	.096	.097
Kansas City	1992	625	0	114	37	6	10	2	63	11	18	9	1	4	0	74	.155	.082	.088

Luis Aquino, 27

Throws: Neutral type, moderate righty

(.112/.096) .104   558L   622R   46ML

		OUTS	RO	1B	2B	3B	HR	HBP	BB	GDP	SB	CS	PO	WP	BK	RUNS	EOB%	RL#	RPA
Kansas City	1990	205	139	39	14	0	6	4	21	11	3	1	1	3	1	24	.124	.084	.086
Kansas City	1991	471	127	104	33	5	10	4	42	9	10	6	1	1	0	64	.168	.096	.097
Kansas City	1992	203	11	62	14	0	5	1	19	8	1	3	0	1	1	33	.169	.104	.112

Juan Berenguer, 38

Throws: Flyball type, extreme righty

(.139/.077) .105   443L   544R

		OUTS	RO	1B	2B	3B	HR	HBP	BB	GDP	SB	CS	PO	WP	BK	RUNS	EOB%	RL#	RPA
Minnesota	1990	301	301	63	11	2	9	2	54	8	12	6	0	5	0	43	.184	.104	.100
Atlanta	1991	193	193	29	7	2	5	3	18	3	3	1	0	0	0	19	.148	.079	.075
Atlanta	1992	100	100	18	8	2	7	1	12	3	5	1	1	2	2	21	.140	.130	.141
Kansas City	1992	134	107	28	10	1	3	1	17	2	3	1	1	2	1	22	.192	.105	.114

Mike Boddicker, 35

Throws: Neutral type, moderate righty

(.119/.105) .112   1050L   995R

		OUTS	RO	1B	2B	3B	HR	HBP	BB	GDP	SB	CS	PO	WP	BK	RUNS	EOB%	RL#	RPA
Boston	1990	684	0	166	38	5	16	10	63	21	13	10	1	10	0	85	.158	.094	.089
Kansas City	1991	542	3	127	41	7	13	13	59	18	17	10	2	3	2	82	.168	.104	.107
Kansas City	1992	260	143	63	22	2	5	8	34	9	13	2	0	2	0	47	.209	.115	.124

Tom Gordon, 25

Throws: Neutral type, neutral righty

(.112/.111) .111   963L   1018R

		OUTS	RO	1B	2B	3B	HR	HBP	BB	GDP	SB	CS	PO	WP	BK	RUNS	EOB%	RL#	RPA
Kansas City	1990	586	0	137	31	7	17	3	98	19	8	10	1	11	0	95	.185	.109	.112
Kansas City	1991	474	208	89	16	8	16	4	81	8	9	7	0	5	0	74	.189	.108	.111
Kansas City	1992	353	202	82	23	2	9	4	51	12	5	7	0	5	2	56	.176	.103	.111

KANSAS CITY ROYALS

Mark Gubicza, 30
Throws: Groundball type, moderate righty
(.124/.104) .114   689L 721R

		OUTS	RO	1B	2B	3B	HR	HBP	BB	GDP	SB	CS	PO	WP	BK	RUNS	EOB%	RL#	RPA
Kansas City	1990	282	0	75	19	2	5	4	34	12	11	2	1	2	1	43	.183	.103	.106
Kansas City	1991	399	0	128	27	3	10	6	41	14	18	6	0	5	0	73	.195	.120	.122
Kansas City	1992	334	0	80	19	3	8	1	33	10	4	4	0	5	1	49	.161	.096	.105

Chris Haney, 24
Throws: Neutral type, extreme lefty
(.092/.133) .125   141L 558R 702ML

		OUTS	RO	1B	2B	3B	HR	HBP	BB	GDP	SB	CS	PO	WP	BK	RUNS	EOB%	RL#	RPA
Montreal	1991	254	0	66	20	2	6	1	42	5	8	6	0	9	0	51	.215	.118	.131
Montreal	1992	114	22	20	12	2	6	4	10	5	6	1	0	5	1	21	.148	.126	.129
Kansas City	1992	126	0	20	9	1	5	0	14	1	3	3	0	0	0	18	.146	.098	.107

Mike Magnante, 27
Throws: Neutral type, extreme reverse lefty
(.138/.098) .109   158L 440R 264ML

		OUTS	RO	1B	2B	3B	HR	HBP	BB	GDP	SB	CS	PO	WP	BK	RUNS	EOB%	RL#	RPA
Kansas City	1991	165	165	36	15	1	3	0	20	5	1	2	0	1	0	23	.177	.098	.099
Kansas City	1992	268	104	91	17	2	5	2	30	13	9	3	0	2	0	49	.191	.113	.123

Rusty Meacham, 24
Throws: Neutral type, moderate righty
(.120/.104) .110   202L 304R 517ML

		OUTS	RO	1B	2B	3B	HR	HBP	BB	GDP	SB	CS	PO	WP	BK	RUNS	EOB%	RL#	RPA
Detroit	1991	83	25	23	8	0	4	0	11	2	1	0	0	0	1	18	.214	.143	.138
Kansas City	1992	305	305	65	15	3	5	1	16	9	0	1	0	4	0	33	.133	.075	.081

Jeff Montgomery, 30
Throws: Neutral type, extreme righty
(.115/.068) .091   531L 531R

		OUTS	RO	1B	2B	3B	HR	HBP	BB	GDP	SB	CS	PO	WP	BK	RUNS	EOB%	RL#	RPA
Kansas City	1990	283	283	57	17	1	6	5	26	2	14	3	1	3	0	38	.181	.096	.098
Kansas City	1991	270	270	60	15	2	6	2	26	7	4	0	0	6	0	37	.177	.097	.098
Kansas City	1992	248	248	49	7	0	5	3	25	7	5	2	0	2	0	27	.146	.075	.081

Hipolito Pichardo, 23
Throws: Groundball type, extreme righty
(.144/.108) .124   263L 327R 502ML

		OUTS	RO	1B	2B	3B	HR	HBP	BB	GDP	SB	CS	PO	WP	BK	RUNS	EOB%	RL#	RPA
Kansas City	1992	431	40	106	31	2	9	3	48	15	11	3	0	3	1	67	.180	.101	.110

Dennis Rasmussen, 33
Throws: Neutral type, moderate reverse lefty
(.109/.101) .102   249L 1301R 579ML

		OUTS	RO	1B	2B	3B	HR	HBP	BB	GDP	SB	CS	PO	WP	BK	RUNS	EOB%	RL#	RPA
San Diego	1990	563	0	157	30	2	28	3	58	13	21	16	0	9	1	96	.156	.117	.117
San Diego	1991	440	0	120	17	6	12	2	46	13	21	6	0	1	1	67	.171	.103	.106
Chicago Cubs	1992	15	3	2	3	0	2	1	1	0	1	1	0	0	0	4	.117	.158	.177
Kansas City	1992	113	0	22	3	0	0	0	6	2	1	6	0	3	0	5	.059	.037	.040

Rick Reed, 28
Throws: Neutral type, extreme reverse righty
(.059/.152) .104   337L 310R 919ML

		OUTS	RO	1B	2B	3B	HR	HBP	BB	GDP	SB	CS	PO	WP	BK	RUNS	EOB%	RL#	RPA
Pittsburgh	1990	161	29	43	13	0	6	1	6	0	8	1	0	0	0	29	.186	.120	.127
Pittsburgh	1991	13	0	4	3	0	1	0	1	1	0	0	0	0	0	3	.165	.168	.166
Kansas City	1992	301	20	72	21	2	10	5	17	11	6	3	3	0	0	41	.123	.092	.099

Bill Sampen, 29
Throws: Neutral type, moderate righty
(.117/.110) .113   541L 541R 170ML

		OUTS	RO	1B	2B	3B	HR	HBP	BB	GDP	SB	CS	PO	WP	BK	RUNS	EOB%	RL#	RPA
Montreal	1990	271	229	75	12	0	7	2	27	4	15	3	0	4	0	45	.194	.107	.114
Montreal	1991	277	155	60	22	1	13	3	39	5	16	8	0	3	1	54	.175	.121	.131
Montreal	1992	190	178	48	9	1	4	1	23	11	11	1	0	1	2	25	.153	.094	.096
Kansas City	1992	59	47	19	1	1	0	3	2	4	4	1	0	1	0	6	.127	.074	.079

Steve Shifflett, 26
Throws: Groundball type, moderate reverse righty
(.094/.100) .098   82L 119R 625ML

		OUTS	RO	1B	2B	3B	HR	HBP	BB	GDP	SB	CS	PO	WP	BK	RUNS	EOB%	RL#	RPA
Kansas City	1992	156	156	40	8	1	6	2	11	9	3	1	0	2	1	22	.118	.095	.103

Kansas City Royals AAA & AA Minor League Ratings

AAA (OMAHA)	AGE	BATS	POSITION	CPA	RUNS	SET-UP	DRIVE-IN	RPA
Sean Berry	26	R	3B	493	56.4	.055	.059	.114
Adam Casillas	27	L	OF\1B	609	58.7	.053	.043	.096
Stu Cole	26	R	SS\OF	438	27.5	.029	.034	.063
Jeff Conine	26	R	1B\OF	459	62.5	.072	.064	.136
Leo Garcia	30	L	OF	250	13.7	.024	.031	.055
Bob Hamelin	25	L	1B	258	34.6	.074	.060	.134
Kevin Koslofski	26	L	OF	305	33.3	.058	.051	.109
Kevin Long	26	L	OF	345	23.5	.033	.035	.068
Luis Medina	29	R	1B	372	38.1	.046	.056	.102
Jose Mota	27	B	2B\SS	515	35.8	.034	.036	.070
Al Pedrique	32	R	SS\3B	215	10.0	.020	.026	.046
Harvey Pulliam	25	R	OF	412	40.4	.045	.053	.098
Rico Rossy	28	R	SS	213	25.3	.068	.051	.119
Terry Shumpert	26	R	2B\SS	228	12.8	.025	.031	.056
Tim Spehr	26	R	C	413	52.5	.071	.056	.127

AA (MEMPHIS)	AGE	BATS	POSITION	CPA	RUNS	SET-UP	DRIVE-IN	RPA
Cesar Bernhardt	23	R	OF\2B	260	11.2	.018	.025	.043
Paco Burgos	25	B	SS	293	13.7	.018	.029	.047
Edgardo Caraballo	21	R	3B	209	13.4	.027	.037	.064
Greg David	25	L	C	275	21.3	.041	.036	.077
Carlos Diaz	28	R	C	179	7.6	.016	.026	.042
Jeff Garber	26	R	OF\SS\3B	368	29.9	.038	.043	.081
Phil Hiatt	23	R	3B\OF	544	50.8	.036	.057	.093
Lance Jennings	21	R	C	156	5.3	.013	.021	.034
Tim Leiper	26	L	OF	284	24.4	.045	.041	.086
Kerwin Moore	22	B	OF	207	20.5	.051	.048	.099
Domingo Mota	23	R	2B	460	31.0	.030	.037	.067
Les Norman	23	R	OF	297	27.9	.048	.046	.094
Darryl Robinson	25	R	1B	384	31.6	.035	.047	.082
Dan Rohrmeier	27	R	OF	506	50.1	.049	.050	.099
Rich Tunison	23	R	1B	144	9.8	.031	.037	.068

AAA Pitchers	Age	Throws	Outs	RPA	AA Pitchers	Age	Throws	Outs	RPA
Brian Ahern	24	R	522	.121	Scott Centala	25	R	130	.126
Jose Bautista	28	R	343	.128	Steve Curry	27	R	485	.132
Jim Campbell	26	L	440	.141	Chip Duncan	27	R	220	.150
Dera Clark	27	R	129	.182	Matt Karchner	25	R	423	.133
Mark Huismann	34	R	371	.134	Danny Miceli	22	R	113	.109
Joel Johnston	25	R	224	.157	Mark Parnell	27	R	146	.190
Reese Lambert	30	L	161	.175	Vladimir Perez	23	R	210	.138
Carlos Maldonado	26	R	225	.115	Ed Pierce	24	L	461	.144
Josias Manzanillo	25	R	431	.139	Ed Puig	27	L	226	.079
Dennis Moeller	25	L	362	.119	Jose Ventura	23	R	553	.123
Dennis Rasmussen	33	L	324	.115	Skip Wiley	25	R	206	.137
Rick Reed	28	R	186	.132					
Mike Roesler	29	R	229	.154					
Rich Sauveur	29	L	352	.102					
Steve Shifflett	26	R	131	.075					

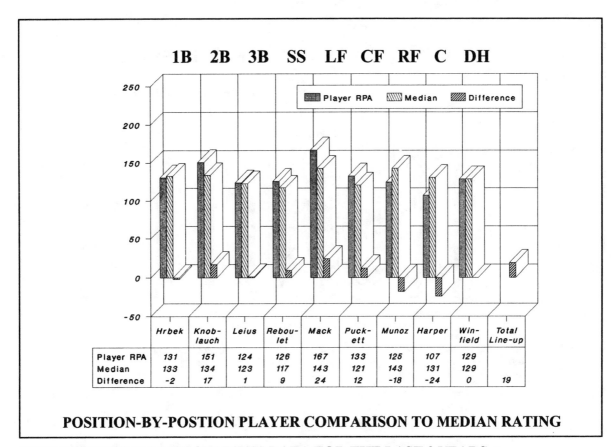

	Hrbek	Knob-lauch	Leius	Rebou-let	Mack	Puck-ett	Munoz	Harper	Win-field	Total Line-up
Player RPA	131	151	124	126	167	133	125	107	129	
Median	133	134	123	117	143	121	143	131	129	
Difference	-2	17	1	9	24	12	-18	-24	0	19

POSITION-BY-POSTION PLAYER COMPARISON TO MEDIAN RATING

DEFENSIVE TEAM AND STADIUM DATA FOR THE LAST 3 YEARS:

TEAM DEFENSE BY POSITION:

		1990	1991	1992	POSITION-BY-POSITION STADIUM CHARACTERISTICS:
1B:	Home	-3.7	+3.2	+3.6	Slightly easy to play
	Away	-3.5	-2.3	-0.8	
2B:	Home	-0.9	+6.0	+3.3	Average
	Away	-4.7	+4.9	+0.9	
3B:	Home	+3.2	+6.8	+4.6	Easy to play
	Away	+3.4	+1.1	+5.8	
SS:	Home	+0.5	+5.1	+5.8	Average
	Away	+1.2	-1.6	+7.1	
LF:	Home	+3.3	+10.6	-7.0	Hard to play
	Away	+3.2	-1.0	+3.7	
CF:	Home	+4.4	-1.4	+0.8	Very hard to play
	Away	-3.0	+3.5	+2.2	
RF:	Home	-2.3	+3.9	-1.4	Extremely hard to play. An avg. of 22.2 RPA pts. per chance difference Home vs. Away.
	Away	-4.8	+2.3	-0.1	
Total Home:		+4.5	+34.2	+9.7	A very difficult outfield!
Total Away:		-8.2	+6.9	+18.8	

Comments: This was the 2nd best defense in the American League and 3rd best overall. Fortunately for the Twins, the loss of Gagne won't hurt the defense, despite Gagne's marvelous defensive ability. Jeff Reboulet looks like the real thing, especially on defense. As difficult as this outfield is, why don't the Twins have a home-field advantage on outfield defense?

MINNESOTA TWINS

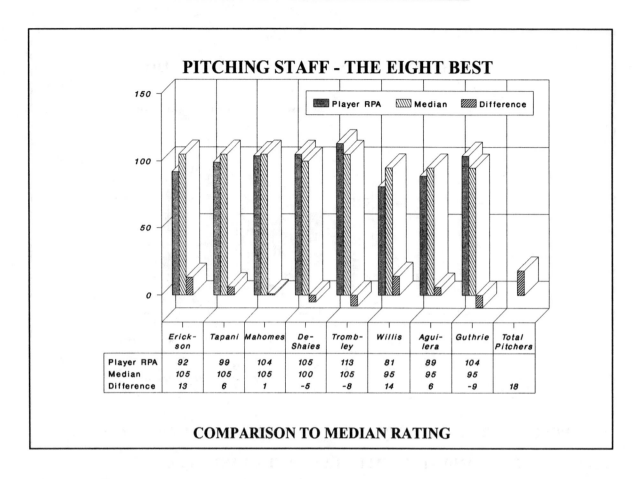

PITCHING STAFF - THE EIGHT BEST

	Erick-son	Tapani	Mahomes	De-Shaies	Tromb-ley	Willis	Agui-lera	Guthrie	Total Pitchers
Player RPA	92	99	104	105	113	81	89	104	
Median	105	105	105	100	105	95	95	95	
Difference	13	6	1	-5	-8	14	6	-9	18

COMPARISON TO MEDIAN RATING

SUGGESTED LINE-UPS (with set-up RPA & drive-in RPA ratings):

Vs: Left-handed Groundball
2B:	C. Knoblauch	75-57
LF:	S. Mack	95-81
3B:	S. Leius	72-65
DH:	D. Winfield	81-80
CF:	K. Puckett	67-66
C:	B. Harper	67-67
1B:	D. McCarty	69-61
RF:	P. Munoz	56-71
SS:	J. Reboulet	62-51

Vs: Neutral Lefty Pitchers
2B:	C. Knoblauch	78-60
LF:	S. Mack	98-84
3B:	S. Leius	78-70
CF:	K. Puckett	75-73
DH:	D. Winfield	77-77
RF:	P. Munoz	64-81
1B:	D. McCarty	69-61
C:	B. Harper	62-62
SS:	J. Reboulet	62-51

Vs: Left-handed Flyball
2B:	C. Knoblauch	82-63
LF:	S. Mack	102-88
3B:	S. Leius	85-76
CF:	K. Puckett	84-83
RF:	P. Munoz	74-93
1B:	K. Hrbek	74-69
DH:	D. Winfield	73-73
C:	D. Parks	58-65
SS:	J. Reboulet	62-51

Vs: Right-handed Groundball
2B:	C. Knoblauch	73-56
LF:	S. Mack	79-66
CF:	K. Puckett	58-57
C:	B. Harper	60-59
DH:	D. Winfield	63-63
1B:	M. Maksudian	62-64
RF:	G. Larkin	53-50
SS:	J. Reboulet	52-41
3B:	S. Leuis	41-35

Vs: Neutral Righty Pitchers
2B:	C. Knoblauch	76-59
LF:	S. Mack	82-69
1B:	K. Hrbek	69-64
CF:	K. Puckett	66-64
DH:	D. Winfield	60-59
C:	M. Maksudian	62-64
RF:	P. Munoz	48-61
SS:	J. Reboulet	52-41
3B:	S. Leuis	47-40

Vs: Right-handed Flyball
2B:	C. Knoblauch	80-62
LF:	S. Mack	86-73
1B:	K. Hrbek	90-83
CF:	K. Puckett	75-74
C:	M. Maksudian	62-64
RF:	P. Munoz	58-73
DH:	D. Winfield	56-55
3B:	S. Leius	53-47
SS:	J. Reboulet	52-41

Comments: This is the 3rd worst offense in the AL. The Twins have a decent amount of hitting ability vs. lefties, but are very vulnerable to righty pitching, particularly groundball & neutral-type righties. Dave McCarty may be a year away, but I couldn't see any other alternative since Hrbek has so much trouble against these types of lefties. This team is going to have to hope that its superior defense can keep them in the race. Even in this weak division, I think that's a long shot.

MINNESOTA TWINS

The "loss" of Greg Gagne ought to be of no great consequence to the fortunes of the Twins. But the Twins don't seem to understand that they already possess the solution. They should leave Scott Leius at third base. Jeff Reboulet appears to be a slightly younger (28 yrs. old) and even better version of Gagne (31 yrs. old). He's an excellent defensive player and certainly ought to be a better hitter than the light-hitting Gagne. Why the Twins didn't protect Reboulet in the Expansion Draft is a mystery to me. The Twins skated by, however, since the Marlins and the Rockies failed to select him.

The biggest problem for the Twins is in the loss of Chili Davis and John Smiley. Even though the Twins signed Dave Winfield to replace Chili Davis, Winfield won't fully make up for what Davis produces. In the case of Smiley, the Twins signed Jim DeShaies to replace him. DeShaies is a good pitcher, but won't bring anything like what Smiley brings to the table.

The Twins' acquisition of Toronto farmhand Mike Maksudian who is a catcher\first baseman was a very good move. He's no star, but he's got a decent bat. He's a solid player.

I don't mean to be totally negative about the Twins' pitching problems with the loss of Smiley, since I do think that Pat Mahomes is an excellent pitcher and Mike Trombley has potential for improvement.

This team's lack of depth showed through when I attempted to fashion the line-ups against righty pitching. There was very little talent available and I ended up using quite unsatisfactory choices for the suggested line-ups. Couldn't this team find some journeyman third baseman to platoon with Scott Leius? It's a major hole that needs to be filled if this team wants to be a serious contender.

The loss of catcher Jay Owens in the Expansion draft might have worried another team, but with Derek Parks and Mike Maksudian this team possesses adequate young talent at that position. By the way, after Jay Owens was selected, why didn't the Twins pull back Parks? They took a chance of losing their two best young catchers. Lenny Webster may have hit well during his short stays in the Majors, but I'm very skeptical about his real ability. I'm not a huge fan of Brian Harper, either. He's also 33 years old. Don't expect too much more out of him.

Why wasn't outfielder Rex DeLaNuez pulled back in the first round of pullbacks at the Expansion draft? He appears to be a better hitter than Gene Larkin and he's only 24 years old. The Twins need outfield depth and DeLaNuez looks like he could be ready for the Majors in about a year at most.

The Twins' pitching prospects in the high minors appear to be very thin or virtually non-existent.

Minnesota's Projected record for 1993: 81--81, good for 4th place in the division.

MINNESOTA TWINS

Randy Bush, 34

Bats Left   15L   584R   177G   118F

L= ....G L   ....F   (.052/.053) .105   .110G .107R .103F = R

		ATBATS	1B	2B	3B	HR	HBP	BB	GDP	SB	CS	ROE	XB	RUNS	EOB%	RL#	SET-UP	DR-IN	RPA
Minnesota	1990	181	30	8	0	6	6	19	2	0	3	1	6	24	.224	.121	.061	.056	.117
Minnesota	1991	165	33	10	1	6	3	21	5	0	2	0	8	26	.240	.146	.075	.065	.140
Minnesota	1992	182	28	8	1	2	2	8	5	1	1	0	4	14	.149	.070	.029	.042	.071

Chili Davis, 32

Bats Both   483L   1144R   432G   373F

L= .125G .137L .151F   (.083/.069) .152   .147G .159R .173F = R

		ATBATS	1B	2B	3B	HR	HBP	BB	GDP	SB	CS	ROE	XB	RUNS	EOB%	RL#	SET-UP	DR-IN	RPA
California	1990	412	79	17	1	12	0	57	14	1	2	6	34	59	.234	.125	.065	.058	.123
Minnesota	1991	534	84	34	1	29	1	82	9	5	7	6	34	95	.242	.166	.084	.073	.157
Minnesota	1992	444	87	27	2	12	3	62	11	4	5	6	41	77	.259	.144	.081	.064	.145

Greg Gagne, 31

Bats Right   387L   954R   397G   283F

L= .098G .103L .109F   (.042/.050) .092   .083G .088R .094F = R

		ATBATS	1B	2B	3B	HR	HBP	BB	GDP	SB	CS	ROE	XB	RUNS	EOB%	RL#	SET-UP	DR-IN	RPA
Minnesota	1990	388	59	22	3	7	1	24	5	8	8	7	35	40	.183	.098	.045	.051	.096
Minnesota	1991	408	74	23	3	8	3	26	15	11	9	8	35	43	.181	.104	.046	.052	.098
Minnesota	1992	439	78	23	0	7	2	19	11	6	8	2	48	41	.157	.086	.037	.049	.086

Brian Harper, 33

Bats Right   398L   1140R   440G   370F

L= .139G .129L .117F   (.060/.058) .118   .124G .114R .102F = R

		ATBATS	1B	2B	3B	HR	HBP	BB	GDP	SB	CS	ROE	XB	RUNS	EOB%	RL#	SET-UP	DR-IN	RPA
Minnesota	1990	479	90	42	3	6	7	17	20	3	2	8	39	55	.197	.107	.051	.054	.105
Minnesota	1991	441	98	28	1	10	6	11	14	1	2	11	26	54	.210	.126	.060	.059	.119
Minnesota	1992	502	120	25	0	9	7	19	15	0	1	6	31	65	.214	.117	.060	.058	.118

Donnie Hill, 32

Bats Both   159L   528R   183G   163F

L= .111G .116L .121F   (.065/.050) .115   .110G .115R .120F = R

		ATBATS	1B	2B	3B	HR	HBP	BB	GDP	SB	CS	ROE	XB	RUNS	EOB%	RL#	SET-UP	DR-IN	RPA
California	1990	352	70	18	2	3	1	28	10	1	2	4	29	38	.214	.099	.049	.048	.097
California	1991	209	40	8	1	1	0	29	1	1	0	2	21	27	.269	.109	.063	.049	.112
Minnesota	1992	51	12	3	0	0	1	5	0	0	0	0	3	7	.291	.124	.073	.052	.125

Kent Hrbek, 32

Bats Left   392L   1194R   432G   358F

L= .074G .107L .147F   (.067/.063) .130   .104G .137R .177F = R

		ATBATS	1B	2B	3B	HR	HBP	BB	GDP	SB	CS	ROE	XB	RUNS	EOB%	RL#	SET-UP	DR-IN	RPA
Minnesota	1990	492	93	26	0	22	7	61	17	5	2	3	30	81	.228	.144	.074	.067	.141
Minnesota	1991	462	90	20	1	20	0	63	15	4	4	1	17	69	.221	.140	.068	.064	.132
Minnesota	1992	394	61	20	0	15	0	62	13	5	2	1	30	61	.218	.127	.065	.062	.127

Chuck Knoblauch, 24

Bats Right   308L   1028R   361G   309F

L= .121G .127L .134F   (.071/.054) .125   .118G .124R .131F = R

		ATBATS	1B	2B	3B	HR	HBP	BB	GDP	SB	CS	ROE	XB	RUNS	EOB%	RL#	SET-UP	DR-IN	RPA
Minnesota	1991	565	128	24	6	1	4	59	8	25	7	5	51	69	.261	.119	.063	.049	.112
Minnesota	1992	600	151	19	6	2	5	87	8	34	14	8	75	97	.292	.137	.080	.057	.137

Gene Larkin, 30

Bats Both   300L   816R   339G   243F

L= .076G .083L .093F   (.053/.050) .103   .103G .110R .120F = R

		ATBATS	1B	2B	3B	HR	HBP	BB	GDP	SB	CS	ROE	XB	RUNS	EOB%	RL#	SET-UP	DR-IN	RPA
Minnesota	1990	401	73	26	4	5	5	40	6	5	3	4	37	54	.246	.122	.064	.055	.119
Minnesota	1991	255	56	14	1	2	1	27	9	2	3	4	20	30	.239	.113	.056	.050	.106
Minnesota	1992	337	58	18	1	6	4	22	7	7	2	2	17	38	.195	.102	.049	.053	.102

Scott Leius, 27

Bats Right   306L   409R   193G   161F

L= .132G .143L .156F   (.057/.051) .108   .071G   .082R   .095F = R

		ATBATS	1B	2B	3B	HR	HBP	BB	GDP	SB	CS	ROE	XB	RUNS	EOB%	RL#	SET-UP	DR-IN	RPA
Minnesota	1990	25	4	1	0	1	0	2	2	0	0	0	0	2	.110	.079	.027	.051	.078
Minnesota	1991	199	43	7	2	5	0	29	4	5	5	3	24	30	.254	.142	.074	.061	.135
Minnesota	1992	409	80	18	2	2	1	34	10	6	5	8	28	44	.217	.094	.048	.046	.094

Shane Mack, 29

Bats Right   465L   1067R   395G   341F

L= .174G .180L .188F   (.086/.072) .158   .143G   .149R   .157F = R

		ATBATS	1B	2B	3B	HR	HBP	BB	GDP	SB	CS	ROE	XB	RUNS	EOB%	RL#	SET-UP	DR-IN	RPA
Minnesota	1990	313	80	10	4	8	5	28	7	13	5	2	35	52	.251	.150	.080	.067	.147
Minnesota	1991	442	84	27	8	18	6	33	11	13	9	3	46	68	.206	.152	.071	.073	.144
Minnesota	1992	600	136	31	6	16	15	63	8	26	14	14	69	117	.278	.168	.096	.072	.168

Pedro Munoz, 24

Bats Right   203L   490R   185G   156F   238ML

L= .116G .134L .156F   (.048/.061) .109   .080G   .098R   .120F = R

		ATBATS	1B	2B	3B	HR	HBP	BB	GDP	SB	CS	ROE	XB	RUNS	EOB%	RL#	SET-UP	DR-IN	RPA
Minnesota	1990	85	18	4	1	0	0	2	3	3	0	2	7	8	.193	.089	.042	.045	.087
Minnesota	1991	138	24	7	1	7	1	9	2	3	0	1	10	21	.200	.151	.070	.073	.143
Minnesota	1992	418	82	16	3	12	1	16	18	4	5	3	24	44	.143	.096	.039	.057	.096

Mike Pagliarulo, 32

Bats Left   149L   803R   291G   207F

L= .101G .111L .125F   (.048/.049) .097   .083G   .093R   .107F = R

		ATBATS	1B	2B	3B	HR	HBP	BB	GDP	SB	CS	ROE	XB	RUNS	EOB%	RL#	SET-UP	DR-IN	RPA
San Diego	1990	398	69	23	2	7	3	36	12	1	3	5	25	47	.208	.103	.052	.051	.103
Minnesota	1991	365	76	20	0	6	3	18	9	1	2	6	29	40	.209	.110	.052	.052	.104
Minnesota	1992	105	17	4	0	0	1	1	1	1	0	4	10	8	.185	.071	.033	.038	.071

Kirby Puckett, 31

Bats Right   492L   1485R   532G   440F

L= .135G .150L .169F   (.069/.067) .136   .117G   .132R   .151F = R

		ATBATS	1B	2B	3B	HR	HBP	BB	GDP	SB	CS	ROE	XB	RUNS	EOB%	RL#	SET-UP	DR-IN	RPA
Minnesota	1990	551	109	40	3	12	3	46	15	5	4	10	55	80	.235	.133	.069	.060	.129
Minnesota	1991	611	145	29	6	15	4	27	27	11	5	13	64	78	.203	.129	.060	.061	.121
Minnesota	1992	639	149	38	4	19	6	31	17	17	7	12	73	106	.226	.149	.078	.072	.150

Luis Quinones, 30

Bats Both   142L   256R   130G   101F   330ML

L= .116G .111L .104F   (.047/.050) .097   .094G   .089R   .082F = R

		ATBATS	1B	2B	3B	HR	HBP	BB	GDP	SB	CS	ROE	XB	RUNS	EOB%	RL#	SET-UP	DR-IN	RPA
Cincinnati	1990	145	26	7	0	2	1	10	3	1	0	1	10	15	.201	.095	.046	.047	.093
Cincinnati	1991	212	36	4	3	4	2	18	2	1	3	2	6	21	.196	.091	.043	.046	.089
Minnesota	1992	5	1	0	0	0	0	0	0	0	0	0	0	0	.142	.050	.020	.030	.050

Jeff Reboulet, 28

Bats Right   33L   128R   27G   59F   663ML

L= ....G ....L ....F   (.055/.044) .099   ....G   .096R   .104F = R

		ATBATS	1B	2B	3B	HR	HBP	BB	GDP	SB	CS	ROE	XB	RUNS	EOB%	RL#	SET-UP	DR-IN	RPA
Minnesota	1992	137	17	7	1	1	1	23	0	3	2	2	14	17	.258	.104	.058	.047	.105

Darren Reed, 27

Bats Right   98L   68R   59G   39F

L= .086G .094L ....F   (.037/.048) .085   .065G   .073R   ....F = R

		ATBATS	1B	2B	3B	HR	HBP	BB	GDP	SB	CS	ROE	XB	RUNS	EOB%	RL#	SET-UP	DR-IN	RPA
Mets	1990	39	2	4	1	1	0	3	0	1	0	0	4	5	.179	.111	.053	.063	.116
Montreal	1992	81	7	2	0	5	1	4	3	0	0	0	2	7	.073	.082	.021	.059	.080
Minnesota	1992	33	4	2	0	0	0	2	0	0	0	0	0	2	.178	.062	.029	.033	.062

MINNESOTA TWINS

Lenny Webster, 27

Bats Right   48L   131R   43G   35F   364ML

L= .119G .123L ....F   (.045/.044) .089   .073G   .077R   ....F = R

		ATBATS	1B	2B	3B	HR	HBP	BB	GDP	SB	CS	ROE	XB	RUNS	EOB%	RL#	SET-UP	DR-IN	RPA
Minnesota	1990	6	1	1	0	0	0	1	0	0	0	0	1	1	.343	.172	.104	.064	.168
Minnesota	1991	34	6	1	0	3	0	6	2	0	0	0	4	6	.196	.173	.078	.083	.161
Minnesota	1992	118	21	10	1	1	0	9	3	0	2	2	8	14	.216	.108	.055	.054	.109

PITCHERS

Throws: Flyball type, extreme reverse righty

Paul Abbott, 25   (.103/.141) .122   195L   204R   384ML

		OUTS	RO	1B	2B	3B	HR	HBP	BB	GDP	SB	CS	PO	WP	BK	RUNS	EOB%	RL#	RPA
Minnesota	1990	104	0	26	9	2	0	1	28	4	10	2	0	1	0	20	.266	.126	.124
Minnesota	1991	142	106	22	10	1	5	0	35	5	6	1	0	5	0	25	.214	.125	.122
Minnesota	1992	33	33	8	2	1	1	1	5	0	2	0	1	1	0	7	.228	.135	.146

Throws: Neutral type, moderate righty

Rick Aguilera, 31   (.092/.076) .084   406L   366R

		OUTS	RO	1B	2B	3B	HR	HBP	BB	GDP	SB	CS	PO	WP	BK	RUNS	EOB%	RL#	RPA
Minnesota	1990	196	196	41	9	0	5	4	13	8	3	0	0	3	0	20	.133	.080	.077
Minnesota	1991	207	207	30	9	2	3	1	24	6	7	0	0	3	0	19	.152	.076	.074
Minnesota	1992	200	200	45	8	0	7	1	13	7	5	0	0	5	0	26	.132	.088	.095

Throws: Neutral type, moderate to severe reverse righty

Willie Banks, 23   (.123/.144) .134   189L   209R   963ML

		OUTS	RO	1B	2B	3B	HR	HBP	BB	GDP	SB	CS	PO	WP	BK	RUNS	EOB%	RL#	RPA
Minnesota	1991	52	15	18	2	0	1	0	12	2	2	0	0	3	0	11	.267	.141	.137
Minnesota	1992	213	18	56	15	3	6	2	37	2	8	4	0	5	1	48	.237	.133	.144

Throws: Neutral type, extreme lefty

Larry Casian, 27   (..../.142) .105   51L   142R   462ML

		OUTS	RO	1B	2B	3B	HR	HBP	BB	GDP	SB	CS	PO	WP	BK	RUNS	EOB%	RL#	RPA
Minnesota	1990	67	10	17	7	0	2	0	4	6	0	0	0	0	0	7	.088	.082	.078
Minnesota	1991	55	55	15	9	0	4	1	5	3	0	0	1	2	0	12	.156	.156	.152
Minnesota	1992	20	20	6	1	0	0	1	0	0	0	0	0	0	0	3	.212	.086	.092

Throws: Groundball type, moderate righty

Scott Erickson, 24   (.098/.092) .095   1128L   984R

		OUTS	RO	1B	2B	3B	HR	HBP	BB	GDP	SB	CS	PO	WP	BK	RUNS	EOB%	RL#	RPA
Minnesota	1990	339	17	81	16	2	9	5	47	14	6	3	1	3	0	46	.171	.100	.095
Minnesota	1991	612	0	132	39	5	13	6	68	22	4	10	0	4	0	73	.152	.092	.090
Minnesota	1992	636	0	145	29	5	18	8	80	31	23	7	0	6	1	90	.150	.092	.100

Throws: Neutral type, moderate reverse lefty

Mark Guthrie, 27   (.111/.102) .104   280L   995R

		OUTS	RO	1B	2B	3B	HR	HBP	BB	GDP	SB	CS	PO	WP	BK	RUNS	EOB%	RL#	RPA
Minnesota	1990	434	29	118	28	0	8	1	36	12	17	12	2	9	0	52	.145	.089	.086
Minnesota	1991	294	129	81	19	5	11	1	39	16	9	5	1	7	0	48	.153	.118	.116
Minnesota	1992	225	225	45	6	1	7	0	16	4	6	2	0	2	0	26	.130	.080	.086

Throws: Flyball type, moderate reverse lefty

Bob Kipper, 28   (.132/.115) .121   220L   447R

		OUTS	RO	1B	2B	3B	HR	HBP	BB	GDP	SB	CS	PO	WP	BK	RUNS	EOB%	RL#	RPA
Pittsburgh	1990	188	184	28	9	0	7	3	25	1	5	3	1	1	5	26	.165	.095	.101
Pittsburgh	1991	180	180	45	12	2	7	0	19	4	7	4	0	0	1	30	.163	.114	.116
Minnesota	1992	116	116	27	5	0	8	3	11	3	1	2	0	1	0	21	.141	.117	.127

MINNESOTA TWINS

Pat Mahomes, 22

Throws: Flyball type, neutral reverse righty

(.110/.111) .110   150L   143R   1162ML

		OUTS	RO	1B	2B	3B	HR	HBP	BB	GDP	SB	CS	PO	WP	BK	RUNS	EOB%	RL#	RPA
Minnesota	1992	209	3	45	19	4	5	0	37	6	9	8	1	2	1	36	.174	.108	.117

John Smiley, 27

Throws: Neutral type, moderate lefty

(.082/.093) .091   401L   1965R

		OUTS	RO	1B	2B	3B	HR	HBP	BB	GDP	SB	CS	PO	WP	BK	RUNS	EOB%	RL#	RPA
Pittsburgh	1990	448	3	110	29	7	15	2	35	9	13	6	0	2	2	73	.164	.110	.116
Pittsburgh	1991	623	13	133	38	6	17	3	44	11	18	13	0	3	1	77	.139	.090	.092
Minnesota	1992	723	0	133	51	4	17	6	65	14	25	16	0	4	0	90	.142	.085	.091

Kevin Tapani, 28

Throws: Neutral type, moderate righty

(.102/.093) .098   1317L   1142R

		OUTS	RO	1B	2B	3B	HR	HBP	BB	GDP	SB	CS	PO	WP	BK	RUNS	EOB%	RL#	RPA
Minnesota	1990	478	0	116	28	8	12	2	27	9	9	9	0	1	0	59	.144	.094	.091
Minnesota	1991	732	0	150	48	4	23	2	40	14	18	3	0	3	3	89	.144	.097	.094
Minnesota	1992	660	0	151	53	5	17	5	46	17	26	11	0	4	0	96	.150	.095	.103

Mike Trombley, 25

Throws: Neutral type, extreme righty

(.148/.086) .115   88L   102R   1468ML

		OUTS	RO	1B	2B	3B	HR	HBP	BB	GDP	SB	CS	PO	WP	BK	RUNS	EOB%	RL#	RPA
Minnesota	1992	139	21	26	12	0	5	1	17	2	2	3	1	0	0	21	.158	.100	.108

Gary Wayne, 30

Throws: Flyball type, moderate to severe lefty

(.091/.124) .115   114L   286R   389ML

		OUTS	RO	1B	2B	3B	HR	HBP	BB	GDP	SB	CS	PO	WP	BK	RUNS	EOB%	RL#	RPA
Minnesota	1990	116	116	25	8	0	5	1	13	4	3	2	0	4	0	17	.146	.106	.103
Minnesota	1991	37	37	7	3	0	1	1	4	1	0	0	0	0	0	5	.184	.102	.102
Minnesota	1992	144	144	30	11	3	2	3	14	2	5	0	0	1	1	24	.210	.105	.114

David West, 28

Throws: Flyball type, moderate reverse lefty

(.142/.136) .137   165L   887R   444ML

		OUTS	RO	1B	2B	3B	HR	HBP	BB	GDP	SB	CS	PO	WP	BK	RUNS	EOB%	RL#	RPA
Minnesota	1990	439	10	81	35	5	21	4	77	16	5	5	0	4	1	76	.179	.123	.119
Minnesota	1991	214	21	35	17	1	13	1	28	3	3	2	0	3	0	38	.167	.127	.127
Minnesota	1992	85	47	24	5	0	3	1	20	1	2	0	0	2	0	22	.281	.149	.161

Carl Willis, 32

Throws: Groundball type, moderate to severe righty

(.094/.063) .075   247L   388R

		OUTS	RO	1B	2B	3B	HR	HBP	BB	GDP	SB	CS	PO	WP	BK	RUNS	EOB%	RL#	RPA
Minnesota	1991	267	267	59	12	1	4	1	17	8	5	3	0	4	1	25	.131	.076	.073
Minnesota	1992	238	238	54	12	3	4	0	10	10	2	1	0	2	1	24	.112	.072	.077

Minnesota Twins AAA & AA Minor League Ratings

AAA (PORTLAND)	AGE	BATS	POSITION	CPA	RUNS	SET-UP	DRIVE-IN	RPA
Bernardo Brito	29	R	OF	620	64.1	.045	.058	.103
Jarvis Brown	25	R	OF	251	24.1	.051	.045	.096
J.T. Bruett	25	L	OF	346	33.2	.054	.042	.096
Shawn Gilbert	27	R	SS\OF	494	37.9	.037	.040	.077
Chip Hale	28	L	2B	554	58.2	.060	.045	.105
Keith Hughes	29	L	OF	249	26.3	.054	.052	.106
Terry Jorgensen	26	R	3B\1B	585	62.4	.054	.053	.107
Terry Lee	30	R	1B	429	38.4	.044	.046	.090
Ed Naveda	26	R	OF	409	29.4	.034	.038	.072
Ray Ortiz	24	L	OF	439	44.2	.048	.053	.101
Derek Parks	24	R	C	284	30.3	.050	.057	.107
Luis Quinones	30	B	3B\2B	330	35.3	.052	.055	.107
Jeff Reboulet	28	R	SS	204	22.2	.062	.047	.109
Danny Sheaffer	31	R	C\OF	484	35.6	.032	.042	.074

AA (ORLANDO)	AGE	BATS	POSITION	CPA	RUNS	SET-UP	DRIVE-IN	RPA
Rick Allen	25	R	SS\2B	267	10.9	.017	.024	.041
Fred Cooley	26	R	DH	150	14.1	.044	.050	.094
Rex DeLaNuez	24	R	OF	524	58.0	.061	.050	.111
Chris DeLarwelle	25	R	1B\3B	332	26.5	.041	.039	.080
Cheo Garcia	24	R	3B\2B	543	34.3	.027	.036	.063
Jay Kvasnicka	25	L	OF	281	19.6	.034	.036	.070
Mica Lewis	25	R	OF\2B	433	40.7	.049	.045	.094
Dan Masteller	24	L	OF\1B	399	33.6	.039	.045	.084
Dave McCarty	23	R	OF\1B	562	64.0	.061	.053	.114
Pat Meares	24	R	SS	324	22.1	.031	.037	.068
Jay Owens	23	R	C	382	36.3	.052	.043	.095
Brian Raabe	25	R	2B	112	7.3	.026	.039	.065
Paul Russo	23	R	3B\1B	486	47.2	.044	.053	.097
Joe Siwa	26	R	C	144	5.3	.015	.022	.037

AAA Pitchers	Age	Throws	Outs	RPA	AA Pitchers	Age	Throws	Outs	RPA
Paul Abbott	25	R	139	.107	Rich Garces	22	R	220	.154
Willie Banks	23	R	225	.108	Ed Gustafson	25	R	438	.167
Larry Casian	27	L	186	.090	Jon Henry	24	R	406	.137
Mike Dyer	26	R	315	.158	Jason Klonoski	25	L	282	.136
Mauro Gozzo	26	R	467	.124	Curtis Leskanic	24	R	504	.143
Greg Johnson	26	R	154	.162	Marc Lipson	26	R	109	.175
Orlando Lind	27	R	254	.129	Bob McCreary	25	R	200	.129
Pat Mahomes	22	R	333	.116	Oscar Munoz	23	R	203	.174
Mike Trombley	25	R	495	.129	Alan Newman	23	L	306	.132
George Tsamis	25	L	491	.143	Carlos Pulido	21	L	301	.135
Rob Wassenaar	27	R	270	.125	Rusty Richards	27	R	253	.135
David West	28	L	305	.133	Fred White	24	R	79	.208
					Bill Wissler	22	R	247	.121

OAKLAND ATHLETICS

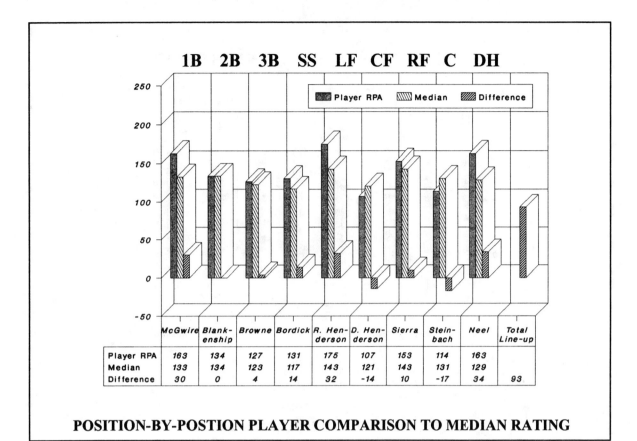

	1B	2B	3B	SS	LF	CF	RF	C	DH	Total Line-up
	McGwire	Blank-enship	Browne	Bordick	R. Hen-derson	D. Hen-derson	Sierra	Stein-bach	Neel	
Player RPA	163	134	127	131	175	107	153	114	163	
Median	133	134	123	117	143	121	143	131	129	
Difference	30	0	4	14	32	-14	10	-17	34	93

POSITION-BY-POSTION PLAYER COMPARISON TO MEDIAN RATING

DEFENSIVE TEAM AND STADIUM DATA FOR THE LAST 3 YEARS:

TEAM DEFENSE BY POSITION:

		1990	1991	1992	POSITION-BY-POSITION STADIUM CHARACTERISTICS:
1B:	Home	-1.1	+1.9	-2.4	Very easy to play
	Away	-0.5	-2.2	+1.9	
2B:	Home	+3.1	-2.8	-0.1	Slightly easy to play
	Away	+5.2	-0.3	-1.4	
3B:	Home	+1.4	+2.9	+1.9	Slightly easy to play
	Away	-4.0	-4.1	+0.6	
SS:	Home	+4.1	+2.1	-6.7	Average (to slightly easy)
	Away	-0.6	-0.7	-1.3	
LF:	Home	+6.9	+4.8	-0.3	Easy to play
	Away	+10.8	+8.7	+0.7	
CF:	Home	+0.7	-8.5	+1.4	Average
	Away	+3.4	+0.8	-0.7	
RF:	Home	-2.4	-2.3	+0.1	Very easy to play
	Away	-2.7	-14.2	-6.0	
Total Home:		+12.7	-1.9	-6.1	Still one of the easiest stadiums to play
Total Away:		+11.6	-12.0	-6.1	defense at.

Comments: After a big defensive downturn in '91, the A's defense continued to be somewhat poor in '92. There should be improvement in '93 in right field, due the replacement of Canseco with Sierra, and at shortstop as Bordick settles in. These improvements, however, will probably be offset by the continued defensive decline of the Hendersons as the natural aging process has its effect on their speed and reactions.

OAKLAND ATHLETICS

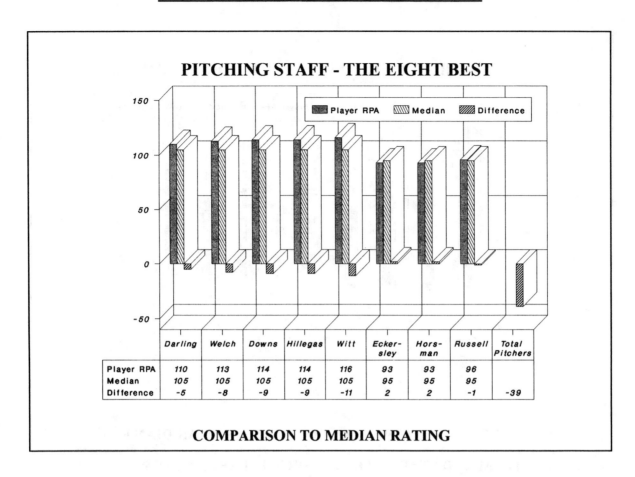

PITCHING STAFF - THE EIGHT BEST

Legend: ■ Player RPA   ▨ Median   ▧ Difference

	Darling	Welch	Downs	Hillegas	Witt	Ecker-sley	Hors-man	Russell	Total Pitchers
Player RPA	110	113	114	114	116	93	93	96	
Median	105	105	105	105	105	95	95	95	
Difference	-5	-8	-9	-9	-11	2	2	-1	-39

COMPARISON TO MEDIAN RATING

SUGGESTED LINE-UPS (with set-up RPA & drive-in RPA ratings):

Vs: Left-handed Groundball
LF:	R. Henderson	99-70
DH:	T. Neel	91-64
SS:	M. Bordick	74-64
1B:	M. McGwire	98-91
RF:	R. Sierra	80-80
CF:	D. Henderson	71-70
3B:	S. Brosius	55-69
2B:	L. Blankenship	70-53
C:	T. Steinbach	57-59

Vs: Neutral Lefty Pitchers
LF:	R. Henderson	107-76
DH:	T. Neel	91-64
SS:	M. Bordick	73-63
1B:	M. McGwire	99-91
RF:	R. Sierra	78-78
CF:	D. Henderson	72-71
C:	T. Steinbach	63-65
3B:	S. Brosius	55-69
2B:	L. Blankenship	67-51

Vs: Left-handed Flyball
LF:	R. Henderson	118-84
DH:	T. Neel	91-64
1B:	M. McGwire	99-92
CF:	D. Henderson	125-124
RF:	R. Sierra	76-75
C:	T. Steinbach	72-73
SS:	M. Bordick	71-62
3B:	S. Brosius	55-69
2B:	L. Blankenship	63-48

Vs: Right-handed Groundball
CF:	R. Henderson	90-64
LF:	T. Neel	101-74
2B:	L. Blankenship	82-62
1B:	M. McGwire	79-73
DH:	H. Baines	66-63
RF:	R. Sierra	69-69
SS:	M. Bordick	58-50
3B:	J. Browne	58-48
C:	T. Steinbach	45-46

Vs: Neutral Righty Pitchers
CF:	R. Henderson	99-69
LF:	T. Neel	101-74
2B:	L. Blankenship	79-60
1B:	M. McGwire	80-73
DH:	H. Baines	67-64
RF:	R. Sierra	67-67
3B:	J. Browne	64-54
C:	T. Steinbach	51-52
SS:	M. Bordick	57-49

Vs: Right-handed Flyball
LF:	R. Henderson	110-77
LF:	T. Neel	101-74
2B:	L. Blankenship	75-57
1B:	M. McGwire	80-74
CF:	D. Henderson	85-85
RF:	R. Sierra	65-64
3B:	J. Browne	71-60
C:	T. Steinbach	59-612
SS:	M. Bordick	55-48

Comments: While the A's still possess the most fearsome offense in the AL, it is nowhere as dominating as in the past, and that should pose some problems for them due to their weak pitching staff with an aging Eckersley. This team could be in big trouble if they don't give Troy Neel substantial playing time. They could even end up with an under .500 winning percentage!

OAKLAND ATHLETICS

Last year I stated that the Oakland A's had the next to worst pitching staff and still picked them to win the western division based upon their fabulous hitting. This year the A's pitching has gone from woeful to awful and I almost picked them to win the division again in '93.

As a matter of fact, I had already decided to pick them to win! But then the Chisox signed Ellis Burks and I went back to my numbers and changed my estimates and the White Sox ended up as the favorites (just barely).

How bad will the A's pitching be in '93? It will be the worst pitching staff in the AL. In fact, the pitching staff of the Florida Marlins will be far and away better than the pitching staff of the A's!

The big losses from the '92 staff were Mike Moore and Jim Corsi. In addition, Dennis Eckersley is getting to that age where he is very likely to begin sliding badly. He's still likely to be relatively effective, but not be the Eckersley of old. Fortunately the A's do have one quality young pitcher in Vince Horsman. The starting staff is a shambles, however. The best starter the A's possess is Ron Darling and he's a below average pitcher at this stage of his career.

We learn this year if Dave Henderson has anything left. Even if he does, it can't be all that much. The A's can only hope to get a year or two of quality play out of him at most.

I really like Troy Neel. He's got a really big bat. He should be given every possible opportunity to show what he can do. The A's will need as many big bats in the line-up as possible, so as to overcome the weakness of the pitching staff.

The trading away of Walt Weiss was no loss for the A's since Mike Bordick is a far superior player, and in addition, I have the impression that Weiss' abilities, both on offense and defense, may be disappearing fast.

Even though the A's lost an important member of their bullpen in Jim Corsi, I think they skated through the Expansion draft relatively unscathed considering what could have happened. I certainly would have protected Troy Neel over Walt Weiss and some of the other players the A's protected. I probably would have placed Marcos Armas on my 15 man protected list as well.

Todd Revenig looks like a very good pitching prospect. He may need a little time at AAA, however.

While the A's still have the best hitting in the AL, the gap has been narrowed severely and if Troy Neel does not get major playing time the A's offense will slide completely out of first place.

I wish to remind our readers of the illusions created by Oakland's home park. It's a pitcher's heaven. Ron Darling may appear to be a very good pitcher, but that's just a park effect. The Texas Rangers, last year and this year may appear to have the best offense, but the A's offense is far superior. It's the park that makes it appear otherwise.

Oakland's Projected record for 1993: 84--78, good for 2nd place in the division.

OAKLAND ATHLETICS

Harold Baines, 33

Bats Left   255L   1327R   464G   349F

L= .119G .121L .123F | (.069/.065) .134 | .134G .136R .138F = R

		ATBATS	1B	2B	3B	HR	HBP	BB	GDP	SB	CS	ROE	XB	RUNS	EOB%	RL#	SET-UP	DR-IN	RPA
Texas	1990	321	69	10	1	13	0	38	13	0	1	2	23	50	.214	.130	.066	.064	.130
Oakland	1990	94	17	5	0	3	0	19	4	0	2	2	3	16	.256	.130	.077	.062	.139
Oakland	1991	488	98	25	1	20	1	50	12	0	1	2	35	83	.223	.134	.075	.069	.144
Oakland	1992	478	87	18	0	16	0	53	11	1	3	5	22	67	.212	.121	.062	.061	.124

Lance Blankenship, 29

Bats Right   280L   540R   240G   198F   156ML

L= .121G .116L .109F | (.074/.056) .130 | .142G .137R .130F = R

		ATBATS	1B	2B	3B	HR	HBP	BB	GDP	SB	CS	ROE	XB	RUNS	EOB%	RL#	SET-UP	DR-IN	RPA
Oakland	1990	136	23	3	0	0	0	20	6	3	2	3	18	12	.208	.070	.038	.038	.076
Oakland	1991	185	35	8	0	3	3	23	2	12	3	4	25	29	.263	.122	.072	.058	.130
Oakland	1992	349	56	24	1	3	6	80	10	21	9	4	42	59	.291	.129	.076	.055	.131

Mike Bordick, 27

Bats Right   211L   620R   216G   200F

L= .133G .131L .128F | (.058/.051) .109 | .103G .101R .098F = R

		ATBATS	1B	2B	3B	HR	HBP	BB	GDP	SB	CS	ROE	XB	RUNS	EOB%	RL#	SET-UP	DR-IN	RPA
Oakland	1990	14	1	0	0	0	0	1	0	0	0	0	0	0	.114	.022	.009	.015	.024
Oakland	1991	235	50	5	1	0	3	14	3	3	4	4	16	22	.211	.077	.041	.041	.082
Oakland	1992	504	125	19	4	3	9	38	10	12	6	5	37	69	.250	.120	.067	.055	.122

Scott Brosius, 26

Bats Right   55L   109R   45G   47F   537ML

L= .135G .134L .133F | (.047/.060) .107 | .094G .093R .092F = R

		ATBATS	1B	2B	3B	HR	HBP	BB	GDP	SB	CS	ROE	XB	RUNS	EOB%	RL#	SET-UP	DR-IN	RPA
Oakland	1991	68	9	5	0	2	0	3	2	3	1	1	4	7	.145	.089	.039	.057	.096
Oakland	1992	87	13	2	0	4	2	2	0	3	0	3	4	12	.186	.128	.061	.068	.129

Jerry Browne, 26

Bats Both   315L   981R   373G   351F   20ML

L= .076G .088L .101F | (.057/.048) .105 | .099G .111R .124F = R

		ATBATS	1B	2B	3B	HR	HBP	BB	GDP	SB	CS	ROE	XB	RUNS	EOB%	RL#	SET-UP	DR-IN	RPA
Cleveland	1990	513	100	26	5	6	2	71	12	12	9	11	70	74	.258	.125	.069	.055	.124
Cleveland	1991	290	58	5	2	1	1	27	5	2	5	2	17	26	.203	.078	.040	.042	.082
Oakland	1992	324	76	12	2	3	4	40	7	3	3	2	19	47	.264	.123	.070	.054	.124

Eric Fox, 29

Bats Both   24L   133R   30G   53F   995ML

L= ....G ....L ....F | (.051/.049) .100 | ....G .105R .075F = R

		ATBATS	1B	2B	3B	HR	HBP	BB	GDP	SB	CS	ROE	XB	RUNS	EOB%	RL#	SET-UP	DR-IN	RPA
Oakland	1992	143	24	5	2	3	0	13	1	3	4	2	13	18	.198	.110	.054	.057	.111

Dave Henderson, 34

Bats Right   334L   865R   387G   245F

L= .148G .190L .256F | (.067/.066) .133 | .069G .111R .177F = R

		ATBATS	1B	2B	3B	HR	HBP	BB	GDP	SB	CS	ROE	XB	RUNS	EOB%	RL#	SET-UP	DR-IN	RPA
Oakland	1990	450	74	28	0	20	1	39	5	3	2	4	39	75	.211	.140	.076	.074	.150
Oakland	1991	572	100	33	0	25	4	55	9	6	7	5	49	96	.214	.132	.072	.070	.142
Oakland	1992	63	8	1	0	0	0	2	0	0	0	1	2	3	.144	.044	.018	.027	.045

Rickey Henderson, 34

Bats Right   424L   1249R   502G   348F

L= .176G .190L .209F | (.105/.074) .179 | .161G .175R .194F = R

		ATBATS	1B	2B	3B	HR	HBP	BB	GDP	SB	CS	ROE	XB	RUNS	EOB%	RL#	SET-UP	DR-IN	RPA
Oakland	1990	489	95	33	3	28	4	95	13	65	15	6	76	134	.284	.206	.127	.093	.220
Oakland	1991	470	90	17	1	18	7	91	7	58	19	11	60	103	.282	.156	.097	.072	.169
Oakland	1992	396	76	18	3	15	6	90	5	48	12	3	47	95	.307	.187	.113	.077	.190

Mike Kingery, 31

Bats Left   42L   336R   111G   79F   402ML

L= ....G .119L ....F | (.040/.043) .083 | .080G .078R .075F = R

		ATBATS	1B	2B	3B	HR	HBP	BB	GDP	SB	CS	ROE	XB	RUNS	EOB%	RL#	SET-UP	DR-IN	RPA
San Francisco	1990	207	53	7	1	0	1	12	1	6	1	3	30	26	.260	.115	.064	.052	.116
San Francisco	1991	110	16	2	2	0	0	14	3	1	0	3	7	11	.219	.072	.041	.039	.080
Oakland	1992	28	3	0	0	0	0	1	1	0	0	1	1	1	.104	.028	.009	.019	.028

OAKLAND ATHLETICS

Carney Lansford, 35
Bats Right   296L   844R   327G   279F

L= .126G .143L .164F   (.061/.054) .115   .090G   .107R   .128F = R

		ATBATS	1B	2B	3B	HR	HBP	BB	GDP	SB	CS	ROE	XB	RUNS	EOB%	RL#	SET-UP	DR-IN	RPA
Oakland	1990	507	117	15	1	3	6	41	10	16	14	8	33	59	.223	.097	.053	.050	.103
Oakland	1991	16	1	0	0	0	0	0	0	0	0	0	0	0	.044	.010	.002	.009	.011
Oakland	1992	496	92	30	1	7	7	43	14	7	2	12	47	67	.235	.117	.063	.055	.118

Mark McGwire, 29
Bats Right   435L   1358R   546G   393F

L= .187G .188L .189F   (.083/.077) .160   .150G   .151R   .152F = R

		ATBATS	1B	2B	3B	HR	HBP	BB	GDP	SB	CS	ROE	XB	RUNS	EOB%	RL#	SET-UP	DR-IN	RPA
Oakland	1990	523	68	16	0	39	7	101	13	2	1	6	39	114	.234	.163	.092	.083	.175
Oakland	1991	483	53	22	0	22	3	90	13	2	1	6	27	79	.226	.119	.066	.062	.128
Oakland	1992	467	61	22	0	42	5	78	10	0	1	5	33	110	.226	.192	.101	.094	.195

Jamie Quirk, 38
Bats Left   72L   488R   158G   134F

L= ....G .125L ....F   (.042/.044) .086   .095G   .082R   .067F = R

		ATBATS	1B	2B	3B	HR	HBP	BB	GDP	SB	CS	ROE	XB	RUNS	EOB%	RL#	SET-UP	DR-IN	RPA
Oakland	1990	121	25	5	1	3	1	13	1	0	0	1	4	20	.258	.136	.081	.065	.146
Oakland	1991	203	48	4	0	1	2	15	7	0	3	0	7	19	.192	.074	.038	.041	.079
Oakland	1992	177	29	7	1	2	3	13	4	0	0	4	8	19	.210	.093	.047	.047	.094

Randy Ready, 32
Bats Right   405L   250R   248G   124F

L= .147G .142L .132F   (.068/.051) .119   .086G   .081R   .071F = R

		ATBATS	1B	2B	3B	HR	HBP	BB	GDP	SB	CS	ROE	XB	RUNS	EOB%	RL#	SET-UP	DR-IN	RPA
Philadelphia	1990	217	42	9	1	1	1	29	3	3	2	2	20	26	.255	.106	.058	.047	.105
Philadelphia	1991	205	39	10	1	1	1	44	5	2	1	3	16	32	.303	.116	.071	.049	.120
Oakland	1992	125	20	2	0	3	0	24	1	1	0	1	7	18	.261	.117	.066	.053	.119

Ruben Sierra, 27
Bats Both   628L   1404R   583G   488F

L= .155G .151L .146F   (.068/.068) .136   .133G   .129R   .124F = R

		ATBATS	1B	2B	3B	HR	HBP	BB	GDP	SB	CS	ROE	XB	RUNS	EOB%	RL#	SET-UP	DR-IN	RPA
Texas	1990	608	115	37	2	16	1	36	15	9	1	5	56	79	.199	.116	.057	.060	.117
Texas	1991	661	129	44	5	25	0	49	17	16	4	7	48	105	.214	.143	.073	.072	.145
Texas	1992	500	89	30	6	14	0	25	9	12	4	2	39	66	.184	.123	.058	.066	.124
Oakland	1992	101	20	4	1	3	0	8	2	2	0	0	9	15	.207	.129	.065	.066	.131

Terry Steinbach, 30
Bats Right   395L   1014R   429G   317F

L= .116G .128L .145F   (.054/.056) .110   .091G   .103R   .120F = R

		ATBATS	1B	2B	3B	HR	HBP	BB	GDP	SB	CS	ROE	XB	RUNS	EOB%	RL#	SET-UP	DR-IN	RPA
Oakland	1990	379	69	15	2	9	4	18	11	0	2	3	28	42	.170	.095	.046	.056	.102
Oakland	1991	456	87	31	1	6	7	18	15	2	2	8	33	53	.198	.095	.050	.052	.102
Oakland	1992	438	89	20	1	12	1	42	20	2	3	6	33	60	.201	.116	.058	.060	.118

Walt Weiss, 29
Bats Both   244L   771R   295G   260F

L= .016G .044L .075F   (.041/.040) .081   .065G   .093R   .124F = R

		ATBATS	1B	2B	3B	HR	HBP	BB	GDP	SB	CS	ROE	XB	RUNS	EOB%	RL#	SET-UP	DR-IN	RPA
Oakland	1990	445	98	17	1	2	4	41	7	9	4	6	44	57	.246	.104	.061	.052	.113
Oakland	1991	133	23	6	1	0	0	12	3	6	0	1	12	14	.213	.080	.044	.044	.088
Oakland	1992	316	60	5	2	0	1	42	10	6	3	1	25	29	.213	.078	.040	.039	.079

Willie Wilson, 37
Bats Both   363L   746R   295G   265F

L= .063G .074L .087F   (.046/.047) .093   .094G   .105R   .118F = R

		ATBATS	1B	2B	3B	HR	HBP	BB	GDP	SB	CS	ROE	XB	RUNS	EOB%	RL#	SET-UP	DR-IN	RPA
Kansas City	1990	307	71	13	3	2	2	29	4	24	6	8	39	47	.269	.133	.077	.059	.136
Oakland	1991	294	52	14	4	0	4	17	11	20	5	2	24	27	.177	.075	.037	.043	.080
Oakland	1992	396	87	15	5	0	1	33	11	28	8	5	34	46	.221	.101	.053	.050	.103

PITCHERS

Throws: Neutral type, righty

John Briscoe, 25
(..../....) .160   45L   51R   710ML

		OUTS	RO	1B	2B	3B	HR	HBP	BB	GDP	SB	CS	PO	WP	BK	RUNS	EOB%	RL#	RPA
Oakland	1991	42	42	6	3	0	3	0	10	3	0	0	0	3	0	8	.152	.121	.123
Oakland	1992	21	0	10	2	0	0	0	9	1	0	1	0	2	0	7	.342	.170	.175

OAKLAND ATHLETICS

Kevin Campbell, 28

Throws: Flyball type, moderate to severe righty

(.129/.099) .113

169L   206R   367ML

		OUTS	RO	1B	2B	3B	HR	HBP	BB	GDP	SB	CS	PO	WP	BK	RUNS	EOB%	RL#	RPA
Oakland	1991	69	69	6	3	0	4	1	14	2	1	0	0	0	0	10	.164	.102	.104
Oakland	1992	195	125	49	12	1	4	0	42	5	2	5	0	2	0	34	.219	.112	.115

Jim Corsi, 31

Throws: Groundball type, extreme righty

(.136/.035) .086

237L   235R   121ML

		OUTS	RO	1B	2B	3B	HR	HBP	BB	GDP	SB	CS	PO	WP	BK	RUNS	EOB%	RL#	RPA
Houston	1991	233	233	60	9	1	6	0	18	9	8	3	0	1	1	29	.132	.081	.088
Oakland	1992	132	132	37	4	1	2	0	16	7	5	5	0	0	0	14	.117	.076	.077

Ron Darling, 32

Throws: Neutral type, moderate reverse righty

(.101/.107) .104

1142L   1028R

		OUTS	RO	1B	2B	3B	HR	HBP	BB	GDP	SB	CS	PO	WP	BK	RUNS	EOB%	RL#	RPA
New York Mets	1990	378	88	92	18	5	20	5	40	3	24	4	5	5	1	70	.174	.126	.125
New York Mets	1991	307	0	65	16	6	9	6	27	4	12	2	3	9	4	41	.172	.108	.096
Montreal	1991	51	0	15	2	2	6	1	5	1	5	0	0	4	0	18	.188	.198	.213
Oakland	1991	225	0	43	12	2	7	2	36	5	7	1	1	3	1	37	.193	.103	.108
Oakland	1992	619	0	134	44	5	15	4	67	15	10	13	1	13	0	85	.159	.095	.097

Kelly Downs, 32

Throws: Neutral type, moderate righty

(.114/.101) .108

689L   623R

		OUTS	RO	1B	2B	3B	HR	HBP	BB	GDP	SB	CS	PO	WP	BK	RUNS	EOB%	RL#	RPA
San Francisco	1990	189	24	40	14	0	2	2	16	3	11	1	0	2	1	24	.187	.088	.089
San Francisco	1991	335	167	69	16	2	12	3	44	10	15	4	0	4	1	53	.164	.098	.109
San Francisco	1992	187	72	50	10	1	4	3	24	3	5	4	0	4	0	33	.202	.103	.114
Oakland	1992	246	43	54	13	1	4	4	43	6	12	4	0	3	1	37	.210	.101	.104

Denis Eckersley, 38

Throws: Flyball type, moderate to severe righty

(.098/.063) .080

424L   425R

		OUTS	RO	1B	2B	3B	HR	HBP	BB	GDP	SB	CS	PO	WP	BK	RUNS	EOB%	RL#	RPA
Oakland	1990	220	220	29	9	1	2	0	3	3	1	2	0	0	0	12	.075	.041	.045
Oakland	1991	228	228	39	8	2	11	1	6	0	8	1	1	1	0	28	.113	.086	.089
Oakland	1992	240	240	45	11	1	5	1	5	3	9	1	0	0	0	22	.120	.071	.072

Goose Gossage, 41

Throws: Neutral type, moderate reverse righty

(.093/.109) .103

113L   203R

		OUTS	RO	1B	2B	3B	HR	HBP	BB	GDP	SB	CS	PO	WP	BK	RUNS	EOB%	RL#	RPA
Texas	1991	121	121	22	6	1	4	3	15	1	2	2	1	3	0	17	.172	.101	.101
Oakland	1992	114	114	25	2	0	5	2	15	2	4	2	0	0	0	17	.165	.102	.105

Shawn Hillegas, 28

Throws: Flyball type, moderate to severe righty

(.131/.096) .113

351L   393R   114ML

		OUTS	RO	1B	2B	3B	HR	HBP	BB	GDP	SB	CS	PO	WP	BK	RUNS	EOB%	RL#	RPA
Chi. White Sox	1990	34	34	3	0	1	0	0	4	0	1	0	0	2	0	2	.164	.054	.056
Cleveland	1991	249	205	47	12	1	7	2	39	6	6	3	0	5	0	35	.181	.099	.099
N.Y. Yankees	1992	235	86	63	17	4	12	0	32	7	15	6	1	2	0	47	.168	.132	.133
Oakland	1992	23	23	5	2	0	1	0	3	2	1	0	0	0	0	3	.112	.097	.099

Rick Honeycutt, 38

Throws: Groundball type, extreme lefty

(.073/.129) .108

214L   344R

		OUTS	RO	1B	2B	3B	HR	HBP	BB	GDP	SB	CS	PO	WP	BK	RUNS	EOB%	RL#	RPA
Oakland	1990	190	190	35	8	1	2	1	20	4	2	3	0	1	1	19	.149	.069	.076
Oakland	1991	113	113	26	6	2	3	2	17	3	5	1	0	0	0	20	.204	.110	.115
Oakland	1992	117	117	32	5	2	3	3	7	4	1	0	2	0	17	.176	.098	.101

Vince Horsman, 25

Throws: Neutral type, moderate lefty

(.087/.102) .095

85L   92R   335ML

		OUTS	RO	1B	2B	3B	HR	HBP	BB	GDP	SB	CS	PO	WP	BK	RUNS	EOB%	RL#	RPA
Toronto	1991	12	12	2	0	0	0	0	2	0	0	0	0	0	0	1	.213	.059	.060
Oakland	1992	130	130	32	4	0	3	0	17	9	0	2	0	1	0	13	.110	.072	.074

OAKLAND ATHLETICS

Mike Moore, 33

Throws: Neutral type, moderate to severe reverse righty

(.084/.118) .101   1343L 1273R

		OUTS	RO	1B	2B	3B	HR	HBP	BB	GDP	SB	CS	PO	WP	BK	RUNS	EOB%	RL#	RPA
Oakland	1990	598	0	141	41	8	14	3	82	23	17	6	0	13	0	104	.182	.105	.119
Oakland	1991	630	0	130	35	0	11	5	104	19	19	12	0	14	0	85	.183	.087	.091
Oakland	1992	669	0	162	43	4	20	8	98	26	19	13	0	22	0	108	.176	.107	.110

Gene Nelson, 32

Throws: Neutral type, extreme righty

(.179/.119) .145   303L 403R

		OUTS	RO	1B	2B	3B	HR	HBP	BB	GDP	SB	CS	PO	WP	BK	RUNS	EOB%	RL#	RPA
Oakland	1990	224	224	39	11	0	5	3	16	10	1	2	0	1	0	20	.098	.064	.069
Oakland	1991	146	146	35	9	4	12	3	22	3	4	1	0	0	0	40	.199	.158	.166
Oakland	1992	155	129	52	8	3	5	0	17	6	4	3	0	2	0	29	.178	.120	.124

Jeff Parrett, 31

Throws: Flyball type, extreme righty

(.135/.089) .111   447L 499R

		OUTS	RO	1B	2B	3B	HR	HBP	BB	GDP	SB	CS	PO	WP	BK	RUNS	EOB%	RL#	RPA
Philadelphia	1990	245	166	62	15	5	10	1	28	8	7	5	2	3	1	40	.149	.115	.115
Atlanta	1990	81	81	23	2	1	1	1	17	2	1	2	1	2	0	12	.215	.104	.097
Atlanta	1991	64	64	24	4	1	2	0	10	1	1	0	0	4	0	16	.268	.159	.147
Oakland	1992	295	295	55	17	2	7	2	39	4	14	4	0	13	0	43	.186	.099	.102

Jeff Russell, 31

Throws: Neutral type, moderate righty

(.096/.087) .091   322L 361R

		OUTS	RO	1B	2B	3B	HR	HBP	BB	GDP	SB	CS	PO	WP	BK	RUNS	EOB%	RL#	RPA
Texas	1990	76	76	15	7	0	1	0	11	2	5	0	0	2	0	11	.210	.100	.102
Texas	1991	238	238	54	6	0	11	1	25	10	1	0	0	6	0	32	.136	.097	.097
Texas	1992	170	170	38	9	1	3	2	19	3	1	2	0	3	0	22	.184	.093	.092
Oakland	1992	29	29	3	1	0	0	0	3	1	0	1	0	0	0	1	.053	.027	.028

Joe Slusarski, 26

Throws: Neutral type, moderate to severe reverse righty

(.113/.148) .130   413L 385R 431ML

		OUTS	RO	1B	2B	3B	HR	HBP	BB	GDP	SB	CS	PO	WP	BK	RUNS	EOB%	RL#	RPA
Oakland	1991	328	9	87	17	3	14	4	51	11	5	5	1	4	0	61	.186	.118	.121
Oakland	1992	228	12	50	17	3	15	6	27	5	6	4	2	0	1	46	.160	.132	.137

Dave Stewart, 35

Throws: Flyball type, moderate righty

(.121/.111) .116   1379L 1448R

		OUTS	RO	1B	2B	3B	HR	HBP	BB	GDP	SB	CS	PO	WP	BK	RUNS	EOB%	RL#	RPA
Oakland	1990	801	0	168	39	3	16	5	82	23	13	6	0	8	0	102	.158	.083	.093
Oakland	1991	678	0	169	44	8	24	9	104	19	23	9	0	12	0	132	.202	.119	.124
Oakland	1992	598	0	116	28	6	25	8	78	14	15	10	1	3	1	90	.157	.104	.107

Bruce Walton, 30

Throws: Neutral type, righty

(..../....) .111   34L 68R 517ML

		OUTS	RO	1B	2B	3B	HR	HBP	BB	GDP	SB	CS	PO	WP	BK	RUNS	EOB%	RL#	RPA
Oakland	1991	39	39	6	2	0	3	1	6	1	2	0	0	3	0	8	.175	.134	.137
Oakland	1992	30	30	12	4	0	1	0	3	0	0	0	0	0	1	9	.278	.172	.175

Bob Welch, 36

Throws: Neutral type, moderate to severe righty

(.117/.087) .103   1237L 1112R

		OUTS	RO	1B	2B	3B	HR	HBP	BB	GDP	SB	CS	PO	WP	BK	RUNS	EOB%	RL#	RPA
Oakland	1990	714	0	140	42	6	26	5	73	25	10	7	0	2	2	103	.138	.094	.104
Oakland	1991	660	0	157	34	4	25	11	88	17	12	16	1	3	2	108	.167	.102	.108
Oakland	1992	371	0	89	11	1	13	2	43	13	8	5	0	1	0	49	.147	.094	.096

Bobby Witt, 28

Throws: Neutral type, neutral righty

(.116/.114) .115   973L 1156R 35ML

		OUTS	RO	1B	2B	3B	HR	HBP	BB	GDP	SB	CS	PO	WP	BK	RUNS	EOB%	RL#	RPA
Texas	1990	666	14	151	31	3	12	4	107	18	36	7	1	11	2	97	.199	.098	.099
Texas	1991	266	13	60	18	2	4	1	73	5	18	4	0	8	0	54	.271	.129	.129
Texas	1992	484	0	109	26	3	14	2	94	19	17	8	0	6	1	77	.191	.110	.109
Oakland	1992	95	0	27	2	0	2	0	18	3	5	2	0	3	0	15	.204	.104	.108

Oakland Athletics AAA & AA Minor League Ratings

AAA (TACOMA)	AGE	BATS	POSITION	CPA	RUNS	SET-UP	DRIVE-IN	RPA
Scott Brosius	26	R	3B	265	24.8	.042	.052	.094
James Buccheri	24	R	OF	229	22.9	.057	.043	.100
Jeff Carter	29	B	OF\2B	460	47.9	.060	.044	.104
Eric Fox	29	B	OF	408	38.9	.049	.046	.095
Webster Garrison	27	R	2B\3B	513	42.5	.038	.045	.083
Dan Grunhard	29	L	OF	398	35.3	.042	.047	.089
Mike Heath	37	R	C\OF	254	14.7	.025	.033	.058
Keith Lockhart	28	L	2B	398	40.3	.052	.049	.101
Henry Mercedes	23	R	C	280	17.7	.030	.033	.063
Troy Neel	27	L	OF	470	76.7	.095	.068	.163
Gus Polidor	31	R	SS	399	27.8	.033	.037	.070
Jack Smith	28	R	SS\2B\3B	359	31.1	.044	.043	.087
Ron Witmeyer	1B	25	L	561	46.2	.041	.041	.082

AA (HUNTSVILLE)	AGE	BATS	POSITION	CPA	RUNS	SET-UP	DRIVE-IN	RPA
Kurt Abbott	23	R	SS	535	45.7	.041	.044	.085
Marcos Armas	23	R	1B	565	61.1	.052	.056	.108
Dean Borrelli	26	R	C	271	15.4	.027	.030	.057
Jorge Brito	26	R	C	124	10.1	.042	.039	.081
Mike Conte	25	R	OF\1B	334	26.2	.041	.037	.078
Kevin Dattola	25	B	OF	369	30.8	.043	.041	.084
Eric Helfand	23	L	C	124	7.9	.027	.037	.064
David Jacas	28	R	OF	491	45.9	.048	.045	.093
Scott Lydy	24	R	OF	461	61.7	.080	.054	.134
Francisco Matos	22	R	2B\SS	167	9.8	.025	.033	.058
Craig Paquette	23	R	3B	564	50.5	.038	.052	.090
Darryl Vice	26	B	2B\3B	587	55.7	.055	.040	.095

AAA Pitchers	Age	Throws	Outs	RPA	AA Pitchers	Age	Throws	Outs	RPA
Dana Allison	26	L	318	.142	Scott Erwin	25	R	107	.140
Jeff Bittiger	30	R	445	.124	Chaon Garland	23	R	127	.196
John Briscoe	25	R	234	.164	Chad Kuhn	26	L	151	.163
Steve Chitren	25	R	186	.166	Dave Latter	26	R	264	.133
Jim Corsi	31	R	88	.087	Mike Mohler	24	L	241	.133
Johnny Guzman	21	L	475	.135	Gavin Osteen	23	L	350	.148
Reggie Harris	24	R	449	.160	Bronswell Patrick	22	R	538	.144
Jeff Musselman	29	L	316	.124	Steve Phoenix	24	R	522	.121
Tim Peek	24	R	263	.131	Todd Revenig	23	R	191	.089
Mike Raczka	30	L	146	.109	Roger Smithberg	26	R	108	.157
Dave Schmidt	35	R	208	.128	Ricky Strebeck	26	R	155	.175
Joe Slusarski	26	R	172	.147	Pat Wernig	27	L	121	.134
Todd Van Poppel	21	R	136	.142	Bill Wilkinson	28	L	101	.253
Bruce Walton	30	R	244	.114					
Weston Weber	28	R	282	.144					
David Zancanaro	23	L	317	.145					

SEATTLE MARINERS

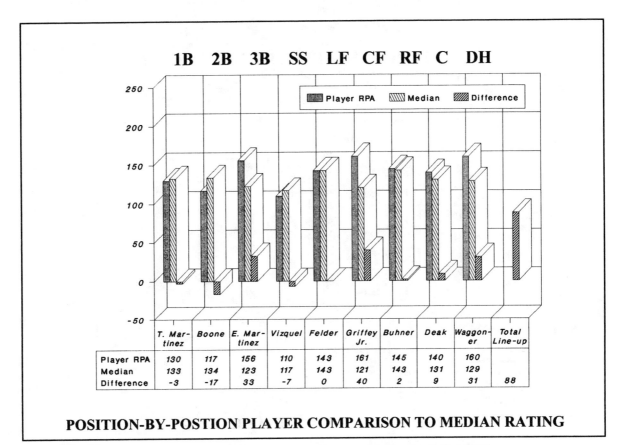

	T. Mar-tinez	Boone	E. Mar-tinez	Vizquel	Felder	Griffey Jr.	Buhner	Deak	Waggon-er	Total Line-up
Player RPA	130	117	156	110	143	161	145	140	160	
Median	133	134	123	117	143	121	143	131	129	
Difference	-3	-17	33	-7	0	40	2	9	31	88

POSITION-BY-POSTION PLAYER COMPARISON TO MEDIAN RATING

DEFENSIVE TEAM AND STADIUM DATA FOR THE LAST 3 YEARS:

TEAM DEFENSE BY POSITION:

POSITION-BY-POSITION STADIUM CHARACTERISTICS:

		1990	1991	1992	STADIUM CHARACTERISTICS
1B:	Home	-0.2	-0.9	+0.6	Easy to play
	Away	-1.5	-1.2	+2.2	
2B:	Home	+0.1	-0.9	-4.1	Slightly hard to play
	Away	+1.4	-3.2	-1.5	
3B:	Home	-0.3	-2.2	+3.6	Average
	Away	+5.6	-1.0	-3.8	
SS:	Home	-3.3	+1.5	-1.0	Average
	Away	-5.5	+1.6	0.0	
LF:	Home	-2.1	-3.1	-0.3	Average
	Away	-3.6	-6.8	-6.5	
CF:	Home	-7.6	-8.5	+3.9	Slightly hard to play
	Away	-7.4	-8.3	+2.6	
RF:	Home	+8.9	+7.7	-4.2	Slightly hard to play
	Away	-0.3	+0.4	-4.0	
Total Home:		-4.5	-6.4	-0.6	
Total Away:		-11.3	-18.5	-11.1	

Comments: All four years of my defensive study have shown the Mariners to have about a 5 or 10 run home field advantage. Too bad they haven't taken advantage of this with superior defensive players. While Seattle's defense was somewhat porous in '92, it marked a strong step forward from the awful defense of '91. The Mariners won't miss Harold Reynolds' glove, since his range has shrunk markedly over the last 2 years.

SEATTLE MARINERS

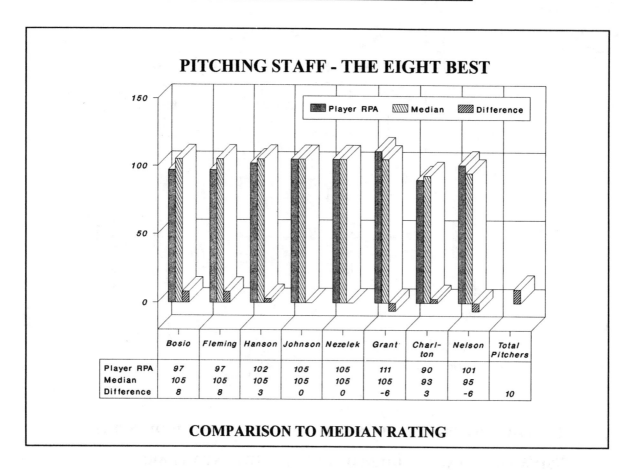

PITCHING STAFF - THE EIGHT BEST

Legend: ■ Player RPA ▨ Median ▨ Difference

	Bosio	Fleming	Hanson	Johnson	Nezelek	Grant	Charl-ton	Nelson	Total Pitchers
Player RPA	97	97	102	105	105	111	90	101	
Median	105	105	105	105	105	105	93	95	
Difference	8	8	3	0	0	-6	3	-6	10

COMPARISON TO MEDIAN RATING

SUGGESTED LINE-UPS (with set-up RPA & drive-in RPA ratings):

Vs: Left-handed Groundball
C:	B. Deak	91-63
3B:	E. Martinez	103-80
CF:	K. Griffey, Jr.	90-89
RF:	J. Buhner	85-87
DH:	H. Cotto	66-66
2B:	B. Boone	57-71
1B:	T. Martinez	45-59
LF:	M. Felder	55-50
SS:	O. Vizquel	40-37

Vs: Neutral Lefty Pitchers
C:	B. Deak	91-63
3B:	E. Martinez	97-76
CF:	K. Griffey, Jr.	90-89
DH:	H. Cotto	70-70
RF:	J. Buhner	79-81
2B:	B. Boone	57-71
1B:	T. Martinez	54-69
LF:	M. Felder	63-58
SS:	O. Vizquel	45-41

Vs: Left-handed Flyball
C:	B. Deak	91-63
3B:	E. Martinez	91-71
LF:	M. Felder	76-70
CF:	K. Griffey, Jr.	90-90
DH:	H. Cotto	74-74
RF:	J. Buhner	72-74
1B:	T. Martinez	62-80
2B:	B. Boone	57-71
SS:	O. Vizquel	50-47

Vs: Right-handed Groundball
C:	B. Deak	81-53
DH:	A. Waggoner	80-60
3B:	E. Martinez	94-73
CF:	K. Griffey, Jr.	81-80
RF:	J. Buhner	71-72
2B:	B. Boone	47-61
1B:	T. Martinez	44-58
LF:	M. Felder	52-47
SS:	O. Vizquel	51-48

Vs: Neutral Righty Pitchers
C:	B. Deak	81-53
DH:	A. Waggoner	80-60
3B:	E. Martinez	88-69
CF:	K. Griffey, Jr.	81-80
RF:	J. Buhner	65-66
1B:	T. Martinez	53-68
LF:	M. Felder	60-55
2B:	B. Boone	47-61
SS:	O. Vizquel	56-52

Vs: Right-handed Flyball
C:	B. Deak	81-53
DH:	A. Waggoner	80-60
3B:	E. Martinez	82-64
LF:	M. Felder	73-67
CF:	K. Griffey, Jr.	81-80
1B:	T. Martinez	61-79
SS:	O. Vizquel	62-57
RF:	J. Buhner	58-59
2B:	B. Boone	47-61

Comments: A very respectable and much improved offense! The keys are the signings of Brian Deak, Aubrey Waggoner and Mike Felder. Deak has a remarkable ability to get on base, despite a low batting average. That's why I've got him leading off. I hope they don't think Mackey Sasser is any type of answer (over Deak) at catcher. This team still needs to find a way to deal with some of the offensive weakness at shortstop since Vizquel is so very weak against lefty pitching.

SEATTLE MARINERS

The Seattle Mariners are one of my three "sleeper" teams for 1993. The other two "sleeper" picks are my choices to win their division. That's not the case here, but the Mariners are not that far away. They could steal the '93 western division title with any kind of luck.

The western division, as stated earlier, will be the most wide-open division in baseball in '93 and the Mariners figure to be right in the middle of the pennant scramble.

What happened to change this ugly duckling of a team into a contender? I don't know the specifics of what they've done, but at times this winter I became convinced they were seriously applying my methods since almost every key 6-year minor league free-agent we (the Montreal Expos) went after was also being pursued by one other club: the Seattle Mariners.

Whatever method they are using, they are using it well. They signed, in my opinion, the top two minor league free agents this winter from what was truly a fabulous bumper crop of quality free agents. Brian Deak is a *premier* hitting Major League catcher. He won't hit for a high batting average, but who cares? He'll be on base constantly and has good power. He doesn't have a strong throwing arm, but more than makes up for it with his bat. Outfielder Aubrey Waggoner is an even better hitter than is Deak. In addition to the above two, the Mariners also signed AA pitcher Andy Nezelek, who had an outstanding year in '92. He might need a little time at AAA, however.

Add to those signing's the acquisition of a premier starting pitcher (Chris Bosio) and a premier outfielder (Mike Felder), plus the services of a talented youngster like Bret Boone and you have the elements for a big change for the better in Seattle.

The trade of Kevin Mitchell for Norm Charlton will help this team, even though I think that the Reds got more value. The Mariner bullpen was a disaster in '92. The only way this team has any chance in '93 is in correcting this problem and Charlton certainly fills the bill. But don't rejoice for the Mariner bullpen. It's still one of the weakest in the Major Leagues, but at least the hemorrhaging is over (provided Charlton stays healthy).

The signing of Greg Litton will help a little, since he's a decent utility player. The signing of Mackey Sasser, however, is more problematical. He's got a world of hitting ability, but is about as undisciplined a hitter as you'll find anywhere. I've essentially written him off as ever living up to the talent he possesses. I think the Mariners would have been better off pursuing someone else in the free-agent market (or retaining the services of Lance Parrish) or simply rely on Bill Haselman to fill that spot.

I was surprised that the Mariners parted with AAA third baseman Frank Bolick. His path was blocked by Edgar Martinez, but everyone can use a big bat like Bolick's. He can flat hit. He's certainly a much better hitter than Pete O'Brien.

Seattle's Projected record for 1993: 82--80, good for 3rd place in the division.

SEATTLE MARINERS

Rich Amaral, 30

Bats Right   46L   82R   24G   42F   887ML

L= ....G   .128L   ....F   (.046/.058) .104   ....G   .091R   ....F = R

		ATBATS	1B	2B	3B	HR	HBP	BB	GDP	SB	CS	ROE	XB	RUNS	EOB%	RL#	SET-UP	DR-IN	RPA
Seattle	1991	16	1	0	0	0	1	1	1	0	0	0	1	0	.090	.018	.006	.012	.018
Seattle	1992	100	20	3	0	1	0	5	4	4	2	1	4	8	.150	.072	.031	.042	.073

Mike Blowers, 27

Bats Right   104L   177R   69G   57F   746ML

L= .107G   .124L   .145F   (.046/.052) .098   .065G   .082R   .103F = R

		ATBATS	1B	2B	3B	HR	HBP	BB	GDP	SB	CS	ROE	XB	RUNS	EOB%	RL#	SET-UP	DR-IN	RPA
Yankees	1990	144	18	4	0	5	1	11	3	1	0	1	8	14	.152	.087	.038	.051	.089
Yankees	1991	35	6	0	0	1	0	4	1	0	0	2	1	4	.226	.102	.053	.049	.102
Seattle	1992	73	10	3	0	1	0	6	3	0	0	0	1	5	.145	.063	.026	.038	.064

Bret Boone, 23

Bats Right   43L   95R   42G   36F   1089ML

L= .068G   .087L   ....F   (.046/.060) .106   .095G   .114R   ....F = R

		ATBATS	1B	2B	3B	HR	HBP	BB	GDP	SB	CS	ROE	XB	RUNS	EOB%	RL#	SET-UP	DR-IN	RPA
Seattle	1992	129	17	4	0	4	1	4	4	1	2	1	7	10	.098	.068	.022	.047	.069

Greg Briley, 27

Bats Left   83L   922R   284G   241F

L= .056G   .068L   .083F   (.044/.051) .095   .085G   .097R   .112F = R

		ATBATS	1B	2B	3B	HR	HBP	BB	GDP	SB	CS	ROE	XB	RUNS	EOB%	RL#	SET-UP	DR-IN	RPA
Seattle	1990	337	58	18	2	5	1	37	6	16	4	4	39	44	.229	.113	.060	.054	.114
Seattle	1991	381	77	17	3	2	0	27	7	23	12	0	24	37	.187	.085	.041	.046	.087
Seattle	1992	200	40	10	0	5	1	4	4	9	2	3	6	24	.176	.108	.050	.060	.110

Jay Buhner, 28

Bats Right   414L   875R   353G   285F

L= .168G   .156L   .142F   (.067/.069) .136   .139G   .127R   .113F = R

		ATBATS	1B	2B	3B	HR	HBP	BB	GDP	SB	CS	ROE	XB	RUNS	EOB%	RL#	SET-UP	DR-IN	RPA
Seattle	1990	163	26	12	0	7	4	16	6	2	2	0	9	24	.197	.129	.063	.066	.129
Seattle	1991	406	54	14	4	27	6	48	10	0	1	2	31	69	.188	.138	.067	.075	.142
Seattle	1992	543	88	16	3	25	6	69	12	0	6	6	19	85	.210	.129	.066	.066	.132

Dave Cochrane, 29

Bats Both   125L   254R   95G   99F   204ML

L= .057G   .089L   .120F   (.044/.044) .088   .055G   .087R   .118F = R

		ATBATS	1B	2B	3B	HR	HBP	BB	GDP	SB	CS	ROE	XB	RUNS	EOB%	RL#	SET-UP	DR-IN	RPA
Seattle	1990	20	3	0	0	0	0	0	0	0	0	0	0	1	.107	.033	.011	.022	.033
Seattle	1991	178	29	13	0	2	1	9	3	0	1	1	7	17	.189	.086	.042	.046	.088
Seattle	1992	152	31	5	0	2	1	12	3	1	0	0	6	17	.209	.096	.049	.048	.097

Henry Cotto, 31

Bats Right   498L   398R   211G   226F

L= .134G   .142L   .150F   (.062/.062) .124   .094G   .102R   .110F = R

		ATBATS	1B	2B	3B	HR	HBP	BB	GDP	SB	CS	ROE	XB	RUNS	EOB%	RL#	SET-UP	DR-IN	RPA
Seattle	1990	355	71	14	3	4	4	20	13	21	3	7	33	39	.198	.099	.049	.051	.100
Seattle	1991	177	40	6	2	6	2	10	7	16	3	3	18	27	.197	.130	.065	.068	.133
Seattle	1992	294	59	11	1	5	1	11	2	23	2	6	29	37	.211	.118	.060	.059	.119

Ken Griffey, Jr., 23

Bats Left   606L   1278R   494G   451F

L= .167G   .167L   .168F   (.078/.077) .155   .149G   .149R   .150F = R

		ATBATS	1B	2B	3B	HR	HBP	BB	GDP	SB	CS	ROE	XB	RUNS	EOB%	RL#	SET-UP	DR-IN	RPA
Seattle	1990	597	122	28	7	22	2	51	12	16	14	3	56	92	.205	.138	.069	.070	.139
Seattle	1991	548	114	42	1	22	1	50	10	18	7	3	59	101	.238	.156	.085	.075	.160
Seattle	1992	565	104	39	4	27	5	29	15	10	5	7	51	95	.192	.149	.073	.078	.151

Dann Howitt, 28

Bats Left   16L   151R   45G   44F   880ML

L= ....G L   ....F   (.048/.055) .103   .074G   .111R   .149F = R

		ATBATS	1B	2B	3B	HR	HBP	BB	GDP	SB	CS	ROE	XB	RUNS	EOB%	RL#	SET-UP	DR-IN	RPA
Oakland	1990	22	2	0	1	0	0	3	0	0	0	1	1	2	.237	.085	.046	.041	.087
Oakland	1991	42	5	1	0	1	0	1	1	0	0	0	2	3	.088	.051	.016	.039	.055
Oakland	1992	48	5	0	0	1	0	4	4	0	0	0	1	2	.057	.033	.007	.027	.034
Seattle	1992	37	4	4	1	1	0	3	2	1	1	0	2	5	.140	.101	.042	.062	.104

Edgar Martinez, 29

Bats Right   527L   1294R   476G   435F

L= .181G   .171L   .160F   (.090/.070) .160   .165G   .155R   .144F = R

		ATBATS	1B	2B	3B	HR	HBP	BB	GDP	SB	CS	ROE	XB	RUNS	EOB%	RL#	SET-UP	DR-IN	RPA
Seattle	1990	487	107	27	2	11	5	71	13	1	4	3	40	82	.271	.142	.081	.062	.143
Seattle	1991	544	117	35	1	14	8	75	19	0	4	7	64	96	.267	.140	.081	.062	.143
Seattle	1992	528	114	46	3	18	4	52	15	14	4	10	50	109	.266	.174	.099	.078	.177

SEATTLE MARINERS

Tino Martinez, 25

Bats Left   168L   553R   185G   185F   532ML

L= .095G .114L .133F **(.049/.063) .112** .093G .112R .131F = R

		ATBATS	1B	2B	3B	HR	HBP	BB	GDP	SB	CS	ROE	XB	RUNS	EOB%	RL#	SET-UP	DR-IN	RPA
Seattle	1990	68	11	4	0	0	0	9	0	0	0	2	3	8	.280	.103	.059	.044	.103
Seattle	1991	112	17	2	0	4	0	11	2	0	0	0	5	12	.171	.092	.042	.052	.094
Seattle	1992	460	81	19	2	16	2	33	24	2	1	2	23	53	.153	.098	.042	.058	.100

John Moses, 35

Bats Both   30L   216R   83G   51F   641ML

L= ....G ....L ....F **(.044/.035) .079** .050G .076R .118F = R

		ATBATS	1B	2B	3B	HR	HBP	BB	GDP	SB	CS	ROE	XB	RUNS	EOB%	RL#	SET-UP	DR-IN	RPA
Minnesota	1990	172	33	3	1	1	2	18	4	2	3	3	19	16	.214	.086	.043	.041	.084
Detroit	1991	21	0	1	0	0	0	2	0	4	0	1	2	1	.178	.056	.025	.030	.055
Seattle	1992	22	2	1	0	0	0	5	0	0	0	1	0	3	.300	.090	.054	.037	.091

Pete O'Brien, 34

Bats Left   414L   1057R   383G   360F

L= .069G .085L .101F **(.048/.056) .104** .095G .111R .127F = R

		ATBATS	1B	2B	3B	HR	HBP	BB	GDP	SB	CS	ROE	XB	RUNS	EOB%	RL#	SET-UP	DR-IN	RPA
Seattle	1990	366	59	18	0	5	2	43	12	0	0	1	19	38	.206	.089	.045	.045	.090
Seattle	1991	560	90	29	3	17	1	37	14	0	1	2	30	65	.173	.099	.046	.056	.102
Seattle	1992	396	58	15	1	14	0	32	8	2	1	6	16	48	.178	.105	.049	.058	.107

Lance Parrish, 36

Bats Right   367L   914R   320G   314F

L= .109G .114L .119F **(.049/.062) .111** .106G .111R .116F = R

		ATBATS	1B	2B	3B	HR	HBP	BB	GDP	SB	CS	ROE	XB	RUNS	EOB%	RL#	SET-UP	DR-IN	RPA
California	1990	470	88	14	0	24	5	42	12	2	2	5	20	70	.198	.134	.064	.067	.131
California	1991	402	56	12	0	19	5	33	7	0	1	1	14	49	.165	.107	.049	.061	.110
California	1992	83	13	2	0	4	0	4	1	0	0	1	0	10	.153	.111	.048	.064	.112
Seattle	1992	192	25	11	1	8	1	17	6	1	1	1	5	25	.165	.109	.049	.062	.111

Harold Reynolds, 32

Bats Both   563L   1403R   504G   464F

L= .107G .095L .082F **(.055/.049) .104** .119G .107R .094F = R

		ATBATS	1B	2B	3B	HR	HBP	BB	GDP	SB	CS	ROE	XB	RUNS	EOB%	RL#	SET-UP	DR-IN	RPA
Seattle	1990	642	116	36	5	5	3	78	9	31	19	9	68	81	.237	.110	.059	.052	.111
Seattle	1991	631	117	34	6	3	5	70	11	28	9	12	66	81	.249	.108	.060	.050	.110
Seattle	1992	458	84	23	3	3	3	44	12	15	12	7	39	51	.209	.095	.048	.048	.096

Jeff Schaefer, 32

Bats Right   165L   198R   116G   82F   43ML

L= .082G .074L .063F **(.025/.039) .064** .064G .056R .045F = R

		ATBATS	1B	2B	3B	HR	HBP	BB	GDP	SB	CS	ROE	XB	RUNS	EOB%	RL#	SET-UP	DR-IN	RPA
Seattle	1990	107	19	3	0	0	2	3	1	4	1	3	10	8	.194	.073	.036	.038	.074
Seattle	1991	164	32	7	1	1	0	5	7	3	1	4	8	14	.165	.073	.033	.042	.075
Seattle	1992	70	5	2	0	1	0	2	2	0	1	1	7	3	.062	.036	.008	.028	.036

Dave Valle, 32

Bats Right   390L   775R   306G   289F

L= .137G .111L .084F **(.045/.048) .093** .110G .084R .057F = R

		ATBATS	1B	2B	3B	HR	HBP	BB	GDP	SB	CS	ROE	XB	RUNS	EOB%	RL#	SET-UP	DR-IN	RPA
Seattle	1990	308	44	15	0	7	7	45	11	1	2	5	22	39	.227	.105	.055	.050	.105
Seattle	1991	324	46	8	1	8	9	34	19	0	2	3	19	30	.159	.073	.033	.042	.075
Seattle	1992	367	62	16	1	9	8	26	7	0	1	6	15	46	.210	.108	.055	.055	.110

Omar Vizquel, 25

Bats Both   300L   990R   337G   291F   27ML

L= .070G .079L .090F **(.048/.045) .093** .092G .101R .112F = R

		ATBATS	1B	2B	3B	HR	HBP	BB	GDP	SB	CS	ROE	XB	RUNS	EOB%	RL#	SET-UP	DR-IN	RPA
Seattle	1990	255	56	3	2	2	0	18	7	4	2	2	15	24	.192	.084	.041	.044	.085
Seattle	1991	426	77	16	4	1	0	45	8	7	2	5	27	44	.226	.086	.046	.042	.088
Seattle	1992	483	118	20	4	0	2	32	14	15	14	5	34	53	.211	.096	.049	.048	.097

PITCHERS

Throws: Groundball type, extreme righty

Jim Acker, 34

(.145/.109) .124   356L   526R

		OUTS	RO	1B	2B	3B	HR	HBP	BB	GDP	SB	CS	PO	WP	BK	RUNS	EOB%	RL#	RPA
Toronto	1990	275	275	72	21	1	9	3	25	6	6	7	0	4	1	42	.166	.110	.108
Toronto	1991	265	204	50	10	1	16	2	31	5	10	3	0	7	0	41	.148	.113	.111
Seattle	1992	92	92	30	11	0	4	0	11	1	1	1	0	1	0	23	.235	.151	.155

SEATTLE MARINERS

Juan Agosto, 34
Throws: Groundball type, neutral lefty
(.112/.113) .113   299L   637R

		OUTS	RO	1B	2B	3B	HR	HBP	BB	GDP	SB	CS	PO	WP	BK	RUNS	EOB%	RL#	RPA
Houston	1990	277	277	70	15	2	4	7	31	5	5	1	0	1	0	45	.214	.097	.107
St. Louis	1991	258	258	67	17	4	4	8	35	14	7	5	0	6	0	43	.176	.096	.109
St. Louis	1992	95	95	28	8	1	2	3	7	5	3	0	0	2	0	18	.183	.105	.123
Seattle	1992	55	47	22	5	0	0	0	3	2	3	0	0	0	0	10	.221	.113	.115

Kevin D. Brown, 26
Throws: Groundball type, extreme lefty
(.074/.148) .132   80L   298R   937ML

		OUTS	RO	1B	2B	3B	HR	HBP	BB	GDP	SB	CS	PO	WP	BK	RUNS	EOB%	RL#	RPA
New York Mets	1990	6	6	2	0	0	0	0	1	0	0	0	0	0	0	1	.268	.095	.095
Milwaukee	1990	63	16	11	2	0	1	1	6	0	1	0	1	2	0	6	.169	.075	.074
Milwaukee	1991	191	24	43	16	1	6	1	32	6	5	4	0	6	0	33	.191	.117	.117
Seattle	1992	9	9	1	1	1	0	3	1	0	0	0	0	0	3	.164	.183	.192

Norm Charlton, 29
Throws: Groundball type, moderate lefty
(.117/.080) .088   308L   1046R

		OUTS	RO	1B	2B	3B	HR	HBP	BB	GDP	SB	CS	PO	WP	BK	RUNS	EOB%	RL#	RPA
Cincinnati	1990	463	152	99	20	2	10	4	66	19	17	4	1	9	1	59	.164	.091	.093
Cincinnati	1991	325	128	69	13	4	6	6	30	10	10	7	0	11	0	35	.140	.080	.077
Cincinnati	1992	244	244	53	18	1	7	3	22	7	15	4	0	8	0	36	.156	.098	.103

Rich DeLucia, 28
Throws: Flyball type, extreme righty
(.150/.088) .118   608L   646R   162ML

		OUTS	RO	1B	2B	3B	HR	HBP	BB	GDP	SB	CS	PO	WP	BK	RUNS	EOB%	RL#	RPA
Seattle	1990	108	0	22	4	2	2	0	9	2	0	1	0	0	0	11	.149	.081	.079
Seattle	1991	546	14	107	35	3	31	4	74	13	4	9	1	10	0	90	.156	.114	.111
Seattle	1992	251	100	60	26	1	13	2	34	6	5	2	1	1	0	54	.195	.134	.138

Brian Fisher, 30
Throws: Flyball type, moderate to severe righty
(.140/.105) .123   207L   198R   661ML

		OUTS	RO	1B	2B	3B	HR	HBP	BB	GDP	SB	CS	PO	WP	BK	RUNS	EOB%	RL#	RPA
Houston	1990	15	15	7	0	1	1	0	0	1	0	0	0	0	0	4	.131	.134	.154
Seattle	1992	274	33	51	20	0	9	1	45	4	6	3	1	3	1	44	.196	.107	.110

Dave Fleming, 23
Throws: Neutral type, neutral reverse lefty
(.103/.101) .101   159L   833R   627ML

		OUTS	RO	1B	2B	3B	HR	HBP	BB	GDP	SB	CS	PO	WP	BK	RUNS	EOB%	RL#	RPA
Seattle	1991	53	18	9	6	1	3	3	3	1	1	0	1	0	8	.106	.107	.104
Seattle	1992	685	0	155	53	4	13	4	57	16	18	14	0	8	1	88	.155	.089	.091

Eric Gunderson, 26
Throws: Flyball type lefty
(..../.146) .138   35L   115R   848ML

		OUTS	RO	1B	2B	3B	HR	HBP	BB	GDP	SB	CS	PO	WP	BK	RUNS	EOB%	RL#	RPA
San Francisco	1990	59	7	19	3	0	2	0	10	0	2	2	1	0	0	12	.209	.122	.124
San Francisco	1991	10	10	4	2	0	0	0	1	0	0	0	0	0	0	3	.307	.162	.162
Seattle	1992	28	28	8	3	0	1	1	2	0	1	3	0	0	2	4	.115	.098	.102

Mark Grant, 29
Throws: Neutral type, moderate to severe righty
(.122/.096) .109   363L   351R

		OUTS	RO	1B	2B	3B	HR	HBP	BB	GDP	SB	CS	PO	WP	BK	RUNS	EOB%	RL#	RPA
San Diego	1990	117	117	30	12	0	5	0	11	4	4	0	0	1	1	22	.181	.126	.125
Atlanta	1990	157	145	44	10	3	4	1	15	4	8	3	0	1	0	25	.179	.113	.107
Seattle	1992	243	67	71	22	1	6	2	20	11	4	2	0	2	0	39	.170	.106	.109

Erik Hanson, 27
Throws: Groundball type, extreme reverse righty
(.076/.130) .102   1239L   1173R

		OUTS	RO	1B	2B	3B	HR	HBP	BB	GDP	SB	CS	PO	WP	BK	RUNS	EOB%	RL#	RPA
Seattle	1990	708	0	151	35	4	15	2	62	17	18	8	1	10	1	79	.148	.085	.083
Seattle	1991	524	0	123	36	7	16	2	54	16	11	10	0	14	1	75	.156	.101	.098
Seattle	1992	560	9	157	34	4	14	7	56	25	15	4	0	6	0	87	.171	.102	.105

SEATTLE MARINERS

Randy Johnson, 29

Throws: Neutral type, extreme lefty

(.070/.107) .103   274L   2385R

		OUTS	RO	1B	2B	3B	HR	HBP	BB	GDP	SB	CS	PO	WP	BK	RUNS	EOB%	RL#	RPA
Seattle	1990	659	0	118	26	4	26	5	118	16	28	8	1	4	2	99	.181	.108	.106
Seattle	1991	604	0	103	32	1	15	12	152	22	18	9	0	12	2	93	.218	.104	.101
Seattle	1992	631	0	106	33	2	13	18	143	14	42	16	0	13	1	100	.218	.101	.105

Calvin Jones, 29

Throws: Flyball type, moderate reverse righty

(.102/.113) .108   182L   259R   145ML

		OUTS	RO	1B	2B	3B	HR	HBP	BB	GDP	SB	CS	PO	WP	BK	RUNS	EOB%	RL#	RPA
Seattle	1991	139	139	28	4	1	0	1	24	6	5	1	0	6	0	14	.185	.071	.069
Seattle	1992	185	170	32	9	1	8	2	46	5	6	3	0	10	0	36	.216	.123	.126

Randy Kramer, 32

Throws: Neutral type, moderate to severe righty

(.150/.128) .139   140L   136R   839ML

		OUTS	RO	1B	2B	3B	HR	HBP	BB	GDP	SB	CS	PO	WP	BK	RUNS	EOB%	RL#	RPA
Pittsburgh	1990	77	50	20	4	0	3	2	5	1	11	2	0	0	0	13	.164	.115	.122
Chicago Cubs	1990	61	42	14	1	2	3	1	10	0	3	0	0	0	0	13	.234	.146	.136
Seattle	1992	49	0	22	6	0	2	1	7	2	3	0	0	0	0	16	.272	.178	.183

Tim Leary, 34

Throws: Groundball type, moderate reverse righty

(.117/.131) .124   1008L   953R

		OUTS	RO	1B	2B	3B	HR	HBP	BB	GDP	SB	CS	PO	WP	BK	RUNS	EOB%	RL#	RPA
N.Y. Yankees	1990	624	0	144	39	1	18	7	77	20	18	8	5	23	0	86	.164	.100	.096
N.Y. Yankees	1991	362	59	96	32	2	20	4	56	13	10	5	0	10	0	75	.195	.141	.133
N.Y. Yankees	1992	291	12	56	19	0	9	4	55	14	17	4	0	7	0	45	.178	.105	.106
Seattle	1992	132	0	35	7	2	3	5	27	4	10	1	0	2	0	29	.255	.132	.136

Jeff Nelson, 26

Throws: Neutral type, extreme righty

(.129/.086) .102   119L   200R   259ML

		OUTS	RO	1B	2B	3B	HR	HBP	BB	GDP	SB	CS	PO	WP	BK	RUNS	EOB%	RL#	RPA
Seattle	1992	243	243	51	10	3	7	6	32	9	4	3	0	2	0	34	.165	.094	.097

Clay Parker, 30

Throws: Groundball type, extreme reverse righty

(.095/.137) .120   180L   260R   555ML

		OUTS	RO	1B	2B	3B	HR	HBP	BB	GDP	SB	CS	PO	WP	BK	RUNS	EOB%	RL#	RPA
N.Y. Yankees	1990	66	23	10	4	0	5	0	6	0	2	0	1	0	0	9	.109	.108	.104
Detroit	1990	153	147	30	7	2	6	1	20	4	6	2	0	3	0	22	.161	.107	.104
Seattle	1992	100	14	29	12	0	6	2	11	4	3	1	0	1	0	24	.191	.145	.150

Dennis Powell, 29

Throws: Neutral type, extreme lefty

(.073/.131) .115   119L   318R   761ML

		OUTS	RO	1B	2B	3B	HR	HBP	BB	GDP	SB	CS	PO	WP	BK	RUNS	EOB%	RL#	RPA
Milwaukee	1990	118	9	46	10	3	0	1	19	2	6	1	1	2	0	28	.279	.144	.144
Seattle	1990	9	9	3	1	1	0	1	2	0	1	0	0	0	0	4	.377	.221	.217
Seattle	1992	171	171	31	13	0	5	3	27	7	3	3	0	2	0	24	.163	.095	.097

Dave Schmidt, 35

Throws: Neutral type, extreme righty

(.158/.101) .140   248L   112R   292ML

		OUTS	RO	1B	2B	3B	HR	HBP	BB	GDP	SB	CS	PO	WP	BK	RUNS	EOB%	RL#	RPA
Montreal	1990	144	144	43	9	3	3	0	8	5	7	1	0	1	0	23	.165	.105	.112
Montreal	1991	13	13	6	1	0	2	0	2	0	0	0	0	0	0	7	.252	.249	.273
Seattle	1992	10	10	5	1	0	1	0	3	0	0	0	0	0	0	5	.340	.250	.258

Mike Schooler, 30

Throws: Neutral type, moderate righty

(.115/.098) .106   270L   297R

		OUTS	RO	1B	2B	3B	HR	HBP	BB	GDP	SB	CS	PO	WP	BK	RUNS	EOB%	RL#	RPA
Seattle	1990	168	168	32	8	2	5	1	11	2	5	1	0	1	0	20	.150	.091	.089
Seattle	1991	103	103	20	2	1	2	0	10	2	3	0	0	2	1	11	.160	.079	.076
Seattle	1992	155	155	41	6	1	7	1	18	3	8	1	0	0	0	29	.188	.121	.124

Russ Swan, 28

Throws: Groundball type, extreme lefty

(.049/.120) .101   252L   683R

		OUTS	RO	1B	2B	3B	HR	HBP	BB	GDP	SB	CS	PO	WP	BK	RUNS	EOB%	RL#	RPA
San Francisco	1990	7	0	6	0	0	0	0	4	0	0	0	0	1	0	4	.491	.255	.258
Seattle	1990	141	20	29	9	1	3	0	16	9	5	0	0	0	1	15	.129	.082	.080
Seattle	1991	236	236	56	17	0	8	0	21	13	7	1	0	8	0	30	.131	.093	.090
Seattle	1992	313	159	70	22	4	8	3	38	9	5	2	0	6	0	50	.186	.105	.108

Seattle Mariners AAA & AA Minor League Ratings

AAA (CALGARY)	AGE	BATS	POSITION	CPA	RUNS	SET-UP	DRIVE-IN	RPA
Rich Amaral	30	R	SS\2B	478	52.3	.064	.045	.109
Kent Anderson	29	R	SS\OF	258	15.4	.030	.030	.060
Mike Blowers	27	R	3B	363	42.6	.064	.053	.117
Frank Bolick	26	B	3B	586	77.0	.069	.062	.131
Bret Boone	23	R	2B	516	589	.061	.053	.114
Jim Bowie	27	L	1B	528	50.7	.049	.047	.096
Dave Brundage	28	L	OF	389	32.9	.048	.037	.085
Benny DiStefano	30	L	OF\1B	127	11.5	.050	.041	.091
Billy Haselman	26	R	OF\C	427	46.3	.053	.055	.108
Chris Howard	26	R	C	347	22.5	.027	.038	.065
Dann Howitt	28	L	OF	366	39.3	.057	.050	.107
John Moses	35	B	OF	286	22.1	.038	.039	.077
Greg Pirkl	22	R	1B	563	49.4	.039	.049	.088
Shane Turner	29	L	OF	287	23.9	.044	.039	.083
Jeff Wetherby	29	L	OF	320	25.2	.039	.040	.079
Ted Williams	27	B	OF	271	18.2	.030	.037	.067

AA (JACKSONVILLE)	AGE	BATS	POSITION	CPA	RUNS	SET-UP	DRIVE-IN	RPA
Jim Campanis	25	R	C	327	28.5	.044	.043	.087
Bert Heffernan	27	L	C	286	26.0	.049	.042	.091
Bobby Holley	25	R	3B\OF	452	45.9	.053	.049	.102
Anthony Manahan	24	R	SS	558	44.1	.037	.042	.079
Tow Maynard	26	R	OF	460	37.0	.040	.040	.080
Mike McDonald	24	L	OF	409	35.4	.041	.046	.087
Mark Merchant	24	L	OF	431	36.7	.039	.046	.085
Marc Newfield	20	R	OF	179	14.4	.037	.043	.080
Jesus Tavarez	21	R	OF	425	27.8	.029	.036	.065
Brian Turang	25	R	2B	550	49.7	.043	.047	.090

AAA Pitchers	Age	Throws	Outs	RPA	AA Pitchers	Age	Throws	Outs	RPA
Shawn Barton	29	L	159	.128	Daven Bond	28	R	152	.143
Kevin D. Brown	26	L	452	.131	Jeff Borski	23	R	103	.163
Rich DeLucia	28	R	121	.093	Jim Converse	21	R	477	.121
Tom Drees	29	L	385	.140	Mark Czarkowski	25	L	296	.116
Mark Grant	29	R	176	.106	Fernando Figueroa	28	L	283	.126
Eric Gunderson	26	L	227	.139	Jim Gutierrez	22	R	162	.158
Andy Hawkins	32	R	388	.132	Brad Holman	24	R	221	.117
Calvin Jones	29	R	98	.118	Troy Kent	25	R	205	.131
Randy Kramer	32	R	192	.161	Brent Knackert	23	R	351	.138
Dave Masters	28	R	271	.158	Paul Perkins	22	R	97	.133
Jim Newlin	26	R	197	.136	Scott Pitcher	24	R	190	.105
Jose Nunez	28	R	115	.136	Kerry Woodson	23	R	267	.137
Mike Remlinger	26	L	289	.164	Clint Zavaras	25	R	368	.173
Pat Rice	29	R	250	.181					
Charles Scott	28	R	254	.128					
Ed VanDeBerg	34	L	130	.186					
Mike Walker	27	R	309	.147					

TEXAS RANGERS

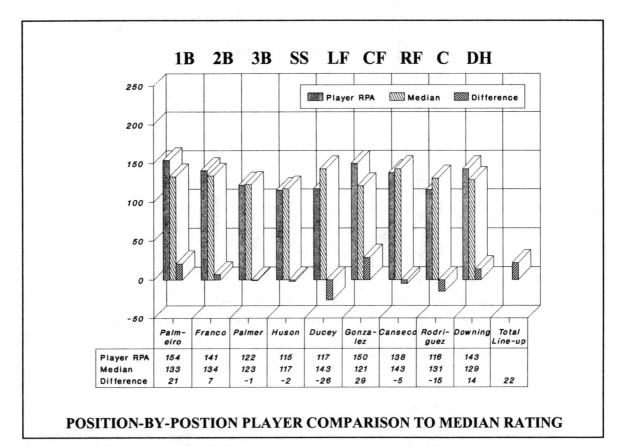

	1B	2B	3B	SS	LF	CF	RF	C	DH	Total Line-up
	Palm-eiro	Franco	Palmer	Huson	Ducey	Gonza-lez	Canseco	Rodri-guez	Downing	
Player RPA	154	141	122	115	117	150	138	116	143	
Median	133	134	123	117	143	121	143	131	129	
Difference	21	7	-1	-2	-26	29	-5	-15	14	22

Legend: Player RPA, Median, Difference

POSITION-BY-POSTION PLAYER COMPARISON TO MEDIAN RATING

DEFENSIVE TEAM AND STADIUM DATA FOR THE LAST 3 YEARS:

TEAM DEFENSE BY POSITION:

		1990	1991	1992	POSITION-BY-POSITION STADIUM CHARACTERISTICS:
1B:	Home	-1.0	+0.2	+1.6	Slightly hard to plaay
	Away	+2.8	+1.8	-5.1	
2B:	Home	+2.9	+0.2	-2.3	Average
	Away	+2.6	-2.0	-4.0	
3B:	Home	-0.4	-0.5	-6.7	Slightly easy to play
	Away	-3.9	+1.2	-3.4	
SS:	Home	+1.2	-3.2	-7.0	Average
	Away	-4.2	-1.6	-0.7	
LF:	Home	+6.5	+5.0	-3.7	Slightly hard to play
	Away	+4.0	-3.9	-4.7	
CF:	Home	+2.8	+1.2	+8.2	Hard to play
	Away	-4.5	+0.3	-7.4	
RF:	Home	-2.9	+2.7	+4.4	Average
	Away	+3.9	+1.3	-2.0	
Total Home:		+9.1	+5.6	-5.5	
Total Away:		+0.7	-2.9	-27.3	

Comments: This is another team where all 4 years have shown a home field defensive advantage, but with nothing much to show for it since this was easily the worst fielding team in the AL in '92. The trade of Sierra for Canseco should only make the defense that much worse in '93! The infield defense, atrocius in '92, should improve in '93 as the kids mature and with the addition of Manuel Lee and with the return of Julio Franco's much maligned (falsely) defense.

TEXAS RANGERS

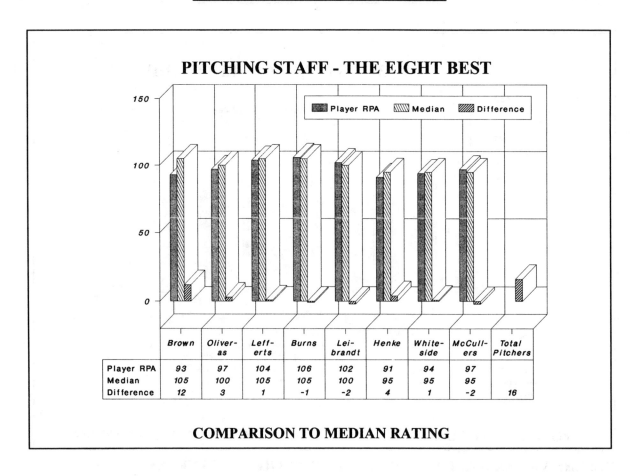

PITCHING STAFF - THE EIGHT BEST

	Brown	Oliver-as	Leff-erts	Burns	Lei-brandt	Henke	White-side	McCull-ers	Total Pitchers
Player RPA	93	97	104	106	102	91	94	97	
Median	105	100	105	105	100	95	95	95	
Difference	12	3	1	-1	-2	4	1	-2	16

COMPARISON TO MEDIAN RATING

SUGGESTED LINE-UPS (with set-up RPA & drive-in RPA ratings):

Vs: Left-handed Groundball
DH:	B. Downing	118-88
2B:	J. Franco	88-76
LF:	K. Belcher	73-65
RF:	J. Canseco	74-79
CF:	J. Gonzalez	72-92
3B:	D. Palmer	81-88
1B:	R. Palmeiro	70-61
SS:	M. Lee	50-46
C:	I. Rodriguez	38-46

Vs: Neutral Lefty Pitchers
DH:	B. Downing	100-75
2B:	J. Franco	92-79
1B:	R. Palmeiro	79-69
RF:	J. Canseco	75-80
3B:	D. Palmer	79-86
CF:	J. Gonzalez	70-88
LF:	K. Belcher	73-65
SS:	J. Huson	58-54
C:	I. Rodriguez	45-54

Vs: Left-handed Flyball
DH:	B. Downing	89-68
2B:	J. Franco	97-83
1B:	R. Palmeiro	90-79
RF:	J. Canseco	76-82
3B:	D. Palmer	77-84
CF:	J. Gonzalez	67-85
LF:	K. Belcher	73-65
SS:	J. Huson	65-61
C:	I. Rodriguez	51-61

Vs: Right-handed Groundball
DH:	B. Downing	89-67
1B:	R. Palmeiro	76-67
2B:	J. Franco	69-61
LF:	R. Ducey	87-85
RF:	J. Canseco	75-80
CF:	J. Gonzalez	67-86
3B:	D. Palmer	64-69
SS:	M. Lee	51-46
C:	I. Rodriguez	38-45

Vs: Neutral Righty Pitchers
DH:	R. Maurer	72-57
2B:	J. Franco	73-64
1B:	R. Palmeiro	85-75
CF:	J. Gonzalez	65-82
RF:	J. Canseco	76-81
3B:	D. Palmer	62-67
LF:	K. Belcher	63-55
SS:	J. Huson	59-54
C:	I. Rodriguez	45-53

Vs: Right-handed Flyball
DH:	R. Maurer	72-57
2B:	J. Franco	78-68
1B:	R. Palmeiro	96-85
RF:	J. Canseco	77-83
CF:	J. Gonzalez	62-79
SS:	J. Huson	66-61
3B:	D. Palmer	60-65
LF:	K. Belcher	63-55
C:	I. Rodriguez	51-60

Comments: The Rangers have one of the stronger line-ups in the AL, but they've sacrificed a lot of defense in order to get it. The exchange of Sierra for Canseco was a perfect illustration of the Ranger penchant of exchanging defensive ability for hitting prowess. Kevin Belcher may be a year away, but the Rangers don't have any other quality outfielders available to fill his position in these line-ups.

TEXAS RANGERS

The Texas Rangers have a good hitting ball club and will have a much improved pitching staff in 1993. Yet I don't think this team will end up with a winning record. The reason is simple: the Rangers' defense is awful.

The Signing of good fielding Manuel Lee will help the defense, but not to the extent that the Rangers require since Jeff Huson is not one of the defensive problems. Lee was signed purely because of Huson's operation and unavailability until mid-season.

Jose Canseco is an American League DH masquerading as an outfielder. The problem for the Rangers is that they already possess an excellent hitting DH in Brian Downing. The Rangers will be forced to play Canseco in the outfield. That is not a pleasant picture.

I listed Kevin Belcher in the proposed line-ups on the opposite page. This was before the Rangers signed Gary Redus. I left Belcher in these line-ups since Belcher's projected RPA numbers and Redus' RPA numbers are quite similar while Redus is probably not an adequate defensive outfielder at this stage of his career.

I don't fully understand why the Rangers signed Gary Redus. As readers of this series of books know, I really like Gary Redus. Gary, however, is no longer a youngster. He can't have much left in the tank. The Rangers have Rob Maurer in the minors. He can hit and brings to the table about exactly what Redus brings to the table.

Despite the loss of Jose Guzman, the signing's of Charlie Leibrandt, Craig Lefferts and Tom Henke improves the previously weak pitching staff immeasurably. Don't overlook the acquisition of Francisco Oliveras. He's an excellent pitcher. I hope he gets an opportunity to be part of the Rangers' starting rotation.

I think that the loss of Scott Chiamparino in the Expansion draft is a big blow to the Rangers. Couldn't they have gotten Nolan Ryan to step aside from the 15 man protected list so as to protect Chiamparino?

I was very disappointed in the RPA rating for Juan Gonzalez. His numbers may look real nice to rotisserie fans, but he's not living up to his ability. He's likely to become a tremendous hitter eventually, but he's nowhere near that goal yet. His 43 home runs in 1992 were completely misleading. His effective on-base%, which has never been very good, plummeted in '92 which caused his overall offensive RPA to only narrowly improve over his '91 figure. He, like teammate Ivan Rodriguez, is an undisciplined hitter who needs to be taught patience at the plate. If these two don't learn patience they'll never live up to their mutual enormous promise.

AA pitcher Dan Smith appears to be an excellent prospect. I hope the Rangers don't rush him. He could be a real good starting pitcher, but probably needs at least a couple of months at AAA. Fortunately for the Rangers, Matt Whiteside seems to have made the jump to the majors from AA successfully and is already the second best reliever on the Rangers. Henke and Whiteside really solidify this bullpen.

Texas' Projected record for 1993: 80–82, good for 5th place in the division.

TEXAS RANGERS

Jose Canseco, 28

Bats Right   418L   1330R   526G   391F

L= .149G .151L .154F   (.074/.079) .153   .151G .153R .156F = R

		ATBATS	1B	2B	3B	HR	HBP	BB	GDP	SB	CS	ROE	XB	RUNS	EOB%	RL#	SET-UP	DR-IN	RPA
Oakland	1990	481	79	14	2	37	5	64	9	19	11	7	38	102	.208	.168	.090	.090	.180
Oakland	1991	572	75	32	1	44	9	70	16	26	8	7	50	116	.194	.155	.080	.086	.166
Oakland	1992	366	57	11	0	22	3	47	15	5	8	4	25	56	.171	.128	.059	.071	.130
Texas	1992	73	9	4	0	4	3	14	1	1	0	0	4	15	.270	.168	.096	.073	.169

Jack Daugherty, 32

Bats Both   151L   494R   200G   154F

L= .062G .071L .083F   (.045/.041) .086   .082G .091R .103F = R

		ATBATS	1B	2B	3B	HR	HBP	BB	GDP	SB	CS	ROE	XB	RUNS	EOB%	RL#	SET-UP	DR-IN	RPA
Texas	1990	310	65	20	2	6	2	22	4	0	0	1	28	45	.239	.128	.069	.060	.129
Texas	1991	144	22	3	2	1	0	15	2	1	0	3	6	14	.215	.084	.043	.041	.084
Texas	1992	127	17	9	0	0	1	15	3	2	1	4	4	13	.236	.088	.047	.041	.088

Mario Diaz, 30

Bats Right   121L   136R   72G   57F   231ML

L= .086G .082L .078F   (.038/.041) .079   .081G .077R .073F = R

		ATBATS	1B	2B	3B	HR	HBP	BB	GDP	SB	CS	ROE	XB	RUNS	EOB%	RL#	SET-UP	DR-IN	RPA
Mets	1990	22	2	1	0	0	0	0	0	0	0	0	0	1	.096	.032	.010	.023	.033
Texas	1991	182	40	7	0	1	0	15	5	0	1	0	18	18	.208	.089	.045	.045	.090
Texas	1992	31	6	1	0	0	0	0	2	0	1	0	1	1	.059	.035	.008	.027	.035

Brian Downing, 42

Bats Right   466L   797R   317G   309F

L= .222G .191L .173F   (.091/.070) .161   .173G .142R .124F = R

		ATBATS	1B	2B	3B	HR	HBP	BB	GDP	SB	CS	ROE	XB	RUNS	EOB%	RL#	SET-UP	DR-IN	RPA
California	1990	330	56	18	2	14	6	48	11	0	0	4	26	58	.247	.149	.079	.067	.146
Texas	1991	407	77	17	2	17	8	51	7	1	1	5	47	74	.254	.154	.086	.070	.156
Texas	1992	320	61	18	0	10	8	60	7	1	0	3	33	65	.300	.165	.098	.068	.166

Monty Fariss, 25

Bats Right   114L   112R   48G   59F   819ML

L= .177G .121L .075F   (.059/.057) .116   .166G .110R .064F = R

		ATBATS	1B	2B	3B	HR	HBP	BB	GDP	SB	CS	ROE	XB	RUNS	EOB%	RL#	SET-UP	DR-IN	RPA
Texas	1991	31	6	1	0	1	0	7	0	0	0	0	1	6	.311	.155	.094	.063	.157
Texas	1992	166	25	7	1	3	2	17	3	0	2	3	7	19	.210	.100	.051	.050	.101

Julio Franco, 31

Bats Right   428L   1032R   461G   335F

L= .166G .173L .182F   (.080/.069) .149   .132G .139R .148F = R

		ATBATS	1B	2B	3B	HR	HBP	BB	GDP	SB	CS	ROE	XB	RUNS	EOB%	RL#	SET-UP	DR-IN	RPA
Texas	1990	582	133	27	1	11	2	79	12	31	12	10	76	97	.269	.138	.078	.061	.139
Texas	1991	589	156	27	3	15	3	57	13	36	12	7	54	105	.263	.156	.088	.070	.158
Texas	1992	107	16	7	0	2	0	13	3	1	2	0	10	12	.193	.099	.048	.052	.100

Jeff Frye, 26

Bats Right   73L   147R   41G   75F   991ML

L= .193G .137L .107F   (.055/.043) .098   .135G .079R .049F = R

		ATBATS	1B	2B	3B	HR	HBP	BB	GDP	SB	CS	ROE	XB	RUNS	EOB%	RL#	SET-UP	DR-IN	RPA
Texas	1992	199	40	9	1	1	3	16	2	1	3	8	21	26	.259	.117	.065	.053	.118

Juan Gonzalez, 23

Bats Right   360L   970R   367G   330F

L= .152G .146L .140F   (.060/.078) .138   .141G .135R .129F = R

		ATBATS	1B	2B	3B	HR	HBP	BB	GDP	SB	CS	ROE	XB	RUNS	EOB%	RL#	SET-UP	DR-IN	RPA
Texas	1990	90	14	7	1	4	2	2	2	0	1	0	4	12	.158	.121	.053	.069	.122
Texas	1991	545	82	34	1	27	5	35	10	4	4	10	30	80	.188	.134	.064	.071	.135
Texas	1992	584	83	24	2	43	5	34	16	0	2	5	33	89	.140	.139	.056	.084	.140

TEXAS RANGERS

Jeff Huson, 28

Bats Left   119L   1011R   328G   251F

L= .098G .108L .122F [(.057/.052) .109] .099G .109R .123F = R

		ATBATS	1B	2B	3B	HR	HBP	BB	GDP	SB	CS	ROE	XB	RUNS	EOB%	RL#	SET-UP	DR-IN	RPA
Texas	1990	396	81	12	2	0	2	46	8	12	4	4	56	43	.239	.092	.050	.043	.093
Texas	1991	268	44	8	3	2	0	39	6	8	4	2	25	29	.222	.092	.048	.045	.093
Texas	1992	318	62	14	3	4	1	39	7	18	6	4	35	45	.239	.123	.066	.057	.123

Al Newman, 32

Bats Both   282L   709R   268G   227F

L= .089G .093L .098F [(.030/.044) .074] .062G .066R .071F = R

		ATBATS	1B	2B	3B	HR	HBP	BB	GDP	SB	CS	ROE	XB	RUNS	EOB%	RL#	SET-UP	DR-IN	RPA
Minnesota	1990	388	80	14	0	0	2	33	7	13	7	4	36	36	.216	.085	.042	.041	.083
Minnesota	1991	246	42	5	0	0	1	23	5	4	6	4	19	16	.184	.064	.028	.032	.060
Texas	1992	246	49	5	0	0	1	34	5	9	7	5	25	25	.235	.088	.047	.042	.089

Rafael Palmeiro, 28

Bats Left   619L   1445R   597G   483F

L= .127G .144L .165F [(.081/.071) .152] .139G .156R .177F = R

		ATBATS	1B	2B	3B	HR	HBP	BB	GDP	SB	CS	ROE	XB	RUNS	EOB%	RL#	SET-UP	DR-IN	RPA
Texas	1990	598	136	35	6	14	3	34	24	3	3	5	50	83	.206	.121	.061	.061	.122
Texas	1991	631	125	49	3	26	6	58	17	4	3	4	55	113	.235	.157	.084	.075	.159
Texas	1992	608	110	27	4	22	10	64	10	2	3	8	47	101	.236	.145	.078	.068	.146

Dean Palmer, 24

Bats Right   259L   661R   231G   236F   258ML

L= .158G .154L .150F [(.064/.068) .132] .122G .118R .114F = R

		ATBATS	1B	2B	3B	HR	HBP	BB	GDP	SB	CS	ROE	XB	RUNS	EOB%	RL#	SET-UP	DR-IN	RPA
Texas	1991	268	24	9	2	15	3	32	4	0	2	2	15	35	.167	.114	.051	.064	.115
Texas	1992	541	73	25	0	26	4	60	9	10	4	9	28	83	.202	.134	.066	.069	.135

Geno Petralli, 32

Bats Left   60L   768R   259G   214F

L= .097G .090L .081F [(.044/.044) .088] .095G .088R .079F = R

		ATBATS	1B	2B	3B	HR	HBP	BB	GDP	SB	CS	ROE	XB	RUNS	EOB%	RL#	SET-UP	DR-IN	RPA
Texas	1990	325	69	13	1	0	3	47	12	0	2	0	18	36	.244	.090	.048	.042	.090
Texas	1991	199	43	8	1	2	0	20	4	2	1	0	12	24	.230	.105	.056	.050	.106
Texas	1992	192	25	12	0	1	0	18	8	0	0	3	5	15	.178	.071	.033	.038	.071

Kevin Reimer, 28

Bats Left   154L   949R   298G   271F

L= .097G .094L .091F [(.060/.066) .126] .134G .131R .128F = R

		ATBATS	1B	2B	3B	HR	HBP	BB	GDP	SB	CS	ROE	XB	RUNS	EOB%	RL#	SET-UP	DR-IN	RPA
Texas	1990	100	14	9	1	2	1	10	3	0	1	2	3	13	.221	.114	.059	.055	.114
Texas	1991	394	64	22	0	20	7	27	10	0	3	0	14	55	.174	.125	.057	.069	.126
Texas	1992	494	82	32	2	16	10	37	10	2	4	1	25	70	.203	.126	.063	.064	.127

Ivan Rodriguez, 21

Bats Right   190L   563R   181G   195F   187ML

L= .071G .086L .099F [(.038/.047) .085] .070G .085R .098F = R

		ATBATS	1B	2B	3B	HR	HBP	BB	GDP	SB	CS	ROE	XB	RUNS	EOB%	RL#	SET-UP	DR-IN	RPA
Texas	1991	280	55	16	0	3	0	5	10	0	1	4	16	24	.160	.080	.035	.046	.081
Texas	1992	420	84	16	1	8	1	22	15	0	0	4	23	44	.177	.096	.045	.052	.097

John Russell, 31

Bats Right   119L   61R   49G   52F   191ML

L= .080G .098L .115F [(.050/.050) .100] .085G .103R .120F = R

		ATBATS	1B	2B	3B	HR	HBP	BB	GDP	SB	CS	ROE	XB	RUNS	EOB%	RL#	SET-UP	DR-IN	RPA
Texas	1990	128	29	4	0	2	0	9	3	1	0	1	7	15	.214	.103	.052	.051	.103
Texas	1991	27	3	0	0	0	0	1	0	0	0	0	3	1	.112	.032	.011	.021	.032
Texas	1992	10	1	0	0	0	1	1	0	0	0	0	0	1	.226	.055	.029	.027	.056

TEXAS RANGERS

Dickie Thon, 34

Bats Right   546L   913R   484G   323F

L= .104G .116L .135F   (.048/.052) .100   .081G   .093R   .112F = R

		ATBATS	1B	2B	3B	HR	HBP	BB	GDP	SB	CS	ROE	XB	RUNS	EOB%	RL#	SET-UP	DR-IN	RPA
Philadelphia	1990	552	109	20	4	8	3	27	14	12	6	8	41	56	.185	.096	.045	.050	.095
Philadelphia	1991	539	105	18	4	9	0	19	9	11	6	11	27	55	.181	.092	.044	.050	.094
Texas	1992	275	46	15	3	4	0	19	2	12	2	1	18	33	.205	.112	.055	.057	.112

PITCHERS

Throws: Flyball type, extreme reverse righty

Gerald Alexander, 24   (.068/.174) .123   204L   224R   439ML

		OUTS	RO	1B	2B	3B	HR	HBP	BB	GDP	SB	CS	PO	WP	BK	RUNS	EOB%	RL#	RPA
Texas	1990	21	6	12	1	1	0	1	5	1	0	0	0	0	0	8	.342	.176	.180
Texas	1991	268	136	64	15	3	11	3	41	6	7	3	0	3	1	50	.200	.125	.126
Texas	1992	5	5	3	1	0	1	0	1	0	0	0	0	0	0	4	.307	.338	.334

Throws: Flyball type, moderate lefty

Floyd Bannister, 37   (.107/.122) .117   89L   165R

		OUTS	RO	1B	2B	3B	HR	HBP	BB	GDP	SB	CS	PO	WP	BK	RUNS	EOB%	RL#	RPA
California	1991	75	75	15	3	2	5	0	9	5	0	1	0	1	0	11	.083	.102	.104
Texas	1992	111	111	25	11	0	3	3	15	1	3	1	0	3	0	21	.232	.127	.126

Throws: Neutral type, extreme lefty

Brian Bohanon, 24   (.054/.135) .122   98L   526R   603ML

		OUTS	RO	1B	2B	3B	HR	HBP	BB	GDP	SB	CS	PO	WP	BK	RUNS	EOB%	RL#	RPA
Texas	1990	102	24	27	6	1	6	2	18	7	1	2	1	1	0	19	.140	.118	.120
Texas	1991	184	0	49	13	0	4	2	23	3	5	0	0	3	1	32	.227	.118	.118
Texas	1992	137	54	41	7	2	7	1	25	4	0	3	0	2	0	30	.206	.143	.141

Throws: Groundball type, moderate righty

Kevin Brown, 27   (.098/.088) .093   1329L   1344R

		OUTS	RO	1B	2B	3B	HR	HBP	BB	GDP	SB	CS	PO	WP	BK	RUNS	EOB%	RL#	RPA
Texas	1990	540	0	127	34	1	13	3	57	24	7	4	1	9	2	69	.150	.089	.090
Texas	1991	632	0	172	40	4	17	13	85	30	5	11	3	12	3	98	.170	.106	.106
Texas	1992	797	0	210	40	1	11	10	74	28	7	12	2	8	2	91	.158	.085	.083

Throws: Flyball type, moderate reverse righty

Todd Burns, 29   (.095/.111) .104   343L   442R   281ML

		OUTS	RO	1B	2B	3B	HR	HBP	BB	GDP	SB	CS	PO	WP	BK	RUNS	EOB%	RL#	RPA
Oakland	1990	236	198	49	17	4	8	0	28	9	1	2	0	5	0	39	.155	.103	.115
Oakland	1991	40	40	5	3	0	2	0	7	2	1	0	0	1	0	6	.144	.097	.102
Texas	1992	309	115	61	26	2	8	4	31	7	1	7	0	5	0	40	.155	.096	.094

Throws: Flyball type, extreme lefty

Don Carman, 33   (.093/.131) .119   169L   345R   692ML

		OUTS	RO	1B	2B	3B	HR	HBP	BB	GDP	SB	CS	PO	WP	BK	RUNS	EOB%	RL#	RPA
Philadelphia	1990	260	248	40	15	1	13	4	31	6	5	1	0	6	1	39	.156	.109	.109
Cincinnati	1991	108	108	24	8	0	8	1	18	1	3	1	0	2	0	24	.209	.151	.142
Texas	1992	7	7	4	0	0	0	0	0	0	0	0	0	0	0	1	.258	.122	.122

Throws: Groundball type, extreme righty

Scott Chiamparino, 26   (.115/.073) .092   159L   188R   205ML

		OUTS	RO	1B	2B	3B	HR	HBP	BB	GDP	SB	CS	PO	WP	BK	RUNS	EOB%	RL#	RPA
Texas	1990	113	0	28	7	0	1	2	12	3	2	3	0	5	0	14	.171	.084	.085
Texas	1991	67	0	22	2	1	0	1	12	4	2	0	0	0	0	11	.210	.111	.112
Texas	1992	76	0	17	5	1	2	0	5	5	1	1	0	1	0	7	.083	.075	.074

TEXAS RANGERS

Jose Guzman, 29

Throws: Neutral type, moderate righty

(.102/.092) .097   742L   880R

		OUTS	RO	1B	2B	3B	HR	HBP	BB	GDP	SB	CS	PO	WP	BK	RUNS	EOB%	RL#	RPA
Texas	1991	509	0	108	33	1	10	4	83	11	12	13	1	8	1	70	.186	.097	.097
Texas	1992	672	0	156	52	4	17	4	73	20	16	15	0	6	0	92	.159	.100	.098

Mike Jeffcoat, 33

Throws: Neutral type, extreme lefty

(.094/.140) .127   240L   629R   134ML

		OUTS	RO	1B	2B	3B	HR	HBP	BB	GDP	SB	CS	PO	WP	BK	RUNS	EOB%	RL#	RPA
Texas	1990	332	131	85	24	1	12	2	23	12	0	6	0	1	0	46	.132	.094	.096
Texas	1991	239	239	78	13	5	8	4	22	9	5	2	0	3	0	46	.190	.127	.127
Texas	1992	59	21	18	6	2	2	0	5	1	0	1	0	0	0	12	.200	.141	.139

Terry Mathews, 28

Throws: Flyball type, extreme righty

(.159/.085) .114   161L   255R   483ML

		OUTS	RO	1B	2B	3B	HR	HBP	BB	GDP	SB	CS	PO	WP	BK	RUNS	EOB%	RL#	RPA
Texas	1991	172	150	29	19	1	5	1	15	2	8	3	0	5	0	25	.165	.105	.105
Texas	1992	127	127	31	13	0	4	1	28	5	0	4	0	2	1	24	.207	.124	.123

Lance McCullers, 28

Throws: Flyball type, moderate to severe reverse righty

(.077/.110) .096   85L   117R   285ML

		OUTS	RO	1B	2B	3B	HR	HBP	BB	GDP	SB	CS	PO	WP	BK	RUNS	EOB%	RL#	RPA
N.Y. Yankees	1990	45	45	10	2	0	2	0	4	0	1	1	0	3	0	7	.161	.107	.104
Detroit	1990	89	79	11	4	1	0	12	0	2	1	0	2	0	10	.174	.085	.082	
Texas	1992	15	15	1	0	0	0	0	8	1	1	0	0	0	0	2	.296	.085	.084

Edwin Nunez, 29

Throws: Neutral type, neutral righty

(.139/.135) .137   277L   415R

		OUTS	RO	1B	2B	3B	HR	HBP	BB	GDP	SB	CS	PO	WP	BK	RUNS	EOB%	RL#	RPA
Detroit	1990	241	241	46	15	0	4	2	31	8	5	2	0	4	0	27	.167	.084	.082
Milwaukee	1991	76	76	16	5	1	6	0	11	1	2	0	0	0	1	18	.192	.156	.157
Milwaukee	1992	41	41	9	2	0	1	0	6	0	0	1	0	0	0	6	.195	.098	.106
Texas	1992	137	137	32	11	3	5	2	16	1	1	1	0	5	0	27	.216	.136	.134

Roger Pavlik, 25

Throws: Flyball type, extreme reverse righty

(.092/.133) .110   149L   119R   611ML

		OUTS	RO	1B	2B	3B	HR	HBP	BB	GDP	SB	CS	PO	WP	BK	RUNS	EOB%	RL#	RPA
Texas	1992	186	3	52	7	4	3	3	34	5	3	8	1	9	0	29	.191	.107	.106

Kenny Rogers, 28

Throws: Neutral type, extreme lefty

(.085/.127) .116   307L   900R

		OUTS	RO	1B	2B	3B	HR	HBP	BB	GDP	SB	CS	PO	WP	BK	RUNS	EOB%	RL#	RPA
Texas	1990	293	247	62	22	3	6	1	37	5	6	1	0	5	0	46	.203	.104	.106
Texas	1991	329	200	82	22	3	14	6	54	11	1	3	2	3	1	63	.196	.127	.127
Texas	1992	236	236	55	17	1	7	0	18	3	2	3	1	4	1	33	.161	.102	.100

Wayne Rosenthal, 27

Throws: Flyball type, moderate to severe reverse righty

(.125/.148) .139   138L   200R   508ML

		OUTS	RO	1B	2B	3B	HR	HBP	BB	GDP	SB	CS	PO	WP	BK	RUNS	EOB%	RL#	RPA
Texas	1991	211	211	45	16	2	9	1	35	1	6	1	0	8	1	45	.231	.140	.140
Texas	1992	14	14	5	1	0	1	0	2	0	1	0	0	1	0	4	.260	.192	.190

Nolan Ryan, 45

Throws: Flyball type, moderate righty

(.101/.081) .092   1118L   1006R

		OUTS	RO	1B	2B	3B	HR	HBP	BB	GDP	SB	CS	PO	WP	BK	RUNS	EOB%	RL#	RPA
Texas	1990	612	0	87	20	12	18	7	72	5	25	9	0	9	1	75	.157	.088	.089
Texas	1991	519	0	62	25	3	12	5	72	6	24	8	1	8	0	55	.157	.080	.081
Texas	1992	472	0	99	27	3	9	12	69	5	26	12	1	9	0	69	.200	.103	.102

Matt Whiteside, 25

Throws: Neutral type, righty

(..../....) .096   54L   58R   178ML

		OUTS	RO	1B	2B	3B	HR	HBP	BB	GDP	SB	CS	PO	WP	BK	RUNS	EOB%	RL#	RPA
Texas	1992	84	84	19	6	0	1	0	9	3	1	0	0	2	0	10	.176	.087	.087

Texas Rangers AAA & AA Minor League Ratings

AAA (OKLAHOMA CITY)	AGE	BATS	POSITION	CPA	RUNS	SET-UP	DRIVE-IN	RPA
Steve Balboni	35	R	DH	524	59.4	.052	.061	.113
Juan Bell	24	B	SS	241	17.0	.032	.039	.071
Bob Brower	32	R	OF	271	15.0	.023	.032	.055
Doug Davis	30	R	C	271	14.5	.023	.031	.054
Mario Diaz	30	R	SS	231	17.4	.034	.041	.075
Monty Fariss	25	R	OF	223	28.5	.067	.061	.128
Jeff Frye	26	R	2B	408	40.7	.057	.043	.100
Chuck Jackson	29	R	OF\3B\SS	532	50.5	.049	.046	.095
Rob Maurer	25	L	1B	581	63.4	.062	.047	.109
Russ McGinnis	29	R	3B\C	431	52.3	.066	.055	.121
Keith Miller	29	B	OF\SS	566	55.3	.055	.043	.098
Dan Peltier	24	L	OF	527	51.6	.052	.046	.098
Paul Postier	28	R	SS	251	15.8	.031	.032	.063
Jim Presley	31	R	3B	195	16.4	.042	.042	.084
Tony Scruggs	26	R	OF	215	14.3	.033	.034	.067
Ray Stephens	30	R	C	267	21.0	.035	.044	.079
Jim Walewander	31	B	2B	144	9.9	.036	.032	.068

AA (TULSA)	AGE	BATS	POSITION	CPA	RUNS	SET-UP	DRIVE-IN	RPA
Kevin Belcher	25	R	OF	473	58.6	.066	.058	.124
Cris Colon	23	B	SS	435	31.3	.034	.038	.072
Rusty Greer	23	L	1B	435	45.0	.057	.047	.104
Donald Harris	25	R	OF	330	27.3	.034	.049	.083
David Hulse	24	L	OF	411	35.7	.043	.044	.087
Pete Kuld	26	R	C	240	23.1	.043	.053	.096
Paul List	27	R	OF	171	16.4	.052	.044	.096
Rod Morris	26	L	OF	399	31.6	.039	.040	.079
Darren Niethammer	27	R	C\1B	131	10.6	.038	.043	.081
Jose Oliva	21	R	3B	494	55.8	.055	.058	.113
John Russell	31	R	C	191	20.8	.048	.061	.109
Luke Sable	27	R	2B\3B\OF	300	21.4	.034	.037	.071
John Shave	25	R	2B	504	43.9	.044	.043	.087

AAA Pitchers	Age	Throws	Outs	RPA	AA Pitchers	Age	Throws	Outs	RPA
Gerald Alexander	24	R	318	.115	Mike Arner	22	R	150	.133
John Barfield	28	L	215	.126	Jeff Bronkey	27	R	259	.108
Kevin Blankenship	29	R	319	.133	Terry Burrows	24	L	252	.112
Brian Bohanon	24	L	253	.115	Hector Fajardo	22	R	96	.111
Rob Brown	25	R	304	.134	Chris Gies	24	R	296	.138
Todd Burns	29	R	127	.093	Bryan Gore	26	L	280	.135
Mike Campbell	28	R	123	.136	Danilo Leon	25	R	104	.067
Don Carman	33	L	413	.114	Kurt Miller	20	R	264	.143
Scott Chiamparino	26	R	150	.096	Robb Nen	23	R	75	.108
Narciso Elvira	25	L	266	.121	David Perez	24	R	179	.146
Steve Fireovid	34	R	314	.123	Brian Romero	24	L	157	.187
Mike Jeffcoat	33	L	96	.112	Dan Smith	23	L	439	.092
Barry Manuel	27	R	163	.170	Matt Whiteside	25	R	135	.100
Roger Pavlik	25	R	353	.104					
Wayne Rosenthal	27	R	185	.143					
Cedric Shaw	25	L	378	.155					

CHICAGO CUBS

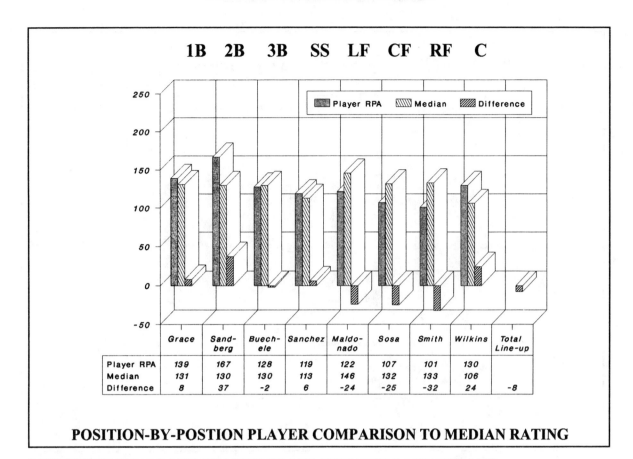

	1B	2B	3B	SS	LF	CF	RF	C	Total Line-up
	Grace	Sand-berg	Buech-ele	Sanchez	Maldo-nado	Sosa	Smith	Wilkins	
Player RPA	139	167	128	119	122	107	101	130	
Median	131	130	130	113	146	132	133	106	
Difference	8	37	-2	6	-24	-25	-32	24	-8

POSITION-BY-POSTION PLAYER COMPARISON TO MEDIAN RATING

DEFENSIVE TEAM AND STADIUM DATA FOR THE LAST 3 YEARS:

TEAM DEFENSE BY POSITION:		1990	1991	1992	POSITION-BY-POSITION STADIUM CHARACTERISTICS:
1B:	Home	+0.9	+1.8	-0.7	Average
	Away	+0.6	+5.6	+2.8	
2B:	Home	+3.5	+4.4	+2.6	Slightly easy to play
	Away	-3.1	+4.1	+3.5	
3B:	Home	-7.0	-0.6	-3.5	Slightly easy to play
	Away	+1.8	-2.6	-7.4	
SS:	Home	+2.9	-3.0	+1.6	Slightly easy to play
	Away	+1.9	-1.6	-1.9	
LF:	Home	+3.2	-0.6	+1.4	Slightly hard to play
	Away	+3.7	+0.5	-3.0	
CF:	Home	-5.6	-8.1	+4.0	Hard to play
	Away	-7.1	-6.4	+0.9	
RF:	Home	-4.4	-9.9	-1.8	Slightly hard to play
	Away	-7.7	-11.4	-2.4	
Total Home:		-6.5	-16.0	+3.5	Has the introduction of nightgames helped
Total Away:		-9.9	-11.8	-7.4	make it easier to play defense here?

Comments: While still a little below average defensively in '92, this still represented a big improvement over '91. The infield defense in '93 could be amongst the best in baseball with the addition of Rey Sanchez & Steve Buechele on the left side of the infield for the full year. The "loss" of Dawson should also help enormously, although Maldonado's no prize fielder either.

CHICAGO CUBS

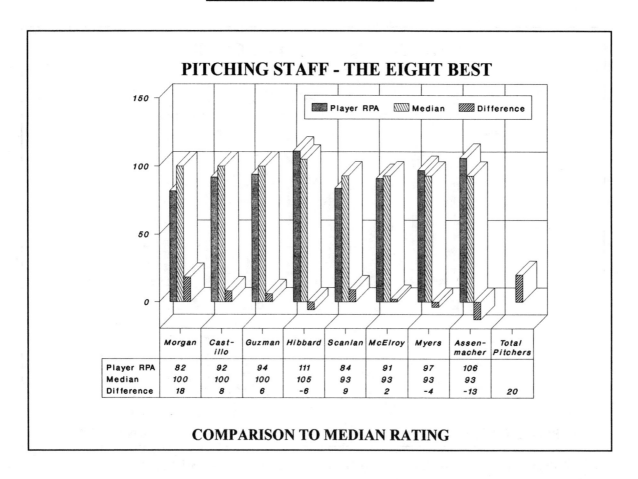

PITCHING STAFF - THE EIGHT BEST

	Morgan	Cast-illo	Guzman	Hibbard	Scanlan	McElroy	Myers	Assen-macher	Total Pitchers
Player RPA	82	92	94	111	84	91	97	106	
Median	100	100	100	105	93	93	93	93	
Difference	18	8	6	-6	9	2	-4	-13	20

COMPARISON TO MEDIAN RATING

SUGGESTED LINE-UPS (with set-up RPA & drive-in RPA ratings):

Vs: Left-handed Groundball
1B:	M. Grace	68-55
2B:	R. Sandberg	79-68
LF:	C. Maldonado	76-70
3B:	S. Buechele	78-76
C:	R. Wilkins	52-52
RF:	K. Roberson	53-60
CF:	S. Sosa	54-72
SS:	R. Sanchez	45-41
Pitcher		

Vs: Neutral Lefty Pitchers
1B:	M. Grace	65-52
2B:	R. Sandberg	83-72
LF:	C. Maldonado	81-75
3B:	S. Buechele	85-83
RF:	K. Roberson	53-60
CF:	S. Sosa	53-70
C:	M. Walbeck	52-48
SS:	R. Sanchez	57-53
Pitcher		

Vs: Left-handed Flyball
1B:	M. Grace	60-48
2B:	R. Sandberg	89-77
SS:	R. Sanchez	79-73
LF:	C. Maldonado	89-82
3B:	S. Buechele	96-94
RF:	D. Smith	57-63
CF:	S. Sosa	51-69
C:	M. Walbeck	52-48
Pitcher		

Vs: Right-handed Groundball
1B:	M. Grace	80-66
2B:	R. Sandberg	80-69
LF:	C. Maldonado	61-56
C:	R. Wilkins	83-82
RF:	K. Roberson	53-60
CF:	S. Sosa	43-59
3B:	D. Strange	55-48
SS:	J. Vizcaino	46-52
Pitcher		

Vs: Neutral Righty Pitchers
1B:	M. Grace	77-63
2B:	R. Sandberg	84-73
LF:	C. Maldonado	66-61
C:	R. Wilkins	69-69
CF:	D. Smith	50-55
RF:	K. Roberson	53-60
SS:	R. Sanchez	50-47
3B:	S. Buechele	51-49
Pitcher		

Vs: Right-handed Flyball
1B:	M. Grace	72-59
2B:	R. Sandberg	90-78
SS:	R. Sanchez	72-67
LF:	C. Maldonado	74-68
3B:	S. Buechele	62-60
RF:	D. Smith	68-73
C:	R. Wilkins	52-51
CF:	W. Wilson	52-52
Pitcher		

Comments: Only the Mets and the two expansion teams have poorer offenses than that listed above. These line-ups could be a lot worse if Walbeck, Roberson and Sanchez don't get the above indicated playing time. Walbeck may need a couple of months (or an entire season) at AAA, however. The Cubs are particularly vulnerable to groundball-type pitchers.

CHICAGO CUBS

Do the Chicago Cubs really believe that the signing's of Willie Wilson and Candy Maldonado really represent progress? Do they really feel that the signing of Randy Myers represents a significant step towards making them a contender?

The only winter deal that the Cubs made which actually makes any sense whatsoever was the signing of Jose Guzman. He's a quality pitcher. Candy Maldonado is a decent player, which is an improvement for the awful Cubs' outfield, but that's nothing to celebrate about. Willie Wilson is too old to make much of a difference. Randy Myers appears to be rapidly going downhill.

That's not much to show for a team that was bad in '92 and then lost a fabulous pitching talent in Greg Maddux this winter. Fortunately for the bad teams in the NL like the Chicago Cubs, the two expansion clubs will spread enough charity around to make these team's final won/loss records look somewhat respectable.

The Cubs do have some quality young players, however. With talented catcher Rick Wilkins settling in and with young Matt Walbeck about a year away, the Cubs have finally solved their catching problems for years to come. The Colorado Rockies did the Cubs a huge favor when they wasted a selection on weak-hitting Joe Girardi in the Expansion draft and got him out of the way of the more talented youngsters. It's another case of addition by subtraction.

Two other good youngsters are at shortstop. They are Rey Sanchez and Jose Vizcaino. The Cubs need to find a way to unload Shawon Dunston, who's no longer a quality player, so as to open up the position for Sanchez to start at shortstop. Vizcaino could start for many other teams, but with the Cubs he can be a very valuable sub.

The outfield, despite the "loss" of that defensive statue in right field (the utterly immobile Andre Dawson) has not been improved all that much by the addition of Maldonado and Wilson. If Kevin Roberson's healthy he ought to be given a shot, but he's not yet shown that he's a big talent. He's the only young outfielder with any promise who has experience at AAA. AA Outfielders Richie Grayum and John Jensen also appear to have some possibilities, but each of them will need at least a year at AAA before they're ready. With the outfield problems that the Cubs have, I certainly would have protected Grayum over pitcher Jim Bullinger in the Expansion draft.

The Cubs did sign one 6-year minor league free-agent outfielder who I think could really help them, if they realize what they have. His name is Eduardo Zambrano. He's possibly the best hitting outfielder they have in the Majors or the high minors.

Even though I've projected the Cubs as finishing eight games in front of the Florida Marlins, I would not be shocked if the Marlins finished in front of the Cubs. The Cubs are a poor team going nowhere, while the Marlins will be a young team with decent talent that could surprise us.

Chicago's Projected record for 1993: 79--83, good for 6th place in the division.

CHICAGO CUBS

Alex Arias, 25

Bats Right   47L   69R   45G   20F   1010ML

L= .103G .104L ....F   (.058/.043) .101   .098G   .099R   ....F = R

		ATBATS	1B	2B	3B	HR	HBP	BB	GDP	SB	CS	ROE	XB	RUNS	EOB%	RL#	SET-UP	DR-IN	RPA
Cubs	1992	99	23	6	0	0	2	11	4	0	0	3	15	15	.280	.116	.071	.052	.123

Steve Buechele, 31

Bats Right   479L   988R   496G   333F

L= .156G .170L .192F   (.063/.061) .124   .088G   .102R   .124F = R

		ATBATS	1B	2B	3B	HR	HBP	BB	GDP	SB	CS	ROE	XB	RUNS	EOB%	RL#	SET-UP	DR-IN	RPA
Texas	1990	251	37	10	0	7	2	26	5	1	0	6	15	31	.214	.105	.054	.052	.106
Texas	1991	416	74	17	2	18	5	35	11	0	4	3	22	58	.190	.124	.060	.065	.125
Pittsburgh	1991	114	18	5	1	4	2	10	3	0	1	2	7	16	.200	.117	.059	.062	.121
Pittsburgh	1992	285	48	14	1	8	2	30	5	0	2	8	18	44	.235	.130	.072	.064	.136
Cubs	1992	239	53	9	3	1	5	16	5	1	1	3	10	30	.239	.103	.058	.051	.109

Kal Daniels, 29

Bats Left   481L   825R   462G   255F

L= .114G .103L .083F   (.061/.060) .121   .142G   .131R   .111F = R

		ATBATS	1B	2B	3B	HR	HBP	BB	GDP	SB	CS	ROE	XB	RUNS	EOB%	RL#	SET-UP	DR-IN	RPA
Los Angeles	1990	450	82	23	1	27	3	67	9	4	4	8	42	98	.255	.179	.102	.083	.185
Los Angeles	1991	461	82	15	1	17	1	59	9	6	1	6	27	70	.230	.127	.068	.062	.130
Los Angeles	1992	104	17	5	0	2	1	10	7	0	0	2	4	11	.172	.083	.040	.048	.088
Cubs	1992	108	17	6	0	4	1	12	3	0	2	0	6	15	.187	.111	.055	.061	.116

Doug Dascenzo, 28

Bats Both   417L   517R   344G   214F

L= .106G .089L .062F   (.047/.046) .093   .114G   .097R   .070F = R

		ATBATS	1B	2B	3B	HR	HBP	BB	GDP	SB	CS	ROE	XB	RUNS	EOB%	RL#	SET-UP	DR-IN	RPA
Cubs	1990	241	46	9	5	1	1	19	3	15	8	1	20	24	.199	.096	.045	.046	.091
Cubs	1991	239	49	11	0	1	2	22	3	14	8	3	29	26	.228	.099	.050	.046	.096
Cubs	1992	376	79	13	4	0	0	25	3	6	9	3	31	39	.207	.086	.045	.046	.091

Andre Dawson, 38

Bats Right   626L   1116R   596G   425F

L= .119G .136L .159F   (.058/.070) .128   .106G   .123R   .146F = R

		ATBATS	1B	2B	3B	HR	HBP	BB	GDP	SB	CS	ROE	XB	RUNS	EOB%	RL#	SET-UP	DR-IN	RPA
Cubs	1990	529	104	28	5	27	2	21	12	16	2	12	48	84	.198	.157	.072	.077	.149
Cubs	1991	563	97	21	4	31	5	19	10	4	5	11	24	76	.163	.129	.055	.070	.125
Cubs	1992	542	99	27	2	22	4	22	13	6	2	9	35	79	.180	.124	.060	.070	.130

Shawon Dunston, 29

Bats Right   425L   745R   354G   298F

L= .104G .113L .123F   (.050/.057) .107   .094G   .103R   .113F = R

		ATBATS	1B	2B	3B	HR	HBP	BB	GDP	SB	CS	ROE	XB	RUNS	EOB%	RL#	SET-UP	DR-IN	RPA
Cubs	1990	545	96	22	8	17	3	14	9	25	5	16	54	67	.183	.122	.054	.062	.116
Cubs	1991	492	87	22	7	12	4	18	9	21	6	6	40	55	.177	.108	.048	.057	.105
Cubs	1992	73	19	3	1	0	0	3	0	2	3	2	5	9	.240	.115	.064	.056	.120

Joe Girardi, 28

Bats Right   335L   453R   290G   190F

L= .106G .111L .119F   (.046/.045) .091   .072G   .077R   .085F = R

		ATBATS	1B	2B	3B	HR	HBP	BB	GDP	SB	CS	ROE	XB	RUNS	EOB%	RL#	SET-UP	DR-IN	RPA
Cubs	1990	419	86	24	2	1	3	6	13	8	3	10	34	36	.186	.087	.039	.043	.082
Cubs	1991	47	7	2	0	0	0	5	0	0	0	2	1	4	.257	.085	.045	.036	.081
Cubs	1992	270	68	3	1	1	1	16	8	0	2	4	8	27	.209	.083	.044	.044	.088

Mark Grace, 28

Bats Left   741L   1293R   681G   517F

L= .119G .113L .104F   (.071/.057) .128   .142G   .136R   .127F = R

		ATBATS	1B	2B	3B	HR	HBP	BB	GDP	SB	CS	ROE	XB	RUNS	EOB%	RL#	SET-UP	DR-IN	RPA
Cubs	1990	589	140	32	1	9	5	54	10	15	6	11	38	86	.267	.137	.073	.057	.130
Cubs	1991	619	128	28	5	8	3	63	6	3	4	9	54	82	.255	.120	.065	.052	.117
Cubs	1992	603	134	37	5	9	4	64	14	6	1	3	38	100	.260	.132	.077	.062	.139

CHICAGO CUBS

Jeff Kunkel, 30
Bats Right 152L 98R 71G 60F 317ML

L= .051G .077L .108F (.027/.039) .066 .023G .049R .080F = R

		ATBATS	1B	2B	3B	HR	HBP	BB	GDP	SB	CS	ROE	XB	RUNS	EOB%	RL#	SET-UP	DR-IN	RPA
Texas	1990	200	19	11	1	3	2	11	7	2	1	2	15	14	.127	.060	.023	.038	.061
Cubs	1992	29	2	2	0	0	0	0	1	0	0	1	1	1	.093	.034	.011	.025	.036

Derrick May, 24
Bats Left 92L 370R 184G 101F 376ML

L= .090G .091L .092F (.043/.057) .100 .101G .102R .103F = R

		ATBATS	1B	2B	3B	HR	HBP	BB	GDP	SB	CS	ROE	XB	RUNS	EOB%	RL#	SET-UP	DR-IN	RPA
Cubs	1990	61	11	3	0	1	0	2	1	1	0	0	4	5	.167	.089	.038	.047	.085
Cubs	1991	22	2	2	0	1	0	2	1	0	0	0	2	2	.140	.100	.038	.057	.095
Cubs	1992	351	77	11	0	8	3	10	9	5	3	4	28	41	.176	.098	.048	.057	.105

Luis Salazar, 36
Bats Right 508L 556R 312G 273F

L= .111G .110L .108F (.036/.053) .089 .075G .074R .072F = R

		ATBATS	1B	2B	3B	HR	HBP	BB	GDP	SB	CS	ROE	XB	RUNS	EOB%	RL#	SET-UP	DR-IN	RPA
Cubs	1990	410	76	13	3	12	4	16	4	3	1	9	22	48	.198	.115	.053	.056	.109
Cubs	1991	333	57	14	1	14	1	14	8	0	3	2	11	36	.148	.104	.042	.059	.101
Cubs	1992	255	39	7	2	5	0	9	10	1	1	6	9	21	.132	.069	.028	.045	.073

Rey Sanchez, 25
Bats Right 123L 178R 119G 68F 555ML

L= .077G .101L .143F (.048/.045) .093 .064G .088R .130F = R

		ATBATS	1B	2B	3B	HR	HBP	BB	GDP	SB	CS	ROE	XB	RUNS	EOB%	RL#	SET-UP	DR-IN	RPA
Cubs	1991	23	6	0	0	0	0	4	0	0	0	0	3	3	.306	.115	.065	.045	.110
Cubs	1992	255	46	14	3	1	3	9	7	2	1	8	18	28	.204	.095	.050	.050	.100

Ryne Sandberg, 33
Bats Right 714L 1321R 680G 519F

L= .152G .160L .171F (.087/.074) .161 .154G .162R .173 = R

		ATBATS	1B	2B	3B	HR	HBP	BB	GDP	SB	CS	ROE	XB	RUNS	EOB%	RL#	SET-UP	DR-IN	RPA
Cubs	1990	615	115	30	3	40	1	42	8	25	8	15	69	112	.209	.176	.084	.083	.167
Cubs	1991	585	110	32	2	26	2	83	9	22	10	10	54	108	.257	.162	.087	.070	.157
Cubs	1992	612	120	32	8	26	1	64	13	17	7	7	59	119	.231	.156	.086	.078	.164

Gary Scott, 24
Bats Right 64L 132R 75G 43F 673ML

L= .101G .097L ....F (.038/.041) .079 .074G .070R .063F = R

		ATBATS	1B	2B	3B	HR	HBP	BB	GDP	SB	CS	ROE	XB	RUNS	EOB%	RL#	SET-UP	DR-IN	RPA
Cubs	1991	79	9	3	0	1	3	9	2	0	1	1	3	7	.196	.073	.034	.036	.070
Cubs	1992	96	11	2	0	2	0	4	3	0	2	6	3	7	.132	.060	.025	.039	.064

Dwight Smith, 29
Bats Left 64L 672R 272G 186F

L= .068G .082L .118F (.048/.053) .101 .079G .103R .139F = R

		ATBATS	1B	2B	3B	HR	HBP	BB	GDP	SB	CS	ROE	XB	RUNS	EOB%	RL#	SET-UP	DR-IN	RPA
Cubs	1990	290	55	15	0	6	2	26	7	11	7	6	23	35	.213	.112	.054	.053	.107
Cubs	1991	167	26	7	2	3	1	9	2	2	3	4	6	16	.183	.092	.042	.047	.089
Cubs	1992	217	44	10	3	3	1	13	1	9	10	2	17	27	.193	.104	.053	.057	.110

Sammy Sosa, 24
Bats Right 477L 723R 365G 300F

L= .115G .112L .109F (.041/.057) .098 .091G .088R .085F = R

		ATBATS	1B	2B	3B	HR	HBP	BB	GDP	SB	CS	ROE	XB	RUNS	EOB%	RL#	SET-UP	DR-IN	RPA
White Sox	1990	532	73	26	10	15	6	29	10	32	17	6	46	59	.152	.102	.043	.059	.102
White Sox	1991	316	43	10	1	10	2	12	5	13	8	5	20	27	.126	.082	.030	.051	.081
Cubs	1992	262	51	7	2	8	4	18	4	15	7	1	22	36	.186	.114	.056	.063	.119

CHICAGO CUBS

Doug Strange, 28
Bats Both   28L   86R   34G   36F   797ML

L= ....G L   ....F   (.052/.045) .097   ....G   .099R   ....F = R

		ATBATS	1B	2B	3B	HR	HBP	BB	GDP	SB	CS	ROE	XB	RUNS	EOB%	RL#	SET-UP	DR-IN	RPA
Cubs	1991	9	3	1	0	0	1	0	0	1	0	0	0	2	.392	.214	.132	.070	.202
Cubs	1992	94	13	1	0	1	0	8	2	1	0	2	3	7	.171	.062	.029	.036	.065

Hector Villanueva, 28
Bats Right   240L   221R   131G   116F   183ML

L= .130G .119L .106F   (.060/.058) .118   .128G .117R .104F = R

		ATBATS	1B	2B	3B	HR	HBP	BB	GDP	SB	CS	ROE	XB	RUNS	EOB%	RL#	SET-UP	DR-IN	RPA
Cubs	1990	114	19	4	1	7	2	2	3	1	0	1	5	15	.138	.127	.048	.073	.121
Cubs	1991	192	29	10	1	13	0	20	3	0	0	6	2	35	.224	.168	.084	.079	.163
Cubs	1992	112	9	6	0	2	0	9	5	0	0	1	6	8	.118	.055	.021	.037	.058

Jose Vizcaino, 24
Bats Both   156L   351R   195G   121F

L= .067G .068L .069F   (.039/.043) .082   .087G .088R .089F = R

		ATBATS	1B	2B	3B	HR	HBP	BB	GDP	SB	CS	ROE	XB	RUNS	EOB%	RL#	SET-UP	DR-IN	RPA
Los Angeles	1990	51	12	1	1	0	0	3	1	1	1	1	4	5	.215	.095	.050	.049	.099
Cubs	1991	145	33	5	0	0	0	5	1	2	1	2	7	12	.212	.084	.041	.041	.082
Cubs	1992	285	49	10	4	1	0	12	4	3	1	5	17	26	.185	.079	.039	.044	.083

Jerome Walton, 27
Bats Right   364L   451R   265G   203F   31ML

L= .078G .087L .099F   (.042/.046) .088   .080G .089R .101F = R

		ATBATS	1B	2B	3B	HR	HBP	BB	GDP	SB	CS	ROE	XB	RUNS	EOB%	RL#	SET-UP	DR-IN	RPA
Cubs	1990	392	83	16	2	2	4	49	4	14	8	6	46	50	.265	.117	.062	.048	.110
Cubs	1991	270	40	13	1	5	3	19	7	7	3	6	23	27	.185	.091	.042	.047	.089
Cubs	1992	55	6	0	1	0	2	9	1	1	2	2	5	5	.222	.067	.036	.034	.070

Rick Wilkins, 25
Bats left   99L   400R   179G   134F   297ML

L= .095G .068L .033F   (.058/.059) .117   .156G .129R .094F = R

		ATBATS	1B	2B	3B	HR	HBP	BB	GDP	SB	CS	ROE	XB	RUNS	EOB%	RL#	SET-UP	DR-IN	RPA
Cubs	1991	203	30	9	0	6	6	17	3	3	3	5	13	25	.212	.109	.054	.052	.106
Cubs	1992	244	48	9	1	8	0	21	6	0	2	4	8	36	.206	.118	.062	.066	.118

PITCHERS

Paul Assenmacher, 32
Throws: Neutral type, moderate to severe lefty

(.077/.112) .100   370L   719R

		OUTS	RO	1B	2B	3B	HR	HBP	BB	GDP	SB	CS	PO	WP	BK	RUNS	EOB%	RL#	RPA
Chicago Cubs	1990	309	306	70	8	2	10	1	28	9	6	4	0	2	0	33	.134	.087	.080
Chicago Cubs	1991	308	308	58	13	4	10	3	25	3	8	5	0	4	0	35	.147	.092	.084
Chicago Cubs	1992	204	204	47	18	1	6	3	21	3	9	2	0	4	0	38	.199	.112	.122

Shawn Boskie, 25
Throws: Neutral type, extreme righty

(.151/.066) .117   782L   532R   218ML

		OUTS	RO	1B	2B	3B	HR	HBP	BB	GDP	SB	CS	PO	WP	BK	RUNS	EOB%	RL#	RPA
Chicago Cubs	1990	293	0	68	21	2	8	1	28	7	6	6	0	3	2	37	.157	.099	.090
Chicago Cubs	1991	387	57	101	29	6	14	5	48	9	4	2	1	1	1	69	.204	.127	.117
Chicago Cubs	1992	275	21	57	25	0	14	4	33	11	2	1	2	5	1	49	.155	.111	.120

Jim Bullinger, 27
Throws: Neutral type, moderate reverse righty

(.118/.137) .127   195L   159R   889ML

		OUTS	RO	1B	2B	3B	HR	HBP	BB	GDP	SB	CS	PO	WP	BK	RUNS	EOB%	RL#	RPA
Chicago Cubs	1992	255	103	49	9	5	9	4	48	7	8	2	0	4	0	47	.201	.109	.120

Frank Castillo, 23
Throws: Neutral type, extreme righty

(.110/.073) .096   790L   488R   98ML

		OUTS	RO	1B	2B	3B	HR	HBP	BB	GDP	SB	CS	PO	WP	BK	RUNS	EOB%	RL#	RPA
Chicago Cubs	1991	335	0	77	23	2	5	0	31	5	7	4	0	5	1	40	.180	.092	.085
Chicago Cubs	1992	616	0	114	42	4	19	6	57	6	18	9	0	11	0	91	.165	.093	.102

CHICAGO CUBS

Mike Harkey, 26

Throws: Neutral type, neutral reverse righty
(.117/.119) .118   569L   367R   101ML

		OUTS	RO	1B	2B	3B	HR	HBP	BB	GDP	SB	CS	PO	WP	BK	RUNS	EOB%	RL#	RPA
Chicago Cubs	1990	521	0	105	29	5	14	7	51	10	8	6	0	8	1	64	.165	.096	.088
Chicago Cubs	1991	56	0	14	4	0	3	0	5	1	2	0	0	1	0	10	.181	.128	.118
Chicago Cubs	1992	114	0	21	6	3	4	1	15	2	3	3	0	3	1	18	.160	.102	.110

Greg Hibbard, 28

Throws: Groundball type, extreme lefty
(.066/.111) .105   304L   2007R

		OUTS	RO	1B	2B	3B	HR	HBP	BB	GDP	SB	CS	PO	WP	BK	RUNS	EOB%	RL#	RPA
Chi. White Sox	1990	633	0	151	34	6	11	6	53	25	11	8	0	2	1	75	.143	.084	.086
Chi. White Sox	1991	582	32	144	27	2	23	2	56	27	6	8	0	1	0	78	.125	.094	.096
Chi. White Sox	1992	528	18	140	25	5	17	7	55	20	9	6	0	1	1	85	.163	.105	.114

Greg Maddux, 26

Throws: Groundball type, extreme righty
(.093/.044) .074   1827L   1169R

		OUTS	RO	1B	2B	3B	HR	HBP	BB	GDP	SB	CS	PO	WP	BK	RUNS	EOB%	RL#	RPA
Chicago Cubs	1990	711	0	186	42	3	11	4	61	27	13	4	3	3	3	80	.159	.088	.081
Chicago Cubs	1991	789	0	171	34	9	18	6	57	14	25	7	5	6	3	85	.147	.086	.079
Chicago Cubs	1992	804	0	153	36	5	7	14	63	19	26	13	1	5	0	77	.140	.064	.069

Chuck McElroy, 25

Throws: Neutral type, moderate lefty
(.087/.093) .091   275L   535R

		OUTS	RO	1B	2B	3B	HR	HBP	BB	GDP	SB	CS	PO	WP	BK	RUNS	EOB%	RL#	RPA
Philadelphia	1990	42	42	17	7	0	0	0	8	1	2	0	0	0	0	12	.316	.167	.166
Chicago Cubs	1991	304	304	55	10	1	7	0	50	6	12	10	0	1	0	31	.152	.081	.074
Chicago Cubs	1992	251	251	46	19	3	5	0	41	2	4	3	0	3	0	42	.213	.101	.110

Mike Morgan, 33

Throws: Groundball type, moderate to severe righty
(.090/.055) .075   1527L   1138R

		OUTS	RO	1B	2B	3B	HR	HBP	BB	GDP	SB	CS	PO	WP	BK	RUNS	EOB%	RL#	RPA
Los Angeles	1990	633	0	156	37	4	19	5	55	19	16	13	0	4	1	88	.145	.095	.100
Los Angeles	1991	709	7	157	22	6	12	3	51	23	24	7	2	6	0	68	.126	.073	.073
Chicago Cubs	1992	720	0	147	39	3	14	3	69	29	6	9	1	11	0	79	.127	.072	.078

Ken Patterson, 28

Throws: Flyball type, moderate lefty
(.101/.118) .113   219L   478R

		OUTS	RO	1B	2B	3B	HR	HBP	BB	GDP	SB	CS	PO	WP	BK	RUNS	EOB%	RL#	RPA
Chi. White Sox	1990	199	199	42	9	1	6	2	33	5	5	3	0	2	0	31	.188	.105	.108
Chi. White Sox	1991	191	191	34	7	2	5	1	34	6	5	3	0	2	0	25	.171	.094	.096
Chicago Cubs	1992	125	116	23	9	2	7	1	21	1	2	3	0	3	1	27	.190	.130	.139

Jeff Robinson, 32

Throws: Groundball type, extreme reverse righty
(.087/.135) .114   403L   501R   60ML

		OUTS	RO	1B	2B	3B	HR	HBP	BB	GDP	SB	CS	PO	WP	BK	RUNS	EOB%	RL#	RPA
N.Y. Yankees	1990	266	187	57	15	2	8	1	31	12	6	5	0	2	0	31	.129	.089	.085
California	1991	171	171	34	13	0	9	2	25	6	4	0	1	10	0	32	.176	.124	.127
Chicago Cubs	1992	234	170	53	15	3	5	2	33	8	9	8	0	8	1	35	.158	.093	.100

Bob Scanlan, 26

Throws: Groundball type, neutral righty
(.086/.083) .085   413L   380R

		OUTS	RO	1B	2B	3B	HR	HBP	BB	GDP	SB	CS	PO	WP	BK	RUNS	EOB%	RL#	RPA
Chicago Cubs	1991	333	125	85	19	5	5	3	37	11	5	7	0	5	1	41	.168	.094	.086
Chicago Cubs	1992	262	262	58	13	1	4	1	24	8	6	3	0	6	4	31	.151	.077	.083

Heathcliff Slocumb, 26

Throws: Groundball type, extreme righty
(.169/.052) .108   202L   218R   177ML

		OUTS	RO	1B	2B	3B	HR	HBP	BB	GDP	SB	CS	PO	WP	BK	RUNS	EOB%	RL#	RPA
Chicago Cubs	1991	188	188	39	10	1	3	3	24	1	12	1	0	9	0	26	.221	.104	.096
Chicago Cubs	1992	108	108	46	3	0	3	1	18	2	4	4	0	1	0	26	.236	.129	.141

Dave Smith, 37

Throws: Groundball type, extreme righty
(.141/.091) .117   221L   200R

		OUTS	RO	1B	2B	3B	HR	HBP	BB	GDP	SB	CS	PO	WP	BK	RUNS	EOB%	RL#	RPA
Houston	1990	181	181	34	5	2	4	0	16	4	4	8	0	5	5	17	.087	.061	.068
Chicago Cubs	1991	99	99	25	4	4	6	1	14	5	3	0	0	1	1	19	.171	.140	.129
Chicago Cubs	1992	43	43	13	1	1	0	0	2	1	2	0	0	0	1	6	.181	.083	.089

Chicago Cubs AAA & AA Minor League Ratings

AAA (IOWA)	AGE	BATS	POSITION	CPA	RUNS	SET-UP	DRIVE-IN	RPA
Alex Arias	25	R	SS\2B	463	45.7	.054	.045	.099
Billy Bates	29	L	2B	291	18.9	.032	.033	.065
Phil Bradley	33	R	OF	313	28.4	.051	.040	.091
Scott Bryant	25	R	1B\OF	372	37.0	.042	.057	.099
Pedro Castellano	22	R	3B	449	35.3	.041	.038	.079
Tony Chance	28	R	OF	488	40.4	.039	.044	.083
Mike Knapp	28	R	C	152	12.5	.040	.042	.082
Jeff Kunkel	30	R	2B	317	23.1	.029	.044	.073
Elvin Paulino	25	L	1B	331	21.5	.029	.036	.065
Jorge Pedre	26	R	C	333	26.2	.037	.042	.079
Fernando Ramsey	27	R	OF	519	33.6	.030	.035	.065
Kevin Roberson	24	B	OF	208	21.3	.048	.055	.103
Jeff Schulz	31	L	1B\OF	337	25.3	.035	.040	.075
Gary Scott	24	R	3B\SS	405	39.2	.049	.048	.097
Doug Strange	28	B	2B\3B	226	20.8	.044	.048	.092
Hector Villanueva	28	R	1B\C	183	18.5	.046	.055	.101
Scott Wade	29	R	OF	263	29.1	.052	.059	.111
Rick Wilkins	25	L	C	177	21.0	.065	.054	.119

AA (CHARLOTTE)	AGE	BATS	POSITION	CPA	RUNS	SET-UP	DRIVE-IN	RPA
Rick Casarotti	26	B	2B	206	12.8	.027	.035	.062
Rusty Crockett	26	R	2B\SS	365	26.3	.037	.035	.072
Phil Dauphin	23	L	OF	577	54.2	.049	.045	.094
Darrin Duffy	27	R	SS\2B	149	7.5	.024	.026	.050
Chris Ebright	25	L	1B	468	49.9	.053	.054	.107
Matt Franco	23	L	3B\1B	374	31.8	.044	.041	.085
Mike Grace	25	R	3B	361	29.6	.039	.043	.082
Richie Grayum	24	L	OF	38.3	40.3	.053	.052	.105
John Jensen	26	L	OF	460	50.3	.058	.051	.109
Jim Robinson	23	R	C	215	18.8	.050	.037	.087
Ozzie Timmons	22	R	OF	137	10.1	.034	.040	.074
Matt Walbeck	23	B	C	426	41.2	.050	.047	.097
Doug Welch	26	R	OF	134	8.9	.027	.039	.066
Billy White	24	R	SS\2B	461	35.0	.038	.038	.076

AAA Pitchers	Age	Throws	Outs	RPA	AA Pitchers	Age	Throws	Outs	RPA
Steve Adkins	28	L	405	.162	Ryan Hawblitzel	21	R	524	.130
Brad Arnsberg	29	R	299	.172	Jessie Hollins	22	R	211	.133
Bill Brennan	29	R	169	.176	Eric Jaques	26	L	199	.123
John Gardner	27	R	367	.150	Jerry Kutzler	27	R	124	.112
Mike Harkey	26	R	92	.155	Mike Sodders	26	L	204	.120
Jeff Hartsock	26	R	520	.122	Dave Stevens	22	R	449	.144
Paul Marak	27	R	290	.129	Dave Swartzbaugh	24	R	495	.122
Scott May	31	R	197	.152	Steve Trachsel	22	R	573	.115
Bill Melvin	26	R	321	.133	Travis Willis	24	R	206	.114
Dave Pavlas	30	R	112	.133					
Laddie Renfroe	30	R	302	.140					
John Salles	25	R	451	.137					
Bob Sebra	31	R	274	.162					
Heathcliff Slocumb	26	R	125	.091					
Julio Strauss	25	R	230	.126					
Turk Wendell	25	R	75	.115					

MONTREAL EXPOS

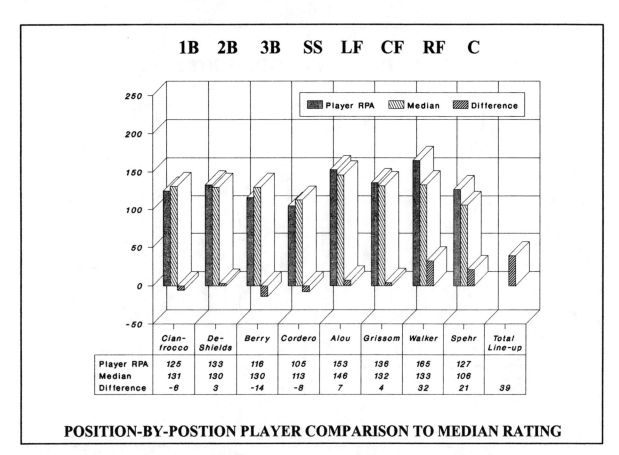

	1B	2B	3B	SS	LF	CF	RF	C
	Cian-frocco	De-Shields	Berry	Cordero	Alou	Grissom	Walker	Spehr	Total Line-up
Player RPA	125	133	116	105	153	136	165	127	
Median	131	130	130	113	146	132	133	106	
Difference	-6	3	-14	-8	7	4	32	21	39

POSITION-BY-POSTION PLAYER COMPARISON TO MEDIAN RATING

DEFENSIVE TEAM AND STADIUM DATA FOR THE LAST 3 YEARS:

TEAM DEFENSE BY POSITION:

POSITION-BY-POSITION STADIUM CHARACTERISTICS:

		1990	1991	1992	
1B:	Home	+0.9	-0.7	-4.3	Slightly hard to play
	Away	+0.4	+1.9	+4.7	
2B:	Home	-0.5	-0.5	+2.2	Hard to play
	Away	-1.1	-1.1	+0.1	
3B:	Home	+2.1	+1.6	+2.6	Easy to play
	Away	+2.4	+2.6	+3.3	
SS:	Home	+0.4	+4.1	-2.3	Average
	Away	-1.4	+0.4	-1.9	
LF:	Home	+8.6	+2.0	-0.9	Average
	Away	-4.1	+0.6	+6.0	
CF:	Home	+13.7	+1.6	+3.9	Average
	Away	+1.3	+2.9	-2.1	
RF:	Home	+1.3	-1.9	-1.3	Average
	Away	+1.4	+5.9	+4.6	
Total Home:		+26.5	+6.2	+0.1	
Total Away:		-1.1	+13.2	+14.7	

Comments: **This young team has preferred to play defense at the away parks. I guess it's because it's the veterans that give a home stadium advantage as they learn the quirks of their home park. This is a very good defensive team. While Spike Owen seemed to lose range in '92, Wil Cordero's defensive debut was not auspicious. His defense, hopefully, will improve with experience.**

MONTREAL EXPOS

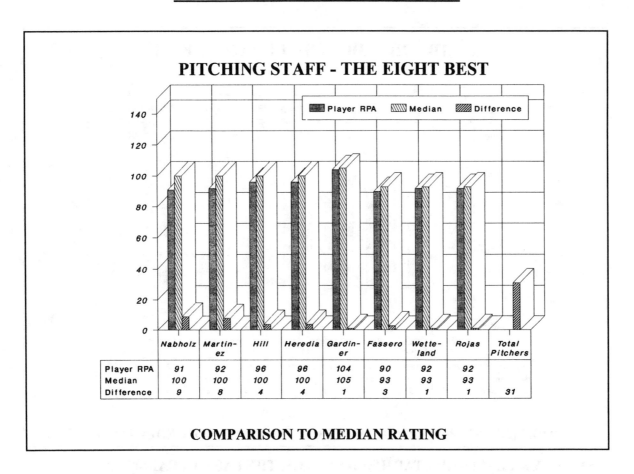

PITCHING STAFF - THE EIGHT BEST

	Nabholz	Martin-ez	Hill	Heredia	Gardin-er	Fassero	Wette-land	Rojas	Total Pitchers
Player RPA	91	92	96	96	104	90	92	92	
Median	100	100	100	100	105	93	93	93	
Difference	9	8	4	4	1	3	1	1	31

Legend: Player RPA, Median, Difference

COMPARISON TO MEDIAN RATING

SUGGESTED LINE-UPS (with set-up RPA & drive-in RPA ratings):

Vs: Left-handed Groundball

C:	T. Spehr	78-62
SS:	W. Cordero	76-62
2B:	D. DeShields	73-65
3B:	F. Bolick	71-64
CF:	M. Grissom	71-71
RF:	L. Walker	67-66
1B:	A. Cianfrocco	67-66
LF:	M. Alou	66-63
Pitcher		

Vs: Neutral Lefty Pitchers

C:	T. Spehr	78-62
SS:	W. Cordero	76-62
3B:	F. Bolick	71-64
RF:	L. Walker	74-74
CF:	M. Grissom	71-71
2B:	D. DeShields	69-63
LF:	M. Alou	64-61
1B:	A. Cianfrocco	67-66
Pitcher		

Vs: Left-handed Flyball

C:	T. Spehr	78-62
SS:	W. Cordero	76-62
3B:	F. Bolick	71-64
RF:	L. Walker	86-86
CF:	M. Grissom	72-71
1B:	A. Cianfrocco	67-66
2B:	D. DeShields	64-58
LF:	M. Alou	60-58
Pitcher		

Vs: Right-handed Groundball

C:	T. Spehr	68-52
2B:	D. DeShields	75-67
3B:	F. Bolick	71-64
CF:	M. Alou	80-77
RF:	L. Walker	70-69
LF:	J. VanderWal	69-69
SS:	W. Cordero	66-52
1B:	G. Colbrunn	64-60
Pitcher		

Vs: Neutral Righty Pitchers

C:	T. Spehr	68-52
2B:	D. DeShields	72-64
3B:	F. Bolick	71-64
CF:	M. Alou	78-75
RF:	L. Walker	77-77
LF:	J. VanderWal	74-73
SS:	W. Cordero	66-52
1B:	G. Colbrunn	64-60
Pitcher		

Vs: Right-handed Flyball

C:	T. Spehr	68-52
2B:	D. DeShields	66-60
3B:	F. Bolick	71-64
CF:	M. Alou	74-72
RF:	L. Walker	89-89
LF:	J. VanderWal	81-81
SS:	W. Cordero	66-52
1B:	G. Colbrunn	64-60
Pitcher		

Comments: The Expos have a very solid offense with no apparent weaknesses, except one glaring one. The Expos don't have a superior lead-off type hitter. They had one in Bret Barberie, but lost him to the Marlins in the expansion draft. Tim Spehr, despite a low batting average, knows how to get on base, which is the main qualification for a lead-off hitter. A big question is whether Frank Bolick can play well enough on defense to keep him in the line-up.

MONTREAL EXPOS

It's sometimes hard to write about a team you work for since you wonder if the reader will think that you're being partial. Last year I referred to the Expos as one of my two "sleeper" teams and I worried how serious I would be taken by the readers. Fortunately, I was proven correct in both cases.

This team is no longer a "sleeper" team. It is getting a lot of attention in the media due to the perception that the Expos are, by default, the favorites to win the eastern division. There has been a lot of criticism of the trades of Tim Wallach, Ivan Calderon & Mark Gardner. I really don't get it. Wallach and Gardner, in my opinion, really cost us the pennant in '92 due to their poor performances. Ivan Calderon played sparingly due to an injury and Moises Alou played marvelously in his absence. So what is it that we lost?

This furor reminds me of the situation last winter when GM Dan Duquette took all those hits from the press for the Galarraga trade.

In my opinion, the Gardner for Tim Spehr trade is a huge steal on the part of the Expos. They unload a pitcher with no value for an excellent young catcher who has good pop in his bat and ability to get on base to fill a position that was a serious problem for the Expos all last season.

Some may argue that the Expos could have gotten more for Calderon, but don't be too critical because Gardiner isn't a "big-name" pitcher. Mike Gardiner is a better pitcher than most people realize. He's certainly a lot better than Mark Gardner. He helps further solidify an already solid pitching staff.

I was stunned by the loss of Bret Barberie in the Expansion draft. He's one of my favorite young players and he'll be a super player with the Florida Marlins. His absence will really hurt since he's one of the best leadoff type hitters around and the Expos don't currently possess a quality leadoff type hitter. DeShields doesn't walk enough to qualify as a true leadoff type hitter. He is better suited to the number two or three slot. I would have protected Barberie over pitcher Kent Bottenfield.

The Expos acquisition of Frank Bolick was a real steal. He's got a very strong bat.

When I did the team evaluations in order to do projections for '93, I was very pleased to see that the acquisitions of Spehr, Bolick and Gardiner really solidified this team. There are no weak points other than the question of how well Wilfredo Cordero's defense will progress. The Expos are easily the solidest team in the division. Then why aren't I picking them to win the division? Because of the lack of "franchise-type" players that can carry a team through hard times. The nearest thing to a "franchise-type" player is Larry Walker.

I wouldn't be too alarmed by my prediction if I were an Expo fan, however. One of the advantages that a team that is solid and deep at every position has is that if the more talented team fails to take proper advantage of the talent it possesses, then the crown almost automatically falls in our lap. And this is very likely to be the case.

Montreal's Projected record for 1993: 86--76, good for 2nd place in the division.

MONTREAL EXPOS

Moises Alou, 26

Bats Right   164L   229R   147G   90F

L= .122G .118L .111F (.068/.066) .134 .150G .146R .139F = R

		ATBATS	1B	2B	3B	HR	HBP	BB	GDP	SB	CS	ROE	XB	RUNS	EOB%	RL#	SET-UP	DR-IN	RPA
Pittsburgh	1990	5	1	0	0	0	0	0	1	0	0	0	0	0	.048	.008	.000	.009	.009
Montreal	1990	15	2	0	1	0	0	0	0	0	0	0	2	1	.128	.072	.029	.047	.076
Montreal	1992	341	57	28	2	9	1	25	5	16	4	2	33	49	.213	.137	.068	.066	.134

Bret Barberie, 25

Bats Both   121L   380R   208G   107F   329ML

L= .112G .107L .098F (.082/.064) .146 .163G .158R .149F = R

		ATBATS	1B	2B	3B	HR	HBP	BB	GDP	SB	CS	ROE	XB	RUNS	EOB%	RL#	SET-UP	DR-IN	RPA
Montreal	1991	136	32	12	2	2	2	18	4	0	0	2	8	28	.311	.164	.104	.069	.173
Montreal	1992	285	54	11	0	1	8	44	4	9	5	1	17	35	.266	.106	.058	.045	.103

Sean Berry, 26

Bats Right   50L   101R   61G   22F   920ML

L= .110G .097L ....F (.053/.056) .109 .128G .115R ....F = R

		ATBATS	1B	2B	3B	HR	HBP	BB	GDP	SB	CS	ROE	XB	RUNS	EOB%	RL#	SET-UP	DR-IN	RPA
Kansas City	1990	23	3	1	1	0	0	2	0	0	0	0	2	2	.213	.097	.049	.048	.097
Kansas City	1991	60	5	3	0	0	1	5	1	0	0	0	4	3	.159	.048	.021	.028	.049
Montreal	1992	57	17	1	0	1	0	1	1	2	1	0	3	7	.199	.119	.057	.060	.117

Ivan Calderon, 30

Bats Right   497L   898R   415G   329F

L= .179G .175L .169F (.073/.070) .143 .130G .126R .120F = R

		ATBATS	1B	2B	3B	HR	HBP	BB	GDP	SB	CS	ROE	XB	RUNS	EOB%	RL#	SET-UP	DR-IN	RPA
White Sox	1990	607	106	44	2	14	1	44	26	32	17	4	48	69	.165	.101	.045	.056	.101
Montreal	1991	470	97	22	3	19	3	49	7	31	17	5	29	84	.222	.143	.080	.075	.155
Montreal	1992	170	26	14	2	3	1	13	4	1	2	1	11	20	.199	.115	.054	.057	.111

Gary Carter, 38

Bats Right   475L   401R   297G   205F

L= .109G .097L .080F (.048/.049) .097 .110G .098R .081F = R

		ATBATS	1B	2B	3B	HR	HBP	BB	GDP	SB	CS	ROE	XB	RUNS	EOB%	RL#	SET-UP	DR-IN	RPA
San Francisco	1990	244	43	10	0	9	1	22	2	1	1	7	14	37	.233	.133	.071	.063	.134
Los Angeles	1991	248	41	14	0	6	7	21	11	2	3	5	14	29	.197	.100	.049	.052	.101
Montreal	1992	285	38	18	1	5	2	29	4	0	4	1	8	30	.196	.098	.045	.049	.094

Rick Cerone, 38

Bats Right   104L   142R   97G   52F   580ML

L= .100G .103L .107F (.056/.050) .106 .103G .106R .110F = R

		ATBATS	1B	2B	3B	HR	HBP	BB	GDP	SB	CS	ROE	XB	RUNS	EOB%	RL#	SET-UP	DR-IN	RPA
Yankees	1990	139	34	6	0	2	0	5	4	0	0	2	8	16	.208	.107	.055	.055	.110
Mets	1991	227	47	13	0	2	1	28	9	1	1	4	9	27	.245	.107	.056	.048	.104
Montreal	1992	63	12	4	0	1	1	3	0	1	2	1	7	8	.211	.118	.057	.057	.114

Archi Cianfrocco, 26

Bats Right   74L   102R   54G   44F   233ML

L= .156G .157L .158F (.058/.058) .116 .111G .112R .113F = R

		ATBATS	1B	2B	3B	HR	HBP	BB	GDP	SB	CS	ROE	XB	RUNS	EOB%	RL#	SET-UP	DR-IN	RPA
Montreal	1992	232	43	5	2	6	1	11	2	3	0	8	15	29	.211	.121	.060	.058	.118

Greg Colbrunn, 23

Bats Right   37L   101R   57G   18F   628ML

L= .086G .090L .096F (.058/.054) .112 .124G .128R .134F = R

		ATBATS	1B	2B	3B	HR	HBP	BB	GDP	SB	CS	ROE	XB	RUNS	EOB%	RL#	SET-UP	DR-IN	RPA
Montreal	1992	168	35	8	0	2	2	5	1	3	2	5	10	19	.223	.113	.057	.053	.110

Wilfredo Cordero, 21

L= .184G .194L ....F (.062/.050) .112 .072G .082R ....F = R

		ATBATS	1B	2B	3B	HR	HBP	BB	GDP	SB	CS	ROE	XB	RUNS	EOB%	RL#	SET-UP	DR-IN	RPA
Montreal	1992	126	31	4	1	2	1	9	3	0	0	3	12	18	.251	.136	.072	.060	.132

MONTREAL EXPOS

Delino DeShields, 23

Bats Left   663L   1170R   634G   418F

L= .126G   .120L   .110F   (.065/.058) .123   .130G   .124R   .114F = R

		ATBATS	1B	2B	3B	HR	HBP	BB	GDP	SB	CS	ROE	XB	RUNS	EOB%	RL#	SET-UP	DR-IN	RPA
Montreal	1990	499	106	28	6	4	4	63	10	42	27	3	52	70	.233	.117	.063	.057	.120
Montreal	1991	563	105	15	4	10	2	93	6	56	26	6	60	84	.240	.115	.066	.057	.123
Montreal	1992	530	121	19	8	7	3	50	10	46	18	1	56	72	.223	.128	.064	.060	.124

Darrin Fletcher, 26

Bats Left   43L   367R   165G   75F   392ML

L= ....G   .114L   ....F   (.037/.047) .084   .090G   .077R   .047F = R

		ATBATS	1B	2B	3B	HR	HBP	BB	GDP	SB	CS	ROE	XB	RUNS	EOB%	RL#	SET-UP	DR-IN	RPA
Los Angeles	1990	1	0	0	0	0	0	0	0	0	0	0	0	0	.000	.000	.000	.000	.000
Philadelphia	1990	22	2	1	0	0	0	1	0	0	0	0	4	1	.135	.048	.019	.029	.048
Philadelphia	1991	136	22	8	0	1	0	5	2	0	1	0	5	10	.160	.069	.031	.039	.070
Montreal	1992	222	40	10	2	2	2	11	8	0	2	0	5	18	.159	.077	.033	.043	.076

Tom Foley, 33

Bats Left   65L   424R   203G   118F

L= .048G   .037L   .017F   (.029/.035) .064   .079G   .068R   .048F = R

		ATBATS	1B	2B	3B	HR	HBP	BB	GDP	SB	CS	ROE	XB	RUNS	EOB%	RL#	SET-UP	DR-IN	RPA
Montreal	1990	164	32	2	1	0	0	10	4	0	1	1	15	12	.172	.063	.029	.036	.065
Montreal	1991	168	23	11	1	0	1	10	4	2	0	3	8	14	.189	.070	.036	.040	.076
Montreal	1992	115	16	3	1	0	1	6	6	3	0	1	1	6	.127	.048	.017	.029	.046

Marquis Grissom, 25

Bats Right   662L   961R   604G   368F

L= .133G   .133L   .134F   (.061/.062) .123   .116G   .116R   .117F = R

		ATBATS	1B	2B	3B	HR	HBP	BB	GDP	SB	CS	ROE	XB	RUNS	EOB%	RL#	SET-UP	DR-IN	RPA
Montreal	1990	288	55	14	2	3	0	25	3	22	4	4	35	38	.232	.114	.062	.056	.118
Montreal	1991	558	111	23	9	6	1	34	8	76	17	11	37	74	.210	.112	.060	.060	.120
Montreal	1992	653	121	39	6	14	5	36	12	78	18	10	66	88	.200	.129	.062	.064	.126

Spike Owen, 31

Bats Both   617L   810R   480G   317F

L= .121G   .126L   .133F   (.057/.053) .110   .092G   .097R   .104F = R

		ATBATS	1B	2B	3B	HR	HBP	BB	GDP	SB	CS	ROE	XB	RUNS	EOB%	RL#	SET-UP	DR-IN	RPA
Montreal	1990	453	72	24	5	5	0	58	6	8	6	9	34	59	.242	.109	.060	.052	.112
Montreal	1991	424	75	22	8	3	1	31	11	2	6	5	29	46	.197	.091	.047	.050	.097
Montreal	1992	386	78	16	3	7	0	47	10	9	4	5	34	54	.238	.127	.066	.057	.123

John VanderWal, 26

Bats Left   48L   253R   115G   71F   569ML

L= .069G   .078L   .093F   (.065/.065) .130   .131G   .140R   .155F = R

		ATBATS	1B	2B	3B	HR	HBP	BB	GDP	SB	CS	ROE	XB	RUNS	EOB%	RL#	SET-UP	DR-IN	RPA
Montreal	1991	61	7	4	1	1	0	1	2	0	0	0	2	4	.108	.066	.023	.044	.067
Montreal	1992	213	37	8	2	4	0	22	2	3	0	1	13	27	.225	.116	.059	.054	.113

Larry Walker, 26

Bats Left   532L   1057R   554G   345F

L= .126G   .141L   .165F   (.072/.073) .145   .132G   .147R   .171F = R

		ATBATS	1B	2B	3B	HR	HBP	BB	GDP	SB	CS	ROE	XB	RUNS	EOB%	RL#	SET-UP	DR-IN	RPA
Montreal	1990	419	61	18	3	19	5	44	8	21	8	4	37	64	.192	.128	.063	.069	.132
Montreal	1991	487	93	30	2	16	5	40	7	14	11	3	37	76	.214	.130	.070	.069	.139
Montreal	1992	528	101	31	4	23	6	31	9	18	6	3	51	85	.203	.155	.074	.076	.150

Tim Wallach, 35

Bats Right   644L   1268R   690G   427F

L= .106G   .111L   .120F   (.048/.051) .099   .088G   .093R   .102F = R

		ATBATS	1B	2B	3B	HR	HBP	BB	GDP	SB	CS	ROE	XB	RUNS	EOB%	RL#	SET-UP	DR-IN	RPA
Montreal	1990	626	122	37	5	21	3	31	12	6	9	10	47	91	.198	.130	.065	.069	.134
Montreal	1991	577	94	22	1	13	6	42	12	2	4	9	34	64	.189	.093	.047	.052	.099
Montreal	1992	537	81	29	1	9	8	48	10	2	2	4	34	58	.206	.101	.049	.049	.098

PITCHERS

Throws: Neutral type, extreme reverse lefty

Brian Barnes, 25
(.152/.099) .109   218L   954R   338ML

		OUTS	RO	1B	2B	3B	HR	HBP	BB	GDP	SB	CS	PO	WP	BK	RUNS	EOB%	RL#	RPA
Montreal	1990	84	0	20	3	0	2	0	7	2	4	0	0	2	0	11	.166	.091	.097
Montreal	1991	480	2	91	24	4	16	6	82	10	20	8	1	5	1	81	.188	.106	.115
Montreal	1992	300	18	53	15	0	9	3	45	7	14	7	0	1	2	39	.159	.094	.095

Throws: Neutral type, righty

Kent Bottenfield, 24
(..../....) .122   67L   62R   1259ML

		OUTS	RO	1B	2B	3B	HR	HBP	BB	GDP	SB	CS	PO	WP	BK	RUNS	EOB%	RL#	RPA
Montreal	1992	97	35	19	5	1	1	1	10	2	3	0	1	0	0	11	.170	.081	.084

Throws: Groundball type, moderate reverse lefty

Jeff Fassero, 29
(.100/.083) .088   171L   390R

		OUTS	RO	1B	2B	3B	HR	HBP	BB	GDP	SB	CS	PO	WP	BK	RUNS	EOB%	RL#	RPA
Montreal	1991	166	166	29	7	2	1	1	16	4	3	1	0	4	0	17	.155	.067	.074
Montreal	1992	257	257	63	12	5	1	2	28	6	12	2	0	7	1	35	.197	.095	.097

Throws: Flyball type, moderate righty

Mark Gardner, 30
(.114/.098) .108   1216L   829R

		OUTS	RO	1B	2B	3B	HR	HBP	BB	GDP	SB	CS	PO	WP	BK	RUNS	EOB%	RL#	RPA
Montreal	1990	458	4	91	21	4	13	9	56	10	16	6	0	2	4	67	.173	.097	.104
Montreal	1991	505	0	99	21	2	17	4	74	8	13	17	0	2	1	71	.154	.092	.100
Montreal	1992	539	13	125	36	3	15	9	58	2	29	11	0	2	0	88	.197	.114	.116

Throws: Groundball type, moderate righty

Gil Heredia, 27
(.101/.089) .096   160L   133R   989ML

		OUTS	RO	1B	2B	3B	HR	HBP	BB	GDP	SB	CS	PO	WP	BK	RUNS	EOB%	RL#	RPA
San Francisco	1991	99	18	19	3	1	4	0	5	4	2	2	0	1	0	10	.060	.064	.075
San Francisco	1992	90	43	23	6	0	3	1	15	4	3	2	0	1	0	16	.178	.106	.117
Montreal	1992	44	29	9	2	0	1	0	4	3	2	1	1	0	0	3	.027	.052	.053

Throws: Groundball type, moderate righty

Ken Hill, 27
(.101/.090) .096   1120L   797R

		OUTS	RO	1B	2B	3B	HR	HBP	BB	GDP	SB	CS	PO	WP	BK	RUNS	EOB%	RL#	RPA
St. Louis	1990	236	11	52	17	3	7	1	32	3	9	4	0	5	0	40	.197	.115	.116
St. Louis	1991	544	0	103	23	6	15	6	63	11	19	11	0	7	1	75	.153	.086	.097
Montreal	1992	654	0	133	36	5	13	3	71	12	30	8	2	11	4	84	.168	.093	.095

Throws: Neutral type, moderate lefty

Bill Krueger, 34
(.093/.112) .109   347L   1644R

		OUTS	RO	1B	2B	3B	HR	HBP	BB	GDP	SB	CS	PO	WP	BK	RUNS	EOB%	RL#	RPA
Milwaukee	1990	387	123	100	22	5	10	3	48	14	9	6	0	8	0	59	.174	.107	.107
Seattle	1991	525	70	141	34	4	15	4	56	19	11	5	4	10	1	78	.166	.103	.100
Minnesota	1992	484	0	114	33	1	18	3	44	13	21	3	1	11	0	81	.165	.108	.117
Montreal	1992	52	27	18	4	1	0	1	7	0	1	1	0	1	0	11	.271	.130	.133

Throws: Neutral type, extreme righty

Bill Landrum, 34
(.131/.091) .111   337L   334R   109ML

		OUTS	RO	1B	2B	3B	HR	HBP	BB	GDP	SB	CS	PO	WP	BK	RUNS	EOB%	RL#	RPA
Pittsburgh	1990	215	215	59	3	3	4	0	16	10	8	2	0	1	1	24	.127	.079	.084
Pittsburgh	1991	229	229	63	7	2	4	0	14	3	9	1	1	3	2	30	.172	.093	.094
Montreal	1992	60	60	19	4	1	3	2	7	2	4	1	0	0	0	14	.202	.150	.152

MONTREAL EXPOS

Dennis Martinez, 37   (.077/.084) .080

Throws: Groundball type, moderate reverse righty

1574L   1047R

		OUTS	RO	1B	2B	3B	HR	HBP	BB	GDP	SB	CS	PO	WP	BK	RUNS	EOB%	RL#	RPA
Montreal	1990	678	0	139	30	6	16	6	40	13	19	9	0	1	1	78	.133	.080	.085
Montreal	1991	666	0	140	32	6	9	4	59	14	22	4	3	3	0	80	.160	.080	.087
Montreal	1992	679	0	134	26	0	12	9	57	9	22	17	3	2	0	64	.133	.073	.074

Chris Nabholz, 25   (.109/.089) .093

Throws: Neutral type, moderate reverse lefty

299L   1366R

		OUTS	RO	1B	2B	3B	HR	HBP	BB	GDP	SB	CS	PO	WP	BK	RUNS	EOB%	RL#	RPA
Montreal	1990	210	0	27	8	2	6	2	31	3	7	3	1	1	1	25	.153	.083	.089
Montreal	1991	461	0	91	35	3	5	2	53	9	15	11	1	3	1	58	.163	.082	.090
Montreal	1992	585	0	129	29	7	11	5	72	21	23	6	1	5	1	76	.165	.093	.095

Mel Rojas, 26   (.100/.085) .093

Throws: Neutral type, moderate righty

418L   322R   221ML

		OUTS	RO	1B	2B	3B	HR	HBP	BB	GDP	SB	CS	PO	WP	BK	RUNS	EOB%	RL#	RPA
Montreal	1990	120	120	22	7	0	5	2	20	1	4	2	0	2	0	22	.201	.116	.123
Montreal	1991	144	144	26	9	3	4	1	12	1	5	1	0	3	0	22	.173	.101	.109
Montreal	1992	302	302	52	15	2	2	2	26	7	12	3	0	2	0	27	.145	.068	.069

Doug Simons, 26   (.073/.129) .108

Throws: Neutral type, extreme lefty

103L   167R   481ML

		OUTS	RO	1B	2B	3B	HR	HBP	BB	GDP	SB	CS	PO	WP	BK	RUNS	EOB%	RL#	RPA
New York Mets	1991	182	176	36	13	1	5	2	14	3	5	4	0	3	0	20	.144	.092	.081
Montreal	1992	16	16	9	3	0	3	1	2	0	0	0	0	1	0	11	.301	.335	.331

Sergio Valdez, 27   (.081/.112) .097

Throws: Neutral type, moderate to severe reverse righty

319L   335R   796ML

		OUTS	RO	1B	2B	3B	HR	HBP	BB	GDP	SB	CS	PO	WP	BK	RUNS	EOB%	RL#	RPA
Atlanta	1990	16	16	5	1	0	0	0	3	1	0	0	0	1	0	2	.222	.100	.094
Cleveland	1990	307	79	65	26	1	17	1	33	9	6	4	0	3	0	53	.151	.119	.120
Cleveland	1991	49	49	11	1	0	3	0	4	1	2	0	0	1	0	7	.141	.112	.110
Montreal	1992	112	112	17	5	1	2	0	11	2	9	1	0	4	0	12	.147	.080	.082

John Wetteland, 26   (.095/.090) .093

Throws: Flyball type, neutral righty

308L   244R

		OUTS	RO	1B	2B	3B	HR	HBP	BB	GDP	SB	CS	PO	WP	BK	RUNS	EOB%	RL#	RPA
Los Angeles	1990	129	73	32	6	0	6	4	14	1	7	2	1	8	0	25	.191	.126	.130
Los Angeles	1991	27	27	4	1	0	0	1	3	1	0	0	0	1	0	2	.160	.055	.055
Montreal	1992	250	250	49	8	1	6	4	33	4	14	3	0	4	0	33	.183	.095	.097

Montreal Expos AAA & AA Minor League Ratings

AAA (INDIANAPOLIS)	AGE	BATS	POSITION	CPA	RUNS	SET-UP	DRIVE-IN	RPA
Shon Ashley	26	R	OF	200	17.5	.046	.042	.088
Eric Bullock	32	L	OF	345	37.6	.058	.051	.109
Greg Colbrunn	23	R	1B	233	26.3	.050	.063	.113
Wil Cordero	21	R	SS	235	24.8	.052	.053	.105
Jim Eppard	32	L	1B\OF	311	32.5	.059	.045	.104
Greg Fulton	29	B	3B\OF\2B	519	42.9	.040	.043	.083
Jerry Goff	28	L	3B	350	37.2	.051	.055	.106
Todd Haney	27	R	2B	240	29.5	.071	.052	.123
Jimmy Kremers	27	L	C	167	12.6	.036	.039	.075
Quinn Mack	27	L	OF	332	26.6	.038	.042	.080
Omer Munoz	26	R	SS\2B	403	22.6	.024	.032	.056
Bob Natal	27	R	C	383	45.2	.060	.058	.118
F.P. Santangelo	25	B	OF\2B	540	48.6	.048	.042	.090
Razor Shines	36	B	1B\3B	209	19.3	.050	.042	.092
Matt Stairs	23	R	OF	464	45.6	.048	.050	.098
Jerry Willard	32	L	C	111	12.6	.059	.054	.113

AA (HARRISBURG)	AGE	BATS	POSITION	CPA	RUNS	SET-UP	DRIVE-IN	RPA
Steve Hecht	27	L	OF\2B	306	30.3	.053	.046	.099
Rick Hirtensteiner	25	L	OF	504	47.2	.048	.046	.094
Bryn Kosco	25	L	3B	380	30.0	.038	.041	.079
Tim Laker	23	R	C	463	46.8	.047	.054	.101
Mike Lansing	24	R	SS	554	56.3	.052	.050	.102
Chris Martin	24	R	2B	448	34.8	.037	.041	.078
Chad McDonald	24	R	3B	212	14.6	.032	.037	.069
Darwin Pennye	26	R	OF	338	27.5	.038	.043	.081
Joe Siddall	25	L	OF\C	327	23.8	.035	.038	.073
Derrick White	23	R	1B	557	57.0	.050	.052	.102
Rondell White	20	R	OF	102	12.1	.062	.057	.119

AAA Pitchers	Age	Throws	Outs	RPA	AA Pitchers	Age	Throws	Outs	RPA
Brian Barnes	25	L	249	.114	Tavo Alvarez	21	R	142	.119
Blaine Beatty	28	L	282	.133	Doug Bochtler	22	R	233	.094
Kent Bottenfield	24	R	457	.117	Mario Brito	26	R	248	.108
Howard Farmer	26	R	252	.131	Travis Buckley	22	R	480	.131
Chris Haney	24	L	252	.132	Mark Chapman	27	R	167	.130
Gil Heredia	27	R	295	.108	Archie Corbin	25	R	346	.148
Jonathan Hurst	26	R	358	.124	Chris Johnson	24	R	427	.153
Bill Landrum	34	R	82	.125	Chris Marchok	28	L	175	.135
Matt Maysey	25	R	201	.132	Mike Mathile	24	R	557	.110
Bill Risley	25	R	287	.153	Chris Myers	23	L	174	.137
Doug Simons	26	L	360	.105	Doug Piatt	27	R	220	.132
Sergio Valdez	27	R	187	.103	Len Picota	26	R	216	.111
David Wainhouse	25	R	138	.140	Chris Pollack	27	L	373	.153
Pete Young	24	R	146	.140					

NEW YORK METS

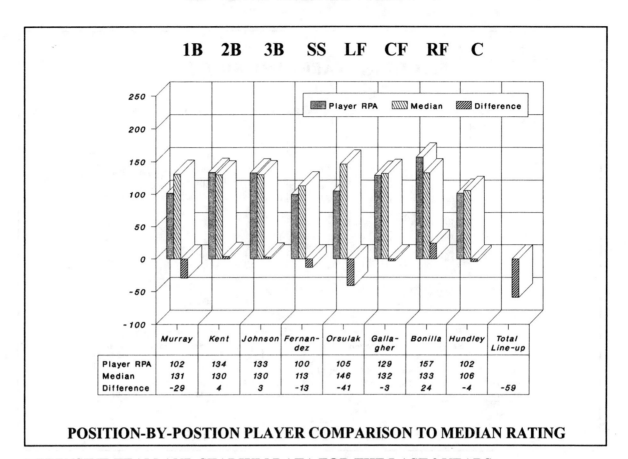

	1B	2B	3B	SS	LF	CF	RF	C	Total Line-up
	Murray	Kent	Johnson	Fernan-dez	Orsulak	Galla-gher	Bonilla	Hundley	
Player RPA	102	134	133	100	105	129	157	102	
Median	131	130	130	113	146	132	133	106	
Difference	-29	4	3	-13	-41	-3	24	-4	-59

POSITION-BY-POSTION PLAYER COMPARISON TO MEDIAN RATING

DEFENSIVE TEAM AND STADIUM DATA FOR THE LAST 3 YEARS:

TEAM DEFENSE BY POSITION:

POSITION-BY-POSITION STADIUM CHARACTERISTICS:

		1990	1991	1992		
1B:	Home	-1.2	-0.1	-3.5		Slightly easy to play
	Away	-1.1	+1.3	-7.1		
2B:	Home	-3.4	-4.4	-1.6		Slightly hard to play
	Away	-6.2	-3.0	-8.3		
3B:	Home	-0.4	-1.3	-2.0		Slightly hard to play
	Away	-2.9	-4.1	-1.0		
SS:	Home	+4.5	-6.3	-4.7		Average
	Away	-7.1	-2.4	+2.0		
LF:	Home	-6.0	+0.2	-8.6		Slightly easy to play
	Away	-8.3	-2.8	-3.3		
CF:	Home	-9.1	-11.2	-3.7		Very easy to play
	Away	-0.1	-7.6	-12.0		
RF:	Home	+3.4	-14.7	-0.7		Average (to slightly easy)
	Away	+2.4	-5.7	+0.2		
Total Home:		-12.2	-37.8	-24.8	Oh No!	
Total Away:		-23.3	-24.3	-29.5	Oh No!	

Comments: Still the undisputed worst defensive club in the Majors. They improved their outfield defense in right field by almost 20 runs from '91 to '92, yet still managed to be almost as bad a defensive horror show in '92 as they were the previous year. The acquisition of Tony Fernandez is not likely to help, however, since he's on the backside of his career and losing range quickly. There doesn't seem to be much help coming from the minors either. This is a truly bad team!

NEW YORK METS

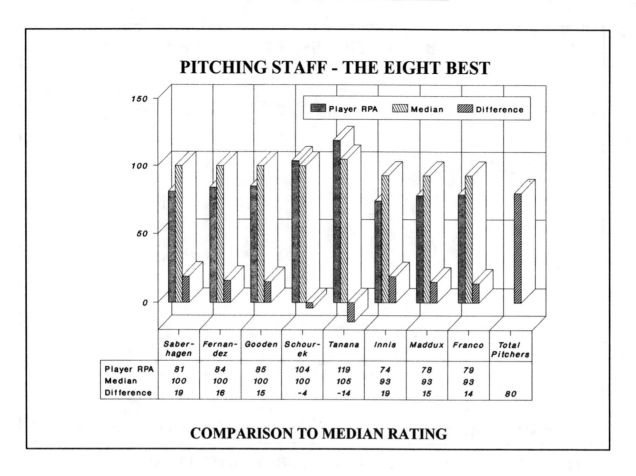

PITCHING STAFF - THE EIGHT BEST

Legend: Player RPA | Median | Difference

	Saber-hagen	Fernan-dez	Gooden	Schour-ek	Tanana	Innis	Maddux	Franco	Total Pitchers
Player RPA	81	84	85	104	119	74	78	79	
Median	100	100	100	100	105	93	93	93	
Difference	19	16	15	-4	-14	19	15	14	80

COMPARISON TO MEDIAN RATING

SUGGESTED LINE-UPS (with set-up RPA & drive-in RPA ratings):

Vs: Left-handed Groundball
RF:	B. Bonilla	63-54
CF:	D. Gallagher	63-58
2B:	J. Kent	65-68
3B:	H. Johnson	50-53
LF:	D. Reed	44-56
1B:	J. McKnight	45-57
SS:	T. Fernandez	49-45
C:	C. O'Brien	43-48
Pitcher		

Vs: Neutral Lefty Pitchers
CF:	D. Gallagher	53-48
RF:	B. Bonilla	72-62
3B:	H. Johnson	58-60
2B:	J. Kent	55-59
1B:	J. McKnight	45-57
C:	T. Hundley	47-59
LF:	D. Reed	44-56
SS:	T. Fernandez	50-46
Pitcher		

Vs: Left-handed Flyball
CF:	V. Coleman	72-63
LF:	J. Orsulak	62-57
RF:	B. Bonilla	87-75
3B:	H. Johnson	70-73
C:	T. Hundley	65-70
1B:	J. McKnight	45-57
SS:	T. Fernandez	52-48
2B:	J. Kent	45-47
Pitcher		

Vs: Right-handed Groundball
LF:	D. Gallagher	64-58
RF:	B. Bonilla	80-69
1B:	E. Murray	64-64
3B:	H. Johnson	63-65
2B:	J. Kent	80-85
CF:	R. Thompson	65-76
SS:	T. Fernandez	55-51
C:	C. O'Brien	52-57
Pitcher		

Vs: Neutral Righty Pitchers
SS:	T. Fernandez	56-52
LF:	J. Orsulak	62-57
RF:	B. Bonilla	89-77
1B:	E. Murray	65-66
3B:	H. Johnson	70-73
2B:	J. Kent	71-75
SS:	T. Fernandez	56-52
C:	T. Hundley	49-62
Pitcher		

Vs: Right-handed Flyball
CF:	V. Coleman	76-66
LF:	J. Orsulak	74-69
RF:	B. Bonilla	104-90
1B:	E. Murray	67-68
3B:	H. Johnson	82-86
C:	T. Hundley	67-73
2B:	J. Kent	60-64
SS:	T. Fernandez	58-54
Pitcher		

Comments: Only the two expansion teams have poorer offenses, and even the Marlins offense is almost as good. Yet the Mets offense probably will be even worse since the Mets are unlikely to platoon Murray, who can't hit lefty pitching, or almost any of the other moves listed above. Why does this management think that they have any chance at the pennant with this putrid offense and the worst defense in the Major Leagues? They had better pay more attention to beating out the Marlins, rather than winning a pennant.

NEW YORK METS

The Mets have the second best pitching staff in the Major Leagues. They have six *high* premier pitchers: three starters (Dwight Gooden, Bret Saberhagen & Sid Fernandez) and three relievers (John Franco, Jeff Innis & Mike Maddux). But I guess the Mets are out to prove, once and for all, that pitching is not as important as it is made out to be, since the cast of characters assembled to backup these six true "All-Stars" are pitiful indeed. The Mets' "offense" is a joke and the Mets' "defense" is a shameful travesty. This is one team whose players ought to take their helmets with them when they play the field.

I can't figure the Mets front office out. Do they really think they can win a pennant with this sad cast of characters? What was that trade for Tony Fernandez all about? The Mets would have you believe that they made a big steal. No way! Tony Fernandez' range is declining at shortstop at about the same rate as his hitting ability is going south. I don't think that there's all that much difference in the overall quality of play between Dick Schofield and Tony Fernandez. For this utter non-improvement at the shortstop position, the Mets gave up a fine pitcher in Wally Whitehurst, who should really blossom away from the disastrous defense he had to pitch in front of for these past two seasons, and they also gave up a fine outfield prospect in D.J. Dozier who I think could be ready right now. Dozier is certainly already better than Vince Coleman, Kevin Bass, Joe Orsulak and Howard Johnson. With all the outfield problems the Mets have, how could they afford to give him away? They certainly have no one else in the high minors that is a serious outfield prospect.

I feel sorry for Bobby Bonilla. He's been taking a lot of typically unfair hits from the ignorant New York press corps ever since he arrived. He'll be taking a lot more unfair blame over the coming season for the "failure" of the Mets to contend. It's not his fault that this team has so little talent, either in the Majors or in the high minors. The front office is solely to blame.

Why in the world does this team think that the signing's of Frank Tanana and Joe Orsulak have any significance whatsoever? It certainly won't make up for the loss of Dave Magadan's bat.

Bobby Jones appears to be a very good pitching prospect and didn't need to be protected since he wasn't eligible in the Expansion draft, but how in the world could this team have left pitcher Jose Martinez exposed in the draft? The Mets AAA Tidewater club was a joke in '92. Now that Jose Martinez, D.J. Dozier and Chris Donnels are gone, there is almost no one in the high minors other than Jones who has any prospect of making a big impact at the Major League level. The farm system, if anything, is in worse shape than the parent club. With the Yankees figuring to contend in '93, the Mets should become the joke of New York.

Is it my imagination, or are the Mets and Red Sox in a heated contest to see who can assemble the oldest (and slowest) team in the Majors?

New York's Projected record for 1993: 80--82, good for 5th place in the division.

NEW YORK METS

Kevin Bass, 33

Bats Both   371L   697R   399G   221F

L= .101G .101L .101F   (.048/.058) .106   .108G .108R .108F = R

		ATBATS	1B	2B	3B	HR	HBP	BB	GDP	SB	CS	ROE	XB	RUNS	EOB%	RL#	SET-UP	DR-IN	RPA
San Francisco	1990	214	37	9	1	7	2	11	5	2	2	3	11	25	.174	.106	.048	.058	.106
San Francisco	1991	361	60	10	4	10	4	28	12	7	4	5	16	43	.174	.093	.046	.056	.102
San Francisco	1992	265	50	11	3	7	1	15	6	7	8	2	7	32	.165	.099	.046	.060	.106
Mets	1992	137	21	12	2	2	0	5	2	7	2	2	11	17	.190	.115	.057	.062	.119

Bobby Bonilla, 29

Bats Both   754L   1099R   632G   401F

L= .115G .132L .160F   (.081/.070) .151   .147G .164R .192F = R

		ATBATS	1B	2B	3B	HR	HBP	BB	GDP	SB	CS	ROE	XB	RUNS	EOB%	RL#	SET-UP	DR-IN	RPA
Pittsburgh	1990	625	97	39	7	32	1	36	11	4	3	9	51	100	.183	.144	.070	.079	.149
Pittsburgh	1991	577	106	44	6	18	2	82	14	2	4	6	55	107	.263	.154	.089	.070	.159
Mets	1992	438	67	23	0	19	1	56	11	4	3	5	33	70	.212	.136	.070	.069	.139

Daryl Boston, 29

Bats left   151L   867R   343G   214F

L= .139G .114L .099F   (.066/.063) .129   .157G .132R .092F = R

		ATBATS	1B	2B	3B	HR	HBP	BB	GDP	SB	CS	ROE	XB	RUNS	EOB%	RL#	SET-UP	DR-IN	RPA
White Sox	1990	1	0	0	0	0	0	0	0	1	0	0	0	0	.000	.000	.000	.000	.000
Mets	1990	366	65	21	2	12	2	26	7	18	8	4	48	54	.193	.123	.060	.070	.130
Mets	1991	255	46	16	4	4	0	30	2	15	8	2	25	36	.238	.129	.067	.059	.126
Mets	1992	289	45	14	2	11	3	32	5	12	7	1	15	43	.198	.128	.064	.067	.131

Vince Coleman, 31

Bats Both   383L   732R   412G   234F

L= .100G .113L .137F   (.063/.055) .118   .107G .120R .144F = R

		ATBATS	1B	2B	3B	HR	HBP	BB	GDP	SB	CS	ROE	XB	RUNS	EOB%	RL#	SET-UP	DR-IN	RPA
St. Louis	1990	497	112	18	9	6	2	34	6	77	21	5	52	68	.217	.125	.063	.061	.124
Mets	1991	278	58	7	5	1	0	39	3	37	16	5	39	36	.241	.115	.060	.053	.113
Mets	1992	229	49	11	1	2	2	24	1	24	11	1	29	32	.234	.121	.066	.059	.125

Chris Donnels, 26

Bats Left   65L   176R   86G   57F   708ML

L= .129G .139L .154F   (.065/.057) .122   .106G .116R .131F = R

		ATBATS	1B	2B	3B	HR	HBP	BB	GDP	SB	CS	ROE	XB	RUNS	EOB%	RL#	SET-UP	DR-IN	RPA
Mets	1991	89	18	2	0	0	0	13	0	1	1	1	4	9	.267	.093	.052	.040	.092
Mets	1992	121	17	4	0	0	0	17	1	1	0	1	8	11	.230	.077	.041	.038	.079

Kevin Elster, 28

Bats Right   311L   442R   251G   134F

L= .100G .100L .099F   (.049/.049) .098   .097G .097R .096F = R

		ATBATS	1B	2B	3B	HR	HBP	BB	GDP	SB	CS	ROE	XB	RUNS	EOB%	RL#	SET-UP	DR-IN	RPA
Mets	1990	314	35	20	1	9	1	28	4	2	0	5	16	38	.193	.101	.052	.055	.107
Mets	1991	348	60	16	2	6	1	34	4	2	3	1	16	39	.213	.103	.051	.050	.101
Mets	1992	18	4	0	0	0	0	0	1	0	0	0	0	1	.097	.038	.013	.027	.040

Tony Fernandez, 30

Bats Both   674L   1359R   676G   383F

L= .094G .096L .100F   (.054/.050) .104   .106G .108R .112F = R

		ATBATS	1B	2B	3B	HR	HBP	BB	GDP	SB	CS	ROE	XB	RUNS	EOB%	RL#	SET-UP	DR-IN	RPA
Toronto	1990	635	127	27	17	4	7	67	17	26	14	6	55	81	.231	.114	.058	.053	.111
San Diego	1991	558	116	27	5	4	0	55	12	23	10	3	52	67	.225	.105	.055	.051	.106
San Diego	1992	622	131	32	4	4	4	52	6	20	20	5	49	73	.224	.106	.053	.050	.103

Dave Gallagher, 32

Bats Right   350L   191R   185G   124F

L= .125G .105L .076F   (.055/.050) .105   .126G .106R .077F = R

		ATBATS	1B	2B	3B	HR	HBP	BB	GDP	SB	CS	ROE	XB	RUNS	EOB%	RL#	SET-UP	DR-IN	RPA
White Sox	1990	75	17	3	1	0	1	3	3	0	1	0	4	7	.179	.079	.037	.043	.080
Baltimore	1990	51	10	1	0	0	0	4	0	1	1	2	6	5	.234	.087	.047	.041	.088
California	1991	270	61	17	0	1	2	24	6	2	4	2	24	33	.242	.107	.059	.051	.110
Mets	1992	175	29	11	1	1	1	19	7	4	5	5	16	19	.207	.093	.048	.048	.096

Todd Hundley, 23

Bats Both   168L   361R   214G   99F   519ML

L= .080G .094L .123F (.042/.055) .097 .085G .099R .128F = R

		ATBATS	1B	2B	3B	HR	HBP	BB	GDP	SB	CS	ROE	XB	RUNS	EOB%	RL#	SET-UP	DR-IN	RPA
Mets	1990	67	8	6	0	0	0	6	1	0	0	1	6	6	.214	.082	.042	.042	.084
Mets	1991	60	6	0	1	1	1	6	3	0	0	0	5	4	.121	.053	.019	.033	.052
Mets	1992	358	51	17	0	7	4	15	8	3	0	1	21	32	.151	.081	.035	.048	.083

Howard Johnson, 32

Bats Both   651L   1047R   559G   319F

L= .107G .122L .147F (.067/.070) .137 .132G .147R .172F = R

		ATBATS	1B	2B	3B	HR	HBP	BB	GDP	SB	CS	ROE	XB	RUNS	EOB%	RL#	SET-UP	DR-IN	RPA
Mets	1990	590	81	37	3	23	0	57	7	34	8	5	61	90	.198	.127	.065	.068	.133
Mets	1991	564	70	34	4	38	1	66	4	30	17	1	40	94	.182	.152	.070	.079	.149
Mets	1992	350	52	19	0	7	2	50	7	22	6	5	23	49	.232	.115	.062	.056	.118

Jeff Kent, 24

Bats Right   104L   240R   99G   89F   538ML

L= .122G .103L .081F (.061/.064) .125 .154G .135R .113F = R

		ATBATS	1B	2B	3B	HR	HBP	BB	GDP	SB	CS	ROE	XB	RUNS	EOB%	RL#	SET-UP	DR-IN	RPA
Toronto	1992	192	24	13	1	8	6	20	3	2	1	3	19	32	.226	.146	.077	.071	.148
Mets	1992	113	15	8	1	3	1	7	2	0	2	0	13	13	.161	.102	.046	.060	.106

Dave Magadan, 30

Bats Left   509L   909R   487G   259F

L= .092G .097L .106F (.079/.053) .132 .147G .152R .161F = R

		ATBATS	1B	2B	3B	HR	HBP	BB	GDP	SB	CS	ROE	XB	RUNS	EOB%	RL#	SET-UP	DR-IN	RPA
Mets	1990	451	108	28	6	6	2	70	11	2	1	3	50	88	.302	.152	.095	.065	.160
Mets	1991	418	81	23	0	4	2	80	5	1	1	6	42	65	.307	.132	.077	.052	.129
Mets	1992	321	78	9	1	3	0	53	6	1	0	3	17	52	.294	.131	.079	.056	.135

Jeff McKnight, 29

Bats Both   86L   129R   72G   52F   418ML

L= .099G .111L .127F (.044/.056) .100 .080G .092R .108F = R

		ATBATS	1B	2B	3B	HR	HBP	BB	GDP	SB	CS	ROE	XB	RUNS	EOB%	RL#	SET-UP	DR-IN	RPA
Baltimore	1990	75	12	2	0	1	1	5	0	0	0	0	13	7	.193	.087	.042	.046	.088
Baltimore	1991	41	6	1	0	0	0	2	2	1	0	0	1	2	.112	.039	.014	.026	.040
Mets	1992	85	17	3	1	2	0	2	2	0	1	0	6	9	.147	.097	.041	.059	.100

Eddie Murray, 36

Bats Both   732L   1161R   648G   383F

L= .078G .081L .085F (.058/.060) .118 .140G .143R .147F = R

		ATBATS	1B	2B	3B	HR	HBP	BB	GDP	SB	CS	ROE	XB	RUNS	EOB%	RL#	SET-UP	DR-IN	RPA
Los Angeles	1990	558	133	22	3	26	1	61	19	8	7	3	56	104	.228	.158	.085	.078	.163
Los Angeles	1991	576	107	23	1	19	0	38	17	10	3	8	21	70	.181	.107	.051	.058	.109
Mets	1992	551	89	37	2	16	0	58	15	4	4	6	30	79	.211	.124	.064	.063	.127

Junior Noboa, 28

Bats Right   236L   79R   121G   63F   20ML

L= .097G .084L .060F (.031/.044) .075 .060G .047R .023F = R

		ATBATS	1B	2B	3B	HR	HBP	BB	GDP	SB	CS	ROE	XB	RUNS	EOB%	RL#	SET-UP	DR-IN	RPA
Montreal	1990	158	33	7	2	0	1	5	2	4	2	1	9	15	.197	.087	.044	.046	.090
Montreal	1991	95	19	3	0	1	0	0	1	2	4	3	4	7	.140	.069	.030	.045	.075
Mets	1992	47	7	0	0	0	1	3	2	0	0	0	5	2	.132	.041	.016	.026	.042

Charlie O'Brien, 31

Bats Right   310L   297R   191G   119F

L= .093G .071L .036F (.038/.042) .080 .111G .089R .054F = R

		ATBATS	1B	2B	3B	HR	HBP	BB	GDP	SB	CS	ROE	XB	RUNS	EOB%	RL#	SET-UP	DR-IN	RPA
Milwaukee	1990	145	18	7	2	0	2	10	3	0	0	5	12	12	.204	.076	.038	.040	.078
Mets	1990	68	8	3	0	0	1	8	1	0	0	2	3	6	.228	.069	.038	.035	.073
Mets	1991	168	23	6	0	2	4	16	5	0	2	1	10	13	.176	.071	.031	.038	.069
Mets	1992	156	19	12	0	2	1	15	4	0	1	3	6	16	.201	.091	.046	.047	.093

Bill Pecota, 32

Bats Right   375L   649R   357G   226F

L= .139G   .130L   .115F   **(.054/.053) .107**   .103G   .094R   .079F = R

		ATBATS	1B	2B	3B	HR	HBP	BB	GDP	SB	CS	ROE	XB	RUNS	EOB%	RL#	SET-UP	DR-IN	RPA
Kansas City	1990	240	36	15	2	5	1	33	5	8	5	7	28	36	.243	.125	.069	.059	.128
Kansas City	1991	398	83	23	2	6	2	35	12	16	7	4	33	53	.219	.114	.060	.058	.118
Mets	1992	269	46	13	0	2	1	22	7	9	3	5	16	27	.201	.087	.044	.046	.090

Willie Randolph, 38

Bats Right   435L   865R   460G   210F

L= .150G   .153L   .158F   **(.075/.053) .128**   .112G   .115R   .120F = R

		ATBATS	1B	2B	3B	HR	HBP	BB	GDP	SB	CS	ROE	XB	RUNS	EOB%	RL#	SET-UP	DR-IN	RPA
Los Angeles	1990	96	21	4	0	1	1	13	3	1	0	2	15	14	.271	.123	.071	.055	.126
Oakland	1990	292	62	9	3	1	1	31	11	6	1	6	32	36	.233	.099	.055	.050	.105
Milwaukee	1991	431	124	14	3	0	0	72	14	4	2	4	48	69	.309	.133	.080	.053	.133
Mets	1992	286	58	11	1	2	4	39	6	1	3	7	25	40	.269	.115	.067	.052	.119

Mackey Sasser, 30

Bats Left   108L   566R   216G   149F

L= .044G   .035L   .022F   **(.042/.051) .093**   .113G   .104R   .091F = R

		ATBATS	1B	2B	3B	HR	HBP	BB	GDP	SB	CS	ROE	XB	RUNS	EOB%	RL#	SET-UP	DR-IN	RPA
Mets	1990	270	63	14	0	6	1	6	7	0	0	3	17	35	.197	.113	.058	.061	.119
Mets	1991	228	41	14	2	5	1	7	6	0	2	4	10	24	.175	.103	.046	.055	.101
Mets	1992	141	26	6	0	2	0	3	4	0	0	1	5	12	.149	.077	.033	.047	.080

Dick Schofield, 30

Bats Right   417L   924R   434G   256F

L= .106G   .102L   .094F   **(.050/.045) .095**   .096G   .092R   .084F = R

		ATBATS	1B	2B	3B	HR	HBP	BB	GDP	SB	CS	ROE	XB	RUNS	EOB%	RL#	SET-UP	DR-IN	RPA
California	1990	310	69	8	1	1	2	49	3	3	4	7	33	42	.292	.117	.067	.048	.115
California	1991	427	84	9	3	0	3	48	3	8	4	7	30	45	.248	.091	.051	.043	.094
California	1992	3	1	0	0	0	0	1	0	0	0	0	0	1	.428	.178	.122	.059	.181
Mets	1992	420	62	18	2	4	5	56	11	11	4	3	27	46	.217	.092	.048	.046	.094

Ryan Thompson, 25

Bats Right   44L   74R   52G   24F   924ML

L= .120G   .090L   ....F   **(.045/.053) .098**   .132G   .102R   ....F = R

		ATBATS	1B	2B	3B	HR	HBP	BB	GDP	SB	CS	ROE	XB	RUNS	EOB%	RL#	SET-UP	DR-IN	RPA
Mets	1992	108	13	7	1	3	0	8	2	2	2	3	5	13	.178	.106	.050	.059	.109

Chico Walker, 34

Bats Both   224L   469R   232G   175F

L= .092G   .100L   .111F   **(.058/.053) .111**   .110G   .118R   .129F = R

		ATBATS	1B	2B	3B	HR	HBP	BB	GDP	SB	CS	ROE	XB	RUNS	EOB%	RL#	SET-UP	DR-IN	RPA
Cubs	1991	374	79	10	1	6	0	31	3	13	5	3	33	43	.219	.106	.053	.050	.103
Cubs	1992	26	3	0	0	0	0	3	0	1	0	0	1	2	.180	.046	.023	.027	.050
Mets	1992	227	53	12	1	4	0	21	9	14	2	1	15	34	.225	.127	.068	.062	.130

PITCHERS

Mark Dewey, 27

Throws: Groundball type, moderate reverse righty

(.115/.128) .121   123L   101R   524ML

		OUTS	RO	1B	2B	3B	HR	HBP	BB	GDP	SB	CS	PO	WP	BK	RUNS	EOB%	RL#	RPA
San Francisco	1990	68	68	16	3	2	1	0	4	2	2	1	0	0	1	8	.135	.083	.084
New York Mets	1992	100	100	30	5	0	2	0	8	3	1	3	0	0	1	12	.144	.088	.085

Sid Fernandez, 30

Throws: Flyball type, moderate to severe reverse lefty

(.101/.076) .081   346L   1371R

		OUTS	RO	1B	2B	3B	HR	HBP	BB	GDP	SB	CS	PO	WP	BK	RUNS	EOB%	RL#	RPA
New York Mets	1990	538	0	81	25	6	18	5	63	4	20	6	0	1	0	70	.165	.093	.093
New York Mets	1991	132	0	28	3	1	4	0	9	1	3	1	0	0	0	13	.148	.087	.077
New York Mets	1992	644	0	104	37	9	12	4	63	5	17	9	0	0	0	71	.162	.084	.082

Tom Filer, 36

Throws: Groundball type, extreme reverse righty

(.071/.166) .127   75L   106R   905ML

		OUTS	RO	1B	2B	3B	HR	HBP	BB	GDP	SB	CS	PO	WP	BK	RUNS	EOB%	RL#	RPA
Milwaukee	1990	66	9	21	3	0	2	0	9	2	1	0	0	2	0	12	.216	.124	.125
New York Mets	1992	66	45	12	3	1	2	0	4	1	3	1	0	1	0	7	.123	.085	.084

NEW YORK METS

John Franco, 32

Throws: Groundballl type, extreme reverse lefty

(.101/.064) .073   151L   477R

		OUTS	RO	1B	2B	3B	HR	HBP	BB	GDP	SB	CS	PO	WP	BK	RUNS	EOB%	RL#	RPA
New York Mets	1990	203	203	50	11	1	4	0	19	5	6	1	0	7	2	28	.178	.094	.095
New York Mets	1991	166	166	48	8	3	2	1	14	6	4	2	0	6	0	20	.171	.097	.086
New York Mets	1992	99	99	16	6	1	1	0	9	6	2	3	0	0	0	6	.054	.049	.048

Paul Gibson, 32

Throws: Neutral type, extreme reverse lefty

(.150/.099) .115   331L   735R

		OUTS	RO	1B	2B	3B	HR	HBP	BB	GDP	SB	CS	PO	WP	BK	RUNS	EOB%	RL#	RPA
Detroit	1990	292	292	63	24	2	10	1	32	7	7	3	0	1	1	45	.173	.110	.108
Detroit	1991	288	288	88	10	4	10	3	40	13	5	5	1	4	0	46	.171	.114	.109
New York Mets	1992	186	172	43	17	3	7	0	25	4	7	3	0	1	0	34	.191	.128	.125

Dwight Gooden, 28

Throws: Groundball type, moderate righty

(.090/.075) .084   1485L   1047R

		OUTS	RO	1B	2B	3B	HR	HBP	BB	GDP	SB	CS	PO	WP	BK	RUNS	EOB%	RL#	RPA
New York Mets	1990	698	0	179	33	7	10	7	67	12	60	16	1	6	3	94	.176	.094	.094
New York Mets	1991	570	0	134	33	6	12	3	54	15	33	16	0	5	2	63	.146	.093	.082
New York Mets	1992	618	0	136	43	7	11	3	63	20	22	11	2	3	1	74	.150	.089	.087

Lee Guetterman, 34

Throws: Groundball type, moderate lefty

(.095/.115) .109   306L   679R

		OUTS	RO	1B	2B	3B	HR	HBP	BB	GDP	SB	CS	PO	WP	BK	RUNS	EOB%	RL#	RPA
N.Y. Yankees	1990	279	279	61	8	5	6	0	19	11	8	2	0	1	1	27	.116	.076	.074
N.Y. Yankees	1991	264	264	64	19	2	6	3	20	11	4	3	0	4	0	32	.144	.090	.085
N.Y. Yankees	1992	68	68	22	7	1	5	0	10	2	1	0	0	1	0	20	.224	.179	.180
New York Mets	1992	130	130	42	9	1	5	1	9	7	4	1	0	3	0	22	.153	.115	.113

Eric Hillman, 26

Throws: Groundball type, lefty

(..../.141) .140   40L   175R   1090ML

		OUTS	RO	1B	2B	3B	HR	HBP	BB	GDP	SB	CS	PO	WP	BK	RUNS	EOB%	RL#	RPA
New York Mets	1992	157	20	47	10	1	9	2	8	6	4	5	0	1	0	25	.113	.111	.109

Jeff Innis, 30

Throws: Groundball type, extreme righty

(.106/.040) .071   347L   402R

		OUTS	RO	1B	2B	3B	HR	HBP	BB	GDP	SB	CS	PO	WP	BK	RUNS	EOB%	RL#	RPA
New York Mets	1990	79	79	13	2	0	4	1	7	6	8	0	0	1	1	7	.058	.073	.072
New York Mets	1991	254	254	51	10	3	2	0	17	6	6	5	0	4	0	19	.121	.065	.057
New York Mets	1992	264	264	67	11	3	4	6	32	14	8	5	0	1	0	31	.151	.086	.084

Barry Jones, 29

Throws: Groundball type, moderate righty

(.102/.095) .098   415L   489R

		OUTS	RO	1B	2B	3B	HR	HBP	BB	GDP	SB	CS	PO	WP	BK	RUNS	EOB%	RL#	RPA
Chi. White Sox	1990	222	222	51	9	0	2	1	26	7	3	2	3	0	1	22	.150	.072	.074
Montreal	1991	266	266	56	10	2	8	1	25	11	8	6	2	1	1	29	.094	.073	.080
Philadelphia	1992	163	163	45	15	2	3	2	20	8	1	1	1	1	2	30	.184	.103	.117
New York Mets	1992	46	46	16	4	0	0	0	8	2	4	0	0	1	0	9	.258	.124	.122

Bret Saberhagen, 28

Throws: Neutral type, moderate righty

(.083/.077) .080   838L   849R

		OUTS	RO	1B	2B	3B	HR	HBP	BB	GDP	SB	CS	PO	WP	BK	RUNS	EOB%	RL#	RPA
Kansas City	1990	405	0	112	20	5	9	1	27	10	2	5	2	1	0	54	.153	.094	.096
Kansas City	1991	589	0	121	28	4	12	9	40	14	9	9	4	8	1	60	.127	.076	.077
New York Mets	1992	293	14	60	14	4	6	4	26	4	6	5	3	1	2	33	.148	.085	.083

Pete Schourek, 23

Throws: Flyball type, moderate reverse lefty

(.121/.103) .108   255L   708R   328ML

		OUTS	RO	1B	2B	3B	HR	HBP	BB	GDP	SB	CS	PO	WP	BK	RUNS	EOB%	RL#	RPA
New York Mets	1991	259	117	55	14	6	7	2	39	1	12	0	0	1	0	42	.233	.127	.112
New York Mets	1992	408	15	95	28	5	9	2	38	12	15	5	0	4	2	56	.164	.099	.097

Anthony Young, 26

Throws: Groundball type, extreme righty

(.145/.090) .121   384L   298R   702ML

		OUTS	RO	1B	2B	3B	HR	HBP	BB	GDP	SB	CS	PO	WP	BK	RUNS	EOB%	RL#	RPA
New York Mets	1991	148	13	35	8	1	4	1	11	4	3	1	0	1	0	17	.155	.095	.084
New York Mets	1992	363	144	94	23	9	8	1	26	10	10	6	1	3	1	50	.153	.101	.098

New York Mets AAA & AA Minor League Ratings

AAA (TIDEWATER)	AGE	BATS	POSITION	CPA	RUNS	SET-UP	DRIVE-IN	RPA
Kevin Baez	25	R	SS	378	24.5	.029	.036	.061
Tim Bogar	26	R	2B\SS\3B	514	39.3	.033	.043	.076
Scott Bradley	32	L	C	187	11.6	.029	.033	.062
Jeromy Burnitz	23	L	OF	488	44.1	.042	.048	.090
Chris Donnels	26	L	3B\1B	345	47.3	.082	.055	.137
D.J. Dozier	27	R	OF	239	29.2	.065	.057	.122
Javier Gonzalez	24	R	C	128	9.8	.031	.045	.076
Terrel Hansen	26	R	1B\OF	439	38.7	.039	.049	.088
Pat Howell	24	B	OF	434	32.2	.035	.039	.074
Mitch Lyden	28	R	1B\C	325	29.8	.037	.055	.092
Lee May	24	B	OF	261	18.2	.033	.07	.070
Jeff McKnight	29	B	OF\1B\2B	418	45.3	.059	.049	.108
Orlando Merced	31	R	C	199	19.7	.043	.056	.099
Keith Smith	31	B	2B\SS	125	7.2	.028	.030	.058
Steve Springer	31	R	3B\2B	461	48.0	.046	.058	.104

AA (BINGHAMPTON)	AGE	BATS	POSITION	CPA	RUNS	SET-UP	DRIVE-IN	RPA
Tom Allison	25	B	SS\2B	149	16.0	.059	.048	.107
Chris Butterfield	25	B	3B	546	53.7	.048	.050	.098
Joe Dellicarri	25	R	SS	391	31.6	.040	.041	.081
Andy Dziadkowiec	25	L	C	119	7.3	.028	.033	.061
Brook Fordyce	22	R	C	479	48.3	.049	.052	.101
Jamie Hoffner	25	L	1B	194	20.8	.051	.056	.107
Tim Howard	23	B	OF	555	53.4	.049	.047	.096
Bert Hunter	25	B	OF	457	41.3	.044	.046	.090
Rob Katzaroff	24	L	OF	505	43.5	.043	.043	.086
Curtis Pride	24	L	OF	444	41.2	.045	.048	.093
Doug Saunders	23	R	2B	497	41.2	.041	.042	.083
Mike White	24	L	OF	185	10.7	.026	.032	.058
Alan Zinter	24	B	1B	511	57.6	.059	.054	.113

AAA Pitchers	Age	Throws	Outs	RPA	AA Pitchers	Age	Throws	Outs	RPA
Mike Birkbeck	31	R	351	.125	Chris Dorn	24	R	214	.123
Doug Cinella	28	R	85	.150	Todd Douma	23	L	441	.141
Mark Dewey	27	R	163	.144	John Johnstone	24	R	448	.126
Frank Eufemia	33	R	89	.146	Bobby Jones	22	R	474	.101
Tom Filer	36	R	301	.122	Greg Langbehn	23	L	213	.127
Eric Hillman	26	L	274	.131	Jose Martinez	21	R	174	.096
Randy Marshall	26	L	455	.139	Andy Reich	23	R	192	.116
Brad Moore	28	R	238	.159	Bryan Rogers	25	R	106	.173
Dale Plummer	27	R	174	.151	Julian Vasquez	24	R	148	.119
Chris Rauth	29	R	364	.159	Joe Vitko	22	R	495	.138
Pete Schourek	23	L	158	.120	Pete Walker	23	R	419	.151
Dave Telgheder	26	R	507	.127					
Tom Wegmann	24	R	403	.117					

PHILADELPHIA PHILLIES

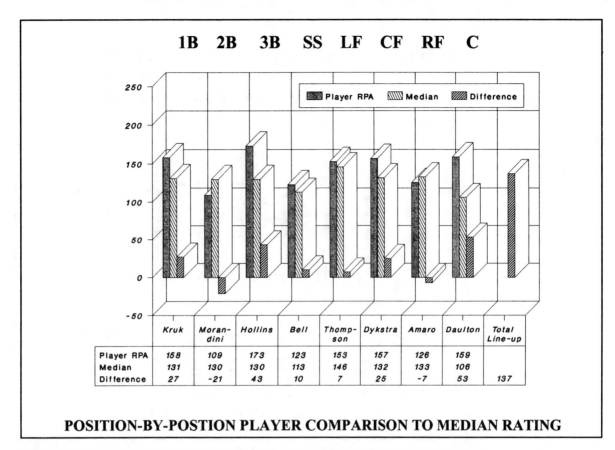

	Kruk	Moran-dini	Hollins	Bell	Thomp-son	Dykstra	Amaro	Daulton	Total Line-up
Player RPA	158	109	173	123	153	157	126	159	
Median	131	130	130	113	146	132	133	106	
Difference	27	-21	43	10	7	25	-7	53	137

POSITION-BY-POSTION PLAYER COMPARISON TO MEDIAN RATING

DEFENSIVE TEAM AND STADIUM DATA FOR THE LAST 3 YEARS:

TEAM DEFENSE BY POSITION:

POSITION-BY-POSITION STADIUM CHARACTERISTICS:

		1990	1991	1992	
1B:	Home	+4.7	+4.2	+2.7	Slightly easy to play
	Away	+0.7	+1.0	+1.0	
2B:	Home	+4.6	+1.6	-0.5	Average
	Away	-0.3	-0.6	+0.5	
3B:	Home	-3.4	-2.1	+2.5	Average
	Away	+2.5	-3.7	-2.6	
SS:	Home	+2.6	+5.7	+6.5	Average (to slightly hard)
	Away	-2.1	-5.5	-3.1	
LF:	Home	-5.9	-6.5	-4.5	Average
	Away	-2.0	-5.7	+6.9	
CF:	Home	+0.7	+1.6	+5.4	Slightly hard to play
	Away	+6.9	+0.7	-0.7	
RF:	Home	+2.1	+0.5	+5.1	Average
	Away	-3.7	+5.1	+1.5	
Total Home:		+5.4	+5.0	+17.2	
Total Away:		+2.0	-8.7	+3.4	

Comments: The Phillies are becoming a very good defensive team. They could get even better in '93 if the marvelous Juan Bell is permitted to play shortstop for the full season and as their young players gain maturity and playing time. This is another stadium where the home team has had a home vs. away defensive advantage for each of the 4 years that I've been rating the defenses. At least in this case, we've got a team that can take advantage of this home park advantage.

PHILADELPHIA PHILLIES

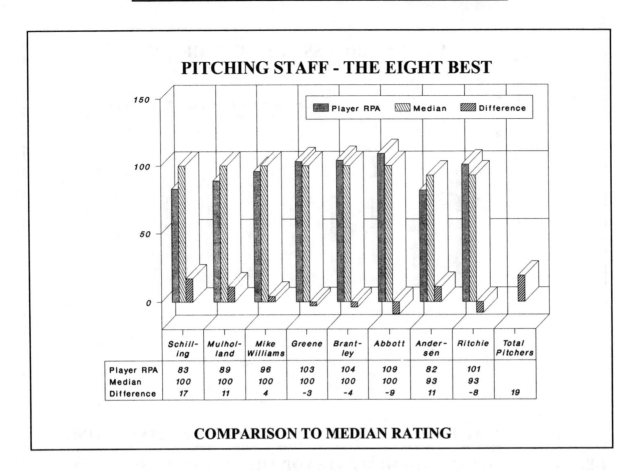

PITCHING STAFF - THE EIGHT BEST

Player RPA   Median   Difference

	Schill-ing	Mulhol-land	Mike Williams	Greene	Brant-ley	Abbott	Ander-sen	Ritchie	Total Pitchers
Player RPA	83	89	96	103	104	109	82	101	
Median	100	100	100	100	100	100	93	93	
Difference	17	11	4	-3	-4	-9	11	-8	19

COMPARISON TO MEDIAN RATING

SUGGESTED LINE-UPS (with set-up RPA & drive-in RPA ratings):

Vs: Left-handed Groundball
CF:	L. Dykstra	80-56
3B:	D. Hollins	123-102
C:	D. Daulton	86-75
1B:	R. Jordan	63-72
LF:	M. Duncan	59-69
RF:	R. Amaro	52-57
2B:	K. Batiste	40-53
SS:	J. Bell	23-31
Pitcher		

Vs: Neutral Lefty Pitchers
CF:	L. Dykstra	93-67
3B:	D. Hollins	121-101
C:	D. Daulton	77-66
1B:	R. Jordan	67-77
LF:	M. Duncan	63-74
RF:	R. Amaro	57-62
2B:	K. Batiste	40-53
SS:	J. Bell	26-34
Pitcher		

Vs: Left-handed Flyball
CF:	L. Dykstra	118-87
C:	T. Pratt	98-67
3B:	D. Hollins	118-98
LF:	W. Chamberlain	81-94
1B:	R. Jordan	73-84
RF:	R. Amaro	69-74
2B:	K. Batiste	40-53
SS:	J. Bell	30-37
Pitcher		

Vs: Right-handed Groundball
CF:	L. Dykstra	81-56
1B:	J. Kruk	95-76
3B:	D. Hollins	78-66
C:	D. Daulton	99-86
LF:	M. Thompson	79-73
2B:	M. Morandini	70-65
RF:	S. Javier	60-51
SS:	J. Bell	40-48
Pitcher		

Vs: Neutral Righty Pitchers
CF:	L. Dykstra	94-67
1B:	J. Kruk	92-73
3B:	D. Hollins	76-65
C:	D. Daulton	89-78
LF:	M. Thompson	78-73
RF:	S. Javier	62-53
2B:	M. Morandini	64-59
SS:	J. Bell	43-51
Pitcher		

Vs: Right-handed Flyball
CF:	L. Dykstra	119-87
1B:	J. Kruk	87-68
3B:	D. Hollins	73-62
C:	D. Daulton	72-62
LF:	M. Thompson	78-72
RF:	R. Amaro	57-61
2B:	M. Morandini	53-48
SS:	J. Bell	46-55
Pitcher		

Comments: **With the above line-ups the Phillies have the best offense in the NL despite carrying Juan Bell for his glove. Will they platoon Jordan & Kruk? The platoon of Kruk & Jordan isn't essential to this team's success, although it would help. With the excellent signing of Milt Thompson the Phillies have turned a huge problem (the outfield) into an asset. One of the biggest side benefits of the Thompson signing will be in getting Kruk out of the outfield.**

PHILADELPHIA PHILLIES

It's a real pleasure to go from a downer essay on the Mets to an essay on one of my three "sleeper" teams for 1993. Your eyes aren't fooling you. Not only are the Phillies a "sleeper" team, they are potentially the strongest of the three! I am picking them to be the surprise winners of the eastern division. In fact, if they use their talent properly, the Phillies are almost as strong as the Atlanta Braves!

How can a team that was so awful in '92 be a contender in '93? The answer lies in a combination of factors. Last year's Philadelphia team was not as bad as it appeared by its record. The Phillies have the top-rated players in the National League at three positions: centerfield (Lenny Dykstra), catcher (Darren Daulton) and third base (Dave Hollins). In addition, the Phillies have one of the top-rated first basemen in John Kruk.

The problem for the Phillies in '92 was that they were in a transition year. Most of the other positions (including the mound) were peopled by youngsters learning the ropes. These kids will make a bigger and better impact this season, and together with a couple of astute free-agent signing's by the front office over this winter, will project the Phillies into the thick of the 1993 pennant race.

Here are some of the key personnel that should help put the Phillies in the race: 1) shortstop Juan Bell. Juan Bell is a terrific defensive player. Even though he's a mediocre hitter at best, he more than makes up for it on defense; 2) outfielder Milt Thompson. Thompson is, like Bell, a terrific defensive player. Unlike Bell,

however, Thompson can hit as well as he fields. He's primarily a platoon-type player due to his inability to hit lefty pitching, but that hardly lessens his immense value to this team since the team possesses matching parts for use against those lefties. 3) the signing of Larry Andersen. Larry's always been one of my top-rated relievers. In fact, he's been about as good as anyone out there for many years. The only question about him, and it's not a small one, is his age. If he can produce quality pitching for another year or two, then his signing is a huge steal for this team. 4) the development of outfielder Ruben Amaro. Ruben's got the defensive tools and his offense should be coming around. He can play. 5) the maturation of pitcher Mike Williams into a premier starter.

What can hold this team back? Lots of things! With this many changes there are almost bound to be mistakes in who gets to play and how often. Already the Phillies have made a counterproductive move in acquiring Danny Jackson. Any amount of pitching time that Jackson and reliever Mitch Williams get will only help the cause of the Montreal Expos.

The signing of minor league free-agent third baseman Jeff Manto was a very good move. He's excellent insurance if Dave Hollins should get hurt. Manto can hit.

What are this team's plans for Todd Pratt? Pratt may be the best hitting catcher who's not starting for a Major League club. His value is enormous, but he doesn't figure to get much playing time with Darren Daulton present.

Philadelphia's Projected record for 1993: 90--72, good for 1st place in the division.

PHILADELPHIA PHILLIES

Ruben Amaro, 27

							Bats Both			185L	271R		217G	88F			624ML	

L= .104G .114L .138F (.048/.051) .099 .079G .089R .113F = R

		ATBATS	1B	2B	3B	HR	HBP	BB	GDP	SB	CS	ROE	XB	RUNS	EOB%	RL#	SET-UP	DR-IN	RPA
California	1991	23	4	1	0	0	0	2	1	0	0	0	0	2	.174	.060	.028	.033	.061
Philadelphia	1992	374	54	15	6	7	9	36	11	11	6	4	24	45	.193	.096	.048	.052	.100

Wally Backman, 33

							Bats Left			67L	568R		210G	123F				

L= .053G .048L .040F (.056/.044) .100 .111G .106R .098F = R

		ATBATS	1B	2B	3B	HR	HBP	BB	GDP	SB	CS	ROE	XB	RUNS	EOB%	RL#	SET-UP	DR-IN	RPA
Pittsburgh	1990	315	66	21	3	2	1	41	5	6	4	5	32	50	.279	.132	.079	.058	.137
Philadelphia	1991	185	33	12	0	0	0	30	2	3	4	3	11	23	.272	.100	.058	.045	.103
Philadelphia	1992	48	12	1	0	0	0	5	3	1	0	1	3	5	.220	.083	.045	.042	.087

Kim Batiste, 24

							Bats Right			92L	81R		74G	36F			767ML	

L= .074G .068L ....F (.030/.042) .072 .082G .076R ....F = R

		ATBATS	1B	2B	3B	HR	HBP	BB	GDP	SB	CS	ROE	XB	RUNS	EOB%	RL#	SET-UP	DR-IN	RPA
Philadelphia	1991	27	6	0	0	0	0	0	0	0	1	0	0	1	.121	.043	.016	.029	.045
Philadelphia	1992	136	23	4	0	1	0	3	7	0	0	5	7	9	.136	.057	.023	.036	.059

Juan Bell, 24

							Bats Both			116L	266R		119G	90F			241ML	

L= .043G .049L .056F (.033/.040) .073 .077G .083R .090F = R

		ATBATS	1B	2B	3B	HR	HBP	BB	GDP	SB	CS	ROE	XB	RUNS	EOB%	RL#	SET-UP	DR-IN	RPA
Baltimore	1990	2	0	0	0	0	0	0	0	0	0	0	1	0	.000	.000	.000	.000	.000
Baltimore	1991	209	24	9	2	1	0	8	1	0	0	1	19	14	.147	.061	.026	.036	.062
Philadelphia	1992	147	25	3	1	1	1	13	1	5	1	3	6	15	.220	.086	.046	.044	.090

Braulio Castillo, 24

							Bats Right			84L	45R		18G	31F			847ML	

L= .089G .077L ....F (.043/.054) .097 .125G .113R ....F = R

		ATBATS	1B	2B	3B	HR	HBP	BB	GDP	SB	CS	ROE	XB	RUNS	EOB%	RL#	SET-UP	DR-IN	RPA
Philadelphia	1991	52	6	3	0	0	0	1	1	1	1	2	3	3	.138	.049	.020	.031	.051
Philadelphia	1992	76	9	3	1	2	0	4	1	1	0	1	5	8	.154	.088	.040	.053	.093

Wes Chamberlain, 26

							Bats Right			296L	466R		316G	134F			300ML	

L= .106G .124L .168F (.049/.059) .108 .080G .098R .142F = R

		ATBATS	1B	2B	3B	HR	HBP	BB	GDP	SB	CS	ROE	XB	RUNS	EOB%	RL#	SET-UP	DR-IN	RPA
Philadelphia	1990	46	8	3	0	2	0	1	0	4	0	2	7	8	.228	.173	.089	.082	.171
Philadelphia	1991	383	60	16	3	13	2	31	8	9	4	5	26	49	.186	.108	.053	.058	.111
Philadelphia	1992	275	44	18	0	9	1	8	7	4	0	4	13	34	.163	.104	.049	.061	.110

Darren Daulton, 30

							Bats Left			481L	948R		529G	289F				

L= .161G .143L .110F (.085/.074) .159 .185G .167R .134F = R

		ATBATS	1B	2B	3B	HR	HBP	BB	GDP	SB	CS	ROE	XB	RUNS	EOB%	RL#	SET-UP	DR-IN	RPA
Philadelphia	1990	459	80	30	1	12	2	63	6	7	1	2	39	73	.258	.141	.077	.062	.139
Philadelphia	1991	285	32	12	0	12	2	37	4	5	0	4	15	39	.206	.113	.058	.058	.116
Philadelphia	1992	485	67	32	5	27	6	77	3	11	3	3	31	110	.260	.173	.102	.081	.183

Mariano Duncan, 29

							Bats Right			595L	833R		554G	311F				

L= .126G .135L .152F (.048/.057) .105 .075G .084R .101F = R

		ATBATS	1B	2B	3B	HR	HBP	BB	GDP	SB	CS	ROE	XB	RUNS	EOB%	RL#	SET-UP	DR-IN	RPA
Cincinnati	1990	435	90	22	11	10	4	20	10	13	7	10	42	62	.215	.137	.068	.066	.134
Cincinnati	1991	333	63	7	4	12	3	12	0	5	4	1	20	39	.175	.112	.049	.059	.108
Philadelphia	1992	574	102	40	3	8	5	17	15	23	3	5	43	66	.181	.098	.048	.055	.103

Lenny Dykstra, 29

							Bats Left			506L	840R		513G	281F				

L= .134G .158L .203F (.093/.066) .159 .135G .159R .204F = R

		ATBATS	1B	2B	3B	HR	HBP	BB	GDP	SB	CS	ROE	XB	RUNS	EOB%	RL#	SET-UP	DR-IN	RPA
Philadelphia	1990	590	145	35	3	9	7	75	5	33	7	4	89	110	.302	.167	.098	.067	.165
Philadelphia	1991	246	52	13	5	3	1	36	1	24	4	6	31	48	.311	.161	.099	.066	.165
Philadelphia	1992	345	80	18	0	6	3	36	1	30	6	4	30	63	.279	.145	.088	.066	.154

PHILADELPHIA PHILLIES

Dave Hollins, 26

Bats Both   374L 606R   418G 199F   283ML

L= .218G .215L .209F (.090/.075) .165 .137G .134R .128F = R

		ATBATS	1B	2B	3B	HR	HBP	BB	GDP	SB	CS	ROE	XB	RUNS	EOB%	RL#	SET-UP	DR-IN	RPA
Philadelphia	1990	114	16	0	0	5	1	7	1	0	0	0	6	11	.137	.090	.035	.054	.089
Philadelphia	1991	151	27	10	2	6	3	16	2	1	1	2	11	29	.256	.159	.089	.073	.162
Philadelphia	1992	586	99	28	4	27	19	72	8	9	6	8	65	119	.252	.157	.091	.074	.165

Stan Javier, 28

Bats Both   415L 510R   314G 187F

L= .093G .097L .103F (.057/.048) .105 .107G .111R .117F = R

		ATBATS	1B	2B	3B	HR	HBP	BB	GDP	SB	CS	ROE	XB	RUNS	EOB%	RL#	SET-UP	DR-IN	RPA
Oakland	1990	33	6	0	2	0	0	3	0	0	0	0	4	4	.229	.109	.063	.058	.121
Los Angeles	1990	276	68	9	4	3	0	35	6	15	7	6	42	46	.270	.139	.081	.063	.144
Los Angeles	1991	176	27	5	3	1	0	16	4	7	1	5	13	17	.207	.086	.043	.044	.087
Los Angeles	1992	58	7	3	0	1	1	4	0	1	2	1	5	6	.173	.084	.040	.048	.088
Philadelphia	1992	276	57	14	1	0	2	31	4	17	1	6	23	39	.276	.114	.068	.052	.120

Ricky Jordan, 27

Bats Right   400L 560R   331G 210F

L= .130G .139L .152F (.051/.058) .109 .078G .087R .100F = R

		ATBATS	1B	2B	3B	HR	HBP	BB	GDP	SB	CS	ROE	XB	RUNS	EOB%	RL#	SET-UP	DR-IN	RPA
Philadelphia	1990	324	52	21	0	5	5	7	9	2	0	5	19	30	.169	.088	.039	.048	.087
Philadelphia	1991	301	49	21	3	9	2	12	11	0	3	2	22	34	.154	.099	.044	.058	.102
Philadelphia	1992	276	61	19	0	4	0	5	8	3	0	7	17	35	.207	.112	.058	.059	.117

John Kruk, 31

Bats Left   608L 1102R   618G 357F

L= .138G .132L .122F (.087/.068) .155 .173G .167R .157F = R

		ATBATS	1B	2B	3B	HR	HBP	BB	GDP	SB	CS	ROE	XB	RUNS	EOB%	RL#	SET-UP	DR-IN	RPA
Philadelphia	1990	443	89	25	8	7	0	53	11	10	6	6	44	67	.249	.134	.073	.060	.133
Philadelphia	1991	538	104	27	6	21	1	51	11	7	0	5	39	91	.229	.143	.077	.069	.146
Philadelphia	1992	507	120	30	4	10	1	84	11	3	5	5	42	104	.300	.156	.097	.067	.164

Steve Lake, 35

Bats Right   203L 100R   104G 73F

L= .048G .075L .113F (.030/.040) .070 .033G .060R .098F = R

		ATBATS	1B	2B	3B	HR	HBP	BB	GDP	SB	CS	ROE	XB	RUNS	EOB%	RL#	SET-UP	DR-IN	RPA
Philadelphia	1990	80	18	2	0	0	1	2	1	0	0	0	1	6	.192	.074	.035	.038	.073
Philadelphia	1991	158	30	4	1	1	0	1	5	0	0	3	7	11	.142	.062	.026	.037	.063
Philadelphia	1992	53	10	2	0	1	0	1	1	0	0	1	0	5	.167	.084	.040	.049	.089

Jim Lindeman, 30

Bats Right   126L 59R   51G 37F   63ML

L= .184G .143L ....F (.068/.054) .122 .117G .076R ....F = R

		ATBATS	1B	2B	3B	HR	HBP	BB	GDP	SB	CS	ROE	XB	RUNS	EOB%	RL#	SET-UP	DR-IN	RPA
Detroit	1990	32	4	1	0	2	0	2	0	0	0	0	3	4	.145	.122	.050	.072	.122
Philadelphia	1991	95	27	5	0	0	0	12	1	0	1	1	9	15	.311	.133	.082	.055	.137
Philadelphia	1992	39	8	1	0	1	0	3	1	0	0	2	3	6	.236	.120	.067	.060	.127

Tom Marsh, 27

Bats Right   69L 61R   45G 29F   430ML

L= .052G .072L ....F (.029/.050) .079 .067G .087R ....F = R

		ATBATS	1B	2B	3B	HR	HBP	BB	GDP	SB	CS	ROE	XB	RUNS	EOB%	RL#	SET-UP	DR-IN	RPA
Philadelphia	1992	125	18	3	2	2	1	2	2	0	2	1	5	9	.117	.068	.026	.045	.071

Mickey Morandini, 26

Bats Left   213L 685R   350G 187F

L= .077G .065L .043F (.054/.050) .104 .128G .116R .094F = R

		ATBATS	1B	2B	3B	HR	HBP	BB	GDP	SB	CS	ROE	XB	RUNS	EOB%	RL#	SET-UP	DR-IN	RPA
Philadelphia	1990	79	14	4	0	1	0	6	1	3	0	0	7	8	.207	.100	.050	.049	.099
Philadelphia	1991	325	65	11	4	1	2	29	7	13	3	5	28	37	.228	.094	.051	.046	.097
Philadelphia	1992	422	93	8	8	3	0	23	4	8	3	7	30	51	.220	.104	.056	.053	.109

PHILADELPHIA PHILLIES

Dale Murphy, 36

Bats Right   461L   847R   438G   265F

L= .112G   .132L   .164F   (.048/.056) .104   .068G   .088R   .120F = R

		ATBATS	1B	2B	3B	HR	HBP	BB	GDP	SB	CS	ROE	XB	RUNS	EOB%	RL#	SET-UP	DR-IN	RPA
Atlanta	1990	349	50	14	0	17	1	30	11	9	2	10	15	47	.178	.118	.054	.063	.117
Philadelphia	1990	214	40	9	1	7	0	17	11	0	1	0	8	24	.158	.099	.043	.056	.099
Philadelphia	1991	544	85	33	1	18	0	45	20	1	0	9	35	69	.186	.106	.052	.057	.109
Philadelphia	1992	62	7	1	0	2	0	1	3	0	0	2	1	4	.075	.053	.015	.042	.057

PITCHERS

Kyle Abbott, 24

Throws: Neutral type, moderate reverse lefty

(.119/.110) .112   149L   490R   868ML

		OUTS	RO	1B	2B	3B	HR	HBP	BB	GDP	SB	CS	PO	WP	BK	RUNS	EOB%	RL#	RPA
California	1991	59	6	16	4	0	2	1	13	3	1	2	0	1	1	11	.194	.121	.123
Philadelphia	1992	400	49	103	16	8	20	1	45	11	9	7	0	9	1	79	.158	.113	.128

Andy Ashby, 25

Throws: Groundball type, moderate righty

(.129/.123) .126   198L   146R   824ML

		OUTS	RO	1B	2B	3B	HR	HBP	BB	GDP	SB	CS	PO	WP	BK	RUNS	EOB%	RL#	RPA
Philadelphia	1991	126	0	25	9	2	5	3	19	2	0	1	0	6	0	24	.211	.124	.125
Philadelphia	1992	111	6	27	7	2	6	1	21	3	4	2	0	2	0	28	.205	.135	.154

Bob Ayrault, 26

Throws: Flyball type, moderate to severe righty

(.139/.107) .123   85L   84R   543ML

		OUTS	RO	1B	2B	3B	HR	HBP	BB	GDP	SB	CS	PO	WP	BK	RUNS	EOB%	RL#	RPA
Philadelphia	1992	130	130	21	9	2	0	1	16	1	3	0	0	0	0	16	.210	.078	.087

Cliff Brantley, 24

Throws: Groundball type, extreme righty

(.127/.081) .107   266L   200R   607ML

		OUTS	RO	1B	2B	3B	HR	HBP	BB	GDP	SB	CS	PO	WP	BK	RUNS	EOB%	RL#	RPA
Philadelphia	1991	95	12	21	4	1	0	2	19	1	6	2	0	2	0	14	.244	.094	.095
Philadelphia	1992	229	90	55	9	1	6	4	54	9	10	5	0	4	1	44	.216	.109	.122

Brad Brink, 27

Throws: Neutral type, righty

(.104/....) .121   106L   73R   651ML

		OUTS	RO	1B	2B	3B	HR	HBP	BB	GDP	SB	CS	PO	WP	BK	RUNS	EOB%	RL#	RPA
Philadelphia	1992	124	6	41	8	2	2	1	11	5	3	2	0	0	0	22	.181	.102	.115

Pat Combs, 26

Throws: Neutral type, moderate to severe reverse lefty

(.148/.125) .130   225L   913R   658ML

		OUTS	RO	1B	2B	3B	HR	HBP	BB	GDP	SB	CS	PO	WP	BK	RUNS	EOB%	RL#	RPA
Philadelphia	1990	550	4	126	36	5	12	4	79	14	11	10	1	9	1	82	.186	.104	.104
Philadelphia	1991	193	11	44	13	0	7	2	42	6	12	2	0	7	0	39	.228	.128	.129
Philadelphia	1992	56	0	14	5	1	0	0	12	1	4	1	0	1	0	11	.260	.120	.128

Jose DeLeon, 32

Throws: Flyball type, extreme righty

(.135/.077) .110   1082L   824R

		OUTS	RO	1B	2B	3B	HR	HBP	BB	GDP	SB	CS	PO	WP	BK	RUNS	EOB%	RL#	RPA
St. Louis	1990	548	0	118	30	5	15	5	77	8	20	12	0	5	0	82	.186	.103	.104
St. Louis	1991	488	0	95	29	5	15	6	60	8	12	12	0	1	1	76	.163	.093	.106
St. Louis	1992	307	64	59	25	4	7	2	42	4	12	4	0	3	0	56	.199	.102	.119
Philadelphia	1992	45	0	15	1	0	0	0	5	1	0	1	0	0	0	6	.192	.077	.086

Tommy Greene, 25

Throws: Flyball type, extreme righty

(.142/.055) .105   757L   569R   96ML

		OUTS	RO	1B	2B	3B	HR	HBP	BB	GDP	SB	CS	PO	WP	BK	RUNS	EOB%	RL#	RPA
Atlanta	1990	37	15	8	1	2	3	1	9	1	1	1	0	0	0	10	.205	.170	.161
Philadelphia	1990	117	6	22	9	0	5	0	16	2	1	4	0	1	0	17	.146	.103	.103
Philadelphia	1991	623	83	119	35	4	19	3	62	9	18	7	1	9	1	82	.160	.093	.093
Philadelphia	1992	193	3	54	14	2	5	0	32	6	13	1	0	1	0	43	.225	.123	.138

PHILADELPHIA PHILLIES

Mike Hartley, 31

Throws: Flyball type, neutral righty

(.127/.123) .125   468L   430R   47ML

		OUTS	RO	1B	2B	3B	HR	HBP	BB	GDP	SB	CS	PO	WP	BK	RUNS	EOB%	RL#	RPA
Los Angeles	1990	238	131	40	8	3	7	2	28	3	14	1	0	3	0	33	.174	.097	.101
Los Angeles	1991	171	171	36	8	2	7	3	30	3	10	1	0	8	1	34	.220	.131	.132
Philadelphia	1991	79	79	15	2	0	4	3	9	2	3	0	0	2	1	12	.171	.107	.108
Philadelphia	1992	165	165	35	12	2	5	2	17	2	8	2	0	4	0	30	.188	.108	.121

Greg Mathews, 30

Throws: Neutral type, extreme reverse lefty

(.190/.105) .125   104L   332R   796ML

		OUTS	RO	1B	2B	3B	HR	HBP	BB	GDP	SB	CS	PO	WP	BK	RUNS	EOB%	RL#	RPA
St. Louis	1990	152	6	36	11	4	2	2	29	5	13	2	1	2	1	28	.223	.119	.119
Philadelphia	1992	157	33	34	13	0	7	1	22	4	3	3	0	1	2	30	.174	.112	.125

Terry Mulholland, 29

Throws: Neutral type, moderate lefty

(.080/.089) .087   433L   2095R

		OUTS	RO	1B	2B	3B	HR	HBP	BB	GDP	SB	CS	PO	WP	BK	RUNS	EOB%	RL#	RPA
Philadelphia	1990	542	28	113	40	4	15	2	35	16	3	3	2	7	2	66	.136	.091	.090
Philadelphia	1991	696	0	167	42	7	15	3	47	16	6	5	4	3	0	87	.152	.087	.088
Philadelphia	1992	687	0	167	43	3	14	3	43	14	2	5	15	3	0	86	.131	.077	.087

Wally Ritchie, 27

Throws: Neutral type, extreme lefty

(.031/.138) .101   124L   238R   163ML

		OUTS	RO	1B	2B	3B	HR	HBP	BB	GDP	SB	CS	PO	WP	BK	RUNS	EOB%	RL#	RPA
Philadelphia	1991	151	151	32	7	1	4	2	12	1	10	0	0	1	0	22	.189	.099	.100
Philadelphia	1992	117	117	29	10	2	3	0	14	6	3	0	0	0	0	21	.174	.105	.118

Ben Rivera, 23

Throws: Neutral type, neutral righty

(.130/.127) .129   272L   195R   724ML

		OUTS	RO	1B	2B	3B	HR	HBP	BB	GDP	SB	CS	PO	WP	BK	RUNS	EOB%	RL#	RPA
Atlanta	1992	46	46	17	2	1	1	2	11	2	2	2	0	0	0	12	.246	.140	.151
Philadelphia	1992	306	31	50	16	4	8	2	30	7	13	2	1	5	0	39	.144	.082	.092

Don Robinson, 35

Throws: Flyball type, extreme righty

(.136/.091) .117   795L   589R

		OUTS	RO	1B	2B	3B	HR	HBP	BB	GDP	SB	CS	PO	WP	BK	RUNS	EOB%	RL#	RPA
San Francisco	1990	473	3	117	36	2	18	1	33	6	19	8	2	2	0	74	.158	.108	.110
San Francisco	1991	364	110	81	25	5	12	1	43	8	10	5	0	1	0	64	.175	.105	.117
California	1992	49	0	15	3	0	1	0	3	4	4	0	0	1	0	6	.116	.087	.089
Philadelphia	1992	131	0	32	10	1	6	1	4	1	7	0	0	0	0	25	.169	.118	.129

Curt Schilling, 26

Throws: Neutral type, moderate righty

(.090/.077) .084   724L   641R

		OUTS	RO	1B	2B	3B	HR	HBP	BB	GDP	SB	CS	PO	WP	BK	RUNS	EOB%	RL#	RPA
Baltimore	1990	138	138	28	9	0	1	0	19	4	1	0	0	0	0	16	.192	.082	.084
Houston	1991	227	227	59	15	3	2	0	32	4	3	4	0	4	1	38	.211	.096	.107
Philadelphia	1992	679	85	120	30	4	11	1	55	10	7	7	0	4	0	71	.142	.067	.076

Mickey Weston, 31

Throws: Groundball type, extreme righty

(.158/.075) .113   52L   62R   1393ML

		OUTS	RO	1B	2B	3B	HR	HBP	BB	GDP	SB	CS	PO	WP	BK	RUNS	EOB%	RL#	RPA
Baltimore	1990	63	41	20	2	0	6	0	5	3	0	0	0	1	0	13	.129	.140	.143
Toronto	1991	6	6	0	1	0	0	0	0	0	0	0	0	0	0	0	.098	.044	.043
Philadelphia	1992	11	0	4	2	0	1	1	1	1	1	0	0	0	0	4	.204	.198	.210

Mike Williams, 24

Throws: Neutral type, righty

(..../....) .099   77L   39R   863ML

		OUTS	RO	1B	2B	3B	HR	HBP	BB	GDP	SB	CS	PO	WP	BK	RUNS	EOB%	RL#	RPA
Philadelphia	1992	86	0	16	9	1	3	0	7	3	1	1	0	0	0	13	.134	.093	.105

Mitch Williams, 28

Throws: Flydball type, neutral lefty

(.108/.110) .110   222L   793R

		OUTS	RO	1B	2B	3B	HR	HBP	BB	GDP	SB	CS	PO	WP	BK	RUNS	EOB%	RL#	RPA
Chicago Cubs	1990	199	180	33	20	3	4	1	44	3	6	0	1	4	2	35	.250	.126	.117
Philadelphia	1991	265	265	39	12	1	4	8	57	3	12	2	1	4	1	38	.235	.096	.096
Philadelphia	1992	243	243	46	16	3	4	6	62	3	9	6	2	5	3	49	.246	.112	.126

Philadelphia Phillies AAA & AA Minor League Ratings

AAA (SCRANTON)	AGE	BATS	POSITION	CPA	RUNS	SET-UP	DRIVE-IN	RPA
Gary Alexander	28	R	1B	447	37.5	.039	.045	.084
Kim Batiste	24	R	SS	285	18.9	.028	.038	.066
Nick Capra	34	R	OF	410	41.4	.055	.046	.101
Braulio Castillo	24	R	OF	439	43.0	.046	.052	.098
Wes Chamberlain	26	R	OF	142	18.7	.071	.061	.132
Bruce Dostal	27	L	OF	355	33.7	.054	.041	.095
Jose Gonzalez	28	R	OF	159	17.8	.062	.050	.112
Greg Legg	32	R	3B\2B	338	25.6	.040	.036	.076
Doug Lindsey	25	R	C	323	21.2	.031	.035	.066
Tom Marsh	27	R	OF	175	15.4	.035	.053	.088
Joe Millette	26	R	SS	285	20.6	.035	.037	.072
Todd Pratt	25	R	C	317	51.0	.096	.065	.161
Victor Rodriguez	31	R	2B\3B	162	11.7	.032	.040	.072
Rick Schu	30	R	3B\2B	458	53.8	.064	.053	.117
Jeff Stone	32	L	OF	255	18.2	.033	.038	.071
Cary Williams	25	R	OF	400	28.7	.031	.041	.072

AA (READING)	AGE	BATS	POSITION	CPA	RUNS	SET-UP	DRIVE-IN	RPA
Pete Alborano	27	L	OF	155	10.2	.029	.037	.066
Steve Bieser	25	B	OF\C	152	11.9	.038	.040	.078
Pat Brady	26	R	OF	288	30.2	.056	.049	.105
John Escobar	23	R	SS\3B	334	21.0	.028	.035	.063
Mickey Hyde	26	R	OF	257	20.2	.039	.039	.078
Jeff Jackson	20	R	OF	126	7.4	.028	.031	.059
Mike Lieberthal	20	R	C	402	29.1	.035	.037	.072
Ron Lockett	23	L	1B\OF	430	26.2	.026	.035	.061
R.A. Neitzel	24	L	2B	305	17.5	.028	.029	.057
Tom Nuneviller	23	R	OF	183	19.9	.056	.053	.109
Ed Rosado	23	B	C\3B	232	22.1	.048	.047	.095
Sean Ryan	23	B	1B	403	35.6	.044	.044	.088
Kevin Stocker	22	B	SS	266	21.7	.042	.040	.082
Sam Taylor	24	L	OF	396	35.1	.041	.048	.089
Tony Trevino	27	R	2B\OF\SS	319	21.0	.032	.034	.066
Casey Waller	25	B	3B	420	37.4	.045	.044	.089

AAA Pitchers	Age	Throws	Outs	RPA	AA Pitchers	Age	Throws	Outs	RPA
Kyle Abbott	24	L	105	.075	Joel Adamson	21	L	177	.167
Andy Ashby	25	R	99	.122	Ron Allen	22	R	93	.130
Bob Ayrault	26	R	76	.134	Andy Carter	24	L	76	.222
Jay Baller	32	R	190	.087	Rocky Elli	25	L	196	.143
Toby Borland	23	R	208	.152	Paul Fletcher	25	R	449	.112
Cliff Brantley	24	R	92	.093	Darrell Goedhart	22	R	259	.134
Brad Brink	27	R	375	.125	Tyler Green	22	R	218	.109
Darrin Chapin	26	R	185	.150	Eric Hill	25	R	294	.161
Pat Combs	26	L	374	.120	Chris Limbach	24	L	249	.114
Greg Mathews	30	L	255	.131	Jeff Patterson	24	R	135	.111
Tim Mauser	26	R	300	.114	Keith Shepherd	24	R	282	.094
Steve Parris	25	R	410	.143	Matt Stevens	25	R	215	.130
Mark Sims	24	L	160	.116	Mike Sullivan	24	R	134	.171
Mickey Weston	31	R	512	.108	Scott Wiegandt	25	L	245	.121
Mike Williams	24	R	325	.111					

PITTSBURGH PIRATES

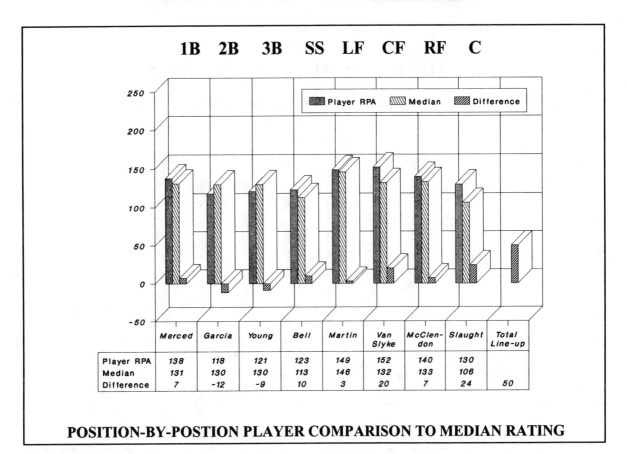

	1B	2B	3B	SS	LF	CF	RF	C	Total Line-up
	Merced	Garcia	Young	Bell	Martin	Van Slyke	McClendon	Slaught	
Player RPA	138	118	121	123	149	152	140	130	
Median	131	130	130	113	146	132	133	106	
Difference	7	-12	-9	10	3	20	7	24	50

POSITION-BY-POSTION PLAYER COMPARISON TO MEDIAN RATING

DEFENSIVE TEAM AND STADIUM DATA FOR THE LAST 3 YEARS:

TEAM DEFENSE BY POSITION:

		1990	1991	1992	POSITION-BY-POSITION STADIUM CHARACTERISTICS:
1B:	Home	+3.7	-4.1	+4.5	Slightly easy to play
	Away	+2.9	-3.0	+4.4	
2B:	Home	+8.3	+7.8	+3.3	Average (to slightly hard)
	Away	-2.4	+0.3	-4.5	
3B:	Home	+3.6	0.0	+1.5	Average
	Away	-0.8	+3.7	+3.0	
SS:	Home	-0.3	-7.9	-2.0	Average
	Away	+4.5	+0.2	-0.9	
LF:	Home	-2.0	-4.1	+6.3	Average
	Away	+7.5	+3.8	+3.8	
CF:	Home	-0.7	+0.5	+4.7	Slightly hard to play
	Away	-1.7	-0.5	-6.8	
RF:	Home	+0.9	-0.6	-6.2	Average
	Away	-7.1	+6.3	+0.2	
Total Home:		+13.5	-8.4	+12.1	
Total Away:		+2.9	+10.8	-0.8	

Comments: There's been a lot of talk about the "loss" of Jose Lind and what it means to the Pirate defense. Lind is a good defensive player, but not a defensive "impact" player. The big loss on defense from the '92 season will be the same loss as on offense: Barry Bonds in left field. Left field provided the Pirates with over a 10 run defensive advantage during the past season.

PITTSBURGH PIRATES

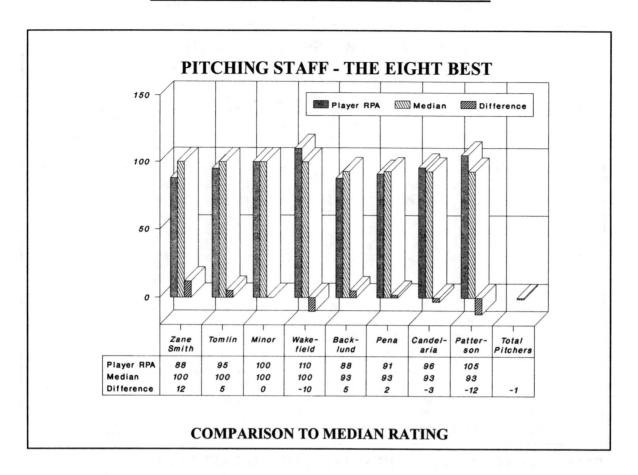

PITCHING STAFF - THE EIGHT BEST

Legend: ■ Player RPA ▨ Median ▨ Difference

	Zane Smith	Tomlin	Minor	Wake-field	Back-lund	Pena	Candel-aria	Patter-son	Total Pitchers
Player RPA	88	95	100	110	88	91	96	105	
Median	100	100	100	100	93	93	93	93	
Difference	12	5	0	-10	5	2	-3	-12	-1

COMPARISON TO MEDIAN RATING

SUGGESTED LINE-UPS (with set-up RPA & drive-in RPA ratings):

Vs: Left-handed Groundball
3B:	K. Young	75-60
CF:	A. Van Slyke	63-51
RF:	L. McClendon	77-65
LF:	A. Martin	72-68
SS:	J. Bell	77-76
C:	T. Prince	58-57
2B:	C. Garcia	63-67
1B:	J. King	45-54
Pitcher		

Vs: Neutral Lefty Pitchers
3B:	K. Young	75-60
CF:	A. Van Slyke	69-55
C:	D. Slaught	65-54
RF:	L. McClendon	78-66
LF:	A. Martin	72-68
SS:	J. Bell	77-76
2B:	C. Garcia	63-67
1B:	J. King	58-70
Pitcher		

Vs: Left-handed Flyball
CF:	A. Van Slyke	77-61
3B:	K. Young	75-60
C:	D. Slaught	88-74
RF:	L. McClendon	80-68
LF:	A. Martin	72-68
SS:	J. Bell	76-76
1B:	J. King	78-91
2B:	C. Garcia	63-67
Pitcher		

Vs: Right-handed Groundball
CF:	A. Van Slyke	95-77
C:	D. Slaught	67-56
1B:	O. Merced	76-65
LF:	A. Martin	82-78
RF:	D. Clark	62-69
SS:	J. Bell	57-56
2B:	C. Garcia	53-57
3B:	J. Wehner	56-45
Pitcher		

Vs: Neutral Righty Pitchers
CF:	A. Van Slyke	100-82
C:	D. Slaught	80-68
1B:	O. Merced	81-70
LF:	A. Martin	82-78
RF:	D. Clark	62-69
SS:	J. Bell	57-56
2B:	C. Garcia	53-57
3B:	J. Wehner	60-48
Pitcher		

Vs: Right-handed Flyball
CF:	A. Van Slyke	107-89
3B:	J. Wehner	66-55
C:	D. Slaught	103-88
1B:	O. Merced	88-77
LF:	A. Martin	82-78
RF:	D. Clark	62-69
SS:	J. Bell	56-56
2B:	C. Garcia	53-57
Pitcher		

Comments: Much as I would have liked to, I couldn't get Lonnie Smith's big bat into these line-ups since he's lost so much range in the outfield and since he probably can't play first base. Even so, this is still one of the best offenses in the NL, despite the loss of Bonds. Fortunately for the Pirates they do have good young talent in Al Martin, Carlos Garcia and Kevin Young to allow this team to be at least respectable in the coming season.

PITTSBURGH PIRATES

Where do you start with a team that lost a player of the quality of Barry Bonds? No team can afford to lose the best player in baseball and expect to contend. So we know the Pirates won't contend. The loss of Doug Drabek can't help either. Does this mean that the Pirates will be a bad team in '93. No, not at all.

Unlike the woeful New York Mets, the Pirates do have quality young players. While the Mets AAA farm club at Tidewater was setting a record for losses in one season, the Pirates AAA farm club was winning the American Association pennant.

Kevin Young (3B), Carlos Garcia (2B) and Al Martin (OF) are all high quality young players. Blas Minor is an excellent young pitcher who I think is ready right now to make an impact at the Major League level. Why this team left Blas Minor exposed in the Expansion draft is beyond me. Fortunately for them, the Colorado Rockies, as they did with so many other clubs, came to the Pirates rescue when they selected Alex Cole. But why didn't the Pirates at least protect Minor in the subsequent round? Brett Backlund is a pitching phenom who might be ready faster than anyone would have believed. He could really be outstanding. Lonnie Smith and Dave Clark are solid veteran players who can help supplement the kids. John Candelaria and Alejandro Pena will strengthen the bullpen.

By the way, the trade of Jose Lind to Kansas City was a huge plus for this team. Carlos Garcia should be a better overall player. Lind can't hit at all. Lind would have had to be almost a superhuman defensive player to overcome his offensive negatives. But Lind is only a good defensive player, not a great defensive player as is purported in the press.

All in all, considering the problems that they faced, I think the Pirates did a marvelous job of repair after losing Bonds and Drabek. It won't be enough to project them into the pennant race, but they will be respectable. What's more importanat is that this team is already on the road to pulling itself together and making itself into a contender in the near future.

I realize that the Pirates needed a utility player to back up Carlos Garcia and Jay Bell. But why Tom Foley? The Pirates did sign Dave Rohde. He's got to be a lot better than Foley!

The signing of Dave Otto may have been a financial boo-boo, but I think it could work out in the Pirates favor. Otto has real ability, but has been very inconsistent. He could really surprise a lot of people and be a real asset as a starting pitcher for this team.

The Pirates shouldn't overlook the abilities of John Wehner. I was surprised to see just how much range Wehner had at third base. He's got a very good glove.

Pitcher Steve Cooke is progressing nicely. He's only 22 years old and is almost ready for the Major Leagues.

Pittsburgh's Projected record for 1993: 82--80, good for 3rd place in the division.

PITTSBURGH PIRATES

Jay Bell, 27

Bats Right   785L   1261R   721G   438F

L= .148G .148L .147F $\boxed{(.062/.061)\ .123}$ .108G .108R .107F = R

		ATBATS	1B	2B	3B	HR	HBP	BB	GDP	SB	CS	ROE	XB	RUNS	EOB%	RL#	SET-UP	DR-IN	RPA
Pittsburgh	1990	583	106	28	7	7	3	65	14	10	6	12	65	79	.237	.114	.063	.055	.118
Pittsburgh	1991	608	108	32	8	16	4	51	15	10	8	6	60	83	.204	.119	.061	.062	.123
Pittsburgh	1992	632	116	36	6	9	4	55	12	7	5	7	53	86	.225	.117	.063	.059	.122

Barry Bonds, 28

Bats Left   780L   1014R   591G   393F

L= .195G .200L .208F $\boxed{(.115/.090)\ .205}$ .204G .209R .217F = R

		ATBATS	1B	2B	3B	HR	HBP	BB	GDP	SB	CS	ROE	XB	RUNS	EOB%	RL#	SET-UP	DR-IN	RPA
Pittsburgh	1990	519	88	32	3	33	3	78	8	52	14	4	58	119	.243	.188	.105	.090	.195
Pittsburgh	1991	510	91	28	5	25	4	82	8	43	13	4	51	108	.257	.174	.099	.080	.179
Pittsburgh	1992	473	72	36	5	34	5	95	9	39	10	1	65	134	.273	.222	.131	.100	.231

Dave Clark, 30

Bats Left   6L   226R   78G   68F   695ML

L= ....G ....L ....F $\boxed{(.057/.064)\ .121}$ .113G .123R .134F = R

		ATBATS	1B	2B	3B	HR	HBP	BB	GDP	SB	CS	ROE	XB	RUNS	EOB%	RL#	SET-UP	DR-IN	RPA
Cubs	1990	171	36	4	2	5	0	7	4	7	1	2	14	20	.180	.115	.050	.058	.108
Kansas City	1991	10	2	0	0	0	0	1	0	0	0	0	0	1	.220	.068	.036	.035	.071
Pittsburgh	1992	33	5	0	0	2	0	6	0	0	0	0	2	6	.234	.152	.085	.076	.161

Alex Cole, 27

Bats Both   113L   266R   141G   107F   436ML

L= .149G .138L .122F $\boxed{(.059/.052)\ .111}$ .116G .105R .089F = R

		ATBATS	1B	2B	3B	HR	HBP	BB	GDP	SB	CS	ROE	XB	RUNS	EOB%	RL#	SET-UP	DR-IN	RPA
Cleveland	1990	227	59	5	4	0	1	28	2	40	12	4	25	35	.273	.135	.076	.059	.135
Cleveland	1991	387	94	17	3	0	1	56	8	27	20	3	45	53	.254	.112	.065	.053	.118
Cleveland	1992	97	19	1	0	0	1	10	2	9	3	1	8	8	.201	.077	.037	.038	.075
Pittsburgh	1992	205	47	3	7	0	0	17	2	7	6	1	21	26	.222	.110	.059	.055	.114

Cecil Espy, 29

Bats Left   278L   686R   314G   208F

L= .104G .099L .092F $\boxed{(.056/.056)\ .112}$ .123G .118R .111F = R

		ATBATS	1B	2B	3B	HR	HBP	BB	GDP	SB	CS	ROE	XB	RUNS	EOB%	RL#	SET-UP	DR-IN	RPA
Texas	1990	71	9	0	0	0	0	10	1	11	5	0	7	4	.140	.047	.019	.028	.047
Pittsburgh	1991	82	15	4	0	1	0	5	0	4	0	0	10	9	.214	.105	.055	.054	.109
Pittsburgh	1992	194	39	7	3	1	0	13	3	6	3	2	11	22	.207	.099	.052	.052	.104

Kirk Gibson, 35

Bats Left   521L   521R   330G   227F   31ML

L= .102G .118L .143F $\boxed{(.066/.063)\ .129}$ .117G .133R .158F = R

		ATBATS	1B	2B	3B	HR	HBP	BB	GDP	SB	CS	ROE	XB	RUNS	EOB%	RL#	SET-UP	DR-IN	RPA
Los Angeles	1990	315	54	20	0	8	3	39	4	26	3	1	29	51	.247	.137	.076	.065	.141
Kansas City	1991	462	70	17	6	16	6	66	9	18	5	2	36	72	.226	.128	.069	.064	.133
Pittsburgh	1992	56	9	0	0	2	0	3	1	3	1	2	4	6	.152	.096	.042	.057	.099

Jeff King, 28

Bats Right   165L   867R   360G   228F

L= .095G .124L .165F $\boxed{(.049/.060)\ .109}$ .066G .095R .136F = R

		ATBATS	1B	2B	3B	HR	HBP	BB	GDP	SB	CS	ROE	XB	RUNS	EOB%	RL#	SET-UP	DR-IN	RPA
Pittsburgh	1990	371	59	17	1	14	1	20	12	3	3	6	23	43	.155	.103	.046	.061	.107
Pittsburgh	1991	109	20	1	1	4	1	11	3	3	1	0	4	14	.183	.108	.052	.060	.112
Pittsburgh	1992	480	74	21	2	14	2	24	8	4	6	6	42	54	.161	.101	.046	.060	.106

Mike LaValliere, 32

Bats Left   165L   867R   360G   228F

L= .119G .122L .126F $\boxed{(.054/.051)\ .105}$ .099G .102R .106F = R

		ATBATS	1B	2B	3B	HR	HBP	BB	GDP	SB	CS	ROE	XB	RUNS	EOB%	RL#	SET-UP	DR-IN	RPA
Pittsburgh	1990	279	54	15	0	3	2	36	6	0	3	2	10	36	.245	.106	.059	.051	.110
Pittsburgh	1991	336	81	11	2	3	2	29	10	2	1	3	13	41	.235	.106	.058	.052	.110
Pittsburgh	1992	293	59	13	1	2	1	30	8	0	3	2	8	33	.220	.096	.051	.049	.100

PITTSBURGH PIRATES

Jose Lind, 28
Bats Right   610L   981R   570G   332F

L= .070G .075L .084F [(.035/.043) .078] .075G .080R .089F = R

		ATBATS	1B	2B	3B	HR	HBP	BB	GDP	SB	CS	ROE	XB	RUNS	EOB%	RL#	SET-UP	DR-IN	RPA
Pittsburgh	1990	514	100	28	5	1	1	16	20	8	0	2	40	45	.168	.078	.036	.045	.081
Pittsburgh	1991	502	108	16	6	3	2	20	20	7	4	8	30	47	.178	.083	.039	.047	.086
Pittsburgh	1992	468	95	14	1	0	1	14	14	3	1	4	25	35	.165	.067	.031	.039	.070

Lloyd McClendon, 33
Bats Right   428L   106R   147G   98F

L= .147G .149L .153F [(.076/.063) .139] .098G .100R .104F = R

		ATBATS	1B	2B	3B	HR	HBP	BB	GDP	SB	CS	ROE	XB	RUNS	EOB%	RL#	SET-UP	DR-IN	RPA
Cubs	1990	107	13	3	0	1	0	12	2	1	0	0	4	7	.175	.063	.027	.033	.060
Pittsburgh	1990	3	0	0	0	1	0	0	0	0	0	0	0	0	.000	.220	.000	.220	.220
Pittsburgh	1991	163	33	7	0	7	2	18	2	2	2	4	9	30	.255	.156	.088	.072	.160
Pittsburgh	1992	190	36	8	1	3	2	28	5	1	3	1	19	27	.240	.116	.065	.056	.121

Orlando Merced, 26
Bats Both   165L   796R   344G   231F

L= .065G .075L .089F [(.071/.061) .132] .134G .144R .158F = R

		ATBATS	1B	2B	3B	HR	HBP	BB	GDP	SB	CS	ROE	XB	RUNS	EOB%	RL#	SET-UP	DR-IN	RPA
Pittsburgh	1990	24	4	1	0	0	0	1	1	0	0	0	2	1	.136	.053	.022	.033	.055
Pittsburgh	1991	411	84	17	2	10	1	60	6	8	5	5	49	68	.264	.139	.080	.063	.143
Pittsburgh	1992	405	61	28	5	6	2	44	6	5	4	1	34	55	.222	.115	.062	.058	.120

Tom Prince, 28
Bats Right   56L   52R   31G   19F   546ML

L= ....G .134L ....F [(.051/.050) .101] ....G .065R ....F = R

		ATBATS	1B	2B	3B	HR	HBP	BB	GDP	SB	CS	ROE	XB	RUNS	EOB%	RL#	SET-UP	DR-IN	RPA
Pittsburgh	1990	10	1	0	0	0	0	1	0	0	1	1	0	0	.155	.036	.016	.021	.037
Pittsburgh	1991	34	5	3	0	1	1	7	3	0	0	1	3	6	.254	.128	.071	.059	.130
Pittsburgh	1992	44	2	2	0	0	0	6	2	1	1	2	2	2	.152	.041	.018	.025	.043

Gary Redus, 36
Bats Right   586L   152R   243G   165F

L= .137G .138L .139F [(.072/.064) .136] .127G .128R .129F = R

		ATBATS	1B	2B	3B	HR	HBP	BB	GDP	SB	CS	ROE	XB	RUNS	EOB%	RL#	SET-UP	DR-IN	RPA
Pittsburgh	1990	227	32	15	3	6	2	33	1	11	6	1	25	37	.241	.135	.075	.065	.140
Pittsburgh	1991	252	41	12	2	7	3	26	0	17	4	5	26	40	.245	.138	.077	.065	.142
Pittsburgh	1992	176	32	7	3	3	0	17	1	11	4	0	20	25	.214	.122	.065	.062	.127

Don Slaught, 34
Bats Right   519L   265R   275G   158F

L= .101G .126L .169F [(.074/.062) .136] .130G .155R .198F = R

		ATBATS	1B	2B	3B	HR	HBP	BB	GDP	SB	CS	ROE	XB	RUNS	EOB%	RL#	SET-UP	DR-IN	RPA
Pittsburgh	1990	230	44	18	3	4	3	25	2	0	1	2	21	40	.275	.149	.088	.066	.154
Pittsburgh	1991	220	46	17	1	1	3	20	6	1	0	4	12	31	.264	.119	.069	.054	.123
Pittsburgh	1992	255	64	17	3	4	2	12	6	2	2	1	15	41	.237	.142	.079	.070	.149

Andy Van Slyke, 32
Bats Left   720L   1095R   591G   389F

L= .118G .128L .142F [(.090/.073) .163] .176G .186R .200F = R

		ATBATS	1B	2B	3B	HR	HBP	BB	GDP	SB	CS	ROE	XB	RUNS	EOB%	RL#	SET-UP	DR-IN	RPA
Pittsburgh	1990	493	91	26	6	17	1	64	6	14	5	8	41	92	.259	.157	.090	.072	.162
Pittsburgh	1991	491	82	24	7	17	4	70	5	10	3	3	53	88	.255	.150	.085	.069	.154
Pittsburgh	1992	614	128	45	12	14	4	54	9	12	5	4	56	115	.256	.162	.094	.075	.169

Gary Varsho, 31
Bats Left   21L   409R   163G   104F

L= ....G ....L ....F [(.060/.062) .122] .115G .122R .132F = R

		ATBATS	1B	2B	3B	HR	HBP	BB	GDP	SB	CS	ROE	XB	RUNS	EOB%	RL#	SET-UP	DR-IN	RPA
Cubs	1990	48	8	4	0	0	0	0	1	2	0	0	5	3	.156	.075	.030	.041	.071
Pittsburgh	1991	187	34	11	2	4	2	17	2	9	2	0	19	28	.230	.128	.069	.063	.132
Pittsburgh	1992	162	23	6	3	4	0	9	2	5	3	2	16	18	.158	.101	.046	.060	.106

PITTSBURGH PIRATES

John Wehner, 25

Bats Right   116L 134R   90G   52F   658ML

L= .088G .095L .108F (.054/.044) .098 .092G .099R .112F = R

		ATBATS	1B	2B	3B	HR	HBP	BB	GDP	SB	CS	ROE	XB	RUNS	EOB	RL#	SET-UP	DR-IN	RPA
Pittsburgh	1991	106	29	7	0	0	0	7	0	3	0	1	8	16	.298	.141	.085	.060	.145
Pittsburgh	1992	123	16	6	0	0	0	10	4	3	0	3	9	9	.181	.065	.031	.036	.067

PITCHERS

Throws: Flyball type, extreme reverse righty

Stan Belinda, 26

(.086/.125) .107   378L 443R

		OUTS	RO	1B	2B	3B	HR	HBP	BB	GDP	SB	CS	PO	WP	BK	RUNS	EOB%	RL#	RPA
Pittsburgh	1990	175	175	33	9	2	4	1	26	5	5	0	0	1	0	26	.189	.099	.104
Pittsburgh	1991	235	235	33	5	2	10	4	31	2	13	3	0	2	0	31	.158	.097	.099
Pittsburgh	1992	214	214	35	13	2	8	0	24	1	12	2	0	1	0	34	.172	.106	.116

Throws: Neutral type, righty

Victor Cole, 24

(..../....) .135   59L 42R 667ML

		OUTS	RO	1B	2B	3B	HR	HBP	BB	GDP	SB	CS	PO	WP	BK	RUNS	EOB%	RL#	RPA
Pittsburgh	1992	69	18	16	6	0	1	0	14	1	2	1	0	1	0	13	.243	.117	.129

Throws: Neutral type, extreme righty

Danny Cox, 33

(.141/.079) .111   355L 323R 166ML

		OUTS	RO	1B	2B	3B	HR	HBP	BB	GDP	SB	CS	PO	WP	BK	RUNS	EOB%	RL#	RPA
Philadelphia	1991	307	37	65	16	3	14	1	37	6	11	7	0	7	1	48	.154	.107	.108
Philadelphia	1992	115	10	34	8	1	3	0	18	2	4	1	0	0	0	26	.234	.121	.139
Pittsburgh	1992	73	73	14	4	0	2	0	7	0	1	0	0	1	0	11	.190	.098	.107

Throws: Neutral type, moderate lefty

Jerry Don Gleaton, 35

(.097/.104) .102   221L 519R 104ML

		OUTS	RO	1B	2B	3B	HR	HBP	BB	GDP	SB	CS	PO	WP	BK	RUNS	EOB%	RL#	RPA
Detroit	1990	248	248	50	7	0	5	3	23	9	3	4	0	2	1	21	.119	.068	.066
Detroit	1991	226	226	52	11	4	7	0	31	7	8	8	2	1	1	29	.131	.095	.091
Pittsburgh	1992	95	95	24	6	0	4	0	16	3	3	3	0	1	0	18	.171	.116	.128

Throws: Neutral type, extreme righty

Doug Drabek, 30

(.107/.061) .089   1697L 1111R

		OUTS	RO	1B	2B	3B	HR	HBP	BB	GDP	SB	CS	PO	WP	BK	RUNS	EOB%	RL#	RPA
Pittsburgh	1990	694	0	134	37	4	15	3	54	11	18	9	3	6	0	79	.141	.081	.085
Pittsburgh	1991	704	0	183	41	5	16	3	56	15	29	15	3	5	0	95	.153	.095	.097
Pittsburgh	1992	770	0	162	35	4	17	6	46	19	18	14	3	11	1	82	.116	.074	.081

Throws: Groundball type, moderate reverse lefty

Danny Jackson, 30

(.115/.109) .110   298L 1336R

		OUTS	RO	1B	2B	3B	HR	HBP	BB	GDP	SB	CS	PO	WP	BK	RUNS	EOB%	RL#	RPA
Cincinnati	1990	352	6	91	13	4	11	2	36	11	15	3	0	3	1	53	.166	.105	.108
Chicago Cubs	1991	212	11	65	15	1	8	1	44	7	8	2	0	1	1	45	.241	.144	.132
Chicago Cubs	1992	339	0	87	21	4	5	3	45	11	15	9	0	1	2	51	.177	.094	.101
Pittsburgh	1992	265	0	73	18	2	1	1	26	6	6	4	0	1	0	39	.192	.092	.103

Throws: Groundball type, extreme righty

Dennis Lamp, 40

(.129/.089) .106   391L 527R

		OUTS	RO	1B	2B	3B	HR	HBP	BB	GDP	SB	CS	PO	WP	BK	RUNS	EOB%	RL#	RPA
Boston	1990	317	302	79	22	3	10	3	22	10	12	4	0	2	0	43	.151	.103	.097
Boston	1991	276	276	67	21	4	8	3	24	14	10	0	0	1	0	39	.155	.105	.101
Pittsburgh	1992	84	84	26	3	1	3	2	5	2	2	2	0	0	1	14	.158	.110	.120

PITTSBURGH PIRATES

Roger Mason, 34

Throws: Flyball type, moderate to severe reverse righty

(.106/.134) .120   233L   228R   521ML

		OUTS	RO	1B	2B	3B	HR	HBP	BB	GDP	SB	CS	PO	WP	BK	RUNS	EOB%	RL#	RPA
Pittsburgh	1991	89	89	15	3	1	2	1	5	1	0	2	0	2	0	8	.110	.068	.069
Pittsburgh	1992	264	264	52	14	3	11	4	25	3	4	5	1	3	0	42	.150	.104	.114

Denny Neagle, 24

Throws: Flyball type, moderate lefty

(.115/.129) .125   127L   325R   438ML

		OUTS	RO	1B	2B	3B	HR	HBP	BB	GDP	SB	CS	PO	WP	BK	RUNS	EOB%	RL#	RPA
Minnesota	1991	60	24	16	8	1	3	0	5	1	2	1	0	1	0	13	.190	.158	.147
Pittsburgh	1992	259	179	54	17	1	9	2	35	2	14	3	0	3	2	48	.202	.118	.129

Vince Palacios, 29

Throws: Flyball type, moderate to severe righty

(.124/.099) .113   309L   299R

		OUTS	RO	1B	2B	3B	HR	HBP	BB	GDP	SB	CS	PO	WP	BK	RUNS	EOB%	RL#	RPA
Pittsburgh	1990	45	45	4	0	0	0	0	2	0	0	0	0	2	0	1	.098	.024	.026
Pittsburgh	1991	245	126	46	10	1	12	1	36	2	3	4	0	6	2	40	.176	.114	.117
Pittsburgh	1992	159	52	44	10	1	1	0	26	6	2	4	0	7	0	25	.195	.097	.107

Bob Patterson, 33

Throws: Flyball type, moderate to severe lefty

(.079/.107) .098   280L   595R

		OUTS	RO	1B	2B	3B	HR	HBP	BB	GDP	SB	CS	PO	WP	BK	RUNS	EOB%	RL#	RPA
Pittsburgh	1990	284	205	63	15	1	9	3	14	8	5	4	0	1	2	34	.120	.085	.090
Pittsburgh	1991	197	187	47	12	1	7	0	14	5	1	5	0	0	0	25	.123	.091	.092
Pittsburgh	1992	194	194	38	12	2	7	0	17	5	1	3	0	3	0	27	.131	.093	.103

Jeff M. Robinson, 31

(.139/.107) .122   687L   734R

		OUTS	RO	1B	2B	3B	HR	HBP	BB	GDP	SB	CS	PO	WP	BK	RUNS	EOB%	RL#	RPA
Detroit	1990	435	0	80	34	4	23	6	79	13	10	9	1	16	1	80	.178	.128	.124
Baltimore	1991	313	20	84	22	1	12	6	49	12	10	5	0	8	0	60	.197	.127	.127
Texas	1992	137	71	34	10	0	6	0	20	5	1	1	0	6	1	25	.185	.123	.122
Pittsburgh	1992	109	5	25	5	1	2	1	15	1	6	4	0	0	0	16	.179	.095	.106

Zane Smith, 32

Throws: Groundball type, moderate lefty

(.070/.084) .082   367L   1851R

		OUTS	RO	1B	2B	3B	HR	HBP	BB	GDP	SB	CS	PO	WP	BK	RUNS	EOB%	RL#	RPA
Montreal	1990	418	3	108	19	3	11	3	38	21	26	2	0	1	0	58	.145	.094	.101
Pittsburgh	1990	228	3	41	6	4	4	0	8	13	1	2	0	1	0	14	.042	.048	.051
Pittsburgh	1991	684	0	179	36	4	15	2	26	27	26	8	0	1	0	76	.118	.081	.083
Pittsburgh	1992	423	6	103	23	4	8	2	16	19	9	4	1	0	0	45	.105	.074	.080

Randy Tomlin, 26

Throws: Groundball type, moderate to severe lefty

(.079/.100) .096   349L   1465R

		OUTS	RO	1B	2B	3B	HR	HBP	BB	GDP	SB	CS	PO	WP	BK	RUNS	EOB%	RL#	RPA
Pittsburgh	1990	233	0	39	17	1	5	1	11	5	2	6	0	1	3	21	.095	.067	.072
Pittsburgh	1991	525	18	127	28	6	9	6	50	15	17	12	1	2	3	66	.153	.089	.090
Pittsburgh	1992	626	6	163	45	7	11	5	38	27	21	8	0	7	2	86	.141	.090	.099

Tim Wakefield, 26

Throws: Neutral type, moderate to severe reverse righty

(.098/.132) .111   224L   135R   1300ML

		OUTS	RO	1B	2B	3B	HR	HBP	BB	GDP	SB	CS	PO	WP	BK	RUNS	EOB%	RL#	RPA
Pittsburgh	1992	276	0	59	12	2	3	1	34	3	4	9	3	3	1	31	.149	.074	.082

Bob Walk, 36

Throws: Groundball type, moderate to severe righty

(.120/.085) .105   890L   652R

		OUTS	RO	1B	2B	3B	HR	HBP	BB	GDP	SB	CS	PO	WP	BK	RUNS	EOB%	RL#	RPA
Pittsburgh	1990	389	7	96	22	1	17	4	34	6	13	9	1	5	3	64	.154	.110	.117
Pittsburgh	1991	345	23	72	21	1	10	5	33	7	7	4	1	11	2	48	.163	.098	.100
Pittsburgh	1992	405	77	93	26	3	10	6	38	13	19	5	1	7	2	61	.159	.098	.109

Pittsburgh Pirates AAA & AA Minor League Ratings

AAA (BUFFALO)	AGE	BATS	POSITION	CPA	RUNS	SET-UP	DRIVE-IN	RPA
Pete Beeler	25	R	C	215	14.7	.029	.039	.068
Dave Clark	30	L	OF	293	41.9	.076	.067	.143
Brian Dorsett	31	R	C\1B	548	64.2	.057	.060	.117
Greg Edge	28	B	SS\2B	411	14.0	.019	.027	.046
Carlos Garcia	25	R	SS	461	54.3	.057	.061	.118
Al Martin	25	L	OF	462	68.9	.076	.073	.149
William Pennyfeather	24	R	OF	382	32.7	.039	.047	.086
Tom Prince	28	R	C	277	30.5	.054	.056	.110
Joe Redfield	31	R	1B\2B\3B	252	22.1	.045	.043	.088
Jeff Richardson	27	R	2B\SS	360	30.2	.040	.044	.084
Jose Tolentino	31	L	1B	245	28.9	.059	.059	.118
Greg Tubbs	30	R	OF	496	52.6	.056	.050	.106
John Wehner	25	R	2B\1B\3B	260	27.5	.052	.054	.106
Kevin Young	23	R	3B	579	70.1	.068	.053	.121
Eddie Zambrano	26	R	OF	456	58.7	.068	.061	.129

AA (CAROLINA)	AGE	BATS	POSITION	CPA	RUNS	SET-UP	DRIVE-IN	RPA
Tony Beasley	26	R	2B\SS	166	12.2	.033	.041	.074
Scott Bullett	25	R	OF	573	47.7	.038	.045	.083
Alberto DeLosSantos	23	R	OF	405	26.7	.030	.036	.066
Mark Johnson	25	L	1B\OF	449	37.0	.041	.041	.082
Austin Manahan	22	R	2B	378	28.4	.035	.040	.075
Keith Osik	24	R	3B\C	504	42.2	.044	.040	.084
Daryl Ratliff	23	R	OF	461	31.0	.033	.034	.067
Mandy Romero	25	B	C	309	19.2	.028	.034	.062
Bruce Schreiber	25	R	SS\2B\3B	292	17.6	.027	.033	.060
Ben Shelton	23	L	1B	455	44.2	.052	.045	.097

AAA Pitchers	Age	Throws	Outs	RPA	AA Pitchers	Age	Throws	Outs	RPA
Darrel Akerfelds	31	R	198	.173	Dave Bird	24	L	398	.143
Joe Ausanio	27	R	251	.109	Steve Buckholz	26	R	139	.218
Brett Backlund	?	R	132	.082	Stan Fansler	27	R	421	.145
John Cerutti	32	L	451	.143	Lee Hancock	25	L	148	.102
Victor Cole	24	R	347	.130	Bobby Hunter	24	R	191	.112
Steve Cooke	22	L	331	.113	Richard Robertson	24	L	374	.118
Danny Cox	33	R	127	.085	Brian Shouse	24	L	232	.110
Mike Dalton	29	L	214	.095	Dennis Tafoya	28	R	257	.109
Eddie Dixon	28	R	210	.144	Dave Tellers	24	R	76	.111
Drew Hall	29	L	114	.122	Ben Webb	25	R	143	.135
Paul Miller	27	R	97	.157	Rick White	24	R	173	.128
Blas Minor	26	R	289	.097	Mike Zimmerman	23	R	459	.148
Mark Petkovsek	27	R	451	.122					
Jim Tracy	27	R	348	.130					
Paul Wagner	25	R	483	.123					
Tim Wakefield	26	R	406	.122					
Mike York	28	R	362	.141					

ST. LOUIS CARDINALS

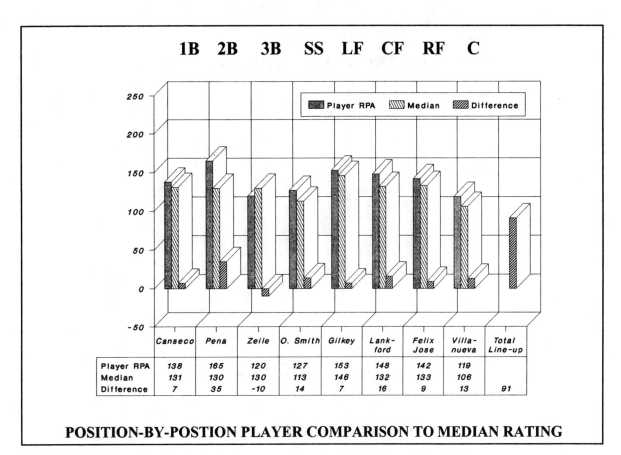

	1B	2B	3B	SS	LF	CF	RF	C
	Canseco	Pena	Zeile	O. Smith	Gilkey	Lank-ford	Felix Jose	Villa-nueva	Total Line-up
Player RPA	138	165	120	127	153	148	142	119	
Median	131	130	130	113	146	132	133	106	
Difference	7	35	-10	14	7	16	9	13	91

POSITION-BY-POSTION PLAYER COMPARISON TO MEDIAN RATING

DEFENSIVE TEAM AND STADIUM DATA FOR THE LAST 3 YEARS:

TEAM DEFENSE BY POSITION:

POSITION-BY-POSITION STADIUM CHARACTERISTICS:

		1990	1991	1992	
1B:	Home	-0.6	+0.7	-1.0	Average
	Away	-0.2	-4.0	-3.1	
2B:	Home	+2.7	+4.5	+4.7	Very easy to play
	Away	-1.5	+2.0	+5.3	
3B:	Home	-1.7	-8.5	+2.0	Slightly easy to play
	Away	+0.4	-2.4	-2.5	
SS:	Home	+4.9	+2.8	+5.8	Slightly hard to play
	Away	+4.0	+4.4	+5.5	
LF:	Home	-5.1	+8.9	+1.9	Average
	Away	-0.2	+6.4	+7.7	
CF:	Home	-4.2	+0.7	+5.6	Slightly hard to play
	Away	+0.5	+7.0	-3.6	
RF:	Home	+4.3	+3.0	+5.7	Very hard to play
	Away	+5.9	0.0	-0.5	
Total Home:		+0.3	+12.1	+24.8	
Total Away:		+8.9	+13.4	+8.9	

Comments: The best defensive team in the National League in '91 got even better in '92 to become the best defensive team in either league. The second base/shortstop combination gave St. Louis a whopping 21.3 run advantage over their opponents this past season. Todd Zeile improved somewhat on defense from his poor defensive play of the previous year.

ST. LOUIS CARDINALS

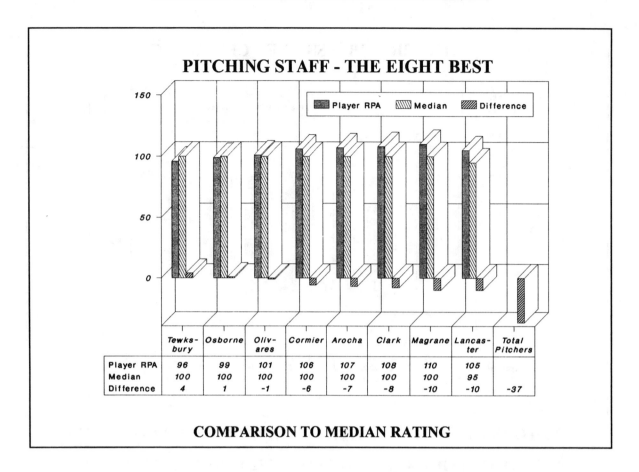

PITCHING STAFF - THE EIGHT BEST

	Tewks-bury	Osborne	Oliv-ares	Cormier	Arocha	Clark	Magrane	Lancas-ter	Total Pitchers
Player RPA	96	99	101	106	107	108	110	105	
Median	100	100	100	100	100	100	100	95	
Difference	4	1	-1	-6	-7	-8	-10	-10	-37

COMPARISON TO MEDIAN RATING

SUGGESTED LINE-UPS (with set-up RPA & drive-in RPA ratings):

Vs: Left-handed Groundball

SS:	O. Smith	60-48
3B:	T. Zeile	76-66
2B:	G. Pena	81-76
RF:	F. Jose	66-64
C:	H. Villanueva	68-66
1B:	O. Canseco	74-74
CF:	R. Lankford	64-67
LF:	B. Gilkey	55-52
Pitcher		

Vs: Neutral Lefty Pitchers

SS:	O. Smith	62-49
3B:	T. Zeile	78-68
2B:	G. Pena	99-92
RF:	F. Jose	76-72
1B:	O. Canseco	74-74
LF:	B. Gilkey	63-60
C:	H. Villanueva	63-60
CF:	R. Lankford	55-59
Pitcher		

Vs: Left-handed Flyball

SS:	O. Smith	64-51
3B:	T. Zeile	82-71
2B:	G. Pena	122-112
LF:	B. Gilkey	79-75
RF:	F. Jose	90-87
1B:	O. Canseco	74-74
CF:	B. Jordan	44-70
C:	T. Pagnozzi	46--55
Pitcher		

Vs: Right-handed Groundball

2B:	J. Oquendo	73-58
3B:	T. Zeile	62-54
C:	H. Villanueva	67-65
1B:	O. Canseco	64-64
CF:	R. Lankford	85-90
LF:	B. Gilkey	56-52
RF:	F. Jose	55-52
SS:	O. Smith	60-48
Pitcher		

Vs: Neutral Righty Pitchers

SS:	O. Smith	62-49
3B:	T. Zeile	64-56
LF:	B. Gilkey	64-60
2B:	G. Pena	67-63
1B:	O. Canseco	64-64
CF:	R. Lankford	77-81
RF:	F. Jose	64-61
C:	H. Villanueva	61-60
Pitcher		

Vs: Right-handed Flyball

SS:	O. Smith	64-51
3B:	T. Zeile	68-59
LF:	B. Gilkey	80-75
2B:	G. Pena	89-84
RF:	F. Jose	79-75
1B:	O. Canseco	64-64
CF:	R. Lankford	64-68
C:	T. Pagnozzi	40-50
Pitcher		

Comments: Hector Villanueva (if he can keep his weight down) and Ozzie Canseco make this a halfway decent offense. Without them, this offense is in big trouble. These two make the Cardinal attack against lefties quite strong. I would have loved to find a way to get Luis Alicea into these line-ups, since he's a quality player, but due to the outstanding ability of Geronimo Pena his career is completely blocked.

ST. LOUIS CARDINALS

Each year I write about how good the St. Louis defense is. 1993 will be no exception. The problem for the Cards is that their pitching , in particular the bullpen, will be be extremely weak. Only the expansion Colorado Rockies will have a weaker staff in the NL. The loss of middle reliever Cris Carpenter in the Expansion draft has really hurt this team which had such a thin staff to begin with.

The signing of Rob Murphy doesn't figure to help. The signing of Les Lancaster could help. He had a terrible year in '92, but had been a very good reliever in previous years.

Lee Smith is no longer the pitcher he's been in previous years. He doesn't figure to be much of a factor in 1993. He's 35 years old and past his prime. The result will be that, in effect, the Cardinals probably will not have a single reliable reliever in '93. The entire burden of the pitching staff will fall upon the starters who will need to take the game into the late innings for the Cards   to have a chance to win. Unfortunately for the Cards, the starting staff is mediocre at best.

I like Ozzie Canseco a lot. I think he's going to be a very good hitter and should be moved to first base so as to play there instead of Rod Brewer. I don't think Rod Brewer is more than a mediocre Major League hitter. I would have protected Luis Alicea in the Expansion Draft instead of Brewer. Alicea is a very good player and would be a fine starting player on most other teams. Unfortunately for Alicea, he finds himself behind Geronimo Pena, one of the top young players in the Major Leagues.

Tom Pagnozzi is an overrated catcher. He's very good defensively, but I've got to sing that same song once again: you've got to judge the whole player! Pagnozzi can't hit. That's very important. Baseball players that can't hit usually hurt your team. The signing of Hector Villanueva could really improve the Cardinal catching situation. He can hit and his defense isn't all that bad, provided he can keep his weight within reasonable bounds.

The loss of a quality outfielder like Milt Thompson would really hurt most teams, but the Cardinals' outfield of Gilkey, Lankford and Jose is one of the best in baseball. They won't be hurt all that much by Thompson's loss.

AAA pitcher Rene Arocha is a good pitcher, but not as outstanding as he's made out to be.

Probably the best young pitcher the Cards have in the high minors is AA pitcher Allen Watson. He could be a very good one. He probably needs a little time at AAA, however. There are at least two other good pitching prospects from the AA Arkansas team. They are Steve Dixon and Gab Ozuna. The latter two were both exposed to the Expansion draft. That may have been unavoidable in the first round of the draft, but I'd have pulled these two back rather than Joe Magrane and Mike Milchin.

St. Louis' Projected record for 1993: 81--81, good for 4th place in the division.

ST. LOUIS CARDINALS

Luis Alicea, 27

Bats Both   112L 264R 158G 71F   222ML

L= .074G .123L .232F [(.057/.056) .113] .060G .109R .218F = R

		ATBATS	1B	2B	3B	HR	HBP	BB	GDP	SB	CS	ROE	XB	RUNS	EOB%	RL#	SET-UP	DR-IN	RPA
St. Louis	1991	68	10	3	0	0	0	8	0	0	1	0	4	4	.213	.069	.038	.036	.074
St. Louis	1992	265	43	9	11	2	4	26	5	2	5	2	12	34	.213	.102	.055	.053	.108

Rod Brewer, 26

Bats Left   34L 118R 53G 24F   918ML

L= ....G .078L ....F [(.053/.046) .099] .077G .105R ....F = R

		ATBATS	1B	2B	3B	HR	HBP	BB	GDP	SB	CS	ROE	XB	RUNS	EOB%	RL#	SET-UP	DR-IN	RPA
St. Louis	1990	25	5	1	0	0	0	0	1	0	0	2	2	2	.202	.079	.039	.040	.079
St. Louis	1991	13	1	0	0	0	0	0	0	0	0	0	0	0	.055	.013	.003	.011	.014
St. Louis	1992	103	25	6	0	0	1	8	1	0	1	0	5	13	.256	.107	.062	.051	.113

Andres Galarraga, 31

Bats Right   504L 878R 502G 299F

L= .086G .095L .111F [(.042/.055) .097] .089G .098R .114F = R

		ATBATS	1B	2B	3B	HR	HBP	BB	GDP	SB	CS	ROE	XB	RUNS	EOB%	RL#	SET-UP	DR-IN	RPA
Montreal	1990	579	99	29	0	20	4	32	14	10	2	7	63	75	.180	.114	.054	.063	.117
Montreal	1991	375	58	13	2	9	2	18	6	5	6	7	22	38	.160	.086	.040	.052	.092
St. Louis	1992	325	53	14	2	10	8	11	8	5	4	2	26	38	.156	.098	.044	.059	.103

Rich Gedman, 33

Bats Left   33L 319R 95G 90F

L= ....G ....L ....F [(.030/.040) .070] .077G .077R .078F = R

		ATBATS	1B	2B	3B	HR	HBP	BB	GDP	SB	CS	ROE	XB	RUNS	EOB%	RL#	SET-UP	DR-IN	RPA
Boston	1990	15	3	0	0	0	1	5	1	0	0	1	1	3	.370	.120	.075	.041	.116
Houston	1990	104	13	7	0	1	0	9	2	0	0	1	3	10	.190	.075	.039	.044	.083
St. Louis	1991	94	6	1	0	3	0	4	2	0	1	1	2	3	.058	.040	.010	.035	.045
St. Louis	1992	105	18	4	0	1	0	10	0	0	0	0	0	11	.220	.086	.047	.045	.092

Bernard Gilkey, 26

Bats Right   402L 774R 389G 248F

L= .100G .116L .147F [(.060/.057) .117] .101G .117R .148F = R

		ATBATS	1B	2B	3B	HR	HBP	BB	GDP	SB	CS	ROE	XB	RUNS	EOB%	RL#	SET-UP	DR-IN	RPA
St. Louis	1990	64	11	5	2	1	0	8	1	6	2	0	7	10	.242	.143	.076	.066	.142
St. Louis	1991	268	44	7	2	5	1	39	14	14	10	3	19	15	.174	.078	.040	.047	.087
St. Louis	1992	384	86	19	4	7	1	38	5	18	13	5	40	63	.240	.132	.074	.065	.139

Pedro Guerrero, 36

Bats Right   363L 191R 193G 114F

L= .077G .094L .120F [(.050/.051) .101] .088G .105R .131F = R

		ATBATS	1B	2B	3B	HR	HBP	BB	GDP	SB	CS	ROE	XB	RUNS	EOB%	RL#	SET-UP	DR-IN	RPA
St. Louis	1990	498	95	31	1	13	1	30	14	1	1	5	28	62	.198	.113	.055	.057	.112
St. Louis	1991	427	95	12	1	8	1	35	12	4	2	7	16	30	.219	.101	.058	.054	.112
St. Louis	1992	146	24	6	1	1	0	8	4	2	2	0	4	11	.149	.066	.029	.040	.069

Rex Hudler, 32

Bats Right   66L 256R 115G 59F   344ML

L= .080G .089L .104F [(.035/.048) .083] .062G .071R .086F = R

		ATBATS	1B	2B	3B	HR	HBP	BB	GDP	SB	CS	ROE	XB	RUNS	EOB%	RL#	SET-UP	DR-IN	RPA
Montreal	1990	3	1	0	0	0	0	0	0	0	0	0	0	0	.237	.101	.056	.049	.105
St. Louis	1990	217	41	11	2	7	2	11	3	18	10	5	21	29	.183	.125	.058	.066	.124
St. Louis	1991	207	34	10	2	1	0	9	1	12	8	3	11	10	.166	.073	.036	.045	.081
St. Louis	1992	98	17	4	0	3	1	2	0	2	7	1	10	9	.109	.082	.030	.056	.086

Tim Jones, 30

Bats Left   ...

L= .055G .059L .066F [(.037/.043) .080] .082G .086R .093F = R

		ATBATS	1B	2B	3B	HR	HBP	BB	GDP	SB	CS	ROE	XB	RUNS	EOB%	RL#	SET-UP	DR-IN	RPA
St. Louis	1990	128	19	7	1	1	1	11	1	3	5	1	10	12	.183	.082	.038	.043	.081
St. Louis	1991	24	2	2	0	0	0	1	0	0	2	0	1	1	.072	.032	.009	.026	.035
St. Louis	1992	145	25	4	0	0	0	10	1	5	2	1	6	11	.186	.067	.032	.037	.069

ST. LOUIS CARDINALS

Brian Jordan, 25

Bats Right — 74L — 135R — 86G — 39F — 410ML

L= .098G .115L ....F — (.035/.060) .095 — .067G .084R ....F = R

		ATBATS	1B	2B	3B	HR	HBP	BB	GDP	SB	CS	ROE	XB	RUNS	EOB%	RL#	SET-UP	DR-IN	RPA
St. Louis	1992	193	22	9	4	5	1	9	6	7	2	0	8	18	.119	.079	.030	.053	.083

Bats Both — 590L — 1049R — 543G — 338F

Felix Jose, 27

L= .125G .143L .172F — (.065/.063) .128 — .102G .120R .149F = R

		ATBATS	1B	2B	3B	HR	HBP	BB	GDP	SB	CS	ROE	XB	RUNS	EOB%	RL#	SET-UP	DR-IN	RPA
Oakland	1990	341	70	12	0	8	5	16	8	8	3	5	32	43	.194	.106	.055	.060	.115
St. Louis	1990	85	15	4	1	3	0	8	1	4	5	1	7	11	.176	.117	.054	.063	.117
St. Louis	1991	568	119	40	6	8	2	42	12	20	14	7	39	46	.225	.116	.066	.062	.128
St. Louis	1992	509	111	22	3	14	1	32	9	28	15	5	35	74	.198	.121	.062	.066	.128

Bats Left — 538L — 888R — 478G — 321F

Ray Lankford, 25

L= .122G .105L .079F — (.065/.067) .132 — .166G .149R .123F = R

		ATBATS	1B	2B	3B	HR	HBP	BB	GDP	SB	CS	ROE	XB	RUNS	EOB%	RL#	SET-UP	DR-IN	RPA
St. Louis	1990	126	22	10	1	3	0	13	1	8	2	0	11	20	.237	.139	.074	.064	.138
St. Louis	1991	566	95	23	15	9	1	40	4	44	22	6	48	39	.186	.103	.053	.060	.113
St. Louis	1992	598	109	40	6	20	5	66	6	42	28	5	56	106	.222	.141	.077	.073	.150

Bats Both — 377L — 630R — 321G — 230F

Jose Oquendo, 28

L= .122G .109L .091F — (.063/.049) .112 — .127G .114R .096F = R

		ATBATS	1B	2B	3B	HR	HBP	BB	GDP	SB	CS	ROE	XB	RUNS	EOB%	RL#	SET-UP	DR-IN	RPA
St. Louis	1990	469	95	17	5	1	0	66	7	1	2	2	33	56	.259	.103	.057	.045	.102
St. Louis	1991	366	72	11	4	1	1	54	5	1	2	7	23	27	.271	.101	.063	.048	.111
St. Louis	1992	35	5	3	1	0	0	4	0	0	0	0	3	5	.259	.120	.069	.055	.124

Bats Right — 494L — 763R — 480G — 249F

Tom Pagnozzi, 30

L= .094G .096L .101F — (.040/.049) .089 — .083G .085R .090F = R

		ATBATS	1B	2B	3B	HR	HBP	BB	GDP	SB	CS	ROE	XB	RUNS	EOB%	RL#	SET-UP	DR-IN	RPA
St. Louis	1990	220	44	15	0	2	1	13	0	1	1	2	17	27	.241	.114	.061	.052	.113
St. Louis	1991	459	90	24	5	2	4	30	10	9	13	3	24	27	.194	.084	.044	.048	.092
St. Louis	1992	485	85	26	3	7	1	19	15	2	5	5	21	47	.160	.083	.038	.049	.087

Bats Both — 199L — 291R — 147G — 119F — 115ML

Geronimo Pena, 25

L= .146G .180L .223F — (.075/.069) .144 — .0850G .119R .162F = R

		ATBATS	1B	2B	3B	HR	HBP	BB	GDP	SB	CS	ROE	XB	RUNS	EOB%	RL#	SET-UP	DR-IN	RPA
St. Louis	1990	45	9	2	0	0	1	4	0	1	1	0	3	5	.237	.091	.048	.043	.091
St. Louis	1991	185	29	8	3	5	5	17	0	15	6	1	24	16	.217	.122	.069	.065	.134
St. Louis	1992	203	42	12	1	7	5	24	1	13	9	1	22	40	.251	.155	.090	.074	.164

Bats Left — 290L — 651R — 280G — 217F

Gerald Perry, 32

L= .054G .078L .109F — (.048/.054) .102 — .089G .113R .144F = R

		ATBATS	1B	2B	3B	HR	HBP	BB	GDP	SB	CS	ROE	XB	RUNS	EOB%	RL#	SET-UP	DR-IN	RPA
Kansas City	1990	465	86	22	2	8	3	35	14	17	6	5	35	53	.193	.100	.049	.054	.103
St. Louis	1991	242	40	8	4	6	0	21	2	15	8	4	19	17	.192	.105	.056	.061	.117
St. Louis	1992	143	25	8	0	1	1	11	3	3	6	0	11	13	.166	.074	.035	.043	.078

Bats Both — 738L — 1065R — 587G — 388F

Ozzie Smith, 38

L= .129G .132L .136F — (.069/.056) .125 — .129G .132R .136F = R

		ATBATS	1B	2B	3B	HR	HBP	BB	GDP	SB	CS	ROE	XB	RUNS	EOB%	RL#	SET-UP	DR-IN	RPA
St. Louis	1990	512	107	21	1	1	2	57	8	32	6	8	63	62	.254	.107	.058	.048	.106
St. Louis	1991	550	121	30	3	3	1	81	8	35	14	4	68	46	.274	.121	.075	.058	.133
St. Louis	1992	518	131	20	2	0	0	55	11	43	12	3	50	72	.252	.110	.064	.053	.117

ST. LOUIS CARDINALS

Milt Thompson, 33

Bats Left   231L 811R   326G   240F

L= .091G .090L .089F   (.074/.067) .141   .157G .156R .155F = R

		ATBATS	1B	2B	3B	HR	HBP	BB	GDP	SB	CS	ROE	XB	RUNS	EOB%	RL#	SET-UP	DR-IN	RPA
St. Louis	1990	418	64	14	7	6	5	34	4	25	6	4	32	46	.201	.099	.048	.050	.098
St. Louis	1991	326	73	16	5	6	0	25	4	16	11	5	39	29	.227	.127	.072	.067	.139
St. Louis	1992	208	47	9	1	4	2	13	3	18	6	9	20	34	.248	.137	.079	.066	.145

Craig Wilson, 28

Bats Right   196L 146R   120G   78F   88ML

L= .069G .084L .106F   (.041/.042) .083   .067G .082R .104F = R

		ATBATS	1B	2B	3B	HR	HBP	BB	GDP	SB	CS	ROE	XB	RUNS	EOB%	RL#	SET-UP	DR-IN	RPA
St. Louis	1990	121	28	2	0	0	0	8	7	0	2	0	11	8	.149	.057	.024	.033	.057
St. Louis	1991	82	12	2	0	0	0	4	2	0	0	3	6	2	.169	.051	.026	.032	.058
St. Louis	1992	106	27	6	0	0	0	8	4	1	2	1	5	13	.224	.095	.052	.049	.101

Tracy Woodson, 30

Bats Right   44L 75R   40G   11F   939ML

L= .182G .151L ....F   (.050/.040) .090   .086G .055R ....F = R

		ATBATS	1B	2B	3B	HR	HBP	BB	GDP	SB	CS	ROE	XB	RUNS	EOB%	RL#	SET-UP	DR-IN	RPA
St. Louis	1992	114	26	8	0	1	1	3	1	0	0	2	4	15	.242	.119	.067	.057	.124

Todd Zeile, 27

Bats Right   541L 1109R   596G   356F   87ML

L= .137G .141L .148F   (.066/.058) .124   .111G .115R .122F = R

		ATBATS	1B	2B	3B	HR	HBP	BB	GDP	SB	CS	ROE	XB	RUNS	EOB%	RL#	SET-UP	DR-IN	RPA
St. Louis	1990	495	78	25	3	15	2	64	11	2	4	2	37	68	.217	.118	.060	.057	.117
St. Louis	1991	565	108	36	3	11	5	59	15	17	12	12	41	48	.235	.117	.068	.061	.129
St. Louis	1992	439	84	18	4	7	0	64	11	7	10	4	36	63	.234	.110	.062	.055	.117

PITCHERS

Cris Carpenter, 27

Throws: Flyball type, neutral reverse righty

(.090/.091) .090   310L   300R

		OUTS	RO	1B	2B	3B	HR	HBP	BB	GDP	SB	CS	PO	WP	BK	RUNS	EOB%	RL#	RPA
St. Louis	1990	24	24	3	0	0	2	0	1	0	1	0	0	0	0	3	.078	.093	.094
St. Louis	1991	198	198	30	17	0	6	0	11	2	3	4	0	1	0	23	.116	.075	.085
St. Louis	1992	264	264	44	13	2	10	4	19	7	11	3	0	5	0	35	.119	.083	.095

Mark Clark, 24

Throws: Neutral type, moderate to severe righty

(.124/.091) .111   335L   222R   837ML

		OUTS	RO	1B	2B	3B	HR	HBP	BB	GDP	SB	CS	PO	WP	BK	RUNS	EOB%	RL#	RPA
St. Louis	1991	67	32	12	2	0	3	0	11	0	5	1	0	2	0	13	.194	.106	.125
St. Louis	1992	340	0	83	18	4	12	0	34	8	17	2	2	4	0	60	.167	.106	.120

Rheal Cormier, 25

Throws: Groundball type, moderate lefty

(.092/.111) .108   184L   823R   563ML

		OUTS	RO	1B	2B	3B	HR	HBP	BB	GDP	SB	CS	PO	WP	BK	RUNS	EOB%	RL#	RPA
St. Louis	1991	203	3	52	16	1	5	2	7	6	1	3	0	2	1	29	.135	.085	.098
St. Louis	1992	558	3	142	34	3	15	5	31	19	11	4	0	4	2	82	.144	.089	.102

Frank DiPino, 36

Throws: Groundball type, moderate to severe lefty

(.102/.131) .119   154L   218R   102ML

		OUTS	RO	1B	2B	3B	HR	HBP	BB	GDP	SB	CS	PO	WP	BK	RUNS	EOB%	RL#	RPA
St. Louis	1990	243	243	63	18	3	8	1	19	5	4	2	0	2	1	40	.177	.113	.113
St. Louis	1992	33	33	7	2	0	0	0	3	0	0	0	0	0	0	4	.207	.072	.083

ST. LOUIS CARDINALS

Joe Magrane, 28

Throws: Groundball type, neutral reverse lefty

(.113/.108) .109

184L   771R   248ML

		OUTS	RO	1B	2B	3B	HR	HBP	BB	GDP	SB	CS	PO	WP	BK	RUNS	EOB%	RL#	RPA
St. Louis	1990	610	0	149	36	9	10	8	52	15	21	16	0	11	1	78	.156	.091	.091
St. Louis	1992	94	0	27	3	2	2	2	15	2	2	1	0	4	0	20	.232	.121	.135

Bob McClure, 39

Throws: Flyball type, extreme lefty

(.074/.150) .114

177L   201R

		OUTS	RO	1B	2B	3B	HR	HBP	BB	GDP	SB	CS	PO	WP	BK	RUNS	EOB%	RL#	RPA
California	1990	21	21	7	0	0	0	0	3	1	2	0	0	0	1	3	.209	.091	.086
California	1991	29	29	10	0	0	3	1	5	0	0	0	0	2	1	10	.251	.203	.206
St. Louis	1991	69	69	19	3	1	1	1	6	2	0	2	0	0	0	10	.152	.081	.094
St. Louis	1992	162	162	33	13	0	6	2	20	8	1	2	1	1	0	25	.133	.089	.103

Omar Olivares, 25

Throws: Groundball type, moderate to severe righty

(.117/.085) .103

941L   698R   158ML

		OUTS	RO	1B	2B	3B	HR	HBP	BB	GDP	SB	CS	PO	WP	BK	RUNS	EOB%	RL#	RPA
St. Louis	1990	148	30	35	7	1	2	2	17	5	2	3	0	1	1	17	.160	.083	.083
St. Louis	1991	502	25	109	22	4	13	5	60	12	10	11	1	3	1	72	.155	.085	.098
St. Louis	1992	591	9	131	35	3	20	4	58	16	11	13	2	2	0	88	.137	.088	.102

Donovan Osborne, 23

Throws: Neutral type, extreme reverse lefty

(.138/.093) .103

155L   568R   696ML

		OUTS	RO	1B	2B	3B	HR	HBP	BB	GDP	SB	CS	PO	WP	BK	RUNS	EOB%	RL#	RPA
St. Louis	1992	537	30	135	39	5	14	2	36	18	15	3	0	6	0	85	.156	.096	.109

Mike Perez, 28

Throws: Neutral type, extreme righty

(.129/.089) .108

220L   255R   225ML

		OUTS	RO	1B	2B	3B	HR	HBP	BB	GDP	SB	CS	PO	WP	BK	RUNS	EOB%	RL#	RPA
St. Louis	1990	41	41	9	3	0	0	0	3	0	2	0	0	0	0	5	.208	.082	.082
St. Louis	1991	51	51	11	6	1	1	1	5	1	2	1	0	0	1	10	.193	.110	.125
St. Louis	1992	279	279	58	6	2	4	1	23	6	5	2	1	4	0	29	.141	.066	.076

Bryn Smith, 37

Throws: Groundball type, moderate to severe righty

(.113/.091) .104

851L   601R   39ML

		OUTS	RO	1B	2B	3B	HR	HBP	BB	GDP	SB	CS	PO	WP	BK	RUNS	EOB%	RL#	RPA
St. Louis	1990	424	1	122	23	4	11	4	29	13	21	4	0	2	0	63	.168	.104	.104
St. Louis	1991	596	0	128	39	5	16	7	42	11	19	8	0	3	1	88	.155	.089	.102
St. Louis	1992	64	56	15	2	0	3	3	4	2	4	0	0	1	0	11	.159	.102	.119

Lee Smith, 35

Throws: Flyball type, moderate to severe Righty

(.108/.080) .097

542L   373R

		OUTS	RO	1B	2B	3B	HR	HBP	BB	GDP	SB	CS	PO	WP	BK	RUNS	EOB%	RL#	RPA
Boston	1990	43	43	10	3	0	0	0	7	0	4	2	0	1	0	5	.207	.092	.086
St. Louis	1990	206	206	41	13	1	3	0	15	2	10	3	0	1	0	23	.158	.081	.081
St. Louis	1991	219	219	54	8	3	5	0	8	3	10	2	0	1	0	30	.144	.083	.096
St. Louis	1992	225	225	46	8	4	4	0	22	4	12	1	0	2	0	32	.170	.084	.098

Bob Tewksbury, 32

Throws: Groundball type, neutral reverse righty

(.088/.093) .090

1272L   928R

		OUTS	RO	1B	2B	3B	HR	HBP	BB	GDP	SB	CS	PO	WP	BK	RUNS	EOB%	RL#	RPA
St. Louis	1990	436	43	105	36	3	7	3	12	9	8	5	0	2	0	51	.145	.087	.086
St. Louis	1991	573	0	143	42	8	13	5	36	19	10	10	0	0	0	83	.142	.089	.100
St. Louis	1992	699	6	159	39	4	15	3	20	25	7	4	0	2	0	77	.111	.070	.081

Todd Worrell, 33

Throws: Flyball type, moderate to severe reverse righty

(.077/.109) .092

130L   115R

		OUTS	RO	1B	2B	3B	HR	HBP	BB	GDP	SB	CS	PO	WP	BK	RUNS	EOB%	RL#	RPA
St. Louis	1992	192	192	34	7	0	4	1	20	3	13	0	0	1	1	25	.171	.079	.092

St. Louis Cards AAA & AA Minor League Ratings

AAA (LOUISVILLE)	AGE	BATS	POSITION	CPA	RUNS	SET-UP	DRIVE-IN	RPA
Rod Brewer	26	L	OF\1B	485	57.1	.061	.057	.118
Ozzie Canseco	28	R	OF	356	49.1	.069	.069	.138
Greg Carmona	24	B	SS	157	7.5	.022	.026	.048
Chuck Carr	24	B	OF	536	55.3	.054	.049	.103
Bien Figueroa	28	R	SS\2B	362	30.4	.045	.039	.084
Curt Ford	32	L	OF	295	32.3	.058	.052	.110
Ed Fulton	26	L	C	289	23.2	.034	.046	.080
Brian Jordan	25	R	OF	168	18.1	.055	.053	.108
Lonnie Maclin	25	L	OF	318	32.5	.057	.045	.102
Geronimo Pena	25	B	2B	115	13.1	.057	.057	.114
Stan Royer	25	R	1B	497	44.5	.042	.048	.090
Jeff Shireman	26	B	2B\SS	212	10.7	.024	.027	.051
Alex Trevino	35	R	C	236	17.5	.036	.038	.074
Tracy Woodson	30	R	3B	450	42.9	.044	.051	.095

AA (ARKANSAS)	AGE	BATS	POSITION	CPA	RUNS	SET-UP	DRIVE-IN	RPA
Joe Aversa	24	B	2B\3B	128	11.4	.051	.038	.089
Brad Beanblossom	25	R	2B	452	26.0	.027	.031	.058
Cliff Brannon	25	R	OF	373	25.5	.030	.038	.068
Rick Christian	25	R	OF	167	7.8	.019	.028	.047
Tripp Cromer	25	R	SS	400	31.6	.035	.044	.079
Steve Fanning	25	R	SS\3B	190	12.5	.029	.037	.066
Jose Fernandez	25	L	C	179	10.4	.027	.031	.058
Julian Martinez	25	R	OF\3B	328	17.2	.022	.030	.052
Jesus Mendez	28	L	1B\OF	330	29.3	.041	.048	.089
Don Prybylinski	24	R	C	220	13.7	.030	.032	.062
Mike Ross	27	R	3B	448	38.9	.042	.045	.087
Odalis Savinon	22	R	OF	118	4.3	.015	.022	.037
John Sellick	27	R	1B	335	31.6	.045	.049	.094
John Thomas	24	L	OF	446	35.9	.034	.046	.080

AAA Pitchers	Age	Throws	Outs	RPA	AA Pitchers	Age	Throws	Outs	RPA
Rene Arocha	26	R	500	.107	Paul Anderson	24	R	369	.125
Jeff Ballard	29	L	482	.118	David Cassidy	26	L	89	.167
Mark Clark	24	R	183	.105	Fidel Compres	27	R	173	.135
Mike Cook	29	R	176	.132	Steve Dixon	23	L	206	.101
Mark Grater	28	R	228	.099	John Ericks	25	R	225	.128
Mike Hinkle	27	R	190	.156	Steffen Majer	27	R	141	.149
Blaise Ilsley	28	L	295	.143	Kevin Meier	26	R	513	.124
Paul Kilgus	30	L	505	.118	Gab Ozuna	23	R	234	.107
Joe Magrane	28	L	160	.157	Rick Shackle	25	R	216	.104
Mike Milchin	24	L	196	.143	Allen Watson	22	L	326	.095
Tim Sherrill	27	L	187	.115	Dennis Wiseman	25	R	438	.121
Tom Urbani	24	L	462	.127					

ATLANTA BRAVES

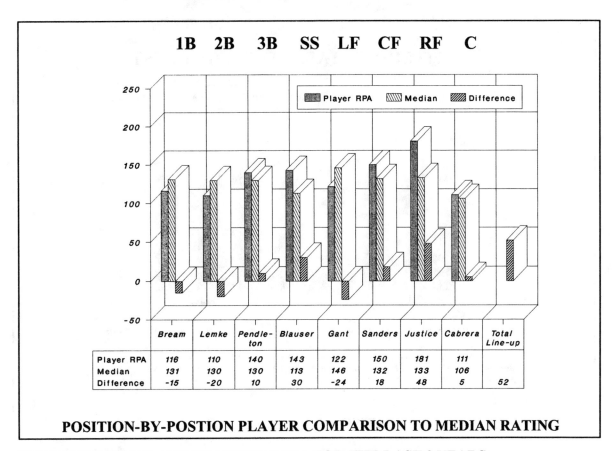

	1B	2B	3B	SS	LF	CF	RF	C	
	Bream	Lemke	Pendle-ton	Blauser	Gant	Sanders	Justice	Cabrera	Total Line-up
Player RPA	116	110	140	143	122	150	181	111	
Median	131	130	130	113	146	132	133	106	
Difference	-15	-20	10	30	-24	18	48	5	52

POSITION-BY-POSTION PLAYER COMPARISON TO MEDIAN RATING

DEFENSIVE TEAM AND STADIUM DATA FOR THE LAST 3 YEARS:

TEAM DEFENSE BY POSITION:

		1990	1991	1992	POSITION-BY-POSITION STADIUM CHARACTERISTICS:
1B:	Home	-3.5	+5.0	-4.2	Average
	Away	-6.5	+0.7	-0.8	
2B:	Home	+5.8	-3.2	+6.1	Average
	Away	-4.1	+5.1	+3.4	
3B:	Home	-6.4	+2.7	-0.4	Hard to play
	Away	-7.6	+2.6	+2.4	
SS:	Home	-0.9	+7.5	+4.0	Hard to play
	Away	-4.0	+2.8	+1.9	
LF:	Home	-3.3	-4.9	-6.1	Average
	Away	+1.7	-7.2	-0.9	
CF:	Home	-3.7	-5.2	+8.5	Slightly easy to play
	Away	+2.3	+2.0	+1.6	
RF:	Home	+2.2	+5.6	+7.2	Slightly easy to play
	Away	-2.7	+0.3	+5.5	
Total Home:		-9.8	+7.5	+15.0	
Total Away:		-20.9	+6.3	+13.0	

Comments: The Braves defense has improved to where it was the 2nd best defense in the NL in '92. The biggest positive change from '91 came in centerfield, which can be attributed to the switch of Otis Nixon into his natural position. RF & CF combined to give the Braves a 22.8 run advantage in '92. It appears that Bream has lost a lot of range at 1B.

ATLANTA BRAVES

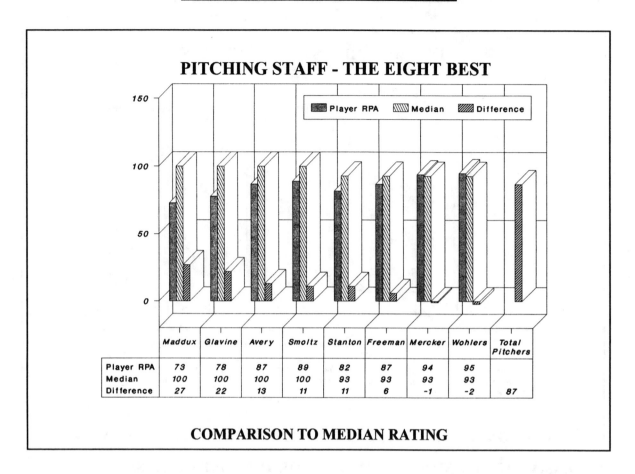

PITCHING STAFF - THE EIGHT BEST

	Maddux	Glavine	Avery	Smoltz	Stanton	Freeman	Mercker	Wohlers	Total Pitchers
Player RPA	73	78	87	89	82	87	94	95	
Median	100	100	100	100	93	93	93	93	
Difference	27	22	13	11	11	6	-1	-2	87

COMPARISON TO MEDIAN RATING

SUGGESTED LINE-UPS (with set-up RPA & drive-in RPA ratings):

Vs: Left-handed Groundball
CF:	O. Nixon	79-65
SS:	J. Blauser	96-82
RF:	D. Justice	102-87
3B:	T. Pendleton	74-76
LF:	R. Gant	72-75
1B:	B. Hunter	67-80
2B:	B. Pecota	68-67
C:	F. Cabrera	49-65
Pitcher		

Vs: Neutral Lefty Pitchers
SS:	J. Blauser	101-86
RF:	D. Justice	90-75
3B:	T. Pendleton	66-68
LF:	R. Gant	73-76
CF:	D. Sanders	64-67
1B:	B. Hunter	71-85
2B:	M. Lemke	56-53
C:	G. Olson	58-56
Pitcher		

Vs: Left-handed Flyball
SS:	J. Blauser	107-92
RF:	D. Justice	71-61
2B:	M. Lemke	70-65
C:	G. Olson	73-69
LF:	R. Gant	74-77
CF:	D. Sanders	82-87
1B:	B. Hunter	76-91
3B:	T. Pendleton	54-56
Pitcher		

Vs: Right-handed Groundball
CF:	O. Nixon	64-54
RF:	D. Justice	100-85
1B:	S. Bream	60-58
3B:	T. Pendleton	74-75
LF:	R. Gant	66-68
C:	F. Cabrera	64-86
SS:	J. Blauser	58-52
2B:	B. Pecota	50-49
Pitcher		

Vs: Neutral Righty Pitchers
RF:	D. Justice	88-73
SS:	J. Blauser	63-56
1B:	S. Bream	66-64
3B:	T. Pendleton	66-67
LF:	R. Gant	67-69
CF:	D. Sanders	69-73
C:	F. Cabrera	57-78
2B:	M. Lemke	46-44
Pitcher		

Vs: Right-handed Flyball
RF:	D. Justice	69-59
SS:	J. Blauser	70-61
1B:	S. Bream	76-74
LF:	R. Gant	68-70
CF:	D. Sanders	87-93
2B:	M. Lemke	60-56
3B:	T. Pendleton	54-55
C:	F. Cabrera	50-66
Pitcher		

Comments: As structured above, this is the 4th best offense in the NL. Greg Olson is not much of a hitter and he's on the downside of his career. It's time to give someone like Cabrera some solid playing time. Cabrera's a much better hitter in any case. If Ryan Klesko is ready, then this may become the best hitting club in the league. And with the fabulous Chipper Jones on the near horizon, this team can expect to be an offensive powerhouse for some time to come.

ATLANTA BRAVES

What can be said about the Atlanta Braves that isn't totally obvious? This is a very strong team with an outstanding pitching staff who then goes out and signs the marvelous Greg Maddux. My reaction was stunned attention. How could you possibly beat this team? Why bother with playing out the 162 game schedule? Just hand them the title now.

Fortunately, as I checked the data, I found out that the Braves will be the deserving favorite in the western division, but not by all that much. In fact, even the eastern division favorite (Philadelphia), in a division supposedly greatly weakened by player defections, was virtually the equal of Atlanta. I felt reassured. There will be a real pennant race after all!

Even though the Braves added Maddux, they had to part with a quality starting pitcher in Charlie Leibrandt. Maddux is superior to Leibrandt, but it would have been a bigger team improvement had Maddux not been replacing such a quality pitcher.

The free-agent signing of Bill Pecota was a plus, but he was just replacing Jeff Treadway, who's about his equal in ability. The loss of Lonnie Smith removes a potent bat from the bench.

The problem for the National League is that the Braves figure to be hugely stronger in a year or so even though they lost minor league free-agent catcher Brian Deak, who I believe is far superior to any catcher on the Braves' Major League roster. I guess they figured that Javy Lopez, their outstanding young catching prospect at AA, would blow by Deak in about a year at most, so that there was no need to keep Deak. I can understand their reasoning, although I find it hard to accept letting such a talent go -- especially when you've been getting by with the likes of journeyman catcher Greg Olson.

The Braves have Ryan Klesko almost ready to take over at first base. He should be a very big power hitter. AA shortstop Chipper Jones could be the next Cal Ripken. He's no more than a year away from Atlanta, and could be ready for the Majors by the All-Star break. As much as Jeff Blauser has improved, there is absolutely no way he'll be able to prevent Jones from taking his job.

Melvin Nieves is one of the top young outfielders. Mike Kelly is a little further away from the Majors in terms of time needed to get here, but he ought to make a strong impact as well. And don't forget that Deion Sanders is still learning the game. He's a young player with enormous potential who's doing his learning at the Major League level. He's already a very good player. He could become a terrific player. I can't believe those people who urged the Braves not to protect Sanders in the Expansion draft!

With a number of good young Atlanta players available to the Colorado Rockies in the second round and third rounds of the Expansion draft, why did the Rockies select light-hitting shortstop Vinny Castilla and marginal pitching prospect Armando Reynoso? I just don't get it.

Atlanta's Projected record for 1993: 90--72, good for 1st place in the division.

ATLANTA BRAVES

Rafael Belliard, 31

Bats Right   188L   557R   258G   175F

L= .075G .067L .055F   (.037/.039) .076   .087G .079R .067F = R

		ATBATS	1B	2B	3B	HR	HBP	BB	GDP	SB	CS	ROE	XB	RUNS	EOB%	RL#	SET-UP	DR-IN	RPA
Pittsburgh	1990	54	8	3	0	0	1	5	2	1	2	0	8	4	.159	.061	.028	.036	.064
Atlanta	1991	353	77	9	2	0	2	20	4	3	1	7	27	32	.227	.090	.044	.041	.085
Atlanta	1992	285	53	6	1	0	3	10	6	0	1	5	13	20	.175	.064	.030	.035	.065

Damon Berryhill, 29

Bats Both   139L   419R   235G   129F

L= .065G .059L .047F   (.036/.053) .089   .105G .099R .087F = R

		ATBATS	1B	2B	3B	HR	HBP	BB	GDP	SB	CS	ROE	XB	RUNS	EOB%	RL#	SET-UP	DR-IN	RPA
Cubs	1990	53	5	4	0	1	0	4	3	0	0	0	3	4	.116	.063	.021	.038	.059
Cubs	1991	159	18	7	0	5	1	10	2	1	2	1	7	14	.141	.081	.032	.046	.078
Atlanta	1991	1	0	0	0	0	0	0	0	0	0	0	0	0	.000	.000	.000	.000	.000
Atlanta	1992	307	43	16	1	10	1	13	4	0	2	0	10	31	.145	.094	.039	.056	.095

Jeff Blauser, 27

Bats Right   475L   755R   419G   308F

L= .173G .182L .194F   (.075/.065) .140   .105G .114R .126F = R

		ATBATS	1B	2B	3B	HR	HBP	BB	GDP	SB	CS	ROE	XB	RUNS	EOB%	RL#	SET-UP	DR-IN	RPA
Atlanta	1990	386	69	24	3	8	5	34	4	3	5	9	28	55	.244	.128	.069	.058	.127
Atlanta	1991	352	63	14	3	11	2	50	4	5	8	7	25	53	.248	.135	.070	.058	.128
Atlanta	1992	343	54	19	3	14	4	44	2	5	5	2	30	61	.238	.152	.081	.071	.152

Sid Bream, 32

Bats Left   185L   968R   414G   257F

L= .060G .072L .092F   (.063/.061) .124   .122G .134R .154F = R

		ATBATS	1B	2B	3B	HR	HBP	BB	GDP	SB	CS	ROE	XB	RUNS	EOB%	RL#	SET-UP	DR-IN	RPA
Pittsburgh	1990	389	65	23	2	15	2	43	6	8	4	3	26	64	.224	.140	.075	.070	.145
Atlanta	1991	265	44	12	0	11	0	20	8	0	4	4	15	31	.166	.109	.046	.058	.104
Atlanta	1992	372	61	25	1	10	1	44	3	6	0	3	20	59	.249	.138	.076	.063	.139

Francisco Cabrera, 26

Bats Right   186L   77R   86G   70F   462ML

L= .108G .093L .074F   (.044/.060) .104   .144G .129R .110F = R

		ATBATS	1B	2B	3B	HR	HBP	BB	GDP	SB	CS	ROE	XB	RUNS	EOB%	RL#	SET-UP	DR-IN	RPA
Atlanta	1990	137	25	5	1	7	0	5	4	1	0	4	4	19	.171	.129	.058	.070	.128
Atlanta	1991	95	13	6	0	4	0	6	5	1	1	1	3	9	.125	.092	.032	.054	.086
Atlanta	1992	10	1	0	0	2	0	1	0	0	0	0	0	2	.092	.224	.069	.155	.224

Ron Gant, 27

Bats Right   608L   1262R   626G   482F

L= .142G .144L .146F   (.067/.068) .135   .129G .131R .133F = R

		ATBATS	1B	2B	3B	HR	HBP	BB	GDP	SB	CS	ROE	XB	RUNS	EOB%	RL#	SET-UP	DR-IN	RPA
Atlanta	1990	575	105	34	3	32	1	50	8	33	16	10	62	104	.209	.163	.081	.080	.161
Atlanta	1991	561	71	35	3	32	5	63	6	34	16	7	51	89	.196	.146	.068	.071	.139
Atlanta	1992	544	96	22	6	17	7	40	10	32	12	13	54	80	.206	.130	.065	.066	.131

Tommy Gregg, 29

Bats Left   31L   367R   129G   90F   147ML

L= ....G .036L .047F   (.053/.054) .107   ....G .113R .124F = R

		ATBATS	1B	2B	3B	HR	HBP	BB	GDP	SB	CS	ROE	XB	RUNS	EOB%	RL#	SET-UP	DR-IN	RPA
Atlanta	1990	239	44	13	1	5	1	16	1	4	3	3	15	30	.218	.116	.059	.056	.115
Atlanta	1991	107	10	8	1	1	1	10	1	2	2	1	9	9	.185	.081	.036	.040	.076
Atlanta	1992	19	4	0	0	1	0	1	1	1	0	1	2	3	.175	.129	.060	.071	.131

Brian Hunter, 24

Bats Right   298L   255R   170G   149F   199ML

L= .136G .145L .156F   (.053/.064) .117   .076G .085R .096F = R

		ATBATS	1B	2B	3B	HR	HBP	BB	GDP	SB	CS	ROE	XB	RUNS	EOB%	RL#	SET-UP	DR-IN	RPA
Atlanta	1991	271	39	16	1	12	1	17	6	0	2	4	17	33	.169	.118	.050	.061	.111
Atlanta	1992	238	28	13	2	14	0	18	2	1	2	3	19	36	.167	.137	.062	.076	.138

ATLANTA BRAVES

Dave Justice, 26

Bats Left   496L   1022R   504G   370F

L= .182G .158L .125F   (.084/.071) .155   .178G .154R .121F = R

		ATBATS	1B	2B	3B	HR	HBP	BB	GDP	SB	CS	ROE	XB	RUNS	EOB%	RL#	SET-UP	DR-IN	RPA
Atlanta	1990	439	71	23	2	28	0	60	2	11	6	2	34	87	.233	.172	.090	.081	.171
Atlanta	1991	396	62	25	1	21	3	56	4	8	8	6	33	71	.243	.162	.083	.072	.155
Atlanta	1992	484	79	19	5	21	2	71	1	2	4	1	38	88	.245	.154	.084	.071	.155

Bats Both   390L   653R   350G   263F

Mark Lemke, 27

L= .084G .104L .130F   (.047/.045) .092   .065G .085R .111F = R

		ATBATS	1B	2B	3B	HR	HBP	BB	GDP	SB	CS	ROE	XB	RUNS	EOB%	RL#	SET-UP	DR-IN	RPA
Atlanta	1990	239	41	13	0	0	0	18	6	0	1	5	18	20	.206	.077	.038	.038	.076
Atlanta	1991	269	48	11	2	2	0	27	9	1	2	4	20	25	.204	.087	.041	.041	.082
Atlanta	1992	427	80	7	4	6	0	39	9	0	3	13	20	47	.215	.097	.050	.048	.098

Bats Both   467L   745R   412G   300F

Otis Nixon, 33

L= .149G .129L .102F   (.065/.054) .119   .133G .113R .086F = R

		ATBATS	1B	2B	3B	HR	HBP	BB	GDP	SB	CS	ROE	XB	RUNS	EOB%	RL#	SET-UP	DR-IN	RPA
Montreal	1990	231	49	6	2	1	0	28	2	50	14	2	27	30	.225	.110	.059	.054	.113
Atlanta	1991	401	108	10	1	0	2	44	5	72	22	8	53	53	.262	.124	.065	.052	.117
Atlanta	1992	456	116	14	2	2	0	39	4	41	18	10	46	62	.248	.122	.066	.056	.122

Bats Right   406L   737R   357G   304F

Greg Olson, 32

L= .094G .118L .146F   (.049/.047) .096   .060G .084R .112F = R

		ATBATS	1B	2B	3B	HR	HBP	BB	GDP	SB	CS	ROE	XB	RUNS	EOB%	RL#	SET-UP	DR-IN	RPA
Atlanta	1990	298	58	12	1	7	2	26	8	1	1	8	24	39	.226	.117	.060	.056	.116
Atlanta	1991	411	68	25	0	6	3	41	13	1	1	8	27	44	.219	.099	.048	.046	.094
Atlanta	1992	302	53	14	2	3	1	30	8	2	1	3	17	33	.214	.097	.049	.048	.097

Bats Both   585L   1220R   614G   426F

Terry Pendleton, 32

L= .154G .138L .114F   (.068/.069) .137   .153G .137R .113F = R

		ATBATS	1B	2B	3B	HR	HBP	BB	GDP	SB	CS	ROE	XB	RUNS	EOB%	RL#	SET-UP	DR-IN	RPA
St. Louis	1990	447	75	20	2	6	1	22	12	7	5	5	32	39	.162	.080	.034	.045	.079
Atlanta	1991	586	123	34	8	22	1	35	16	10	3	6	44	88	.210	.144	.069	.068	.137
Atlanta	1992	640	138	39	1	21	0	29	16	5	3	8	48	95	.203	.135	.067	.069	.136

Bats Left   93L   507R   223G   157F   142ML

Deion Sanders, 25

L= .095G .122L .160F   (.064/.067) .131   .106G .133R .171F = R

		ATBATS	1B	2B	3B	HR	HBP	BB	GDP	SB	CS	ROE	XB	RUNS	EOB%	RL#	SET-UP	DR-IN	RPA
Yankees	1990	133	14	2	2	3	1	13	2	8	2	3	19	13	.170	.088	.040	.049	.089
Atlanta	1991	110	14	1	2	4	0	12	1	11	3	1	8	12	.168	.105	.044	.055	.099
Atlanta	1992	303	64	6	14	8	2	18	5	26	11	7	34	50	.208	.150	.075	.075	.150

Bats Right   429L   691R   365G   245F

Lonnie Smith, 37

L= .156G .153L .149F   (.081/.060) .141   .138G .135R .131F = R

		ATBATS	1B	2B	3B	HR	HBP	BB	GDP	SB	CS	ROE	XB	RUNS	EOB%	RL#	SET-UP	DR-IN	RPA
Atlanta	1990	466	97	27	9	9	6	55	2	10	11	8	53	82	.279	.155	.088	.065	.153
Atlanta	1991	353	70	19	1	7	9	47	4	9	5	12	37	58	.296	.148	.082	.057	.139
Atlanta	1992	158	23	8	2	6	3	16	1	4	0	1	17	26	.230	.146	.077	.070	.147

Bats Left   162L   821R   322G   243F

Jeff Treadway, 29

L= .132G .132L .133F   (.053/.050) .103   .097G .097R .098F = R

		ATBATS	1B	2B	3B	HR	HBP	BB	GDP	SB	CS	ROE	XB	RUNS	EOB%	RL#	SET-UP	DR-IN	RPA
Atlanta	1990	474	101	20	2	11	3	24	10	3	4	4	33	57	.198	.111	.054	.056	.110
Atlanta	1991	306	76	17	2	3	2	22	8	2	2	4	31	40	.249	.126	.065	.054	.119
Atlanta	1992	126	21	6	1	0	0	5	3	1	2	1	2	9	.154	.064	.027	.037	.064

ATLANTA BRAVES

PITCHERS

Throws: Neutral type, moderate lefty

Steve Avery, 22 (.083/.095) .093   412L   1799R

		OUTS	RO	1B	2B	3B	HR	HBP	BB	GDP	SB	CS	PO	WP	BK	RUNS	EOB%	RL#	RPA
Atlanta	1990	297	6	86	25	3	7	2	43	5	20	8	0	5	1	55	.218	.128	.120
Atlanta	1991	631	0	131	33	4	21	3	65	16	21	11	0	4	1	77	.145	.095	.089
Atlanta	1992	701	0	165	31	6	14	0	68	16	42	14	0	7	3	93	.155	.089	.096

Throws: Neutral type, moderate righty

Mike Bielecki, 33 (.097/.087) .093   989L   731R

		OUTS	RO	1B	2B	3B	HR	HBP	BB	GDP	SB	CS	PO	WP	BK	RUNS	EOB%	RL#	RPA
Chicago Cubs	1990	504	51	131	35	9	13	5	59	11	17	9	2	11	0	79	.189	.115	.107
Chicago Cubs	1991	516	69	112	30	9	18	2	48	15	17	9	2	6	0	65	.136	.098	.090
Atlanta	1991	5	5	1	1	0	0	0	2	0	0	0	0	0	0	2	.377	.168	.168
Atlanta	1992	242	21	54	16	5	2	1	26	7	8	2	1	4	0	33	.176	.091	.098

Throws: Neutral type, moderate to severe lefty

Mark Davis, 32 (.113/.148) .140   197L   638R   142ML

		OUTS	RO	1B	2B	3B	HR	HBP	BB	GDP	SB	CS	PO	WP	BK	RUNS	EOB%	RL#	RPA
Kansas City	1990	206	170	45	16	1	9	4	49	5	15	0	0	6	0	52	.260	.155	.160
Kansas City	1991	188	103	37	11	1	6	1	39	6	4	3	0	1	0	31	.197	.111	.112
Kansas City	1992	109	38	25	10	1	6	0	28	2	8	1	0	1	0	32	.258	.169	.182
Atlanta	1992	50	50	14	5	0	3	1	11	1	0	0	0	4	1	16	.271	.177	.192

Throws: Groundball type, extreme righty

Marvin Freeman, 29 (.107/.066) .085   295L   347R

		OUTS	RO	1B	2B	3B	HR	HBP	BB	GDP	SB	CS	PO	WP	BK	RUNS	EOB%	RL#	RPA
Philadelphia	1990	97	58	24	3	2	5	3	12	1	2	3	0	4	0	18	.179	.129	.130
Atlanta	1990	47	47	7	0	0	0	2	3	1	2	0	0	0	0	2	.140	.042	.040
Atlanta	1991	144	144	29	6	0	2	2	12	6	2	2	0	4	0	11	.120	.066	.061
Atlanta	1992	193	193	44	9	1	7	1	22	6	7	5	0	4	0	28	.138	.095	.103

Throws: Neutral type, moderate to severe reverse lefty

Tom Glavine, 26 (.102/.072) .079   643L   2167R

		OUTS	RO	1B	2B	3B	HR	HBP	BB	GDP	SB	CS	PO	WP	BK	RUNS	EOB%	RL#	RPA
Atlanta	1990	643	0	165	45	4	18	1	68	23	22	9	0	8	1	91	.164	.104	.098
Atlanta	1991	740	0	143	35	6	17	2	63	19	18	10	0	10	2	75	.134	.080	.076
Atlanta	1992	675	0	150	37	4	6	2	63	18	13	10	0	5	0	76	.156	.076	.082

Throws: Neutral type, neutral lefty

Charlie Leibrandt, 36 (.088/.093) .092   496L   1851R

		OUTS	RO	1B	2B	3B	HR	HBP	BB	GDP	SB	CS	PO	WP	BK	RUNS	EOB%	RL#	RPA
Atlanta	1990	487	0	114	38	3	9	4	32	10	21	3	1	4	3	62	.171	.096	.091
Atlanta	1991	689	0	151	38	5	18	4	53	6	35	11	4	5	3	85	.157	.095	.090
Atlanta	1992	579	6	144	34	4	9	5	38	6	28	16	3	3	2	75	.152	.086	.093

Throws: Neutral type, moderate to severe reverse lefty

Kent Mercker, 24 (.113/.090) .097   221L   556R

		OUTS	RO	1B	2B	3B	HR	HBP	BB	GDP	SB	CS	PO	WP	BK	RUNS	EOB%	RL#	RPA
Atlanta	1990	145	145	31	5	1	6	2	21	1	5	4	0	2	0	22	.179	.110	.104
Atlanta	1991	220	162	40	9	2	5	1	32	5	10	0	0	4	1	28	.190	.097	.092
Atlanta	1992	205	205	37	10	0	4	3	34	4	12	2	0	6	0	30	.202	.095	.103

ATLANTA BRAVES

Alejandro Pena, 33

Throws: Flyball type, moderate to severe reverse righty

(.067/.099) .084   377L   402R

		OUTS	RO	1B	2B	3B	HR	HBP	BB	GDP	SB	CS	PO	WP	BK	RUNS	EOB%	RL#	RPA
New York Mets	1990	228	228	54	11	2	4	1	17	3	11	0	0	0	0	30	.185	.094	.092
New York Mets	1991	189	189	48	9	1	5	0	15	4	8	4	0	1	2	22	.149	.095	.084
Atlanta	1991	58	58	10	0	0	1	0	3	2	0	0	0	0	0	3	.080	.045	.044
Atlanta	1992	126	126	28	5	0	7	0	8	5	5	1	0	0	0	17	.099	.093	.101

Jeff Reardon, 37

Throws: Flyball type, moderate righty

(.114/.094) .104   342L   336R

		OUTS	RO	1B	2B	3B	HR	HBP	BB	GDP	SB	CS	PO	WP	BK	RUNS	EOB%	RL#	RPA
Boston	1990	154	154	23	11	0	5	1	15	2	8	1	0	0	0	18	.157	.093	.088
Boston	1991	178	178	32	11	2	9	1	13	2	3	1	0	0	0	25	.146	.109	.104
Boston	1992	127	127	35	11	1	6	1	7	5	2	0	0	0	0	21	.155	.121	.116
Atlanta	1992	47	47	14	0	0	0	1	1	1	2	0	0	0	0	4	.163	.065	.070

Armando Reynoso, 26

Throws: Neutral type, righty

(..../....) .119   61L   64R   1237ML

		OUTS	RO	1B	2B	3B	HR	HBP	BB	GDP	SB	CS	PO	WP	BK	RUNS	EOB%	RL#	RPA
Atlanta	1991	70	3	15	4	3	4	3	9	2	1	1	5	2	0	10	.094	.108	.103
Atlanta	1992	23	8	5	4	0	2	1	1	2	0	1	1	0	0	3	.017	.079	.085

Pete Smith, 26

Throws: Neutral type, extreme righty

(.140/.074) .112   479L   345R   654ML

		OUTS	RO	1B	2B	3B	HR	HBP	BB	GDP	SB	CS	PO	WP	BK	RUNS	EOB%	RL#	RPA
Atlanta	1990	231	0	56	10	0	11	0	22	7	9	3	0	2	1	32	.140	.104	.098
Atlanta	1991	144	15	28	13	2	5	0	19	4	13	1	0	1	4	24	.186	.122	.116
Atlanta	1992	237	6	47	11	2	3	0	26	1	8	2	2	2	1	29	.179	.084	.090

John Smoltz, 25

Throws: Neutral type, extreme righty

(.115/.057) .091   1679L   1152R

		OUTS	RO	1B	2B	3B	HR	HBP	BB	GDP	SB	CS	PO	WP	BK	RUNS	EOB%	RL#	RPA
Atlanta	1990	694	0	150	31	5	20	1	87	16	31	10	2	14	3	90	.164	.098	.092
Atlanta	1991	689	0	145	38	7	16	3	76	18	14	13	2	20	2	80	.151	.090	.084
Atlanta	1992	740	0	145	39	5	17	5	75	10	11	7	2	17	1	99	.168	.090	.097

Mike Stanton, 25

Throws: Neutral type, moderate reverse lefty

(.094/.078) .084   207L   381R

		OUTS	RO	1B	2B	3B	HR	HBP	BB	GDP	SB	CS	PO	WP	BK	RUNS	EOB%	RL#	RPA
Atlanta	1990	21	21	14	1	0	1	1	2	0	2	0	0	1	0	9	.337	.223	.210
Atlanta	1991	234	234	45	9	2	6	1	15	7	9	1	0	0	0	22	.123	.077	.073
Atlanta	1992	191	191	42	11	0	6	2	18	5	1	2	2	3	0	26	.142	.090	.097

Randy St. Claire, 32

Throws: Groundball type, extreme reverse righty

(.075/.128) .107   72L   106R   557ML

		OUTS	RO	1B	2B	3B	HR	HBP	BB	GDP	SB	CS	PO	WP	BK	RUNS	EOB%	RL#	RPA
Atlanta	1991	86	86	21	6	0	4	0	6	1	1	3	0	4	0	12	.132	.105	.098
Atlanta	1992	46	46	11	5	0	1	0	5	2	0	0	1	0	0	7	.151	.093	.101

Mark Wohlers, 22

Throws: Groundball type, moderate to severe righty

(.113/.090) .101   99L   106R   378ML

		OUTS	RO	1B	2B	3B	HR	HBP	BB	GDP	SB	CS	PO	WP	BK	RUNS	EOB%	RL#	RPA
Atlanta	1991	59	59	10	5	1	1	2	10	3	5	0	0	0	0	9	.201	.107	.101
Atlanta	1992	106	106	25	3	0	0	1	10	5	3	1	0	1	0	9	.138	.058	.063

Atlanta Braves AAA & AA Minor League Ratings

AAA (RICHMOND)	AGE	BATS	POSITION	CPA	RUNS	SET-UP	DRIVE-IN	RPA
Francisco Cabrera	26	R	C\1B	324	30.6	.043	.051	.094
Ramon Caraballo	23	B	2B	544	47.4	.042	.045	.087
Vinny Castilla	25	R	SS	493	34.9	.030	.041	.071
Brian Deak	25	R	C	304	42.4	.084	.056	.140
Nick Esasky	32	R	1B	119	14.9	.063	.063	.126
Tommy Gregg	29	L	OF	147	16.1	.063	.046	.109
Ryan Klesko	21	L	1B	477	46.9	.044	.054	.098
Jeff Manto	28	R	3B	522	63.9	.067	.055	.122
Keith Mitchell	23	R	OF	479	42.0	.047	.041	.088
Bobby Moore	27	R	OF	343	24.1	.033	.037	.070
Mike Mordecai	25	R	SS\2B	381	30.5	.038	.042	.080
Boi Rodriguez	26	L	3B	315	42.6	.067	.068	.135
Sean Ross	25	L	OF	410	34.7	.036	.049	.085
Andy Tomberlin	26	L	OF	457	48.9	.055	.052	.107

AA (GREENVILLE)	AGE	BATS	POSITION	CPA	RUNS	SET-UP	DRIVE-IN	RPA
Ed Alicea	25	B	OF\2B	369	33.1	.045	.045	.090
Mike Bell	24	L	1B	487	45.5	.047	.046	.093
Ed Giovanola	23	L	3B	300	29.2	.052	.046	.098
Chipper Jones	20	B	SS	282	38.8	.069	.069	.138
Mike Kelly	22	R	OF	553	60.6	.052	.058	.110
Pat Kelly	25	R	3B\2B	373	28.6	.040	.037	.077
Javy Lopez	22	R	C	479	57.6	.060	.060	.120
Melvin Nieves	21	B	OF	412	57.8	.075	.065	.140
Jose Olmeda	24	B	2B	383	31.4	.041	.041	.082
Eduardo Perez	24	R	C\1B	312	21.9	.031	.039	.070
Tony Tarasco	22	L	OF	526	48.5	.040	.052	.092
Aubrey Waggoner	26	L	OF	334	53.4	.094	.066	.160

AAA Pitchers	Age	Throws	Outs	RPA	AA Pitchers	Age	Throws	Outs	RPA
Brian Bark	24	L	291	.125	Pedro Borbon	26	L	282	.109
Kevin Coffman	27	R	388	.116	Dennis Burlingame	23	R	455	.132
Pat Gomez	24	L	356	.130	Donnie Elliot	24	R	418	.114
Tom McCarthy	31	R	278	.107	Mike Hostetler	22	R	242	.145
Greg McMichael	26	R	410	.116	Judd Johnson	26	L	208	.112
David Nied	24	R	504	.113	Andy Nezelek	27	R	341	.095
Dale Polley	28	L	169	.114	Don Strange	25	R	180	.086
Armando Reynoso	26	R	508	.121	Marcos Vasquez	24	R	220	.148
Nap Robinson	26	R	491	.118	Preston Watson	25	R	220	.112
Pete Smith	26	R	328	.086	Brad Woodall	23	L	118	.084
Randy St. Claire	32	R	215	.139					
Billy Taylor	31	R	237	.114					
Mark Wohlers	22	R	103	.150					

CINCINNATI REDS

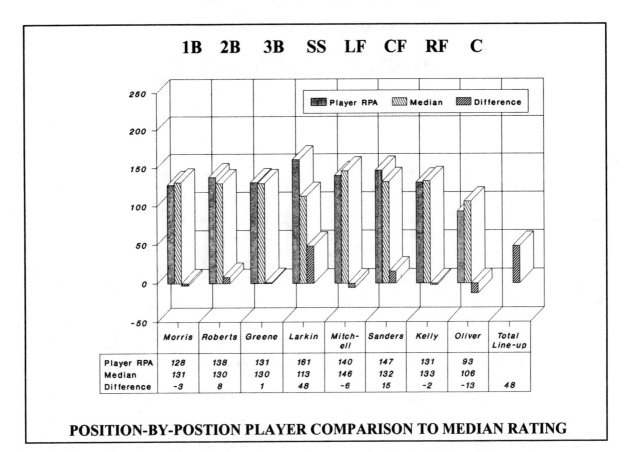

	1B	2B	3B	SS	LF	CF	RF	C
	Morris	Roberts	Greene	Larkin	Mitch-ell	Sanders	Kelly	Oliver	Total Line-up
Player RPA	128	138	131	161	140	147	131	93	
Median	131	130	130	113	146	132	133	106	
Difference	-3	8	1	48	-6	15	-2	-13	48

POSITION-BY-POSTION PLAYER COMPARISON TO MEDIAN RATING

DEFENSIVE TEAM AND STADIUM DATA FOR THE LAST 3 YEARS:

TEAM DEFENSE BY POSITION:

POSITION-BY-POSITION STADIUM CHARACTERISTICS:

		1990	1991	1992	
1B:	Home	-1.2	+0.8	-0.5	Average
	Away	-1.7	-3.2	-2.2	
2B:	Home	+2.4	+2.1	+2.0	Average
	Away	-1.6	-4.6	-0.9	
3B:	Home	+5.0	-0.1	-0.6	Easy to play
	Away	+5.7	-1.5	-3.7	
SS:	Home	+6.5	-0.9	+1.8	Slightly easy to play
	Away	+3.6	-3.5	+3.0	
LF:	Home	+4.2	+1.1	-2.7	Average
	Away	+2.2	-0.2	+0.8	
CF:	Home	-0.8	+2.9	+4.8	Slightly easy to play
	Away	+4.6	-4.9	-4.5	
RF:	Home	-0.9	+5.6	+2.8	Average
	Away	+4.8	+5.9	+6.2	
Total Home:		+15.2	+11.5	+7.5	
Total Away:		+17.6	-12.0	-1.2	

Comments: The Reds continued their slide towards defensive mediocrity in '92. With Paul O'Neill traded, the Reds had better play Roberto Kelley in left field where he's substantially above average. He's had big defensive problems in CF, however. The Reds need to find a quality second baseman which could allow them to put the marvelous Bip Roberts in the outfield. Bip's a very good second baseman, but he's a truly outstanding outfielder.

CINCINNATI REDS

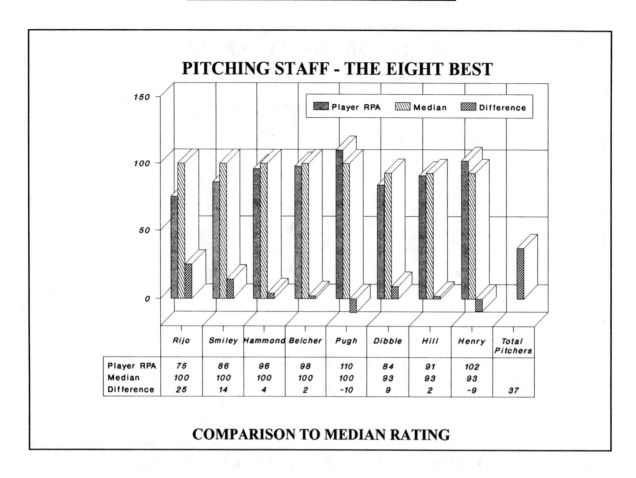

PITCHING STAFF - THE EIGHT BEST

Legend: Player RPA | Median | Difference

	Rijo	Smiley	Hammond	Belcher	Pugh	Dibble	Hill	Henry	Total Pitchers
Player RPA	75	86	96	98	110	84	91	102	
Median	100	100	100	100	100	93	93	93	
Difference	25	14	4	2	-10	9	2	-9	37

COMPARISON TO MEDIAN RATING

SUGGESTED LINE-UPS (with set-up RPA & drive-in RPA ratings):

Vs: Left-handed Groundball
2B:	B. Roberts	68-54
SS:	B. Larkin	101-84
CF:	R. Sanders	98-89
LF:	K. Mitchell	106-100
3B:	C. Sabo	73-79
RF:	R. Kelly	64-69
1B:	T. Costo	60-70
C:	T. Afenir	56-63
Pitcher		

Vs: Neutral Lefty Pitchers
2B:	B. Roberts	65-51
SS:	B. Larkin	104-87
CF:	R. Sanders	92-84
LF:	K. Mitchell	97-94
RF:	R. Kelly	68-73
3B:	C. Sabo	73-80
1B:	T. Costo	60-70
C:	T. Afenir	56-63
Pitcher		

Vs: Left-handed Flyball
SS:	B. Larkin	109-91
CF:	R. Sanders	85-76
LF:	K. Mitchell	88-84
RF:	R. Kelly	73-79
3B:	C. Sabo	74-80
1B:	T. Costo	60-70
C:	T. Afenir	56-63
2B:	B. Roberts	59-46
Pitcher		

Vs: Right-handed Groundball
SS:	B. Larkin	73-58
2B:	B. Roberts	82-67
1B:	H. Morris	75-65
CF:	R. Sanders	72-64
LF:	K. Mitchell	78-75
3B:	W. Greene	65-66
RF:	R. Kelly	51-55
C:	T. Afenir	46-53
Pitcher		

Vs: Neutral Righty Pitchers
SS:	B. Larkin	76-61
2B:	B. Roberts	79-64
1B:	H. Morris	80-70
CF:	R. Sanders	66-59
LF:	K. Mitchell	71-67
3B:	W. Greene	65-66
RF:	R. Kelly	55-59
C:	T. Afenir	46-53
Pitcher		

Vs: Right-handed Flyball
2B:	B. Roberts	73-59
SS:	B. Larkin	85-70
1B:	H. Morris	87-77
3B:	W. Greene	65-66
RF:	G. Varsho	64-66
LF:	R. Kelly	60-65
CF:	R. Sanders	58-52
C:	T. Afenir	46-53
Pitcher		

Comments: Scott Bradley, Jeff Reed & Joe Oliver are an extremely weak catching trio. That's why Troy Afenir is listed in all the above line-ups. He's not a premium player, but at least he's got a little pop in his bat while being adequate defensively. Willie Greene is one of the top prospects in the Majors and I think he's already as good as Sabo. Only the Phillies in the NL have a better offense (barely) than the line-ups listed above.

CINCINNATI REDS

I was concerned that the Braves would be my runaway choice for the western division pennant, but I was pleasantly surprised to see that the Reds were serious pennant contenders after I ran through my data. I shouldn't have been all that surprised, however. This is essentially the same team as last year when I picked them to beat out the Braves rather easily.

While the acquisition of pitcher John Smiley is only a replacement for Greg Swindell, I like Smiley a little more than Swindell, even though both are excellent pitchers.

I don't know what the Reds intend to do with Chris Sabo. There is no way he should hold the third base job for more than this coming year since Willie Greene is already at least his equal as a player and will be blowing right by Sabo in the near future.

Why did the Reds protect Joe Oliver in the Expansion draft? He's another one of these catchers that I just don't understand how they keep their job. He and Jeff Reed are a pretty sorry pair of catchers for a team that expects to contend. Even the Reds AAA catcher (Troy Afenir), while no ball of fire, is superior to either of them. The Reds have gone several years without addressing this serious problem. Failure to seriously deal with this problem is probably the single most important reason why I'm not selecting the Reds to win the division. I would have protected Chris Hammond (or even Trevor Hoffman) instead.

The trade of Norm Charlton for Kevin Mitchell is a curious one to me. Mitchell, in my mind, is the more valuable commodity, yet when I looked at the Mariners and the Reds as *teams*, in each case I came away with the impression that Norm Charlton was the player who better met the immediate needs of each team. The loss of Charlton could really hurt this team.

The trade of Paul O'Neill for Roberto Kelly isn't as important a trade as the Mitchell\Charlton trade, but I do think the Reds marginally lost out in this deal. O'Neill overall is a slightly more valuable player and that value goes up if the team utilizing his services uses him in a strict platoon.

Tim Costo is a good prospect, but he probably needs some time at AAA, perhaps more than one entire season. I only used Costo in the proposed lineups on the opposite page since Hal Morris is such a futile hitter vs. lefties and Costo was the only available bat I could find to platoon at first.

The signing of 6-year minor league free-agent pitcher Bo Kennedy was a good move. He's got some ability. AA DH Kevin Garner looks like he's got a big bat and is a more advanced hitter than is the much younger Tim Costo, but with Costo on the same team he didn't get playing time at first base. What's his future in this organization?

The Reds have two farm hands who, as relievers, were really stellar performers in '92. Scott Service and Jerry Spradlin could both make an important impact in the Reds thin bullpen now that Norm Charlton has departed. If either of them do make a quality difference, then the Mitchell trade would really have paid off.

Cincinnati's Projected record for 1993: 87--75, good for 3rd place in the division.

CINCINNATI REDS

Freddie Benavides, 26

Bats Right   118L   130R   80G   64F   357ML

L= .062G .078L .098F (.030/.034) .064 .035G .051R .071F = R

		ATBATS	1B	2B	3B	HR	HBP	BB	GDP	SB	CS	ROE	XB	RUNS	EOB%	RL#	SET-UP	DR-IN	RPA
Cincinnati	1991	63	17	1	0	0	1	0	1	1	0	1	7	6	.213	.089	.044	.042	.086
Cincinnati	1992	173	28	10	1	1	1	6	3	0	2	2	12	15	.169	.078	.035	.043	.078

Scott Bradley, 32

Bats Left   41L   410R   138G   93F

L= ....G .076L ....F (.043/.038) .081 .060G .081R .112F = R

		ATBATS	1B	2B	3B	HR	HBP	BB	GDP	SB	CS	ROE	XB	RUNS	EOB%	RL#	SET-UP	DR-IN	RPA
Seattle	1990	233	42	9	0	1	0	13	6	0	1	1	14	17	.170	.069	.031	.038	.069
Seattle	1991	172	28	7	0	0	0	17	2	0	0	3	10	15	.224	.074	.040	.036	.076
Seattle	1992	1	0	0	0	0	0	1	0	0	0	0	0	0	.500	.136	.100	.041	.141
Cincinnati	1992	5	2	0	0	0	0	1	0	0	0	0	1	1	.403	.195	.130	.067	.197

Glenn Braggs, 30

Bats Right   487L   457R   315G   187F

L= .126G .133L .146F (.059/.060) .119 .097G .104R .117F = R

		ATBATS	1B	2B	3B	HR	HBP	BB	GDP	SB	CS	ROE	XB	RUNS	EOB%	RL#	SET-UP	DR-IN	RPA
Milwaukee	1990	113	20	5	0	3	3	10	1	5	3	1	11	15	.216	.119	.062	.059	.121
Cincinnati	1990	201	44	9	1	6	3	25	3	3	4	1	17	33	.255	.147	.079	.064	.143
Cincinnati	1991	250	44	10	0	11	2	20	4	11	3	3	19	35	.198	.128	.060	.063	.123
Cincinnati	1992	266	36	16	3	8	2	31	10	3	1	2	27	36	.196	.114	.056	.059	.115

Jeff Branson, 25

Bats Left   8L   114R   67G   25F   627ML

L= ....G ....L ....F (.042/.046) .088 .088G .093R ....F = R

		ATBATS	1B	2B	3B	HR	HBP	BB	GDP	SB	CS	ROE	XB	RUNS	EOB%	RL#	SET-UP	DR-IN	RPA
Cincinnati	1992	115	26	7	1	0	0	3	4	0	1	1	11	11	.187	.089	.043	.047	.090

Darnell Coles, 30

Bats Right   242L   152R   92G   108F   463ML

L= .119G .116L .114F (.055/.057) .112 .109G .106R .104F = R

		ATBATS	1B	2B	3B	HR	HBP	BB	GDP	SB	CS	ROE	XB	RUNS	EOB%	RL#	SET-UP	DR-IN	RPA
Seattle	1990	107	15	5	1	2	1	3	1	0	0	0	4	9	.152	.081	.035	.047	.082
Detroit	1990	108	19	2	0	1	0	11	3	0	4	2	5	8	.169	.066	.030	.036	.066
San Francisco	1991	14	3	0	0	0	0	0	1	0	0	0	1	1	.075	.032	.010	.026	.036
Cincinnati	1992	141	28	11	2	3	0	3	1	1	1	3	11	21	.220	.139	.073	.068	.141

Billy Doran, 34

Bats Both   426L   920R   474G   283F

L= .091G .118L .162F (.062/.053) .115 .086G .113R .157F = R

		ATBATS	1B	2B	3B	HR	HBP	BB	GDP	SB	CS	ROE	XB	RUNS	EOB%	RL#	SET-UP	DR-IN	RPA
Houston	1990	344	70	21	2	6	0	70	2	18	10	7	34	73	.315	.152	.101	.067	.168
Cincinnati	1990	59	13	8	0	1	0	7	1	5	1	0	8	12	.300	.187	.107	.075	.182
Cincinnati	1991	361	81	12	2	6	0	45	4	5	4	5	20	50	.264	.123	.067	.052	.119
Cincinnati	1992	387	65	16	2	8	0	55	11	7	4	5	21	51	.226	.109	.057	.053	.110

Gary Green, 30

Bats Right   62L   67R   46G   42F   346ML

L= .052G .051L .049F (.027/.032) .059 .067G .066R .064F = R

		ATBATS	1B	2B	3B	HR	HBP	BB	GDP	SB	CS	ROE	XB	RUNS	EOB%	RL#	SET-UP	DR-IN	RPA
Texas	1990	88	16	3	0	0	0	6	2	1	1	1	3	6	.183	.064	.030	.034	.064
Texas	1991	20	2	1	0	0	0	1	0	0	0	0	0	1	.148	.046	.019	.028	.047
Cincinnati	1992	12	3	1	0	0	0	0	0	0	0	1	3	2	.318	.170	.103	.068	.171

Willie Greene, 21

Bats Left   31L   73R   49G   19F   406ML

L= ....G ....L ....F (.057/.058) .115 .136G .139R ....F = R

		ATBATS	1B	2B	3B	HR	HBP	BB	GDP	SB	CS	ROE	XB	RUNS	EOB%	RL#	SET-UP	DR-IN	RPA
Cincinnati	1992	93	16	5	2	2	0	10	1	0	3	0	9	13	.205	.118	.059	.060	.119

CINCINNATI REDS

Roberto Kelly, 28

Bats Right   587L   1286R   540G   429F

L= .129G .137L .148F | (.057/.061) .118 | .102G .110R .121F = R

		ATBATS	1B	2B	3B	HR	HBP	BB	GDP	SB	CS	ROE	XB	RUNS	EOB%	RL#	SET-UP	DR-IN	RPA
Yankees	1990	641	132	32	4	15	4	33	7	42	20	5	66	85	.195	.119	.059	.063	.122
Yankees	1991	486	86	22	2	20	5	43	14	32	9	9	39	72	.200	.129	.063	.066	.129
Yankees	1992	580	115	31	2	10	4	37	19	28	6	7	50	71	.199	.109	.053	.056	.109

Barry Larkin, 28

Bats Right   623L   1191R   633G   382F

L= .181G .187L .196F | (.083/.068) .151 | .126G .132R .141F = R

		ATBATS	1B	2B	3B	HR	HBP	BB	GDP	SB	CS	ROE	XB	RUNS	EOB%	RL#	SET-UP	DR-IN	RPA
Cincinnati	1990	614	147	25	6	7	7	46	14	30	5	8	63	85	.247	.129	.068	.058	.126
Cincinnati	1991	464	89	27	4	20	3	54	7	24	6	5	46	84	.249	.160	.084	.070	.154
Cincinnati	1992	533	112	32	6	12	4	55	13	15	4	10	41	92	.258	.146	.082	.066	.148

Dave Martinez, 28

Bats Left   258L   1025R   437G   288F

L= .095G .100L .108F | (.061/.057) .118 | .117G .122R .130F = R

		ATBATS	1B	2B	3B	HR	HBP	BB	GDP	SB	CS	ROE	XB	RUNS	EOB%	RL#	SET-UP	DR-IN	RPA
Montreal	1990	391	80	13	5	11	1	22	8	13	11	7	39	51	.184	.117	.056	.064	.120
Montreal	1991	396	87	18	5	7	3	17	3	16	11	10	27	56	.221	.124	.068	.063	.131
Cincinnati	1992	393	72	20	5	3	0	38	6	12	10	5	34	47	.217	.103	.053	.051	.104

Kevin Mitchell, 30

Bats Right   421L   978R   395G   329F

L= .206G .191L .172F | (.079/.075) .154 | .153G .138R .119F = R

		ATBATS	1B	2B	3B	HR	HBP	BB	GDP	SB	CS	ROE	XB	RUNS	EOB%	RL#	SET-UP	DR-IN	RPA
San Francisco	1990	524	91	24	2	35	2	49	8	4	7	7	34	95	.201	.159	.079	.081	.160
San Francisco	1991	371	54	13	1	27	5	35	6	2	3	13	18	74	.205	.152	.084	.085	.169
Seattle	1992	360	70	24	0	9	3	31	4	0	2	4	26	56	.242	.135	.074	.063	.137

Hal Morris, 27

Bats Left   354L   953R   435G   307F

L= .064G .074L .088F | (.067/.059) .126 | .135G .145R .159F = R

		ATBATS	1B	2B	3B	HR	HBP	BB	GDP	SB	CS	ROE	XB	RUNS	EOB%	RL#	SET-UP	DR-IN	RPA
Cincinnati	1990	309	73	22	3	7	1	17	12	9	3	2	33	45	.215	.137	.068	.066	.134
Cincinnati	1991	478	104	33	1	14	1	39	4	10	4	3	40	76	.250	.148	.077	.065	.142
Cincinnati	1992	395	77	21	3	6	2	37	12	6	7	4	20	49	.211	.105	.054	.053	.107

Joe Oliver, 27

Bats Right   534L   670R   457G   235F

L= .110G .107L .103F | (.037/.051) .088 | .076G .073R .067F = R

		ATBATS	1B	2B	3B	HR	HBP	BB	GDP	SB	CS	ROE	XB	RUNS	EOB%	RL#	SET-UP	DR-IN	RPA
Cincinnati	1990	364	53	23	0	8	2	22	6	1	2	2	26	36	.176	.095	.043	.050	.093
Cincinnati	1991	269	36	11	0	11	0	13	14	0	0	2	2	22	.103	.074	.024	.047	.071
Cincinnati	1992	485	95	25	1	10	1	16	12	2	3	3	22	52	.171	.097	.044	.054	.098

Jeff Reed, 30

Bats Left   64L   457R   151G   142F

L= .133G .148L .164F | (.046/.045) .091 | .068G .083R .099F = R

		ATBATS	1B	2B	3B	HR	HBP	BB	GDP	SB	CS	ROE	XB	RUNS	EOB%	RL#	SET-UP	DR-IN	RPA
Cincinnati	1990	175	32	8	1	3	0	19	4	0	1	4	9	22	.233	.113	.058	.052	.110
Cincinnati	1991	270	52	15	2	3	1	20	6	0	1	2	13	29	.214	.098	.049	.047	.096
Cincinnati	1992	25	4	0	0	0	0	0	1	0	0	1	2	1	.109	.038	.013	.025	.038

Bip Roberts, 29

Bats Both   574L   1120R   618G   342F

L= .120G .114L .103F | (.073/.059) .132 | .147G .141R .130F = R

		ATBATS	1B	2B	3B	HR	HBP	BB	GDP	SB	CS	ROE	XB	RUNS	EOB%	RL#	SET-UP	DR-IN	RPA
San Diego	1990	556	124	36	3	9	6	54	8	46	12	14	82	96	.275	.153	.087	.066	.153
San Diego	1991	424	100	13	3	3	4	37	6	26	11	8	35	55	.245	.112	.062	.052	.114
Cincinnati	1992	532	128	34	6	4	2	58	7	44	20	7	74	90	.269	.145	.082	.064	.146

CINCINNATI REDS

Chris Sabo, 30

Bats Right   625L   1036R   599G   327F

L= .152G .153L .154F   (.060/.065) .125   .107G   .108R   .109F = R

		ATBATS	1B	2B	3B	HR	HBP	BB	GDP	SB	CS	ROE	XB	RUNS	EOB%	RL#	SET-UP	DR-IN	RPA
Cincinnati	1990	567	88	38	2	25	4	54	8	25	13	8	63	89	.208	.145	.070	.071	.141
Cincinnati	1991	582	111	35	3	26	6	41	13	19	9	6	49	90	.204	.140	.067	.068	.135
Cincinnati	1992	344	50	19	3	12	1	29	12	4	5	5	21	43	.169	.108	.049	.060	.109

Reggie Sanders, 25

Bats Right   214L   268R   151G   108F   349ML

L= .178G .167L .152F   (.073/.066) .139   .127G   .116R   .101F = R

		ATBATS	1B	2B	3B	HR	HBP	BB	GDP	SB	CS	ROE	XB	RUNS	EOB%	RL#	SET-UP	DR-IN	RPA
Cincinnati	1991	40	7	0	0	1	0	0	1	1	2	1	5	2	.066	.054	.013	.040	.053
Cincinnati	1992	385	60	26	6	12	4	46	6	16	7	3	40	66	.233	.143	.076	.069	.145

PITCHERS

Bobby Ayala, 23

Throws: Groundball type, righty

(..../....) .141   67L   52R   1094ML

		OUTS	RO	1B	2B	3B	HR	HBP	BB	GDP	SB	CS	PO	WP	BK	RUNS	EOB%	RL#	RPA
Cincinnati	1992	87	0	22	10	0	1	1	11	4	2	3	1	0	0	12	.147	.087	.092

Scott Bankhead, 29

Throws: Flyball type, moderate reverse righty

(.105/.121) .113   288L   320R

		OUTS	RO	1B	2B	3B	HR	HBP	BB	GDP	SB	CS	PO	WP	BK	RUNS	EOB%	RL#	RPA
Seattle	1990	39	0	11	4	1	2	0	7	0	3	1	0	1	0	11	.247	.175	.172
Seattle	1991	182	54	48	16	1	8	2	19	5	8	0	0	0	0	35	.198	.131	.127
Cincinnati	1992	212	212	39	10	4	4	3	24	3	5	0	0	6	0	30	.194	.094	.100

Tim Belcher, 31

Throws: Neutral type, extreme righty

(.112/.066) .093   1367L   1001R

		OUTS	RO	1B	2B	3B	HR	HBP	BB	GDP	SB	CS	PO	WP	BK	RUNS	EOB%	RL#	RPA
Los Angeles	1990	459	0	95	19	5	17	2	48	11	11	7	2	6	1	62	.139	.096	.099
Los Angeles	1991	628	0	150	26	3	10	2	72	15	17	10	0	7	0	77	.170	.086	.087
Cincinnati	1992	683	3	134	42	8	17	3	78	9	6	11	1	3	1	95	.170	.093	.098

Tom Bolton, 30

Throws: Goundball type, moderate to severe lefty

(.101/.133) .126   283L   996R

		OUTS	RO	1B	2B	3B	HR	HBP	BB	GDP	SB	CS	PO	WP	BK	RUNS	EOB%	RL#	RPA
Boston	1990	359	39	85	19	1	6	3	44	16	7	5	0	1	1	40	.155	.085	.080
Boston	1991	330	49	94	22	4	16	1	49	18	5	2	0	3	0	62	.176	.130	.124
Boston	1992	87	74	25	8	1	0	2	13	3	4	0	0	2	1	15	.251	.119	.115
Cincinnati	1992	139	16	38	4	1	9	2	21	5	1	1	0	3	1	30	.181	.131	.139

Keith Brown, 28

Throws: Neutral type, extreme righty

(.143/.098) .121   68L   64R   905ML

		OUTS	RO	1B	2B	3B	HR	HBP	BB	GDP	SB	CS	PO	WP	BK	RUNS	EOB%	RL#	RPA
Cincinnati	1990	34	34	10	0	0	2	0	3	2	0	2	0	0	0	3	.027	.072	.072
Cincinnati	1991	36	36	11	3	1	0	0	5	0	3	2	0	1	0	6	.218	.111	.102
Cincinnati	1992	24	0	5	3	0	2	0	5	2	0	0	0	0	0	6	.155	.142	.150

Tom Browning, 32

Throws: Flyball type, neutral lefty

(.107/.108) .108   496L   1733R

		OUTS	RO	1B	2B	3B	HR	HBP	BB	GDP	SB	CS	PO	WP	BK	RUNS	EOB%	RL#	RPA
Cincinnati	1990	683	0	161	44	6	24	5	39	6	12	10	1	5	1	101	.157	.104	.107
Cincinnati	1991	691	0	164	40	5	32	4	52	13	21	6	1	3	1	104	.155	.109	.103
Cincinnati	1992	261	0	67	28	7	6	2	21	10	11	1	2	3	1	47	.174	.115	.121

Greg Cadaret, 30

Throws: Neutral type, moderate to severe lefty

(.080/.114 .106   356L   1078R

		OUTS	RO	1B	2B	3B	HR	HBP	BB	GDP	SB	CS	PO	WP	BK	RUNS	EOB%	RL#	RPA
N.Y. Yankees	1990	364	280	80	27	5	8	1	59	10	6	17	0	14	0	50	.159	.098	.094
N.Y. Yankees	1991	365	275	77	21	4	8	2	53	14	11	8	0	3	1	44	.157	.090	.085
N.Y. Yankees	1992	311	116	73	17	2	12	2	67	9	19	7	0	5	1	61	.211	.127	.128

CINCINNATI REDS

Rob Dibble, 28

Throws: Neutral type, neutral righty

(.083/.082) .083   524L   439R

		OUTS	RO	1B	2B	3B	HR	HBP	BB	GDP	SB	CS	PO	WP	BK	RUNS	EOB%	RL#	RPA
Cincinnati	1990	294	294	45	13	1	3	1	31	8	20	3	0	3	1	26	.139	.067	.068
Cincinnati	1991	247	247	50	9	3	5	0	23	1	16	5	0	5	0	28	.163	.086	.082
Cincinnati	1992	211	211	38	5	2	3	2	29	3	8	2	1	6	0	24	.177	.079	.083

Steve Foster, 26

Throws: Neutral type, moderate to severe righty

(.125/.101) .112   119L   130R   513ML

		OUTS	RO	1B	2B	3B	HR	HBP	BB	GDP	SB	CS	PO	WP	BK	RUNS	EOB%	RL#	RPA
Cincinnati	1991	42	42	5	1	0	1	0	4	1	0	0	0	0	0	3	.111	.055	.051
Cincinnati	1992	150	140	37	8	3	4	0	12	4	1	1	0	1	0	22	.161	.098	.103

Chris Hammond, 26

Throws: Groundball type, moderate reverse lefty

(.105/.094) .097   249L   808R

		OUTS	RO	1B	2B	3B	HR	HBP	BB	GDP	SB	CS	PO	WP	BK	RUNS	EOB%	RL#	RPA
Cincinnati	1990	34	0	8	3	0	2	0	11	1	1	1	0	1	3	10	.256	.173	.175
Cincinnati	1991	299	12	69	17	2	4	2	45	13	8	3	1	3	0	36	.175	.087	.083
Cincinnati	1992	442	9	108	20	8	13	3	49	11	7	4	4	6	0	69	.166	.100	.106

Dwayne Henry, 30

Throws: Flyball type, extreme righty

(.120/.078) .099   384L   386R

		OUTS	RO	1B	2B	3B	HR	HBP	BB	GDP	SB	CS	PO	WP	BK	RUNS	EOB%	RL#	RPA
Atlanta	1990	115	115	28	9	1	3	0	25	2	4	4	0	2	1	21	.222	.124	.117
Houston	1991	203	203	33	10	1	7	2	32	3	7	3	1	5	0	31	.174	.094	.104
Cincinnati	1992	251	251	37	14	4	4	1	38	3	6	2	0	12	0	34	.194	.091	.095

Milt Hill, 27

Throws: Neutral type, extreme reverse righty

(.062/.118) .091   94L   104R   561ML

		OUTS	RO	1B	2B	3B	HR	HBP	BB	GDP	SB	CS	PO	WP	BK	RUNS	EOB%	RL#	RPA
Cincinnati	1991	100	100	26	8	1	1	0	6	4	4	4	0	1	0	9	.108	.073	.067
Cincinnati	1992	60	60	10	3	1	1	1	3	1	1	0	0	0	0	6	.145	.074	.078

Tim Pugh, 25

Throws: Neutral type, moderate righty

(.121/.102) .112   91L   85R   1480ML

		OUTS	RO	1B	2B	3B	HR	HBP	BB	GDP	SB	CS	PO	WP	BK	RUNS	EOB%	RL#	RPA
Cincinnati	1992	136	0	32	11	2	2	1	10	5	1	1	1	0	0	17	.147	.085	.090

Jose Rijo, 27

Throws: Groundball type, exteme righty

(.096/.045) .075   1382L   999R

		OUTS	RO	1B	2B	3B	HR	HBP	BB	GDP	SB	CS	PO	WP	BK	RUNS	EOB%	RL#	RPA
Cincinnati	1990	591	0	103	34	4	10	2	77	10	19	4	6	2	5	70	.169	.086	.087
Cincinnati	1991	613	0	120	33	4	8	3	51	15	16	3	4	2	4	58	.146	.073	.069
Cincinnati	1992	633	0	140	26	4	15	3	43	16	17	12	2	2	1	68	.120	.076	.080

Scott Ruskin, 29

Throws: Neutral type, moderate reverse lefty

(.124/.113) .117   301L   501R

		OUTS	RO	1B	2B	3B	HR	HBP	BB	GDP	SB	CS	PO	WP	BK	RUNS	EOB%	RL#	RPA
Pittsburgh	1990	143	143	39	8	1	2	2	25	5	14	1	0	3	1	27	.231	.118	.126
Montreal	1990	83	83	20	3	0	2	0	7	2	6	1	0	0	0	11	.151	.087	.093
Montreal	1991	191	191	36	15	2	4	3	28	1	7	3	0	5	0	34	.215	.109	.119
Cincinnati	1992	161	161	40	10	0	6	1	16	2	5	3	0	1	0	27	.175	.108	.114

Greg Swindell, 27

Throws: Flyball type, moderate lefty

(.082/.091) .089   455L   2193R

		OUTS	RO	1B	2B	3B	HR	HBP	BB	GDP	SB	CS	PO	WP	BK	RUNS	EOB%	RL#	RPA
Cleveland	1990	644	0	169	41	8	27	1	45	14	3	12	0	3	2	101	.148	.110	.111
Cleveland	1991	714	0	168	48	4	21	3	30	15	9	11	2	3	1	86	.128	.089	.089
Cincinnati	1992	641	3	156	37	3	14	2	37	15	17	9	1	3	2	79	.142	.085	.089

Cincinnati Reds AAA & AA Minor League Ratings

AAA (NASHVILLE)	AGE	BATS	POSITION	CPA	RUNS	SET-UP	DRIVE-IN	RPA
Troy Afenir	29	R	C\1B\OF	143	15.4	.050	.057	.107
Geronimo Berroa	27	R	OF	511	64.6	.062	.065	.127
Jeff Branson	25	L	SS\3B\2B	133	16.0	.060	.060	.120
Mickey Brantley	31	R	OF	436	44.3	.053	.049	.102
Jacob Brumfield	27	R	OF	237	26.1	.057	.053	.110
Scott Coolbaugh	26	R	3B	454	43.3	.046	.049	.095
Ruben Escalera	28	L	OF	309	24.8	.040	.040	.080
Gary Green	30	R	SS	346	19.1	.024	.031	.055
Mark Howie	30	R	2B\3B\SS	381	25.3	.029	.037	.066
Russ Morman	30	R	1B	427	52.9	.064	.060	.124
Jeff Small	27	R	2B	550	41.9	.034	.042	.076
Dwight Taylor	32	L	OF	296	20.7	.032	.038	.070
Todd Trafton	28	R	OF\1B	434	51.3	.062	.056	.118
Dan Wilson	23	R	C	406	30.5	.036	.039	.075
Rick Wrona	29	R	C\OF	126	9.8	.034	.043	.077

AA (CHATTANOOGA)	AGE	BATS	POSITION	CPA	RUNS	SET-UP	DRIVE-IN	RPA
Benny Colvard	26	R	OF	403	37.3	.042	.051	.093
Tim Costo	23	R	1B	493	56.1	.052	.062	.114
Darren Cox	25	R	C	358	24.8	.032	.036	.068
Kiki Diaz	28	R	SS	606	46.7	.042	.035	.077
Chris Estep	26	R	OF	191	16.4	.047	.039	.086
Kevin Garner	27	L	DH	271	36.5	.067	.068	.135
Willie Greene	21	L	3B	406	45.8	.056	.057	.113
Ty Griffin	25	B	2B	420	38.0	.048	.042	.090
Cesar Hernandez	26	R	OF	358	30.3	.041	.044	.085
Frank Kremblas	26	R	2B\1B	303	18.8	.029	.033	.062
Brian Lane	23	R	3B	238	21.7	.044	.047	.091
Scott Pose	25	L	OF	601	63.3	.058	.047	.105
Glenn Sutko	24	R	C	217	18.0	.035	.048	.083

AAA Pitchers	Age	Throws	Outs	RPA	AA Pitchers	Age	Throws	Outs	RPA
Keith Brown	28	R	449	.115	Mike Anderson	26	R	515	.114
Bob Buchanan	31	L	147	.148	Bobby Ayala	23	R	488	.137
Chris Bushing	25	R	242	.152	Dan Freed	26	R	170	.135
Brian Fisher	30	R	167	.125	Matt Grott	25	L	121	.145
Steve Foster	26	R	151	.130	Rodney Imes	26	R	267	.154
Milt Hill	27	R	223	.095	Rusty Kilgo	26	L	95	.098
Trevor Hoffman	25	R	285	.114	Larry Luebbers	23	R	262	.124
Tony Menendez	27	R	320	.124	David Lynch	27	L	157	.096
Gino Minutelli	28	L	474	.153	Johnny Ray	25	R	171	.121
Ross Powell	24	L	452	.108	Scott Robinson	24	R	249	.121
Tim Pugh	25	R	509	.119	John Roper	21	R	362	.145
Mo Sanford	26	R	446	.148	Jason Satre	22	R	174	.143
Jose Segura	29	R	95	.123	Jerry Spradlin	25	R	196	.071
Scott Service	25	R	285	.090	Kevin Tatar	24	R	164	.111
Joey Vierra	26	L	263	.103					

HOUSTON ASTROS

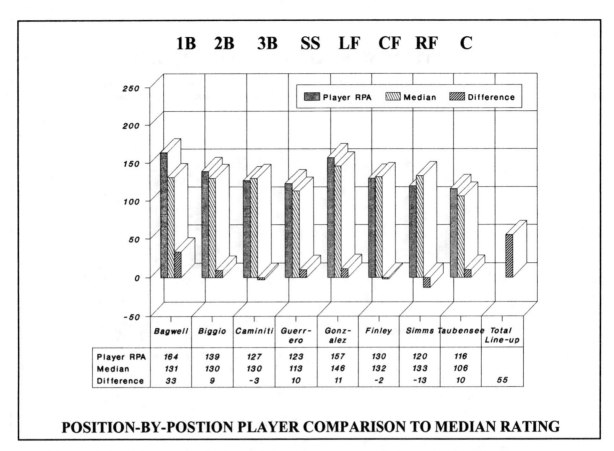

	1B	2B	3B	SS	LF	CF	RF	C
	Bagwell	Biggio	Caminiti	Guerr-ero	Gonz-alez	Finley	Simms	Taubensee	Total Line-up
Player RPA	164	139	127	123	157	130	120	116	
Median	131	130	130	113	146	132	133	106	
Difference	33	9	-3	10	11	-2	-13	10	55

POSITION-BY-POSTION PLAYER COMPARISON TO MEDIAN RATING

DEFENSIVE TEAM AND STADIUM DATA FOR THE LAST 3 YEARS:

TEAM DEFENSE BY POSITION:

		1990	1991	1992	POSITION-BY-POSITION STADIUM CHARACTERISTICS:
1B:	Home	+2.6	+3.1	+2.0	Average
	Away	+0.1	-2.8	+2.5	
2B:	Home	+3.6	-0.4	+3.3	Hard to play
	Away	-2.5	-6.7	-6.6	
3B:	Home	+3.6	+3.1	+4.9	Average
	Away	-1.2	+3.8	-0.9	
SS:	Home	-7.1	+0.6	+0.1	Average (to slightly hard)
	Away	-10.4	-6.2	-5.4	
LF:	Home	+0.6	+12.1	+9.6	Easy to play
	Away	+2.0	-1.7	0.0	
CF:	Home	+3.7	-4.0	+7.8	Slightly hard to play
	Away	-3.9	-0.8	-4.5	
RF:	Home	+1.6	+0.6	-9.8	Average
	Away	+3.2	-2.6	-10.3	
Total Home:		+8.6	+15.1	+17.9	
Total Away:		-12.7	-17.0	-25.3	

Comments: What a huge home field defensive advantage! The Astros have had the home field advantage on defense for each of the 4 years I've done this study. The past 3 yrs. they have *averaged* over 32 runs per season advantage on defense. That's almost 4/10 of a run per game! Eric Anthony had better improve his defense. He's killing this team.

HOUSTON ASTROS

PITCHING STAFF - THE EIGHT BEST

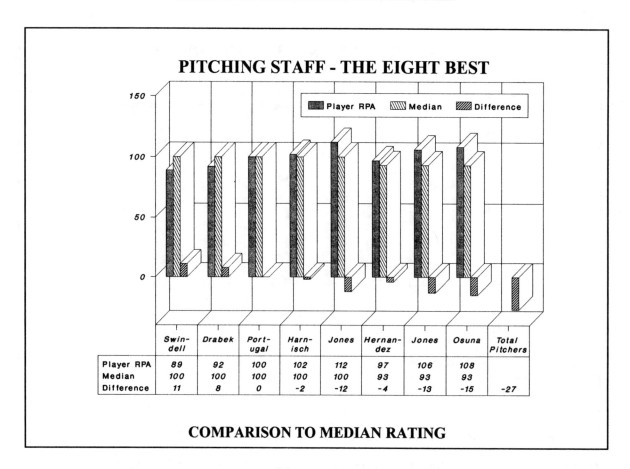

	Swin-dell	Drabek	Port-ugal	Harn-isch	Jones	Hernan-dez	Jones	Osuna	Total Pitchers
Player RPA	89	92	100	102	112	97	106	108	
Median	100	100	100	100	100	93	93	93	
Difference	11	8	0	-2	-12	-4	-13	-15	-27

COMPARISON TO MEDIAN RATING

SUGGESTED LINE-UPS (with set-up RPA & drive-in RPA ratings):

Vs: Left-handed Groundball
2B:	C. Biggio	81-61
3B:	C. Donnels	73-63
1B:	J. Bagwell	101-83
RF:	M. Simms	67-63
SS:	C. Candaele	62-62
CF:	S. Finley	58-52
C:	E. Taubensee	48-51
LF:	L. Gonzalez	40-46
Pitcher		

Vs: Neutral Lefty Pitchers
2B:	C. Biggio	82-62
1B:	J. Bagwell	103-85
CF:	S. Finley	58-52
RF:	M. Simms	67-63
C:	E. Taubensee	57-60
SS:	J. Guerrero	60-63
3B:	K. Caminiti	61-67
LF:	L. Gonzalez	57-66
Pitcher		

Vs: Left-handed Flyball
2B:	C. Biggio	83-63
RF:	M. Simms	67-63
1B:	J. Bagwell	106-88
C:	E. Taubensee	71-75
3B:	K. Caminiti	77-84
LF:	L. Gonzalez	82-93
SS:	A. Cedeno	66-90
CF:	S. Finley	57-52
Pitcher		

Vs: Right-handed Groundball
2B:	C. Biggio	83-63
1B:	J. Bagwell	79-64
3B:	C. Donnels	60-53
CF:	S. Finley	77-69
SS:	J. Guerrero	60-63
C:	E. Taubensee	48-51
RF:	K. Rhodes	45-44
LF:	L. Gonzalez	44-50
Pitcher		

Vs: Neutral Righty Pitchers
2B:	C. Biggio	84-64
1B:	J. Bagwell	81-66
CF:	S. Finley	77-69
SS:	J. Guerrero	60-63
C:	E. Taubensee	57-60
LF:	L. Gonzalez	60-69
RF:	K. Rhodes	56-55
3B:	K. Caminiti	51-56
Pitcher		

Vs: Right-handed Flyball
2B:	C. Biggio	85-65
1B:	J. Bagwell	84-69
CF:	S. Finley	78-69
RF:	K. Rhodes	72-71
C:	E. Taubensee	71-75
LF:	L. Gonzalez	86-97
SS:	A. Cedeno	80-108
3B:	K. Caminiti	67-73
Pitcher		

Comments: This is a relatively solid offense. It is vulnerable, however, to groundball-type pitchers, particularly righties. Juan Guerrero can hit, but I'm not sure he has enough range at shortstop. This team needs to find a solid right fielder. Once this team solves its problems at shortstop and right field it'll be ready to take the next step forward (to contention).

HOUSTON ASTROS

Over this winter I suspected that the Astros were fooling themselves into believing they were contenders when they signed Doug Drabek and Greg Swindell and when I checked my data my suspicions were fully confirmed.

Even with the addition of excellent pitchers like Drabek and Swindell, the Astros pitching staff figures to be one of the worst in the National League. Only the Cardinals and the woeful Rockies staffs will be worse in '93.

The Astros defense, even though they have good players at certain positions, is also nothing to write home about while the offense will be about average in strength. There's no single area of strength on this team. The Astros are still in the midst of their rebuilding mode. They'll just have to hope that their young kids continue to develop so that they can contend in the near future.

I really feel sorry for Chris Donnels. He belongs in the Major Leagues and could be starting for a number of teams. When the Florida Marlins took him in the Expansion draft I thought he finally got his big break, but then the Marlins signed Donnels' nemesis, Dave Magadan, who again blocked his route to a Major League job. Now he's with the Astros and sitting behind Ken Caminiti. Now it doesn't look like he'll get that starting job any time soon. It was a smart move by the Astros to pick him up. He'll give them quality depth at third base.

The signing of Jim Lindeman should also help the Astros. He's got a good bat off the bench. The signing of Jose Uribe has only very marginal value. The signing's of Kevin Bass, Chris James and Jack Daugherty have no value whatsoever. Why the Astros even bothered with these washed-up players is beyond me. They should be concentrating on developing their young players instead.

I hope that all the talk about how the Astros got ripped-off in the Kenny Lofton for Eddie Taubensee trade is given as little credence as possible. If anything, despite the fact that Lofton is a quality player, I think the Astros came out at least even in the deal, if not the winners. Taubensee can play! He's not spectacular, but when you compare him to the other catchers in this league he comes out smelling of roses and that's how you really measure value. Without a quality catcher like Taubensee filling the vacated catcher position when Biggio moved to second base, it would have made the Biggio switch to second base totally counter productive. As it stands, even with the presence of Taubensee, I'm still not sure that the switch was a wise move.

Eric Anthony is a defensive disaster in right field. Karl Rhodes and Mike Simms appear to be at least adequate hitters. Shouldn't they be given a shot at the right field job? They couldn't be worse than Anthony!

There were any number of players in the Astros high minors that I would have protected in the Expansion draft over Eric Anthony. But why if you're building for the future did the Astros also protect 35 year old Doug Jones? These were two wasted spots on the 15 man protected list that could have been used to protect young talent.

Houston's Projected record for 1993: 80--82, good for 5th place in the division.

HOUSTON ASTROS

Eric Anthony, 25

Bats Left   298L   584R   107G   139F   359ML

L= .092G .098L .106F (.050/.060) .110 .110G .116R .124F = R

		ATBATS	1B	2B	3B	HR	HBP	BB	GDP	SB	CS	ROE	XB	RUNS	EOB%	RL#	SET-UP	DR-IN	RPA
Houston	1990	239	28	8	0	10	2	26	4	5	0	4	12	33	.190	.105	.055	.061	.116
Houston	1991	118	11	6	0	1	0	11	2	1	0	0	6	8	.159	.057	.027	.035	.062
Houston	1992	440	70	15	1	19	1	33	7	5	4	7	20	65	.179	.112	.058	.067	.125

Jeff Bagwell, 24

Bats Right   489L   846R   486G   298F

L= .173G .177L .183F (.083/.068) .151 .132G .136R .142F = R

		ATBATS	1B	2B	3B	HR	HBP	BB	GDP	SB	CS	ROE	XB	RUNS	EOB%	RL#	SET-UP	DR-IN	RPA
Houston	1991	554	118	26	4	15	13	70	12	7	4	8	48	106	.273	.140	.088	.067	.155
Houston	1992	586	102	34	6	18	12	71	17	10	6	7	46	108	.238	.130	.078	.069	.147

Craig Biggio, 27

Bats Right   713L   1218R   662G   421F

L= .137G .139L .141F (.081/.061) .142 .141G .143R .145F = R

		ATBATS	1B	2B	3B	HR	HBP	BB	GDP	SB	CS	ROE	XB	RUNS	EOB%	RL#	SET-UP	DR-IN	RPA
Houston	1990	555	123	24	2	4	3	52	11	25	15	7	36	73	.230	.100	.058	.053	.111
Houston	1991	546	130	23	4	4	2	50	2	19	6	13	56	89	.281	.127	.081	.060	.141
Houston	1992	613	129	32	3	6	7	85	5	38	16	8	65	109	.277	.126	.081	.061	.142

Ken Caminiti, 29

Bats Both   743L   1041R   616G   359F

L= .106G .126L .159F (.054/.060) .114 .085G .105R .138F = R

		ATBATS	1B	2B	3B	HR	HBP	BB	GDP	SB	CS	ROE	XB	RUNS	EOB%	RL#	SET-UP	DR-IN	RPA
Houston	1990	541	105	20	2	4	0	41	15	9	4	5	46	57	.195	.081	.044	.047	.091
Houston	1991	574	99	30	3	13	5	39	18	4	5	4	33	69	.180	.093	.048	.055	.103
Houston	1992	506	103	31	2	13	1	31	14	10	4	1	43	76	.196	.114	.062	.066	.128

Casey Candaele, 31

Bats Both   458L   683R   396G   260F

L= .126G .120L .112F (.050/.049) .099 .091G .085R .077F = R

		ATBATS	1B	2B	3B	HR	HBP	BB	GDP	SB	CS	ROE	XB	RUNS	EOB%	RL#	SET-UP	DR-IN	RPA
Houston	1990	262	58	8	6	3	1	26	4	7	6	4	25	40	.242	.119	.070	.061	.131
Houston	1991	461	90	20	7	4	0	33	5	9	3	5	25	58	.223	.100	.058	.053	.111
Houston	1992	320	54	12	1	1	3	21	5	7	1	4	12	31	.199	.074	.040	.043	.083

Andujar Cedeno, 23

Bats Right   155L   352R   196G   120F   687ML

L= .028G .072L .144F (.040/.054) .094 .060G .104R .176F = R

		ATBATS	1B	2B	3B	HR	HBP	BB	GDP	SB	CS	ROE	XB	RUNS	EOB%	RL#	SET-UP	DR-IN	RPA
Houston	1990	8	0	0	0	0	0	0	0	0	0	0	0	0	.000	.000	.000	.000	.000
Houston	1991	251	37	13	2	9	1	8	3	4	3	4	18	31	.156	.101	.048	.065	.113
Houston	1992	220	21	13	2	2	3	12	1	2	0	0	12	20	.163	.066	.034	.042	.076

Steve Finley, 27

Bats Left   568L   1252R   595G   404F

L= .105G .105L .104F (.068/.062) .130 .141G .141R .140F = R

		ATBATS	1B	2B	3B	HR	HBP	BB	GDP	SB	CS	ROE	XB	RUNS	EOB%	RL#	SET-UP	DR-IN	RPA
Baltimore	1990	464	96	16	4	3	2	29	8	22	12	7	41	48	.200	.094	.047	.048	.095
Houston	1991	596	124	28	10	8	2	37	8	34	18	9	57	83	.211	.110	.062	.060	.122
Houston	1992	607	130	29	13	5	3	52	10	44	10	5	60	99	.241	.122	.073	.064	.137

Luis Gonzalez, 25

Bats Left   229L   735R   326G   224F   50ML

L= .077G .114L .168F (.056/.064) .120 .085G .122R .176F = R

		ATBATS	1B	2B	3B	HR	HBP	BB	GDP	SB	CS	ROE	XB	RUNS	EOB%	RL#	SET-UP	DR-IN	RPA
Houston	1990	21	2	2	0	0	0	1	0	0	0	0	1	2	.173	.065	.031	.038	.069
Houston	1991	473	70	28	9	13	8	36	9	10	7	4	25	67	.196	.111	.059	.063	.122
Houston	1992	387	62	19	3	10	2	21	6	7	8	6	24	49	.172	.096	.050	.059	.109

HOUSTON ASTROS

Juan Guerrero, 25

Bats Right   67L   67R   41G   31F   542ML

L= ....G   .108L   ....F   (.056/.058) .114   ....G   .121R   ....F = R

		ATBATS	1B	2B	3B	HR	HBP	BB	GDP	SB	CS	ROE	XB	RUNS	EOB%	RL#	SET-UP	DR-IN	RPA
Houston	1992	125	18	4	2	1	1	8	0	1	0	1	6	13	.197	.083	.044	.046	.090

Pete Incaviglia, 28

Bats Right   492L   865R   472G   299F

L= .114G .128L .151F   (.056/.059) .115   .094G   .108R   .131F = R

		ATBATS	1B	2B	3B	HR	HBP	BB	GDP	SB	CS	ROE	XB	RUNS	EOB%	RL#	SET-UP	DR-IN	RPA
Texas	1990	529	72	27	0	24	9	40	18	3	5	6	29	65	.160	.105	.046	.060	.106
Detroit	1991	337	48	12	1	11	1	36	6	1	3	5	10	38	.193	.103	.048	.053	.101
Houston	1992	349	59	22	1	11	3	23	6	2	3	3	20	53	.197	.114	.063	.066	.129

Chris Jones, 27

Bats Right   99L   65R   50G   43F   751ML

L= .060G .076L .095F   (.042/.048) .090   .096G   .112R   .131F = R

		ATBATS	1B	2B	3B	HR	HBP	BB	GDP	SB	CS	ROE	XB	RUNS	EOB%	RL#	SET-UP	DR-IN	RPA
Cincinnati	1991	89	21	1	2	2	0	2	2	2	1	1	4	10	.175	.106	.046	.056	.102
Houston	1992	63	8	2	1	1	0	7	1	3	0	1	3	8	.206	.091	.051	.052	.103

Rafael Ramirez, 33

Bats Right   410L   496R   300G   205F

L= .100G .092L .080F   (.039/.044) .083   .083G   .075R   .063F = R

		ATBATS	1B	2B	3B	HR	HBP	BB	GDP	SB	CS	ROE	XB	RUNS	EOB%	RL#	SET-UP	DR-IN	RPA
Houston	1990	445	92	19	3	2	1	15	9	10	5	11	29	47	.199	.086	.047	.048	.095
Houston	1991	233	44	10	0	1	0	12	3	3	3	0	10	20	.178	.071	.035	.042	.077
Houston	1992	176	37	6	0	1	1	6	5	0	0	5	14	18	.198	.081	.044	.047	.091

Karl Rhodes, 24

Bats left   48L   204R   77G   54F   751ML

L= .026G .048L .080F   (.045/.045) .090   .078G   .100R   .132F = R

		ATBATS	1B	2B	3B	HR	HBP	BB	GDP	SB	CS	ROE	XB	RUNS	EOB%	RL#	SET-UP	DR-IN	RPA
Houston	1990	86	13	6	1	1	0	10	1	4	1	1	9	13	.238	.112	.066	.058	.124
Houston	1991	136	24	3	1	1	1	11	3	2	2	2	7	13	.189	.072	.038	.042	.080
Houston	1992	4	0	0	0	0	0	0	0	0	0	0	0	0	.000	.000	.000	.000	.000

Ernest Riles, 32

Bats Left   39L   522R   187G   120F   237ML

L= ....G   .078L   ....F   (.046/.052) .098   .108G   .100R   .088F = R

		ATBATS	1B	2B	3B	HR	HBP	BB	GDP	SB	CS	ROE	XB	RUNS	EOB%	RL#	SET-UP	DR-IN	RPA
San Francisco	1990	155	20	2	1	8	0	23	2	0	0	1	13	23	.201	.122	.061	.062	.123
Oakland	1991	281	43	8	4	5	1	28	8	3	3	2	18	30	.179	.082	.041	.048	.089
Houston	1992	61	14	1	0	1	0	2	0	1	0	0	3	7	.198	.096	.052	.054	.106

Scott Servais, 25

Bats Right   167L   100R   81G   65F   247ML

L= .092G .079L .063F   (.038/.042) .080   .095G   .082R   .066F = R

		ATBATS	1B	2B	3B	HR	HBP	BB	GDP	SB	CS	ROE	XB	RUNS	EOB%	RL#	SET-UP	DR-IN	RPA
Houston	1991	37	3	3	0	0	0	4	0	0	1	1	0	3	.200	.062	.033	.034	.067
Houston	1992	205	40	9	0	0	5	9	7	0	0	1	9	18	.189	.068	.036	.040	.076

Mike Simms, 25

Bats Right   88L   97R   66G   38F   822ML

L= .144G .137L ....F   (.057/.054) .111   .094G   .087R   ....F = R

		ATBATS	1B	2B	3B	HR	HBP	BB	GDP	SB	CS	ROE	XB	RUNS	EOB%	RL#	SET-UP	DR-IN	RPA
Houston	1990	13	2	1	0	1	0	0	1	0	0	0	2	2	.052	.101	.021	.087	.108
Houston	1991	123	17	5	0	3	0	18	2	1	0	1	10	17	.224	.098	.057	.053	.110
Houston	1992	24	4	1	0	1	1	2	1	0	0	0	4	4	.189	.107	.058	.064	.122

Eddie Taubensee, 24

Bats Left   67L   335R   167G   100F   406ML

L= .128G .146L .175F   (.052/.054) .106   .080G   .098R   .127F = R

		ATBATS	1B	2B	3B	HR	HBP	BB	GDP	SB	CS	ROE	XB	RUNS	EOB%	RL#	SET-UP	DR-IN	RPA
Cleveland	1991	66	13	2	1	0	0	4	1	0	0	0	4	6	.199	.081	.042	.044	.086
Houston	1992	297	46	15	0	5	2	28	4	2	1	0	14	36	.202	.089	.050	.051	.101

HOUSTON ASTROS

Denny Walling, 38

Bats Left   15L   180R   74G   32F

L= ....G ....L ....F (.025/.029) .054 .064G .060R ....F = R

		ATBATS	1B	2B	3B	HR	HBP	BB	GDP	SB	CS	ROE	XB	RUNS	EOB%	RL#	SET-UP	DR-IN	RPA
St. Louis	1990	127	22	5	0	1	0	8	5	0	0	0	5	9	.156	.066	.028	.036	.064
Texas	1991	44	3	1	0	0	2	3	3	0	0	0	2	1	.093	.023	.007	.017	.024
Houston	1992	3	1	0	0	0	0	0	0	0	0	0	0	0	.237	.089	.061	.053	.114

Eric Yelding, 27

Bats Right   362L 497R 293G 141F   372ML

L= .090G .091L .092F (.032/.040) .072 .058G .059R .060F = R

		ATBATS	1B	2B	3B	HR	HBP	BB	GDP	SB	CS	ROE	XB	RUNS	EOB%	RL#	SET-UP	DR-IN	RPA
Houston	1990	511	115	9	5	1	0	38	11	64	28	6	65	54	.181	.082	.043	.048	.091
Houston	1991	276	54	11	1	1	0	10	4	11	10	0	18	22	.149	.065	.030	.042	.072
Houston	1992	8	2	0	0	0	0	0	0	0	0	0	0	1	.178	.064	.033	.039	.072

Gerald Young, 28

Bats Both   185L 249R 168G 103F   91ML

L= .092G .109L .137F (.051/.047) .098 .072G .089R .117F = R

		ATBATS	1B	2B	3B	HR	HBP	BB	GDP	SB	CS	ROE	XB	RUNS	EOB%	RL#	SET-UP	DR-IN	RPA
Houston	1990	154	21	4	1	1	0	20	3	6	3	5	12	16	.212	.076	.043	.043	.086
Houston	1991	142	26	3	1	1	0	24	3	16	5	1	21	19	.233	.095	.056	.050	.106
Houston	1992	76	12	1	1	0	0	10	2	6	2	1	14	8	.197	.075	.040	.043	.083

PITCHERS

Willie Blair, 27

Throws: Neutral type, neutral righty

(.114/.111) .112   380L 380R 719ML

		OUTS	RO	1B	2B	3B	HR	HBP	BB	GDP	SB	CS	PO	WP	BK	RUNS	EOB%	RL#	RPA
Toronto	1990	206	116	43	15	4	4	1	24	2	5	2	0	3	0	32	.201	.107	.107
Cleveland	1991	108	17	43	8	0	7	1	10	7	1	1	0	1	0	25	.166	.145	.145
Houston	1992	236	121	50	16	3	5	2	23	7	6	4	1	2	0	33	.147	.083	.095

Joe Boever, 32

Throws: Neutral type, moderate reverse righty

(.098/.106) .102   594L 630R

		OUTS	RO	1B	2B	3B	HR	HBP	BB	GDP	SB	CS	PO	WP	BK	RUNS	EOB%	RL#	RPA
Atlanta	1990	127	127	23	11	0	6	0	25	2	6	2	0	2	0	23	.207	.129	.122
Philadelphia	1990	138	138	28	9	0	0	0	14	2	6	1	0	1	2	14	.188	.077	.077
Philadelphia	1991	295	295	62	15	3	10	0	43	2	12	2	1	6	1	50	.204	.113	.114
Houston	1992	334	334	85	13	2	3	4	36	7	7	5	0	4	0	46	.185	.079	.092

Ryan Bowen, 24

Throws: Groundball type, moderate to severe righty

(.154/.122) .140   266L 210R 1005ML

		OUTS	RO	1B	2B	3B	HR	HBP	BB	GDP	SB	CS	PO	WP	BK	RUNS	EOB%	RL#	RPA
Houston	1991	215	6	56	13	0	4	3	35	5	12	1	0	8	1	42	.234	.111	.123
Houston	1992	101	6	30	9	1	8	2	27	2	5	3	1	5	0	39	.247	.173	.205

Tom Edens, 31

Throws: Groundball type, moderate reverse righty

(.091/.110) .102   331L 479R 668ML

		OUTS	RO	1B	2B	3B	HR	HBP	BB	GDP	SB	CS	PO	WP	BK	RUNS	EOB%	RL#	RPA
Milwaukee	1990	267	180	68	12	1	8	4	30	6	9	6	0	1	0	39	.170	.102	.102
Minnesota	1991	99	8	22	8	2	2	0	9	1	2	1	0	1	0	15	.189	.110	.110
Minnesota	1992	229	229	53	8	3	1	2	33	9	15	5	0	5	0	28	.168	.079	.086

Pete Harnisch, 26

Throws: Flyball type, extreme righty

(.120/.079) .103   1491L 1015R

		OUTS	RO	1B	2B	3B	HR	HBP	BB	GDP	SB	CS	PO	WP	BK	RUNS	EOB%	RL#	RPA
Baltimore	1990	566	0	133	33	6	17	1	81	11	18	10	1	2	2	93	.187	.111	.114
Houston	1991	650	0	122	28	5	14	5	80	6	27	6	0	5	2	92	.186	.088	.097
Houston	1992	620	0	119	37	8	18	5	61	8	27	6	0	4	1	103	.172	.091	.109

Butch Henry, 24

Throws: Neutral type, moderate reverse lefty

(.136/.116) .120   149L 525R 671ML

		OUTS	RO	1B	2B	3B	HR	HBP	BB	GDP	SB	CS	PO	WP	BK	RUNS	EOB%	RL#	RPA
Houston	1992	497	0	126	38	5	16	1	34	10	10	7	0	2	2	87	.162	.099	.115

HOUSTON ASTROS

Xavier Hernandez, 27

Throws: Groundball type, moderate righty

(.107/.087) .097   503L   460R   151ML

		OUTS	RO	1B	2B	3B	HR	HBP	BB	GDP	SB	CS	PO	WP	BK	RUNS	EOB%	RL#	RPA
Houston	1990	187	172	41	11	0	8	4	19	3	8	3	0	6	0	33	.172	.108	.118
Houston	1991	189	96	48	12	0	6	0	25	4	7	2	0	0	0	33	.194	.109	.117
Houston	1992	333	333	63	11	2	5	3	35	5	10	4	0	5	0	40	.163	.071	.082

Doug Jones, 35

Throws: Groundball type, moderate righty

(.107/.087) .097   529L   479R   135ML

		OUTS	RO	1B	2B	3B	HR	HBP	BB	GDP	SB	CS	PO	WP	BK	RUNS	EOB%	RL#	RPA
Cleveland	1990	253	253	46	13	2	5	2	18	13	3	1	0	2	0	22	.101	.067	.067
Cleveland	1991	190	97	55	23	2	7	0	12	5	4	0	0	1	0	38	.194	.134	.132
Houston	1992	335	335	74	14	3	5	5	12	7	5	4	0	2	1	37	.131	.066	.077

Jimmy Jones, 28

Throws: Groundball type, extreme righty

(.130/.082) .111   804L   546R

		OUTS	RO	1B	2B	3B	HR	HBP	BB	GDP	SB	CS	PO	WP	BK	RUNS	EOB%	RL#	RPA
N.Y. Yankees	1990	150	68	51	13	0	8	1	23	9	9	1	0	3	0	34	.198	.148	.143
Houston	1991	406	21	111	18	5	9	3	48	9	18	6	0	4	0	72	.193	.101	.114
Houston	1992	418	8	90	27	5	13	5	36	11	20	5	0	4	1	66	.157	.097	.108

Darryl Kile, 24

Throws: Neutrall type, moderate to severe righty

(.138/.109) .126   701L   494R   250ML

		OUTS	RO	1B	2B	3B	HR	HBP	BB	GDP	SB	CS	PO	WP	BK	RUNS	EOB%	RL#	RPA
Houston	1991	461	74	95	28	5	16	6	80	7	12	3	0	5	4	92	.220	.117	.128
Houston	1992	376	0	84	26	6	8	4	59	8	6	3	1	3	4	72	.212	.105	.121

Rob Mallicoat, 28

Throws: Neutral type, moderate to severe reverse lefty

(.125/.103) .112   81L   127R   546ML

		OUTS	RO	1B	2B	3B	HR	HBP	BB	GDP	SB	CS	PO	WP	BK	RUNS	EOB%	RL#	RPA
Houston	1991	70	70	15	5	0	2	2	12	3	1	1	0	1	0	11	.190	.103	.108
Houston	1992	71	71	16	6	2	2	5	17	2	3	1	0	2	0	20	.276	.145	.164

Rob Murphy, 32

Throws: Neutral type, extreme lefty

(.058/.139) .108   264L   436R

		OUTS	RO	1B	2B	3B	HR	HBP	BB	GDP	SB	CS	PO	WP	BK	RUNS	EOB%	RL#	RPA
Boston	1990	171	171	58	16	1	10	1	29	5	5	3	0	4	0	44	.227	.167	.158
Seattle	1991	144	144	28	12	3	4	1	15	2	5	0	0	4	0	24	.199	.113	.111
Houston	1992	167	167	43	8	3	2	0	17	3	4	1	0	4	0	27	.196	.090	.106

Al Osuna, 27

Throws: Flyball type, neutral reverse lefty

(.110/.107) .108   221L   403R

		OUTS	RO	1B	2B	3B	HR	HBP	BB	GDP	SB	CS	PO	WP	BK	RUNS	EOB%	RL#	RPA
Houston	1990	34	34	5	3	1	1	3	5	3	0	1	1	3	0	4	.084	.080	.086
Houston	1991	245	245	40	13	1	5	3	41	5	2	0	0	3	1	35	.204	.089	.097
Houston	1992	185	185	37	7	0	8	1	33	4	4	1	0	3	1	35	.196	.105	.122

Mark Portugal, 30

Throws: Neutral type, neutral reverse righty

(.097/.098) .097   1082L   780R

		OUTS	RO	1B	2B	3B	HR	HBP	BB	GDP	SB	CS	PO	WP	BK	RUNS	EOB%	RL#	RPA
Houston	1990	590	0	137	28	1	21	4	63	16	23	9	1	6	0	90	.153	.094	.104
Houston	1991	505	14	112	29	3	19	2	54	15	12	7	0	4	1	77	.151	.097	.105
Houston	1992	304	3	52	13	4	7	1	38	10	7	6	0	1	1	36	.130	.071	.083

Shane Reynolds, 24

Throws: Groundball type, righty

(..../....) .130   67L   45R   1278ML

		OUTS	RO	1B	2B	3B	HR	HBP	BB	GDP	SB	CS	PO	WP	BK	RUNS	EOB%	RL#	RPA
Houston	1992	76	15	26	11	3	2	0	5	2	6	1	0	1	1	21	.220	.153	.166

Brian Williams, 23

Throws: Neutral type, moderate to severe righty

(.133/.110) .124   270L   170R   558ML

		OUTS	RO	1B	2B	3B	HR	HBP	BB	GDP	SB	CS	PO	WP	BK	RUNS	EOB%	RL#	RPA
Houston	1991	36	0	9	0	0	2	1	4	2	1	2	0	0	0	4	.054	.073	.078
Houston	1992	289	0	64	16	2	10	0	41	9	7	3	0	2	1	49	.173	.100	.113

Houston Astros AAA & AA Minor League Ratings

AAA (TUCSON)	AGE	BATS	POSITION	CPA	RUNS	SET-UP	DRIVE-IN	RPA
Rod Booker	34	L	SS\3B	324	24.6	.039	.037	.076
Andujar Cedeno	23	R	SS	307	29.0	.044	.050	.094
Gary Cooper	28	R	3B\1B	526	54.2	.053	.050	.103
Trent Hubbard	28	R	2B	476	49.0	.057	.046	.103
Chris Jones	27	R	OF	194	23.4	.063	.058	.121
Barry Lyons	32	R	C\1B	297	24.2	.037	.044	.081
John Massarelli	26	R	OF\C	265	20.9	.039	.040	.079
Joe Mikulik	29	R	OF	351	25.6	.032	.041	.073
Andy Mota	26	R	2B\OF\3B	348	22.9	.029	.037	.066
Rick Parker	29	R	OF	357	41.9	.063	.054	.117
Karl Rhodes	24	L	OF	395	42.2	.060	.047	.107
Ernest Riles	32	L	1B\3B	237	25.8	.062	.047	.109
Mike Simms	25	R	OF\1B	482	54.9	.061	.053	.114
Scooter Tucker	26	R	C	331	28.5	.045	.041	.086

AA (JACKSON)	AGE	BATS	POSITION	CPA	RUNS	SET-UP	DRIVE-IN	RPA
Willie Ansley	23	R	OF	144	14.4	.057	.043	.100
Jeff Baldwin	27	L	OF	205	20.9	.055	.047	.102
Jeff Ball	23	R	3B\1B	317	21.2	.029	.038	.067
Kevin Dean	25	R	OF	325	26.5	.040	.042	.082
Tony Eusebio	25	R	C	378	38.0	.051	.049	.100
Dave Hajek	25	R	3B\2B	362	31.8	.046	.042	.088
Frank Kellner	25	B	2B\SS	526	40.1	.037	.039	.076
Lance Madsen	24	R	3B\OF	378	38.6	.048	.054	.102
Scott Makarewicz	25	R	C\1B	379	39.1	.052	.051	.103
Orlando Miller	23	R	SS	443	39.4	.041	.048	.089
Ray Montgomery	23	R	OF	160	8.6	.022	.032	.054
Howard Prager	25	L	1B\OF	379	39.3	.057	.047	.104
Lee Sammons	24	R	OF	316	27.0	.044	.041	.085

AAA Pitchers	Age	Throws	Outs	RPA	AA Pitchers	Age	Throws	Outs	RPA
Willie Blair	27	R	158	.106	Harold Allen	27	L	367	.157
Ryan Bowen	24	R	367	.136	Jim Bruske	28	R	238	.135
Mike Capel	31	R	247	.103	Fred Costello	26	R	160	.109
Chris Gardner	23	R	332	.148	Brian Griffiths	24	R	291	.154
Jason Grimsley	25	R	374	.144	Dean Hartgraves	26	L	464	.121
Jeff Juden	21	R	441	.138	Keith Helton	27	L	231	.118
Darryl Kile	24	R	169	.128	Bob Hurta	27	L	201	.141
Rob Mallicoat	28	L	151	.085	Todd Jones	24	R	210	.149
Shane Reynolds	24	R	426	.114	Jim Lewis	22	R	213	.125
Rich Scheid	27	L	277	.117	Ken Luckham	23	R	219	.154
Matt Turner	25	R	300	.108	Edward Ponte	25	R	138	.176
Dave Veres	26	R	158	.122	Matt Rambo	25	L	100	.080
Brian Williams	23	R	210	.136	Rich Simon	27	R	205	.167
Rodney Windes	26	L	273	.138	Donnie Wall	25	R	367	.133

LOS ANGELES DODGERS

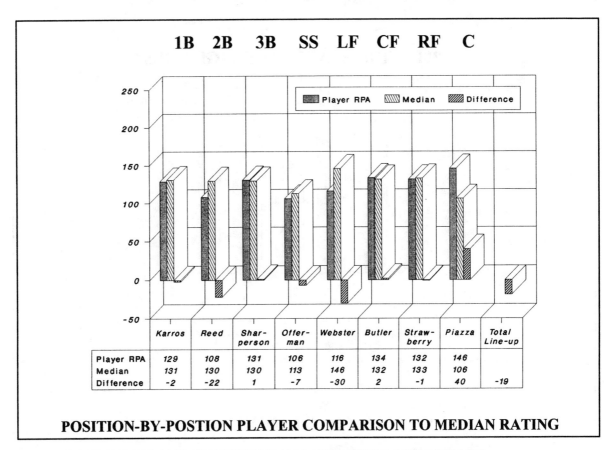

	1B	2B	3B	SS	LF	CF	RF	C	
	Karros	Reed	Shar-person	Offer-man	Webster	Butler	Straw-berry	Piazza	Total Line-up
Player RPA	129	108	131	106	116	134	132	146	
Median	131	130	130	113	146	132	133	106	
Difference	-2	-22	1	-7	-30	2	-1	40	-19

POSITION-BY-POSTION PLAYER COMPARISON TO MEDIAN RATING

DEFENSIVE TEAM AND STADIUM DATA FOR THE LAST 3 YEARS:

TEAM DEFENSE BY POSITION:

POSITION-BY-POSITION STADIUM CHARACTERISTICS:

		1990	1991	1992	
1B:	Home	+3.5	+0.4	+2.9	Very hard to play
	Away	+2.6	+2.8	-1.0	
2B:	Home	-2.4	-1.4	-3.6	Average (to slightly hard)
	Away	-3.0	-2.5	-3.3	
3B:	Home	+3.5	-0.4	+1.8	Very hard to play
	Away	-5.8	+10.2	-3.8	
SS:	Home	+3.6	+4.5	-2.2	Average (to slightly hard)
	Away	-3.7	+1.4	-4.2	
LF:	Home	+0.4	-7.4	-1.7	Slightly easy to play
	Away	+1.6	-5.4	-12.6	
CF:	Home	+6.6	+4.0	-4.2	Very easy to play
	Away	+2.3	+3.1	-1.2	
RF:	Home	+2.7	+1.8	-3.1	Average (to slightly easy)
	Away	-3.6	-6.6	-8.8	
Total Home:		+17.9	+1.5	-10.1	A big contrast between the infield and the
Total Away:		-9.6	+3.0	-35.0	outfield conditions for the players.

Comments: Despite the small away park defensive advantage in '91, the overall 4 yr. totals show a whopping 74.6 run home stadium defensive advantage (18.9 runs per yr.) for the Dodgers! Too bad the '92 Dogers were only eclipsed by the Mets as the worst defensive team in the Majors. They certainly weren't able to take any real advantage of this stadium effect. The outfield was the major culprit, with even Brett Butler slipping badly.

LOS ANGELES DODGERS

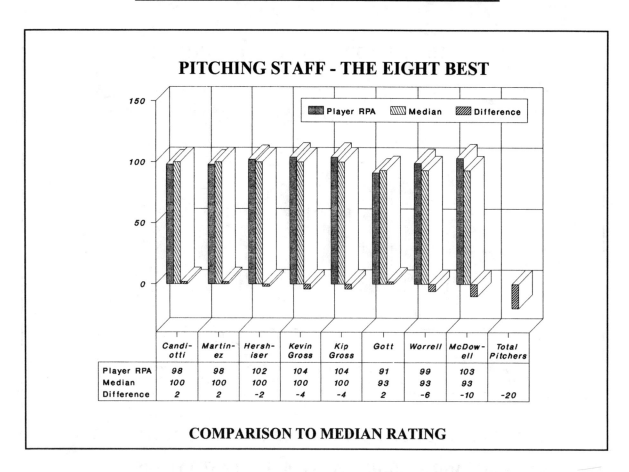

PITCHING STAFF - THE EIGHT BEST

Legend: Player RPA | Median | Difference

	Candi-otti	Martin-ez	Hersh-iser	Kevin Gross	Kip Gross	Gott	Worrell	McDow-ell	Total Pitchers
Player RPA	98	98	102	104	104	91	99	103	
Median	100	100	100	100	100	93	93	93	
Difference	2	2	-2	-4	-4	2	-6	-10	-20

COMPARISON TO MEDIAN RATING

SUGGESTED LINE-UPS (with set-up RPA & drive-in RPA ratings):

Vs: Left-handed Groundball
CF:	B. Butler	68-46
3B:	M. Sharperson	91-72
SS:	J. Offerman	61-54
C:	M. Piazza	85-75
RF:	M. Webster	60-60
LF:	B. Ashley	57-68
1B:	E. Karros	59-72
2B:	J. Reed	56-49
Pitcher		

Vs: Neutral Lefty Pitchers
CF:	B. Butler	73-49
3B:	M. Sharperson	79-61
C:	M. Piazza	85-75
RF:	M. Webster	65-64
LF:	B. Ashley	57-68
1B:	E. Karros	59-72
2B:	J. Reed	57-51
SS:	J. Offerman	54-48
Pitcher		

Vs: Left-handed Flyball
CF:	B. Butler	78-54
2B:	J. Reed	59-52
C:	M. Piazza	85-75
RF:	M. Webster	70-70
LF:	B. Ashley	57-68
1B:	E. Karros	60-72
3B:	T. Wallach	54-57
SS:	J. Offerman	46-41
Pitcher		

Vs: Right-handed Groundball
CF:	B. Butler	79-55
3B:	M. Sharperson	75-58
SS:	J. Offerman	65-57
C:	M. Piazza	75-65
RF:	D. Strawberry	81-79
1B:	E. Karros	57-69
2B:	J. Reed	59-52
LF:	B. Ashley	47-58
Pitcher		

Vs: Neutral Righty Pitchers
CF:	B. Butler	83-59
SS:	J. Offerman	58-51
C:	M. Piazza	75-65
RF:	D. Strawberry	81-80
1B:	E. Karros	57-69
2B:	J. Reed	60-54
3B:	L. Harris	55-52
LF:	B. Ashley	47-58
Pitcher		

Vs: Right-handed Flyball
CF:	B. Butler	89-63
2B:	J. Reed	62-55
C:	M. Piazza	75-65
RF:	D. Strawberry	82-81
3B:	D. Hansen	68-76
LF:	M. Webster	54-54
1B:	E. Karros	57-70
SS:	J. Offerman	50-44
Pitcher		

Comments: The above pitiful sets of line-ups only beats out the even more pitiful Cubs, Mets and the two expansion teams. Eric Davis appears to be done. We'll know this year if he is through. Brett Butler (and perhaps Darryl Strawberry also) can't have too much fuel left in his tank either. If it weren't for youngsters Mike Piazza, Eric Karros, Billy Ashley and Jose Offerman, this offense would be truly awful.

LOS ANGELES DODGERS

There are three large market teams in the National League: The New York Mets, the Chicago Cubs and these Los Angeles Dodgers. Each of these teams seems to be attempting to prove that money and intelligence don't mix.

With all those quality Major League and minor league players shifting teams and organizations, one would think that some of them would have ended up with these three franchises. But if you put all three teams' moves together, and only looked at those signings that had some positive value, these moves would generate very little real value.

The Dodgers did make some moves, of course, that had *some* positive value. But, of course, they were marginal at best. These marginally positive acquisitions were Jody Reed, Todd Worrell, Lance Parrish and Wally Ritchie. Why in the world they want Tim Wallach or Cory Snyder is beyond me. The signing of Kevin Elster doesn't make any sense since he was never much of a shortstop to begin with, even before his injury.

Since the Dodgers made no real moves this winter that will more than marginally help them, we need to see if they've got some youngsters that have real promise. In this case, unlike the Mets who have virtually nothing in the high minors, the Dodgers do have some quality youngsters.

Catcher Mike Piazza will be one of the best young players arriving on the scene in the Majors in '93. He's going to make a few All-Star teams before he's through.

Raul Mondesi is probably about a year away, but he has real promise. Billy Ashley also probably needs a little more time at AAA, but is also a good prospect. AA Outfielder Garey Ingram and first baseman Murph Proctor could also be only about a year away. Pitcher Pedro Martinez had a bit of an off year at Albuquerque in '92, but I still think he's about ready to make an impact at the Major League level. AA Pitcher Steve Allen looks like a real good prospect. He could only be a year away as well.

All in all it doesn't look so bad for the Dodgers about a year or two from now as the kids start arriving. Right now, however, only Mike Piazza is a sure thing and that's not enough to improve this horrible team so as to make it at least respectable in '93. Fortunately for the Dodgers, the woeful Colorado Rockies and not the much better Florida Marlins are in their division. If it were the Marlins, they might have the fight of their lives to stay out of last place.

The Dodgers have to keep Henry Rodriguez out of the outfield. He's strictly a first baseman.

I would have protected second baseman Eric Young (or pitcher Steve Allen) over Carlos Hernandez in the Expansion draft. With Piazza present, what's Hernandez' future? Hernandez doesn't appear to be more than a second-string type player in any case. Do the Dodgers really believe that Jody Reed is a long-term answer at second base? My defensive rating for Young is very poor, but this is a small sample and it's not unusual for youngsters when they first come up to have poor defensive ratings. While there's no guarantee, he may improve on defense.

Los Angeles' Projected record for 1993: 77--85, good for 6th place in the division.

LOS ANGELES DODGERS

Dave Anderson, 32

Bats Right   216L 224R 149G 111F   266ML

L= .087G .080L .070F ☐(.035/.050) .085 .096G .089R .079F = R

		ATBATS	1B	2B	3B	HR	HBP	BB	GDP	SB	CS	ROE	XB	RUNS	EOB%	RL#	SET-UP	DR-IN	RPA
San Francisco	1990	100	28	5	1	1	0	3	2	1	2	2	8	14	.235	.127	.068	.060	.128
San Francisco	1991	226	47	5	2	2	0	10	8	2	4	3	16	20	.158	.071	.034	.045	.079
Los Angeles	1992	84	17	4	0	3	0	4	3	0	4	1	6	10	.131	.098	.040	.063	.103

Billy Ashley, 22

Bats Right   31L 71R 28G 37F   514ML

L= ....G ....L ....F ☐(.045/.056) .101 ....G .052R ....F = R

		ATBATS	1B	2B	3B	HR	HBP	BB	GDP	SB	CS	ROE	XB	RUNS	EOB%	RL#	SET-UP	DR-IN	RPA
Los Angeles	1992	95	14	5	0	2	0	5	2	0	0	0	5	9	.155	.085	.038	.050	.088

Todd Benzinger, 29

Bats Both   464L 696R 414G 260F

L= .082G .085L .091F ☐(.043/.049) .092 .093G .096R .102F = R

		ATBATS	1B	2B	3B	HR	HBP	BB	GDP	SB	CS	ROE	XB	RUNS	EOB%	RL#	SET-UP	DR-IN	RPA
Cincinnati	1990	376	74	14	2	5	4	15	3	3	4	5	25	38	.199	.098	.047	.049	.096
Cincinnati	1991	123	17	3	2	1	0	8	2	2	0	1	5	9	.166	.067	.029	.035	.064
Kansas City	1991	293	66	15	3	2	3	15	5	2	7	2	21	33	.210	.103	.053	.053	.106
Los Angeles	1992	293	48	16	2	4	0	14	6	2	4	2	17	29	.164	.085	.040	.050	.090

Brett Butler, 35

Bats Left   856L 1240R 656G 491F

L= .123G .131L .141F ☐(.084/.059) .143 .143G .151R .161F = R

		ATBATS	1B	2B	3B	HR	HBP	BB	GDP	SB	CS	ROE	XB	RUNS	EOB%	RL#	SET-UP	DR-IN	RPA
San Francisco	1990	622	160	20	9	3	6	89	3	51	23	11	92	108	.301	.146	.086	.060	.146
Los Angeles	1991	615	162	13	5	2	1	104	3	38	30	9	90	96	.292	.129	.077	.054	.131
Los Angeles	1992	553	143	14	11	3	3	93	4	41	26	9	63	104	.299	.148	.092	.064	.156

Eric Davis, 30

Bats Right   408L 757R 408G 254F

L= .124G .130L .139F ☐(.063/.057) .120 .108G .114R .123F = R

		ATBATS	1B	2B	3B	HR	HBP	BB	GDP	SB	CS	ROE	XB	RUNS	EOB%	RL#	SET-UP	DR-IN	RPA
Cincinnati	1990	453	66	26	2	24	2	54	7	21	3	7	52	80	.224	.159	.081	.075	.156
Cincinnati	1991	285	46	10	0	11	5	43	4	14	2	1	18	44	.243	.131	.068	.058	.126
Los Angeles	1992	267	47	8	1	5	3	34	9	19	2	4	13	36	.224	.108	.059	.055	.114

Dave Hansen, 24

Bats Left   60L 387R 154G 126F   310ML

L= .025G .051L .083F ☐(.044/.050) .094 .073G .101R .133F = R

		ATBATS	1B	2B	3B	HR	HBP	BB	GDP	SB	CS	ROE	XB	RUNS	EOB%	RL#	SET-UP	DR-IN	RPA
Los Angeles	1990	7	1	0	0	0	0	0	0	0	0	0	1	0	.101	.036	.012	.026	.038
Los Angeles	1991	56	10	4	0	1	0	2	2	1	0	2	3	6	.195	.102	.050	.054	.104
Los Angeles	1992	341	56	11	0	6	1	31	9	0	2	4	8	35	.185	.085	.042	.048	.090

Lenny Harris, 28

Bats Left   187L 1142R 443G 282F

L= .071G .069L .066F ☐(.050/.048) .098 .105G .103R .102F = R

		ATBATS	1B	2B	3B	HR	HBP	BB	GDP	SB	CS	ROE	XB	RUNS	EOB%	RL#	SET-UP	DR-IN	RPA
Los Angeles	1990	431	109	16	4	2	1	27	8	15	10	13	52	58	.245	.119	.067	.056	.123
Los Angeles	1991	429	103	16	1	3	5	32	16	12	3	5	44	50	.225	.101	.054	.049	.103
Los Angeles	1992	347	83	11	0	0	1	21	10	19	8	5	17	35	.204	.086	.045	.046	.091

Carlos Hernandez, 25

Bats Right   145L 87R 63G 61F   380ML

L= .073G .102L .131F ☐(.041/.050) .091 .044G .073R .102F = R

		ATBATS	1B	2B	3B	HR	HBP	BB	GDP	SB	CS	ROE	XB	RUNS	EOB%	RL#	SET-UP	DR-IN	RPA
Los Angeles	1990	20	3	1	0	0	0	0	0	0	0	1	2	2	.191	.073	.037	.040	.077
Los Angeles	1991	14	2	1	0	0	1	0	2	1	0	0	2	1	.071	.040	.010	.030	.040
Los Angeles	1992	173	38	4	0	3	4	10	8	0	1	0	3	18	.174	.085	.041	.049	.090

LOS ANGELES DODGERS

Eric Karros, 25

Bats Right   245L   366R   204G   167F   558ML

L= .122G .122L .123F [(.054/.065) .119] .117G .117R .118F = R

		ATBATS	1B	2B	3B	HR	HBP	BB	GDP	SB	CS	ROE	XB	RUNS	EOB%	RL#	SET-UP	DR-IN	RPA
Los Angeles	1991	14	0	1	0	0	0	1	0	0	0	0	0	0	.113	.029	.010	.019	.029
Los Angeles	1992	545	89	30	1	20	2	34	15	2	6	9	30	73	.173	.113	.054	.065	.119

Bats Both   309L   487R   250G   214F   341ML

Jose Offerman, 24

L= .104G .091L .076F [(.050/.045) .095] .111G .098R .083F = R

		ATBATS	1B	2B	3B	HR	HBP	BB	GDP	SB	CS	ROE	XB	RUNS	EOB%	RL#	SET-UP	DR-IN	RPA
Los Angeles	1990	58	8	0	0	1	0	3	0	1	0	1	6	4	.156	.069	.030	.041	.071
Los Angeles	1991	113	20	2	0	0	1	23	5	3	2	8	11	11	.246	.078	.043	.036	.079
Los Angeles	1992	534	110	20	8	1	0	53	5	23	17	4	37	65	.225	.101	.055	.052	.107

Bats Left   16L   140R   63G   34F   891ML

Henry Rodriguez, 25

L= ....G ....L ....F [(.038/.050) .088] .067G .079R ....F = R

		ATBATS	1B	2B	3B	HR	HBP	BB	GDP	SB	CS	ROE	XB	RUNS	EOB%	RL#	SET-UP	DR-IN	RPA
Los Angeles	1992	146	22	7	0	3	0	8	2	0	0	0	7	15	.164	.085	.040	.051	.091

Bats Left   345L   927R   431G   267F

Mike Scioscia, 34

L= .082G .091L .106F [(.056/.051) .107] .104G .113R .128F = R

		ATBATS	1B	2B	3B	HR	HBP	BB	GDP	SB	CS	ROE	XB	RUNS	EOB%	RL#	SET-UP	DR-IN	RPA
Los Angeles	1990	435	78	25	0	12	3	41	11	4	1	5	33	61	.219	.121	.064	.061	.125
Los Angeles	1991	345	65	16	2	8	3	44	5	4	3	4	15	51	.252	.126	.070	.058	.128
Los Angeles	1992	348	65	6	3	3	1	28	9	3	2	5	14	34	.193	.081	.042	.044	.086

Bats Right   642L   377R   317G   246F

Mike Sharperson, 31

L= .165G .142L .112F [(.074/.057) .131] .135G .112R .082F = R

		ATBATS	1B	2B	3B	HR	HBP	BB	GDP	SB	CS	ROE	XB	RUNS	EOB%	RL#	SET-UP	DR-IN	RPA
Los Angeles	1990	357	87	14	2	3	1	40	5	15	6	4	45	54	.267	.129	.075	.059	.134
Los Angeles	1991	216	45	11	2	2	1	25	2	1	3	2	15	30	.259	.119	.067	.053	.120
Los Angeles	1992	317	71	21	0	3	0	46	9	2	3	4	29	52	.276	.130	.079	.059	.138

Bats Left   577L   790R   403G   280F

Darryl Strawberry, 30

L= .125G .126L .128F [(.074/.072) .146] .160G .161R .163F = R

		ATBATS	1B	2B	3B	HR	HBP	BB	GDP	SB	CS	ROE	XB	RUNS	EOB%	RL#	SET-UP	DR-IN	RPA
Mets	1990	542	94	18	1	37	4	55	5	15	8	7	41	105	.207	.160	.084	.085	.169
Los Angeles	1991	505	80	22	4	28	3	71	8	10	9	2	38	90	.218	.149	.077	.074	.151
Los Angeles	1992	156	24	8	0	5	1	15	2	3	2	4	11	23	.217	.123	.067	.063	.130

Bats Both   464L   515R   288G   259F

Mitch Webster, 33

L= .125G .134L .145F [(.059/.058) .117] .093G .102R .113F = R

		ATBATS	1B	2B	3B	HR	HBP	BB	GDP	SB	CS	ROE	XB	RUNS	EOB%	RL#	SET-UP	DR-IN	RPA
Cleveland	1990	437	72	20	6	12	3	19	5	22	9	6	41	52	.174	.112	.051	.061	.112
Cleveland	1991	32	4	0	0	0	0	3	0	2	3	2	1	2	.144	.041	.018	.025	.043
Pittsburgh	1991	97	9	3	4	1	0	8	3	0	0	0	4	8	.140	.069	.028	.043	.071
Los Angeles	1991	74	14	5	1	1	0	9	0	0	1	0	9	11	.262	.133	.075	.059	.134
Los Angeles	1992	262	47	12	5	6	2	24	1	11	5	1	15	41	.225	.131	.071	.067	.138

Bats Right   70L   73R   53G   41F   945ML

Eric Young, 25

L= .079G .106L .142F [(.047/.045) .092] .051G .078R .114F = R

		ATBATS	1B	2B	3B	HR	HBP	BB	GDP	SB	CS	ROE	XB	RUNS	EOB%	RL#	SET-UP	DR-IN	RPA
Los Angeles	1992	132	32	1	0	1	0	8	3	6	1	3	8	15	.215	.095	.051	.049	.100

LOS ANGELES DODGERS

PITCHERS

Pedro Astacio, 23

Throws: Groundball type, moderate righty

(.123/.112) .118   141L   558R   702ML

		OUTS	RO	1B	2B	3B	HR	HBP	BB	GDP	SB	CS	PO	WP	BK	RUNS	EOB%	RL#	RPA
Los Angeles	1992	246	0	69	8	2	1	2	16	12	5	3	0	1	0	23	.132	.068	.070

John Candelaria, 39

Throws: Flyball type, extreme lefty

(.056/.096) .082   198L   357R

		OUTS	RO	1B	2B	3B	HR	HBP	BB	GDP	SB	CS	PO	WP	BK	RUNS	EOB%	RL#	RPA
Minnesota	1990	175	159	35	10	1	9	0	7	2	2	0	0	3	0	24	.135	.105	.101
Toronto	1990	64	41	21	7	2	2	2	8	2	4	1	0	2	0	17	.237	.160	.160
Los Angeles	1991	101	101	18	9	1	3	0	9	6	1	3	0	1	1	10	.071	.073	.073
Los Angeles	1992	76	76	16	2	1	1	0	10	0	2	0	0	1	0	10	.217	.094	.095

Tom Candiotti, 35

Throws: Neutral type, moderate righty

(.095/.083) .089   1348L   1229R

		OUTS	RO	1B	2B	3B	HR	HBP	BB	GDP	SB	CS	PO	WP	BK	RUNS	EOB%	RL#	RPA
Cleveland	1990	606	19	154	30	0	23	6	54	17	18	7	0	9	3	90	.158	.105	.106
Cleveland	1991	325	0	64	14	4	6	2	28	3	10	3	1	6	0	37	.165	.087	.085
Toronto	1991	389	0	75	27	6	6	4	44	6	16	5	2	5	0	51	.179	.094	.093
Los Angeles	1992	611	5	125	35	4	13	3	58	17	30	5	1	9	2	75	.155	.088	.089

Tim Crews, 31

Throws: Neutral type, moderate to severe righty

(.119/.084) .102   524L   515R

		OUTS	RO	1B	2B	3B	HR	HBP	BB	GDP	SB	CS	PO	WP	BK	RUNS	EOB%	RL#	RPA
Los Angeles	1990	322	294	70	16	3	9	1	18	6	8	3	1	2	0	39	.135	.088	.091
Los Angeles	1991	228	228	50	17	1	7	0	8	2	10	2	2	3	1	29	.137	.094	.094
Los Angeles	1992	234	198	76	10	3	6	2	11	3	12	6	0	3	0	37	.168	.106	.109

Jim Gott, 33

Throws: Groundball type, moderate to severe righty

(.101/.066) .084   461L   436R

		OUTS	RO	1B	2B	3B	HR	HBP	BB	GDP	SB	CS	PO	WP	BK	RUNS	EOB%	RL#	RPA
Los Angeles	1990	186	186	44	9	1	5	0	27	5	2	2	0	4	0	29	.186	.104	.108
Los Angeles	1991	228	228	50	6	2	5	1	25	6	8	0	0	6	3	29	.174	.090	.091
Los Angeles	1992	264	264	61	6	1	4	1	28	6	6	5	0	9	3	29	.155	.077	.078

Kevin Gross, 31

Throws: Neutral type, extreme righty

(.136/.057) .099   1119L   965R

		OUTS	RO	1B	2B	3B	HR	HBP	BB	GDP	SB	CS	PO	WP	BK	RUNS	EOB%	RL#	RPA
Montreal	1990	490	50	131	29	2	9	4	58	7	31	5	0	4	1	84	.213	.110	.117
Los Angeles	1991	347	190	98	13	2	10	2	44	6	15	6	0	3	0	57	.196	.111	.112
Los Angeles	1992	614	12	136	30	5	11	3	67	12	18	9	0	4	2	78	.171	.089	.091

Kip Gross, 28

Throws: Groundball type, extreme righty

(.125/.077) .103   264L   225R   632ML

		OUTS	RO	1B	2B	3B	HR	HBP	BB	GDP	SB	CS	PO	WP	BK	RUNS	EOB%	RL#	RPA
Cincinnati	1990	19	19	6	0	0	0	0	2	0	1	1	0	0	0	2	.167	.072	.073
Cincinnati	1991	257	105	72	12	1	8	0	38	11	8	3	0	5	1	40	.181	.108	.103
Los Angeles	1992	71	53	25	5	1	1	0	9	3	2	1	0	1	1	13	.209	.119	.120

Orel Hershiser, 34

Throws: Groundball type, extreme righty

(.121/.061) .094   770L   647R

		OUTS	RO	1B	2B	3B	HR	HBP	BB	GDP	SB	CS	PO	WP	BK	RUNS	EOB%	RL#	RPA
Los Angeles	1990	76	0	21	4	0	1	1	4	1	0	1	0	0	1	10	.174	.088	.092
Los Angeles	1991	336	0	89	18	2	3	5	26	8	11	2	2	2	4	42	.179	.089	.089
Los Angeles	1992	632	0	149	42	3	15	8	56	19	13	7	0	10	0	87	.163	.095	.097

LOS ANGELES DODGERS

Jay Howell, 37

Throws: **Neutral type, moderate reverse righty**

(.075/.095) .084   353L   290R

		OUTS	RO	1B	2B	3B	HR	HBP	BB	GDP	SB	CS	PO	WP	BK	RUNS	EOB%	RL#	RPA
Los Angeles	1990	198	198	45	8	1	5	6	17	6	10	1	0	4	1	28	.169	.096	.100
Los Angeles	1991	153	153	26	8	2	3	1	8	1	3	1	0	0	0	16	.145	.077	.078
Los Angeles	1992	140	140	36	3	0	2	1	13	1	7	1	0	3	1	18	.196	.089	.091

Ramon Martinez, 24

Throws: **Flyball type, extreme righty**

(.121/.072) .101   1418L   1035R

		OUTS	RO	1B	2B	3B	HR	HBP	BB	GDP	SB	CS	PO	WP	BK	RUNS	EOB%	RL#	RPA
Los Angeles	1990	703	0	124	38	7	22	4	62	11	22	13	2	3	3	86	.133	.088	.091
Los Angeles	1991	661	0	138	33	1	18	7	65	6	16	9	1	6	0	86	.171	.093	.094
Los Angeles	1992	452	0	98	30	2	11	5	65	7	19	7	0	9	0	73	.202	.106	.110

Roger McDowell, 32

Throws: **Groundball type, extreme righty**

(.125/.065) .097   575L   518R

		OUTS	RO	1B	2B	3B	HR	HBP	BB	GDP	SB	CS	PO	WP	BK	RUNS	EOB%	RL#	RPA
Philadelphia	1990	259	259	73	15	2	2	2	26	16	7	2	0	1	1	30	.152	.085	.085
Philadelphia	1991	177	177	46	14	0	1	2	20	5	6	1	0	1	0	25	.207	.094	.094
Los Angeles	1991	127	127	28	6	2	3	0	8	5	6	3	0	1	0	13	.098	.076	.076
Los Angeles	1992	251	251	88	10	2	3	1	29	9	3	2	0	4	1	41	.208	.107	.108

Bob Ojeda, 35

Throws: **Groundball type, extreme lefty**

(.054/.107) .096   391L   1535R

		OUTS	RO	1B	2B	3B	HR	HBP	BB	GDP	SB	CS	PO	WP	BK	RUNS	EOB%	RL#	RPA
New York Mets	1990	354	148	83	26	4	10	2	36	11	14	11	3	2	3	47	.131	.092	.092
Los Angeles	1991	568	0	131	31	4	15	3	61	12	23	15	0	4	2	76	.156	.095	.095
Los Angeles	1992	499	0	126	29	6	8	1	73	15	20	15	1	3	0	71	.173	.095	.097

Steve Searcy, 28

Throws: **Groundball type, moderate Lefty**

(.137/.148) .145   143L   443R   381ML

		OUTS	RO	1B	2B	3B	HR	HBP	BB	GDP	SB	CS	PO	WP	BK	RUNS	EOB%	RL#	RPA
Detroit	1990	226	32	53	13	1	9	0	48	9	9	5	0	3	0	40	.191	.121	.118
Detroit	1991	122	65	36	7	1	8	0	30	5	2	1	0	4	0	32	.232	.166	.160
Philadelphia	1991	91	91	18	7	2	2	0	13	1	5	0	0	1	1	16	.222	.117	.118
Philadelphia	1992	31	31	10	2	1	0	0	8	1	0	1	0	0	0	7	.259	.120	.133

Steve Wilson, 28

Throws: **Flyball type, moderate lefty**

(.102/.118) .113   282L   644R   482ML

		OUTS	RO	1B	2B	3B	HR	HBP	BB	GDP	SB	CS	PO	WP	BK	RUNS	EOB%	RL#	RPA
Chicago Cubs	1990	417	179	94	23	6	17	2	37	5	6	8	0	2	1	59	.157	.108	.100
Chicago Cubs	1991	37	37	9	3	0	1	0	4	1	1	0	0	0	0	5	.190	.108	.101
Los Angeles	1991	25	25	1	0	0	0	0	4	2	0	0	0	0	0	0	.025	.012	.012
Los Angeles	1992	200	200	52	13	3	6	1	22	9	4	1	0	7	0	33	.170	.110	.111

Los Angeles Dodgers AAA & AA Minor League Ratings

AAA (ALBUQUERQUE)	AGE	BATS	POSITION	CPA	RUNS	SET-UP	DRIVE-IN	RPA
Billy Ashley	22	R	OF	514	52.8	.043	.060	.103
Tony Barron	26	R	OF	428	44.7	.048	.056	.104
Rafael Bournigal	26	R	SS	439	34.4	.039	.039	.078
Jerry Brooks	25	R	OF	519	49.8	.047	.049	.096
Tom Goodwin	24	L	OF	360	35.8	.055	.045	.100
Jeff Hamilton	28	R	3B	182	16.4	.041	.049	.090
Matt Howard	25	R	2B	516	37.6	.035	.038	.073
Luis Martinez	26	R	3B\SS	195	13.9	.034	.037	.071
Raul Mondesi	21	R	OF	218	23.8	.051	.058	.109
Jose Munoz	25	B	3B\OF\2B	497	36.1	.034	.039	.073
Julio Peguero	24	B	OF	412	31.2	.038	.038	.076
Mike Piazza	24	R	C	535	77.9	.078	.068	.146
Eddie Pye	25	R	3B\2B	241	20.4	.042	.042	.084
Henry Rodriguez	25	L	1B\OF	408	43.5	.051	.056	.107
Brian Traxler	25	L	1B	446	44.5	.049	.051	.100
Don Wakamatsu	29	R	C	191	19.5	.056	.046	.102
Eric Young	25	R	2B	397	41.5	.056	.048	.104

AA (SAN ANTONIO)	AGE	BATS	POSITION	CPA	RUNS	SET-UP	DRIVE-IN	RPA
Jorge Alvarez	24	R	2B\3B\OF	333	26.9	.037	.044	.081
Bryan Baar	24	R	C	216	11.0	.019	.032	.051
Tim Barker	24	R	SS	389	36.8	.051	.044	.095
Mike Busch	24	R	3B\OF	463	45.8	.045	.054	.099
Anthony Collier	22	L	OF	147	9.8	.029	.037	.066
John Deutsch	26	L	1B	241	19.1	.036	.043	.079
Scott Doffek	24	L	OF\3B	217	17.4	.037	.043	.080
Garey Ingram	22	R	OF	242	28.2	.067	.050	.117
Ron Maurer	24	R	3B\SS	250	18.8	.037	.038	.075
Chris Morrow	23	L	OF	332	23.4	.030	.040	.070
Murph Proctor	23	B	1B	260	28.0	.058	.050	.108
Lance Rice	26	B	C	214	16.2	.037	.039	.076
Vernon Spearman	23	L	OF	203	16.7	.040	.042	.082

AAA Pitchers	Age	Throws	Outs	RPA	AA Pitchers	Age	Throws	Outs	RPA
Pedro Astacio	23	R	296	.142	Steve Allen	26	R	237	.093
Albert Bustillos	24	R	152	.121	Bill Bene	25	R	96	.141
Balvino Galvez	28	R	268	.117	Jason Brosnan	24	L	123	.258
Kip Gross	28	R	323	.093	Ray Calhoun	23	R	129	.127
Greg Hansell	21	R	483	.136	Omar Daal	20	L	203	.157
Brian Holton	33	R	122	.126	Javier DeLaHoya	22	R	76	.162
Mike James	25	R	302	.123	Mike Mimbs	23	L	389	.161
Pedro Martinez	21	R	376	.116	Brian Piotrwicz	25	R	89	.110
Jamie McAndrew	25	R	239	.134	Jody Treadwell	24	R	228	.127
Lance McCullers	28	R	208	.100	Bill Wengert	25	R	151	.138
Mark Mimbs	23	L	393	.122	Todd Williams	21	R	132	.116
Jim Neidlinger	28	R	437	.121					
Chris Nichting	26	R	362	.118					
Dan Opperman	24	R	75	.126					
Steve Searcy	28	L	253	.148					
Zak Shinall	24	R	246	.132					
Dennis Springer	27	R	552	.137					
Mike Wilkins	26	R	265	.129					

SAN DIEGO PADRES

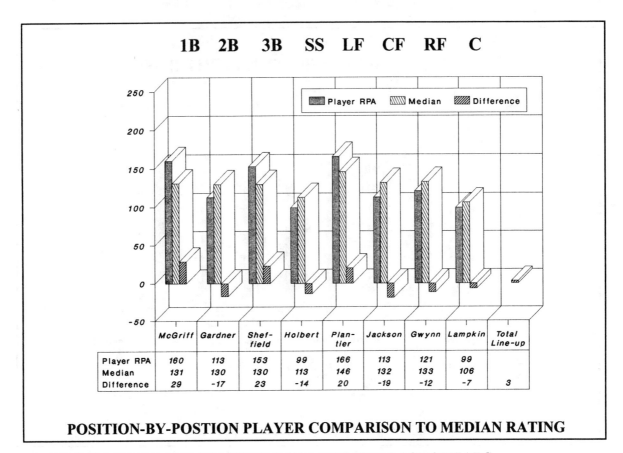

	1B McGriff	2B Gardner	3B Shef-field	SS Holbert	LF Plan-tier	CF Jackson	RF Gwynn	C Lampkin	Total Line-up
Player RPA	160	113	153	99	166	113	121	99	
Median	131	130	130	113	146	132	133	106	
Difference	29	-17	23	-14	20	-19	-12	-7	3

POSITION-BY-POSTION PLAYER COMPARISON TO MEDIAN RATING

DEFENSIVE TEAM AND STADIUM DATA FOR THE LAST 3 YEARS:

TEAM DEFENSE BY POSITION:

POSITION-BY-POSITION STADIUM CHARACTERISTICS:

		1990	1991	1992	
1B:	Home	+1.9	+0.2	-4.0	Average (to slightly easy)
	Away	-1.6	-1.6	+2.1	
2B:	Home	+5.0	-0.5	-5.6	Slightly easy to play
	Away	-5.0	-2.5	-6.7	
3B:	Home	-2.9	-6.7	+4.2	Average
	Away	+3.6	+3.4	-0.4	
SS:	Home	-3.7	-3.8	-5.1	Average
	Away	+1.1	+2.3	-1.8	
LF:	Home	-1.2	+4.3	-2.0	Slightly hard to play
	Away	+3.6	+6.6	-1.0	
CF:	Home	-4.6	+9.5	+2.8	Average
	Away	+2.6	+8.0	-10.5	
RF:	Home	-2.2	-0.1	+6.2	Average
	Away	+1.0	-0.9	+4.8	
Total Home:		+0.3	+2.9	-3.5	
Total Away:		+8.9	+15.3	-13.4	

Comments: A big shift from a good defensive team in '91 to a poor defensive team in '92. Second base, shortstop, LF & CF were the main culprits. My line-ups show AA shortstop Ray Holbert as the replacement for the departed Tony Fernandez. Fernandez wasn't much of a loss, since his range declined badly in '92. Craig Shipley doesn't seem to be able to handle the position, however, while Holbert looks like a real strong prospect, although he may be a year away.

SAN DIEGO PADRES

PITCHING STAFF - THE EIGHT BEST

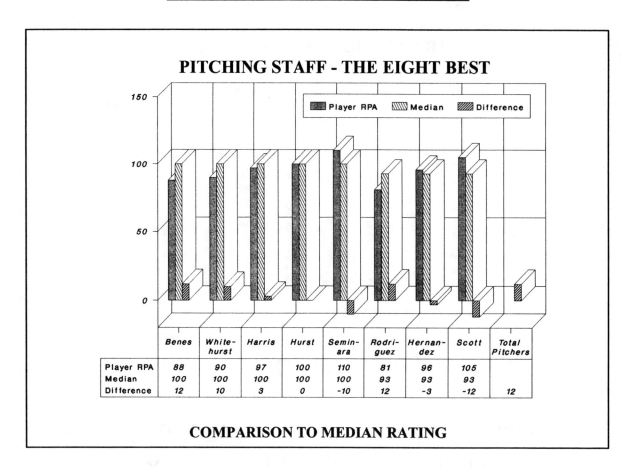

	Benes	White-hurst	Harris	Hurst	Semin-ara	Rodri-guez	Hernan-dez	Scott	Total Pitchers
Player RPA	88	90	97	100	110	81	96	105	
Median	100	100	100	100	100	93	93	93	
Difference	12	10	3	0	-10	12	-3	-12	12

COMPARISON TO MEDIAN RATING

SUGGESTED LINE-UPS (with set-up RPA & drive-in RPA ratings):

Vs: Left-handed Groundball
2B:	J. Gardner	59-41
LF:	D. J. Dozier	71-63
RF:	T. Gwynn	62-57
1B:	F. McGriff	80-73
3B:	G. Sheffield	83-86
SS:	R. Holbert	61-53
C:	D. Walters	54-59
CF:	D. Jackson	52-66
Pitcher		

Vs: Neutral Lefty Pitchers
LF:	D. Sherman	72-48
RF:	D. J. Dozier	71-63
1B:	F. McGriff	78-71
2B:	T. Teufel	66-66
3B:	G. Sheffield	77-81
SS:	R. Holbert	61-53
C:	D. Walters	54-59
CF:	D. Jackson	53-66
Pitcher		

Vs: Left-handed Flyball
LF:	D. Sherman	72-48
RF:	D. J. Dozier	71-63
1B:	F. McGriff	74-68
2B:	T. Teufel	93-93
3B:	G. Sheffield	70-72
CF:	D. Jackson	54-67
SS:	R. Holbert	61-53
C:	D. Walters	54-59
Pitcher		

Vs: Right-handed Groundball
LF:	D. Sherman	82-58
2B:	J. Gardner	69-51
RF:	P. Plantier	89-78
1B:	F. McGriff	95-86
3B:	G. Sheffield	78-81
CF:	D. Jackson	47-61
C:	T. Lampkin	53-53
SS:	R. Holbert	51-43
Pitcher		

Vs: Neutral Righty Pitchers
LF:	D. Sherman	82-58
2B:	J. Gardner	69-51
RF:	P. Plantier	94-83
1B:	F. McGriff	93-84
3B:	G. Sheffield	73-75
CF:	D. Jackson	48-61
C:	T. Lampkin	53-53
SS:	R. Holbert	51-43
Pitcher		

Vs: Right-handed Flyball
LF:	D. Sherman	82-58
2B:	J. Gardner	69-51
1B:	F. McGriff	89-81
RF:	P. Plantier	99-88
3B:	G. Sheffield	65-67
CF:	D. Jackson	49-62
C:	T. Lampkin	53-53
SS:	R. Holbert	51-43
Pitcher		

Comments: The above six line-ups would give the Padres a decent offense. Unfortunately, the Padres actual line-ups will probably little resemble them. This means that the actual Padre offense used in the coming season is likely to be poor. Ray Holbert may need a couple of months at AAA, but what alternative do the Padres have? Craig Shipley? Get real!

SAN DIEGO PADRES

It could be worse. With all the talent that has left the San Diego Padres over the winter, it could have been a lot worse. But the Padres did get some good talent in return for some, but not all of the losses.

The biggest losses have been to the pitching staff. The Mike Maddux for Roger Mason trade was a joke. Maddux is one of the best relievers in baseball. I would have trouble justifying Roger Mason's presence on a AAA farm team let alone a Major League squad! The losses of Larry Andersen and Jim DeShaies also hurts enormously since the Padres have nothing to show for it. But the trade of an excellent reliever in Jose Melendez was a huge steal by the Padres since they got a terrific young hitter in the person of Phil Plantier. This could be as big a steal as the Gary Sheffield steal last year.

The trade of Tony Fernandez for Wally Whitehurst and D.J. Dozier also completely favors the Padres. Fernandez is on the down side of his career while Whitehurst is an excellent pitcher and Dozier a fine outfield prospect who ought to (but probably won't) be given some playing time in the outfield with the Padres this season. Dozier's main problem will be the continued problem that this team has in evaluating Tony Gwynn's value. Gwynn may be the most overrated player in the Majors. I ask you: if the Padres have had such a good pitching staff and they had five "All-Stars" on the squad last year, why weren't they serious contenders? The answer is that two of those so-called "All-Stars" belonged on the "All-Overrated" team: Tony Gwynn and Benito Santiago. The Padres should trade Gwynn (gasp!) while they

can still get top value for him. There are plenty of teams out there who'll be fooled by the illusions created by his high batting averages and be willing to give up real talent for Gwynn's "All-Star" services. For now, in the proposed line-ups on the opposite page, I've projected Darrell Sherman and D.J. Dozier into the rightfield position currently held by Gwynn.

This brings me to the "loss" of Benito Santiago. This "loss" paves the way for Dan Walters to take his place. Walters is not, at this stage of his career, anything to write home about, but he appears to be (along with Tom Lampkin) a substantial improvement over Santiago.

Ray Holbert looks like a real good prospect at shortstop. He played at AA Wichita last year and would normally be expected to move up to AAA this year. But with the Padres only having the awful Craig Shipley available at the Major League level, the Padres may have to try and force-feed Holbert. They would be taking the chance of setting him back in his development, but what choice do the Padres have?

The Colorado Rockies again came to the rescue of another team when they selected, and wasted a pick on Jerald Clark, while passing over pitchers Rich Rodriguez and Wally Whitehurst and quality AA prospects Ray Holbert, Jay Gainer (1B) and Paul Gonzalez (3B) in the Expansion draft. The Rockies' excuse can't be that they were going for youth since Clark is 29 years old. The Rockies then passed over Holbert, Gainer and Gonzalez in the second round to take a marginal pitching prospect in Lance Painter. Go Figure!

San Diego's Projected record for 1993: 81--81, good for 4th place in the division.

SAN DIEGO PADRES

Oscar Azocar, 27

Bats Left   68L   348R   164G   96F   395ML

L= .079G .070L .055F | (.031/.037) .068 | .077G .068R .053F = R

		ATBATS	1B	2B	3B	HR	HBP	BB	GDP	SB	CS	ROE	XB	RUNS	EOB%	RL#	SET-UP	DR-IN	RPA
Yankees	1990	214	40	8	0	5	1	2	1	7	1	3	6	22	.171	.098	.045	.055	.100
San Diego	1991	57	12	2	0	0	1	0	1	2	0	1	3	5	.188	.075	.036	.040	.076
San Diego	1992	168	26	6	0	0	0	8	3	1	1	4	9	11	.172	.060	.026	.032	.058

Dann Bilardello, 33

Bats Right   32L   74R   34G   22F   152ML

L= ....G ....L ....F | (.039/.042) .081 | ....G .085R ....F = R

		ATBATS	1B	2B	3B	HR	HBP	BB	GDP	SB	CS	ROE	XB	RUNS	EOB%	RL#	SET-UP	DR-IN	RPA
Pittsburgh	1990	37	2	0	0	0	0	3	0	0	0	2	2	1	.161	.033	.015	.019	.034
San Diego	1991	26	4	2	1	0	0	3	0	0	0	0	3	4	.266	.126	.072	.066	.128
San Diego	1992	33	3	1	0	0	0	3	1	0	0	0	2	1	.130	.038	.014	.023	.037

Jerald Clark, 29

Bats Right   355L   694R   394G   210F

L= .102G .097L .088F | (.045/.053) .098 | .103G .098R .089F = R

		ATBATS	1B	2B	3B	HR	HBP	BB	GDP	SB	CS	ROE	XB	RUNS	EOB%	RL#	SET-UP	DR-IN	RPA
San Diego	1990	101	17	4	1	5	0	5	3	0	0	2	7	14	.165	.126	.056	.070	.126
San Diego	1991	369	58	16	0	10	6	29	10	2	1	4	13	41	.188	.096	.046	.051	.097
San Diego	1992	496	80	22	6	12	4	19	7	3	1	5	18	54	.175	.102	.045	.054	.099

Paul Faries, 27

Bats Right   73L   131R   72G   35F   513ML

L= .140G .110L ....F | (.039/.041) .080 | .093G .063R ....F = R

		ATBATS	1B	2B	3B	HR	HBP	BB	GDP	SB	CS	ROE	XB	RUNS	EOB%	RL#	SET-UP	DR-IN	RPA
San Diego	1990	37	6	1	0	0	1	4	0	0	1	2	4	4	.261	.088	.049	.039	.088
San Diego	1991	130	19	3	1	0	1	14	5	3	1	3	6	9	.189	.062	.030	.032	.062
San Diego	1992	11	4	1	0	0	0	1	0	0	0	0	3	3	.377	.226	.145	.080	.225

Tony Gwynn, 32

Bats Left   692L   1053R   622G   329F

L= .123G .116L .104F | (.061/.057) .118 | .127G .120R .108F = R

		ATBATS	1B	2B	3B	HR	HBP	BB	GDP	SB	CS	ROE	XB	RUNS	EOB%	RL#	SET-UP	DR-IN	RPA
San Diego	1990	573	134	29	10	4	1	24	13	17	8	6	48	70	.214	.113	.058	.055	.113
San Diego	1991	530	126	27	11	4	0	26	11	8	9	9	39	69	.227	.119	.062	.058	.120
San Diego	1992	520	129	27	3	6	0	34	13	3	7	3	44	68	.225	.119	.060	.056	.116

Darrin Jackson, 29

Bats Right   445L   698R   413G   243F

L= .116G .117L .119F | (.049/.062) .111 | .106G .107R .109F = R

		ATBATS	1B	2B	3B	HR	HBP	BB	GDP	SB	CS	ROE	XB	RUNS	EOB%	RL#	SET-UP	DR-IN	RPA
San Diego	1990	113	23	3	0	3	0	4	1	3	0	2	7	13	.195	.111	.054	.057	.111
San Diego	1991	359	60	12	1	21	2	25	5	5	3	9	28	57	.191	.141	.069	.074	.143
San Diego	1992	587	101	23	5	17	4	22	21	14	3	4	32	60	.146	.094	.038	.054	.092

Tom Lampkin, 28

Bats Left   11L   142R   57G   32F   591ML

L= ....G ....L ....F | (.046/.046) .092 | .107G .092R ....F = R

		ATBATS	1B	2B	3B	HR	HBP	BB	GDP	SB	CS	ROE	XB	RUNS	EOB%	RL#	SET-UP	DR-IN	RPA
San Diego	1990	63	12	0	1	1	0	3	2	0	1	1	6	5	.143	.075	.030	.045	.075
San Diego	1991	58	7	3	1	0	0	3	0	0	0	1	2	4	.189	.071	.034	.038	.072
San Diego	1992	17	4	0	0	0	1	6	0	2	0	0	3	4	.418	.166	.108	.053	.161

Fred McGriff, 28

Bats Left   722L   1168R   620G   350F

L= .149G .145L .138F | (.085/.077) .162 | .177G .173R .166F = R

		ATBATS	1B	2B	3B	HR	HBP	BB	GDP	SB	CS	ROE	XB	RUNS	EOB%	RL#	SET-UP	DR-IN	RPA
Toronto	1990	557	110	21	1	35	2	82	7	5	3	6	47	117	.258	.185	.100	.080	.180
San Diego	1991	528	96	19	1	31	2	79	14	4	1	9	28	102	.242	.160	.087	.075	.162
San Diego	1992	531	83	30	4	35	1	73	14	8	6	6	23	104	.218	.166	.083	.079	.162

SAN DIEGO PADRES

Benito Santiago, 27

Bats Right   486L   933R   524G   282F

L= .100G .105L .114F   (.036/.053) .089   .076G   .081R   .090F = R

		ATBATS	1B	2B	3B	HR	HBP	BB	GDP	SB	CS	ROE	XB	RUNS	EOB%	RL#	SET-UP	DR-IN	RPA
San Diego	1990	344	69	8	5	11	3	25	4	5	6	2	28	47	.199	.123	.060	.063	.123
San Diego	1991	580	113	22	3	17	4	18	21	8	11	5	32	58	.141	.091	.037	.055	.092
San Diego	1992	386	66	21	0	10	0	20	14	2	6	2	18	37	.144	.087	.035	.050	.085

Craig Shipley, 29

Bats Right   81L   122R   73G   55F   251ML

L= .100G .108L .119F   (.037/.042) .079   .051G   .059R   .070F = R

		ATBATS	1B	2B	3B	HR	HBP	BB	GDP	SB	CS	ROE	XB	RUNS	EOB%	RL#	SET-UP	DR-IN	RPA
San Diego	1991	91	21	3	0	1	1	2	1	0	1	1	5	9	.197	.093	.046	.048	.094
San Diego	1992	105	20	6	0	0	0	1	2	1	1	2	4	8	.171	.072	.032	.038	.070

Phil Stephenson, 32

Bats Left   41L   262R   106G   70F   246ML

L= ....G .124L ....F   (.055/.047) .102   .122G   .099R   .064F = R

		ATBATS	1B	2B	3B	HR	HBP	BB	GDP	SB	CS	ROE	XB	RUNS	EOB%	RL#	SET-UP	DR-IN	RPA
San Diego	1990	182	24	9	1	4	0	29	3	2	2	2	14	23	.229	.108	.057	.051	.108
San Diego	1991	7	2	0	0	0	0	2	0	0	0	0	0	1	.380	.138	.090	.050	.140
San Diego	1992	71	8	2	1	0	0	10	0	0	0	1	2	6	.229	.074	.037	.034	.071

Gary Sheffield, 24

Bats Right   413L   955R   466G   309F

L= .158G .147L .131F   (.069/.071) .140   .148G   .137R   .121F = R

		ATBATS	1B	2B	3B	HR	HBP	BB	GDP	SB	CS	ROE	XB	RUNS	EOB%	RL#	SET-UP	DR-IN	RPA
Milwaukee	1990	487	102	30	1	10	3	43	11	25	12	7	50	71	.228	.128	.069	.062	.131
Milwaukee	1991	175	18	12	2	2	3	18	3	5	5	2	11	17	.186	.084	.040	.044	.084
San Diego	1992	557	114	34	3	33	6	43	19	5	7	5	37	102	.203	.162	.078	.080	.158

Kurt Stillwell, 27

Bats Both   387L   997R   453G   299F

L= .085G .087L .090F   (.046/.047) .093   .094G   .096R   .099F = R

		ATBATS	1B	2B	3B	HR	HBP	BB	GDP	SB	CS	ROE	XB	RUNS	EOB%	RL#	SET-UP	DR-IN	RPA
Kansas City	1990	506	84	35	4	3	4	38	11	0	2	6	54	56	.215	.098	.051	.049	.100
Kansas City	1991	385	78	17	1	6	1	28	8	3	4	8	25	46	.217	.106	.056	.053	.109
San Diego	1992	379	66	15	3	2	1	17	6	4	1	4	15	32	.183	.078	.036	.040	.076

Tim Teufel, 34

Bats Right   386L   487R   316G   183F

L= .107G .139L .193F   (.055/.055) .110   .055G   .087R   .141F = R

		ATBATS	1B	2B	3B	HR	HBP	BB	GDP	SB	CS	ROE	XB	RUNS	EOB%	RL#	SET-UP	DR-IN	RPA
Mets	1990	175	22	11	0	10	0	14	5	0	0	3	16	26	.167	.127	.059	.073	.132
Mets	1991	34	3	0	0	1	0	2	0	1	1	0	0	2	.080	.049	.013	.035	.048
San Diego	1991	307	43	16	0	11	1	45	8	8	2	7	18	46	.230	.124	.065	.060	.125
San Diego	1992	246	39	10	0	6	1	28	7	2	1	4	10	29	.207	.102	.050	.050	.100

Jim Vatcher, 26

Bats Right   71L   51R   35G   46F   788ML

L= ....G .113L .078F   (.055/.043) .098   ....G   .076R   .041F = R

		ATBATS	1B	2B	3B	HR	HBP	BB	GDP	SB	CS	ROE	XB	RUNS	EOB%	RL#	SET-UP	DR-IN	RPA
Philadelphia	1990	46	10	1	0	1	0	4	1	0	0	2	2	6	.247	.123	.066	.055	.121
Atlanta	1990	27	5	1	1	0	0	1	0	0	0	0	0	3	.205	.095	.047	.047	.094
San Diego	1991	20	4	0	0	0	0	4	0	1	0	1	2	3	.331	.114	.071	.044	.115
San Diego	1992	16	3	1	0	0	0	3	0	0	0	1	2	3	.359	.146	.091	.053	.144

Dan Walters, 26

Bats Right   64L   130R   60G   41F   471ML

L= .108G .071L ....F   (.046/.050) .096   .145G   .108R   ....F = R

		ATBATS	1B	2B	3B	HR	HBP	BB	GDP	SB	CS	ROE	XB	RUNS	EOB%	RL#	SET-UP	DR-IN	RPA
San Diego	1992	179	29	11	1	4	2	10	3	1	0	1	8	21	.195	.110	.052	.056	.108

SAN DIEGO PADRES

Kevin Ward, 31

Bats Right   174L   117R   97G   64F

L= .134G .116L .096F   (.032/.045) .077   .036G   .018R   .000F = R

		ATBATS	1B	2B	3B	HR	HBP	BB	GDP	SB	CS	ROE	XB	RUNS	EOB%	RL#	SET-UP	DR-IN	RPA
San Diego	1991	107	15	7	2	2	1	9	3	1	4	1	7	11	.167	.092	.041	.052	.093
San Diego	1992	147	21	5	0	3	2	14	8	2	3	1	5	12	.138	.067	.026	.040	.066

PITCHERS

Throws: Groundball type, extreme righty

Larry Andersen, 39

(.104/.030) .068   347L   330R

		OUTS	RO	1B	2B	3B	HR	HBP	BB	GDP	SB	CS	PO	WP	BK	RUNS	EOB%	RL#	RPA
Houston	1990	221	221	52	6	1	2	1	19	5	12	2	0	2	0	25	.162	.072	.080
Boston	1990	66	66	16	2	0	0	1	3	1	4	1	0	2	0	5	.155	.066	.062
San Diego	1991	141	141	34	5	0	0	0	10	2	6	2	0	1	0	13	.162	.066	.067
San Diego	1992	105	105	22	2	0	2	1	6	1	7	1	0	0	0	10	.145	.072	.070

Throws: Flyball type, moderate righty

Andy Benes, 25

(.095/.084) .090   1524L   1056R

		OUTS	RO	1B	2B	3B	HR	HBP	BB	GDP	SB	CS	PO	WP	BK	RUNS	EOB%	RL#	RPA
San Diego	1990	577	6	126	24	9	18	1	64	14	23	5	0	2	5	82	.165	.102	.101
San Diego	1991	669	0	141	24	6	23	4	52	11	10	11	0	3	4	83	.137	.089	.091
San Diego	1992	694	0	171	39	6	14	5	55	12	20	11	2	1	1	88	.164	.092	.089

Throws: Flyball type, extreme reverse lefty

Jim DeShaies, 32

(.185/.081) .099   328L   1546R

		OUTS	RO	1B	2B	3B	HR	HBP	BB	GDP	SB	CS	PO	WP	BK	RUNS	EOB%	RL#	RPA
Houston	1990	628	0	126	34	5	21	8	75	8	21	9	2	3	3	101	.175	.100	.109
Houston	1991	483	0	96	36	5	19	1	67	12	21	14	1	0	5	78	.152	.103	.110
San Diego	1992	288	0	69	16	1	6	1	31	7	6	10	2	1	2	32	.134	.081	.079

Throws: Groundball type, moderate to severe reverse righty

Dave Eiland, 26

(.097/.132) .113   300L   244R   520ML

		OUTS	RO	1B	2B	3B	HR	HBP	BB	GDP	SB	CS	PO	WP	BK	RUNS	EOB%	RL#	RPA
N.Y. Yankees	1990	91	0	18	8	3	2	0	5	1	1	0	0	0	0	13	.174	.106	.103
N.Y. Yankees	1991	218	31	52	20	5	10	3	22	13	6	1	0	0	0	36	.146	.117	.111
San Diego	1992	81	0	22	8	2	1	0	5	2	4	0	0	0	1	13	.198	.112	.109

Throws: Groundball type, extreme reverse righty

Gene Harris, 28

(.086/.143) .119   146L   206R   305ML

		OUTS	RO	1B	2B	3B	HR	HBP	BB	GDP	SB	CS	PO	WP	BK	RUNS	EOB%	RL#	RPA
Seattle	1990	114	114	15	10	1	5	1	25	3	5	0	0	2	0	22	.217	.131	.128
Seattle	1991	40	40	10	4	0	1	0	7	1	0	0	0	1	0	8	.238	.119	.119
Seattle	1992	27	27	4	1	0	3	0	6	1	0	0	0	0	1	6	.157	.147	.152
San Diego	1992	64	53	13	2	0	0	1	9	1	4	0	0	1	1	7	.218	.079	.078

Throws: Neutral type, extreme righty

Greg W. Harris, 29

(.114/.068) .095   862L   587R

		OUTS	RO	1B	2B	3B	HR	HBP	BB	GDP	SB	CS	PO	WP	BK	RUNS	EOB%	RL#	RPA
San Diego	1990	352	352	68	16	2	6	4	36	6	8	2	0	2	3	40	.174	.085	.084
San Diego	1991	399	0	83	17	0	16	1	21	3	13	8	0	2	0	48	.123	.088	.090
San Diego	1992	354	0	81	18	1	13	2	33	4	18	5	1	2	1	51	.166	.102	.100

Throws: Groundball type, moderate to severe righty

Jeremy Hernandez, 26

(.109/.084) .097   102L   93R   545ML

		OUTS	RO	1B	2B	3B	HR	HBP	BB	GDP	SB	CS	PO	WP	BK	RUNS	EOB%	RL#	RPA
San Diego	1991	43	43	6	2	0	0	0	5	1	0	0	0	2	0	3	.160	.054	.056
San Diego	1992	110	110	31	3	1	4	1	6	1	3	1	0	0	0	16	.169	.103	.100

SAN DIEGO PADRES

Bruce Hurst, 34

Throws: Neutral type, moderate reverse lefty

(.101/.090) .092   483L   2133R

		OUTS	RO	1B	2B	3B	HR	HBP	BB	GDP	SB	CS	PO	WP	BK	RUNS	EOB%	RL#	RPA
San Diego	1990	671	0	128	35	4	21	1	58	21	19	7	1	7	1	75	.125	.084	.083
San Diego	1991	665	0	153	30	1	17	3	56	14	11	6	4	5	1	81	.149	.086	.088
San Diego	1992	652	0	167	31	3	22	0	48	8	18	10	2	4	3	90	.157	.099	.097

Mike Maddux, 31

Throws: Groundball type, neutral righty

(.075/.070) .073   394L   376R

		OUTS	RO	1B	2B	3B	HR	HBP	BB	GDP	SB	CS	PO	WP	BK	RUNS	EOB%	RL#	RPA
Los Angeles	1990	62	52	18	3	0	3	1	4	4	2	1	0	2	0	9	.103	.098	.102
San Diego	1991	296	278	61	10	3	4	1	24	7	5	7	0	5	0	27	.124	.068	.069
San Diego	1992	239	224	60	7	2	2	0	20	5	15	3	0	4	1	26	.166	.080	.078

Jose Melendez, 27

Throws: Flyball type, extreme righty

(.115/.060) .088   375L   361R   238ML

		OUTS	RO	1B	2B	3B	HR	HBP	BB	GDP	SB	CS	PO	WP	BK	RUNS	EOB%	RL#	RPA
Seattle	1990	16	16	5	1	0	2	1	3	0	1	0	0	1	0	7	.270	.236	.232
San Diego	1991	281	114	49	16	1	11	1	21	2	1	6	0	3	2	34	.129	.088	.090
San Diego	1992	268	224	64	9	0	9	3	13	5	3	4	1	1	1	29	.124	.081	.079

Randy Myers, 30

Throws: Flyball type, extreme reverse lefty

(.131/.082) .094   302L   902R

		OUTS	RO	1B	2B	3B	HR	HBP	BB	GDP	SB	CS	PO	WP	BK	RUNS	EOB%	RL#	RPA
Cincinnati	1990	260	260	45	7	1	6	3	30	4	2	4	0	2	1	27	.151	.078	.079
Cincinnati	1991	396	185	87	18	3	8	1	75	14	4	7	0	2	1	52	.188	.094	.088
San Diego	1992	239	239	61	16	0	7	1	31	6	2	3	0	5	0	38	.190	.105	.104

Rich Rodriguez, 29

Throws: Groundball type, moderate reverse lefty

(.086/.075) .079   289L   556R

		OUTS	RO	1B	2B	3B	HR	HBP	BB	GDP	SB	CS	PO	WP	BK	RUNS	EOB%	RL#	RPA
San Diego	1990	143	143	40	10	0	2	1	12	9	4	2	0	1	1	16	.132	.082	.081
San Diego	1991	240	225	46	11	1	8	0	36	12	6	4	0	4	1	29	.129	.087	.088
San Diego	1992	273	261	58	14	1	4	0	25	7	6	5	0	1	1	27	.141	.072	.071

Tim Scott, 26

Throws: Groundball type, extreme righty

(.152/.065) .106   77L   87R   603ML

		OUTS	RO	1B	2B	3B	HR	HBP	BB	GDP	SB	CS	PO	WP	BK	RUNS	EOB%	RL#	RPA
San Diego	1991	3	3	1	1	0	0	0	0	0	0	1	0	0	0	0	.040	.016	.016
San Diego	1992	113	113	27	5	3	4	1	15	3	6	1	0	0	1	20	.189	.117	.115

Frank Seminara, 25

Throws: Groundball type, extreme righty

(.147/.070) .112   227L   188R   1118ML

		OUTS	RO	1B	2B	3B	HR	HBP	BB	GDP	SB	CS	PO	WP	BK	RUNS	EOB%	RL#	RPA
San Diego	1992	301	0	78	12	3	5	3	43	11	10	6	1	1	1	39	.173	.090	.088

Wally Whitehurst, 28

Throws: Groundball type, moderate righty

(.094/.084) .089   619L   562R

		OUTS	RO	1B	2B	3B	HR	HBP	BB	GDP	SB	CS	PO	WP	BK	RUNS	EOB%	RL#	RPA
New York Mets	1990	197	197	49	8	1	5	0	7	5	3	3	1	2	0	20	.108	.075	.074
New York Mets	1991	400	78	101	24	5	12	4	22	12	9	8	0	3	4	47	.133	.097	.085
New York Mets	1992	291	139	66	25	4	4	4	28	11	9	3	0	2	1	39	.170	.096	.094

San Diego Padres AAA & AA Minor League Ratings

AAA (LAS VEGAS)	AGE	BATS	POSITION	CPA	RUNS	SET-UP	DRIVE-IN	RPA
Paul Faries	27	R	3B\SS\2B	513	41.5	.041	.040	.081
Jeff Gardner	28	L	2B	517	58.2	.068	.045	.113
Kevin Higgins	25	L	OF\3B	409	28.3	.035	.034	.069
Chris Jelic	29	R	OF\3B	363	25.8	.034	.037	.071
Tom Lampkin	28	L	C	411	40.6	.055	.044	.099
Luis Lopez	22	B	SS	429	23.5	.024	.031	.055
Steve Pegues	24	R	OF	397	31.1	.034	.044	.078
Darrell Sherman	25	L	OF	592	75.2	.075	.052	.127
Dave Staton	24	R	OF\1B	389	42.0	.051	.057	.108
Phil Stephenson	32	L	OF	246	31.9	.073	.057	.130
Jim Vatcher	27	R	OF	323	35.2	.059	.050	.109
Guillermo Velasquez	24	L	1B	564	58.1	.055	.048	.103
Dan Walters	26	R	C	144	17.5	.070	.052	.122

AA (WICHITA)	AGE	BATS	POSITION	CPA	RUNS	SET-UP	DRIVE-IN	RPA
Steve Bethea	25	B	SS\3B\2B	297	28.3	.052	.043	.095
Jay Gainer	26	L	1B	426	55.3	.063	.067	.130
Mark Gieseke	25	B	1B	273	26.5	.049	.048	.097
Paul Gonzalez	23	L	3B	494	51.7	.051	.054	.105
Vince Harris	25	B	OF\2B	282	28.2	.053	.047	.100
Ray Holbert	22	R	SS	354	35.1	.053	.046	.099
Dwayne Hosey	25	B	OF	480	48.1	.050	.050	.100
Brian Johnson	24	R	C	277	27.7	.052	.048	.100
Pedro Lopez	23	R	C	344	27.9	.037	.044	.081
Steve Martin	25	R	OF	259	15.8	.025	.036	.061
Tim McWilliam	26	R	OF	177	13.9	.036	.043	.079
J.D. Noland	24	L	OF	496	43.6	.041	.047	.088
Mat Witkowski	22	R	2B	495	42.4	.042	.044	.086

AAA Pitchers	Age	Throws	Outs	RPA	AA Pitchers	Age	Throws	Outs	RPA
Doug Brocail	25	R	517	.117	Renay Bryand	26	L	182	.170
Terry Bross	26	R	257	.107	Mark Ettles	26	R	205	.126
Rick Davis	26	R	134	.110	Scott Fredrickson	25	R	220	.132
Jim DeShaies	32	L	174	.125	Joey Hamilton	22	R	104	.111
Dave Eiland	26	R	191	.119	Steve Hoeme	25	R	107	.181
Gene Harris	28	R	103	.134	Kelly Lifgren	24	R	257	.145
Jeremy Hernandez	26	R	167	.106	Mike Linskey	26	L	409	.147
Mark Knudson	32	R	441	.130	Pedro Martinez	24	L	505	.128
Adam Peterson	27	R	302	.118	Lance Painter	25	L	490	.130
A.J. Sager	27	R	180	.163	Royal Thomas	23	R	376	.177
Scott Sanders	23	R	479	.150	Dean Wilkins	26	R	161	.155
Erik Schullstrom	23	R	396	.141					
Tim Scott	26	R	84	.071					
Frank Seminara	25	R	242	.122					
Don Vesling	26	L	174	.158					
Tim Worrell	25	R	567	.113					

SAN FRANCISCO GIANTS

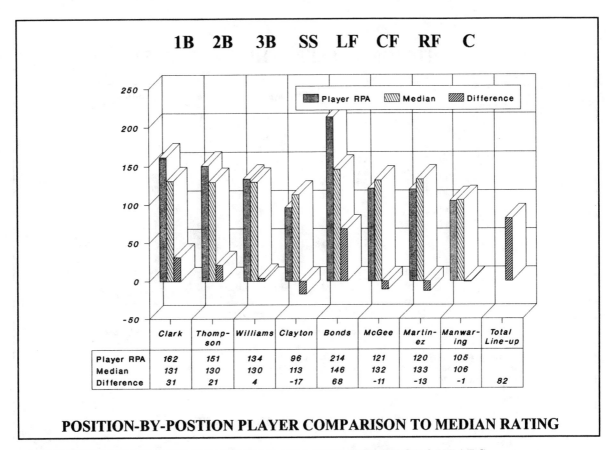

	1B	2B	3B	SS	LF	CF	RF	C	
	Clark	Thomp-son	Williams	Clayton	Bonds	McGee	Martin-ez	Manwar-ing	Total Line-up
Player RPA	162	151	134	96	214	121	120	105	
Median	131	130	130	113	146	132	133	106	
Difference	31	21	4	-17	68	-11	-13	-1	82

POSITION-BY-POSTION PLAYER COMPARISON TO MEDIAN RATING

DEFENSIVE TEAM AND STADIUM DATA FOR THE LAST 3 YEARS:

TEAM DEFENSE BY POSITION:

POSITION-BY-POSITION STADIUM CHARACTERISTICS:

		1990	1991	1992	
1B:	Home	-0.1	-2.6	+2.3	Very easy to play
	Away	+0.9	-1.0	-1.5	
2B:	Home	+2.0	+1.6	-1.8	Easy to play
	Away	-0.6	-2.2	+4 2	
3B:	Home	+2.8	+3.1	+6.1	Slightly easy to play
	Away	+5.0	-1.2	-4.6	
SS:	Home	+0.6	-0.9	-0.4	Slightly easy to play
	Away	+1.3	+1.8	+1.4	
LF:	Home	+5.2	+0.9	+1.6	Hard to play
	Away	-5.4	-1.2	0.0	
CF:	Home	+4.2	+8.1	+12.1	Average (to slightly hard)
	Away	-4.4	-3.4	-8.8	
RF:	Home	-3.0	+7.7	-0.1	Average
	Away	+2.3	+1.9	-4.2	
Total Home:		+11.7	+17.9	+20.7	
Total Away:		-0.9	-5.3	-13.6	

Comments: As reported previously, the Giants have a huge home park advantage on defense. Their total 4-yr. advantage came to an incredible 102.1 runs (25.5 runs per season), which is over 3/10 of a run per game over the 4 years! All but 17 runs of the differential came in the outfield, which is no surprise to those who've heard all the years of stories about the Candlestick Park winds.

SAN FRANCISCO GIANTS

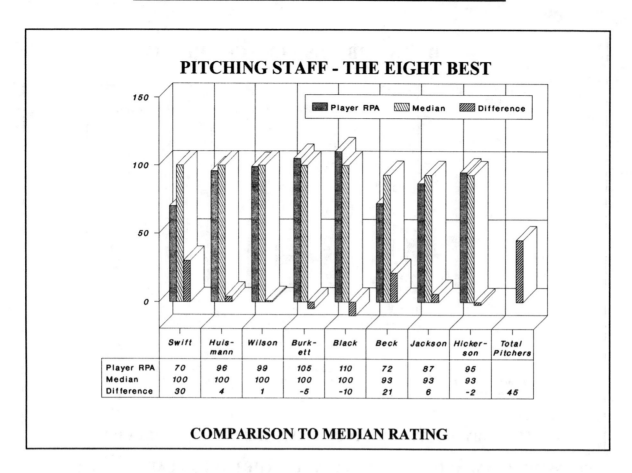

PITCHING STAFF - THE EIGHT BEST

Legend: Player RPA | Median | Difference

	Swift	Huis-mann	Wilson	Burk-ett	Black	Beck	Jackson	Hicker-son	Total Pitchers
Player RPA	70	96	99	105	110	72	87	95	
Median	100	100	100	100	100	93	93	93	
Difference	30	4	1	-5	-10	21	6	-2	45

COMPARISON TO MEDIAN RATING

SUGGESTED LINE-UPS (with set-up RPA & drive-in RPA ratings):

Vs: Left-handed Groundball
CF:	W. McGee	64-58
2B:	R. Thompson	75-68
LF:	B. Bonds	112-87
1B:	W. Clark	74-67
C:	K. Manwaring	62-61
3B:	M. Williams	55-74
RF:	T. Wood	60-50
SS:	R. Clayton	53-61
Pitcher		

Vs: Neutral Lefty Pitchers
RF:	D. Lewis	59-48
1B:	W. Clark	76-68
LF:	B. Bonds	115-89
2B:	R. Thompson	82-73
3B:	M. Williams	56-75
CF:	W. McGee	60-54
C:	K. Manwaring	58-57
SS:	R. Clayton	55-64
Pitcher		

Vs: Left-handed Flyball
RF:	D. Lewis	68-57
2B:	R. Thompson	97-78
LF:	B. Bonds	119-93
1B:	W. Clark	79-71
3B:	M. Williams	58-77
SS:	R. Clayton	61-71
CF:	W. McGee	54-48
C:	K. Manwaring	51-50
Pitcher		

Vs: Right-handed Groundball
RF:	T. Wood	70-60
CF:	W. McGee	63-56
2B:	R. Thompson	67-59
LF:	B. Bonds	116-92
1B:	W. Clark	92-83
3B:	M. Williams	53-71
C:	K. Manwaring	48-48
SS:	R. Clayton	40-47
Pitcher		

Vs: Neutral Righty Pitchers
RF:	T. Wood	70-60
2B:	R. Thompson	73-65
LF:	B. Bonds	119-94
1B:	W. Clark	94-84
3B:	M. Williams	54-72
CF:	W. McGee	58-53
SS:	R. Clayton	42-50
C:	K. Manwaring	44-44
Pitcher		

Vs: Right-handed Flyball
RF:	D. Lewis	67-57
2B:	R. Thompson	83-75
LF:	B. Bonds	123-98
1B:	W. Clark	97-87
CF:	D. Martinez	69-65
3B:	M. Williams	56-74
SS:	R. Clayton	48-57
C:	K. Manwaring	37-37
Pitcher		

Comments: The addition of Barry Bonds makes this one of the more potent offenses in the NL. The Giants could use a lefty-swinging catcher to platoon with Manwaring. Ditto with Clayton at shortstop. The Giants also need a true lead-off type hitter to set up their big guns, and McGee (or Lewis or Wood) isn't the answer to that problem.

SAN FRANCISCO GIANTS

It's amazing what the signing of the best player in baseball can do for a team! Some people say that one player doesn't mean that much. Usually they are right, but not in the case of a player of the quality of Barry Bonds. Just look at Rickey Henderson's career. Wherever he's gone, his team is almost always in contention. In some player's cases the fact that their team is in contention has just been good fortune. In the cases of Henderson and Barry Bonds it's because they are the best players of this period and they can carry a team into contention. Let's put it this way: put Barry Bonds on the Cleveland Indians and the Indians would be very serious contenders!

The only other move of any significance by the Giants over the winter (they couldn't have had much money left after signing Bonds) was the signing of outfielder Dave Martinez. He should have some value in a platoon role, but nothing more than that.

I really don't get what the Giants were doing when they assembled their 15 man protected list for the Expansion draft. The Giants had some of the best young pitching talent around and left most of it exposed. This time the Rockies didn't save the Giants' butts as first Florida, taking Pat Rapp, then Colorado, taking Steve Reed, took two of these prime talents. Fortunately for the Giants, Rick Huismann was not selected. He had a sensational year as a starting pitcher at Phoenix last season. He could be the best of the three. I'd have protected these three fine pitchers over Mike Benjamin, Jeff Brantley and Kevin Rogers.

Also exposed was AA third baseman Adell Davenport. I can understand why Florida chose catcher Steve Decker in the second round of the draft, but I'd have taken Davenport instead. He looks like a better prospect since he can hit, although he's probably at least a year away from the Majors.

Steve Hosey's '92 season was a little disappointing, but I expect him to bounce back this year. Ted Wood did a little better and should get some playing time with the Giants this season.

I was glad to see that Francisco Oliveras is no longer with the Giants. I don't feel that he got the fair shot at a starting role that he should have been given. Hopefully he'll get that shot with Texas, although the awful Ranger defense could do him in.

The Giants appear to have some interesting pitching prospects from the AA Shreveport team of '92. Perhaps the most intriguing is 21 year old Louis Pote. He could be a real good one! Carl Hanselman and Chris Hancock also look like promising pitching prospects. Both Hanselman and Hancock were exposed in the Expansion draft although Hancock was pulled back after the second round. My only criticism is that I'd have probably pulled them both back after the first round (instead of John Patterson and Kevin McGeHee).

San Francisco's Projected record for 1993: 88--74, good for 2nd place in the division.

SAN FRANCISCO GIANTS

Mike Benjamin, 27

Bats Right   101L   152R   97G   39F   368ML

L= .087G .085L ....F   (.027/.042) .069   .061G   .059R   ....F = R

		ATBATS	1B	2B	3B	HR	HBP	BB	GDP	SB	CS	ROE	XB	RUNS	EOB%	RL#	SET-UP	DR-IN	RPA
San Francisco	1990	56	6	3	1	2	0	2	2	1	0	2	3	6	.139	.095	.039	.057	.096
San Francisco	1991	106	8	3	0	2	2	5	1	3	0	2	7	7	.135	.057	.025	.037	.062
San Francisco	1992	75	9	2	1	1	0	3	1	1	0	0	2	5	.127	.060	.024	.040	.064

Will Clark, 28

Bats Left   724L   1209R   532G   497F

L= .137G .140L .146F   (.085/.076) .161   .171G   .174R   .180F = R

		ATBATS	1B	2B	3B	HR	HBP	BB	GDP	SB	CS	ROE	XB	RUNS	EOB%	RL#	SET-UP	DR-IN	RPA
San Francisco	1990	600	128	25	5	19	3	53	7	8	2	8	60	99	.245	.145	.079	.067	.146
San Francisco	1991	565	102	32	7	29	2	39	5	4	2	5	27	107	.214	.151	.085	.082	.167
San Francisco	1992	513	97	40	1	16	4	50	5	12	7	4	34	94	.247	.144	.084	.071	.155

Royce Clayton, 22

Bats Right   112L   271R   185G   62F   773ML

L= .100G .105L .118F   (.039/.047) .086   .073G   .078R   .091F = R

		ATBATS	1B	2B	3B	HR	HBP	BB	GDP	SB	CS	ROE	XB	RUNS	EOB%	RL#	SET-UP	DR-IN	RPA
San Francisco	1991	26	2	1	0	0	0	1	1	0	0	0	0	1	.075	.023	.007	.018	.025
San Francisco	1992	321	57	7	4	4	0	23	11	8	5	8	21	33	.175	.080	.039	.047	.086

Craig Colbert, 27

Bats Right   64L   79R   50G   36F   308ML

L= .025G .066L ....F   (.034/.039) .073   .037G   .078R   ....F = R

		ATBATS	1B	2B	3B	HR	HBP	BB	GDP	SB	CS	ROE	XB	RUNS	EOB%	RL#	SET-UP	DR-IN	RPA
San Francisco	1992	126	21	5	2	1	0	9	8	1	0	3	5	12	.162	.073	.034	.043	.077

Steve Decker, 27

Bats Right   126L   238R   115G   82F   645ML

L= .105G .107L .110F   (.040/.048) .088   .076G   .078R   .081F = R

		ATBATS	1B	2B	3B	HR	HBP	BB	GDP	SB	CS	ROE	XB	RUNS	EOB%	RL#	SET-UP	DR-IN	RPA
San Francisco	1990	54	11	2	0	3	0	1	1	0	0	1	0	8	.167	.132	.059	.074	.133
San Francisco	1991	233	35	7	1	5	3	15	7	0	2	2	8	22	.154	.073	.034	.046	.080
San Francisco	1992	43	6	1	0	0	1	6	0	0	0	1	2	4	.259	.078	.046	.037	.083

Mike Felder, 30

Bats Both   295L   690R   354G   221F

L= .105G .121L .146F   (.061/.056) .117   .099G   .115R   .140F = R

		ATBATS	1B	2B	3B	HR	HBP	BB	GDP	SB	CS	ROE	XB	RUNS	EOB%	RL#	SET-UP	DR-IN	RPA
Milwaukee	1990	237	53	7	2	3	0	22	0	20	9	6	40	35	.247	.130	.072	.061	.133
San Francisco	1991	348	76	10	6	0	1	28	1	21	6	5	39	46	.246	.104	.062	.053	.115
San Francisco	1992	322	72	13	3	4	2	20	3	14	8	2	28	44	.216	.110	.060	.058	.118

Chris James, 30

Bats Right   437L   863R   449G   257F

L= .095G .106L .125F   (.045/.050) .095   .078G   .089R   .108F = R

		ATBATS	1B	2B	3B	HR	HBP	BB	GDP	SB	CS	ROE	XB	RUNS	EOB%	RL#	SET-UP	DR-IN	RPA
Cleveland	1990	528	110	32	4	12	4	27	11	4	3	9	49	74	.221	.130	.067	.062	.129
Cleveland	1991	437	81	16	2	5	4	16	9	3	4	8	23	41	.179	.084	.041	.047	.088
San Francisco	1992	248	41	10	4	5	2	12	2	2	4	5	13	30	.189	.101	.052	.056	.108

Mark Leonard, 28

Bats Left   38L   276R   119G   52F   336ML

L= ....G   .031L ....F   (.058/.058) .116   .134G   .128R   .115F = R

		ATBATS	1B	2B	3B	HR	HBP	BB	GDP	SB	CS	ROE	XB	RUNS	EOB%	RL#	SET-UP	DR-IN	RPA
San Francisco	1990	17	1	1	0	1	0	3	0	0	0	0	3	3	.208	.137	.069	.069	.138
San Francisco	1991	129	21	7	1	2	1	11	3	0	1	0	8	15	.193	.090	.047	.051	.098
San Francisco	1992	128	19	7	0	4	3	16	3	0	1	0	4	19	.216	.111	.060	.058	.118

SAN FRANCISCO GIANTS

Darren Lewis, 25

Bats Right   237L   422R   245G   125F   548ML

L= .089G .098L .116F   (.053/.044) .097   .088G   .097R   .115F = R

		ATBATS	1B	2B	3B	HR	HBP	BB	GDP	SB	CS	ROE	XB	RUNS	EOB%	RL#	SET-UP	DR-IN	RPA
Oakland	1990	35	8	0	0	0	1	7	2	2	0	0	1	4	.264	.088	.053	.042	.095
San Francisco	1991	222	46	5	3	1	2	36	1	13	8	5	26	35	.279	.113	.072	.054	.126
San Francisco	1992	320	64	8	1	1	1	29	3	28	9	6	30	36	.221	.092	.050	.047	.097

Greg Litton, 27

Bats Right   243L   272R   200G   124F   95ML

L= .118G .111L .101F   (.043/.051) .094   .086G   .079R   .069F = R

		ATBATS	1B	2B	3B	HR	HBP	BB	GDP	SB	CS	ROE	XB	RUNS	EOB%	RL#	SET-UP	DR-IN	RPA
San Francisco	1990	204	39	9	1	1	1	11	5	1	1	1	18	18	.187	.080	.038	.043	.081
San Francisco	1991	127	14	7	1	1	1	11	2	0	2	2	9	11	.177	.070	.034	.041	.075
San Francisco	1992	140	23	5	0	4	0	11	2	0	1	0	5	16	.175	.095	.045	.054	.099

Kirt Manwaring, 27

Bats Right   224L   376R   218G   118F

L= .118G .110L .096F   (.046/.047) .093   .091G   .083R   .069F = R

		ATBATS	1B	2B	3B	HR	HBP	BB	GDP	SB	CS	ROE	XB	RUNS	EOB%	RL#	SET-UP	DR-IN	RPA
San Francisco	1990	13	1	0	1	0	0	0	0	0	0	0	1	1	.093	.057	.017	.040	.057
San Francisco	1991	178	31	9	0	0	3	9	2	1	1	3	9	17	.210	.074	.041	.041	.082
San Francisco	1992	349	66	10	5	4	5	29	12	2	1	5	15	41	.206	.092	.049	.049	.098

Willie McGee, 34

Bats Both   572L   1147R   574G   357F

L= .129G .121L .109F   (.063/.056) .119   .126G   .118R   .106F = R

		ATBATS	1B	2B	3B	HR	HBP	BB	GDP	SB	CS	ROE	XB	RUNS	EOB%	RL#	SET-UP	DR-IN	RPA
St. Louis	1990	501	128	32	5	3	1	32	9	28	9	7	72	75	.257	.137	.075	.061	.136
Oakland	1990	113	26	3	2	0	0	10	4	3	0	3	17	15	.243	.108	.062	.053	.115
San Francisco	1991	497	118	30	3	4	2	31	11	17	11	12	45	72	.240	.116	.068	.059	.127
San Francisco	1992	474	118	20	2	1	1	26	7	13	6	4	39	59	.232	.104	.058	.053	.111

John Patterson, 25

Bats Both   26L   85R   48G   17F   917ML

L= ....G L   ....F   (.040/.050) .090   .078G   .082R   ....F = R

		ATBATS	1B	2B	3B	HR	HBP	BB	GDP	SB	CS	ROE	XB	RUNS	EOB%	RL#	SET-UP	DR-IN	RPA
San Francisco	1992	103	17	1	1	0	1	5	2	5	2	2	7	7	.160	.059	.027	.035	.062

Cory Snyder, 30

Bats Right   456L   616R   409G   212F

L= .117G .106L .085F   (.047/.056) .103   .112G   .101R   .080F = R

		ATBATS	1B	2B	3B	HR	HBP	BB	GDP	SB	CS	ROE	XB	RUNS	EOB%	RL#	SET-UP	DR-IN	RPA
Cleveland	1990	438	58	27	3	14	2	18	11	1	4	7	28	45	.148	.097	.040	.057	.097
White Sox	1991	117	15	4	0	3	0	5	5	0	0	5	7	9	.138	.074	.029	.043	.072
Toronto	1991	49	6	0	1	0	0	3	1	0	0	0	2	2	.128	.042	.016	.025	.041
San Francisco	1992	390	67	22	2	14	2	21	10	4	4	4	26	54	.174	.114	.055	.066	.121

Robby Thompson, 30

Bats Right   542L   1069R   557G   315F

L= .143G .155L .175F   (.076/.068) .144   .126G   .138R   .158F = R

		ATBATS	1B	2B	3B	HR	HBP	BB	GDP	SB	CS	ROE	XB	RUNS	EOB%	RL#	SET-UP	DR-IN	RPA
San Francisco	1990	498	82	22	3	15	6	33	9	14	4	10	46	65	.199	.116	.057	.059	.116
San Francisco	1991	492	81	24	5	19	6	61	5	14	7	7	46	91	.241	.140	.083	.071	.154
San Francisco	1992	443	75	25	1	14	8	42	8	5	9	8	49	70	.218	.123	.068	.064	.132

Jose Uribe, 33

Bats Both   273L   589R   290G   181F

L= .112G .104L .090F   (.041/.047) .088   .089G   .081R   .067F = R

		ATBATS	1B	2B	3B	HR	HBP	BB	GDP	SB	CS	ROE	XB	RUNS	EOB%	RL#	SET-UP	DR-IN	RPA
San Francisco	1990	415	88	8	6	1	0	16	8	5	9	5	37	34	.171	.075	.034	.042	.076
San Francisco	1991	231	38	8	4	1	0	14	2	3	5	3	15	21	.180	.075	.038	.045	.083
San Francisco	1992	162	27	9	1	2	0	11	3	2	2	1	14	18	.185	.090	.045	.050	.095

SAN FRANCISCO GIANTS

Matt D. Williams, 27

Bats Right   571L   1301R   661G   371F

L= .124G   .126L   .130F   (.053/.070) .123   .119G   .121R   .125F = R

		ATBATS	1B	2B	3B	HR	HBP	BB	GDP	SB	CS	ROE	XB	RUNS	EOB%	RL#	SET-UP	DR-IN	RPA
San Francisco	1990	617	109	27	2	33	7	24	13	7	4	7	48	88	.166	.130	.058	.072	.130
San Francisco	1991	589	95	24	5	34	6	27	11	5	5	13	25	95	.170	.130	.064	.079	.143
San Francisco	1992	529	82	13	5	20	6	28	15	7	7	6	34	62	.143	.094	.041	.060	.101

PITCHERS

Rod Beck, 24

Throws: Neutral type, moderate reverse righty

(.071/.080) .075   277L   265R   280ML

		OUTS	RO	1B	2B	3B	HR	HBP	BB	GDP	SB	CS	PO	WP	BK	RUNS	EOB%	RL#	RPA
San Francisco	1991	157	157	36	11	2	4	1	11	4	2	3	0	0	0	22	.142	.088	.097
San Francisco	1992	276	276	49	8	1	4	2	13	2	2	4	0	5	2	24	.123	.058	.064

Bud Black, 35

Throws: Neutral type, moderate reverse lefty

(.109/.099) .101   484L   1907R

		OUTS	RO	1B	2B	3B	HR	HBP	BB	GDP	SB	CS	PO	WP	BK	RUNS	EOB%	RL#	RPA
Cleveland	1990	573	0	124	28	2	17	4	57	9	11	7	0	6	1	77	.166	.097	.097
Toronto	1990	47	6	6	2	0	2	1	3	0	1	1	0	0	0	5	.114	.079	.080
San Francisco	1991	643	0	140	31	5	25	4	63	20	14	11	1	6	6	94	.134	.092	.102
San Francisco	1992	531	0	122	27	6	23	1	48	16	7	14	2	3	7	79	.116	.089	.101

Jeff Brantley, 29

Throws: Neutral type, neutral righty

(.104/.103) .104   630L   460R

		OUTS	RO	1B	2B	3B	HR	HBP	BB	GDP	SB	CS	PO	WP	BK	RUNS	EOB%	RL#	RPA
San Francisco	1990	260	260	66	8	0	3	3	27	8	7	4	1	0	3	28	.158	.076	.077
San Francisco	1991	286	286	56	13	1	8	5	42	6	17	2	0	6	0	46	.196	.100	.110
San Francisco	1992	275	213	47	12	0	8	3	40	6	4	1	0	3	1	39	.179	.087	.097

Dave Burba, 26

Throws: Neutral type, moderate to severe righty

(.136/.109) .122   232L   248R   639ML

		OUTS	RO	1B	2B	3B	HR	HBP	BB	GDP	SB	CS	PO	WP	BK	RUNS	EOB%	RL#	RPA
Seattle	1990	24	24	8	0	0	0	1	2	1	1	0	0	0	0	3	.199	.081	.080
Seattle	1991	110	74	19	7	2	6	0	11	5	1	0	1	0	0	15	.106	.098	.095
San Francisco	1992	212	76	59	15	2	4	2	29	7	4	1	0	1	1	40	.212	.108	.120

John Burkett, 28

Throws: Neutral type, moderate to severe righty

(.118/.083) .104   1459L   989R

		OUTS	RO	1B	2B	3B	HR	HBP	BB	GDP	SB	CS	PO	WP	BK	RUNS	EOB%	RL#	RPA
San Francisco	1990	612	9	148	33	2	18	4	54	14	18	7	1	3	3	85	.161	.097	.098
San Francisco	1991	620	5	171	31	2	19	10	58	14	17	16	3	5	0	99	.159	.096	.107
San Francisco	1992	569	0	140	34	7	13	4	39	13	17	7	0	0	0	84	.159	.090	.101

Larry Carter, 27

Throws: Flyball type, righty

(.112/....) .127   86L   55R   1414ML

		OUTS	RO	1B	2B	3B	HR	HBP	BB	GDP	SB	CS	PO	WP	BK	RUNS	EOB%	RL#	RPA
San Francisco	1992	99	0	16	9	3	6	0	18	3	1	1	0	2	0	22	.181	.138	.147

Bryan Hickerson, 29

Throws: Flyball type, moderate to severe lefty

(.078/.100) .093   156L   371R   262ML

		OUTS	RO	1B	2B	3B	HR	HBP	BB	GDP	SB	CS	PO	WP	BK	RUNS	EOB%	RL#	RPA
San Francisco	1991	150	57	39	11	0	3	0	14	6	6	4	0	2	0	20	.138	.086	.093
San Francisco	1992	262	250	47	19	1	7	1	19	8	1	6	0	4	1	29	.106	.072	.079

SAN FRANCISCO GIANTS

Mike Jackson, 28
Throws: Flyball type, extreme righty
(.108/.070) .086   413L   558R

		OUTS	RO	1B	2B	3B	HR	HBP	BB	GDP	SB	CS	PO	WP	BK	RUNS	EOB%	RL#	RPA
Seattle	1990	232	232	47	9	0	8	2	32	5	12	2	0	9	2	34	.180	.105	.103
Seattle	1991	266	266	46	10	3	5	6	23	5	5	0	0	3	0	28	.165	.079	.077
San Francisco	1992	246	246	52	14	3	7	4	23	9	6	3	1	1	0	34	.138	.086	.096

Francisco Oliveras, 29
Throws: Flyball type, extreme righty
(.115/.070) .095   381L   302R   250ML

		OUTS	RO	1B	2B	3B	HR	HBP	BB	GDP	SB	CS	PO	WP	BK	RUNS	EOB%	RL#	RPA
San Francisco	1990	166	137	34	5	3	5	2	15	3	6	2	1	2	1	21	.146	.091	.092
San Francisco	1991	238	223	49	7	1	12	1	18	6	5	9	0	2	2	28	.079	.079	.086
San Francisco	1992	134	39	20	10	0	11	1	8	6	0	3	0	0	0	17	.041	.084	.093

Jim Pena, 28
Throws: Flyball type, lefty
(..../.123) .135   59L   129R   536ML

		OUTS	RO	1B	2B	3B	HR	HBP	BB	GDP	SB	CS	PO	WP	BK	RUNS	EOB%	RL#	RPA
San Francisco	1992	132	101	31	13	1	4	1	15	2	1	0	1	0	0	26	.205	.112	.127

Dave Righetti, 34
Throws: Neutral type, extreme lefty
(.061/.113) .099   216L   616R

		OUTS	RO	1B	2B	3B	HR	HBP	BB	GDP	SB	CS	PO	WP	BK	RUNS	EOB%	RL#	RPA
N.Y. Yankees	1990	159	159	32	6	2	8	2	24	4	0	0	0	2	0	27	.185	.120	.116
San Francisco	1991	215	215	48	12	0	4	3	22	5	8	4	0	1	1	29	.164	.084	.093
San Francisco	1992	235	179	59	13	3	4	0	31	7	7	4	0	6	2	38	.182	.093	.105

Kevin Rogers, 24
Throws: Flyball type, lefty
(..../.140) .122   24L   118R   1228ML

		OUTS	RO	1B	2B	3B	HR	HBP	BB	GDP	SB	CS	PO	WP	BK	RUNS	EOB%	RL#	RPA
San Francisco	1992	102	0	31	2	0	4	1	12	3	1	2	0	2	0	18	.169	.101	.113

Bill Swift, 31
Throws: Groundball type, extreme righty
(.086/.043) .065   741L   713R

		OUTS	RO	1B	2B	3B	HR	HBP	BB	GDP	SB	CS	PO	WP	BK	RUNS	EOB%	RL#	RPA
Seattle	1990	384	230	104	27	0	4	7	15	17	0	2	0	8	3	41	.145	.081	.079
Seattle	1991	271	271	64	6	1	3	1	22	19	1	1	0	2	1	19	.092	.055	.053
San Francisco	1992	494	60	115	19	4	6	3	40	26	5	4	0	0	1	49	.119	.064	.071

Trevor Wilson, 26
Throws: Groundball type, moderate lefty
(.093/.102) .100   401L   1455R

		OUTS	RO	1B	2B	3B	HR	HBP	BB	GDP	SB	CS	PO	WP	BK	RUNS	EOB%	RL#	RPA
San Francisco	1990	331	41	63	13	0	11	1	46	10	3	8	0	5	2	39	.136	.082	.084
San Francisco	1991	606	69	123	32	5	13	5	73	18	8	12	0	5	3	80	.152	.081	.091
San Francisco	1992	462	0	105	25	4	18	6	59	19	6	7	0	2	7	77	.153	.097	.110

San Francisco Giants AAA & AA Minor League Ratings

AAA (PHOENIX)	AGE	BATS	POSITION	CPA	RUNS	SET-UP	DRIVE-IN	RPA
Mark Bailey	31	B	C\1B	111	19.6	.106	.070	.176
Mike Benjamin	27	R	SS	115	11.0	.049	.047	.096
Joel Chimelis	25	R	3B\2B	496	51.2	.050	.053	.103
Royce Clayton	22	R	SS	217	15.3	.030	.040	.070
Craig Colbert	27	R	3B	148	13.0	.042	.046	.088
Jamie Cooper	26	B	OF	409	26.8	.031	.035	.066
Steve Decker	27	R	C	519	46.7	.044	.046	.090
Steve Hosey	23	R	OF	518	50.8	.047	.051	.098
Erik Johnson	27	R	SS\2B	260	14.0	.024	.030	.054
Mark Leonard	28	L	OF	164	25.1	.092	.061	.153
Dan Lewis	25	L	1B	480	44.7	.043	.050	.093
Darren Lewis	25	R	OF	179	9.1	.021	.030	.051
Rob Nelson	28	L	1B	297	33.9	.062	.052	.114
Dave Patterson	28	R	3B\1B	434	38.5	.049	.040	.089
John Patterson	25	B	2B\OF	403	40.0	.050	.048	.098
Gregg Ritchie	28	L	OF	229	24.9	.065	.044	.109
Andres Thomas	29	R	SS	121	9.3	.035	.042	.077
Ted Wood	25	L	OF	475	55.4	.064	.053	.117

AA (SHREVEPORT)	AGE	BATS	POSITION	CPA	RUNS	SET-UP	DRIVE-IN	RPA
Clay Bellinger	24	R	SS	489	34.0	.028	.041	.069
Eric Christopherson	23	R	C	313	29.2	.047	.046	.093
Todd Crosby	27	B	2B	257	13.4	.024	.028	.052
Ron Crowe	25	R	OF\3B	297	20.6	.031	.038	.069
Adell Davenport	25	R	3B\1B	483	58.0	.057	.063	.120
Mike Easley	25	L	1B	222	12.9	.027	.031	.058
Dan Fernandez	26	R	C	207	13.7	.031	.035	.066
Steve Finken	26	R	2B\3B	108	10.4	.048	.049	.097
Ron Jones	28	L	OF	225	21.4	.047	.048	.095
Jason McFarlin	22	L	OF	114	9.7	.041	.044	.085
Jerome Nelson	25	B	OF	321	25.2	.039	.040	.079
Reed Peters	27	R	OF	323	34.9	.056	.052	.108
Reuben Smiley	24	L	OF	385	34.5	.043	.047	.090
Pete Weber	25	L	OF	470	48.6	.054	.049	.103

AAA Pitchers	Age	Throws	Outs	RPA	AA Pitchers	Age	Throws	Outs	RPA
Johnny Ard	25	R	339	.150	Dan Carlson	22	R	558	.125
Dave Burba	26	R	223	.140	Chris Hancock	23	L	148	.106
Larry Carter	27	R	556	.131	Carl Hanselman	22	R	240	.103
Jerry Don Gleaton	35	L	78	.093	Vince Herring	25	L	93	.155
Rick Huismann	23	R	478	.096	Kevin McGehee	23	R	475	.128
Craig McMurtry	33	R	389	.133	Jim Myers	23	R	167	.139
Francisco Oliveras	29	R	184	.110	Louis Pote	21	R	113	.080
Jim Pena	28	L	117	.148	Salomon Torres	20	R	487	.134
Dan Rambo	26	R	303	.126	Mark Yockey	24	L	150	.135
Pat Rapp	25	R	363	.106					
Steve Reed	26	R	180	.089					
Kevin Rogers	24	L	512	.107					
Rob Taylor	26	R	271	.120					

SECTION VI

THE EXPANSION TEAMS

COLORADO ROCKIES

As you can imagine, I looked forward to the Expansion draft with great anticipation. I read *Baseball Weekly* and *Baseball America* to get as much information as possible on what were the plans and strategies of the two new teams.

My mouth was watering at all the fabulous talent that would be available. I was convinced that either, or even both, expansion clubs would be able to select quality players and possibly even be contenders right off the bat! It boggled the mind as to who you would pick first, since there was so much talent out there.

In my conversations with those that seemed to have some information pertaining to the thinking of the Marlins and the Rockies front offices, I came to the conclusion that the Rockies were going to be the team that does all the right things because they would be using some of the modern statistical methods available, while the Marlins would be mired in the old traditional methods and end up with much less talent than they could have had. Boy was I in for a surprise!

I was _not_ one of those fortunates (or is it _unfortunates?_) who was able to watch the draft on TV. I didn't even get the opportunity to listen to the radio reports since I was at work, and when I got home I immediately plunged into working on this book. In any case, I kind of felt that I would have a more balanced view of the overall picks for each team if I saw all the picks at the same time the next day in the newspaper.

By now, if you've read the previous pages, you know that I was stunned by just how awful were the picks made by the Colorado Rockies. In almost every case the Rockies' choice was stunningly bad. Fortunately for them the numbers of good players available was quite large and they inevitably came up with an occasional good selection.

You've heard my gripes, now here's my listing of those players chosen by the Rockies that were worth picking (in order of ability):

1. Eric Wedge, catcher\first base (from Boston)
2. Steve Reed, pitcher (San Francisco)
3. Keith Shepherd, pitcher (Philadelphia)
4. David Nied, pitcher (Atlanta)
5. Jim Tatum, third base (Milwaukee)
6. Brett Merriman, pitcher (California)
7. Denis Boucher, pitcher (Cleveland)
8. Darren Holmes, pitcher (Milwaukee)
9. Jay Owens, catcher (Minnesota)
10. Doug Bochtler, pitcher (Montreal)

The rest of the Rockies' picks were essentially wasted. Why anyone would draft (or trade for) journeyman players like Jerald Clark, Joe Girardi, Charlie Hayes, Dante Bichette and Alex Cole is beyond me. Players of this caliber are always available on the waiver wire and at the end of spring training when rosters are being trimmed.

One bad choice in particular stands out in my mind, not primarily due to the player chosen (Andy Ashby, pitcher for the Phillies), who has some slight ability and could possibly be a good pitcher eventually. But it stands out due to the player not taken: catcher Todd Pratt. Pratt had a huge year in 1992. I would have selected him before any of the above 10 players.

Colorado's Projected record for 1993: 61--101, good for last place in the division.

FLORIDA MARLINS

Had it not been for the atrocious selections of the Colorado Rockies, I wouldn't have been that impressed by the selections of the Florida Marlins, considering all the talent available. But after seeing the Rockies' picks, I was full of praise for Dave Dombrowski and the Marlin front office. Their draft choices may not have been spectacular, but they were professional and they were generally understandable.

The Marlins' draft choices will make this team far better than the Rockies this year and even better in future years. Where the play of the Rockies will be an embarrassment in '92, the Marlins should be competitive.

It was easy to rate the best of the Rockies' picks since I had only to differentiate between 10 quality selections. Here are the quality Marlins choices in order of ability:

1. Bret Barberie, infielder (Montreal)
2. Jeff Conine, first base (Kansas City)
3. Nigel Wilson, outfielder (Toronto)
4. Scott Chiamparino, pitcher (Texas)
5. Pat Rapp, pitcher (San Francisco)
6. Kip Yaughn, pitcher (Baltimore)
7. Jose Martinez, pitcher (N.Y. Mets)
8. Kerwin Moore, outfielder (Kansas City)
9. Cris Carpenter, pitcher (St. Louis)
10. Bryan Harvey, pitcher (California)
11. Rob Natal, catcher (Montreal)
12. Jim Corsi, pitcher (Oakland)
13. Jeff Tabaka, pitcher (Milwaukee)
14. Chuck Carr, outfielder (St. Louis)
15. Junior Felix, outfielder (California)
16. Trevor Hoffman, pitcher (Cincinnati)
17. Steve Decker, catcher (San Francisco)

In addition to these 17 quality players, the Marlins chose some players, like the Indians Darrell Whitmore and the Yankees' Carl Everett, from the lower minors. They also may be very good players.

The Marlins' work didn't stop on draft day. Since draft day the Rockies have only signed two players of any value: outfielder Jim Olander (Milwaukee) and second baseman Trent Hubbard (Houston Astros). Both were minor league free-agents. Olander is the more significant signing. Hubbard has value primarily as a sub. He's only a marginally decent player, but that's not bad for the Rockies. As for the Marlins, they signed a quality third baseman in Dave Magadan. The Marlins had originally chosen Chris Donnels who was also a quality performer, but who was let go after the signing of Magadan. The Marlins traded for Alex Arias, who, while having some defensive liabilities, has a good bat for a shortstop. The Marlins also signed a good minor league free-agent pitcher in Matt Turner (Houston). They also signed a good hitting minor league free-agent outfielder, Geronimo Berroa (Cincinnati).

The Marlins have been very aggressive, and aggressiveness will lead to some mistakes. I think Walt Weiss' career may be over. The Marlins would have been very much better off had they selected Troy Neel from Oakland and not gotten involved in the deal making to get Weiss. In addition, as stated earlier in this book, I don't think much of Benito Santiago. The Marlins would have been better off going with the young catchers selected in the draft.

Florida's Projected record for 1993: 72--90, good for last place in the division.

SECTION VII

ESSAYS

WHO WERE THE REAL MVP'S IN 1992?

This is the second annual set of the "Boerum Street Press Awards" to the top players in baseball. As stated in last year's edition, "the post-season awards process is often based more on hype, prejudice, packherd mentality and subjective opinion and rooting interest than it is on an objective assessment. That doesn't make it bad, however. It just makes it very often incorrect. The process of arguing over who's the best this or that has enlivened many people's lives since time immemorial. It's a fun thing to do. The problem is that some richly deserving players are often overlooked, sometimes for an entire career. That part of the process is bad".

The criteria for these awards will be based on the objective data and analysis found in this book. The awards, however, are not based upon the performances for the past two years combined as usually utilized in this book. What we are dealing with here are the annual awards for performance during the 1992 season alone.

It is a pretty simple process. Much of it you can already figure out from the earlier explanation of player stats in the front of the book. While these awards are based on objective data and analysis, they must be somewhat subjective since we'll have to balance *quality* of the actual performance against *quantity* of the actual production.

We need to know how well a player did each time he came to the plate and we need to know how many runs he produced. If a first baseman, let's say, has an RPA of .150, that only tells us the quality of his hitting. If he had only 200 computed plate appearances, then the quantity of his offense would be 200 times .150, which equals 30 runs. If he was a poor fielder and his 1992 defensive performance was rated at -15, we need to subtract from his offensive production that which he returned to the opposition with his poor defense.

A defensive RPA of -15 means that .015 runs were given back by this player for each of his plate appearances. His adjusted RPA then goes from .150 to .135. Since .015 is a 10% reduction in the original .150 rating we can reduce the 30 runs produced by this same factor. The "effective" runs produced becomes 27 (30 less 3). These awards use the quantity of runs produced balanced against the quality of each at-bat.

What follows is a position by position listing of the winner and runner-up's) in the RPA Award standings. :

AMERICAN LEAGUE:

First Base:	RPA	Runs	Defense	adj. Runs
Frank Thomas	.195	139	- 1	138
Mark McGwire	.195	110	+2	111

Frank Thomas is selected to receive the RPA award as best first baseman in the AL in 1992.

Second Base:	RPA	Runs	Defense	adj. Runs
Roberto Alomar	.167	109	- 7	104
Chuck Knoblauch	.137	97	+6	101

The RPA award goes to Roberto Alomar as the best second baseman in the AL in 1992.

Third Base:	RPA	Runs	Defense	adj. Runs
Edgar Martinez	.177	109	- 4	107
Robin Ventura	.144	100	+18	113

Robin Ventura's defense put him over the top last year. It almost did so again this year. Martinez' 33 pt. RPA lead was narrowed to only 11 pts. after taking into account defense, but that was just enough to edge out Ventura despite producing six fewer runs. The RPA Award goes to Edgar Martinez for best third baseman in the AL in 1992.

Shortstop:	RPA	Runs	Defense	adj. Runs
Pat Listach	.134	85	+18	96
Mike Bordick	.122	69	+13	76

A clear choice. The RPA Award for best shortstop in the AL in 1992 is given to Pat Listach.

Left field:	RPA	Runs	Defense	adj. Runs
Brady Anderson	.160	115	+17	127
Tim Raines	.164	104	+12	112

Anderson is the clear choice despite Raines' slight initial RPA advantage. The RPA Award goes to Brady Anderson as the best left fielder in the AL in 1992.

Centerfield:	RPA	Runs	Defense	adj. Runs
Devon White	.127	88	+32	110
Ken Griffey, Jr.	.151	95	+10	101
Kirby Puckett	.150	106	+2	107

Devon White started out fifth in centerfield in terms of RPA, but after adjusting for his defense during 1992, White ended up as the top run producer and very nearly the tops in RPA. For the second year in a row the RPA award goes to Devon White as the best center fielder in the AL in 1992.

WHO WERE THE REAL MVP'S IN 1992?

Right field:	RPA	Runs	Defense	adj. Runs
Rob Deer	.163	74	+25	85
Danny Tartabull	.182	95	-12	89

A total surprise! The RPA award goes to Rob Deer as the best right fielder in the AL in 1992.

Catcher:	RPA	Runs	Defense	adj. Runs
Mickey Tettleton	.160	102	0	102
Chris Hoiles	.173	64	-11	60

An easy choice despite Hoiles' initial 11 pt. advantage in RPA. For the second year in a row the RPA award goes to Mickey Tettleton as the best catcher in the AL in 1992.

DH:	RPA	Runs
Paul Molitor	.165	113
Dave Winfield	.167	109

A very close choice. The RPA award goes to Paul Molitor as the top DH in the AL in 1992.

NATIONAL LEAGUE:

First Base:	RPA	Runs	Defense	adj. Runs
Jeff Bagwell	.147	108	+7	113
John Kruk	.164	104	- 2	103
Fred McGriff	.162	104	- 6	100
Will Clark	.155	94	+4	96

An extremely close four-way race. The RPA award goes to Jeff Bagwell as the top first baseman in the NL in 1992.

Second Base:	RPA	Runs	Defense	adj. Runs
Ryne Sandberg	.164	119	+10	126
Craig Biggio	.142	109	- 7	104
Geronimo Pena	.164	40	+18	44

Ryne Sandberg wins an easy victory. For the second straight year the RPA award goes to Ryne Sandberg as the best second baseman in the NL in 1992.

Third Base:	RPA	Runs	Defense	adj. Runs
Dave Hollins	.165	119	+2	120
Gary Sheffield	.158	102	+9	108

A narrow but clear choice. The RPA award goes to Dave Hollins as the best third baseman in the NL in 1992.

Shortstop:	RPA	Runs	Defense	adj. Runs
Barry Larkin	.148	92	+13	100
Ozzie Smith	.117	72	+23	86
Jeff Blauser	.152	61	+7	64

Another clear choice. The RPA award goes to Barry Larkin as the best shortstop in the NL in 1992.

Left field:	RPA	Runs	Defense	adj. Runs
Barry Bonds	.231	134	+4	136
Bip Roberts	.146	90	+29	108

Bonds is the clear choice once again. For the second straight year the RPA award goes to Barry Bonds as the best left fielder in the NL in 1992.

Centerfield:	RPA	Runs	Defense	adj. Runs
Andy Van Slyke	.169	115	-9	109
Ray Lankford	.150	106	0	106

The RPA award goes to Andy Van Slyke as the best center fielder in the NL in 1992.

Right field:	RPA	Runs	Defense	adj. Runs
Dave Justice	.155	88	+24	102
Larry Walker	.150	85	+6	88

A clear choice. Who would have thought that Justice's defense would be the thing that puts him over the top? This is the second straight year that Larry Walker was the runner-up. The RPA award goes to Dave Justice as the best right fielder in the NL in 1992.

Catcher:	RPA	Runs	Defense	adj. Runs
Darren Daulton	.183	110	+1	111
Don Slaught	.149	41	0	41

A very easy choice once again. The RPA award for best catcher in the NL in 1992 goes to Darren Daulton.

As far as league MVP goes, our choice is based on who gave his team the greatest advantage over the opposition during the season. The AL choice is Pat Listach winning narrowly over Mickey Tettleton. The NL MVP was more difficult to determine since Daulton had such a huge advantage over Slaught at the catcher position. Slaught's numbers are misleading, however, since he was a platoon player. Once you add the other half of his platoon to his numbers the difference isn't as great. Barry Bonds wins the RPA award as the 1992 National League MVP.

MY BATTING AVERAGE MEANS NOTHING

In the last edition of this book I created the ".525 Club" and the ".375 Club". This feature will be continued here and in future editions. This essay lists the hitters in each league whose batting averages have been most at variance with their RPA's. In other words, a list of those with a lot of "air" in their batting averages (the .375 Club), who tend to be hitters that have no power and/or are totally undisciplined at the plate, and a list of those who were the most productive per each point of batting average (the .525 Club). The latter set of hitters tends to be your big power hitters and/or those hitters who are the most disciplined hitters in baseball.

As stated last year, there are two main frustrations that I have when trying to explain to the average fan why one particular player is not as good as another, or vice versa. These frustrations come in the form of the batting average and the error. While I consider the error one of the most useless stats in all of sports, the batting average at least has some relationship to real ability. This relationship, however, is tenuous. The batting average can hide a multiple of sins or create the false impression that a productive good hitter is a bad hitter merely on the basis of his low batting average or vice versa. The Tony Gwynn vs. Rob Deer comparison is the best current example of this problem. Hitters like Gwynn have what I like to call "empty averages". Once you get past the high number there is absolutely nothing behind them. To be at all productive as a hitter, a member of the .375 club would have to have a very high batting average and even then, as in the case of Tony Gwynn, they tend to be only marginally productive.

What follows are the lists of the members the .525 club and the .375 club for the 1992 season. Let's take a mythical hitter. Say he hit .300 in 1992 and had an RPA of .140. If we divide his .140 RPA by his .300 batting average we would get a run production per point of batting average of .4666 RPA points. This player would not end up in either club since he would be among the majority of players between the .525 club and the .375 club.

Note: players exactly at .525 or .375 are not included since these are the dividing lines. The lists include all players who performed in 1992 and who had at

least 300 at-bats. The player with the highest or lowest rating, depending upon the type of list, is placed at the top of each group:

AMERICAN LEAGUE:

The ".525 CLUB"

Player	Batting Average	RPA	Product. per point
Mark McGwire	.268	.195	.728
Danny Tartabull	.266	.182	.684
Mickey Tettleton	.238	.160	.672
Rickey Henderson	.283	.190	.671
Rob Deer	.247	.163	.660
Kevin McReynolds	.247	.157	.636
Frank Thomas	.323	.195	.604
Brian Downing	.278	.166	.597
Brady Anderson	.271	.160	.590
Dean Palmer	.229	.135	.590
Dave Winfield	.290	.167	.576
Cecil Fielder	.244	.139	.570
Greg Vaughn	.228	.129	.566
Randy Milligan	.240	.135	.562
Tim Raines	.294	.164	.558
Lou Whitaker	.278	.155	.558
Jose Canseco	.244	.136	.557
Mike MacFarlane	.234	.128	.547
Rafael Palmeiro	.268	.146	.545
Lance Blankenship	.241	.131	.544
Candy Maldonado	.272	.148	.544
Jay Buhner	.243	.132	.543
Roberto Alomar	.310	.167	.539
Juan Gonzalez	.260	.140	.538
Shane Mack	.315	.168	.533

The ".375 CLUB"

Player	Batting Average	RPA	Product. per point
Billy Hatcher	.249	.081	.325
Gary DiSarcina	.247	.081	.328
Omar Vizquel	.294	.097	.330
Luis Polonia	.286	.097	.339
Tony Pena	.241	.082	.340
Luis Sojo	.272	.093	.342
Mark Lewis	.264	.091	.345
Greg Gagne	.246	.086	.350
Pedro Munoz	.270	.096	.356

MY BATTING AVERAGE MEANS NOTHING

The AL ".375 CLUB" (continued):

Player	Batting Average	RPA	Product. per point
Billy Ripken	.230	.082	.357
Dante Bichette	.287	.104	.362
Thomas Howard	.277	.101	.365
Lance Johnson	.279	.102	.366
Jody Reed	.247	.091	.368
Scott Livingstone	.282	.104	.369
Steve Sax	.236	.088	.373
Walt Weiss	.212	.079	.373
Ivan Rodriguez	.260	.097	.373

NATIONAL LEAGUE:

The ".525 CLUB"

Player	Batting Average	RPA	Product. per point
Barry Bonds	.311	.231	.743
Darren Daulton	.270	.183	.678
Dave Hollins	.270	.165	.611
Dave Justice	.256	.155	.605
Jeff Blauser	.262	.152	.580
Fred McGriff	.286	.162	.566
Bobby Bonilla	.249	.139	.558
Ryne Sandberg	.304	.164	.539
Jeff Bagwell	.273	.147	.538
Reggie Sanders	.270	.145	.537
Sid Bream	.261	.139	.533
Howard Johnson	.223	.118	.529

THE ".375 CLUB"

Player	Batting Average	RPA	Product. per point
Jose Lind	.235	.070	.298
Kurt Stillwell	.227	.076	.335
Lenny Harris	.271	.091	.336
Benito Santiago	.251	.085	.339
Tom Pagnozzi	.249	.087	.349
Doug Dascenzo	.255	.091	.357
Joe Oliver	.270	.098	.363
Tony Gwynn	.317	.116	.366
Darrin Jackson	.249	.092	.369
Willie McGee	.297	.111	.374

There are only 10 National League players who make the ".375 Club", but four of them are from one team:

the San Diego Padres. Do the Padres seek out undisciplined hitters, or is it just coincidence?

I had the impression, before I did this listing, that those in the ".525 Club" would have lower batting averages as a group from those listed as members of the ".375 Club". It only stands to reason that I would think this since the members of the ".525 Club" are members of this exclusive group based on their relatively low batting average vs. their RPA's, while the members of the ".375 Club" are members of their exclusive club based on their relatively high batting average as compared to their RPA. The problem is, it ain't necessarily so! When you check the above listings you'll find a startling fact: the members of the ".525 Club" have higher batting averages than the members of the ".375 Club"! The median batting average for the 37 members of the ".525 Club" listed above is .268 while the median batting average for the 28 members of the ".375 Club" is .258. In other words, a member of the ".375 Club" is a member of a club that includes the worst hitters in the game.

Since it is clear that the ".375 Club" identifies the collection of worst hitters in the game, Jose Lind's .070 RPA rating for the 1992 season, combined with his .298 RPA production per batting average point, marks him out as the worst hitter in the Majors last season. Are you listening, Kansas City?

THE PLAYERS & PITCHERS WITH THE GREATEST PLATOON DIFFERENCE

This is another listing that began in last year's edition and will be continued in future editions. It is an assembling of the data already contained in this book for the purposes of seeing who's got the biggest difference in RPA ratings when facing lefties or righties. The players from both leagues will be combined. It really doesn't matter to us which league the player performs in. This is an individual thing with no real league meanings. The only requirement for inclusion in these lists is that the player or pitcher needs to have faced both lefty and righty opponents a minimum total of at least 250 times each way, and have a difference of at least 44 points.

BATTERS WHO FARE BETTER AGAINST RIGHT-HANDED PITCHERS:

Player	RPA vs. Lefty	RPA vs. Righty	difference in points
Hal Morris	.074	.145	71
Paul O'Neill	.082	.146	64
Eddie Murray	.081	.143	62
Andy Van Slyke	.128	.186	58
Dave Magadan	.097	.152	55
Wade Boggs	.095	.145	50
Luis Polonia	.072	.116	44
Wally Joyner	.103	.147	44
Ray Lankford	.105	.149	44

BATTERS WHO FARE BETTER AGAINST LEFT-HANDED PITCHERS:

Player	RPA vs. Lefty	RPA vs. Righty	difference in points
Jack Clark	.199	.107	92
Cecil Fielder	.209	.119	90
Rob Deer	.202	.120	82
Dave Hollins	.215	.134	81
Dave Henderson	.190	.111	79
Frank Thomas	.245	.170	75
Jesse Barfield	.139	.070	69
Steve Buechele	.170	.102	68
Jeff Blauser	.182	.114	68
Scott Leius	.143	.082	61
Randy Ready	.142	.081	61
Brian Hunter	.145	.085	60

Continued from previous column:

Player	RPA vs. Lefty	RPA vs. Righty	difference in points
Barry Larkin	.187	.132	55
Paul Molitor	.203	.148	55
Bob Melvin	.112	.059	53
Kevin Mitchell	.191	.138	53
Tim Teufel	.139	.087	52
Ricky Jordan	.139	.087	52
Jim Leyritz	.153	.102	51
Mariano Duncan	.135	.084	51
Danny Tartabull	.220	.170	50
Brian Downing	.191	.142	49
Ivan Calderon	.175	.126	49
Kevin Seitzer	.147	.099	48
Chris Sabo	.153	.108	45
Randy Milligan	.159	.115	44
Dale Murphy	.132	.088	44

PITCHERS WHO FARE BETTER AGAINST RIGHT-HANDED BATTERS:

Player	RPA vs. Lefty	RPA vs. Righty	difference in points
Jim DeShaies	.185	.081	104
Tommy Greene	.142	.055	87
Shawn Boskie	.151	.066	85
Kevin Gross	.136	.057	79
Larry Andersen	.104	.030	74
Jeff Innis	.106	.040	66
Pete Smith	.140	.074	66
Mike Timlin	.131	.066	65
Danny Cox	.141	.079	62
Juan Berenguer	.139	.077	62
Rich DeLucia	.150	.088	62
Orel Hershiser	.121	.061	60
Roger McDowell	.125	.065	60
Gene Nelson	.179	.119	60
Mark Eichhorn	.112	.053	59
John Smoltz	.115	.057	58
Jose DeLeon	.135	.077	58
Steve Olin	.112	.056	56
Jose Melendez	.115	.060	55
Anthony Young	.145	.090	55
Jose Rijo	.096	.045	51
Paul Gibson	.150	.099	51

Continued from previous page:

Player	RPA vs. Lefty	RPA vs. Righty	difference in points
Randy Myers	.131	.082	49
Ramon Martinez	.121	.072	49
Greg Maddux	.093	.044	49
Jeff Montgomery	.115	.068	47
Doug Drabek	.107	.061	46
Greg W. Harris	.114	.068	46
Tim Belcher	.112	.066	46
Jeff Parrett	.135	.089	46
Francisco Oliveras	.115	.070	45
John Habyan	.104	.059	45
Don Robinson	.136	.091	45

Isn't it very interesting to note that Jim DeShaies, the pitcher with the most extreme difference in the above listing, is a reverse-type pitcher! He's a lefty who's simply annihilated by lefty hitters.

Player	RPA vs. Lefty	RPA vs. Righty	difference in points
Rick Reed	.059	.152	93
Rob Murphy	.058	.139	81
Russ Swan	.049	.120	71
Bill Wegman	.066	.130	64
Frank Tanana	.060	.114	54
Erik Hanson	.076	.130	54
Mark Williamson	.079	.132	53
Bob Ojeda	.054	.107	53
Jeff Robinson	.087	.135	48
Chuck Crim	.092	.139	47
Greg Hibbard	.066	.111	45

Does lightning strike twice in the same spot? For this listing it has, and it's no mere coincidence. Once again, the pitcher with the most extreme difference in the above listing is a reverse-type pitcher! Rick Reed is a righty who murders lefty hitters while being crushed by righty hitters. Major League managers need to understand that they are making a huge mistake if they fail to take into account the fact that there are many reverse-type pitchers.

THE MYTH OF THE GOOD OLD DAYS

How many times have you heard an individual or media person assert that baseball was better in the good old days? If you're a long time baseball fan the answer may be: "too many times!". I know that I get very frustrated when some ignoramus in the media makes this claim. While it is sometimes excusable when an older fan, thinking of her or his childhood heroes, says that baseball was better when she or he was younger, I'm a lot less understanding when it comes to the press who should know better since they are the so-called "experts".

The main argument that these people use is that today's game has been watered down. They point to the incontrovertible fact that there are many more Major League teams today, and then claim that in the old days most of these players would be in the minors. Every time there is a Major League expansion the cry of "watered down talent" is heard everywhere, even though it is complete nonsense.

When I was a youngster I thought that baseball players Roberto Clemente, Jackie Robinson, Willie Mays and Sandy Koufax, football running back Jim Brown and basketball's Bill Russell were the greatest players to ever play their respective games and, in fact as I'll show later, I could have been right! But it would no longer be true today, no matter how much I would wish that my childhood heroes be acknowledged by today's youth as the "all-time greatest players in the game".

There is a very disturbing aspect to this question, however. When the press talks about the greatest players in the history of baseball three players from the New York Yankees are inevitably mentioned: Babe Ruth, Lou Gehrig and Joe Dimaggio. When I hear this from the press all I can think about is the incredible arrogance of the media person involved and, above all, I know that he or she is a racist.

I will show, with the assistance of historical population statistics, that the old-time baseball players had to be inferior to the players in the current game. But even comparing players of that old-time period to one another is truly impossible since there was a color bar against black performers.

How can it be assumed that Babe Ruth, as good as he was when being compared to other white ballplayers, was better than every black ballplayer? It can't be done except by a racist who assumes that only the white game was legitimate.

Baseball is no different from all the other major team sports. With the increase in the technological base and the resultant leisure time together with the improvements in communication and the ability to travel, our team sports, like the rest of the entertainment industry, have enjoyed explosive growth and qualitative improvement over the course of this century.

In the same way as the movies have gone from silent films to talkies and now culminate in the multimillion dollar megafilms of today, so sports and the people who play them have developed into the modern game of today. Football players and basketball players have gotten bigger, faster, quicker, their skills are more greatly refined, and this is equally true for the modern baseball players.

While the above argument that I make seems patently obvious and true to me, let me add one last piece of information to completely blow the assertion of these racist media people out of the water: *the population base for the game of baseball has expanded to such an extent that we actually have many fewer teams today, per quantity of population, than we did in the so-called "good old days"!*

That's right! Even without taking into consideration the fact that the population of the country and the world was more rural, more illiterate, had less leisure time, couldn't travel as easily and consequently attendance at Major League baseball games was a fraction of what it is today, it can be shown that the players of today have to be better than the old-timers merely based upon the increase in the overall population base.

Today's players come from all over North America, the Caribbean, Central America, Venezuela and even Australia. Soon, players from Europe will be entering the Major Leagues. Probably the first arrivals will be Dutch. This is a far cry from the "good old days" when Major League players came almost exclusively from the white, English-speaking population of North America.

For the purpose of this essay, I grabbed the *Rand McNally Illustrated Atlas of the World* that sits on my bookshelf and used the data therein entitled "Historical Population of the World". The period covered is 1650 to 1989. We, of course, are only concerned with the current century for which this atlas has breakdowns for each continent for the years 1900, 1914, 1920, 1939, 1950 and 1989.

Even though our game is beginning to quickly expand to other continents, I'll only use the figures listed under the category of North America in this atlas to prove my point.

Here's the raw population data:		
Year	Total Population	White Population
1900	106 million	75 million?
1914	141 million	100 million?
1920	147 million	104 million?
1939	186 million	135 million?
1950	219 million	150 million?
1989	420 million	

The white population estimates are just my best-guess. These are my own estimates based on the *Rand McNally* overall population numbers. I didn't think that I needed to go to all the trouble of searching out the exact totals since it would not really have much effect on the arguments listed herein. My estimates are relatively conservative in any case. If anything, the more accurate population numbers for whites would likely be even more supportive of the point made in this essay.

<u>1.</u> A fourfold overall population increase from 1900 to 1989, but actually a five and one-half-fold increase when looking only at the white population vs. the total population base for baseball today.

<u>2.</u> A threefold overall increase from 1914 (and 1920) to 1989, but actually a more than fourfold increase when only taking into account the whites.

<u>3.</u> A twofold overall population increase from 1950 to 1989, but actually an almost threefold increase when only taking into account the 1950 North American white population.

Even ignoring the obvious fact that a goodly part of the population was physically excluded from the Major Leagues (even in 1950 there were only a tiny handful of black players in the Majors) during the years prior to 1989 that are listed above, the number of Major League teams should have been increased much more than they have been, in order to maintain the proportions of teams to population.

Until the first Major League expansion in the early '60's the total number of Major League franchises was stuck at 16 with 8 in each league. If we take 1900 as the base period then we ought to have 64 (4 times 16) Major League teams. If we use 1914 or 1920 as the base, then we should have 48 teams (3 times 16). If we use 1950 as the base then we should have 32 Major League teams.

If we use the white population figures as a base then we should have the following number of Major League teams:

For 1900:   88 teams (5½ time 16)
For 1914-1920: 64 teams (4 times 16)
For 1939-1950: 48 teams (3 times 16)

Despite the increase in the population base, despite the increase in attendance, despite the development of technology (including sports science), despite the increase in leisure time and the overall explosive growth in all areas of the entertainment industry, the current Major League expansion brings us to only 28 Major League Franchises. That is shameful and a product of the monopoly status that the "Lords of Baseball" got through the U.S. Congress. We ought not to cry over the supposed dilution of talent but rather demand the doubling of the number of Major League franchises so that all those major metropolitan centers that are denied Major League baseball can have a team to call their own. The people in those cities have a right to as much sports entertainment as everyone else!

CAN WE TELL WHEN A HITTER IS BEGINNING TO LOSE IT?

While I was working with the data for this book I thought I saw a pattern developing when I was working with the groundball/flyball ratings for this edition and checking the current numbers vs. those in last year's edition. It appeared to me that more often than seemed to be by chance, hitters who were dropping off the hitting radar screens and heading toward oblivion often seemed to be having sudden and precipitous drops in their groundball RPA's vs. their flyball RPA's.

I decided to use all the computed RPA's from this edition and compare every hitter's groundball RPA to that same hitter's flyball RPA and categorize the resultant differences by age. Take Barry Bonds' data on page 230, for instance. He is listed as 28 years old with a groundball RPA to flyball RPA difference of minus 13 points. I took every play and listed these difference by age.

Here's the chart of what I found:

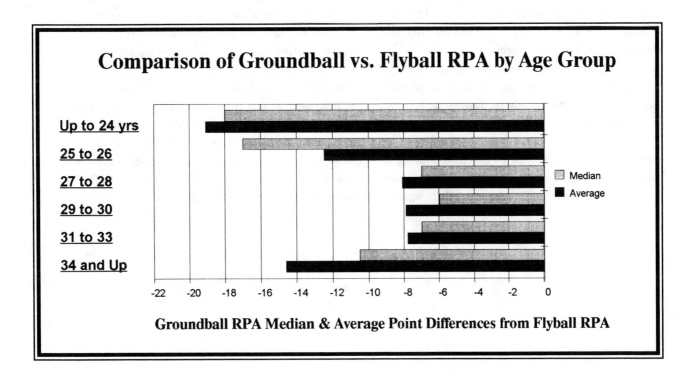

Comparison of Groundball vs. Flyball RPA by Age Group

Groundball RPA Median & Average Point Differences from Flyball RPA

If this suspicion were proven to be correct then we would have an incredibly important marker to indicate which players were about to self-destruct.

Not having an inordinate amount of time to prepare this edition (in fact I'm behind schedule as I write this!) I had to find a shortcut to the answer, or at least make a study that would indicate whether or not my surmise had some actual basis.

Data for the above chart:			
Age Group	No. of Hitters	Median	Average
Up to 24 yrs.	39	-18	-19.1
25 to 26 yrs.	65	-17	-12.5
27 to 28 yrs.	91	-7	-8.1
29 to 30 yrs.	76	-6	-7.9
31 to 33 yrs.	92	-7	-7.8
34 yrs. and up.	56	-10.5	-14.6

CAN WE TELL WHEN A HITTER IS BEGINNING TO LOSE IT?

Wow! It sure looks like a real nice and clear pattern. The sample size is not large enough to be absolutely sure of the conclusions that may be drawn from this data, but the sample size is not all that small either. The sample size won't prevent us from making the suggested inferences that the data seems to reveal.

Before I pose some theories as to why the above pattern seems to exist, we need to make some inference as to what, as far as the hitter is concerned, is the main difference between a groundball-type pitcher and a flyball-type pitcher. Flyball pitchers tend to pitch higher in the strike zone. They are usually fastball pitchers. Groundball pitchers depend upon breaking pitches which are thrown lower in the strike zone. Therefore, hitters who have a larger RPA deficit against groundball-type pitchers are those that prefer hitting the fastball as opposed to the curve ball or other breaking pitch.

From this supposition, which I don't think many of you will argue against, the pattern in the above chart is easy to read. The large deficit against groundball-type pitchers for the youngest hitters indicates that they're still learning to hit the breaking pitch. The middle group of the above ages indicates a plateau is reached until about the age of 33 when the hitter starts to be vulnerable once again to the curve ball. They say that a player starts to lose his reflexes, and that's probably part of the story, but I think the other part of the story is that he starts to lose his sharp vision. He can no longer pick up the spin on the breaking pitch as quickly as when he was younger. If it were merely a matter of his reflexes he ought to be going in the opposite direction. The slower moving breaking pitch should be easier to hit than the fastball if merely the reflexes were involved, but the pattern shown above indicates the opposite.

That explains, I believe, why hitters who lose it tend to disappear so fast from the scene. No amount of exercise can bring back one's eyesight. Our beautiful game calls for the most excellent ability in terms of hand to eye coordination. Once a hitter begins to lose the ability to pick up the spin on the ball, it becomes a slippery slope to oblivion.

THE LIST OF REVERSE-TYPE PITCHERS

Last year I discovered that it wasn't good enough to merely list the RPA breakdowns for each pitcher against lefty and righty hitters. I found that I needed a centralized listing of those pitchers who were of the reverse-type. It's hard to get the significance of this new category without this centralized listing. When it is clear that we're not just speaking about a few pitchers and we can show that many pitchers have extreme reverse tendencies then we demonstrate to ourselves and to those who will pay attention that this is important information.

What follows are these listings with the most extreme pitchers listed at the top (minimum of 100 batters faced each way):

Reverse-type Lefties:

Name	RPA vs. Lefties	RPA vs. Righties	Diff. in Points
Jim DeShaies	.185	.081	104
Greg Mathews	.190	.105	85
Neal Heaton	.164	.105	59
Brian Barnes	.152	.099	53
Paul Gibson	.150	.099	51
Randy Myers	.131	.082	49
Donovan Osborne	.138	.093	45
Mike Magnante	.138	.098	40
Jim Abbott	.119	.080	39
John Franco	.101	.064	37
Tom Glavine	.102	.072	30
Sid Fernandez	.101	.076	25
Kent Mercker	.113	.090	23
Pat Combs	.148	.125	23
Chuck Finley	.125	.103	22
Chris Nabholz	.109	.089	20
Butch Henry	.136	.116	20
Pete Schourek	.121	.103	18
Jeff Fassero	.100	.083	17
Steve Frey	.117	.100	17
Bob Kipper	.132	.115	17
Mike Stanton	.094	.078	16
Derek Lilliquist	.115	.102	13
Jesse Orosco	.114	.102	12
Bruce Hurst	.101	.090	11

Reverse-type lefties continued from previous column:

Name	RPA vs. Lefties	RPA vs. Righties	Diff. in Points
Rich Rodriguez	.086	.075	11
Scott Ruskin	.124	.113	11
Bud Black	.109	.099	10
Kyle Abbott	.119	.110	9
Mark Guthrie	.111	.102	9
Dennis Rasmussen	.109	.101	8
David West	.142	.136	6
Danny Jackson	.115	.109	6
Joe Magrane	.113	.108	5
Dan Plesac	.113	.108	5
Dennis Cook	.106	.104	2
Dave Otto	.111	.110	1

Reverse-type Righties:

Name	RPA vs. Lefties	RPA vs. Righties	Diff. in Points
Gerald Alexander	.068	.174	106
Rick Reed	.059	.152	93
John Doherty	.050	.132	82
Bill Wegman	.066	.130	64
John Kiely	.072	.132	60
Gene Harris	.086	.143	57
Scott Lewis	.094	.149	55
Erik Hanson	.076	.130	54
Mark Williamson	.079	.132	53
Jeff Robinson	.087	.135	48
Chuck Crim	.092	.139	47
Clay Parker	.095	.137	42
Roger Pavlik	.092	.133	41
Stan Belinda	.086	.125	39
Paul Abbott	.103	.141	38
Joe Slusarski	.113	.148	35
Dave Eiland	.097	.132	35
Tim Wakefield	.098	.132	34
Mike Moore	.084	.118	34
Cal Eldred	.087	.120	33
Todd Worrell	.077	.109	32
Alejandro Pena	.067	.099	32
Sergio Valdez	.081	.112	31
Darren Holmes	.087	.116	29
Roger Mason	.106	.134	28
John Dopson	.085	.112	27
Ben McDonald	.101	.124	23

THE LIST OF REVERSE-TYPE PITCHERS

Reverse-type righties continued from previous page:

Name	RPA vs. Lefties	RPA vs. Righties	Diff. in Points
Gregg Olson	.077	.100	23
Wayne Rosenthal	.125	.148	23
Mike Mussina	.077	.099	22
Willie Banks	.123	.144	21
Jay Howell	.075	.095	20
Jim Bullinger	.118	.137	19
Kurt Knudsen	.100	.119	19
Alex Fernandez	.102	.121	19
Tom Edens	.091	.110	19
Todd Burns	.095	.111	16
Mike Gardiner	.095	.11	16
Scott Bankhead	.105	.121	16
Tim Leary	.117	.131	14
Bert Blyleven	.106	.119	13
Mark Dewey	.115	.128	13
Calvin Jones	.102	.113	11
Bob Milacki	.110	.120	10

Reverse-type righties continued from previous column:

Name	RPA vs. Lefties	RPA vs. Righties	Diff. in Points
Bryan Harvey	.079	.089	10
Juan Guzman	.086	.095	9
Rod Beck	.071	.080	9
Joe Boever	.098	.106	8
Ricky Bones	.120	.128	8
Dennis Martinez	.077	.084	7
Ron Robinson	.107	.114	7
Jim Austin	.096	.103	7
Steve Shifflett	.094	.100	6
Ron Darling	.101	.107	6
Bob Tewksbury	.088	.093	5
Rich Monteleone	.088	.091	3
Mike Harkey	.117	.119	2
Pat Mahomes	.110	.111	1
Cris Carpenter	.090	.091	1
Mark Portugal	.097	.098	1
Jose Mesa	.119	.120	1
Roberto Hernandez	.096	.097	1

The above numbers are not to be construed as cast in stone. They will shift somewhat from year to year just in the same way that batting averages and RPA's shift from year to year. It should be expected that many of those pitchers with very tiny, single-digit reverse RPA's could end up off this list next year, while on the other hand some may end up with much more severe reverse-type RPA numbers.

THE ACCURACY OF MINOR LEAGUE RPA'S

In last year's edition of this series I had an essay showing that the minor league RPA ratings, as shown in that book, are as accurate as the year to year RPA ratings for Major League hitters and pitchers.

There was one question left unanswered in the essay. It was clear from the essay that the premier minor league player and pitcher RPA ratings were accurate. I had used the four-page AAA and AA minor league leader board as the source of the minor league players to be checked on. This was done since I did not have unlimited time to prepare the book or unlimited space in the book for a full-sized study.

The question left unanswered was whether these premier minor leaguers were asymptomatic of their fellow minor league players and pitchers. "Sure", a critic could say about last year's study, "the premier player can make the transition with relative ease but many minor leaguers come into the Majors every year and fail to stick. You are skewing your study by not including them. In addition, you are skewing the data by not including those minor leaguers not on your leader board who made the successful transition to the Majors. They were a surprise to you and should have shown a substantial divergence from your projected RPA's".

This sort of argument is quite legitimate and even necessary. It is all too easy to skew results by being selective in the types of data you choose. Every study must have some criteria, and these criteria have to be selected through some subjective manner. In actual fact, no one has challenged me or even questioned (to my knowledge) the accuracy of last year's study on minor league to Major League RPA's. I want, however, to dispel any doubts about the accuracy and usefulness of these ratings before any challenges are raised to this study.

This essay, therefore, is intended to be the answer to that challenge. I decided to list the RPA ratings for *every* Major League hitter and *every* Major League pitcher who met the minimum requirements of 100 computed plate appearances (for the hitters) or 50 innings pitched in either 1991 or 1992 in the Majors and minors in either of the two years. In other words, if a pitcher had over 50 innings pitched at AAA in 1991 *or* 1992 and over 50 innings pitched in the Majors in either 1991 *or* 1992 then his name and his ratings would be listed below.

Comparison of the Major League vs. minor league RPA ratings for hitters with at least 100 computed plate appearances (CPA's) in the Majors in either 1991 *or* 1992 and 100 CPA's in the minors in either 1991 *or* 1992:

Note: where either the minor league *or* Major League ratings have both 1991 and 1992 figures, then the two RPA ratings are averaged. For instance, Mike Simms (the third player listed below) had an RPA rating in the minors in 1991 of .107 and a rating of .114 in 1992. The average of these two ratings is used for comparison to the .110 RPA rating that Simms earned in the Majors in 1991.

Player	Major League 1992 RPA	Major League 1991 RPA	Minor League 1992 RPA	Minor League 1991 RPA	Diff. in pts.
Gary DiSarcina	.081	----	----	.081	0
Lee Stevens	.099	----	----	.099	0
Mike Simms	----	.110	.114	.107	0
Steve Lyons	----	.093	.092	----	1
Chad Kreuter	.091	----	----	.090	1
Dave Nilsson	.113	----	.108	.116	1
Eric Yelding	----	.072	.073	----	1
Eric Karros	.119	----	----	.121	2
Bob Zupcic	.106	----	----	.108	2
Andujar Cedeno	.076	.113	.094	.091	2
Ruben Amaro	.100	----	----	.098	2
Henry Rodriguez	.091	----	.107	.071	2
Greg Colbrunn	.110	----	.113	----	3
Scott Livingstone	.104	.125	----	.111	3
Kevin Koslofski	.119	----	.109	.122	4
Scott Servais	.076	----	----	.080	4
Reggie Sanders	.145	----	----	.141	4
Royce Clayton	.086	----	.070	.095	4
Lance Blankenship	.131	.130	----	.135	5
Carlos Hernandez	.090	----	----	.095	5
Jeff Reboulet	.105	----	.109	.091	5
Juan Bell	.090	.062	.071	----	5
Craig Colbert	.077	----	.088	.056	5
Leo Gomez	.135	.121	----	.134	6
Pedro Munoz	.096	.143	----	.113	6
Karl Rhodes	----	.080	.107	.066	6
Jeff Kent	.106	.148	----	.120	7
Paul Sorrento	.121	----	----	.128	7
Eddie Taubensee	.101	----	----	.108	7
Ed Sprague	----	.116	.123	----	7

Continued from previous page:

Player	Major League 1992 RPA	1991 RPA	Minor League 1992 RPA	1991 RPA	Diff. in pts.
Archi Cianfrocco	.118	----	----	.111	7
Rick Wilkins	.118	.106	.119	.119	7
John Wehner	.067	.145	.106	.090	8
Dave Hansen	.090	----	----	.098	8
Craig Shipley	.070	----	----	.078	8
John Orton	.097	----	.102	.076	8
Eric Anthony	.125	.062	----	.102	8
Jeff Branson	.090	----	.120	.078	9
Bernie Williams	.125	.107	.127	.124	9
Dan Walters	.108	----	.122	.077	9
Mark Lewis	.091	.080	----	.076	9
Esteban Beltre	.061	----	.070	.071	9
Hector Villanueva	.058	.163	.101	----	9
Rey Sanchez	.100	----	----	.091	9
Wes Chamberlain	.110	.111	.132	.067	11
Jim Leyritz	.146	----	----	.135	11
Derek Bell	.111	----	----	.122	11
Tom Marsh	.071	----	.088	.077	11
Jose Offerman	.107	.079	----	.082	11
Luis Sojo	.093	.089	.080	----	11
Dave Cochrane	.097	.088	----	.081	11
Rico Rossy	.089	----	.119	.083	12
Kim Batiste	.059	----	.066	.079	13
Ryan Thompson	.109	----	.120	.071	14
Eric Fox	.111	----	.095	.100	14
Cecil Espy	.104	----	----	.118	14
Mike Kingery	----	.080	.094	----	14
Mario Diaz	----	.090	.075	----	15
Oscar Azocar	.058	----	----	.073	15
Deion Sanders	.150	.099	----	.109	15
Rod Brewer	.113	----	.118	.079	15
Steve Decker	----	.080	.090	.103	16
Mark Leonard	.118	.098	.153	.095	16
Phil Plantier	.106	.202	----	.170	16
Turner Ward	----	.094	.103	.119	17
Mike Benjamin	----	.062	.096	.063	17
Brian Jordan	.083	----	.108	.095	18
Craig Worthington	----	.114	.096	----	18
Luis Quinones	----	.089	.107	----	18
Derrick May	.105	----	----	.087	18
Scott Cooper	.123	----	----	.104	19
Paul Faries	----	.062	.081	----	19

Continued from previous column:

Player	Major League 1992 RPA	1991 RPA	Minor League 1992 RPA	1991 RPA	Diff. in pts.
Dean Palmer	.135	.115	----	.144	19
Monty Fariss	.101	----	.128	.113	19
Ernest Riles	----	.089	.109	----	20
Jeff Tackett	.095	----	----	.074	21
Chad Curtis	.122	----	----	.101	21
Damion Easley	.094	----	.080	.066	21
John Jaha	.121	----	.159	.128	22
Eric Young	.100	----	.104	.080	22
Sammy Sosa	.119	.081	----	.123	23
Andy Stankiewicz	.106	----	----	.083	23
Mo Vaughn	.116	.103	.111	.153	23
Jeff Frye	.118	----	.100	.089	24
Darrin Fletcher	.076	.070	----	.097	24
Wilfredo Cordero	.132	----	.105	.110	25
Freddie Benavides	.078	----	----	.053	25
Tim Jones	.069	----	----	.095	26
Brian Hunter	.138	.111	----	.097	27
Ivan Rodriguez	.097	.081	----	.061	28
Skeeter Barnes	.105	.130	----	.146	29
John Valentin	.133	----	.103	.105	29
Chito Martinez	.119	.148	----	.163	30
Juan Guerrero	.090	----	----	.120	30
Hensley Meulens	----	.088	.118	----	30
Terry Shumpert	----	.087	.056	----	31
John Patterson	.062	----	.098	.089	31
John VanderWal	.113	----	----	.145	32
Todd Hundley	.083	----	----	.116	33
Tommy Gregg	----	.076	.109	----	33
Kenny Lofton	.128	----	----	.094	34
Reggie Jefferson	----	.085	.132	.106	34
Tino Martinez	.100	.094	----	.131	34
Geronimo Pena	.164	.134	.114	----	35
Rich Amaral	.073	----	.109	.110	36
Lenny Webster	.109	----	----	.073	36
Warren Newson	.125	.148	----	.173	37
Darren Lewis	.097	.126	.051	.098	37
Tracy Woodson	.124	----	.095	.077	38
Dave Hollins	.165	.162	----	.124	39
Jim Thome	.089	----	.146	.113	40
Bret Boone	.069	----	.114	.107	41
Pat Kelly	.105	.093	----	.146	47
Pat Listach	.134	----	----	.082	52

THE ACCURACY OF MINOR LEAGUE RPA'S

Continued from previous page:

Player	Major League 1992 RPA	1991 RPA	Minor League 1992 RPA	1991 RPA	Diff. in pts.
Chris Donnels	.079	----	.137	.134	56
Luis Alicea	.108	----	----	.166	58
Darnell Coles	.141	----	----	.083	58

> The Results for the hitters are as follows:
> Total of 117 hitters of which:
> 44 were within 10 RPA points (37.6%)
> 61 were within 15 RPA points (52.1%)
> 75 were winthin 20 RPA points (64.1%)

> **Comparison of the Major League vs. minor league RPA ratings for pitchers with at least 150 outs created in the Majors in either 1991 _or_ 1992 and a total of 150 outs created in the minors in either 1991 _or_ 1992:**

Pitcher	Major League 1992 RPA	1991 RPA	Minor League 1992 RPA	1991 RPA	Diff. in pts.
Steve Shifflett	.103	----	----	.103	0
Roger Pavlik	.106	----	.104	----	2
Chris Haney	.118	.131	.132	.110	3
John Wetteland	.097	----	----	.094	3
Kurt Knudsen	.118	----	----	.115	3
Brian Bohanon	----	.118	.115	.116	3
Darryl Kile	.121	.128	.128	----	4
Dave Eiland	----	.111	.119	.111	4
Scott Kamieniecki	.103	.105	----	.100	4
Sam Militello	.102	----	.097	----	5
Terry Mathews	----	.105	----	.111	6
Jose Mesa	.110	.133	----	.115	6
Steve Searcy	----	.142	.148	----	6
David West	----	.127	.133	----	6
Dave Otto	.132	.093	----	.119	7
Arthur Rhodes	.095	----	.116	.089	7
Wayne Rosenthal	.140	----	.143	.121	8
Pat Mahomes	.117	----	.116	.103	8
Dave Burba	.120	----	.140	.116	8
Rod Beck	.064	.097	----	.072	8
Brian Barnes	.095	.115	.114	----	9
Ryan Bowen	----	.123	.136	.129	9
Pat Combs	----	.129	.120	----	9

Continued from previous column:

Pitcher	Major League 1992 RPA	1991 RPA	Minor League 1992 RPA	1991 RPA	Diff. in pts.
Dennis Rasmussen	----	.106	.115	----	9
Jeff Nelson	.097	----	----	.107	10
Butch Henry	.115	----	----	.125	10
Kip Gross	----	.103	.093	----	10
Wilson Alvarez	.125	.098	----	.121	10
Joe Grahe	.087	.120	----	.114	11
Gerald Alexander	----	.126	.115	----	11
Mike Magnante	.123	.099	----	.099	12
Willie Blair	.095	----	.106	.108	12
Donovan Osborne	.109	----	----	.096	13
Denny Neagle	.129	----	----	.116	13
Rick Reed	.099	----	.132	.094	14
Jose Melendez	.079	.090	----	.098	14
Kevin Campbell	.115	----	----	.101	14
Jim Bullinger	.120	----	----	.134	14
Ricky Bones	.143	.104	----	.109	14
Mark Clark	.120	----	.105	.104	16
Pete Schourek	.097	.112	.120	----	16
Doug Henry	.124	----	----	.108	16
Juan Guzman	.090	.083	----	.103	17
Bruce Ruffin	.149	.094	----	.138	17
Joe Slusarski	.137	.121	.147	----	18
Roger Mason	.114	----	----	.133	19
Rheal Cormier	.102	.098	----	.119	19
Brian Fisher	.110	----	.125	.134	19
Jeff Johnson	.125	.113	.081	.119	19
Steve Wilson	.111	----	----	.130	19
Kevin Ritz	.119	----	----	.139	20
Cliff Brantley	.122	----	----	.102	20
Steve Foster	.103	----	.130	.116	20
Dennis Cook	.114	----	----	.093	21
Willie Banks	.144	----	.108	.139	21
Kevin D. Brown	----	.117	.131	.147	22
Bryan Hickerson	.079	.093	----	.109	23
Julio Valera	.105	----	----	.128	23
Brian Williams	.113	----	.136	.136	23
Francisco Oliveras	----	.086	.110	----	24
Scott Aldred	.147	.117	.174	.139	24
Mike Mussina	.080	.080	----	.104	24
Doug Simons	----	.081	.105	----	24
Bob Milacki	.137	.092	.139	----	25
Dave Fleming	.091	----	----	.116	25

THE ACCURACY OF MINOR LEAGUE RPA'S

Continued from previous page:

Pitcher	Major League 1992 RPA	Major League 1991 RPA	Minor League 1992 RPA	Minor League 1991 RPA	Diff. in pts.
Pat Hentgen	.143	----	----	.118	25
Tom Edens	.086	----	----	.112	26
Dennis Powell	.097	----	----	.124	27
Kyle Abbott	.128	----	----	.101	27
Cal Eldred	.081	----	.098	.120	28
Eric Hillman	.109	----	.131	.151	32
Frank Seminara	.088	----	.122	.120	33
Mike Gardiner	.105	.111	----	.074	34
Bob Wickman	.095	----	.116	.144	35
Dave Haas	.115	----	.136	.166	36
Tim Wakefield	.082	----	.122	.115	36
Hipolito Pichardo	.110	----	----	.147	37
Scott Lewis	----	.154	.121	.112	38
John Doherty	.078	----	----	.127	39
John Kiely	.079	----	----	.118	39
Roberto Hernandez	.075	----	----	.114	39
Rod Nichols	.117	.089	.143	----	40
Mike Fetters	.074	----	----	.116	42
Rusty Meacham	.081	----	----	.125	44
Pete Smith	.090	----	.086	.188	47
Anthony Young	.098	----	----	.148	50
Mel Rojas	.069	----	----	.127	58
Ben Rivera	.092	----	----	.152	60
Derek Lilliquist	.066	----	----	.126	60
Alan Mills	.082	----	----	.146	64
Pedro Astacio	.070	----	.142	.128	65

> **The results for the pitchers are as follows:**
> **Total of 91 pitchers of which:**
> **28 were within 10 points (30.8%)**
> **39 were within 15 points (42.9%)**
> **53 were winthin 20 points (58.2%)**

Last year's study, using the smaller number of players and pitchers, had a median year to year difference in RPA of 17 points for the minor league hitters, 19 points for the Major League hitters, 14.5 points for the minor league pitchers and 12 points for the Major League pitchers. This was a very satisfying result. The medians for the pitchers and hitters listed above are in the same general range. The median for the hitters listed above is 15 RPA points. The median for the pitchers is 19 points.

I've been a little more cautious with my RPA ratings for the minor league pitchers as compared to the RPA ratings for the minor league hitters, and it shows in the above two listings. Of these 91 pitchers, only 30 of them had worse RPA's at the Major League level as compared to their minor league RPA's. Fully sixty of these 91 pitchers actually had better RPA figures at the Major League level as compared to the minor league RPA's they earned, and one had an identical minor league and Major League RPA.

This conservative approach is the most likely reason that these pitchers *appear* to be a little less consistent when coming to the Majors as compared to the hitters listed in the previous group. The small difference in consistency between the minor league pitcher and the minor league hitter ratings, therefore, is most probably an artifact created by my conservative pitcher RPA ratings.

PLAYER
INDEX

PLAYER INDEX

Abbott, Jim 27, 68, 141, 144, 307
Abbott, Kurt 178, 224
Abbott, Kyle 69, 77, 226, 307, 312
Abbott, Paul 74, 168, 170, 307
Abner, Shawn 58, 148, 150
Acker, Jim 72, 183
Adams, Dave 146
Adamson, Joel 226
Adkins, Steve 202
Afenir, Troy 252, 253, 258
Agosto, Juan 72, 184
Aguayo, Luis 98
Aguilera, Rick 72, 168
Ahern, Brian 162
Akerfelds, Darrel 234
Alborano, Pete 226
Aldred, Scott 71, 109, 112, 114, 311
Aldrete, Mike 106
Alexander, Gary 226
Alexander, Gerald 74, 192, 194, 307, 311
Alexander, Manny 90
Alfonzo, Edgar 78, 146
Alicea, Ed 250, 311
Alicea, Luis 51, 237, 238, 310
Allaire, Karl 114
Allanson, Andy 62, 64, 118, 122
Allen, Chad 106
Allen, Harold 266
Allen, Rick 170
Allen, Ron 226
Allen, Steve 79, 269, 274
Allison, Dana 178
Allison, Tom 78, 218
Allred, Beau 76, 106
Alomar, Roberto 50, 132, 133, 134, 297, 299
Alomar, Sandy Jr. 62, 64, 101, 102
Alou, Moises 57, 204, 205, 206
Alvarez, Clemente 154
Alvarez, Jorge 274
Alvarez, Jose 138
Alvarez, Tavo 210
Alvarez, Wilson 70, 152, 311
Amaral, Rich 52, 76, 182, 186, 310
Amaro, Ruben 61, 220, 221, 222, 309
Andersen, Larry 74, 221, 277, 280, 301
Anderson, Brady 56, 83, 84, 86, 297, 299
Anderson, Dave 53, 270
Anderson, Garret 146
Anderson, Kent 186
Anderson, Mike 79, 258
Anderson, Paul 242
Ansley, Willie 226
Anthony, Eric 61, 82, 259, 261, 262, 310
Appier, Kevin 68, 160
Aquino, Luis 68, 157, 160
Ard, Johnny 290
Arias, Alex 55, 198, 202, 293
Armas, Marcos 173, 178
Armstrong, Jack 69, 104
Arner, Mike 194
Arnsberg, Brad 74, 104, 202
Arocha, Rene 77, 237, 242
Ashby, Andy 71, 224, 226, 292
Ashley, Billy 61, 268, 269, 270, 274
Ashley, Shon 210
Assenmacher, Paul 73, 200
Astacio, Pedro 70, 272, 274, 312
August, Don 114
Ausanio, Joe 77, 234

Ausmus, Brad 125, 130
Austin, Jim 72, 119, 308
Aversa, Joe 242
Avery, Steve 39, 45, 69, 248
Ayala, Bobby 71, 256, 258
Ayrault, Bob 74, 224, 226
Azocar, Oscar 57, 278, 310
Baar, Bryan 274
Backlund, Brett 77, 229, 234
Backman, Wally 51, 222
Baerga, Carlos 42, 50, 100, 102
Baez, Kevin 218
Bagwell, Jeff 49, 260, 262, 298, 300
Bailes, Scott 74, 144
Bailey, Mark 290
Baines, Harold 66, 172, 174
Bair, Doug 146
Balboni, Steve 194
Baldwin, Jeff 266
Ball, Jeff 266
Ballard, Jeff 242
Baller, Jay 77, 226
Bankhead, Scott 73, 256, 308
Banks, Willie 71, 77, 168, 170, 308, 311
Bannister, Floyd 74, 192
Barbara, Don 141, 146
Barberie, Bret 3, 53, 205, 206, 293
Barfield, Jesse 60, 126, 301
Barfield, John 194
Bark, Brian 250
Barker, Tim 78, 274
Barnes, Brian 69, 208, 210, 307, 311
Barnes, Skeeter 52, 108, 110, 310
Barnwell, Richard 130
Barrett, Tom 98
Barron, Tony 274
Barton, Shawn 186
Bass, Kevin 57, 213, 214, 261
Batchelor, Richard 130
Bates, Billy 202
Batiste, Kim 55, 220, 222, 226, 310
Bautista, Jose 162
Beams, Mike 98
Bean, Billy 146
Beanblossom, Brad 242
Beasley, Chris 146
Beasley, Tony 234
Beatty, Blaine 210
Beck, Rod 73, 288, 308, 311
Beeler, Pete 234
Belcher, Kevin 78, 188, 189, 194
Belcher, Tim 69, 256, 302
Belinda, Stan 73, 232, 307
Bell, Derek 56, 131, 132, 133, 134, 310
Bell, Eric 74, 104, 106
Bell, George 66, 148, 149, 150
Bell, Jay 55, 228, 229, 230
Bell, Juan 55, 194, 219, 220, 221, 222, 309
Bell, Mike 250
Belle, Albert 42, 66, 100, 102
Belliard, Rafael 55, 246
Bellinger, Clay 290
Beltre, Esteban 54, 150, 154, 310
Benavides, Freddie 55, 254, 310
Bene, Bill 274
Benes, Andy 69, 280
Benjamin, Mike 55, 285, 286, 290, 310
Bennett, Erik 146
Benzinger, Todd 49, 270

Bere, Jason 79, 154
Berenguer, Juan 72, 160, 301
Bergman, Dave 48, 110
Bergman, Sean 109, 114
Bernhardt, Cesar 162
Berroa, Geronimo 76, 258, 293
Berry, Sean 53, 162, 206
Berryhill, Damon 63, 65, 246
Berumen, Andres 157
Bethea, Steve 78, 98, 282
Bichette, Dante 61, 117, 118, 292, 300
Bielecki, Mike 69, 101, 248
Bieser, Steve 226
Biggio, Craig 51, 260, 261, 262, 298
Bilardello, Dann 63, 65, 278
Bird, Dave 234
Birkbeck, Mike 218
Bishop, James 154
Bittiger, Jeff 178
Black, Bud 69, 288, 307
Blair, Willie 70, 264, 266, 311
Blankenship, Kevin 194, 299
Blankenship, Lance 50, 172, 174, 309
Blauser, Jeff 55, 244, 245, 246, 298, 300, 301
Blohm, Pete 138
Blosser, Greg 78, 92, 93, 98
Blowers, Mike 52, 182, 186
Blyleven, Bert 68, 144, 146, 308
Bochtler, Doug 79, 210, 292
Boddicker, Mike 68, 160
Boever, Joe 73, 264, 308
Bogar, Tim 218
Boggs, Wade 52, 94, 124, 301
Bohanon, Brian 71, 192, 194, 311
Bolick, Frank 76, 181, 186, 204, 205
Bolton, Rodney 154
Bolton, Tom 70, 109, 256
Bond, Daven 186
Bonds, Barry 8, 57, 93, 157, 227, 229, 230, 284, 285, 298, 300, 305
Bones, Ricky 68, 119, 308, 311
Bonilla, Bobby 61, 212, 213, 214, 300
Booker, Rod 266
Boone, Bret 50, 76, 180, 181, 182, 186, 310
Borbon, Pedro 79, 250
Borders, Pat 62, 64, 134
Bordick, Mike 54, 171, 172, 173, 174, 297
Borland, Toby 226
Borrelli, Dean 178
Borski, Jeff 186
Bosio, Chis 68, 117, 120, 181
Boskie, Shawn 69, 200, 301
Boston, Daryl 57, 214
Bottenfield, Kent 71, 205, 208, 210
Boucher, Denis 71, 77, 101, 104, 106, 292
Bournigal, Rafael 274
Bowen, Ryan 71, 264, 266, 311
Bowie, Jim 186
Bradkey, Phil 202
Bradley, Scott 63, 65, 218, 254
Brady, Pat 226
Braggs, Glenn 57, 254
Braley, Jeff 79, 109, 114
Brannon, Cliff 242
Branson, Jeff 51, 254, 258, 310
Brantley, Cliff 70, 224, 226, 311
Brantley, Jeff 73, 285, 288

PLAYER INDEX

Brantley, Mickey 258
Bream, Sid 49, 243, 244, 246, 300
Brennan, Bill 202
Brett, George 66, 157, 158
Brewer, Rod 49, 237, 238, 242, 310
Briley, Greg 56, 182
Brink, Brad 71, 224, 226
Briscoe, John 74, 175, 178
Brito, Bernardo 170
Brito, Jorge 178
Brito, Mario 79, 210
Brocail, Doug 282
Brogna, Rico 109, 114
Bronkey, Jeff 79, 194
Brooks, Hubie 66, 142
Brooks, Jerry 274
Brosius, Scott 52, 172, 174, 178
Brosnan, Jason 274
Bross, Terry 77, 282
Brower, Bob 194
Brown, Daren 138
Brown, Jarvis 170
Brown, Keith 74, 256, 258
Brown, Kevin 68, 192
Brown, Kevin D. 71, 184, 186, 311
Brown, Rob 194
Brown, Tim 138
Brown, Tony 146
Browne, Jerry 52, 172, 174
Browning, Tom 69, 256
Bruett, J.T. 170
Brumfield, Jacob 258
Brumley, Mike 98
Brunansky, Tom 60, 94
Brundage, Dave 186
Bruske, Jim 266
Bryand, Renay 282
Bryant, Scott 202
Buccheri, James 178
Buchanan, Bob 258
Buckholz, Steve 234
Buckley, Travis 210
Buechele, Steve 53, 195, 196, 198, 301
Buford, Damon 90
Buhner, Jay 60, 180, 182, 299
Bullett, Scott 234
Bullinger, Jim 70, 197, 200, 308, 311
Bullock, Eric 210
Burba, Dave 71, 288, 290, 311
Burgos, Paco 162
Burke, Tim 72, 128
Burkett, John 69, 288
Burks, Ellis 58, 94, 148, 149, 173
Burlingame, Dennis 250
Burnitz, Jeromy 218
Burns, Todd 70, 192, 194, 308
Burrows, Terry 79, 194
Busby, Wayne 154
Busch, Mike 274
Bush, Randy 66, 166
Bushing, Chris 258
Bustillos, Albert 274
Butcher, Mike 74, 144, 146
Butler, Brett 59, 267, 268, 270
Butterfield, Chris 218
Byington, John 122
Byrd, Jim 98
Byrd, Paul 106
Cabrera, Francisco 63, 65, 244, 246, 250
Caceres, Edgar 78, 122

Cadaret, Greg 73, 256
Cairo, Sergio 90
Calderon, Ivan 56, 92, 93, 205, 206, 301
Calhoun, Ray 274
Caminiti, Ken 53, 260, 261, 262
Campanis, Jim 186
Campbell, Darrin 154
Campbell, Jim 162
Campbell, Kevin 72, 176, 311
Campbell, Mike 194
Campos, Frank 154
Canale, George 76, 106
Candaele, Casey 55, 260, 262
Candelaria, John 74, 229, 272
Candiotti, Tom 69, 272
Cangelosi, John 56, 110
Canseco, Jose 60, 171, 187, 188, 189, 190, 299
Canseco, Ozzie 76, 236, 237, 242
Capel, Mike 77, 266
Capra, Nick 226
Caraballo, Edgardo 162
Caraballo, Ramon 250
Carey, Paul 90
Carlson, Dan 290
Carman, Don 74, 192, 194
Carmona, Greg 242
Carpenter, Bubba 130
Carpenter, Cris 73, 237, 240, 293, 308
Carper, Mark 130
Carr, Chuck 242, 293
Carreon, Mark 56, 110
Carter, Andy 226
Carter, Gary 63, 65, 206
Carter, Glenn 122
Carter, Jeff 154, 178
Carter, Joe 60, 132, 134
Carter, Larry 71, 288, 290
Carter, Mike 122
Carter, Steve 114
Casarotti, Rick 202
Casian, Larry 74, 77, 168, 170
Casillas, Adam 162
Cassidy, David 242
Castaldo, Vince 122
Castellano, Pedro 202
Castilla, Vinny 245, 150
Castillo, Braulio 61, 222, 226
Castillo, Frank 69, 200
Castillo, Tony 114
Castleberry, Kevin 78, 154
Cedeno, Andujar 55, 260, 262, 266, 309
Cedeno, Domingo 138
Centala, Scott 162
Cepicky, Scott 154
Cerone, Rick 63, 65, 206
Cerutti, John 234
Chamberlain, Wes 61, 220, 222, 226, 310
Chance, Tony 202
Chapin, Darrin 226
Chapman, Mark 210
Charland, Colin 106
Charlton, Norm 73, 181, 184, 253
Chiamparino, Scott 71, 77, 189, 192, 194, 293
Chick, Bruce 98
Chimelis, Joel 290
Chitren, Steve 178
Christian, Rick 242
Christopher, Mike 77, 106

Christopherson, Eric 290
Cianfrocco, Archi 49, 204, 206, 310
Cinella, Doug 218
Clark, Dave 61, 76, 228, 229, 230, 234
Clark, Dera 162
Clark, Jack 66, 92, 94, 301
Clark, Jerald 57, 277, 278, 292
Clark, Mark 69, 240, 242, 311
Clark, Phil 109
Clark, Terry 106
Clark, Will 49, 284, 286, 298
Clayton, Royal 130
Clayton, Royce 55, 284, 286, 290, 309
Clemens, Roger 68, 96
Clements, Pat 74, 88
Coachman, Pete 146
Cobb, Marvin 146
Cochrane, Dave 62, 64, 182, 310
Cockrell, Alan 106
Coffman, Kevin 250
Colbert, Craig 63, 65, 286, 290, 309
Colbrunn, Greg 49, 204, 206, 210, 309
Cole, Alex 57, 229, 230, 292
Cole, Stu 162
Cole, Victor 71, 232, 234
Coleman, Vince 59, 212, 213, 214
Coles, Darnell 52, 254, 311
Collier, Anthony 274
Colombino, Carlo 106
Colon, Cris 194
Colvard, Benny 258
Combs, Pat 71, 224, 226, 307, 311
Compres, Fidel 242
Cone, David 68, 133, 136, 157
Conine, Jeff 49, 76, 157, 158, 162, 293
Conroy, Brian 98
Conte, Mike 178
Converse, Jim 186
Cook, Andy 130
Cook, Dennis 68, 104, 307, 311
Cook, Mike 242
Cooke, Steve 77, 234
Coolbaugh, Scott 258
Cooley, Fred 170
Coomer, Ron 154
Cooper, Gary 266
Cooper, Jamie 290
Cooper, Scott 48, 92, 94, 310
Cora, Joey 50, 148, 150
Corbett, Sherm 114
Corbin, Archie 210
Cordero, Wil 55, 76, 203, 204, 205, 206, 210, 310
Cormier, Rheal 69, 240, 311
Cornelius, Brian 114
Correia, Ron 146
Corsi, Jim 72, 173, 176, 178, 293
Costello, Fred 266
Costo, Tim 78, 252, 253, 258
Cotto, Henry 56, 180, 182
Cox, Danny 70, 133, 232, 234, 301
Cox, Darren 258
Crabbe, Bruce 138
Crews, Tim 73, 272
Crim, Chuck 72, 145, 302, 307
Crockett, Rusty 202
Cromer, Tripp 242
Cromwell, Nate 138
Cron, Chris 76, 154
Crosby, Todd 290

316

PLAYER INDEX

Cross, Jesse 138
Crowe, Ron 290
Crowley, Terry 106
Cruz, Ivan 114
Curry, Steve 162
Curtis, Chad 58, 140, 141, 142, 310
Cuyler, Milt 58, 108, 109, 110
Czajkowski, Jim 122
Czarkowski, Mark 186
Daal, Omar 274
Dabney, Fred 154
Dahman, Brian 152
Dalton, Mike 77, 234
Daniels, Kal 57, 198
Darling, Ron 68, 173, 176, 308
Darwin, Danny 68, 96
Dascenzo, Doug 59, 198, 300
Dattola, Kevin 178
Daugherty, Jack 56, 190, 261
Daulton, Darren 63, 65, 220, 221, 222, 298, 300
Dauphin, Phil 202
Davenport, Adell 78, 285, 290
David, Greg 162
Davidson, Mark 106
Davis, Alvin 66, 142
Davis, Butch 138
Davis, Chili 66, 140, 141, 165, 166
Davis, Doug 194
Davis, Eric 57, 270
Davis, Glenn 66, 84, 86
Davis, Mark 73, 248
Davis, Rick 282
Davis, Russ 78, 124, 125, 130
Davis, Storm 72, 88
Dawson, Andre 60, 91, 92, 93, 195, 197, 198
Dean, Kevin 266
Deak, Brian 76, 180, 181, 245, 150
De Butch, Mike 114
De Cillis, Dean 114
Decker, Steve 63, 65, 285, 286, 290, 293, 310
Deer, Rob 6, 7, 60, 108, 298, 299, 301
De Jardin, Bobby 130
De Kneef, Mike 98
De La Hoya, Javier 274
De La Nuez, Rex 78, 165, 170
De La Rosa, Francisco 130
De La Rosa, Juan 138
De Larwelle, Chris 170
De Leon, Jose 69, 224, 301
Delgado, Carlos 133
Dell, Tim 122
Dellicarri, Joe 218
De Los Santos, Luis 234
DeLucia, Rich 68, 184, 186, 301
Dempsey, Rick 62, 64, 86
Denson, Drew 154
De Shaies, Jim 69, 165, 277, 280, 282, 301, 302, 307
De Shields, Delino 51, 204, 205, 206, 207
De Silva, John 114
Deutsch, John 274
De Varez, Cesar 90
Devereaux, Mike 58, 84, 86
Dewey, Mark 74, 216, 218, 308
Diaz, Alex 122
Diaz, Carlos 162
Diaz, Kiki 258

Diaz, Mario 54, 190, 194, 310
Dibble, Rob 73, 257
Dickerson, Bobby 90
Diggs, Tony 122
Di Pino, Frank 74, 240
Di Poto, Jerry 106
Di Sarcina, Gary 54, 140, 142, 299, 309
Di Stefano, Benny 186
Dixon, Colin 98
Dixon, Eddie 234
Dixon, Steve 79, 237, 242
Dodson, Bo 122
Doffek, Scott 274
Doherty, John 68, 109, 112, 307, 312
Donnels, Chris 53, 76, 213, 214, 218, 260, 261, 293, 311
Dopson, John 68, 77, 96, 98, 307
Doran, Billy 51, 254
Dorn, Chris 218
Dorsett, Brian 234
Dostal, Bruce 226
Douma, Todd 218
Downing, Brian 66, 188, 190, 299, 301
Downs, Kelly 68, 176
Dozier, D.J. 76, 213, 218, 276, 277
Drabek, Doug 69, 157, 229, 232, 261, 302
Drahman, Brian 74, 154
Draper, Mike 130
Drees, Tom 186
Ducey, Rob 56, 142, 188
Duffy, Darrin 202
Duncan, Chip 162
Duncan, Mariano 57, 220, 222, 301
Dunne, Mike 74, 152, 154
Dunston, Shawon 55, 197, 198
Dyer, Mike 170
Dykstra, Lenny 59, 220, 221, 222
Dzaidkowiec, Andy 218
Easley, Damion 52, 142, 146, 310
Easley, Mike 290
Ebright, Chris 202
Eckersley, Denis 72, 173, 176
Edenfield, Ken 146
Edens, Tom 72, 264, 308, 312
Edge, Greg 234
Edmonds, Jim 139, 140, 141, 146
Edwards, Wayne 138
Eenhoorn, Robert 130
Eichhorn, Mark 72, 136, 301
Eiland, Dave 71, 280, 282, 307, 311
Eisenreich, Jim 60, 158
Eiterman, Tom 106
Eldred, Cal 70, 77, 120, 122, 307, 312
Elli, Rocky 2, 226
Elliot, Donnie 79, 250
Elster, Kevin 55, 214, 269
Elvira, Narciso 194
Embree, Alan 79, 101, 106
Epley, Daren 106
Eppard, Jim 210
Ericks, John 242
Erickson, Scott 68, 168
Erwin, Scott 178
Esasky, Nick 250
Escalera, Ruben 258
Escobar, John 226
Espinoza, Alvaro 106
Espy, Cecil 61, 230, 310
Estep, Chris 258
Ettles, Mark 282

Eufemia, Frank 218
Eusebio, Tony 78, 266
Everett, Carl 125, 293
Fajardo, Hector 194
Fanning, Steve 242
Fansler, Stan 234
Faries, Paul 51, 278, 282, 310
Fariss, Monty 57, 76, 190, 194, 310
Farmer, Howard 210
Farr, Steve 72, 125, 128
Farrell, Mike 79, 122
Fassero, Jeff 73, 208, 307
Faulkner, Craig 122
Felder, Mike 56, 180, 181, 286
Felix, Junior 59, 141, 142, 293
Fermin, Felix 54, 102
Fernandez, Alex 68, 77, 152, 154, 308
Fernandez, Dan 290
Fernandez, Jose 242
Fernandez, Sid 14, 69, 213, 216, 307
Fernandez, Tony 55, 211, 212, 213, 214, 275, 277
Ferretti, Sam 90
Fetters, Mike 72, 120, 312
Fielder, Cecil 48, 108, 109, 110, 299, 301
Figueroa, Bien 242
Figueroa, Fernando 186
Filer, Tom 71, 216, 218
Finken, Steve 290
Finley, Chuck 68, 145, 307
Finley, Steve 59, 260, 262
Finn, John 78, 122
Finnvold, Gar 98
Fireovid, Steve 194
Fischer, Tom 98
Fisher, Brian 70, 184, 258
Fisk, Carlton 40, 41, 62, 64, 150
Fitzgerald, Dave 122
Fitzgerald, Mike 62, 64, 142
Flaherty, John 98
Flanagan, Mike 72, 88
Fleming, Dave 68, 184, 311
Fletcher, Darrin 63, 65, 207, 310
Fletcher, Paul 79, 226
Fletcher, Scott 50, 92, 93, 117, 118
Flora, Kevin 76, 140, 141, 146
Florence, Don 98
Flores, Miguel 106
Foley, Tom 55, 207, 229
Ford, Curt 242
Fordyce, Brook 78, 218
Fortugno, Tim 71, 145, 146
Fossas, Tony 74, 96
Foster, Lindsay 154
Foster, Steve 73, 257, 258, 311
Fox, Eric 58, 174, 178, 310
Franco, John 74, 213, 217, 307
Franco, Julio 50, 187, 188, 190
Franco, Matt 202
Fraser, Willie 146
Frazier, Lou 114
Fredrickson, Scott 282
Freed, Dan 258
Freeman, Marvin 73, 248
Frey, Steve 74, 145, 307
Frohwirth, Todd 72, 85, 88
Frye, Jeff 50, 190, 194, 310
Fryman, Travis 54, 108, 110
Fulton, Ed 242
Fulton, Greg 210

PLAYER INDEX

Gaetti, Gary 52, 142
Gagne, Greg 54, 155, 156, 157, 163, 165, 166, 299
Gainer, Jay 78, 277, 282
Galarraga, Andres 3, 49, 205, 238
Gallagher, Dave 59, 212, 214
Gallego, Mike 50, 124, 126
Galvez, Balvino 274
Gant, Ron 57, 244, 246
Gantner, Jim 50, 118
Garber, Jeff 162
Garces, Rich 170
Garcia, Carlos 76, 228, 229, 234
Garcia, Cheo 170
Garcia, Leo 162
Garcia, Mike 114
Garcia, Ramon 154
Garcia, Victor 106
Gardella, Mike 106
Gardiner, Mike 68, 93, 96, 205, 308, 312
Gardner, Chris 266
Gardner, Jeff 76, 276, 282
Gardner, John 202
Gardner, Mark 69, 157, 205, 208
Garland, Chaon 178
Garner, Kevin 77, 253, 258
Garrison, Webster 178
Gedman, Rich 63, 65, 238
George, Chris 122
Geren, Bob 98
Giannelli, Ray 138
Gibson, Kirk 61, 230
Gibson, Paul 73, 217, 301, 307
Gies, Christopher 194
Gieseke, Mark 282
Gilbert, Shawn 170
Gilkey, Bernard 57, 236, 237, 238
Gillette, Mike 114
Giovanola, Ed 250
Girardi, Joe 63, 65, 197, 198, 292
Gladden, Dan 56, 108, 111
Glavine, Tom 69, 248, 307
Gleaton, Jerry Don 73, 232, 290
Goedhart, Darrell 226
Goff, Jerry 210
Gohr, Greg 109, 114
Gomez, Chris 114
Gomez, Leo 52, 84, 85, 86, 309
Gomez, Pat 250
Gonzales, Larry 146
Gonzales, Rene 52, 143
Gonzalez, Denny 98
Gonzalez, Frank 114
Gonzalez, Javier 218
Gonzalez, Jose 60, 143, 226
Gonzalez, Juan 58, 188, 189, 190, 299
Gonzalez, Luis 57, 260, 262
Gonzalez, Paul 78, 277, 282
Gooden, Dwight 13, 69, 213, 217
Goodwin, Tom 274
Gordon, Tom 68, 160
Gore, Brian 194
Gossage, Goose 74, 176
Gott, Jim 73, 272
Gozzo, Mauro 170
Grace, Mark 49, 196, 198
Grace, Mike 202
Graham, Greg 98
Grahe, Joe 70, 145, 311
Grant, Mark 70, 184, 186

Grater, Mark 77, 242
Grayum, Richie 197, 202
Grebeck, Craig 54, 148, 149, 150
Green, Gary 55, 254, 258
Green, Otis 122
Green, Tyler 226
Greene, Tommy 69, 224, 301
Greene, Willie 53, 78, 252, 253, 254, 258
Greenwell, Mike 56, 92, 93, 94
Greer, Ken 130
Greer, Rusty 194
Gregg, Tommy 59, 246, 250, 310
Griffey, Ken Jr. 58, 180, 182, 297
Griffin, Alfredo 54, 132, 133, 134
Griffin, Ty 78, 258
Griffiths, Brian 266
Grimsley, Jason 266
Grissom, Marquis 59, 204, 207
Groom, Buddy 71, 112, 114
Gross, Kevin 69, 272, 301
Gross, Kip 71, 77, 274, 311
Grott, Matt 258
Gruber, Kelly 52, 133, 134, 140, 141
Grunhard, Dan 178
Gubicza, Mark 68, 161
Guerrero, Juan 55, 260, 263, 310
Guerrero, Mike 122
Guerrero, Pedro 49, 238
Guerrero, Sandy 122
Guetterman, Lee 73, 217
Gustafson, Ed 170
Guillen, Ozzie 54, 150
Guinn, Brian 154
Gullickson, Bill 40, 42, 68, 112
Gunderson, Eric 74, 184, 186
Guthrie, Mark 72, 168, 307
Gutierrez, Jim 186
Gutierrez, Ricky 90
Guzman, Johnny 178
Guzman, Jose 68, 189, 193, 197
Guzman, Juan 68, 133, 136, 308, 311
Gwynn, Chris 60, 158
Gwynn, Tony 6, 7, 61, 276, 277, 278, 299, 300
Haas, David 71, 109, 112, 114, 312
Habyan, John 72, 125, 128, 302
Hajek, Dave 266
Hale, Chip 170
Hall, Darren 138
Hall, Drew 234
Hall, Joe 154
Hall, Mel 39, 45, 56, 126
Hamelin, Bob 76, 156, 157, 162
Hamilton, Daryl 60, 116, 118
Hamilton, Jeff 274
Hamilton, Joey 282
Hammond, Chris 69, 253, 257
Hancock, Chris 285, 290
Hancock, Lee 234
Haney, Chris 70, 161, 210, 311
Haney, Todd 76, 210
Hansell, Greg 274
Hanselman, Carl 79, 285, 290
Hansen, Dave 53, 268, 270, 310
Hansen, Terrel 218
Hanson, Erik 68, 184, 302, 307
Hare, Shawn 76, 108, 109, 114
Harkey, Mike 71, 201, 202, 308
Harnisch, Pete 69, 264
Harper, Brian 62, 64, 164, 165, 166

Harris, Donald 194
Harris, Gene 74, 280, 282, 307
Harris, Greg 72, 97
Harris, Greg W. 69, 280, 302
Harris, Lenny 51, 268, 270, 300
Harris, Reggie 178
Harris, Robert 154
Harris, Vince 282
Hartgraves, Dean 266
Hartley, Mike 73, 225
Hartsock, Jeff 202
Harvey, Bryan 72, 145, 293, 308
Haselman, Billy 181, 186
Hatcher, Billy 56, 93, 94, 299
Hathaway, Hilly 79, 141, 146
Hatteberg, Scott 98
Hawblitzel, Ryan 202
Hawkins, Andy 186
Hayes, Charlie 39, 53, 125, 126, 292
Hayes, Von 60, 143
Heath, Mike 178
Heaton, Neal 72, 120, 307
Hecht, Steve 210
Heffernan, Bert 186
Helfand, Eric 178
Helton, Keith 266
Henderson, Dave 58, 171, 172, 173, 174, 301
Henderson, Rickey 56, 93, 171, 172, 174, 285, 299
Henke, Tom 72, 133, 136, 189
Henneman, Mike 72, 109, 112
Henry, Butch 69, 264, 307, 311
Henry, Doug 72, 117, 120, 311
Henry, Dwayne 73, 257
Henry, Jim 114
Henry, Jon 170
Hentgen, Pat 72, 136, 312
Heredia, Gil 71, 77, 208, 210
Hernandez, Carlos 63, 65, 269, 270, 309
Hernandez, Cesar 258
Hernandez, Jeremy 74, 280, 282
Hernandez, Jose 54, 102, 106
Hernandez, Kiki 78, 130
Hernandez, Roberto 72, 152, 308, 312
Hernandez, Xavier 73, 265
Herring, Vince 290
Hershiser, Orel 69, 272, 301
Hertensteiner, Rick 210
Hesketh, Joe 68, 97
Hiatt, Phil 162
Hibbard, Greg 69, 201, 302
Hickerson, Bryan 73, 288, 311
Higgins, Kevin 282
Hill, Donnie 50, 166
Hill, Eric 226
Hill, Glenallen 56, 100, 102
Hill, Ken 3, 69, 208
Hill, Milt 74, 77, 257, 258
Hillegas, Shawn 70, 130, 176
Hilleman, Charles 122
Hillman, Eric 71, 217, 218, 312
Hinkle, Mike 242
Hitchcock, Sterling, 130
Hodges, Darren 130
Hoeme, Steve 282
Hoffman, Jeff 130
Hoffman, Trevor 253, 258, 293
Hoffner, Jamie 218
Hoiles, Chris 62, 64, 84, 86, 298

PLAYER INDEX

Holbert, Ray 78, 275, 276, 277, 282
Holcomb, Scott 130
Holland, Tim 90
Holley, Bobby 78, 186
Hollins, Dave 53, 220, 221, 223, 298, 300, 301, 310
Hollins, Jesse 202
Holman, Brad 186
Holmes, Darren 72, 117, 120, 292, 307
Holton, Brian 274
Holzemer, Mark 146
Honeycutt, Rick 74, 176
Horn, Sam 66, 84, 85, 86
Horsman, Vince 74, 173, 176
Hosey, Dwayne 282
Hosey, Steve 285, 290
Hostetler, Mike 250
Hough, Charlie 69, 153
Housie, Wayne 98
Howard, Chris 186
Howard, Dave 54, 157, 158
Howard, Matt 274
Howard, Thomas 56, 100, 102, 300
Howard, Tim 218
Howe, Steve 74, 128
Howell, Jay 74, 273, 308
Howell, Pat 218
Howie, Mark 258
Howitt, Dann 60, 182, 186
Hoy, Peter 98
Hrbek, Kent 48, 164, 166
Hubbard, Trent 266, 293
Hudek, John 154
Hudler, Rex 51, 238
Huff, Mike 60, 148, 150
Hughes, Keith 170
Huisman, Mark 162
Huisman, Rick 77, 285, 290
Hulett, Tim 52, 86
Hulse, David 194
Humphreys, Mike 130
Hundley, Todd 63, 65, 212, 215, 310
Hunter, Bert 218
Hunter, Bobby 234
Hunter, Brian 49, 244, 246, 301, 310
Hunter, Jim 122
Hurst, Bruce 69, 281, 307
Hurst, Jody 108, 109, 114
Hurst, Jonathan 210
Hurta, Bob 266
Huson, Jeff 54, 188, 189, 191
Hutton, Mark 130
Hyde, Mickey 226
Ignasiak, Mike 77, 122
Ilsley, Blaise 242
Imes, Rodney 258
Incaviglia, Pete 57, 263
Ingram, Garey 78, 269, 274
Ingram, Riccardo 114
Innis, Jeff 73, 213, 217, 301
Irvine, Daryl 74, 77, 97, 98
Jacas, Dave 178
Jackson, Chuck 194
Jackson, Danny 69, 221, 232, 307
Jackson, Darrin 59, 276, 278, 300
Jackson, Jeff 226
Jackson, John 146
Jackson, Kenny 122
Jackson, Mike 73, 289
Jacoby, Brook 52, 102

Jaha, John 48, 76, 116, 117, 118, 122, 310
James, Chris 57, 261, 286
James, Dion 60, 126
James, Mike 274
James, Todd 146
Jaques, Eric 202
Jaster, Scott 78, 154
Javier, Stan 59, 220, 223
Jeffcoat, Mike 71, 193, 194
Jefferies, Gregg 52, 155, 156, 158
Jefferson, Reggie 48, 76, 100, 102, 106, 310
Jelic, Chris 282
Jennings, Doug 90
Jennings, Lance 162
Jensen, John 197, 202
Jeter, Shawn 154
Johnson, Brian 78, 106, 282
Johnson, Chris 210
Johnson, Dave 114
Johnson, Erik 290
Johnson, Greg 170
Johnson, Howard 6, 29, 59, 212, 213, 215, 300
Johnson, Jeff 70, 77, 128, 130, 311
Johnson, Judd 250
Johnson, Lance 58, 147, 151, 300
Johnson, Mark 234
Johnson, Randy 68, 185
Johnston, Joel 162
Johnstone, John 218
Jones, Barry 73, 217
Jones, Bobby 78, 146, 213, 218
Jones, Calvin 72, 185, 186, 308
Jones, Chipper 78, 245, 250
Jones, Chris 61, 263, 266
Jones, Doug 73, 261, 265
Jones, Jimmy 69, 265
Jones, Ron 290
Jones, Tim 55, 238, 310
Jones, Todd 266
Jones, Tracy 154
Jordan, Brian 61, 236, 239, 242, 310
Jordan, Ricky 220, 223, 301
Jorgensen, Terry 170
Jose, Felix 61, 236, 237, 239
Joyner, Wally 48, 156, 158, 301
Juden, Jeff 266
Justice, Dave 61, 244, 247, 298, 300
Kaiser, Jeff 114
Kamieniecki, Scott 68, 125, 128, 311
Kapesser, Bob 122
Karchner, Matt 162
Karkovice, Ron 62, 64, 148, 151
Karros, Eric 49, 268, 271, 309
Katzaroff, Rob 218
Kellner, Frank 266
Kelly, Mike 245, 250
Kelly, Pat 50, 124, 126, 250, 310
Kelly, Roberto 57, 251, 252, 253, 255
Kennedy, Bo 79, 154, 253
Kent, Jeff 51, 212, 215, 309
Kent, Troy 186
Key, Jimmy 68, 133, 136
Keyser, Brian 154
Kiefer, Mark 122
Kiely, John 72, 112, 114, 307, 312
Kilgo, Rusty 79, 258

Kilgus, Paul 242
King, Eric 68, 112
King, Jeff 53, 228, 230
Kingery, Mike 60, 174, 310
Kingwood, Tyrone 114
Kipila, Jeff 78, 146
Kipper, Bob 74, 168, 307
Kirby, Wayne 76, 106
Kiser, Garland 106
Kizziah, Daren 138
Klesko, Ryan 245, 250
Kline, Doug 114
Klonoski, Jason 170
Kmak, Joe 122
Knackert, Brent 186
Knapp, Mike 202
Knoblauch, Chuck 50, 164, 166, 297
Knoblauh, Jay 130
Knorr, Randy 132, 133, 138
Knudsen, Kurt 72, 112, 308
Knudson, Mark 282
Komminsk, Brad 154
Kosco, Bryn 210
Koslofski, Kevin 60, 156, 157, 158, 162, 309
Kraemer, Joe 146
Kramer, Randy 71, 185, 186
Kramer, Tom 106
Kremblas, Frank 258
Kremers, Jimmy 210
Kreuter, Chad 62, 64, 109, 111, 309
Krueger, Bill 69, 109, 208
Kruk, John 49, 220, 221, 223, 298
Kuhn, Chad 178
Kuld, Pete 194
Kunkel, Jeff 55, 199, 202
Kutzler, Jerry 202
Kvasnicka, Jay 170
Lake, Steve 63, 65, 223
Laker, Tim 78, 210
Lambert, Reese 162
Lamp, Dennis 73, 232
Lampkin, Tom 63, 65, 276, 277, 278, 282
Lancaster, Les 72, 113, 237
Landrum, Bill 74, 208, 210
Landrum, Cedric 122
Lane, Brian 258
Langbehn, Greg 218
Langston, Mark 68, 145
Lankford, Ray 59, 236, 237, 239, 298, 301
Lansford, Carney 52, 175
Lansing, Mike 78, 210
Larkin, Barry 55, 252, 255, 298, 301
Larkin, Gene 60, 165, 166
Latter, Dave 178
LaValliere, Mike 63, 65, 230
Lawton, Marcus 146
Layana, Tim 90
Leach, Terry 72, 153
Leary, Tim 68, 185, 308
Lee, Derek 154
Lee, Manuel 54, 132, 133, 134, 187, 188, 189
Lee, Mark 122
Lee, Terry 170
Lefferts, Craig 68, 88, 189
Leftwich, Phillip 146
Legg, Greg 226
Leibrandt, Charlie 69, 189, 245, 248

PLAYER INDEX

Leinen, Pat 90
Leiper, Tim 162
Leiter, Al 138
Leiter, Mark 68, 109, 113
Leius, Scott 52, 164, 165, 167, 301
Lemke, Mark 8, 51, 244, 247
Leon, Danilo 79, 194
Leonard, Mark 57, 76, 286, 290, 310
Leskanic, Curtis 170
Levis, Jesse 76, 100, 101, 106
Lewis, Alan 122
Lewis, Dan 290
Lewis, Darren 59, 284, 287, 290, 310
Lewis, Jim 90, 266
Lewis, Mark 54, 99, 100, 101, 103, 299, 310
Lewis, Mica 170
Lewis, Scott 71, 145, 146, 312
Leyritz, Jim 62, 64, 124, 125, 126, 301
Liddell, Dave 90
Liebert, Allen 154
Lieberthal, Mike 226
Lienhard, Steve 122
Lifgren, Kelly 282
Lilliquist, Derek 72, 104, 307, 312
Limbach, Chris 226
Lind, Jose 50, 155, 156, 227, 229, 231, 300
Lind, Orlando 170
Lindeman, Jim 61, 223, 261
Lindsey, Doug 226
Linskey, Mike 282
Linton, Doug 71, 136, 138
Lipson, Marc 170
Liriano, Nelson 76, 106
List, Paul 194
Listach, Pat 54, 115, 116, 117, 118, 297, 310
Litton, Greg 51, 181, 287
Livernois, Derek 98
Livingstone, Scott 52, 108, 111, 300, 309
Lloyd, Graeme 79, 117, 138
Lockett, Ron 226
Lockhart, Keith 178
Lofton, Kenny 58, 99, 100, 101, 103, 261, 310
Lofton, Rodney 90
Long, Kevin 162
Lo Nigro, Greg 154
Lopez, Javy 78, 245, 250
Lopez, Luis 282
Lopez, Pedro 282
Lovelace, Vance 114
Lo Vullo, Torey 76, 130, 140, 141
Luckham, Ken 266
Luebbers, Larry 258
Lumley, Mike 79, 109, 114
Lyden, Mitch 218
Lydy, Scott 78, 178
Lynch, David 79, 258
Lyons, Barry 266
Lyons, Steve 58, 92, 93, 95, 98, 309
Maas, Kevin 66, 124, 125, 126
MacDonald, Bob 72, 136
MacFarlane, Mike 62, 64, 156, 159, 299
Mack, Quin 210
Mack, Shane 56, 164, 167, 299
Maclin, Lonnie 242
Maddux, Greg 69, 125, 197, 201, 245, 302

Maddux, Mike 73, 213, 277, 281
Madsen, Lance 78, 266
Magadan, Dave 53, 213, 215, 261, 293, 301
Magallanes, Ever 154
Magnante, Mike 70, 157, 161, 307, 311
Magrane, Joe 71, 237, 241, 242, 307
Mahomes, Pat 71, 165, 169, 170, 308, 311
Majer, Steffen 242
Makarewicz, Scott 78, 266
Maksudian, Mike 138, 164, 165
Maldonado, Candy 57, 131, 133, 134, 195, 196, 197, 299
Maldonado, Carlos 162
Mallicoat, Rob 74, 77, 265, 266
Manahan, Anthony 186
Manahan, Austin 234
Manon, Ramon 130
Manto, Jeff 76, 221, 250
Manuel, Barry 194
Manwaring, Kirt 63, 65, 284, 287
Manzanillo, Josias 162
Marak, Paul 202
Marchok, Chris 210
Marsh, Tom 61, 223, 226, 310
Marshall, Randy 218
Martel, Ed 130
Martin, Al 76, 228, 229, 234
Martin, Chris 210
Martin, Norberto 154
Martin, Steve 282
Martinez, Carlos 48, 84, 103
Martinez, Chito 60, 85, 87, 310
Martinez, Dave 59, 255, 284, 285
Martinez, David 122
Martinez, Dennis 69, 209, 308
Martinez, Domingo 138
Martinez, Edgar 52, 180, 181, 182, 297
Martinez, Jose 79, 213, 218, 293
Martinez, Julian 242
Martinez, Luis 274
Martinez, Pedro 269, 274, 282
Martinez, Ramon 69, 273, 302
Martinez, Ray 146
Martinez, Tino 48, 180, 183, 310
Marzano, John 62, 64, 92, 95
Mason, Roger 73, 233, 277, 307, 311
Massarelli, John 266
Masse, Billy 130
Masteller, Dan 170
Masters, Dave 186
Mathews, Greg 71, 225, 226, 307
Mathews, Terry 74, 193, 311
Mathile, Mike 79, 210
Matos, Fransisco 178
Mattingly, Don 48, 124, 125, 127
Maurer, Rob 188, 189, 194
Maurer, Ron 274
Mauser, Tim 226
May, Derrick 57, 199, 310
May, Lee 218
May, Scott 202
Maynard, Tow 186
Mayne, Brent 62, 64, 157, 159
Maysey, Matt 210
McAndrew, Jamie 274
McCarthy, Tom 77, 250
McCarty, Dave 78, 164, 170
McCaskill, Kirk 153
McClellan, Paul 122

McClendon, Lloyd 61, 228, 231
McClure, Bob 73, 241
McConnell, Walt 146
McCreary, Bob 170
McCullers, Lance 74, 77, 193, 274
McDonald, Ben 68, 88, 307
McDonald, Chad 210
McDonald, Mike 186
McDowell, Jack 68, 153
McDowell, Roger 73, 273, 301
McElroy, Chuck 73, 201
McFarlin, Jason 290
McGee, Willie 59, 284, 287, 300
McGeHee, Kevin 285, 290
McGinnis, Russ 76, 156, 157, 194
McGraw, Tom 122
McGriff, Fred 49, 276, 278, 298, 300
McGwire, Mark 48, 172, 175, 297, 299
McKaskill, Kirk 68
McKnight, Jeff 51, 212, 215, 218
McLemore, Mark 50, 87
McMichael, Greg 250
McMurtry, Craig 290
McNeely, Jeff 98
McRae, Brian 58, 156, 159
McReynolds, Kevin 56, 155, 156, 159, 299
McWilliam, Tim 282
Meacham, Rusty 72, 161
Meadows, Scott 90
Meares, Pat 170
Medina, Luis 162
Meier, Kevin 242
Melendez, Jose 73, 93, 277, 281, 301, 311
Melvin, Bill 202, 301
Melvin, Bob 62, 64, 92, 159
Mendenhall, Kirk 114
Mendez, Jesus 242
Menendez, Tony 258
Mengel, Brad 138
Menhart, Paul 138
Merced, Orlando 49, 218, 228, 231
Mercedes, Henry 178
Mercedes, Luis 60, 84, 85, 87, 90
Merchant, Mark 186
Mercker, Kent 73, 248, 307
Merigliano, Frank 154
Merriman, Brett 77, 141, 146, 292
Merullo, Matt 62, 64, 151
Mesa, Jose 68, 104, 308, 311
Meulens, Hensley 52, 76, 124, 127, 130, 310
Miceli, Danny 162
Mieske, Matt 116, 122
Mikulik, Joe 266
Milacki, Bob 68, 89, 90, 308, 311
Milchin, Mike 237, 242
Militello, Sam 71, 77, 128, 130, 311
Miller, Brent 90
Miller, Dave 90
Miller, Keith 50, 156, 157, 159, 194
Miller, Kurt 194
Miller, Orlando 266
Miller, Paul 234
Millette, Joe 226
Milligan, Randy 48, 85, 87, 299, 301
Mills, Alan 72, 89, 312
Milstein, Dave 98
Mimbs, Mark 274
Mimbs, Mike 274

PLAYER INDEX

Minchey, Nate 78, 93, 98
Minor, Blas 77, 229, 234
Minutelli, Gino 258
Miranda, Angel 117, 122
Mitchell, Keith 250, 252, 255, 301
Mitchell, Kevin 57, 181, 253
Mlicki, Dave 71, 104, 106
Moeller, Dennis 162
Mohler, Mike 178
Molitor, Paul 66, 117, 118, 132, 133, 298, 301
Mondesi, Raul 269, 274
Mongiello, Mike 154
Montalvo, Rob 138
Monteleone, Rich 72, 125, 129, 308
Montgomery, Jeff 72, 161, 302
Montgomery, Ray 266
Montoyo, Charlie 116, 122
Monzon, Jose 138
Moore, Bobby 250
Moore, Brad 218
Moore, Kerwin, 162, 293
Moore, Marcus 138
Moore, Mike 68, 109, 173, 177, 307
Morandini, Mickey 51, 220, 223
Mordecai, Mike 250
Morgan, Mike 69, 201
Morman, Russ 258
Morris, Hal 49, 252, 253, 255, 301
Morris, Jack 45, 68, 137
Morris, John 66, 143
Morris, Rod 194
Morrow, Chris 274
Morton, Kevin 98
Moses, John 56, 183, 186
Mosley, Tony 98
Mota, Andy 266
Mota, Carlos 106
Mota, Domingo 162
Mota, Jose 162
Mouton, Lyle 130
Moyer, Jamie 77, 114
Mulholland, Terry 69, 225
Mulliniks, Rance 66, 135
Munoz, Jose 274
Munoz, Mike 74, 113
Munoz, Omer 210
Munoz, Oscar 170
Munoz, Pedro 60, 164, 167, 299, 309
Munoz, Roberto 130
Murphy, Dale 61, 224, 301
Murphy, Rob 73, 237, 265, 302
Murray, Eddie 49, 212, 215, 301
Musselman, Jeff 178
Mussina, Mike 68, 85, 89, 308, 311
Musolino, Mike 146
Mutis, Jeff 71, 104, 106
Myers, Chris 210
Myers, Greg 62, 64, 140, 143
Myers, Jim 290
Myers, Randy 73, 197, 281, 302, 307
Nabholz, Chris 69, 209, 307
Naehring, Tim 54, 92, 95
Nagy, Charles 40, 42, 68, 105
Natal, Rob 210, 293
Navarro, Jaime 68, 120
Naveda, Ed 170
Neagle, Denny 73, 233, 311
Neel, Troy 76, 172, 173, 178, 293
Neidlinger, Jim 274

Neitzel, R.A. 226
Nelson, Gene 72, 177, 301
Nelson, Jeff 72, 185, 311
Nelson, Jerome 290
Nelson, Rob 290
Nen, Robb 194
Newfield, Marc 186
Newlin, Jim 186
Newman, Al 50, 191
Newman, Alan 170
Newson, Warren 60, 148, 151, 310
Nezelek, Andy 79, 181, 250
Nichols, Rod 68, 105, 106, 312
Nichting, Chris 274
Nied, David 77, 250, 292
Nielsen, Jerry 79, 130, 41
Niethammer, Darren 194
Nieves, Melvin 78, 245, 250
Nilsson, Dave 62, 64, 116, 117, 118, 122, 309
Nixon, Donell 106
Nixon, Otis 59, 243, 244, 247
Noboa, Junior 51, 215
Nokes, Matt 62, 64, 127
Noland, J.D. 282
Nolte, Eric 122
Norman, Les 162
Norris, Bill 98
Novoa, Rafael 79, 122
Nuneviller, Tom 226
Nunez, Edwin 72, 193
Nunez, Jose 186
Obando, Sherman 78, 84, 85, 125, 130
Oberkfell, Ken 50, 143, 146
O'Brien, Charlie 63, 65, 212, 215
O'Brien, Pete 48, 181, 183
O'Donoghue, John 77, 85, 90
Offerman, Jose 55, 268, 271, 310
Ogea, Chad 101, 106
Ogliaruso, Mike 138
O'Halloran, Greg 138
Ohlms, Mark 79, 133, 138
Ojala, Kirt 130
Ojeda, Bob 69, 101, 273, 302
Olander, Jim 122, 293
O'Leary, Troy 78, 116, 122
Olerud, John 48, 132, 133, 135
Olin, Steve 72, 105, 301
Oliva, Jose (Joe) 78, 194
Olivares, Omar 69, 241
Oliver, Joe 63, 65, 253, 255, 300
Oliveras, Francisco 71, 189, 285, 289, 290, 302, 311
Olmeda, Jose 250
Olmstead, Reed
Olsen, Steve 154
Olson, Greg 63, 65, 244, 245, 247
Olson, Gregg 72, 89, 308
O'Neill, Paul 60, 124, 127, 251, 253, 301
Opperman, Dan 274
Oquendo, Jose 51, 236, 239
Oquist, Mike 90
Orosco, Jesse 74, 120, 307
Osik, Keith 234
Orsulak, Joe 60, 85, 87, 212, 213
Ortiz, Junior 62, 64, 103
Ortiz, Ray 170
Orton, John 62, 64, 140, 143, 146, 310
Osborne, Donovan 69, 241, 307, 311
Osteen, Dave 178

Osuna, Al 73, 265
Otto, Dave 70, 77, 105, 106, 229, 307, 311
Owens, Jay 165, 170, 292
Owen, Spike 54, 124, 203, 207
Ozuna, Gab 79, 237, 242
Pagliarulo, Mike 52, 167
Pagnozzi, Tom 63, 65, 236, 237, 239, 300
Painter, Gary 98
Painter, Lance 277, 282
Palacios, Vicente 71, 233
Pall, Donn 72, 153
Palmeiro, Rafael 48, 188, 191, 299
Palmer, Dean 52, 188, 191, 299, 310
Pappas, Erik 154
Paquette, Craig 178
Parent, Mark 62, 64, 84, 87, 90
Paris, Juan 98
Parker, Clay 71, 185, 307
Parker, Rick 266
Parks, Derek 164, 165, 170
Parnell, Mark 162
Parrett, Jeff 72, 177, 302
Parris, Steve 226
Parrish, Lance 62, 64, 181, 183, 269
Pasqua, Dan 60, 148, 151
Patrick, Bronswell 178
Patterson, Bob 73, 233
Patterson, Dave 290
Patterson, Jeff 226
Patterson, John 51, 285, 287, 290, 310
Patterson, Ken 73, 201
Paulino, Elvin 202
Pavlas, Dave 202
Pavlik, Roger 71, 77, 193, 194, 307, 311
Peck, Steve 79, 146
Pecota, Bill 53, 216, 244, 245
Pederson, Stu 138
Pedre, Jorge 202
Pedrique, Al 162
Peek, Tim 178
Peguero, Julio 274
Pegues, Steve 282
Peltier, Dan 194
Pena, Alejandro 73, 229, 249
Pena, Geronimo 51, 236, 237, 239, 242, 298, 310
Pena, Jim 289, 290
Pena, Tony 62, 64, 92, 93, 95, 299
Pendleton, Terry 53, 244, 247
Pennington, Brad 77, 85, 90
Pennye, Darwin 210
Pennyfeather, William 234
Perez, David 194
Perez, Eduardo 146, 250
Perez, Melido 68, 129
Perez, Mike 73, 241
Perez, Robert 138
Perez, Vladimir 162
Perezchica, Tony 52, 100, 101, 103
Perkins, Paul 186
Perry, Gerald 49, 239
Perschke, Greg 154
Peters, Reed 290
Peterson, Adam 282
Petkovsek, Mark 234
Petralli, Geno 62, 64, 191
Pettis, Gary 58, 111
Pevey, Marty 114
Phillips, J. R. 146
Phillips, Tony 50, 107, 108, 111

PLAYER INDEX

Phoenix, Steve 178
Piatt, Doug 210
Piazza, Mike 76, 268, 269, 274
Pichardo, Hipolito 68, 161, 311
Picota, Len 210
Pierce, Ed 162
Piotrwicz, Brian 274
Pirkl, Greg 186
Pitcher, Scott 186
Plantier, Phil 61, 93, 95, 276, 277, 310
Pledger, Kinnis 154
Plesac, Dan 72, 121, 307
Plummer, Dale 218
Plunk, Eric 72, 105
Plympton, Jeff 98
Polidor, Gus 178
Pollack, Chris 210
Polley, Dale 250
Polonia, Luis 56, 139, 141, 143, 299, 301
Ponte, Edward 266
Poole, Jim 74, 89, 90
Popplewell, Tom 130
Portugal, Mark 69, 265, 308
Pose, Scott 258
Postier, Paul 194
Pote, Louis 79, 285, 290
Powell, Dennis 72, 185, 312
Powell, Ross 77, 258
Power, Ted 72, 105
Prager, Howard 266
Pratt, Todd 76, 220, 221, 226, 292
Presley, Jim 194
Pride, Curtis 218
Prince, Tom 63, 65, 228, 231, 234
Proctor, Murph 269, 274
Prybylinski, Don 242
Puckett, Kirby 58, 164, 167, 297
Pugh, Tim 71, 257, 258
Puig, Ed 79, 157, 162
Pulido, Carlos 170
Pulliam, Harvey 162
Pye, Eddie 274
Quantrill, Paul 74, 97, 98
Quinlan, Tom 138
Quinones, Luis 50, 167, 170, 310
Quirk, Jamie 62, 64, 175
Raabe, Brian 170
Raczka, Mike 178
Radinsky, Scott 72, 153
Raines, Tim 56, 148, 151, 297, 299
Rambo, Dan 290
Rambo, Matt 79, 266
Ramirez, Rafael 55, 263
Ramos, Ken 78, 100, 101, 106
Ramsey, Fernando 202
Randolph, Willie 51, 216
Rapp, Pat 77, 285, 290, 293
Rasmussen, Dennis 70, 161, 162, 307, 311
Ratliff, Daryl 234
Rauth, Chris 218
Ray, Johnny 258
Ready, Randy 50, 175, 301
Reardon, Jeff 73, 249
Reboulet, Jeff 54, 76, 163, 164, 165, 167, 170, 309
Redfield, Joe 234
Redington, Tom 154
Redus, Gary 49, 189, 231
Reed, Darren 61, 167, 212

Reed, Jeff 63, 65, 253, 255
Reed, Jody 51, 95, 268, 269, 300
Reed, Rick 70, 161, 162, 302, 307, 311
Reed, Steve 77, 285, 290, 292
Reich, Andy 218
Reimer, Kevin 56, 116, 117, 191
Reimink, Rob 114
Remlinger, Mike 186
Renfroe, Laddie 202
Revenig, Todd 79, 173, 178
Reynolds, Harold 50, 84, 85, 179, 183
Reynolds, Shane 71, 265, 266
Reynoso, Armando 71, 245, 249, 250
Rhodes, Arthur 70, 89, 90, 311
Rhodes, Karl 61, 260, 261, 263, 266, 309
Rice, Lance 274
Rice, Pat 186
Richards, Dave 122
Richards, Rusty 170
Richardson, Jeff 234
Ridenour, Dana 146
Righetti, Dave 73, 289
Rightnowar, Ron 114
Rijo, Jose 69, 257, 301
Riles, Ernest 53, 263, 266, 310
Riley, Ed 98
Ripken, Billy 50, 87, 300
Ripken, Cal 54, 83, 84, 85, 87, 245
Risley, Bill 210
Ritchie, Gregg 290
Ritchie, Wally 74, 225, 269
Ritz, Kevin 70, 109, 113, 311
Rivera, Ben 70, 225, 312
Rivera, Lino 92
Rivera, Luis 54, 95
Robbins, Doug 85, 90
Roberson, Kevin 196, 197, 202
Roberts, Bip 57, 251, 252, 255, 298
Robertson, Jason 130
Robertson, Richard 79, 234
Robertson, Rod 114
Robinson, Darryl 162
Robinson, Don 70, 225, 302
Robinson, Jeff 73, 201, 302, 307
Robinson, Jeff M. 70, 233
Robinson, Jim 202
Robinson, Nap 250
Robinson, Ron 71, 121, 308
Robinson, Scott 258
Rodriguez, Boi 76, 250
Rodriguez, Carlos 130
Rodriguez, Henry 61, 269, 271, 274, 309
Rodriguez, Ivan 62, 64, 188, 189, 191, 300, 310
Rodriguez, Rich 73, 277, 281, 307
Rodriguez, Ruben 98
Rodriguez, Victor 226
Roesler, Mike 162
Rogers, Brian 218
Rogers, Kenny 72, 193
Rogers, Kevin 71, 77, 285, 289, 290
Rohde, Dave 50, 103, 106, 229
Rohrmeier, Dan 162
Rojas, Mel 73, 209, 312
Rojas, Ricky 114
Romero, Brian 194
Romero, Mandy 234
Roper, John 258
Rosado, Ed 226
Rosario, Dave 130

Rosario, Victor 114
Roscoe, Greg 106
Rose, Bobby 50, 144
Rosenthal, Wayne 74, 193, 194, 308, 311
Ross, Mike 242
Ross, Sean 250
Rossy, Rico 54, 76, 159, 162, 310
Roth, Greg 90
Rowland, Rich 109, 114
Royer, Stan 242
Ruffin, Bruce 70, 121, 122, 311
Ruffin, Johnny 154
Rumsey, Dan 78, 140, 146
Ruskin, Scott 73, 257
Russell, Jeff 72, 177
Russell, John 62, 64, 78, 191, 194
Russo, Paul 170
Ryan, Ken 98
Ryan, Nolan 40, 41, 68, 189, 193
Ryan, Sean 226
Saberhagen, Bret 69, 213, 217
Sable, Luke 194
Sabo, Chris 53, 252, 253, 256, 301
Sager, A.J. 282
Salazar, Luis 53, 199
Salles, John 202
Salmon, Tim 76, 140, 141, 146
Sammons, Lee 266
Sampen, Bill 72, 161
Samuel, Juan 51, 159
Sanchez, Rey 55, 195, 196, 197, 199, 310
Sandberg, Ryne 51, 196, 199, 298, 300
Sanders, Al 98
Sanders, Deion 59, 244, 245, 247, 310
Sanders, Reggie 59, 252, 256, 300, 309
Sanders, Scott 282
Sanders, Tracy 78, 101, 106
Sanderson, Scott 68, 129
Sanford, Mo 258
Santangelo, F.P. 210
Santiago, Benito 63, 65, 277, 279, 293, 300
Santovenia, Nelson 33, 62, 64, 151, 154
Sarbaugh, Mike 106
Sasser, Mackey 63, 65, 181, 216
Satre, Jason 258
Saunders, Doug 218
Sauveur, Rich 77, 162
Savinon, Odalis 242
Sax, Dave 130
Sax, Steve 50, 147, 149, 151, 300
Scanlan, Bob 73, 201
Scarsone, Steve 84, 85, 90
Schaefer, Jeff 54, 183
Scheid, Rich 266
Schilling, Curt 69, 225
Schmidt, Dave 74, 178, 185
Schofield, Dick 55, 213, 216
Schooler, Mike 72, 185
Schourek, Pete 69, 217, 218, 307, 311
Schreiber, Bruce 234
Schu, Rick 226
Schullstrom, Erik 282
Schulz, Jeff 202
Schunk, Jerry 138
Schwarz, Jeff 77, 154
Scioscia, Mike 63, 65, 271
Scott, Charles 186
Scott, Gary 53, 199, 202
Scott, Shawn 138

PLAYER INDEX

Scott, Tim 74, 77, 281, 282
Scruggs, Tony 194
Scudder, Scott 70, 105
Searage, Ray 146
Searcy, Steve 74, 273, 274, 311
Sebra, Bob 202
Segui, David 48, 84, 85, 88
Segura, Jose 258
Seitzer, Kevin 52, 116, 119, 301
Sele, Aaron 98
Sellers, Rick 114
Sellick, John 242
Seminara, Frank 70, 281, 282, 312
Servais, Scott 63, 65, 263, 309
Service, Scott 77, 253, 258
Shackle, Rick 79, 242
Shamburg, Ken 122
Sharperson, Mike 53, 268, 271
Shave, John 194
Shaw, Cedric 194
Shaw, Jeff 74, 105, 106
Shea, John 138
Sheaffer, Danny 170
Sheffield, Gary 53, 276, 277, 279, 298
Shelby, John 98
Shelton, Ben 234
Shepherd, Keith 79, 226, 292
Sherman, Darrell 76, 276, 277, 282
Sherrill, Tim 242
Shields, Tommy 90
Shifflett, Steve 72, 77, 157, 161, 162, 308, 311
Shikles, Larry 98
Shinall, Zak 274
Shines, Razor 210
Shipley, Craig 55, 275, 277, 279, 310
Shireman, Jeff 242
Shouse, Brian 79, 234
Shumpert, Terry 50, 160, 162, 310
Siddall, Joe 210
Sierra, Ruben 60, 171, 172, 175, 187
Silvestri, Dave 76, 130
Simms, Mike 61, 260, 261, 263, 266, 309
Simon, Rich 266
Simons, Doug 74, 77, 209, 210, 311
Sims, Mark 226
Siwa, Joe 170
Slaught, Don 63, 65, 228, 231, 298
Slocumb, Heathcliff 74, 201, 202
Slusarski, Joe 70, 177, 178, 311
Small, Aaron 138
Small, Jeff 258
Smiley, John 68, 165, 169, 253
Smiley, Reuben 290
Smith, Bryn 69, 241
Smith, Dan 79, 189, 194
Smith, Dave 74, 201
Smith, Dwight 59, 196, 199
Smith, Greg 114
Smith, Jack 178
Smith, Keith 218
Smith, Lee 73, 237, 241
Smith, Lonnie 57, 229, 245, 247
Smith, Mark 90
Smith, Ozzie 28, 55, 236, 239, 298
Smith, Pete 70, 77, 249, 250, 301
Smith, Tim 98
Smith, Willie 106
Smith, Zane 69, 233
Smithberg, Roger 178

Smoltz, John 69, 249, 301
Snider, Van 98
Snow, J.T. 76, 130, 140, 141
Snyder, Cory 61, 269, 287
Sodders, Mike 202
Soff, Ray 146
Sojo, Luis 50, 144, 146, 299, 310
Soper, Mike 106
Sorrento, Paul 48, 100, 103, 309
Sosa, Sammy 59, 196, 199, 310
Sparks, Don 78, 130
Sparks, Greg 114
Sparks, Steve 122
Spearman, Vernon 274
Spehr, Tim 76, 157, 162, 204, 205
Spiers, Bill 54, 116, 117, 119
Spradlin, Jerry 79, 253, 258
Sprague, Ed 62, 64, 76, 132, 133, 135, 138, 309
Springer, Dennis 274
Springer, Russ 130, 141
Springer, Steve 218
Stairs, Matt 210
Stanford, Don 130
Stankiewicz, Andy 54, 124, 127, 310
Stanley, Mike 62, 64, 124, 127
Stanton, Mike 73, 249, 307
Staton, Dave 282
St. Claire, Randy 74, 249, 250
Steinbach, Terry 62, 64, 172, 175
Stephan, Todd 90
Stephens, Ray 194
Stephens, Ron 154
Stephenson, Phil 57, 76, 279, 282
Stevens, Lee 48, 144, 309
Stevens, Matt 226
Stewart, Dave 68, 133, 177
Stieb, Dave 70, 137
Stillwell, Kurt 51, 279, 300
Stinnet, Kelly 106
Stocker, Kevin 226
Stone, Jeff 226
Stottlemyre, Todd 68, 133, 137
Strange, Don 79, 196, 250
Strange, Doug 53, 200, 202
Strauss, Julio 202
Strawberry, Darryl 61, 271
Strebeck, Ricky 178
Stubbs, Franklin 48, 119
Suero, William 122
Sullivan, Mike 226
Surhoff, B.J. 62, 64, 117, 119
Sutcliffe, Rick 45, 68, 89
Sutko, Glenn 258
Sveum, Dale 54, 152
Swan, Russ 72, 185, 302
Swartzbaugh, Dave 202
Swift, Bill 69, 289
Swindell, Greg 69, 253, 257, 261
Swingle, Paul 146
Tabaka, Jeff 79, 117, 122, 293
Tabler, Pat 48, 135
Tackett, Jeff 62, 64, 88, 310
Tafoya, Dennis 79, 234
Tanana, Frank 68, 113, 213, 302
Tapani, Kevin 68, 169
Tarasco, Tony 250
Tartabull, Danny 39, 45, 60, 124, 125, 127, 298, 299, 301
Tatar, Kevin 258

Tatum, Jim 116, 117, 122, 292
Tatum, Willie 78, 98
Taubensee, Eddie 63, 65, 101, 260, 261, 263, 309
Tavarez, Jesus 186
Taylor, Billy 250
Taylor, Dwight 258
Taylor, Rob 290
Taylor, Sam 226
Taylor, Scott 98, 122
Taylor, Terry 78, 146
Tedder, Scott 154
Tejero, Fausto 146
Telford, Anthony 90
Telgheder, Dave 218
Tellers, Dave 234
Terrell, Walt 68, 113
Tettleton, Mickey 62, 64, 108, 111, 298, 299
Teufel, Tim 51, 276, 279, 301
Tewksbury, Bob 69, 241, 308
Thigpen, Bobby 72, 153
Thomas, Andres 290
Thomas, Frank 48, 148, 152, 297, 299, 301
Thomas, John 242
Thomas, Larry 78, 149, 154
Thomas, Royal 282
Thome, Jim 52, 78, 100, 101, 103, 106, 310
Thompson, Milt 57, 220, 221, 237, 240
Thompson, Rich 212
Thompson, Robby 51, 284, 287
Thompson, Ryan 59, 138, 216, 310
Thon, Dickie 54, 192
Thoutsis, Paul 98
Thurman, Gary 60, 156, 160
Timlin, Mike 72, 137, 301
Timmons, Ozzie 202
Tingley, Ron 62, 64, 140, 144
Tinsley, Lee 106
Tolentino, Jose 234
Tollison, David 138
Tomberlin, Andy 250
Tomlin, Randy 69, 233
Torres, Salomon 290
Townley, Jason 138
Trachsel, Steve 79, 202
Tracy, Jim 234
Trammell, Alan 54, 111
Traxler, Brian 274
Treadway, Jeff 51, 245, 247
Treadwell, Jody 274
Trevino, Alex 242
Trevino, Tony 226
Trice, Wally 106
Trlicek, Rick 138
Trombley, Mike 71, 165, 169, 170
Tsamis, George 170
Tubbs, Greg 234
Tucker, Scooter 266
Tunison, Rich 162
Turang, Brian 78, 186
Turek, Joe 106
Turner, Matt 77, 266, 293
Turner, Shane 186
Twardoski, Mike 76, 98
Tyler, Brad 90
Uhrhan, Kevin 98
Urbani, Tom 242

PLAYER INDEX

Uribe, Jose 55, 261, 287
Valdez, Efrain 122
Valdez, Sergio 74, 209, 210, 307
Valentin, John 54, 76, 92, 95, 98, 310
Valentin, Jose 122
Valera, Julio 68, 145, 311
Valle, Dave 62, 64, 183
Van Burkleo, Ty 146
Vandeberg, Ed 186
Vanderwal, John 57, 204, 207, 310
Vann, Brandy 122
Van Poppel, Todd 178
Van Slyke, Andy 59, 228, 231, 298, 301
Vargas, Hector 78, 130
Varsho, Gary 61, 231, 252
Vasquez, Julian 218
Vasquez, Marcos 250
Vatcher, Jim 61, 279, 282
Vaughn, Greg 56, 116, 117, 119, 299
Vaughn, Mo 48, 92, 96, 98, 310
Velarde, Randy 39, 45, 54, 124, 125, 127
Velasquez, Guillermo 282
Ventura, Jose 162
Ventura, Robin 52, 148, 149, 152, 297
Veres, Dave 266
Vesling, Don 282
Vice, Darryl 78, 178
Vidmar, Don 146
Viera, John 130
Vierra, Joey 77, 258
Villanueva, Hector 63, 65, 200, 202, 236, 237, 310
Viola, Frank 68, 97
Vizcaino, Jose 55, 196, 197, 200
Vizquel, Omar 54, 180, 183, 299
Voigt, Jack 76, 85, 90
Wade, Scott 202
Waggoner, Aubrey 78, 180, 181, 250
Wagner, Paul 234
Wainhouse, David 210
Wakamatsu, Don 274
Wakefield, Tim 70, 233, 234, 307, 312
Walbeck, Bob 69, 233
Walbeck, Matt 196, 197, 202
Walewander, Jim 194
Walk, Bob 69, 233
Walker, Chico 53, 216
Walker, Larry 61, 204, 205, 207, 298
Walker, Mike 114, 186
Walker, Pete 218
Wall, Donnie 266
Wallach, Tim 3, 53, 205, 207, 268, 269
Waller, Casey 226
Walling, Denny 53, 264
Walter, Gene 138
Walters, Dan 63, 65, 276, 277, 279, 282, 310
Walters, Dave 98
Walton, Bruce 6, 74, 177, 178
Walton, Jerome 57, 200
Wapnick, Steve 154
Ward, Anthony 138
Ward, Duane 72, 137
Ward, Kevin 57, 280
Ward, Turner 60, 135, 138, 310
Warren, Brian 79, 109, 114
Washington, Kyle 90
Wasinger, Mark 146
Wassenaar, Rob 170
Watson, Allen 79, 237, 242

Watson, Preston 250
Wayne, Gary 74, 169
Wearing, Melvin 90
Weathers, Dave 138
Webb, Ben 234
Weber, Pete 290
Webster, Lenny 62, 64, 165, 167, 310
Webster, Mitch 61, 268, 271
Wedge, Eric 76, 93, 98, 292
Wegman, Bill 68, 121, 302, 307
Wegmann, Tom 218
Wehner, John 53, 76, 228, 229, 232, 234, 310
Weiss, Walt 55, 173, 175, 293, 300
Welch, Bob 68, 177
Wells, David 68, 137
Wendell, Turk 202
Wengert, Bill 274
Wernig, Pat 178
Wertz, Bill 79, 101, 106
West, David 71, 169, 170, 307, 311
Weston, Mickey 71, 77, 225, 226
Wetherby, Jeff 186
Wetteland, John 73, 209, 311
Whitaker, Lou 50, 107, 108, 111, 299
White, Billy 202
White, Charlie 154
White, Derrick 210
White, Devon 58, 132, 135, 297
White, Fred 170
White, Mike 218
White, Rick 234
White, Rondell 210
Whitehurst, Wally 69, 213, 277, 281
Whiten, Mark 60, 100, 103
Whiteside, Matt 74, 79, 189, 193, 194
Wickander, Kevin 74, 105
Wickman, Bob 71, 129, 130, 312
Wiegandt, Scott 226
Wilkerson, Curt 50, 156, 160
Wilkins, Dean 282
Wilkins, Mike 274
Wilkins, Rick 63, 65, 196, 197, 200, 202, 310
Wilkinson, Bill 178
Willard, Jerry 210
Williams, Bernie 58, 76, 123, 124, 128, 130, 310
Williams, Brian 70, 265, 266, 311
Williams, Cary 226
Williams, Gerald 124, 130
Williams, Kenny 122
Williams, Matt D. 53, 284, 288
Williams, Mike 71, 77, 221, 225, 226
Williams, Mitch 73, 221, 225
Williams, Reggie 146
Williams, Ted 186
Williams, Todd 274
Williams, Woody 138
Williamson, Mark 74, 89, 302, 307
Willis, Carl 72, 169
Willis, Marty 114
Wilson, Brandon 154
Wilson, Craig 53, 240
Wilson, Dan 258
Wilson, Nigel 78, 133, 138, 293
Wilson, Steve 73, 273, 311
Wilson, Trevor 69, 289
Wilson, Willie 58, 175, 196, 197
Windes, Rodney 266

Winfield, Dave 40, 66, 133, 135, 164, 165, 298, 299
Winningham, Herm 58, 96
Wiseman, Dennis 242
Wishnevski, Rob 122
Wissler, Bill 170
Witkowski, Mat 282
Witmeyer, Ron 178
Witt, Bobby 68, 177
Wohlers, Mark 74, 82, 249, 250
Wolak, Jerry 154
Wolf, Steve 114
Wood, Ted 284, 285, 290
Woodall, Brad 79, 250
Woodson, Kerry 186
Woodson, Tracy 53, 240, 242, 310
Worrell, Tim 77, 282
Worrell, Todd 73, 241, 269, 307
Worthington, Craig 52, 103, 106, 310
Wrona, Rick 258
Yacopino, Ed , 90
Yan, Julian 138
Yaughn, Kip 79, 85, 293
Yelding, Eric 55, 154, 264, 309
Yockey, Mark 290
York, Mike 234
Young, Anthony 69, 217, 301, 312
Young, Cliff 146
Young, Curt 71, 129, 130
Young, Eric 51, 269, 271, 274, 310
Young, Gerald 59, 264
Young, Kevin 76, 228, 229, 234
Young, Matt 70, 97
Young, Pete 210
Yount, Robin 58, 116, 119
Zambrano, Eddie 76, 234
Zancanaro, David 178
Zappelli, Mark 146
Zavaras, Clint 186
Zeile, Todd 53, 235, 236, 240
Zimmerman, Mike 234
Zinter, Alan 78, 218
Zosky, Eddie 133, 138
Zupcic, Bob 56, 92, 96, 309

324